AF323521

GEOMETRIC COMPUTATION

Lecture Notes Series on Computing Vol. 11

GEOMETRIC COMPUTATION

editors

Falai Chen
University of Science and Technology of China, China

Dongming Wang
Université Pierre et Marie Curie — CNRS, France

World Scientific

NEW JERSEY · LONDON · SINGAPORE · BEIJING · SHANGHAI · HONG KONG · TAIPEI · CHENNAI

Published by

World Scientific Publishing Co. Pte. Ltd.
5 Toh Tuck Link, Singapore 596224
USA office: Suite 202, 1060 Main Street, River Edge, NJ 07661
UK office: 57 Shelton Street, Covent Garden, London WC2H 9HE

British Library Cataloguing-in-Publication Data
A catalogue record for this book is available from the British Library.

GEOMETRIC COMPUTATION

ISBN 981-238-799-4

Editor: Tjan Kwang Wei

Printed in Singapore.

PREFACE

Algebraic methods have remarkable applications in the areas of automated geometric reasoning, computer aided geometric design and modeling, and computer graphics. These methods have been developed mostly in the area of computer algebra. The interaction between algebraic computation and the above-mentioned areas of modern engineering geometry has existed for several decades, yet in a loose form. To facilitate this interaction, an informal Seminar on Geometric Computation was held in Hefei, China in April 2002 (see http://www-calfor.lip6.fr/~wang/SGC2002). It brought together active researchers working on different subjects to survey their work, to present their ideas, views and recent results, and to discuss future development and cooperation. The seminar was very successful and it had attracted over 50 participants.

The interest of the audience in the seminar talks motivated our attempt in collecting the presented papers and other relevant work in a coherent volume. The idea of compiling this volume for formal publication was supported enthusiastically by most of the speakers and several other distinguished researchers who were invited to the seminar but were not able to make their trip. The authors were encouraged to prepare their articles in two categories: tutorial surveys and original research papers. All the submissions underwent a careful review-revision process, and it is hoped that this book, with 14 chapters coming out of these submissions, has reached the usual standard of formally reviewed volumes.

The book comprises three closely related parts: the first is devoted mainly to curve and surface modeling, and it contains a general survey on theoretical and practical applications of algebraic methods and three specialized surveys on surface blending, parametrization, and implicitization, followed by four research papers. The second part is concentrated on geometric reasoning, with one tutorial survey on Clifford algebra approaches, another on automated deduction in real geometry, and one research article. The last part is highlighted by a chapter that outlines a theory of real approximation, based on a generalization of the central idea of exact geometric computation. The book ends with one paper on A-resultant quotients and another on face recognition, which show how computer algebra and artificial intelligence meet geometry in the era of computation.

The contents of the book, though fundamental and focused, cross three major areas of research: symbolic and algebraic computation, automated reasoning, and computer aided geometric design. They are also related to numerical and scientific computing, computer aided design, and computer graphics. The design and graphic aspects of the book may even extend its readership to the industry of geometric engineering. We hope that this book will offer the reader a valuable source of reference and an easy access to the intersection of these highly relevant disciplines.

The editors wish to thank all the authors for their valuable contributions and the referees for their timely help. We acknowledge the generous support provided by the Department of Mathematics, University of Science and Technology of China for the above-mentioned seminar.

Hefei and Paris
September 2003

Falai Chen
Dongming Wang

CONTENTS

CHAPTER 1

ALGEBRAIC METHODS IN COMPUTER AIDED GEOMETRIC DESIGN: THEORETICAL AND PRACTICAL APPLICATIONS

Laureano González-Vega[*], Ioana Necula[*], Sonia Pérez-Díaz[†], Juana Sendra[‡],
and J. Rafael Sendra[†]

[*]*Universidad de Cantabria, Dpto. de Matemáticas, Estad. y Comput., Spain*
[‡]*Universidad Carlos III, Departamento de Matemáticas, Spain*
[†]*Universidad de Alcalá, Departamento de Matemáticas, Spain*
E-mail: {gonzalezl,neculai}@unican.es, jsendra@math.uc3m.es,
{rafael.sendra,sonia.perez}@uah.es

In this chapter, we show how to adapt algebraic techniques to deal with some problems, such as implicitization or parameterization, in computer aided geometric design that involve floating-point real numbers. In addition, applications to the offsetting and blending problems are also considered.

1. Introduction

The usefulness of computer aided design and computer aided modeling (CAD/CAM) systems as a means of increasing the efficiency of the design process is nowadays uncontested. Advantages such as

- reduction of lead times,
- quality improvements, and
- cost reduction by saving time spent for implementing engineering changes in the design process

are often cited as the major benefits resulting from the introduction of specialized software for CAD/CAM. From a mathematical point of view almost all the CAD/CAM problems are related to the manipulation of geometric objects, mainly curves, surfaces and their combinations, in two or three-dimensional space. Since these geometric objects may be represented implicitly or parametrically through polynomials or rational functions, it is clear that computer aided geometric design (CAGD) must intersect com-

1

puter algebra, algebraic geometry, and real algebraic geometry.

In this chapter, we briefly survey some results and techniques from these related areas for symbolic and symbolic-numeric manipulation of curves and surfaces and discuss their applications in CAGD. Since some chapters[48,61] of this volume are devoted to symbolic algorithms for curves and surfaces, our discussions will be focused mainly on the approximate version of the problems as well as their applications. More precisely, we will address

- implicitization and parametrization problems in the case when approximate objects are under consideration,
- applications such as computing with implicit curves, offsetting and blending in CAGD, and
- some examples on the practical performance of algebraic techniques in CAGD.

For a complete and comprehensive introduction to CAGD, the reader is referred to the first few chapters in the book[23] by Farin and others.

2. Implicitization and Parametrization Problems

Algebraic curves and surfaces, especially rational curves and surfaces, are the main geometric objects in CAGD. In many practical applications parametric representation of varieties are used,[5,6,41,46] but in some situations the availability of implicit equations is required or even an implicit equation may be produced as output of a geometric operation since the new geometric object does not necessarily have a parametric representation. These facts have motivated the emergence of a research area devoted to the construction of conversion algorithms, namely parametrization and implicitization algorithms,[6,42,48,61] for algebraic varieties.

This section is devoted to analyzing the problem of adapting symbolic and algebraic algorithms of implicitization and parameterization for the (more real) case where the involved coefficients of polynomials are floating-point real numbers. For a description of different ways of dealing with the implicitization problem in the case of exact coefficients (using Gröbner bases, resultants, moving curves and surfaces, *etc.*), see Chapter 4 in this volume[48] or the paper[59] by Sederberg. Similarly, for a description of symbolic parametrization algorithms see Chapter 3 in this volume.[61]

2.1. *Implicitization: Exact versus Approximate*

One of the main problems arising in the manipulation of curves and surfaces in CAGD consists in finding efficient algorithms for computing the implicit equations of curves and surfaces parametrized by rational functions (see for example the books[14,15] by Cox and others, or Chapters 5 and 7 in the book[41] by Hoffmann). This is due, for example, to the fact that for tracing the considered curve or surface the parametric representation is the most convenient, while for determining in an efficient way the position of a point on the curve or surface, the implicit equation is desired.

The implicitization problem for hypersurfaces (curves in the real plane or surfaces in the three-dimensional real space for real applications) parametrized in a rational way can be stated in the following terms: let $\mathcal{V}$ be a hypersurface in $\mathbb{R}^n$ ($n = 2$ or $n = 3$ in real applications) parametrized by

$$x_i = \frac{f_i(t_1, \dots, t_{n-1})}{g_i(t_1, \dots, t_{n-1})}, \quad i \in \{1, \dots, n\},$$

where f_i and g_i belong to $\mathbb{R}[t_1, \dots, t_{n-1}]$ with $\gcd(f_i, g_i) = 1$. The implicitization problem for $\mathcal{V}$ consists in finding a non-zero element $\mathcal{R}_\mathcal{V}(x_1, \dots, x_n)$ in $\mathbb{R}[x_1, \dots, x_n]$ with the smallest possible total degree such that

$$\mathcal{R}_\mathcal{V}\left(\frac{f_1(t_1, \dots, t_{n-1})}{g_1(t_1, \dots, t_{n-1})}, \dots, \frac{f_n(t_1, \dots, t_{n-1})}{g_n(t_1, \dots, t_{n-1})}\right) = 0.$$

More general formulations of the implicitization problem for arbitrary parametric varieties can be found in the papers by Alonso *et al.*,[1] Canny and Manocha,[9] Chionh,[11] Gao and Chou,[30] González-Vega,[34] and Kalkbrener.[47]

The implicitization problem can be seen as a problem in elimination theory and therefore it can be approached by elimination techniques such as Gröbner bases and characteristic sets. Nevertheless, alternative methods can be applied. Next example, extracted from the paper[34] by the first author, shows a non-standard way of computing the implicit equation of a rational surface avoiding the use of Gröbner bases or resultants (i.e., determinants of polynomial matrices). In fact, it can be viewed as a way of computing the corresponding determinant by computing the traces of the powers of the considered matrix.

Example 1: The parametric equations of a bicubic surface $\mathcal{B}$ are

$$x(u,v) = 3v(v-1)^2 + (u-1)^3 + 3u,$$
$$y(u,v) = 3u(u-1)^2 + v^3 + 3v,$$
$$z(u,v) = -3u(u^2 - 5u + 5)v^3 - 3(u^3 + 6u^2 - 9u + 1)v^2$$
$$+ v(6u^3 + 9u^2 - 18u + 3) - 3u(u-1).$$

We look for an implicit equation $\mathcal{H}_\mathcal{B}$ for $\mathcal{B}$. The first two equations, denoted by H_1 and H_2 (and the third one will be denoted by H_3), do not have the desired structure in order to apply the *ad-hoc* technique presented in the paper[34] by the first author, but an easy linear combination of them, namely

$$F_1 = \frac{-H_1 + 3H_2}{8} = u^3 + \frac{3v^2}{4} - \frac{15u^2}{8} + \frac{3v}{4} + \frac{3u}{8} - \frac{3y}{8} + \frac{x}{8} + \frac{1}{8},$$

$$F_2 = \frac{3H_1 - H_2}{8} = v^3 - \frac{9v^2}{4} - \frac{3u^2}{8} + \frac{3v}{4} + \frac{15u}{8} + \frac{y}{8} - \frac{3x}{8} - \frac{3}{8},$$

gives a good shape for the polynomial system to be dealt with. This means that any polynomial in $\mathbb{Q}[x,y][u,v]$ can be written in a unique way modulo F_1 and F_2 as a $\mathbb{Q}[x,y]$-linear combination of monomials $u^i v^j$ (the so-called normal form modulo F_1 and F_2) with total degree strictly smaller than 3.

In this particular case the equation $\mathcal{H}_\mathcal{B}$ has the following structure:

$$\mathcal{H}_\mathcal{B}(x,y,z) = z^9 + \sum_{i=1}^{9} r_i(x,y)z^{9-i} = \prod_{F_1(\Delta)=0, F_2(\Delta)=0} (z - H_3(\Delta)), \quad (1)$$

where Δ represents a zero of the system $F_1 = 0$, $F_2 = 0$ with coordinates in the algebraic closure of $\mathbb{Q}(x,y)$.

The computation of the $r_i(x,y)$ is performed by computing the *Newton sums* of order 9, $\mathbf{S}_k(x,y)$ ($k \in \{1,\dots,9\}$), for the equation (1):

$$\mathbf{S}_k(x,y) = \sum_{F_1(\Delta)=0, F_2(\Delta)=0} (H_3(\Delta))^k.$$

For that, the *Jacobian determinant* of F_1 and F_2 is first computed:

$$\mathbf{Jac}(u,v) = 9v^2u^2 - \frac{27}{2}vu^2 + \frac{9}{4}u^2 - \frac{45}{4}v^2u + 18vu - \frac{9}{4}u + \frac{9}{8}v^2 - \frac{9}{2}v - \frac{9}{8}.$$

Denote by ℓ_{ij} ($0 \le i,j \le 2$) the coefficient of u^2v^2 in the normal form of the polynomial $u^i v^j \mathbf{Jac}$ modulo F_1 and F_2; then every $\mathbf{S}_k(x,y)$ is determined by the following expression:

$$\mathbf{S}_k(x,y) = \sum_{i,j=0}^{2} c_{ij}^{(k)} \ell_{ij},$$

where the $c_{ij}^{(k)}$ are the coefficients of the normal form of H_3^k with respect to F_1 and F_2:

$$(H_3(s,t))^k = \sum_{i,j=0}^{2} c_{ij}^{(k)} u^i v^j \qquad \mathrm{mod} \ \langle F_1, F_2 \rangle.$$

Finally the desired result is obtained by using the classical *Newton identities* of the univariate case. The first two coefficients in $\mathcal{H}_{\mathcal{B}}(x, y, z)$ are

$$\mathbf{r}_1(x, y) = -\frac{233469x}{2048} + \frac{188595y}{2048} - \frac{112832595}{262144} - \frac{81x^2}{64} + \frac{135xy}{32} - \frac{81y^2}{64},$$

$$\mathbf{r}_2(x, y) = -\frac{20972672709381x}{536870912} + \frac{17975329363179y}{536870912} - \frac{729y^4}{8192} - \frac{729x^4}{8192}$$

$$+ \frac{1215x^3y}{2048} + \frac{1215xy^3}{2048} - \frac{4105971x^3}{65536} + \frac{3129597y^3}{65536}$$

$$+ \frac{14456151x^2y}{65536} - \frac{13181049xy^2}{65536} + \frac{48101467761xy}{8388608}$$

$$- \frac{38812918311y^2}{16777216} - \frac{22656991982391171}{137438953472} - \frac{1}{2}\left(\frac{233469x}{2048}\right.$$

$$+ \frac{112832595}{262144} + \frac{81x^2}{64} - \frac{188595y}{2048} - \frac{135xy}{32} + \left.\frac{81y^2}{64}\right).$$

$$\left(-\frac{233469x}{2048} + \frac{188595y}{2048} + \frac{135xy}{32} - \frac{81y^2}{64} - \frac{112832595}{262144}\right.$$

$$\left.- \frac{81x^2}{64}\right) - \frac{4779x^2y^2}{4096} - \frac{54187594407x^2}{16777216} + \cdots.$$

The computing time was less than 5 seconds by using Maple 9 on a PowerPC G4 dual processor at 1MHz (the implicitization time for the previous bicubic spline was 1500 seconds by using Gröbner bases; see the book[41] by Hoffmann). The size of the file containing the full implicit equation of $\mathcal{B}$ is around 600 Kb.

It is important to mention that, in many cases, computer algebra packages can hardly verify the obtained result by substituting the parametric equations of $\mathcal{B}$ into the computed implicit equation and obtaining 0 as result. However, since the parametric equations are available, it is very easy to verify that several hundreds of points randomly generated on $\mathcal{B}$ satisfy the computed implicit equation.

Other problems with a similar formulation to the implicitization problem described above, and where the solution is obtained by eliminating some variables from the initial equations, are listed below (see the book by Hoffmann[41]).

- Computation of offset curves and surfaces.
- Computation of constant-radius blending surfaces.
- Computation of the convolution of two plane curves or surfaces.

- Computation of the common tangent of two plane curves.
- Computation of the inversion formula for parametric surfaces.

These geometrical operations are often used for generating the boundary of configuration space obstacles, in order to construct collision-free motion paths for translating objects.

Two main difficulties are encountered when one uses the usual elimination techniques (resultants, Gröbner bases, triangular sets, *etc.*) offered by computer algebra to deal with the variable elimination problems mentioned above. For example the implicitization of a rational surface defined by

$$x = \frac{X(u,v)}{W(u,v)}, \quad y = \frac{Y(u,v)}{W(u,v)}, \quad z = \frac{Z(u,v)}{W(u,v)}$$

appearing in a real-world problem is difficult to achieve by directly applying resultants or Gröbner bases because, first, it is usually a very costly algebraic operation (due mainly to the sizes of the intermediate coefficients or the size of the involved matrices) and, second, the coefficients of the polynomials in the parametrization are usually floating-point real numbers (not allowing the use of Gröbner bases, for example, or producing stability or robustness problems in the computation of the determinant of a polynomial matrix).

These difficulties can be currently overcome in practice for some particular (mainly low degree) cases in two different ways.

- By using multivariate resultants (see the paper by Canny and Manocha[9]), the implicit equation is described as a non-evaluated determinant. Then any question about the considered surface, requiring the implicit equation, is reduced to a Numerical Linear Algebra question over such a matrix (usually an eigenvalue problem).
- By taking into account that, in general, a concrete object to be modeled is made by several hundreds (or thousands) of small patches, all of them sharing the same algebraic structure. For such an object a database is constructed containing the implicit equation of every class of patch appearing in its definition. This database must also contains the inversion formulae (providing the parameters in terms of the Cartesian coordinates) and must be pruned to avoid specialization problems. Moreover the database for a specific object is kept into a bigger and general database for further use (see the paper[19] by Espinola and others).

For this reason, a first option for the study of numeric implicitization algorithms is the precomputation of the implicit representation of the algebraic models of the patches, defined in a generic way by means of parameters. This approach, called *"generic implicitization"*, generates databases which allow a quickly problem solving. For instance, the implicit equation of the parametric surface of the form

$$x = a_1 v^2 + a_2 v, \quad y = b_1 u^2 + b_2, \quad z = c_1 uv + c_2 u + c_3 v \tag{2}$$

is

$$
\begin{aligned}
&c_1^4 x^2 y^2 - 2c_1^2 a_1 b_1 xyz^2 + b_1^2 a_1^2 z^4 + (-2c_1^4 b_2 - 2c_1^2 b_1 c_3^2)x^2 y \\
&\quad + (2c_1^3 c_2 a_2 - 2c_1^2 c_2^2 a_1)xy^2 + (2b_1 c_1^2 c_3 a_2 - 8c_1 b_1 a_1 c_2 c_3)xyz \\
&\quad + (2c_1^2 a_1 b_1 b_2 - 2a_1 c_3^2 b_1^2)xz^2 + (2b_1 c_1 a_2 a_1 c_2 - 2b_1 a_1^2 c_2^2 \\
&\quad - b_1 c_1^2 a_2^2)yz^2 + 2a_1 a_2 b_1^2 c_3 z^3 + (c_1^4 b_2^2 + 2c_1^2 b_2 c_3^2 b_1 + c_3^4 b_1^2)x^2 \\
&\quad + (4c_1^2 c_2^2 b_2 a_1 - 2c_2 c_1 a_2 b_1 c_3^2 - 2b_1 a_1 c_2^2 c_3^2 - 4c_1^3 c_2 b_2 a_2)xy \\
&\quad + (-2c_1^2 a_2 b_1 c_3 b_2 + 8c_2 c_1 a_1 b_2 c_3 b_1 - 2a_2 b_1^2 c_3^3)xz \\
&\quad + (-2c_2^3 c_1 a_1 a_2 + c_2^4 a_1^2 + c_2^2 c_1^2 a_2^2)y^2 - 2c_2^2 a_1 a_2 b_1 c_3 yz \\
&\quad + (a_2^2 b_1^2 c_3^2 - 2c_2 c_1 a_1 b_2 b_1 a_2 + c_1^2 b_2 b_1 a_2^2 + 2c_2^2 a_1^2 b_1 b_2)z^2 \\
&\quad + (2c_2 c_1 a_2 b_1 c_3^2 b_2 + 2c_2 c_1^3 b_2^2 a_2 - 2c_2^2 c_1^2 a_1 b_2^2 + 2c_2^2 a_1 b_2 c_3^2 b_1)x \\
&\quad + (4c_1 a_2 c_2^3 a_1 b_2 - 2a_1^2 c_2^4 b_2 - 2c_1^2 a_2^2 c_2^2 b_2 - c_2^2 a_2^2 b_1 c_3^2)y \\
&\quad + 2c_2^2 a_1 a_2 b_1 c_3 b_2 z + c_2^4 a_1^2 b_2^2 - 2c_2^3 c_1 a_1 b_2^2 a_2 + c_2^2 a_2^2 b_1 c_3^2 b_2 \\
&\quad + c_2^2 c_1^2 b_2^2 a_2^2 = 0
\end{aligned}
\tag{3}
$$

for almost all the values of the undetermined parameters a_i, b_i and c_i.

The database may also contain the conditions which imply that the previous representation provides after specialization a bad implicit equation: for instance, if a_1 is considered to be equal to 0 in the previous representation, then the resulting implicit equation after specialization is

$$(c_1^2 y - c_3^2 b_1 - c_1^2 b_2) \cdot (c_1^2 x^2 y - (b_2 c_1^2 + b_1 c_3^2)x^2 + \cdots - a_2^2 c_2^2 b_2) = 0,$$

which contains not only the implicit equation of the surface in (2) with $a_1 = 0$, but also the extraneous factor corresponding (if $c_1 \neq 0$) to the equation of the plane

$$y = (c_3^2 b_1 + c_1^2 b_2)/c_1^2.$$

Even in this case this "bad" implicit equation can be useful since the availability of the parametric representation allows one to discard in practice those points coming from the extraneous factor.

Moreover, the database should contain the algebraic expressions which describe u and v in function of x, y and z. For the surface defined by (2), whose implicit equation appears in (3), the value of v in function of x, y

and z is given by the formula

$$v = \frac{b_1 a_1 z^2 - c_1^2 xy + (b_1 c_3^2 + c_1^2 b_2)x - a_1 c_2^2 y + a_1 c_2^2 b_2}{2b_1 a_1 c_3 z + (2a_1 c_2 c_1 - c_1^2 a_2)y - 2a_1 c_2 c_1 b_2 + a_2 b_1 c_3^2 + c_1^2 a_2 b_2}.$$

The main drawback of the first approach is due to the existence of base points, i.e., solutions of the polynomial system

$$X(u,v) = 0, \quad Y(u,v) = 0, \quad Z(u,v) = 0, \quad W(u,v) = 0,$$

since their existence implies the vanishing of the determinant defining the implicit equation. This problem is solved for some instances by looking for an appropriate submatrix of full rank in the resultant matrix defining the implicit equation.[50] In the general case the computation of the greatest common divisor of several determinants of submatrices in order get the right implicit equation is required.

It is also not easy to deal in advance with specialization problems: up to this moment these are detected by substituting several points in the surface, uniformly generated by the parametrization, into the candidate to be the implicit equation.

The main drawback provided by the second approach is due to the fact that some algebraic structures arising in the database construction are very complicated and the implicit equation cannot be generated or cannot be easily used because of its huge size. Namely:

$$x = \frac{X(u,v)}{W(u,v)}, \quad y = \frac{Y(u,v)}{W(u,v)}, \quad z = \frac{Z(u,v)}{W(u,v)}$$

with

$$W(u,v) = \sum_{j=0}^{3} (A_j v^2 + B_j v + C_j) u^j$$

and

$$U(u,v) = \sum_{j=0}^{3} (\alpha_j^{(i)} v^2 + \beta_j^{(i)} v + \gamma_j^{(i)}) u^j$$

for $U \in \{X, Y, Z\}, i \in \{x, y, z\}$. Thus, this strategy has no practical applicability for such cases as the general bicubic patches, since in these cases the generic implicit equation is too complex to be used in practice.

A way of solving this problem is using techniques to reduce the degree of the considered surface. This degree reduction could affect the parametrization and the implicit equation as well. In the first case, by using a set of techniques already usual in geometric design, the considered surface is approximated by another one with parametrizations of lower degrees, which allows the use of the precomputed implicit equations in the database. In the second case, an upper bound for the total degree of the implicit equation of the considered surface is determined and established from the beginning. Then, for each patch, the coefficients of the implicit equation are obtained such that the error produced in the computations is smaller than the tolerance chosen to solve the problem.

It is important to mention that the algorithms sketched here involve techniques for computing singular values, formal expansion at infinity of rational functions constructed with the parametrization of the initial curve or surface, rewriting symmetric polynomials in terms of the solutions of certain equation systems like in our initial example, *etc.*

For instance, in the case of reducing the degree of the implicit equation, it is possible to reduce even the number of components/patches of the considered curve or surface (see the paper[18] by Dokken or for a similar formulation in the paper[13] by Corless and others). If the curve to be implicitized is defined by

$$\begin{pmatrix} x(u) \\ y(u) \end{pmatrix} = \begin{cases} (u, u^2) & \text{if } u > 0, \\ (u, -u^2) & \text{if } u \leq 0 \end{cases}$$

with $u \in [-1, 1]$, and the total degree of the implicit equation is bounded by 3, then by using the Bernstein bases and computing the singular values of the matrix generated by replacing the parametrizations in the implicit equation to be computed, the following is obtained as the implicit equation:

$$\begin{aligned} &-0.14338002021536847 y^3 + 0.50872225217688360 x y^2 \\ &- 0.14431972674994731 y - 0.698331431396000062 x^2 y \\ &+ 0.0170228763995723399 x + 0.460281533430831 x^3 = 0. \end{aligned}$$

In Fig. 1 the initial parametric curve and the curve associated to the implicit equation are displayed, these two curves being indistinguishable. In this case, using the Bernstein basis is essential; however, using the habitual power basis does not produce the correct result with respect to the accuracy of the obtained result.

Another strategy consists in replacing the computations of resultants or Gröbner bases by developing evaluation outlines which supply directly the implicit equation. For instance, if the curve to be implicitized is defined by the polynomial parametrization

$$x = f(u), \quad y = g(u),$$

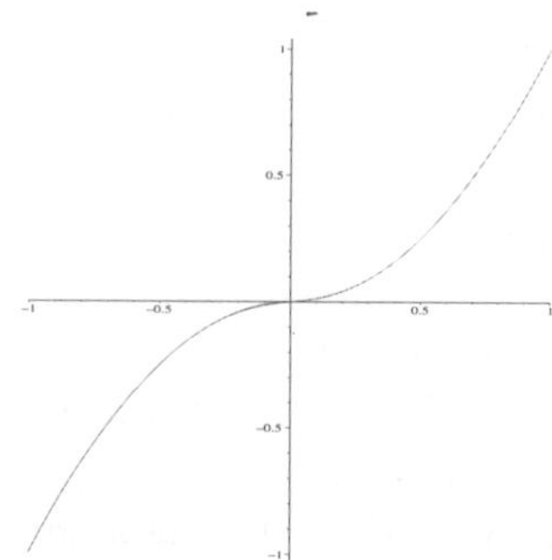

Fig. 1.   Approximated implicitization

then its implicit equation is given by the "formula"

$$\prod_{f(\alpha)-x=0} (y - g(\alpha)),$$

where the solutions of the equation $f(\alpha) - x = 0$ are considered in the algebraic closure of $\mathbb{K}(x)$ (where $\mathbb{K}$ is the base field). Using Newton identities together with the Laurent expansion of the rational functions

$$\frac{f'(x)g(x)^k}{f(x)}$$

one gets the desired result, without computing any determinant (which could be a difficult task when the coefficients of $f(t)$ and $g(t)$ are given in an approximated form) or Gröbner bases. Another alternative, that one may take into account, is to compute the Puiseux expansion of the solutions of the equation $f(u) - x = 0$ (seen as equation in u) and to use the product to recover the implicit equation.

2.2. *Parametrization: Exact versus Approximate*

Although many authors[61] have addressed the problem of globally and symbolically parametrizing algebraic curves and surfaces, only few results have been achieved for the case of approximate algebraic varieties. Piecewise parametrizations are provided in the papers by Corless *et al.*,[12] Gahleitner *et al.*[29] and Hartmann[38] by means of combination of both algebraic and numerical techniques for solving differential equations and rational B-spline manipulations. In the paper[7] by Bajaj and Royappa, the problem of finding a global approximate parametrization is studied for the case of approximate irreducible conics, rational cubics and quadrics. In the paper[54] by Pérez-Díaz and others, the results of Bajaj and Royappa[7] are generalized to the special case of curves parametrizable by lines.

The statement of the problem for the approximate case is slightly different from that of the classical symbolic parametrization problem (see Chapter 3[61] in this volume). Intuitively speaking, one is given an irreducible affine algebraic plane real curve $\mathcal{C}$, that may or may not be rational, and a tolerance $\epsilon > 0$, and the problem consists in computing a rational curve $\overline{\mathcal{C}}$, and its parametrization, such that almost all points of the rational curve $\overline{\mathcal{C}}$ are in the *"vicinity"* of $\mathcal{C}$. The notion of vicinity may be introduced as the offset region limited by the external and internal offsets to $\mathcal{C}$ at distance ϵ, and therefore the problem consists in finding, if possible, a rational curve $\overline{\mathcal{C}}$ lying within the offset region of $\mathcal{C}$.

For instance, suppose that we are given a tolerance $\epsilon = 0.001$ and the quartic $\mathcal{C}$ defined by

$$x^4 + 2y^4 + 1.001x^3 + 3x^2y - y^2x - 3y^3 + 0.001y^2 - 0.001x - 0.001y - 0.001.$$

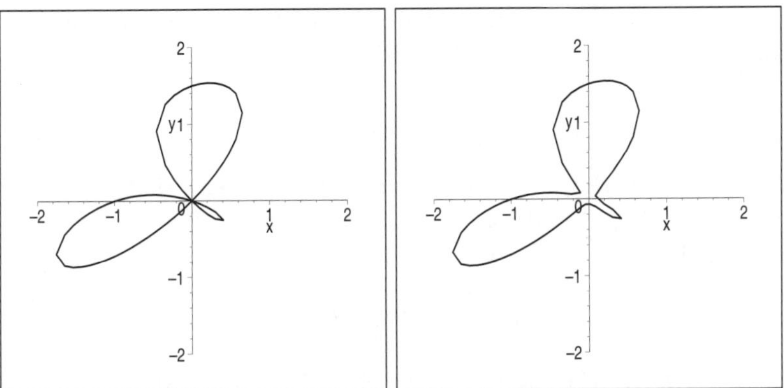

Fig. 2.   Curve $\mathcal{C}$ (right) and curve $\overline{\mathcal{C}}$ (left)

Note that $\mathcal{C}$ has genus 3, and therefore the input curve is not rational. Thus, an answer to the problem is given by the quartic $\overline{\mathcal{C}}$ defined by

$$x^4 + 2.y^4 + 1.001x^3 + 3.x^2y - y^2x - 3.y^3 + 10^{-6}y^2$$
$$- .6243761996 \cdot 10^{-13}x - .6260915576 \cdot 10^{-13}y$$
$$+ .9744187291 \cdot 10^{-23} - .3522924910 \cdot 10^{-16}x^2$$
$$+ .9991263887 \cdot 10^{-6}xy$$

that can be parametrized by $\overline{\mathcal{P}}(t) = (\overline{p}_1(t), \overline{p}_2(t))$, where

$$\overline{p}_1 = -.487671 \cdot$$
$$\frac{2.0526 - 2.05055t^2 + 6.15167t + .512063 \cdot 10^{-6}t^4 - 6.15167t^3}{1 + 2t^4},$$

$$\overline{p}_2 = .487671 \cdot$$
$$\frac{-2.05260t + 2.05055t^3 - 6.15167t^2 + 6.15167t^4 + .256287 \cdot 10^{-6}}{1 + 2t^4}.$$

One may check that $\mathcal{C}$ and $\overline{\mathcal{C}}$ in Fig. 2 are close.

In the following, we briefly describe the ideas in the paper[54] by Pérez-Díaz and others for parametrizing approximate curves by lines. More precisely, given a tolerance $\epsilon > 0$ and an algebraic plane real curve $\mathcal{C}$ defined by an ϵ-irreducible polynomial $f(x, y) \in \mathbb{C}[x, y]$ of degree d, and having an ϵ-singularity of multiplicity $d - 1$ (see below for the notion of ϵ-singularity, and the paper[12] by Corless and others for the concept of ϵ-irreducibility), the algorithm we describe computes a proper parametrization of a rational curve that is exactly parametrizable by lines (see Chapter 3[61] in this volume for the notion of properness). Furthermore, the error analysis shows that under certain initial conditions that ensures that points are projectively well defined, the output curve lies within the offset region of $\mathcal{C}$ at distance at most

$$2 \cdot \sqrt{2} \cdot \epsilon^{1/(2d)} \cdot e^2.$$

We start with the notion of ϵ-singularity. We say that $\overline{P} \in \mathbb{C}^2$ is an *ϵ-affine singularity* of multiplicity r of an algebraic plane curve defined by a polynomial $f(x, y) \in \mathbb{R}[x, y]$ if, for $0 \leq i + j \leq r - 1$,

$$\left| \frac{\partial^{i+j} f}{\partial^i x \partial^j y}(\overline{P}) \right| / \|f\| < \epsilon,$$

where $\|f\|$ denotes the infinity norm of f. Now, let $\mathcal{C}$ be an ϵ-irreducible (over $\mathbb{C}$) real algebraic curve of degree d having an ϵ-singularity $\overline{P} = (\overline{a}, \overline{b})$ of multiplicity $d - 1$ (for checking the existence and actual computation of ϵ-singularities see the paper[54] by Pérez-Díaz and others), and let $f(x, y)$ be its defining polynomials. Then the following theorems hold.

Theorem 2: Let $\overline{p}_1(t)$ be the root in $\mathbb{R}(t)$ of the quotient of $f(x, tx + \overline{b} - \overline{a}t)$ and $(x - \overline{a})^{d-1}$, and let $\overline{p}_2(t) = t\overline{p}_1(t) + \overline{b} - t\overline{a}$. Then the implicit equation of the rational curve $\overline{\mathcal{C}}$ defined by the parametrization $\overline{P}(t) = (\overline{p}_1(t), \overline{p}_2(t))$ is

$$\overline{f}(x, y) = f(x, y) - T(x, y),$$

where $T(x, y)$ is the Taylor expansion up to order $d - 1$ of $f(x, y)$ at $\overline{P}$.

Theorem 3: $\overline{C}$ is contained in the offset region of C at distance at most

$$2 \cdot \sqrt{2} \cdot \epsilon^{\frac{1}{2d}} \cdot e^2.$$

The following example illustrates the results stated in the previous theorems.

Example 4: (Refer to the paper[54] by Pérez-Díaz and others). We consider $\epsilon = 0.001$ and the curve C of degree 6 defined by the polynomial

$$f(x, y) = y^6 + x^6 + 2.yx^4 - 2.y^4x + 10^{-3}x + .10^{-3}y + 2 \cdot 10^{-3} + 10^{-3}x^4.$$

The point $\overline{P} = (.1875000000 \cdot 10^{-5}, -.50000002 \cdot 10^{-3})$ is an ϵ-singularity of multiplicity 5. Applying Theorem 2 one gets the curve $\overline{C}$ defined by the polynomial

$$\begin{aligned}
\overline{f}(x, y) = & -.1250000464 \cdot 10^{-12}x + .1125000100 \cdot 10^{-14}y \\
& + .9999999873 \cdot 10^{-3}x^4 + 2.yx^4 - 2.y^4x - .1000000173 \cdot 10^{-8}yx \\
& + y^6 + x^6 - .7500000036 \cdot 10^{-8}x^3 + .2499999700 \cdot 10^{-8}y^3 \\
& + .2109375029 \cdot 10^{-13}x^2 - .3000000180 \cdot 10^{-12}y^4 \\
& + .2812500000 \cdot 10^{-11}y^2 + .1562500311 \cdot 10^{-18} \\
& - .1500000000 \cdot 10^{-4}x^3y - .4000000160 \cdot 10^{-2}xy^3 \\
& + .4218750000 \cdot 10^{-10}yx^2 - .3000000240 \cdot 10^{-5}y^2x,
\end{aligned}$$

and its parametrization $\overline{P}(t) = (\overline{p}_1(t), \overline{p}_2(t))$, where

$$\overline{p}_1 = \frac{-2t + .300000012 \cdot 10^{-2}t^5 + .1875 \cdot 10^{-5}t^6 + 2.t^4 - .9375 \cdot 10^{-5}}{1 + t^6},$$

$$\overline{p}_2 = \frac{-.48875002 \cdot 10^{-3} - 2t^4 - .300000012 \cdot 10^{-2}t^5 + 2t - .50000002 \cdot 10^{-3}t^6}{1 + t^6}.$$

The reader may compare the input curve and the rational output curve in Fig. 3.

3. Applications in CAGD

As we have mentioned, CAGD is a natural frame for applications of algebraic curves and surfaces. In this section four of these applications, namely computing with real plane curves defined implicitly, dealing with offset curves and surfaces including the consideration of topological problems and blending several surfaces, are analyzed.

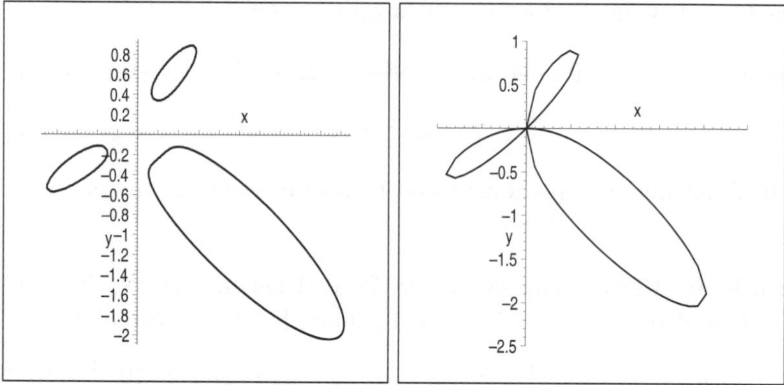

Fig. 3.   Curve $\mathcal{C}$ (left) and curve $\overline{\mathcal{C}}$ (right)

3.1. *Implicit Real Curves Plotting*

A very common problem in CAD systems is the resolution of topological questions when dealing with geometric entities defined by algebraic objects. Probably the simplest one is the determination of the topology of an algebraic curve defined by its implicit equation. For instance, for the polynomial

$$\begin{aligned}
f(x,y) =\ & 279756.0x - 559692.0xy^2 + 279936.0xy^4 + 15588.0y^2x^3 \\
& + 217.0x^5 - 745286.4y^215583.0x^3 + 26043.6x^2 - 2303.9x^4 \\
& + 35.9x^6 + 370656.0y^4 - 72774.0y^2x^2 + 2589.4y^2x^4 \\
& + 1296.0y^6 + 46728.0y^4x^2 + 373334.3900,
\end{aligned}$$

its real drawing appears on the left of Fig. 4. This picture (only quantitative) does not allow one to determine which is the real configuration of the considered curve, while the graph appearing on the right of Fig. 4 gives the right qualitative information looked for. This graph can be computed in a very fast way (a few seconds) by using the algorithms presented by González-Vega and others[35,36] and can be used to resolve topological problems (see Subsection 3.3).

The problem of computing the graph (even topologically) of a planar algebraic curve defined implicitly has received a special attention from computer algebra, since it has been responsible of many advances regarding subresultants, real root counting, infinitesimal computations, *etc.* From the first papers[2,32,58] in computer algebra and real algebraic geometry dealing with this problem, the interested reader can find, in the papers by Cellini *et al.*,[10] Cucker *et al.*,[16] Feng,[26] González-Vega *et al.*[35,36] and Hong,[45] how

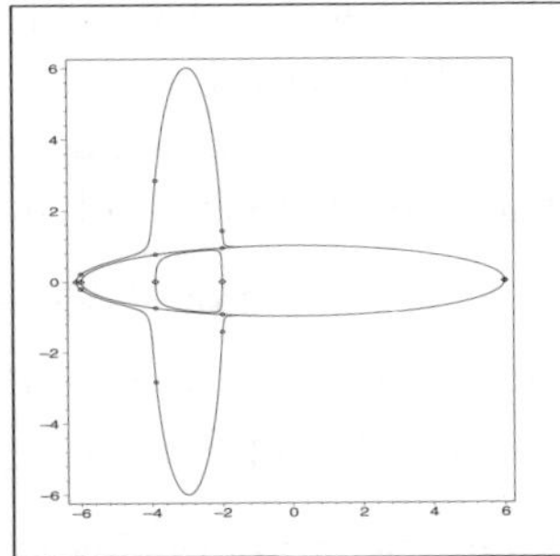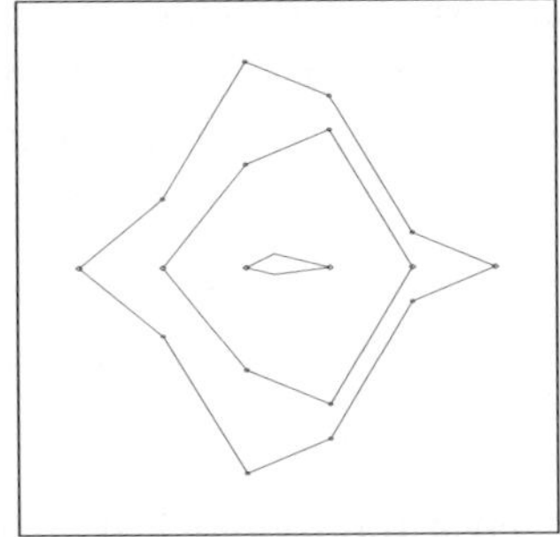

Fig. 4.   Topological resolution of implicitly defined algebraic curves: $f(x, y) = 0$

the theoretical and practical complexities of the algorithms dealing with this problem have been dramatically improved.

The usual strategy to compute the graph (even topologically) of a planar algebraic curve defined implicitly by a polynomial $f(x, y) \in \mathbb{R}[x, y]$ proceeds in the following way.

Step I: Compute the discriminant $R(x)$ of f with respect to y and characterize the real roots α_i of $R(x)$: $\alpha_1 < \cdots < \alpha_r$.

Step II: For every α_i, compute the real roots $\beta_{i,j}$ of $f(\alpha_i, y)$: $\beta_{i,1} < \cdots < \beta_{i,s_i}$.

Step III: For every α_i and $\beta_{i,j}$, compute the number of half-branches to the right and to the left of the point $(\alpha_i, \beta_{i,j})$.

Following the paper[36] by González-Vega and others and in order to avoid the numerical problems arising from the computation of the roots of $R(x)$ and of every $f(\alpha_i, y)$ which always has multiple roots, before starting the computations, a generic linear change of variables is performed in order to have the following condition for every $\alpha \in \mathbb{R}$:

$$\#\left\{\beta \in \mathbb{R} : f(\alpha, \beta) = 0, \frac{\partial f}{\partial y}(\alpha, \beta) = 0\right\} \le 1.$$

This assures that for every real root α_i of $R(x)$, there is only one critical point of the curve in the vertical line $x = \alpha_i$, whose y-coordinate can be rationally described in terms of α_i. Moreover this allows one to symbolically construct, from every $f(\alpha_i, y)$, a squarefree polynomial $g_i(\alpha_i, y)$ whose real roots need to be computed in order to finish with the so-called Step II. Step III is thus accomplished by merely computing the number of real roots of the squarefree polynomials $f(\gamma_i, y)$ ($i \in \{0, 1, \dots, r + 1\}$) with $\gamma_0 = -\infty$, $\gamma_{r+1} = \infty$ and γ_i being any real number in the open interval (α_i, α_{i+1}).

These computations provide a graph of the considered curve which is very helpful when the curve is going to be traced numerically, since we know exactly how to proceed when coming closer to a complicated point.

A more complicated example is given by the squarefree polynomial

$$g(x,y) = y^8 + y^7 + (-7x - 8)y^6 + (21x^2 - 7)y^5 + (-35x^3 + 35x + 20)y^4$$
$$+ (35x^4 - 70x^2 + 14)y^3 + (-21x^5 + 70x^3 - 42x - 16)y^2$$
$$+ (7x^6 - 35x^4 + 42x^2 - 7)y - x^7 + 7x^5 - 14x^3 + 7x + 2.$$

In Fig. 5, both the topological structure and the true drawing of the real algebraic plane curve defined by f are displayed. The real drawing of the curve is obtained by using the information contained in the graph providing the topological structure.

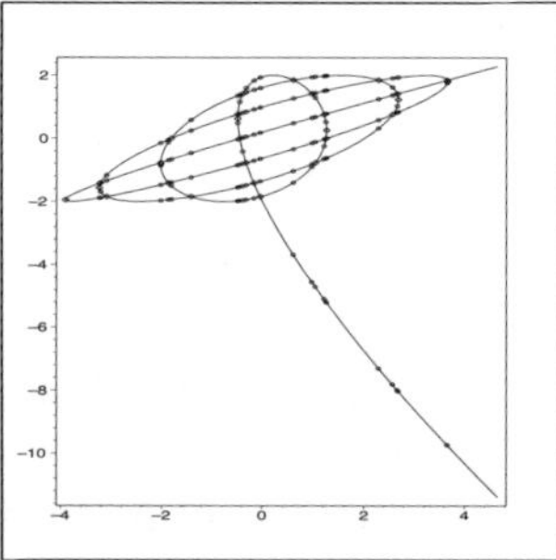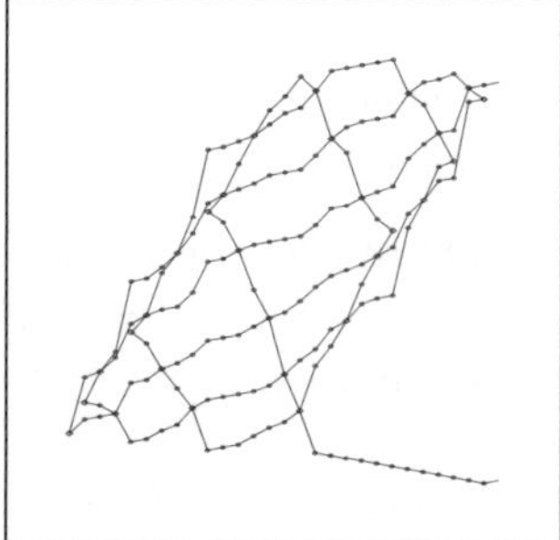

Fig. 5.   Topological resolution of implicitly defined algebraic curves: $g(x,y) = 0$

3.2. *Offsetting*

Given an algebraic variety, in practice a curve or a surface, in some computer aided geometric design applications one needs to compute its offsets. That is, one considers a geometric manipulation of the original variety that generates a new algebraic variety. This offsetting construction essentially consists in computing the envelope $\mathcal{O}_d(\mathcal{V})$ of a system of hyperspheres with fixed, but probably undetermined, distance d and centered at the points of the original algebraic set $\mathcal{V}$ (for a formal definition of offsets see for instance the paper[3] by Arrondo and others). Alternatively, one may see the offset $\mathcal{O}_d(\mathcal{V})$ to a hypersurface $\mathcal{V}$, at distance d, as the Zariski closure of the constructible set consisting of the intersection points of the hyperspheres of radius d centered at each point $P \in \mathcal{V}_0$ and the normal line to $\mathcal{V}$ at P, where $\mathcal{V}_0 \subset \mathcal{V}$ is the set of regular points of $\mathcal{V}$ that have non-zero isotropic normal vectors to $\mathcal{V}$. In Fig. 6 we illustrate the offsetting of the parabola $y = x^2$ at distance 1.

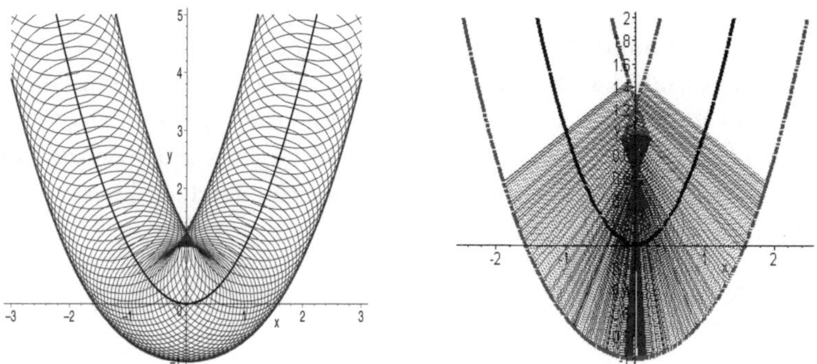

Fig. 6.   Offsetting of $y = x^2$ at $d = 1$

Some interesting problems concerning offsets, and related to Algebraic Geometry, have been addressed by many authors. In particular, implicitization problems,[40,41,65] parametrization problems,[3,49,55,56,63] analysis of topological, algebraic, and geometric properties of the offset in terms of the corresponding properties of the initial variety[4,24,25,62], *etc.*, have been considered.

In this section we report on the characterization of the unirationality of offsets and on the direct parametrization algorithm for offsets to rational surfaces following the ideas in the papers by Arrondo *et al.*[3] and by Sendra and Sendra;[63] a similar treatment can be done for the case of plane curves (see the paper[3] by Arrondo and others or Sendra's Ph.D. thesis[60]).

Unirationality of offsets to surfaces can be characterized by means of the notion of *Rational Pythagorean Hodograph* (RPH) and, more effectively, by means of the concept of *reparametrizing hypersurface* (see the paper[3] by Arrondo and others, and the paper[56] by Pottmann). These concepts do not depend on the distance. They depend only on the initial surface. More precisely, let

$$\mathcal{P}(\bar{t}) = (P_1(\bar{t}), P_2(\bar{t}), P_3(\bar{t}))$$

be a rational parametrization of a surface $\mathcal{V}$. Then, we say that $\mathcal{P}(\bar{t})$ is RPH if the normal vector

$$\mathcal{N}(\bar{t}) = (N_1(\bar{t}), N_2(\bar{t}), N_3(\bar{t}))$$

associated with $\mathcal{P}(\bar{t})$ satisfies the condition

$$N_1(\bar{t})^2 + N_2(\bar{t})^2 + N_3(\bar{t})^2 = m(\bar{t})^2,$$

where $m(\bar{t})$ is a rational function.

On the other hand, let $\mathcal{N}(\bar{t}) = (N_1(\bar{t}), N_2(\bar{t}), N_3(\bar{t}))$ be the normal vector of $\mathcal{V}$ associated with $\mathcal{P}(\bar{t})$ (we assume, without loss of generality, that $N_2(\bar{t})$ in not identically zero). Then, we define the *reparametrizing surface of the offset $\mathcal{O}_d(\mathcal{V})$ to $\mathcal{V}$ associated with $\mathcal{P}(\bar{t})$* as the surface defined by the primitive part, w.r.t. x_3, of the numerator of the irreducible expression of the rational function

$$x_3^2 \sum_{i=2}^{3} N_i^2(x_1, x_2) - N_2^2(x_1, x_2) - 2\, x_3\, N_1(x_1, x_2)\, N_2(x_1, x_2).$$

We denote by $\mathcal{G}_\mathcal{P}(\mathcal{V})$ the reparametrizing surface of $\mathcal{O}_d(\mathcal{V})$ associated with $\mathcal{P}(\bar{t})$.

In this situation, one deduces[3] the following characterization of the rationality.

Theorem 5: The following statements are equivalent:

(1) $\mathcal{V}$ is rational and there exists an RPH parametrization of $\mathcal{V}$.
(2) All the components of $\mathcal{O}_d(\mathcal{V})$ are rational.
(3) There exists a proper parametrization $\mathcal{P}$ of $\mathcal{V}$ such that $\mathcal{G}_\mathcal{P}(\mathcal{V})$ has, at least, one rational component. Furthermore, if

$$\varphi(t_1, t_2) = (\varphi_1(t_1, t_2), \varphi_2(t_1, t_2), \varphi_3(t_1, t_2))$$

is a rational parametrization of one component of $\mathcal{G}_\mathcal{P}(\mathcal{V})$, then the parametrization $\mathcal{P}(\varphi_1(t_1, t_2), \varphi_2(t_1, t_2))$ is RPH.
(4) For all proper parametrizations $\mathcal{P}$ of $\mathcal{V}$, $\mathcal{G}_\mathcal{P}(\mathcal{V})$ has, at least, one rational component.

In addition, from the analysis of unirationality presented by Arrondo and others[3], one deduces that offsets of rational surfaces have the following behavior: they are reducible with two rational components, or they are rational, or irreducible and non-rational. Furthermore, we can derive[3] criteria to distinguish among these cases.

Theorem 6: (Criterion of double rationality). Let $\mathcal{V}$ be rational; then the following statements are equivalent:

(1) There exists an RPH proper parametrization of $\mathcal{V}$.

(2) All proper parametrizations of $\mathcal{V}$ are RPH.

(3) $\mathcal{O}_d(\mathcal{V})$ is reducible.

(4) There exists a proper parametrization $\mathcal{P}$ of $\mathcal{V}$ such that $\mathcal{G}_\mathcal{P}(\mathcal{V})$ is reducible.

(5) For all proper parametrizations $\mathcal{P}$ of $\mathcal{V}$, $\mathcal{G}_\mathcal{P}(\mathcal{V})$ is reducible.

(6) There exists a proper parametrization $\mathcal{P}$ of $\mathcal{V}$ such that $\mathcal{G}_\mathcal{P}(\mathcal{V})$ has two rational components.

(7) For all proper parametrizations $\mathcal{P}$ of $\mathcal{V}$, $\mathcal{G}_\mathcal{P}(\mathcal{V})$ has two rational components.

Theorem 7: (Criterion of rationality). Let $\mathcal{V}$ be rational; then the following statements are equivalent:

(1) There exists an RPH rational parametrization of $\mathcal{V}$, but there does not exist a proper RPH rational parametrization of $\mathcal{V}$.

(2) $\mathcal{O}_d(\mathcal{V})$ is rational (and therefore irreducible).

(3) There exists a proper parametrization $\mathcal{P}$ of $\mathcal{V}$ such that $\mathcal{G}_\mathcal{P}(\mathcal{V})$ is rational.

(4) For all proper parametrizations $\mathcal{P}$ of $\mathcal{V}$, $\mathcal{G}_\mathcal{P}(\mathcal{V})$ is rational.

From these results one may derive an algorithm that deduces the rationality of the components of the offset to a rational surface given parametrically and that, in the affirmative case, obtains a rational parametrization. We illustrate these ideas by the following example.

Example 8: (See the paper[63] by Sendra and Sendra). Let $\mathcal{V}$ be the surface in $\mathbb{C}^3$ defined by

$$F(y_1, y_2, y_3) = 16\, y_1^4 - 3\, y_2^2\, y_3^4 - y_3^6 - y_2^6 - 3\, y_3^2\, y_2^4.$$

$\mathcal{V}$ can be properly parametrized as

$$\mathcal{P}(t_1, t_2) = \left(\frac{t_2^3}{2}, \frac{(-1 + t_1^2)\, t_2^2}{t_1^2 + 1}, \frac{2\, t_1\, t_2^2}{t_1^2 + 1} \right).$$

First, we compute the normal vector of $\mathcal{V}$ associated with $\mathcal{P}$:

$$\mathcal{N}(t_1, t_2) = \left(\frac{4\, t_2^3}{t_1^2 + 1}, \frac{-3\, t_2^4\, (-1 + t_1^2)}{(t_1^2 + 1)^2}, \frac{-6\, t_1\, t_2^4}{(t_1^2 + 1)^2} \right)$$

and we check that

$$\|\mathcal{N}(t_1, t_2)\| = \frac{t_2^3\, \sqrt{16 + 9\, t_2^2}}{(t_1^2 + 1)} \notin \mathbb{C}(t_1, t_2).$$

Therefore, $\mathcal{P}$ is not RPH. As a consequence, $\mathcal{O}_d(\mathcal{V})$ is irreducible. In order to study whether $\mathcal{O}_d(\mathcal{V})$ is rational, we compute the reparametrizing surface

$$H = -3x_2 + 6x_2 x_1^2 + 3x_2 x_3 + 3x_2 x_3 x_1^4 + 6x_2 x_3 x_1^2 - 3x_2 x_1^4 + 8x_3 x_1^4 - 8x_3,$$

which is a rational surface and can be parametrized by

$$\mathcal{R} = (R_1, R_2, R_3) = \left(t_1, \frac{-3\,t_2\,(t_1^4 - 1)}{8\,(t_2 + 2\,t_2\,t_1^2 + t_2\,t_1^4 - 1 + 2\,t_1^2 - t_1^4)}, t_2 \right).$$

In this situation, we conclude that $\mathcal{O}_d(\mathcal{V})$ is rational and that it can be parametrized as

$$\mathcal{S}(t_1, t_2) = \mathcal{P}(R_1, R_2) + d\,\frac{R_3\,\mathcal{N}(R_1, R_2)}{M_1(R_1, R_2)\,R_3 + M_2(R_1, R_2)},$$

where $M_1(t_1, t_2)$ and $M_2(t_1, t_2)$ are the numerators of the first and second components of the normal vector $\mathcal{N}(t_1, t_2)$.

3.3. *Topological Problems*

The resolution of topological problems in CAGD constitutes the main source of qualitative information, which guides the major part of the computation processes. In this section we present one problem in which the determination of the topology represents an indispensable step before starting the purely numeric resolution.

The problem is connected with the determination of the situations when changes of topology (between the topology of the considered curve or surface and the topology of the offset) appear. In the particular case of the parabola $y = x^2$, it can be proved that the topological change of the distance d offset curve appears when $d = 1/2$.

The implicit equation of the distance $d > 0$ offset of the parabola $y = x^2$ is

$$\begin{aligned}
&16x^6 + 16x^4 y^2 - 40x^4 y - 32x^2 y^3 + (1 - 48d^2)x^4 + (-32d^2 + 32)x^2 y^2 \\
&+ 16y^4 + (8d^2 - 2)x^2 y + (-32d^2 - 8)y^3 + (-20d^2 + 48d^4)x^2 \\
&+ (-8d^2 + 1 + 16d^4)y^2 + (8d^2 + 32d^4)y - 8d^4 - 16d^6 - d^2 = 0
\end{aligned}$$

and its discriminant with respect to the variable y is

$$x(64x^6 + (48 - 192d^2)x^4 + (192d^4 + 336d^2 + 12)x^2 - 64d^6 - 12d^2 + 48d^4 + 1).$$

Then, the offset of the parabola is not topologically a parabola when the polynomial

$$64x^3 + (48 - 192d^2)x^2 + (192d^4 + 336d^2 + 12)x - 64d^6 - 12d^2 + 48d^4 + 1$$

$$\tag{4}$$

has a real positive root. By using the Sturm–Habicht sequence together with the techniques developed by the first author,[33] we conclude that:

- The number of real roots of the polynomial (4) is determined by the behavior of the polynomials

$$[1, 1, -d^2, -d^4(4d^2 + 1)^2].$$

  In this case, the number is always equal to 1 (for any d).
- The number of real positive roots of the polynomial (4) is determined by the behavior of the polynomials

$$[1, (2d - 1)(2d + 1), -d^2(20d^2 + 1)(4d^2 + 5),$$
$$-d^4(4d^2 + 1)^2(2d - 1)^3(2d + 1)^3].$$

  In this case, the number is always equal to 0 for any $d \in (0, 1/2)$.

The topological variation of the offsets of the parabola for different values of d is presented in Fig. 7. The isolated point appearing for $d = 0$ coincides with the parabola focal point and appears in the cases corresponding to $d \in (0, 1/2)$ from the complex part: if

$$u = \pm\sqrt{1 + 4d^2},$$

then the parametrization of the offset

$$x(u) = u \pm \frac{2du}{\sqrt{1 + 4u^2}}, \quad y(u) = u^2 \mp \frac{d}{\sqrt{1 + 4u^2}}$$

gives the point $(0, d^2 + 1/4)$. However, the point $(0, d^2 + 1/4)$ (when $d \in (0, 1/2)$) may be seen as exceptional points of the offset to the parabola, because it is not generated from a real point of the curve considered initially.

3.4. *Blending*

Computing blending and modeling surfaces is one of the central problems in CAGD.[41,46] In many applications, objects are modeled as a collection of several surfaces whose pieces join smoothly. This situation leads directly to the blending problem in the sense that a blending surface is a surface that provides a smooth transition between distinct geometric features of an object.[27,43,44,66]

More precisely, if one is given a collection of surfaces $V_1, \ldots, V_n$ (*primary surfaces*) to be blended, and a collection of auxiliary surfaces $U_1, \ldots, U_n$ (*clipping surfaces*), then the blending problem deals with the computation of a surface V (*blending surface*) containing the space curves $C_i = U_i \cap V_i$

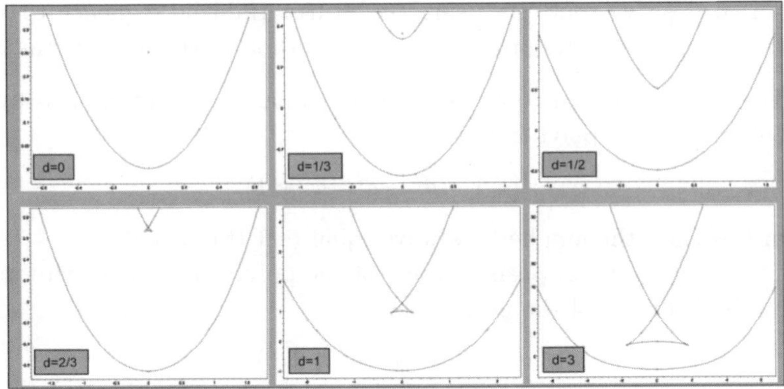

Fig. 7.   Topological variation for the offsets of the parabola $y = x^2$

(*clipping curves*), such that V meets each V_i at C_i with "certain" smooth conditions. Such conditions may be introduced with the notion of G^k-continuity (see the Ph.D. thesis[17] by DeRose).

Intuitively speaking, the G^k-continuity consists in requiring that the Taylor expansions at C_i of the different pieces of the object agree till certain order with the corresponding Taylor expansion of the blending surface. In particular, let $C \subset V_1 \cap V_2$ be an irreducible curve such that V_1, V_2 are smooth at all but finitely many points on C. Then, we say that V_1 meets V_2 with G^k-*continuity* if there exists parametrizations $\mathcal{P}_1$, $\mathcal{P}_2$ of V_1, V_2 respectively such that all partial derivatives of $\mathcal{P}_1$ and $\mathcal{P}_2$ up to order k agree along C. If the surfaces V_1, V_2 are not rational, then the G^k-continuity of V_1, V_2 along an irreducible curve $C \subset V_1 \cap V_2$ can be introduced by requiring that there exists two polynomials $A(x_1, x_2, x_3)$, $B(x_1, x_2, x_3)$, not identically zero along C, such that all derivatives of $AF_1 - BF_2$ up to order k vanish along C, where F_1 and F_2 are the implicit equations of V_1 and V_2 respectively (see the paper[67] by Warren). When the considered surfaces are rational, both definitions of G^k-continuity (for the parametric and the implicit cases) agree (see the paper[31] by Garrity and Warren).

In Fig. 8, we illustrate an example of blending where the primary surfaces are a cylinder, a cone and a sphere, and the clipping surfaces are planes parallel to the floor.

The blending problem may be approached from two different points of view, namely, implicitly[44,67] where an implicit expression of the solution is computed, or parametrically[28,39,51,52,53,57,64] where parametric outputs are reached. Furthermore, a second consideration, depending on whether

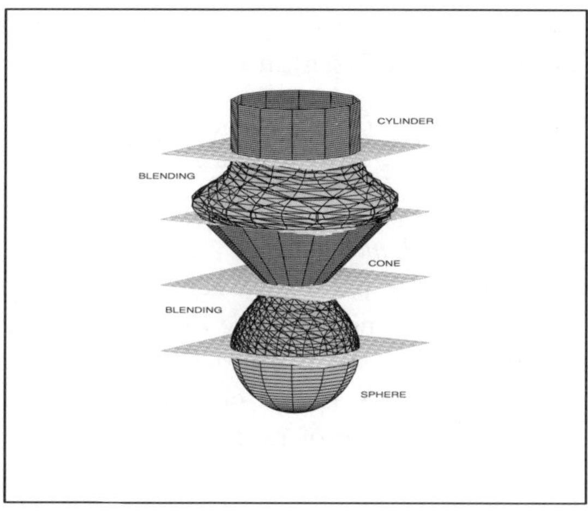

Fig. 8. Primary surfaces (cylinder, cone, sphere), clipping surfaces (planes parallel to the floor), and blending surface

symbolic[46,64] or numerical[8,27,37,46] techniques are used, can be made.

For the implicit blending problem, Hoffmann and Hopcroft proved that using the potential method[44] one may compute all possible implicit solutions for the case of two quadrics with G^1-continuity. Afterwards, Warren[66] extended these results to the general case, stating that all solutions are in the intersection of some polynomial ideals generated by the implicit equations of V_i, and powers of the equations of U_i. This result (that we will refer to as Hoffmann–Warren's theorem) gives a description of the space of solutions for the surface blending problem.

For the symbolic parametric version of the blending problem, one considers that surfaces and curves are rational and that they are given by parametrizations. More precisely, in this case, one is given $k \in \mathbb{N}$ and a pair $\mathcal{S} = (\overline{P}, \overline{s})$, where

- $\overline{\mathcal{P}} = (\mathcal{P}_1(t, h), \ldots, \mathcal{P}_n(t, h)) \in (\mathbb{K}(t, h)^3)^n$, $\mathbb{K}$ is an algebraically close field, and $\mathcal{P}_i(t, h)$ is a regular parametrization of the primary surface V_i in C_i (that is, for almost all points $P_i \in C_i$ such that there exists $(t_0, h_0) \in \mathbb{K}^2$ with $P_i = \mathcal{P}_i(t_0, h_0)$, the vectors

$$\{\partial \mathcal{P}_i(t_0, h_0)/\partial h,\ \partial \mathcal{P}_i(t_0, h_0)/\partial t\}$$

are linearly independent),
- $\overline{s} = (s_0, \ldots, s_{n-1}) \in \mathbb{K}^n$ is a vector of n different elements such that $\mathcal{Q}_i(t) = \mathcal{P}_i(t, s_{i-1})$ parametrizes the clipping curve C_i,

and one looks for parametric solutions, $\mathcal{T}(t,h)$, for $\mathcal{S}$ with G^k-continuity; i.e., a regular parametrization $\mathcal{T}(t,h)$ in C_i such that for $i = 1,\ldots,n$,

$$\frac{\partial^j \mathcal{T}}{\partial^j h}(t, s_{i-1}) = \frac{\partial^j \mathcal{P}_i}{\partial^j h}(t, s_{i-1}), \quad j = 0,\ldots,k$$

(see DeRose's Ph.D. thesis,[17] or the paper[53] by Pérez-Díaz and Sendra). A pair $\mathcal{S}$ as above is called a *blending data*.

In this situation, the set of parametric solutions of the blending is also algebraically well structured, and therefore there exists a "parametric version" of Hoffmann–Warren's theorem. Pérez-Díaz and Sendra[53] have shown that for a given blending data $\mathcal{S}$, the set of all parametric solutions can be directly related to a free module of rank 3. More precisely, one has the following theorem.

Theorem 9: Let $\mathcal{T}_p(t,h)$ be a particular parametric solution of the parametric blending problem. Then, the set of all the parametric solutions for $\mathcal{S}$ with G^k-continuity can be expressed as

$$\mathcal{T}_p(t,h) + \prod_{i=0}^{n-1} (h - s_i)^{k+1} \cdot \left(\frac{N_1}{M_1}, \frac{N_2}{M_2}, \frac{N_3}{M_3} \right),$$

where $N_i, M_i \in \mathbb{K}[t,h]$ and $\gcd\left(\prod_{i=0}^{n-1}(h - s_i), M_i \right) = 1$.

Therefore, taking into account this result, the problem of computing all rational G^k blendings for several surfaces is reduced to the determination of a particular parametric solution. There are several methods that approach this problem.[28,39,52] The following two theorems[53] show how to compute particular solutions for the blending data $\mathcal{S}$ with G^k-continuity.

Theorem 10: Let $u_1,\ldots,u_n \in \mathbb{K} \setminus \{0,1\}$ and for $i = 1,\ldots,n$ let

$$f_i(h) = \frac{u_i \prod_{j=1}^{i-2} (h - s_{j-1})^{k+1} \prod_{j=i-1, j\neq i}^{n} (s_{j-1} - h)^{k+1}}{(1 - u_i)(h - s_{i-1})^{k+1} + u_i \prod_{j=1}^{i-2} (h - s_{j-1})^{k+1} \prod_{j=i-1, j\neq i}^{n} (s_{j-1} - h)^{k+1}}.$$

Then, a parametric solution for $\mathcal{S}$ with G^k-continuity is given by

$$\mathcal{T}_p(t,h) = f_1(h)\mathcal{P}_1(t,h) + \cdots + f_n(h)\mathcal{P}_n(t,h).$$

Theorem 11: A parametric solution for $\mathcal{S}$ with G^k-continuity is given by

$$\mathcal{T}_p(t,h) = \sum_{i=1}^{n}\sum_{\ell=0}^{k} \frac{1}{\ell!}\left[\frac{\partial^\ell}{\partial^\ell h}\left(\frac{(h-s_{i-1})^{k+1}}{\prod_{i=1}^{n}(h-s_{i-1})^{k+1}}\right)\right]_{s_{i-1}} \frac{\prod_{i=1}^{n}(h-s_{i-1})^{k+1}}{(h-s_{i-1})^{k+1-\ell}}\,\mathcal{Q}_i(t)$$

$$+ \sum_{i=1}^{n}\sum_{j=1}^{k} \frac{\partial^j \mathcal{P}_i}{\partial^j h}(t,s_{i-1}) \sum_{\ell=0}^{k-j} \frac{1}{\ell!j!}\left[\frac{\partial^\ell}{\partial^\ell h}\left(\frac{(h-s_{i-1})^{k+1}}{\prod_{i=1}^{n}(h-s_{i-1})^{k+1}}\right)\right]_{s_{i-1}}$$

$$\cdot \frac{\prod_{i=1}^{n}(h-s_{i-1})^{k+1}}{(h-s_{i-1})^{k+1-j-\ell}}.$$

Combining the above results one may derive an algorithm to compute all parametric solutions for a blending data $\mathcal{S}$. In the following example we illustrate these ideas.

Example 12: Let V_i, $i = 1,\ldots,4$, be the primary surfaces parametrized by

$$\mathcal{P}_1(t,h) = \left(\frac{t^2-1}{2(t^2+1)}, h+4, \frac{t+6+6t^2}{t^2+1}\right),$$

$$\mathcal{P}_2(t,h) = \left(\frac{t^2-1}{t^2+1}, h+2, \frac{2t}{t^2+1}\right),$$

$$\mathcal{P}_3(t,h) = \left(\frac{t^2-1}{t^2+1}, 2 - \frac{3(h-2)(5t^2+5-6t)}{4(t^2+1)}, \frac{2t}{t^2+1}\right),$$

$$\mathcal{P}_4(t,h) = \left(\frac{t^2-1}{t^2+1}, \frac{2t}{t^2+1}, 2 + \frac{4(h-3)(-t+t^2+1)}{t^2+1}\right),$$

and the clipping curves C_i, $i = 1,\ldots,4$, be defined by

$$\mathcal{Q}_1(t) = \mathcal{P}_1(t,0), \quad \mathcal{Q}_2(t) = \mathcal{P}_2(t,1), \quad \mathcal{Q}_3(t) = \mathcal{P}_3(t,2), \quad \mathcal{Q}_4(t) = \mathcal{P}_4(t,3).$$

We consider the problem of blending four surfaces with G^1-continuity. By applying Theorem 11 to the rational blending data

$$\mathcal{S} = ((\mathcal{P}_1,\mathcal{P}_2,\mathcal{P}_3,\mathcal{P}_4),(0,1,2,3)),$$

Fig. 9.   Primary surfaces and blending surface with G^1-continuity

one gets the following blending surface for $\mathcal{S}$ with G^1-continuity (see Fig. 9):

$$
\begin{aligned}
\mathcal{T}_p(t,h) = \ & (-1/216(t^2-1)(-129h^6+11h^7+602h^5-1410h^4+1691h^3 \\
& -873h^2-108)/(t^2+1), \\
& -1/432(-1728-432h+4044th^6-398th^7+28248th^4-15596th^5 \\
& +h^7+7224h^4-432ht^2-10823h^3+210h^6-2066h^5+7596th^2 \\
& -23894th^3+6318h^2t^2-10823h^3t^2+6318h^2+h^7t^2-1728t^2 \\
& +7224h^4t^2-2066h^5t^2+210h^6t^2)/(t^2+1), \\
& 1/108(648+108t+33th^6-th^7+822th^4-256th^5+56h^7-7872h^4 \\
& +9674h^3-678h^6+3266h^5+729th^2-1219th^3-5094h^2t^2 \\
& +9674h^3t^2-5094h^2+56h^7t^2+648t^2-7872h^4t^2+3266h^5t^2 \\
& -678h^6t^2)/(t^2+1)).
\end{aligned}
$$

Thus, by Theorem 9 all the parametric solutions for $\mathcal{S}$ with G^1-continuity are

$$
\mathcal{T}_p(t,h) + h^2(h-1)^2(h-2)^2(h-3)^2 \left(\frac{N_1}{M_1}, \frac{N_2}{M_2}, \frac{N_3}{M_3} \right),
$$

where $N_i, M_i \in \mathbb{K}[t,h]$ and $\gcd(h(h-1)(h-2)(h-3), M_i) = 1$.

Another interesting problem in this context is the computation and characterization of existence of polynomial parametric solutions because they avoid the unstable numerical behavior of the denominators when tracing the surface. In this situation, one may state the result analogous to Theorem 9 for the polynomial case (see the paper[53] by Pérez-Díaz and Sendra).

Theorem 13: Let $\mathcal{T}_p^{\mathrm{Pol}}(t,h)$ be a particular polynomial solution of the parametric blending problem. Then, the set of all the parametric polynomial solutions for $\mathcal{S}$ with G^k-continuity can be expressed as

$$\mathcal{T}_p^{\mathrm{Pol}}(t,h) + \prod_{i=0}^{n-1}(h-s_i)^{k+1} \cdot (R_1, R_2, R_3)\,, \quad \text{where } R_i \in \mathbb{K}[t,h].$$

Moreover, a criterion to decide whether there exist parametric polynomial solutions is stated in the paper[53] by Pérez-Díaz and Sendra. In addition, Theorem 11 always reaches a polynomial parametrization if there exists any. More precisely, one has the following theorem.

Theorem 14: There exist parametric polynomial solutions for $\mathcal{S}$ with G^k-continuity if and only if the rational functions

$$\frac{\partial^j \mathcal{P}_i}{\partial^j h}(t, s_{i-1}), \quad j = 0, \ldots, k, \ i = 1, \ldots, n,$$

are polynomials. Furthermore, Theorem 11 outputs a parametric polynomial solution for $\mathcal{S}$, if there exists any.

4. Practical Performance of Algebraic Techniques in CAGD

This last section contains two examples where some of the algebraic techniques presented in the previous sections are being successfully applied in practice to solve two real problems in the company CANDEMAT devoted to constructing bids for the automotive industry.

4.1. *Sectioning B-spline Surfaces*

A successful application of the generic implicitization procedures described in Subsection 2.1 has been the sectioning of a B-spline surface, i.e., the intersection of the considered surface with a plane.

When the user needs, for instance, to section a surface, its type is determined (in our case, the type of the surface defined by (2) is polynomial of degrees

$$x : [u \to 0, v \to 2], \quad y : [u \to 2, v \to 0], \quad z : [u \to 1, v \to 1])$$

and then the database is accessed, in order to obtain the generic algebraic expression (in our case, the equation in (3)). By evaluating this expression, and taking into account the concrete values of the parameters for the considered surface, the implicit equations are obtained.

Consider all the patches (implicitly represented) defining the B-spline surface to be sectioned by the plane $x = k$. For each patch, and with the equation $x(u, v) = k$, we compute the intersection of this curve (in the u–v domain) with the boundary of the definition domain (i.e., starting with $u = 0$, and then $u = 1$, $v = 0$ and $v = 1$, usually two points are determined at most). By evaluating these points in the parametrization we obtain the extremes of the section on the B-spline surface. With each point computed before, and by using the implicit equation, every component of the section is discretized (always inside the plane $x = k$). The points computed before are interpolated by using a cubic spline curve representing the section of the considered patch. The previous steps are repeated for every patch of the considered surface (see the papers[20,21] by Espinola and others).

When topological problems appear, the algorithms described in Subsection 3.1 are applied in order to resolve the configuration problems (for example the appearing of closed components).

Figure 10 shows how the sectioning looks like, by using the generic implicitization, of a concrete object in the CAD/CAM environment CSIS of the company CANDEMAT.

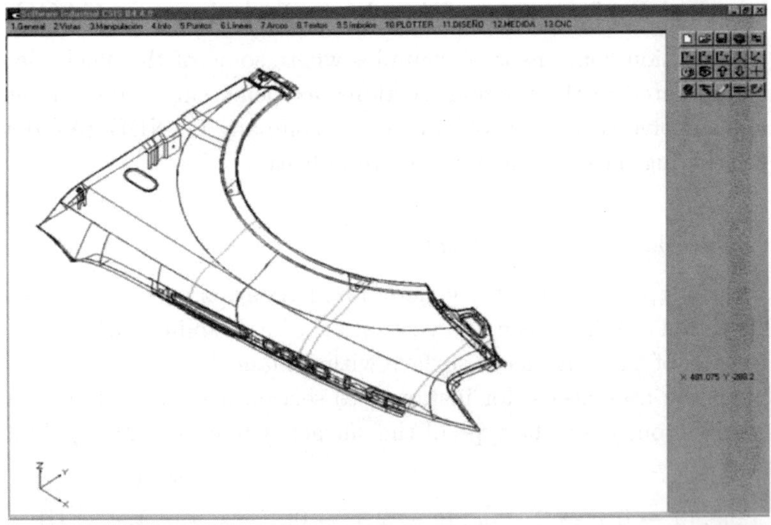

Fig. 10.　Sectioning an implicit B-spline surface

4.2. *Shape Error Control*

The availability of shape error measurement tools is an obvious necessity in the field of quality control in industry, where parts are made according to a theoretical mathematical model. When dealing with surfaces the objective is to establish whether or not the shape of a specific area is correct in terms of the theoretical definition of the mathematical entity irrespective of its position in 3D space.

In our case a theoretical model, and an actual one made from the first as reference, are available. The measuring of errors is based on corresponding points in the theoretical surface model and the actual surface. The points are previously chosen for the detection of faults in regions of the actual surface. The points are given in two different positions in 3D space and one tries to find a Euclidean transformation between them, allowing the evaluation of errors in such a way that it is guaranteed that the tolerances specified by the standards are verified.

The method (see the paper[22] by Espinola and others for more details) finds the rigid motion, moving the first set of points as close as possible to the second one. This is made by introducing a non-linear least-squares problem where the unknowns to be determined are the parameters of the rigid motion (the translation and the three angles of the rotation). The structure of this non-linear least-squares problem allows its resolution in closed form by using several symbolic methods (and the computer algebra system Maple). Thus the error is computed by applying this optimal rigid motion to the first set of points and then making the differences.

Figure 11 shows how the algorithm sketched above works in practice in the software CSIS of the company CANDEMAT.

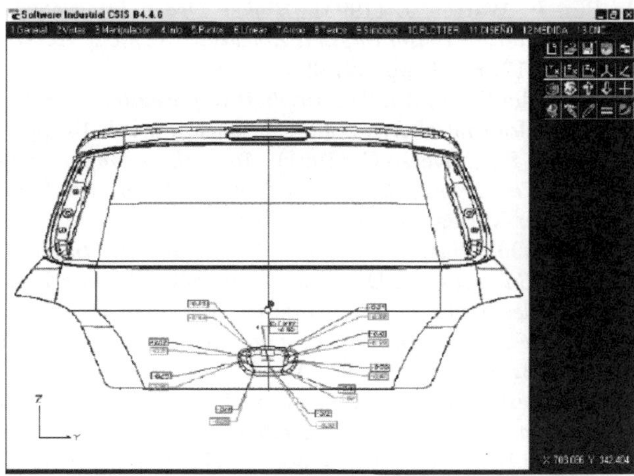

Fig. 11.   Shape error computation

Acknowledgments

This work was supported by the Spanish projects BFM2002-04402-C02-01 (the last three authors), BFM2002-04402-C02-02 (the first and second authors) and by the EU funded project GAIA II (IST-2001-35512). The authors would like to thank the referees for their valuable comments and relevant suggestions on the originally submitted manuscript.

References

1. Alonso C., Gutierrez J., Recio T. (1995). *An Implicitization Algorithm with Fewer Variables*. Computer Aided Geometric Design vol. 12, no. 3, pp. 251–258.
2. Arnon D., McCallum S. (1988). *A Polynomial Time Algorithm for the Topological Type of a Real Algebraic Curve*. Journal of Symbolic Computation vol. 5, pp. 213–236.
3. Arrondo E., Sendra J., Sendra J. R. (1997). *Parametric Generalized Offsets to Hypersurfaces*. Journal of Symbolic Computation vol. 23, pp. 267–285.
4. Arrondo E., Sendra J., Sendra J. R. (1999). *Genus Formula for Generalized Offset Curves*, Journal of Pure and Applied Algebra vol. 136, no. 3, pp. 199–209.
5. Bajaj C. (1993). *The Emergence of Algebraic Curves and Surfaces in Geometric Design*. Directions in Geometric Computing, R. Martin (ed.), pp. 1–29. Information Geometers Press, Winchester, UK.
6. Bajaj C. (ed.) (1994). *Algebraic Geometry and its Applications*. Springer-Verlag, Berlin Heidelberg New York.
7. Bajaj C., Royappa A. (2000). *Parametrization in Finite Precision*. Algorithmica vol. 27, no. 1, pp. 100–114.
8. Bajaj C., Ihm I., Warren J. (1993). *Higher Order Interpolation and Least Squares Approximation Using Implicit Algebraic Surfaces*. ACM Transactions on Graphics vol. 12, no. 4, pp. 327–347.
9. Canny F., Manocha D. (1992). *The Implicit Representation of Rational Parametric Surfaces*. Journal of Symbolic Computation vol. 13, pp. 485–510.
10. Cellini P., Gianni P., Traverso C. (1991). *Algorithms for the Shape of Semialgebraic Sets: A New Approach*. Lecture Notes in Computer Science vol. 539, pp. 1–18, Springer-Verlag, Berlin Heidelberg.
11. Chionh E. W. (1990). *Base Points, Resultants, and the Implicit Representation of Rational Surfaces*. Ph.D. thesis, University of Waterloo, Canada.
12. Corless R. M., Giesbrecht M. W., Kotsireas I. S., van Hoeij M., Watt S. M. (2001). *Towards Factoring Bivariate Approximate Polynomials*. Proc. ISSAC 2001, Mourrain B. (ed.), pp. 85–92. ACM Press, New York.
13. Corless R. M., Giesbrecht M. W., Kotsireas I. S., Watt S. M. (2000). *Numerical Implicitization of Parametric Hypersurfaces with Linear Algebra*. Lecture Notes in Artificial Intelligence vol. 1930, pp. 174–183. Springer-Verlag, Berlin Heidelberg.
14. Cox D., Little J., O'Shea D. (1993). *Ideals, Varieties and Algorithms*. Un-

dergraduate Texts in Mathematics. Springer-Verlag, Berlin Heidelberg New York.

15. Cox D., Little J., O'Shea D. (1998). *Using Algebraic Geometry*. Graduate Texts in Mathematics vol. 185. Springer-Verlag, Berlin Heidelberg New York.

16. Cucker F., González-Vega L., Rosello F. (1991). *On Algorithms for Real Algebraic Plane Curves*. Effective Methods in Algebraic Geometry, Mora T., Traverso C. (eds.), Progress in Mathematics vol. 94, pp. 63–88. Birkhäuser, Boston.

17. DeRose A. D. (1985). *Geometric Continuity: A Parametrization Independent Measure of Continuity for Computer Aided Geometric Design*. Ph.D. thesis, Computer Science Department, University of California, Berkeley, USA.

18. Dokken T. (2001). *Approximate Implicitization*. Mathematical Methods in CAGD, pp. 81–102. Vanderbilt University Press.

19. Espinola J., González-Vega L., Nécula I. (2001). *Algebraic Methods for Sectioning Parametric Surfaces*. Computer Algebra in Scientific Computing CASC-01, Lectures Notes in Computer Science XII, pp. 283–295. Springer-Verlag, Berlin Heidelberg.

20. Espinola J., González-Vega L., Nécula I. (2002). *An Algorithm for the Approximate Conversion of Rational B-spline Curves/Surfaces to Integral B-spline Curves/Surfaces and its Implementation*. Preprint, Universidad de Cantabria, Spain.

21. Espinola J., González-Vega L., Nécula I. (2001). *A Symbolic/Numeric Toolbox for Computer Aided Geometric Design*. To appear in the Annals of the University of Timisoara, Mathematics and Computer Science Series.

22. Espinola J., González-Vega L., Puig-Pey J. (2002). *Shape Error Determination for CAD/CAM Quality Control*. Preprint, Universidad de Cantabria, Spain.

23. Farin G., Hoschek J., Kim M.-S. (2002). *Handbook of Computer Aided Geometric Design*. North-Holland.

24. Farouki R. T., Neff C. A. (1990). *Analytic Properties of Plane Offset Curves*. Computer Aided Geometric Design vol. 7, pp. 83–99.

25. Farouki R. T., Neff C. A. (1990). *Algebraic Properties of Plane Offset Curves*. Computer Aided Geometric Design vol. 7, pp. 100–127.

26. Feng H. (1992). *Decomposition and Computation of the Topology of Plane Real Algebraic Curves*. Ph.D. thesis, The Royal Institute of Technology, Stockholm, Sweden.

27. Feng Y., Chen F., Deng J., Chen C., Tang X. (2003). *Constructing Piecewise Algebraic Blending Surfaces*. Geometric Computation, Chen F., Wang D. (eds.), pp. 34–64. World Scientific, Singapore New Jersey.

28. Filip D. J. (1989). *Blending Parametric Surfaces*. ACM Transactions on Graphics vol. 8, no. 3, pp. 164–173.

29. Gahleitner J., Jüttler B., Schicho J. (2002). *Approximate Parameterization of Planar Cubic Curve Segments*. Proc. 5th International Conference on Curves and Surfaces (Saint-Malo, 2002), pp. 1–13. Nashboro Press, Nashville, TN.

30. Gao X. S., Chou S. C. (1992). *Implicitization of Rational Parametric Equations*. Journal of Symbolic Computation vol. 14, pp. 459–470.

31. Garrity T., Warren J. (1991). *Geometric Continuity.* Computer Aided Geometric Design vol. 8, pp. 51–65.
32. Gianni P., Traverso C. (1983). *Shape Determination of Real Curves and Surfaces.* Ann. Univ. Ferrara Sez VII Sec. Math. vol. XXIX, pp. 87–109.
33. González-Vega L. (1998). *A Combinatorial Algorithm Solving Some Quantifier Elimination Problems.* Quantifier Elimination and Cylindrical Algebraic Decomposition, pp. 365–375. Texts Monogr. Symb. Comput., Springer-Verlag, Wien New York.
34. González-Vega L. (1997). *Implicitization of Parametric Curves and Surfaces by Using Multidimensional Newton Formulae.* Journal of Symbolic Computation vol. 23, pp. 137–152.
35. González-Vega L., El Kahoui M. (1996). *An Improved Upper Complexity Bound for the Topology Computation of a Real Algebraic Plane Curve.* Journal of Complexity vol. 12, pp. 527–544.
36. González-Vega L., Necula I. (2002). *Efficient Topology Determination of Implicitly Defined Algebraic Plane Curves.* Computer Aided Geometric Design vol. 19, no. 9, pp. 719–743.
37. Hartmann E. (1988). *Numerical Implicitization for Intersection and G^n-Continuous Blending of Surfaces.* Computer Aided Geometric Design vol. 15, pp. 377–397.
38. Hartmann. E. (2000). *Numerical Parameterization of Curves and Surfaces.* Computer Aided Geometry Design vol. 17, pp. 251–266.
39. Hartmann E. (2001). *Parametric G^n-Blending of Curves and Surfaces.* Visual Computer vol. 17, pp. 1–13.
40. Hoffmann C. M. (1990). *Algebraic and Numerical Techniques for Offsets and Blends*, Computation of Curves and Surfaces, Dahmen W., Gasca M., Michelli C. A. (eds.), pp. 499–528. Kluwer Academic Publishers, Dordrecht.
41. Hoffmann C. M. (1993). *Geometric and Solid Modeling.* Morgan Kaufmann Publ., Inc.
42. Hoffmann C. M., Sendra J. R., Winkler F. (1997). *Parametric Algebraic Curves and Applications.* Journal of Symbolic Computation vol. 23, Special Issue on Parametric Curves and Applications.
43. Hoffmann C. M., Hopcroft J. (1986). *Quadratic Blending Surfaces.* Computer Aided Geometric Design vol. 18, pp. 301–307.
44. Hoffmann C. M., Hopcroft J. (1987). *The Potential Method for Blending Surfaces and Corners.* Geometric Modeling, Farin G. (ed.). SIAM, Philadelphia.
45. Hong H. (1996). *An Efficient Method for Analyzing the Topology of Plane Real Algebraic Curves.* Mathematics and Computers in Simulation vol. 42, nos. 4–6, pp. 571–582.
46. Hoschek J., Lasser D. (1993). *Fundamentals of Computer Aided Geometric Design.* A. K. Peters Wellesley MA., Ltd.
47. Kalkbrener M. (1991). *Implicitization of Rational Parametric Curves and Surfaces.* Proc. AAECC-8, Lecture Notes in Computer Science, pp. 249–259.
48. Kotsireas I. S. (2003). *Panorama of Methods for Exact Implicitization of Algebraic Curves and Surfaces.* Geometric Computation, Chen F., Wang D. (eds.), pp. 126–155. World Scientific, Singapore New Jersey.

49. Lü W. (1995). *Offset-Rational Parametric Plane Curves*, Computer Aided Geometric Design vol. 12, pp. 601–617.

50. Manocha D. (1992). *Algebraic and Numeric Techniques for Modelling and Robotics*. Ph.D. dissertation, University of California, Berkeley, USA.

51. Pérez-Díaz S. (2003). *Variedades Paramétricas: Algoritmos y Aplicaciones en Blending Geométrico*. Ph.D. thesis, Universidad de Alcalá, Spain.

52. Pérez-Díaz S., Sendra J. R. (2001). *Parametric G^1 Blending of Several Surfaces*. Computer Algebra in Scientific Computing CASC-01, Lectures Notes in Computer Science XII, pp. 445–461. Springer-Verlag, Berlin Heidelberg.

53. Pérez-Díaz S., Sendra J. R. (2003). *Computing All Parametric Solutions for Blending Parametric Surfaces*. Journal of Symbolic Computation vol. 36, no. 6, pp. 925–964.

54. Pérez-Díaz S., Sendra J., Sendra J. R. (2003). Parametrizations of Approximate Algebraic Curves by Lines. Special issue of Theoretical Computer Science on Algebraic-Numeric Algorithms. To appear.

55. Peternell M., Pottmann H. (1998). *A Laguerre Geometric Approach to Rational Offsets*. Computer Aided Geometric Design vol. 15, pp. 223–249.

56. Pottmann H. (1995). *Rational Curves and Surfaces with Rational Offsets*. Computer Aided Geometric Design vol. 12, pp. 175–192.

57. Pottman H., Wallner J. (1997). *Rational Blending Surfaces between Quadrics*. Computer Aided Geometric Design vol. 14, pp. 407–419.

58. Roy M.-F. (1996). *Basic Algorithms in Real Algebraic Geometry and Their Complexity: From Sturm's Theorem to the Existential Theory of Reals*. Lectures in Real Geometry, pp. 1–67. de Gruyter Exp. Math. 23, de Gruyter.

59. Sederberg T. W. (1998). *Applications to Computer Aided Geometric Design*. Applications of Computational Algebraic Geometry, Proceedings of Symposia in Applied Mathematics vol. 53, pp. 67–89. AMS, Providence.

60. Sendra J. (1999). *Algoritmos Efectivos para la Manipulación de Offsets de Hipersuperficies*. Ph.D. thesis, Universidad Politécnica de Madrid, Spain.

61. Sendra J. R. (2003). *Rational Curves and Surfaces: Algorithms and Some Applications*. Geometric Computation, Chen F., Wang D. (eds.), pp. 65–125. World Scientific, Singapore New Jersey.

62. Sendra J., Sendra J. R. (2000). *Algebraic Analysis of Offsets to Hypersurfaces*. Mathematische Zeitschrift vol. 234, pp. 697–719.

63. Sendra J., Sendra J. R. (2000). *Rationality Analysis and Direct Parametrization of Generalized Offsets to Quadrics*. Applicable Algebra in Engineering, Communication and Computing vol. 11, no. 2, pp. 111–139.

64. Vida J., Martin R. R., Varady T. (1994). *A Survey of Blending Methods Using Parametric Surfaces*. Computer Aided Design vol. 26, pp. 341–365.

65. Wang D. (2003). *Implicitization and Offsetting via Regular Systems*. Geometric Computation, Chen F., Wang D. (eds.), pp. 156–176. World Scientific, Singapore New Jersey.

66. Warren J. (1986). *On Algebraic Surfaces Meeting with Geometric Continuity*. Ph.D. thesis, Cornell University, USA.

67. Warren J. (1989). *Blending Algebraic Surfaces*. ACM Transactions on Graphics vol. 8, no. 4, pp. 263–278.

CHAPTER 2

CONSTRUCTING PIECEWISE ALGEBRAIC BLENDING SURFACES

Yuyu Feng, Falai Chen, Jiansong Deng, Changsong Chen,
and Xing Tang

Department of Mathematics
University of Science and Technology of China
Hefei, Anhui 230026, P. R. China
E-mail: {fengyy, chenfl, dengjs}@ustc.edu.cn

Constructing algebraic blending surfaces is an important problem in geometric modeling. In this chapter, we review some methods for this problem and summarize the main results on the construction of piecewise algebraic surfaces investigated recently by members of our group.

This chapter is organized into seven sections. We begin with a brief introduction to the problem of surface blending, followed by some notations and preliminary knowledge from computational algebraic geometry which will be used in later sections. We then discuss four methods — direct method, Gröbner basis method, Wu's method, and syzygy module method — for constructing piecewise algebraic blending surfaces. We also provide many examples to illustrate these methods with comparison. The chapter is concluded with a few remarks.

1. Introduction

Blending is a modeling technique for constructing smooth transitional surfaces between given surfaces. This technique has wide applications in many different areas such as mechanical design and manufacture, computer graphics and animation, and geometric modeling. It has been used in particular for filling surface holes, smoothing corners and edges, and making computer animation.

In the past twenty years, many researchers have worked on this subject and obtained fertile results. According to the representations of the constructing transitional surfaces, blending methods can be classified into many categories, such as parametric methods and implicit methods. In this

34

chapter, we only discuss methods for algebraic surface blending. Readers interested in other blending methods are suggested to refer to the paper[32] by Vida and others. In particular, the chapter[30] written by Sendra in this book has a section about parametric blending of surfaces.

The classical method for blending two intersecting surfaces works by replacing the intersection curve and its vicinity with part of a canal surface that is generated by a rolling ball and which has G^1 continuous contact to the initial surfaces.[27] Hoffmann and Hopcroft[20] proposed a general algorithm for blending surfaces by means of the potential method. Li and others[21] suggested to use functional splines to blend surfaces. Allen, Dutta,[1] and Pratt[25] constructed blending surfaces using cyclides and supercyclides. Wu and Zhou[34] applied the method of Gröbner bases to algebraic surface blending. Other blending methods using algebraic surfaces include Liming skill,[24] substituting method,[26] and those given in the references.[14,18,19,35] All the above-mentioned methods produce algebraic blending surfaces of high degree in general and some of them cannot be easily generalized to blend surfaces with higher-order contact.

The main drawback to blend several surfaces using a single algebraic surface is that the blending surface has high algebraic degree, especially for the case where high order of contact with the initial surfaces is required. Algebraic blending surfaces of high degree are complex in topology and it is hard to control their shapes. These surfaces are computationally more expansive in subsequent geometric operations.

An approach to overcome the drawback is to use a *piecewise* algebraic surface (PAS for short) instead of a single algebraic surface. The idea of PAS comes from Sederberg[28,29] and was applied by Bajaj, Dahmen, Thamm-Schwar, Hartmann, Xu, and others in interpolation and free-form modeling.[2,3,4,12,39,40] In this chapter, we focus on blending algebraic surfaces using PAS and discuss four different methods: the direct method, the Gröbner basis method, Wu's method, and the syzygy module method, which may be used effectively to deal with the problem.

2. Notations and Preliminaries

In this section, we introduce some notations and recall a few basic concepts from computational algebraic geometry. Two good references are the books[10,11] by Cox and others. In Subsection 2.2, the definition of geometric continuity is introduced. As for the details of geometric continuity, please refer to the paper[17] by Garrity and Warren.

2.1. *Monomial Orders and Gröbner Bases*

Let $K[x] := K[x_1, \ldots, x_n]$ denote the ring of polynomials in $x_1, \ldots, x_n$ over some field K. Any polynomial $f \in K[x]$ can be written as $f = \sum_\alpha a_\alpha x^\alpha$, where

$\alpha := (\alpha_1, \ldots, \alpha_n) \in \mathbb{Z}_+^n$ is a multiple index of nonnegative integers,

$x^\alpha := x_1^{\alpha_1} \ldots x_n^{\alpha_n}$ is a monomial in $K[x]$,

$|\alpha| := \alpha_1 + \alpha_2 + \cdots + \alpha_n$ is the length of the multiple index α, and

$\deg(f) := \max\{|\alpha| : a_\alpha \neq 0\}$ is the total degree of f.

To manipulate the polynomials in $K[x]$, we need to order monomials. Two commonly used orders are the *lexicographic* order (denoted by *lex*) and the *graded reverse lexicographic* order (denoted by *grlex*) defined below.

Definition 1: We order

- $x^\alpha >_{\text{lex}} x^\beta$ if the left-most nonzero entry of the vector $\alpha - \beta \in \mathbb{Z}_+^n$ is positive, and
- $x^\alpha >_{\text{grlex}} x^\beta$ if $|\alpha| > |\beta|$, or $|\alpha| = |\beta|$ and $\alpha >_{\text{lex}} \beta$.

For example, $(0, 3, 4) <_{\text{lex}} (1, 2, 0)$, but $(0, 3, 4) >_{\text{grlex}} (1, 2, 0)$. We further introduce

- $\text{mdeg}(f) := \max\{\alpha \in Z_+^n : a_\alpha \neq 0\}$, called the *multiple degree* of f,
- $\text{LC}(f) := a_{\text{mdeg}(f)} \in K$, called the *leading coefficient* of f,
- $\text{LM}(f) := x^{\text{mdeg}(f)}$, called the *leading monomial* of f, and
- $\text{LT}(f) := \text{LC}(f)\,\text{LM}(f)$, called the *leading term* of f,

for any polynomial $f \in K[x]$.

Consider, for instance,

$$f = \sum_\alpha a_\alpha x^\alpha = xy^3 z + xy^2 z^2 + 2x^2 z^2$$

and let the variables be ordered as $x > y > z$. Then we have the following table:

	$\text{mdeg}(f)$	$\text{LC}(f)$	$\text{LM}(f)$	$\text{LT}(f)$
lex order	$(2, 0, 2)$	2	$x^2 z^2$	$2x^2 z^2$
grlex order	$(1, 3, 1)$	1	$xy^3 z$	$xy^3 z$

We next define the concepts of ideal and variety.

Definition 2: A subset $I \subset K[x]$ is an *ideal* if $0 \in I$, and $f, g \in I$ and $h \in K[x]$ imply that $f + g \in I$ and $hf \in I$.

If $f_1, \ldots, f_s \in K[x]$, then $\langle f_1, \ldots, f_s \rangle := \{h_1 f_1 + \cdots + h_s f_s : h_i \in K[x]\}$ is an ideal generated by $f_1, \ldots, f_s$. The set of generators $f_1, \ldots, f_s$ is called a *basis* of the ideal.

Definition 3: A variety is the set of common zeros of a set of polynomials $f_1, \ldots, f_s$, i.e.,

$$V(f_1, \ldots, f_s) := \{(a_1, \ldots, a_n) \in K^n : f_i(a_1, \ldots, a_n) = 0, \ 1 \le i \le s\}.$$

For any ideal I, the corresponding variety is defined as

$$V(I) = \{(a_1, \ldots, a_n) \in K^n : f(a_1, \ldots, a_n) = 0, \ \forall f \in I\}.$$

A variety V is said to be *reducible* if it can be expressed as the union of two true subvarieties of V. Otherwise, it is said to be *irreducible*.

An ideal may be generated by different sets of polynomials in the ideal. There are some well-behaved generating sets which are known as Gröbner bases.

Definition 4: Fix a monomial order. A finite subset $G = \{g_1, \ldots, g_t\}$ of an ideal I is called a *Gröbner basis* of I if

$$\langle \mathrm{LT}(g_1), \ldots, \mathrm{LT}(g_t) \rangle = \langle \mathrm{LT}(I) \rangle.$$

Gröbner bases possess many nice properties. We will need the property stated in the following proposition.

Proposition 5: *Let $G = \{g_1, \ldots, g_t\}$ be a Gröbner basis of an ideal $I \subset K[x]$ and $f \in K[x]$. Then there exists a unique $r \in K[x]$ satisfying the following two conditions:*

(a) *no term of r is divisible by one of $\mathrm{LT}(g_1), \ldots, \mathrm{LT}(g_t)$;*
(b) *there is an element $g \in I$ such that $f = g + r$.*

2.2. *Geometric Continuity of Algebraic Surfaces*

Geometric continuity provides an important characterization for the smoothness of geometric entities.

Definition 6:[17] Let $V(f)$ and $V(g)$ be two algebraic surfaces which intersect transversally at an irreducible algebraic curve C. We say that $V(f)$ and $V(g)$ *meet with G^k rescaling continuity* along the common curve C if

- $V(f)$ and $V(g)$ are smooth along C except at a finite number of points;
- there exist two polynomials $a(x, y, z), b(x, y, z)$, which are not identically zero over C, such that af and bg are G^k continuous on C.

A general characterization of G^k continuity for two algebraic surfaces on their common boundary is stated in the following theorem.

Theorem 7:[17] Let $V(f)$ and $V(h)$ be two algebraic surfaces which intersect transversally at an irreducible algebraic curve $C := V(f) \cap V(h)$. Then the surface $V(f)$ and $V(g)$ meet with G^k continuity along the common curve C if and only if there are polynomials $\alpha(x, y, z) \neq 0$ and $\beta(x, y, z)$ such that $g = \alpha f + \beta h^{k+1}$.

In practical applications, $V(h)$ is often assumed to be a plane. In this case, we have the following result.

Corollary 8:[5] *Assume that an algebraic surface $g = 0$ of degree n and an algebraic surface $f = 0$ of degree m $(n \geq m)$ meet along a common algebraic curve in a plane $\pi = 0$. If there exist polynomials $\alpha(x, y, z)$ of degree $n - m$ and $\beta(x, y, z)$ of degree $n - k - 1$ such that $g = \alpha f + \beta \pi^{k+1}$, then the algebraic surfaces $g = 0$ and $f = 0$ meet with G^k continuity along the common curve.*

Now we can formulate the problem we are going to study in this chapter as follows.

Problem 1: We are given m initial algebraic surfaces $f_i = 0$ and other m corresponding auxiliary surfaces $h_i = 0$, where $f_i, h_i \in \mathbb{R}[x, y, z]$, $i = 1, \ldots, m$. Suppose that $f_i = 0$ and $h_i = 0$ intersect transversally at a curve $C_i = V(f_i, h_i)$ for $i = 1, \ldots, m$. The problem is to find a (piecewise) algebraic surface $g = 0$ such that $g = 0$ meets $f_i = 0$ with G^k continuity along the curve C_i for $i = 1, \ldots, m$.

We shall present four different approaches to solve this problem in the following sections.

3. Direct Method

We start with a simple example, which demonstrates the advantage of constructing blending surfaces with PAS. Two more examples will be provided to show the construction process and a short discussion will also be given. The main results in this section can be found in the papers[5,6,7] by Chen and others.

Example 9: Given two circular cylinders

$$f_1 = y^2 + z^2 - \frac{1}{25} = 0, \quad f_2 = x^2 + z^2 - \frac{1}{25} = 0$$

(whose axes are perpendicular to each other) and two auxiliary planes

$$h_1 = x - \frac{3}{5} = 0, \quad h_2 = y - \frac{5}{4} = 0,$$

find a cubic algebraic surface $g = 0$ which meets f_i with G^1 continuity along the circular sections $C_i = V(f_i, h_i)$, $i = 1, 2$.

Chen and others[7] have proved that there is no cubic algebraic surface $g = 0$ satisfying the above requirements, so we now try to construct a blending surface with one degree higher. A quartic blending surface $g = 0$ in general has six free parameters and it is rather difficult to choose suitable values for the parameters to get a reasonable blending surface. Figure 1 shows one blending surface after many trials, which is obviously undesirable.

Fig. 1.   An undesirable blending surface

In order to construct a blending surface using PAS, we choose an intermediate plane $h_3 = y - 3/5 = 0$. Our intention is to construct two pieces of cubic algebraic surfaces $V(g_1)$ and $V(g_2)$ that meet with G^1 continuity at $V(f_1, h_1)$ with $V(f_1)$ and at $V(f_2, h_2)$ with $V(f_2)$, respectively. Meanwhile, $V(g_1)$ and $V(g_2)$ meet with G^1 continuity at $V(h_3)$. It has been shown by Chen and others[7] that there is one solution

$$g_1 = (5x + 5y - 6)\left(y^2 + z^2 - \frac{1}{25}\right) + (5x + 5y)\left(x - \frac{3}{5}\right)^2,$$

$$g_2 = z^2 + x^2 - \frac{1}{25}.$$

The corresponding piecewise algebraic blending surface is shown in Fig. 2.

Fig. 2.   Simple pipe surface blending

The above example illustrates some advantages of using piecewise algebraic surfaces to blend algebraic surfaces. First, the blending surface has a lower degree and thus is topologically simpler. Second, there are fewer free parameters in the general solutions, which makes the control of shape easier.

The general approach for constructing piecewise algebraic blending surfaces may be summarized as follows.[5]

(1) According to the given initial surfaces and transversal surfaces (or planes), determine the defining region for the PAS. Some heuristic rules should be applied into the step.
(2) Form a system of algebraic equations from the geometric continuity conditions for each pair of adjacent piecewise surface patches.
(3) Solve the system of algebraic equations to obtain piecewise algebraic surfaces with some free parameters.
(4) Adjust the free parameters to control the shape of the blending surface. There are many ways to implement this object, but none is fit for any cases.

Let us explore these steps separately. The first important step of constructing blending surfaces is space partition, i.e., subdividing the space where the blending surface lies into tetrahedrons or prisms. Unfortunately, there is no general approach to do so; only some heuristic rules may be applied. The reader is referred to the paper[5] by Chen and others for details.

The second step is to set up a system of algebraic equations satisfied by the blending surface. Suppose that we are given l algebraic surfaces $f_i = 0$,

$i = 1, \ldots, l$. The blending surface consists of r surface patches $g_j = 0$, $j = 1, \ldots, r$ (or equivalently, the defining region consists of r tetrahedrons or prisms). We assume that all the surface patches $g_j = 0$ have the same degree n ($\geq \deg(f_i)$). Since the blending surface meets each $V(f_i)$ along the planar curve $V(f_i) \cap V(h_i)$ with G^k continuity, according to Corollary 8, we require

$$g_j = \gamma_i f_i + \beta_i h_i^{k+1},$$

where $V(h_i)$ is the auxiliary plane corresponding to $V(f_i)$, and γ_i and β_i are unknown polynomials of degrees $n - \deg(f_i)$ and $n - k - 1$, respectively. On the other hand, the adjacent surface patches $V(g_i)$ and $V(g_j)$, which have the same degree, meet along a planar curve $V(g_i) \cap \pi_i$ with G^k continuity, we require

$$g_j = g_i + \alpha_i \pi_i^{k+1},$$

where π_i is some plane and α_i is a polynomial of degree $n - k - 1$ for each i. Moreover, at each common vertex where several surface patches meet, a conformability condition must be satisfied. Without loss of generality, we assume that $V(g_i)$ ($i = 1, \ldots, m$) are consecutive surface patches meeting at a common vertex V, and $V(g_i)$ and $V(g_{i+1})$ share a common plane π_i (see Fig. 3); then

$$\sum_{i=1}^{m} \alpha_i \pi_i^{k+1} = 0.$$

If there are s common vertices in the defining region, then there are s corresponding conformability conditions.

Thus a system of algebraic equations with polynomials α_i, β_i and γ_i as unknowns is obtained. These equations are linear in the unknowns with coefficients being polynomials involving f_i and π_i. They can be converted into a system of linear equations with the coefficients of α_i, β_i, and γ_i as unknowns. After solving this system of linear equations with the help of some computer algebra system, say Maple, the piecewise algebraic blending surface is constructed.

In what follows, we provide two examples to detail the construction process.

Example 10: Given three cylinders

$$\begin{cases} f_1 = y^2 + z^2 - r_1^2 = 0, & x > h_1 > r_1 > 0, \\ f_2 = z^2 + x^2 - r_2^2 = 0, & y > h_2 > r_2 > 0, \\ f_3 = x^2 + y^2 - r_3^2 = 0, & z > h_3 > r_3 > 0, \end{cases}$$

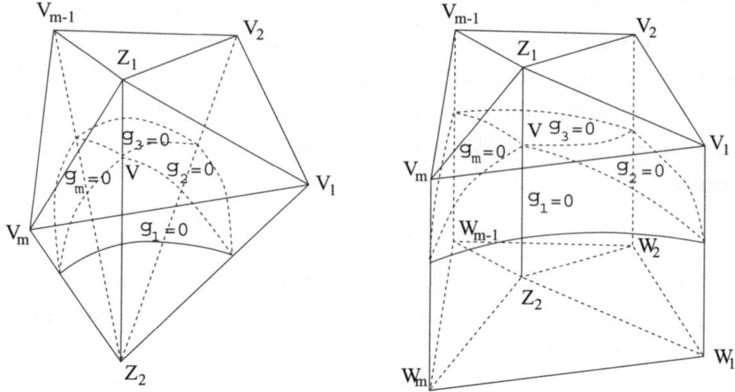

Fig. 3. Surface patches meeting at a common vertex

whose axes are perpendicular to each other, we seek a G^k continuous PAS
in the region

$$\{(x, y, z) : |x| \le h_1, |y| \le h_2, |z| \le h_3\}$$

which meets $f_1 = 0$, $f_2 = 0$, and $f_3 = 0$ at

$$F_1 = x - h_1 = 0, \quad F_2 = y - h_2 = 0, \quad F_3 = z - h_3 = 0$$

with G^k continuity, respectively.

Space partition. For this particular problem, the defining region of
the blending surface can be determined as follows. Choose three surface
patches $g_1 = 0$, $g_3 = 0$, and $g_5 = 0$ to meet the three cylinders with G^k
continuity, respectively. Now we need other three surface patches $g_2 = 0$,
$g_4 = 0$, and $g_6 = 0$ which serve as the transitional surfaces between $g_1 = 0$,
$g_3 = 0$, and $g_5 = 0$. Thus in total we need six surface patches to compose
the blending surface. Since the transversal planes $F_i = 0$ $(i = 1, 2, 3)$ of the
three cylinders intersect at one common point, the defining region of the
blending surface can be defined as the composition of six tetrahedrons as
shown in Fig. 4.

Let $\pi_i = 0$ be the plane passing through Z_1, Z_2, and V_i for $i = 1, \ldots, 6$
and let $T_i = Z_1 Z_2 V_{i-1} V_i$, $i = 1, \ldots, 6$; then

$$\pi_4 = \pi_1 : \quad h_2 h_3 x - 2h_1 h_3 y + h_1 h_2 z = 0,$$
$$\pi_5 = \pi_2 : \quad -2h_2 h_3 x + h_1 h_3 y + h_1 h_2 z = 0,$$
$$\pi_6 = \pi_3 : \quad -h_2 h_3 x - h_1 h_3 y + 2h_1 h_2 z = 0.$$

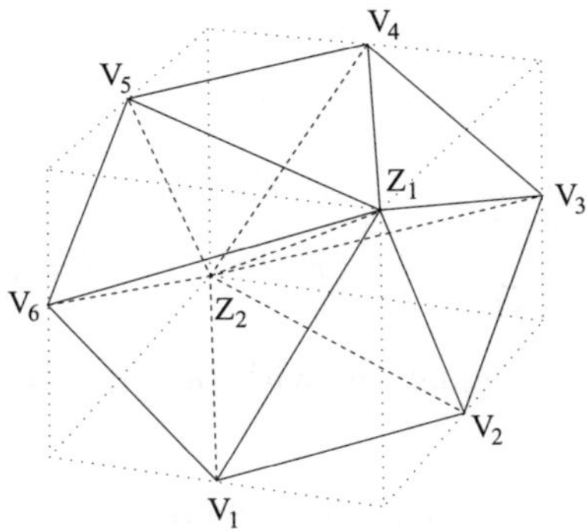

Fig. 4.   Tetrahedron partition of the defining region

Setup of the system of algebraic equations. Assume that the surface patch in the tetrahedron T_i is defined by $g_i = 0$ and that g_i satisfies

$$g_{i+1} = g_i + \alpha_i \pi_i^{k+1}, \quad i = 1, \ldots, 6,$$

where α_i $(i = 1, \ldots, 6)$ are polynomials of degree $n - k - 1$ in x, y, z. By the conformability condition, α_i $(i = 1, \ldots, 6)$ satisfy

$$\sum_{i=1}^{6} \alpha_i \pi_i^{k+1} = 0.$$

On the other hand, $g_1 = 0, g_3 = 0$, and $g_5 = 0$ meet $f_1 = 0, f_2 = 0$. and $f_3 = 0$ with G^k continuity, respectively, so

$$\begin{cases} g_1 = \gamma_1 f_1 + \beta_1 F_1^{k+1}, \\ g_3 = \gamma_2 f_2 + \beta_2 F_2^{k+1}, \\ g_5 = \gamma_3 f_3 + \beta_3 F_3^{k+1}, \end{cases}$$

where β_i $(i = 1, 2, 3)$ are polynomials of degree $n - k - 1$ and γ_i $(i = 1, 2, 3)$ are polynomials of degree $n - 2$. This leads to a system of equations

$$\sum_{i=1}^{6} \alpha_i \pi_i^{k+1} = 0,$$

$$\gamma_1 f_1 + \beta_1 F_1^{k+1} + \alpha_1 \pi_1^{k+1} + \alpha_2 \pi_2^{k+1} = \gamma_2 f_2 + \beta_2 F_2^{k+1}, \tag{1}$$

$$\gamma_1 f_1 + \beta_1 F_1^{k+1} - \alpha_6 \pi_6^{k+1} + \alpha_5 \pi_5^{k+1} = \gamma_3 f_3 + \beta_3 F_3^{k+1}.$$

44 *Feng et al.*

Assuming that

$$\alpha_i = \sum_{0 \le r+s+t \le n-k-1} a^i_{rst} x^r y^s z^t, \quad i = 1, \dots, 6,$$

$$\beta_i = \sum_{0 \le r+s+t \le n-k-1} b^i_{rst} x^r y^s z^t, \quad i = 1, \dots, 3,$$

$$\gamma_i = \sum_{0 \le r+s+t \le n-2} c^i_{rst} x^r y^s z^t, \quad i = 1, \dots, 3,$$

we get a system of linear equations with $(a^i_{rst})^6_{i=1}$, $(b^i_{rst})^3_{i=1}$, and $(c^i_{rst})^3_{i=1}$ as unknowns.

Solutions of PAS. Solving the system of equations, we obtain the following expressions for the PAS $g = 0$:

$$\begin{cases} g_1 = \gamma_1 f_1 + \beta_1 F_1^{k+1} = 0, \\ g_2 = \gamma_1 f_1 + \beta_1 F_1^{k+1} + \alpha_1 \pi_1^{k+1} = 0, \\ g_3 = \gamma_2 f_2 + \beta_2 F_2^{k+1} = 0, \\ g_4 = \gamma_2 f_2 + \beta_2 F_2^{k+1} + \alpha_3 \pi_3^{k+1} = 0, \\ g_5 = \gamma_3 f_3 + \beta_3 F_3^{k+1} = 0, \\ g_6 = \gamma_3 f_3 + \beta_3 F_3^{k+1} + \alpha_5 \pi_5^{k+1} = 0. \end{cases}$$

As an example, we take

$$n = 4, \quad k = 2, \quad h_1 = h_2 = h_3 = \frac{3}{5}, \quad r_1 = r_2 = r_3 = \frac{1}{5}.$$

Then there are three free parameters in the solution, and one solution is shown in Fig. 5.

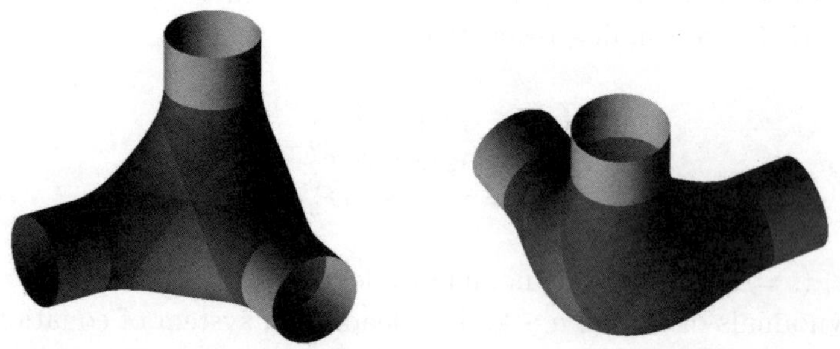

Fig. 5.   Blending three cylinders (from two different views)

Determination of free parameters. In general the blending surface is not unique, and often there exist several linearly independent solutions.

Among these solutions, only some are suitable for practical needs. It is thus important to be able to choose suitable free parameters to control the shape of the blending surface. Some techniques to deal with this issue will be discussed in Sections 4 and 6. For a local adjustment of the shape, one may consult the paper[5] by Chen and others. Figure 6 shows the effects by adjusting free parameters.

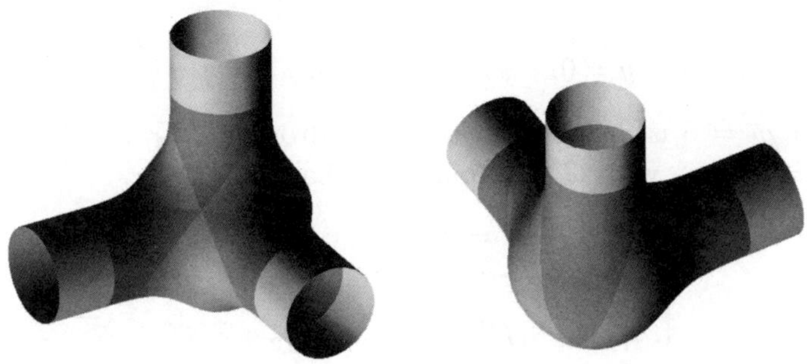

Fig. 6.　Effect of adjusting free parameters (from two different views)

Example 11: (Bajaj's corner[2]). Consider a corner formed by three faces that consist of the first quadrant of the xy, yz, zx planes. The three edges of the corner are smoothed by two cones

$$f_1 = 10yz - 25z^2 + 40z - y^2 + 10xy - 8y - 25x^2 + 40x - 16 = 0,$$
$$f_2 = 4z^2 + 4xz - 12z + 4y^2 + 4xy - 12y + x^2 - 6x + 9 = 0$$

and a circular cylinder $f_3 = (x - 1)^2 + (y - 1)^2 - 1 = 0$.

The intersections of the three quadrics respectively with three planes

$$F_1 = y - 1 = 0, \quad F_2 = x - 1 = 0, \quad F_3 = z - 1 = 0$$

are three circles C_1, C_2, and C_3. We look for a surface $g(x, y, z) = 0$ which smoothly interpolates the three intersection curves and fills the hole generated by the three curves. Furthermore, we require that g meets $f_i{=}0$ respectively along the three curves with G^1 continuity.

Bajaj and others[2] used a quintic algebraic surface to blend the three surfaces $f_i = 0$ with G^1 continuity and showed that the quintic surface has the lowest degree. Here we use a piecewise quartic surface to smoothly interpolate the C_i and fill the hole generated by C_i, $i = 1, 2, 3$.

Let the defining region be three tetrahedrons meeting at a common vertex as shown in Fig. 7. We wish to fill the hole with three quartic surface patches meeting at this vertex.

We select points

$$V_1 = (1, 1, -2), \quad V_2 = (1, -2, 1), \quad V_3 = (-2, 1, 1),$$
$$V_0 = (0, 0, 0), \quad \mathbb{Z}_0 = (1, 1, 1).$$

The transversal planes are

$$\pi_1 = x - y = 0, \quad \pi_2 = x - z = 0, \quad \pi_3 = y - z = 0.$$

Note that $g_i = 0$ is defined in the tetrahedron $\mathbb{Z}_0 V_0 V_{i-1} V_i$. Since $g_i = 0$ meets $f_i = 0$ at F_i with G^1 continuity, we have

$$\begin{cases} \sum_{i=1}^{3} \alpha_i \pi_i^2 = 0, \\ \gamma_1 f_1 + \beta_1 F_1^2 + \alpha_1 \pi_1^2 = \gamma_2 f_2 + \gamma_2 F_2^2, \\ \gamma_1 f_1 + \beta_1 F_1^2 - \alpha_3 \pi_3^2 = \gamma_3 f_3 + \gamma_3 F_3^2, \end{cases} \tag{2}$$

where $\alpha_i, \beta_i, \gamma_i$ are polynomials of degree 2.

We convert the system (2) of equations into a system of linear equations with the coefficients of monomials in $\alpha_i, \beta_i, \gamma_i$ as unknowns. The resulting system contains 105 equations and 90 unknowns, and their solutions have 13 free parameters. One of the solutions is

$$\begin{cases} g_1 = \gamma_1 f_1 + \beta_1 F_1^2, \\ g_2 = \gamma_2 f_2 + \beta_2 F_2^2, \\ g_3 = \gamma_3 f_3 + \beta_3 F_3^2, \end{cases}$$

where

$$\begin{cases}
\gamma_1 = 300x^2 - 2184y^2 - 252xy - 300xz + 120yz - 720x + 3600y - 192z, \\
\beta_1 = -68760x^2 + 756y^2 - 59040z^2 + 16516xy + 39264xz - 5916yz \\
\qquad + 116108x + 18949y + 120720z - 114444, \\
\gamma_2 = 7770x^2 - 2370y^2 + 4695xy + 1875xz - 750yz - 20235x + 5490y \\
\qquad + 1200z, \\
\beta_2 = -17546x^2 - 58230y^2 - 52320z^2 - 32391xy - 18927xz - 16710yz \\
\qquad + 80855x + 140826y + 112992z - 11444, \\
\gamma_3 = -7500x^2 - 9480y^2 + 57360z^2 + 9300xy + 7500xz - 3500yz \\
\qquad 15000x + 31440y - 109920x, \\
\beta_3 = -64860x^2 - 73080y^2 + 12z^2 + 21672xy + 5500xz - 2988yz \\
\qquad + 112628x + 258796y + 48024z - 11444.
\end{cases}$$

The corresponding surface is shown in Fig. 8.

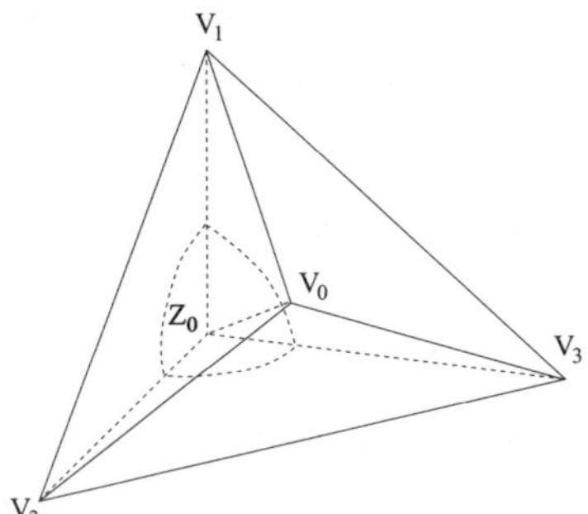

Fig. 7.   Space partition for the hole

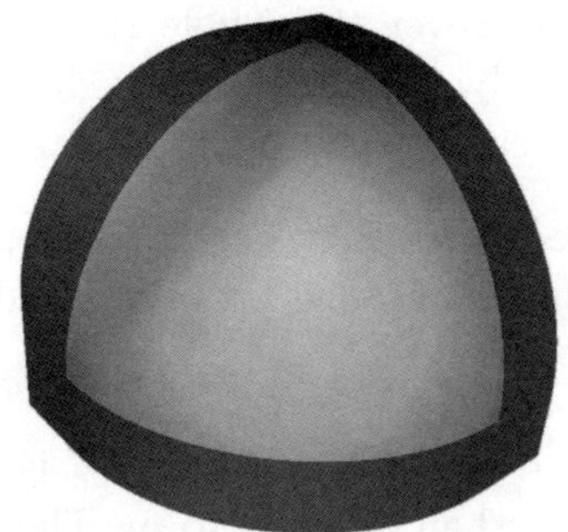

Fig. 8.   Filling hole with three quartic surface patches

We can also use 7 patches of cubic algebraic surfaces to smoothly fill the hole. Details can be found in the paper[7] by Chen and others.

The above examples show that the PAS method for constructing blending surface has some advantages. As we have already pointed out, piecewise algebraic blending surfaces have much lower degree than a single blending surface. Moreover, PAS are easier to trim and control than the blending surfaces generated by other methods. Currently we are relying on a trial-and-error approach for the determination of the degree of the blending surface. How to determine the degree in advance? The methods of Gröbner bases and syzygy modules discussed in Sections 4 and 6 will give us some idea.

4. Gröbner Basis Method

The method of Gröbner bases is an important tool for handling systems of polynomial equations. In this section, we apply this method to the problem of algebraic surface blending. It allows us to find algebraic blending surfaces of lowest degree.

According to Theorem 7 and Corollary 8, we know that any polynomial in the ideal

$$I = \bigcap_{j=1}^{n} \langle f_j, h_j^{k+1} \rangle \tag{3}$$

is a solution to Problem 1. In the paper[33] by Warren, the author approaches the blending problem by computing suitable elements in the former ideal intersection by determining families of solutions for special cases that basically cover the whole spectrum. However, we are interested in finding the polynomials of lowest degree in I. The following theorem solves this problem.

Theorem 12:[22] Let $G = \{g_1, \ldots, g_s\}$ be a Gröbner basis of the ideal I under the graded lex order, and suppose that

$$\overline{G} = \{g_i \in G : \deg(g_i) \leq m\} = \{g_1, \ldots, g_t\} \quad (t \leq s)$$

and $I_m = I \cap P_m$, where P_m is the set of all the polynomials whose degree is less than or equal to m. Then $I_m = \langle g_1, \ldots, g_t \rangle \cap P_m$. Furthermore, any $f \in I_m$ can be represented as $f = \sum_{i=1}^{t} a_i g_i$ with $\deg(a_i g_i) \leq \deg(f)$.

Based on this theorem, we can describe the main algorithmic steps for constructing blending surfaces using Gröbner basis computation as follows.

(1) Compute the Gröbner basis of the ideal $I = \bigcap_{j=1}^{n} \langle f_j, h_j^{k+1} \rangle$ under the graded lex order. Let g_i $(i = 1, \ldots, r)$ be the elements of the Gröbner basis with the lowest degree.
(2) By Theorem 12, the algebraic blending surfaces of lowest degree is given by $g = \sum_{i=1}^{r} \lambda_i g_i$, where λ_i are constants.
(3) Choose suitable free parameters to adjust the shape of the blending surface.

The following example serves to illustrate these steps.

Example 13: Given two spheres

$$g_1 = (x+2)^2 + y^2 + z^2 - 4, \qquad h_1 = x + 2,$$
$$g_2 = (x-1)^2 + y^2 + z^2 - 1, \qquad h_2 = x - 1,$$

we want to construct a blending surface smoothly joining the two spheres with G^2 continuity along the curves $V(g_i, h_i)$, $i = 1, 2$.

To find a blending surface of lowest degree, we first compute the Gröbner basis of the ideal

$$I = \langle g_1, h_1^3 \rangle \cap \langle g_2, h_2^3 \rangle$$

under the graded lex order. From the book[10] by Cox and others, we know that

$$\langle g_1, h_1^3 \rangle \cap \langle g_2, h_2^3 \rangle = \langle tg_1, th_1^3, (1-t)g_2, (1-t)h_2^3 \rangle \cap K[x, y, z]$$

Direct computation yields

$$\langle g_1, h_1^3 \rangle \cap \langle g_2, h_2^3 \rangle = \langle -8 + 12x + 6x^2 - 11x^3 - 3x^4 + 3x^5 + x^6,$$

$$-32 + 28x - 29x^2 + 27y^2 + 27z^2 - 4x^3 + 8x^4 + 2x^5\rangle$$

and the Gröbner basis of this ideal with respect to the graded lex order is $G = \{p_1, p_2, p_3\}$, where

$$p_1 = -16 + 28x - 15x^2 + x^3 + 2x^4 + 9y^2 - 9xy^2 + 9z^2 - 9xz^2,$$
$$p_2 = -16 + 36x + 3x^2 - 5x^3 + 3y^2 - 15xy^2 - 6x^2y^2 + 3z^2 - 15xz^2$$
$$-6x^2z^2,$$
$$p_3 = -16 + 12x - 3x^2 + x^3 + 21y^2 - 9xy^2 - 6y^4 + 21z^2 - 9xz^2$$
$$-12y^2z^2 - 6z^4.$$

Thus the blending surfaces of lowest degree take the form

$$f(x, y, z) = \lambda_1 p_1 + \lambda_2 p_2 + \lambda_3 p_3,$$

where λ_i $(i = 1, 2, 3)$ are arbitrary constants. There are different ways to choose values for the parameters to meet various requirements. For example, we can require the blending surface to interpolate a certain set $\mathcal{P}$ of points. Taking

$$\mathcal{P} = \left\{ \left(0, \tfrac{1}{2}, 0\right), \left(\tfrac{1}{2}, \tfrac{\sqrt{3}}{2}, 0\right) \right\},$$

we get the blending surface shown in Fig. 9.

Fig. 9.   A blending surface which interpolates the point set $\mathcal{P}$ with G^2 continuity

We can also use least-square approximation to control the shape of $V(f)$. For example, if we take three sets of points as

$$\mathcal{P}_1 = \left\{ \left(0, \tfrac{1}{2}, 0\right), \left(\tfrac{1}{2}, \tfrac{\sqrt{3}}{2}, 0\right), \left(\tfrac{2}{5}, \tfrac{4}{5}, 0\right), \left(1 - \tfrac{1}{\sqrt{2}}, \tfrac{1}{\sqrt{2}}, 0\right), \left(-1, \sqrt{3}, 0\right), \right.$$
$$\left. \left(-\tfrac{4}{5}, \tfrac{8}{5}, 0\right), \left(-2 + \sqrt{2}, \sqrt{2}, 0\right) \right\},$$

$$\mathcal{P}_2 = \left\{ \left(0, \frac{4}{5}, 0\right), \left(\frac{1}{2}, \frac{\sqrt{3}}{2}, 0\right), \left(\frac{2}{5}, \frac{4}{5}, 0\right), \left(1 - \frac{1}{\sqrt{2}}, \frac{1}{\sqrt{2}}, 0\right), \left(-1, \sqrt{3}, 0\right), \right.$$
$$\left. \left(-\frac{4}{5}, \frac{8}{5}, 0\right), (-2 + \sqrt{2}, \sqrt{2}, 0) \right\},$$
$$\mathcal{P}_3 = \left\{ (0, 1, 0), \left(\frac{1}{2}, \frac{\sqrt{3}}{2}, 0\right), \left(\frac{2}{5}, \frac{4}{5}, 0\right), (-1, \sqrt{3}, 0), \left(-\frac{4}{5}, \frac{8}{5}, 0\right), \right.$$
$$\left. (-2 + \sqrt{2}, \sqrt{2}, 0) \right\},$$

then we get three blending surfaces $f_i = 0$ ($i = 1, 2, 3$) respectively, as shown in Fig. 10.

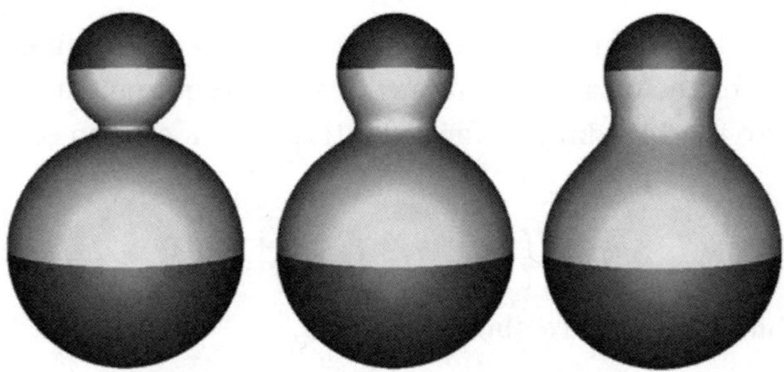

Fig. 10. A G^2 blending surface with least-square approximation to different sets of points

Example 14: Construct a teapot surface.

In this example, we describe an approach to modeling a teapot with PAS. The teapot surface is composed of lid, body, spout, and handle which are pieced together with G^1 or G^2 continuity. The lid is constructed by one quartic and two quadratic PAS with G^2 continuity. The body is composed of two quadratic algebraic surfaces and the spout consists of two cubic algebraic surfaces with G^1 continuity. Finally, one quartic algebraic surface is taken for the handle. The details can be found in the master thesis[22] of Lou. Figure 11 shows the teapot model.

In summary, the method of Gröbner bases provides a powerful tool for the construction of blending surfaces of lowest degree. All the blending surfaces are expressed with several free parameters. These free parameters can be determined by interpolating or least-square approximation to a set of points.

Fig. 11.   A teapot consisting of eight algebraic surface patches

5. Wu's Method

The method of Gröbner bases introduced in the preceding section can find algebraic blending surfaces of lowest degree in general, but its computational cost is very high. Wu and Wang[38] proposed a different approach based on irreducible ascending sets and pseudo-division for the problem of algebraic surface blending. This new approach is much more efficient than the approach based on Gröbner bases and can find algebraic blending surfaces of lowest degree in most cases. However, the method of Wu and Wang still has some drawbacks. First, it is not easy to generalize the method to the case where the blending surface and the initial surface have high-order contact. Second, the intersection curve along which the blending surface and the initial surface meet is required to be irreducible. Third, a single piece of algebraic surface is used to blend several given surfaces; thus the degree of the blending surface may have to be high.

The idea of Wu and Wang has been extended by the present authors.[9] We can get rid of all the restraints imposed by their method:[38] the order of contact of the blending surface and the initial surface can be arbitrarily high; the intersection curve at which the blending surface touches the initial surface can be reducible; piecewise algebraic surfaces of low degree can also be used as blending surfaces, if necessary. The drop of restraints makes the method more flexible and useful for the construction of blending surfaces.

Now we recall some basic concepts used in Wu's method. Let $f \in K[x_1, \ldots, x_n]$ be a polynomial with $\deg_{x_n}(f) > 0$; then f can be written in the form:

$$f = f_0 x_n^d + \cdots + f_1 x_n + f_d,$$

where $f_i \in K[x_1, \ldots, x_{n-1}]$. We call x_n the *leading variable* and f_0 the *initial* of f. For any other polynomial $g \in K[x_1, \ldots, x_n]$, pseudo-dividing g

by f with respect to x_n results in

$$f_0^s g = qf + r,$$

where $q, r \in K[x_1, \ldots, x_n]$, $\deg_{x_n}(r) < d$, and s is a nonnegative integer. The polynomial r is called the *pseudo-remainder* of g with respect to f. Pseudo-division is a key operation underlying Wu's method.

Definition 15: Let $A = \{p_1, \ldots, p_m\}$ be a set of nonzero polynomials in $K[x_1, \ldots, x_n]$ with

$$p_i = I_{i,0} x_{c_i}^{d_i} + I_{i,1} x_{c_i}^{d_i - 1} + \cdots + I_{i,d_i}, \quad i = 1, \ldots, m.$$

A is called an *ascending set* if the following conditions are satisfied:

(1) $0 < c_1 < \cdots < c_m$,
(2) $I_{i,j} \in K[x_1, \ldots, x_{c_i - 1}]$,
(3) $\forall i > j$, $\deg_{x_j}(p_i) < \deg_{x_j}(p_j)$.

For any polynomial $g \in K[x_1, \ldots, x_n]$, one can pseudo-divide g by the polynomials in $A = \{p_1, \ldots, p_m\}$ with respect to their leading variables as follows:

$$I_{m,0}^{s_m} g = q_m p_m + r_{m-1},$$
$$I_{m-1,0}^{s_{m-1}} r_{m-1} = q_{m-1} p_{m-1} + r_{m-2},$$
$$\cdots \cdots$$
$$I_{1,0}^{s_1} r_1 = q_1 p_1 + r_0.$$

From the above equalities, we get

$$I_{1,0}^{s_1} \cdots I_{m,0}^{s_m} \cdot g = q_1 p_1 + \cdots + q_m p_m + r, \tag{4}$$

where s_i are some nonnegative integers and $q_i \in K[x_1, \ldots, x_{c_i}]$, $i = 1, \ldots, m$. We call $r \in K[x_1, \ldots, x_n]$ the *pseudo-remainder* of g with respect to A and write $r = \mathrm{prem}(g, A)$. It is easy to see that r has the following property:

$$\deg_{x_{c_i}}(r) < \deg_{x_{c_i}}(p_i), \quad i = 1, \ldots, m.$$

For any given set of polynomials, one can always transform it into an ascending set by means of pseudo-division (4). The details can found in the works[37,36] by Wu.

Our method for solving the problem of surface blending is based on pseudo-division. It consists of the following algorithmic steps.

(1) Express the polynomial g to be determined in the form:

$$g = \sum_{0 \le i+j+l \le d} g_{ijl} x^i y^j z^l,$$

where g_{ijl} are unknowns and d is the degree of g.

(2) Choose an appropriate monomial order for the variables x, y, z and transform the polynomial set $\{f_i, h_i^{k+1}\}$ into an ascending set A_i for $i = 1, \ldots, m$.

(3) Pseudo-divide g by the polynomials in A_i and let $r_i = \operatorname{prem}(g, A_i)$ for $i = 1, \ldots, m$; each $r_i \in \mathbb{R}[x, y, z]$ is a polynomial whose coefficients are linear combinations of g_{ijl}.

(4) Set $r_i = 0$ for $i = 1, \ldots, m$, i.e., equate all the coefficients of r_i to 0. A system E of linear equations with g_{ijl} as unknowns is thus obtained.

(5) Solve the system E of linear equations. If E has just one trivial solution $g_{ijl} = 0$, then increase the degree of the polynomial g and go to step (1). Otherwise, select a suitable solution among all the solutions.

The following theorem ensures that the above steps produce a solution to the problem in question.

Theorem 16:[9] Let g be a solution obtained according to the above algorithmic steps. Then the algebraic surface $g = 0$ meets $f_i{=}0$ with G^k continuity.

In the rest of this section, we present two examples[9] to illustrate our method for constructing algebraic blending surfaces. In these examples, the equations $f_i = 0$ represent the initial surfaces to be blended, $h_i = 0$ the auxiliary surfaces, and $g = 0$ is the blending surface.

Example 17: Let

$$\begin{aligned}
f_1 &= [y^2 + (z-2)^2 - 1][y^2 + (z+2)^2 - 1], & h_1 &= x - 2, \\
f_2 &= y^2 + z^2 - 2, & h_2 &= x + 2.
\end{aligned}$$

We want to find a quintic surface $g = 0$ such that $g = 0$ blends $f_i = 0$ ($i = 1, 2$) with G^1 continuity. Assume, for simplicity, that $g = 0$ is symmetric with respect to the planes xy and xz. Note that $f_1 = 0$ is the union of two cylinders and thus is reducible. The intersection curve $V(f_1, h_1)$ is the union of two circles and is also reducible.

It is easy to see that both $A_1 = \{h_1^2, f_1\}$ and $A_2 = \{h_2^2, f_2\}$ are ascending sets with respect to the order $x > y > z$. According to the above algorithmic steps, one can obtain a system of 56 linear equations in 50 unknowns. This system has six families of solutions. One solution is given by

$$
\begin{aligned}
g = {} & -88xy^4 - 1604x - 176xy^2z^2 + 7x^2z^2 + 7x^5 + 7x^2 - 420z^2 + 7x^4 \\
& - 1124y^2 - 88xz^4 - 169x^2y^2 + 484xy^2 + 1188xz^2 - 28x^3y^2 \\
& - 28x^3z^2 + 1260.
\end{aligned}
$$

Figure 12 depicts the blending surface defined by $g = 0$.

Example 18: This example from Bajaj[2] has been considered in Example 11. Here Wu's method is used to construct a piecewise quartic surface to blend $f_i = 0$ $(i = 1, 2, 3)$ with G^1 continuity. The surfaces $f_i = 0$ and planes $F_i = 0$ $(i = 1, 2, 3)$ are defined as in Example 11.

Let $p_1 = x - y$, $p_2 = z - x$, and $p_3 = y - z$. We want to construct three quartic algebraic surfaces $g_1 = 0$, $g_2 = 0$, and $g_3 = 0$ such that for $i = 1, 2, 3$,

(1) $g_i = 0$ meets $f_i = 0$ along C_i with G^1 continuity, and
(2) $g_i = 0$ meets $g_{i+1} = 0$ on $p_i = 0$ with G^1 continuity, where the subscripts are modulo 3.

By condition (2), we can assume that

$$
\begin{aligned}
g_2 &= g_1 + \alpha_1 p_1^2, \\
g_3 &= g_2 + \alpha_2 p_2^2, \\
g_1 &= g_3 + \alpha_3 p_3^2,
\end{aligned}
\tag{5}
$$

where $\alpha_i = b_{0,i} + b_{1,i}x + b_{2,i}y + b_{3,i}z$. From these three equations, a conformability condition

$$
\alpha_1 p_1^2 + \alpha_2 p_2^2 + \alpha_3 p_3^2 = 0
\tag{6}
$$

must hold.

From $\{f_i, F_i^2\}$, we can compute three ascending sets A_i $(i = 1, 2, 3)$ under the order $x > y > z$. Setting $\mathrm{prem}(g_i, A_i) \equiv 0$ for $i = 1, 2, 3$ leads to a system of linear equations with b_{ij} as unknowns. The solution of this system has 10 free parameters. A suitable choice of free parameters gives

$$
\begin{aligned}
g_1 = {} & 2z^2xy + 2x^2y - 580x^2yz - 6496yz - 4306xy - 4842xz + 645x^2z \\
& + 1088xy^2 + 1358xz^2 + 3265y^2z + 1708z^2y + 1090x^3y + 1425x^3z \\
& + 1068y^3x - 538y^3z - 737x^2y^2 - 1295x^2z^2 + 546y^2z^2 + 1425xz^3 \\
& - 528yz^3 - 14146 - 15395x^2 - 4657y^2 - 9319z^2 + 5710x^3 \\
& - 2684y^3 + 853z^3 - 1295x^4 + 534y^4 + 1471xy^2z - 4274xyz
\end{aligned}
$$

$$+ 19190x + 14538y + 16924z,$$

$$g_2 = g_1 + 2(606x + 606y - 1212z + 5x^2 - y^2 - 7z^2 + 9xy + 5yz - 11xz) \cdot$$
$$(x - y)^2,$$

$$g_3 = g_1 - 2(606x - 606y + 13x^2 + y^2 - z^2 - 11xy - 3yz + xz)(y - z)^2.$$

The blending surface corresponding to this solution is shown in Fig. 13

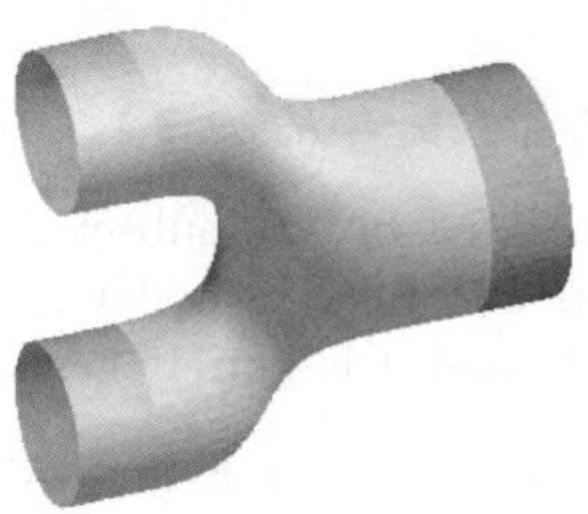

Fig. 12.   Blending three cylinders

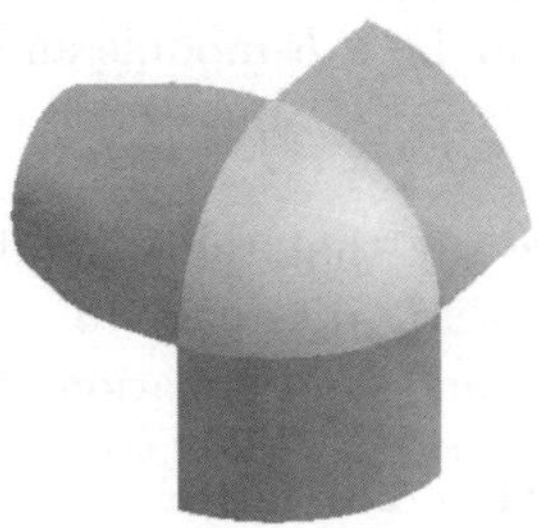

Fig. 13.   Smoothing Bajaj's corner

From the above examples, one can see that Wu's method is powerful for constructing algebraic blending surfaces in various situations. In general it can find blending surfaces of lowest degree and is much more efficient than the method of Gröbner bases. However, Wu's method cannot determine the lowest degree of the blending surfaces in advance. This is a problem that needs further investigation.

6. Syzygy Module Method

In this section, we introduce the method of syzygy modules for blending several algebraic surfaces. This method allows us to find all the blending surfaces of lowest degree theoretically.

6.1. *Syzygy Modules*

Let us begin with some elementary knowledge about syzygy modules.

Definition 19:[11] Let R is a commutative ring with identity. A module over a ring R (or R-module) is a set M together with a binary operation, usually written as addition, and an operation of R on M, called (scalar) multiplication, satisfying the following conditions:

(1) M is an Abelian group under addition;

(2) For $a, b \in R$ and $f, g \in M$,

$$a(f + g) = af + ag, \quad (a + b)f = af + bf, \quad (ab)f = a(bf);$$

(3) if 1 is the multiplicative identity in R, then $1f = f$ for all $f \in M$.

Throughout this section, R will stand for the polynomial ring $K[x]$ over an infinite field K.

Let M be a R-module and $F \subset M$. If

$$M = \langle F \rangle := \{ f = a_1 f_1 + \cdots + a_n f_n : f_i \in F, a_i \in R, \forall i = 1, \ldots n \},$$

then we say that the R-module M is generated by the subset F, or F generates M. It is easy to show that R^m is a R-module under the usual addition and multiplication of vectors in R^m, and it is finitely generated.

Definition 20: Let $\mathbf{F} = (\mathbf{f}_1, \ldots \mathbf{f}_s)$ be an s-tuple, where $\mathbf{f}_i \in R^m$, $i = 1, \ldots, s$. The set

$$\varphi := \left\{ (a_1, a_2, \ldots a_s)^T \in \mathbb{R}^s : \sum_{i=1}^{s} a_i \mathbf{f}_i = \mathbf{0} \right\}$$

is called a *syzygy module* of $(\mathbf{f}_1, \ldots \mathbf{f}_s)$ and denoted by $\mathrm{Syz}(\mathbf{f}_1, \ldots \mathbf{f}_s)$.

From Definition 20, we see that the syzygy module $\mathrm{Syz}(\mathbf{f}_1, \ldots \mathbf{f}_s)$ is identical to the solution space of the system of polynomial equations $\sum_{i=1}^{s} a_i \mathbf{f}_i = \mathbf{0}$.

6.2. *Monomial Orders and Gröbner Bases for Modules*

As for ideals, one can compute Gröbner bases for modules.

Let us first agree that a monomial m in R^m is an element of the form $x^\alpha \mathbf{e}_i$ for some i, where $\mathbf{e}_i$ is the standard basis vector. Any element $\mathbf{f} \in R^m$ can be written in a unique way as a k-linear combination of monomials $\mathbf{m}_i$:

$$\mathbf{f} = \sum_{i=1}^{n} c_i \mathbf{m}_i,$$

where $c_i \in k, c_i \neq 0$. For example, in $K[x, y]^3$

$$\mathbf{f} = \begin{pmatrix} 5xy^2 - y^{10} + 3 \\ 4x^3 + 2y \\ 16x \end{pmatrix} = 5xy^2 \mathbf{e}_1 - y^{10} \mathbf{e}_1 + 3\mathbf{e}_1 + 4x^3 \mathbf{e}_2 + 2y\mathbf{e}_2 + 16x\mathbf{e}_3,$$

which is a k-linear combination of monomials.

Some of the most common and useful monomial orders on R^m come by extending the monomial order on R. There are two natural ways to do this, once we have chosen an order on the standard basis vectors. We will always use the "top-down" ordering on the entries in a column:

$$\mathbf{e}_1 > \mathbf{e}_2 > \cdots > \mathbf{e}_m.$$

Definition 21: Let $>$ be any monomial order on R.

(1) (TOP extension of $>$) We order $x^\alpha \mathbf{e}_i >_{\text{TOP}} x^\beta \mathbf{e}_j$ if $x^\alpha > x^\beta$, or $x^\alpha = x^\beta$ and $i < j$.

(2) (POT extension of $>$) We order $x^\alpha \mathbf{e}_i >_{\text{POT}} x^\beta \mathbf{e}_j$ if $i < j$, or $i = j$ and $x^\alpha > x^\beta$.

Once we have an order $>$ on monomials, we can write any element $\mathbf{f} \in \mathbb{R}^m$ as a sum of terms

$$\mathbf{f} = \sum_{i=1}^{t} c_i \mathbf{m}_i$$

with $c_i \neq 0$ and $\mathbf{m}_1 > \cdots > \mathbf{m}_l$. Then we define

$$\mathrm{LC}_>(\mathbf{f}) = c_1, \quad \mathrm{LT}_>(\mathbf{f}) = \mathbf{m}_1, \quad \mathrm{LM}_>(\mathbf{f}) = c_1 \mathbf{m}_1.$$

Now we are ready to define the Gröbner basis for a module.

Definition 22: Let M be a submodule of R^m and $>$ a monomial order. A finite collection $G = \{\mathbf{g}_1, \ldots, \mathbf{g}_s\} \subset M$ is called a *Gröbner basis* for M if $\langle \mathrm{LT}(M) \rangle = \langle \mathrm{LT}(\mathbf{g}_1), \ldots, \mathrm{LT}(\mathbf{g}_s) \rangle$.

In order to apply the method of syzygy modules to surface blending, we need the following theorem. It allows us to obtain algebraic blending surfaces of lowest degree.

Theorem 23:[31] Let $M \subset R^m$ be a submodule and $>$ a TOP extension on R^m of the grand lex order on R. Suppose that $G = \{\mathbf{g}_1, \ldots, \mathbf{g}_s\}$ is a Gröbner basis for M and $\bar{G} = G \cap P_m^n = \{\mathbf{g}_1, \ldots, \mathbf{g}_t\}$, where P_m^n is the m-dimensional vector space, whose elements are polynomials of degree less than or equal to n. Then

$$M_m := M \cap P_m^n = \langle \mathbf{g}_1, \ldots, \mathbf{g}_t \rangle \cap P_m^n.$$

Furthermore, any $f \in M_m$ can be written as

$$\mathbf{f} = \sum_{i=1}^{t} a_i \mathbf{g}_i$$

with $\deg(a_i \mathbf{g}_i) \leq m$.

6.3. *Syzygy Module Method for Surface Blending*

From Section 3, we see that the problem of surface blending can be reduced to the problem of solving systems of linear equations in the unknown polynomials. Such systems can be solved by computing Gröbner bases for syzygy modules. We use two examples to illustrate the idea.

Example 24: Give two elliptic pipe surfaces

$$f_1 = \frac{y^2}{a_1^2} + \frac{z^2}{b_1^2} - 1 = 0, \quad x \geq h_1 > h_2,$$

$$f_2 = \frac{y^2}{a_2^2} + \frac{z^2}{b_2^2} - 1 = 0, \quad x \leq h_2$$

having the same axis and two planes

$$F_1 = x - h_1 = 0, \quad F_2 = y - h_2 = 0,$$

construct an algebraic surface $f = 0$ that blends these two pipe surfaces with G^k continuity.

According to Theorem 7 and Corollary 8, the G^k blending surface $f = 0$ has to satisfy

$$f = \alpha_1 f_1 + \beta_1 F_1^{k+1} = \alpha_2 f_2 + \beta_2 F_2^{k+1}$$

with $\alpha_i, \beta_i \in R[x, y, z]$, $i = 1, 2$. It follows that

$$\alpha_1 f_1 - \alpha_2 f_2 + \beta_1 F_1^{k+1} - \beta_2 F_2^{k+1} = 0.$$

This polynomial equation (with $\alpha_1, \alpha_2, \beta_1, \beta_2$ as unknowns) can be solved by computing the syzygy

$$\mathrm{Syz}(f_1, -f_2, F_1^{k+1}, -F_2^{k+1}).$$

We take $a_1 = b_2 = 2, a_2 = b_1 = 3, h_1 = -h_2 = 6$ as an example. In this specific case, the generators of $\mathrm{Syz}(f_1, -f_2, F_1^2, -F_2^2)$ may be computed as follows:

$$\begin{pmatrix} \alpha_1 \\ \alpha_2 \\ \beta_1 \\ \beta_2 \end{pmatrix} = \begin{pmatrix} -3456x \\ -7776x \\ 65z^2 - 180 \\ 65z^2 - 180 \end{pmatrix}, \begin{pmatrix} 4y^2 + 9z^2 - 36 \\ 9y^2 + 4z^2 - 36 \\ 0 \\ 0 \end{pmatrix}$$

$$\begin{pmatrix} 7776x \\ 3456x \\ 65y^2 - 180 \\ 65y^2 - 180 \end{pmatrix}, \begin{pmatrix} 36x^2 - 432x + 1296 \\ 0 \\ -9y^2 - 4z^2 + 36 \\ 0 \end{pmatrix}$$

$$\begin{pmatrix} 144x^2 - 1728x + 5184 \\ 324x^2 - 3888x + 11664 \\ 65z^2 - 180 \\ 0 \end{pmatrix}, \begin{pmatrix} 0 \\ 0 \\ x^2 + 12x + 36 \\ x^2 - 12x + 36 \end{pmatrix}.$$

These six generators produce six quartic algebraic surfaces

$$\xi_i = \alpha_{1,i} f_1 + \beta_{1,i} F_1^2, \quad i = 1, \ldots 6,$$

where $\alpha_{1,i}, \beta_{1,i}$ denote α_1, β_1 in the ith generator respectively. Hence all the blending surfaces of lowest degree can be written as

$$f = \sum_{i=1}^{6} \rho_i \xi_i,$$

where ρ_i $(i = 1, \ldots, 6)$ are constants. Figure 14 shows the blending surface with $\rho_1 = \rho_3 = 1$ and $\rho_i = 0$ for $i \neq 1, 3$.

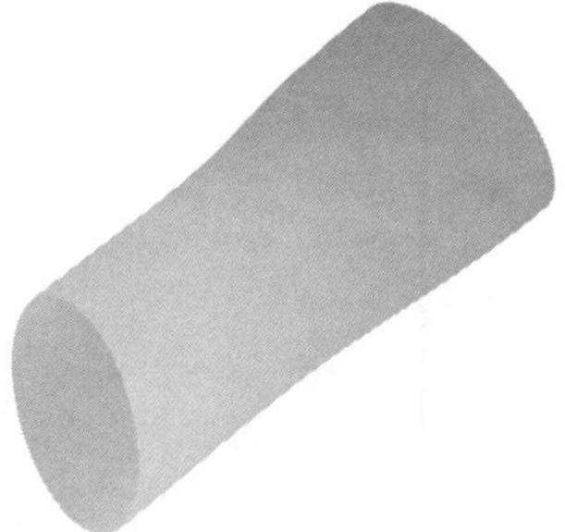

Fig. 14. G^1 blending two ellipse pipe surfaces having the same axis

Example 25: Now we resolve the problem of blending three pipe surfaces discussed in Example 10 using the method of syzygy modules.

We use the same space partition as in Example 10. The problem of finding a piecewise algebraic blending surface is equivalent to computing $\mathrm{Syz}(M)$, where

$$M = \begin{pmatrix} \pi_1^{k+1} & \pi_2^{k+1} & \pi_3^{k+1} & \pi_4^{k+1} & \pi_5^{k+1} & \pi_6^{k+1} & 0 \\ \pi_1^{k+1} & \pi_2^{k+1} & 0 & 0 & 0 & 0 & F_1^{k+1} \\ 0 & 0 & 0 & 0 & -\pi_5^{k+1} & -\pi_6^{k+1} & F_1^{k+1} \end{pmatrix}$$

$$\begin{pmatrix} 0 & 0 & 0 & 0 & 0 \\ -F_2^{k+1} & 0 & f_1 & -f_2 & 0 \\ 0 & -F_3^{k+1} & f_1 & 0 & -f_3 \end{pmatrix}$$

Taking $k = 1$, $h_1 = h_2 = h_3 = 3/5$, and $r_1 = r_2 = r_3 = 1/5$, we can obtain three generators of $\mathrm{Syz}(M)$

$$
\begin{pmatrix} \alpha_1 \\ \alpha_2 \\ \alpha_3 \\ \alpha_4 \\ \alpha_5 \\ \alpha_6 \\ \beta_1 \\ \beta_2 \\ \beta_3 \\ \gamma_1 \\ \gamma_2 \\ \gamma_3 \end{pmatrix} =
\begin{pmatrix}
-5x - 35y - 5z + 27 \\
35x + 5y + 5z - 27 \\
-5x - 5y - 35z + 27 \\
5x + 35y + 5z - 27 \\
-35x - 5y - 5z + 27 \\
5x + 5y + 35z - 27 \\
-135x + 135y + 135z - 81 \\
135x - 135y + 135z - 81 \\
135x + 135y - 135z - 81 \\
0 \\
0 \\
0
\end{pmatrix},
\begin{pmatrix}
-5x - 5y - 5z + 3 \\
5x + 5y + 5z - 3 \\
-5x - 5y - 5z + 3 \\
5x + 5y + 5z - 3 \\
-5x - 5y - 5z + 3 \\
5x + 5y + 5z - 3 \\
-15x + 15y + 15z - 10 \\
15x - 15y + 15z - 10 \\
15x + 15y - 15z - 10 \\
30x - 1 \\
30y - 1 \\
30z - 1
\end{pmatrix},
$$

$$
\begin{pmatrix}
1 \\
-1 \\
1 \\
-1 \\
1 \\
-1 \\
5x + 5y + 5z \\
5x + 5y + 5z \\
5x + 5y + 5z \\
5x + 5y + 5z - 9 \\
5x + 5y + 5z - 9 \\
5x + 5y + 5z - 9
\end{pmatrix},
$$

which have the lowest degree. If we choose the third generator, then the corresponding six pieces of the blending surface are given by the following polynomials

$$g_1 = (5x + 5y + 5z - 9)\left(y^2 + z^2 - 1/25\right) + (5x + 5y + 5z)\left(x - 3/5\right)^2,$$

$$g_2 = (5x + 5y + 5z - 9)\left(y^2 + z^2 - 1/25\right) + (5x + 5y + 5z)\left(x - 3/5\right)^2$$
$$+ (x - 2y + z)^2,$$

$$g_3 = (5x + 5y + 5z - 9)\left(z^2 + x^2 - 1/25\right) + (5x + 5y + 5z)\left(y - 3/5\right)^2,$$

$$g_4 = (5x + 5y + 5z - 9)\left(z^2 + x^2 - 1/25\right) + (5x + 5y + 5z)\left(y - 3/5\right)^2$$
$$+ (-x - y + 2z)^2,$$

$$g_5 = (5x + 5y + 5z - 9)\left(x^2 + y^2 - 1/25\right) + (5x + 5y + 5z)(z - 3/5)^2,$$

$$g_6 = (5x + 5y + 5z - 9)\left(x^2 + y^2 - 1/25\right) + (5x + 5y + 5z)(z - 3/5)^2$$
$$+ (-2x + y + z)^2.$$

The corresponding blending surface is shown in Fig. 15.

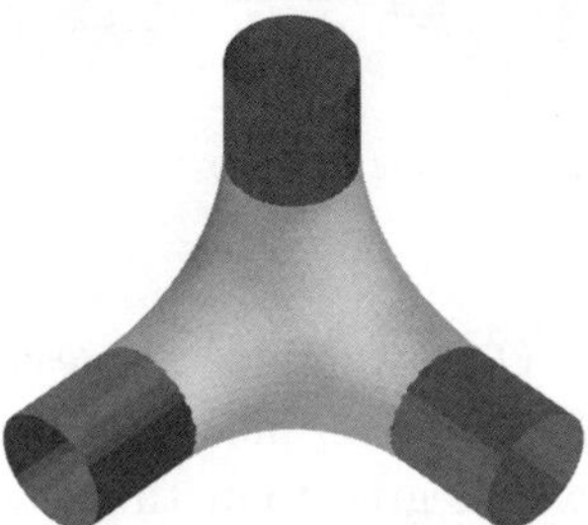

Fig. 15.   A piecewise cubic algebraic surface blending three pipe surfaces with G^1 continuity

Compared with the result in Section 3, the solutions of the polynomial system obtained here are much simpler, and in a certain sense they are the simplest. Moreover, we have three generators, corresponding to three blending surfaces ξ_i $(i = 1, 2, 3)$. Their linear combination

$$f = \rho_1\xi_1 + \rho_2\xi_2 + \rho_3\xi_3$$

contains two free parameters; one can adjust the shape of the blending surface by changing the free parameters.

For the case $k = 2$, the same kind of argument shows that the syzygy module also has three quadratic generators. The general formulation of the blending surface can be written as

$$f = \sum_{i=1}^{3} \rho_i\xi_i,$$

where ξ_i is the algebraic blending surface corresponding to one of the generator for each i. If we take $\rho_1 = 0$, $\rho_2 = 20$, and $\rho_3 = 1$, then the final G^2 blending surface looks as in Fig. 16.

7. Concluding Remark

In this survey, we have summarized several approaches that allows us to construct a piecewise algebraic surface to blend several given algebraic sur-

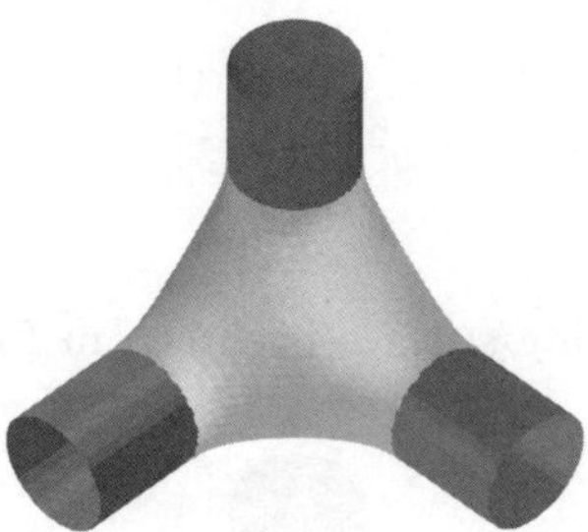

Fig. 16.   A piecewise quartic algebraic surface blending three pipe surfaces with G^2 continuity

faces with G^k continuity. Our examples suggest some advantages of using PAS as blending surfaces. First, piecewise blending algebraic surfaces in general have much lower degree than the blending surfaces generated by other methods. In particular, when the methods of Gröbner bases and syzygy modules are used, we can get blending surfaces of lowest degree theoretically. Second, our method works for any order of geometric continuity. Third, all the blending surfaces of lowest degree are obtained with some free parameters that may be chosen for adjusting the shape of the blending surfaces. Furthermore, the expression of blending surfaces using the syzygy module method is relatively simple.

However, there is still much work that needs to be done. For example, how to automatically construct the defining region of PAS? Currently, we can only solve the problem for each specific situation. How to choose values for the free parameters in the solutions and how to avoid multiple sheets of the algebraic surface patches? These are some of the questions that are worth further study.

Acknowledgments

This work is supported by the Outstanding Youth Grant of the NSF of China (NO. 60225002), the NKBRSF on Mathematics Mechanization (NO. G1998030600), the TRAPOYT in Higher Education Institute of MOE of China, the National Natural Science Foundation of China (NO. 10201030), and the Doctoral Program of MOE of China (NO. 20010358003).

References

1. S. Allen and D. Dutta, Supercyclides and blending, *Comput. Aided Geom. Design* 14, 637–652, 1997.

2. C. L. Bajaj and I. Ihm, C^1 smoothing of polyhedra with implicit algebraic splines, *Comput. Graphics* 26, 79–88, 1992.

3. C. L. Bajaj, The emergence of algebraic curves and surfaces in geometric design, in *Directions in Geometric Computing* (R. Martin, ed.), pp. 1–29, Information Geometers Press, 1993.

4. C. L. Bajaj, J. Chen, and G. Xu, Modeling with cubic A-patches, *ACM Trans. Graphics* 14, 103–133, 1995.

5. C. S. Chen, F. L. Chen, and Y. Y. Feng, Blending quadric surfaces with piecewise algebraic surfaces, *Graphics Models* 63, 212–223, 2001.

6. C. S. Chen, F. L. Chen, J. S. Deng, and Y. Y. Feng, Filling holes with piecewise algebraic surfaces, in *Computer Mathematics*, Lecture Notes Series on Computing 8, pp. 182–191, World Scientific, Singapore New Jersey, 2000.

7. C. S. Chen, *Modeling with Piecewise Algebraic Surfaces* (in Chinese), Ph.D. dissertation, University of Science and Technology of China, 2000.

8. F. L. Chen, *Geometric Continuity, Blending and Intersection of Algebraic Surfaces* (in Chinese), Ph.D. dissertation, University of Science and Technology of China, 1994.

9. F. L. Chen, J. S. Deng, and Y. Y. Feng, Algebraic surface blending using Wu's method, in *Computer Mathematics*, Lecture Notes Series on Computing 8, pp. 172–181, World Scientific, Singapore New Jersey, 2000.

10. D. Cox, J. Little, and D. O'Shea, *Ideas, Varieties and Algorithms — An Introduction to Computational Algebraic Geometry* (2nd edn.), Springer-Verlag, New York, 1997.

11. D. Cox, J. Little, and D. O'Shea, *Using Algebraic Geometry*, Springer-Verlag, New York, 1998.

12. W. Dahmen and T. M. Thamm-Schwar, Cubicoids: Modeling and visualization, *Comput. Aided Geom. Design* 10, 89–108, 1993.

13. J. S. Deng, *A Study of Piecewise Algebraic Surfaces in Computer Aided Geometric Design* (in Chinese), Ph.D. dissertation, University of Science and Technology of China, 1998.

14. G. C. Feng, H. J. Ren, and Y. S. Zhou, Blending several implicit algebraic surfaces, in *Mathematics Mechanization and Applications* (X.-S. Gao and D. Wang, eds.), pp. 461–490, Academic Press, London, 2000.

15. Y. Y. Feng, X. M. Wang, and J. S. Deng, Total degree division in polynomial module and its application in CAGD (I), *J. of China University of Science and Technology* 30/3, 263–269, 2000.

16. Y. Y. Feng, C. S. Chen, and J. S. Deng, Total degree division in polynomial module and its application in CAGD (II), *J. of China University of Science and Technology* 30/4, 379–386, 2000.

17. T. Garrity and J. Warren, Geometric continuity, *Comput. Aided Design* 8, 51–65, 1991.

18. E. Hartmann, A marching method for the triangulation of surfaces, *Visual Comput.* 14, 95–108, 1998.

19. E. Hartmann, Implicit G^n-blending of vertices, *Comput. Aided Geom. Design* 18, 267–285, 2001.

20. C. Hoffmann and J. Hopcroft, Quadratic blending surfaces, *Comput. Aided*

Design 18, 301–307, 1986.

21. J. Li, J. Hoschek, and E. Hartmann, G^{n-1} functional splines for interpolation and approximation of curves, surfaces and solids, *Comput. Aided Geom. Design* 7, 209–220, 1989.

22. W. P. Lou, *Algebraic Surface Blending Using Gröbner Bases* (in Chinese), Master thesis, University of Science and Technology of China, 2000.

23. W. P. Lou, Y. Y. Feng, F. L. Chen, and J. S. Deng, The method of Gröbner bases for constructing algebraic blending surfaces (in Chinese), *Chinese J. Computers* 25/6, 599–605, 2002.

24. A. E. Middleditch and K. H. Sears, Blending surfaces for set theoretic volume modeling system, *Comput. Graphics* 19, 161–170, 1985.

25. M. J. Pratt, Quartic supercyclides I: Basic theory, *Comput. Aided Geom. Design* 14, 671–692, 1997.

26. A. Rockwood and J. Owen, Blending surfaces in solid modeling, in *Geometric Modeling: Algorithm and New Trends* (G. Farin, ed.), SIAM, Philadelphia, 1985.

27. J. R. Rossignac and A. G. Requicha, Constant radius blending in solid modeling, *Comput. Mech. Eng.* 3, 65–73, 1984.

28. T. W. Sederberg, Piecewise algebraic surface patches, *Comput. Aided Geom. Design* 2, 53–60, 1985.

29. T. W. Sederberg, Techniques for cubic algebraic surfaces (part two), *IEEE Comput. Graphics Appl.* 10, 12–21, 1990.

30. J. R. Sendra, Rational curves and surfaces: Algorithms and some applications, in *Geometric Computation* (F. Chen and D. Wang, eds.), pp. 65–125, World Scientific, Singapore New Jersey, 2003.

31. X. Tang, *Modeling with Algebraic Surfaces* (in Chinese), Ph.D. dissertation, University of Science and Technology of China, 2002.

32. J. Vida, R. R. Martin, and T. Varady, A survey of blending methods that use parametric surfaces, *Computer Aided-Design* 26/5, 341–365, 1994.

33. J. Warren, Blending algebraic surfaces, *ACM Trans. Graphics* 8, 263–278, 1989.

34. T. Wu, W. Gao, and G. Feng, Blending of implicit algebraic surfaces, in *Proc. ASCM '95* (H. Shi and H. Kobayashi, eds.), pp. 125–131, Scientists Inc., Tokyo, 1995.

35. T. Wu and Y. Zhou, On blending of several quadratic algebraic surfaces, *Comput. Aided Geom. Design* 17, 759–766, 2000.

36. W.-T. Wu, On zeros of algebraic equations — An application of Ritt principles, *Kexue Tongbao* 31, 1–5, 1986.

37. W.-T. Wu, *Mechanical Theorem Proving in Geometries: Basic Principles*, Springer-Verlag, Wien New York, 1994.

38. W.-T. Wu and D. K. Wang, On the algebraic surface-fitting problem in CAGD (in Chinese), *Math. Practice and Theory* 3, 26–31, 1994.

39. G. Xu, H. C. Huang, and C. L. Bajaj, C^1 modeling with A-patches from rational trivariate functions, *Comput. Aided Geom. Design* 18, 221–243, 2001.

40. G. Xu, C. L. Bajaj, and S. Evans, C^1 modeling with hybrid multiple-sided A-patches, Preprint, 2003.

CHAPTER 3

RATIONAL CURVES AND SURFACES: ALGORITHMS AND SOME APPLICATIONS

J. Rafael Sendra

Departamento de Matemáticas
Universidad de Alcalá
E28871 Alcalá de Henares, Madrid, Spain
E-mail: Rafael.Sendra@uah.es

In this chapter we survey symbolic algorithms for dealing with rational algebraic curves and surfaces as well as some applications. More precisely we describe algorithms for deciding the rationality of algebraic curves and surfaces, and we show how to parametrize them. In addition, we study how to parametrize and reparametrize curves under different criteria of optimality such as the degree, the field of parametrization, its polynomiality and normality character. Parametrization and reparametrization algorithms for the case of real curves are also considered, and so is the inversion problem for proper parametrizations. Finally, we briefly describe some applications of algebraic curves and surfaces such as plotting, offsetting and blending.

1. Introduction

The theoretical development of scientific computation (numerical-symbolic), and the computing feasibility provided by the recent technological advances in software and hardware, have implied an increasing interest in the field of application for the fundamentals and algorithms for curves and surfaces. This phenomenon has motivated a reciprocal relationship of interest between the fields of applications and development of constructive methods in algebraic geometry.

In this tutorial chapter we survey symbolic algorithms for dealing with rational algebraic curves and surfaces as well as some applications; for a more complete treatment on applications see Chapter 1 in this volume. Rational curves or surfaces are algebraic curves or algebraic surfaces that can be parametrized rationally, i.e., by means of a vector of rational functions,

65

where not all components are constant.

Not all algebraic curves and surfaces can be rationally parametrized. Thus the first problem one has to consider is the rationality analysis which is approached by means of the genus for the case of curves and by means of the arithmetic genus and the plurigenus for surfaces. Once the rationality has been decided we focus our attention on the problem of computing a rational parametrization. This question can be approached by means of anticanonical divisors or by adjoints; we will give references for the first method and describe the adjoint method for curves and surfaces.

Other conversion problems are the implicitization or the inversion of rational parametrizations. Implicitization consists in determining, from a given rational parametrization, the implicit equation of the hypersurface it defines. This problem can be translated into an elimination problem and therefore standard techniques such as Gröbner bases or characteristic sets can be applied. Nevertheless, many authors have addressed the specific problem for curves and surfaces with other particular techniques such as resultants or multi-resultants, and moving lines or curves. Here, we do not consider the implicitization problem since a survey[49] by Kotsireas on that topic appears in this volume. The other conversion problem is the inversion of rational parametrizations. In this case, the problem consists in computing explicit rational formulas for the inverse mapping of a birational parametrization, and therefore finding which parameter value must be substituted in the parametrization in order to generate a particular point on the variety.

Once conversion algorithms have been described we focus our attention on the problem of finding optimal parametrizations for algebraic curves, mentioning also some of the few contributions for the surface case. The optimality will be analyzed from a geometric point of view (i.e., achieving optimal degree in the output) or algebraically (i.e., expressing the coefficients of the parametrization on the smallest possible field extension of the ground field). In addition, optimality will be studied from two different points of view, namely assuming that the geometric object is given either implicitly or parametrically. We will also mention the related problems for real curves and surfaces and discuss the question of finding normal parametrization, i.e., parametrizations being surjective.

In the last part of the chapter, we will briefly illustrate how rational curves and surfaces can be used in some applications; for further details we refer to Chapter 1 of this volume by González-Vega and others.[36] More precisely, we will discuss the problem of plotting algebraic real curves, the problem of offsetting, that basically consists in computing parallel curves and surfaces, and the problem of blending where algebraic surfaces providing a smooth transition among distinct geometric features of an object are computed.

The structure of the chapter is as follows. Section 2 is devoted to basic concepts and algorithms on plane algebraic curves. In Section 3 we study rational curves from a theoretical and algorithmic point of view. Section 4 focuses on the parametrization methods for rational plane curves. In Section 5 we study the concept of properness and show how to approach the inversion problem. Section 6 deals with reparametrization algorithms for rational plane curves given parametrically. In Section 7 we analyze and present algorithms for the special case of real plane curves. Section 8 is devoted to the basic notions on algebraic surfaces as well as to the parametrization procedures for surfaces. In Section 9 we briefly describe some applications of curves and surfaces.

2. Algebraic Plane Curves

In this section we introduce the terminology as well as some basic results on algebraic curves. For a further analysis, proofs, *etc.*, we refer to basic textbooks[14,30,97] on algebraic curves.

Throughout this chapter we use the following **notation**: $\mathbb{K}$ is an algebraically closed field of characteristic zero, and as usual the affine plane $\mathbb{K}^2$ will be embedded into the projective plane $\mathbb{P}^2(\mathbb{K})$ by identifying the point $(a, b) \in \mathbb{K}^2$ with the point $(a : b : 1) \in \mathbb{P}^2(\mathbb{K})$. These points are sometimes called the points at finite distance of $\mathbb{P}^2(\mathbb{K})$. In addition to the points at finite distance, $\mathbb{P}^2(\mathbb{K})$ contains points at infinity, namely the points with projective coordinates $(a : b : 0)$, where a, b are not simultaneously zero. Similarly for $\mathbb{K}^3$ and $\mathbb{P}^3(\mathbb{K})$.

We start with the definition of affine and projective plane curves.

Definition 1: An *affine plane algebraic curve* over $\mathbb{K}$ is defined as the set

$$\mathcal{C} = \{(a, b) \in \mathbb{K}^2 \mid f(a, b) = 0\}$$

for a non-constant squarefree polynomial $f(x, y) \in \mathbb{K}[x, y]$. We call f the *defining polynomial* of $\mathcal{C}$ (of course, a polynomial $g = c f$, for some nonzero $c \in \mathbb{K}$, defines the same curve, so f is unique only up to multiplication by nonzero constants). We will write f as

$$f(x, y) = f_d(x, y) + f_{d-1}(x, y) + \cdots + f_0(x, y)$$

where $f_k(x, y)$ is a homogeneous polynomial (form) of degree k, and $f_d(x, y)$ is nonzero. The polynomials f_k are called the *homogeneous components* of f, and d is called the *degree* of C. Curves of degree one are called *lines*, of degree two *conics*, of degree three *cubics, etc.*

If $f = \prod_{i=1}^{n} f_i$, where f_i are the irreducible factors of f, we say that the affine curve defined by each polynomial f_i is a *component* of C. Furthermore, the curve C is said to be *irreducible* if its defining polynomial is irreducible.

Sometimes we will need to consider curves with multiple components. This means that the given definition has to be extended to non-squarefree polynomials; i.e., polynomials of the form $f = \prod_{i=1}^{n} f_i^{e_i}$, where f_i are the irreducible factors of f, and $e_i \in \mathbb{N}$ are their multiplicities. In this situation, the curve defined by f is the curve defined by its squarefree part, i.e., by $\prod_{i=1}^{n} f_i$, but the component generated by f_i carries multiplicity e_i. Whenever we use this generalization, we will always explicitly say so.

Definition 2: A *projective plane algebraic curve* over $\mathbb{K}$ is defined as the set

$$C = \{(a : b : c) \in \mathbb{P}^2(\mathbb{K}) \mid F(a, b, c) = 0\}$$

for a non-constant squarefree homogeneous polynomial $F(x, y, z) \in \mathbb{K}[x, y, z]$. We call F the *defining polynomial* of C (of course, a polynomial $G = cF$ for some nonzero $c \in \mathbb{K}$ defines the same curve, so F is unique only up to multiplication by nonzero constants).

Similarly to the affine case, one may introduce the concepts of degree, components and irreducibility for projective curves. Also, as in the case of affine curves, we will sometimes need to refer to multiple components of a projective plane curve. Again, this notion is introduced by extending the concept of curve to arbitrary forms. We will also explicitly indicate this generalization when we make use of it.

Associated to every affine curve there is a projective curve (its projective closure). If the affine curve C is defined by the polynomial $f(x, y)$, then its projective closure is the projective curve C^* defined by the homogenization $F(x, y, z)$ of $f(x, y)$. Therefore, if

$$f(x, y) = f_d(x, y) + f_{d-1}(x, y) + \cdots + f_0(x, y)$$

is the decomposition of f into forms, then

$$F(x, y, z) = f_d(x, y) + f_{d-1}(x, y)z + \cdots + f_0(x, y)z^d,$$

and

$$C^* = \{(a : b : c) \in \mathbb{P}^2(\mathbb{K}) \mid F(a, b, c) = 0\}.$$

Every point (a, b) on $\mathcal{C}$ corresponds to a point $(a : b : 1)$ on $\mathcal{C}^*$, and every additional point on $\mathcal{C}^*$ is a point at infinity. In other words, the first two coordinates of the additional points are the nontrivial solutions of $f_d(x, y)$. Thus, the curve $\mathcal{C}^*$ has only finitely many points at infinity. Of course, a projective curve, not associated to an affine curve, could have $z = 0$ as a component and therefore have infinitely many points at infinity.

On the other hand, associated to every projective curve there are infinitely many affine curves. We may take any line in $\mathbb{P}^2(\mathbb{K})$ as the line at infinity, move it to $z = 0$ by a linear change of coordinates, and then dehomogenize. But in practice we mostly use dehomogenizations provided by taking the axes as lines at infinity.

2.1. *Singular Points*

Singular points play an important role in the theory of algebraic curves. In the following, some basic notions and results are reviewed. Let $\mathcal{C}$ be an irreducible affine plane curve over $\mathbb{K}$ defined by $f(x, y) \in \mathbb{K}[x, y]$, and let $P = (a, b) \in \mathcal{C}$; then the *multiplicity* of $\mathcal{C}$ at P (denoted by $\text{mult}_P(\mathcal{C})$) is defined as the order of the lowest non-vanishing term in the Taylor expansion of f at P (it can be easily proved that this notion is independent of the choice of coordinates). Therefore, P is of multiplicity r on $\mathcal{C}$ if and only if all the derivatives of f up to and including the $(r - 1)$-th vanish at P but at least one r-th derivative does not vanish at P. On the other hand, the *tangents* to $\mathcal{C}$ at P are the lines through P corresponding to the roots of

$$\sum_{i=0}^{r} \binom{r}{i} \frac{\partial^r f}{\partial x^i \partial y^{r-i}}(P)(x - a)^i (y - b)^{r-i} = 0$$

and are counted with multiplicities equal to the multiplicities of the corresponding roots of this equation. If $\mathcal{C}$ is reducible, say $f = \prod_{i=1}^{n} f_i^{e_i}$ with f_i irreducible, then $\text{mult}_P(\mathcal{C}) = \sum_{i=1}^{n} e_i \text{mult}_P(\mathcal{C}_i)$, where $\mathcal{C}_i$ is the component defined by f_i. Furthermore, if L is a tangent to $\mathcal{C}_i$ with multiplicity r_i, then L is tangent to $\mathcal{C}$ with multiplicity $\sum_{i=1}^{n} e_i r_i$. In this situation, a point $P \in \mathcal{C}$ is said to be *simple* if $\text{mult}_P(\mathcal{C}) = 1$. If $\text{mult}_P(\mathcal{C}) = r > 1$, then we say that P is a *singular point* of multiplicity r or an *r-fold point*; if $r = 2$, then P is called a *double* point, and if $r = 3$ a *triple* point, *etc.* Similarly, by a *non-singular* curve we mean a curve with no singular point.

To analyze the singularities, one introduces the notion of ordinary singularity, that depends on the multiplicities of the tangents. More precisely, a singular point of multiplicity r is *ordinary* if the r tangents to C at P are distinct, and *non-ordinary* otherwise. Moreover, from the previous definitions it follows that if $f(x,y) = f_d(x,y) + \cdots + f_r(x,y)$, with $r > 0$ and $f_r \neq 0$, then the origin is an r-fold point of C, and the curve defined by $f_r(x,y)$ has the tangents to C at the origin as its components. Furthermore, if $r \geq 2$, then the origin is an ordinary singularity of C if and only if the discriminant of $f_r(x,1)$ is not zero, assuming that $y = 0$ is not tangent to C.

Now, as far as projective curves are concerned all these definitions also apply, since every point at infinity can be transformed to a point at finite distance by a change of coordinates. Furthermore, in terms of projective coordinates, using Euler's formula, the singular points can be characterized as follows: $P \in C^\star$ is an r-fold point if and only if all the $(r-1)$-th derivatives of F (where F is the homogenization of f), but not all the r-th derivatives, vanish at P. Thus, $P \in C^\star$ is a singularity if and only if

$$\frac{\partial F}{\partial x}(P) = \frac{\partial F}{\partial y}(P) = \frac{\partial F}{\partial z}(P) = 0.$$

In particular, it follows that a projective algebraic plane curve without multiple components can have only finitely many singular points. We will denote by $\mathrm{Sing}(C)$ or $\mathrm{Sing}(C^\star)$ the singular locus of the curve.

In order to compute the affine singularities one just has to find the finitely many solutions of the system of algebraic equations

$$\left\{ f = 0, \frac{\partial f}{\partial x} = 0, \frac{\partial f}{\partial y} = 0 \right\},$$

and to determine the singularities at infinity one can dehomogenize $F(x,y,z)$ with respect to one variable or analyze the finitely many points of the curve at infinity. Also, one can look for the nonzero solutions of

$$\left\{ \frac{\partial F}{\partial x} = 0, \frac{\partial F}{\partial y} = 0, \frac{\partial F}{\partial z} = 0 \right\}.$$

Furthermore, in order to analyze the character of a singularity (i.e., whether it is ordinary or not), one may study the multiplicity of the factors in the equation defining the tangents.

An important result about singularities (see for instance the books by Fulton[30] and Walker[97]) is the fact that, if C is a projective irreducible curve of degree d, then

$$(d-1)(d-2) \geq \sum_{P \in \mathcal{C}} \mathrm{mult}_P(\mathcal{C})(\mathrm{mult}_P(\mathcal{C}) - 1).$$

Moreover, if $\mathcal{C}$ is reducible with no multiple components, then the bound is $d(d-1)$.

Example 3: Let $\mathcal{C}$ be the affine plane curve over $\mathbb{C}$ (see Fig. 1) defined by the polynomial

$$\begin{aligned}
f(x,y) = {}& -4\,y^4\,x^2 + 2\,y^7\,x^2 + y^9 + 3\,y^7 - 9\,y^6\,x^2 - 2\,x^8 + 2\,x^8\,y + 3\,x^4\,y^5 \\
& - y^6 + 4\,x^6\,y^3 - 7\,x^6\,y^2 + 5\,x^6\,y + 10\,x^2\,y^5 - 11\,x^4\,y^4 + 9\,x^4\,y^3 \\
& - 4\,x^4\,y^2 + y^3 x^2 - 3\,y^8
\end{aligned}$$

and $\mathcal{C}^\star$ the projective curve associated to $\mathcal{C}$. The degree of the curve is 9. First, we compute the finitely many points at infinity of the curve. We

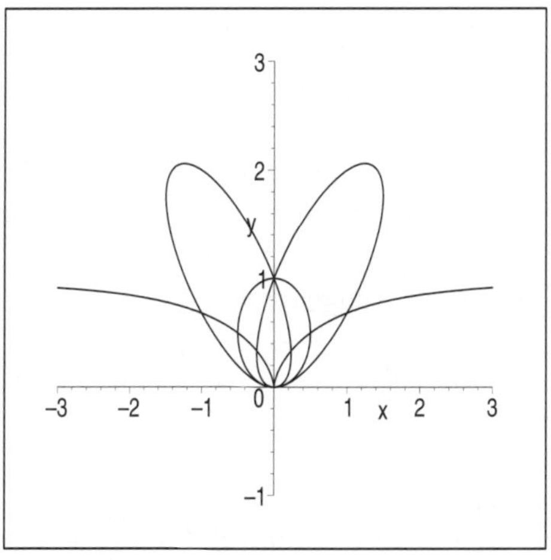

Fig. 1.   Real part of $\mathcal{C}$

observe that $F(x,y,0) = y(2x^4 + y^4)(y^2 + x^2)^2$ does not vanish identically, so the line $z = 0$ is not a component of $\mathcal{C}^\star$. In fact, the points at infinity are $(1 : 0 : 0), (1 : \alpha : 0)$ and the cyclic points $(1 : \pm i : 0)$, where $\alpha^4 + 2 = 0$. Now, we proceed to determine and analyze the singularities. Solving the system

$$\left\{ \frac{\partial F}{\partial x} = 0, \frac{\partial F}{\partial y} = 0, \frac{\partial F}{\partial z} = 0 \right\},$$

we find that the singular points of the projective curve $\mathcal{C}^\star$ are

$$P_1^\pm = (1 : \pm i : 0), \qquad P_2 = (0 : 0 : 1), \quad P_3^\pm = \left(\pm\frac{1}{3\sqrt{2}} : \frac{1}{3} : 1\right),$$

$$P_4^\pm = \left(\pm\frac{1}{2}, \frac{1}{2} : 1\right), \quad P_5 = (0 : 1 : 1), \quad P_\alpha^\pm = (\pm 1 : \alpha : 1),$$

where $\alpha^3 + \alpha - 1 = 0$. So $\mathcal{C}^\star$ has 14 singular points (see Fig. 1).

We now compute the multiplicity and the tangents at each singular point. For this purpose, we determine the first non-vanishing term in the corresponding Taylor expansion. The result of this computation is:

- $\mathrm{mult}_{P_1^\pm}(\mathcal{C}^\star) = 2$; the tangents are

$$2y \mp z \mp 2ix = 0, \quad 2y \pm z \mp 2ix = 0.$$

- $\mathrm{mult}_{P_2}(\mathcal{C}^\star) = 5$; $y = 0$ is a triple tangent and $x = 0$ a double tangent.
- $\mathrm{mult}_{P_3^\pm}(\mathcal{C}^\star) = 2$; the tangents are

$$8x \pm \sqrt{2}z \mp 7\sqrt{2}y = 0, \quad 28x \mp 5\sqrt{2}z \pm \sqrt{2}y = 0.$$

- $\mathrm{mult}_{P_4^\pm}(\mathcal{C}^\star) = 2$; the tangents are $2x \mp z = 0$, $2x \mp 4y \pm z = 0$.
- $\mathrm{mult}_{P_5}(\mathcal{C}^\star) = 3$; the tangents are $y - z = 0$ and the two linear factors of $3x^2 + 2yz - y^2 - z^2 = 0$.
- $\mathrm{mult}_{P_\alpha^\pm}(\mathcal{C}^\star) = 2$; the tangents are

$$\left(\pm 1 \pm \frac{1}{2}\alpha \pm \frac{1}{2}\alpha^2\right) z + x + \left(\mp\frac{5}{2} \mp \frac{1}{2}\alpha \mp 2\alpha^2\right) y = 0$$

and

$$\left(\mp\frac{35}{146} + \mp\frac{23}{73}\alpha \pm \frac{1}{73}\alpha^2\right) z + x + \left(\mp\frac{65}{146} \mp \frac{1}{73}\alpha \mp \frac{111}{146}\alpha^2\right) y = 0.$$

From the tangents one deduces that all these singular points are ordinary, except the affine origin $(0 : 0 : 1)$. On the other hand, factoring f over $\mathbb{C}$ we get

$$f(x, y) = (x^2 + y^2 - y)(y^3 + y - x^2)(y^4 - 2y^3 + y^2 - 3yx^2 + 2x^4).$$

Therefore, $\mathcal{C}$ decomposes into a union of a conic, a cubic, and a quartic (see Fig. 1). Furthermore, $(0 : 0 : 1)$ is a double point on the quartic, a double point on the cubic, and a simple point on the conic. Thus, the multiplicity of $\mathcal{C}^\star$ at $(0 : 0 : 1)$ is 5. $(0 : 1 : 1)$ is a double point on the quartic and a simple point on the conic. Hence, the multiplicity of C^* at $(0 : 1 : 1)$ is 3. In addition, the points

$$\left(\pm \frac{1}{2} : \frac{1}{2} : 1 \right)$$

are simple points on the conic and the cubic, and

$$\left(\pm \frac{1}{3\sqrt{2}} : \frac{1}{3} : 1 \right)$$

are simple points on the quartic and the cubic. Similarly, the points $(\pm 1 : \alpha : 1)$ are also simple points on the quartic and the cubic (two of them are real, and four of them complex). Finally, the cyclic points are simple points on the cubic and the conic. Hence, all these singular points are double points on C^*.

2.2. *Intersection of Curves*

In this subsection we deal with the problem of computing the intersection of two plane curves and we introduce the notion of multiplicity of intersection. The intersection of two algebraic plane curves over $\mathbb{K}$ either is a finite set of points or contains a curve. In fact, the intersection contains a 1-dimensional component, i.e., a curve, if and only if the gcd (greatest common divisor) of the corresponding defining polynomials is not constant, or equivalently if both curves have a common component; namely the gcd. Therefore, crossing out the common components in both curves, the problem is reduced to the case of two curves without common components. Furthermore, since we are working in the affine plane, the problem can be solved by means of resultants.

Let C and D be two projective plane curves defined by the forms F and G, respectively, such that $\gcd(F, G) = 1$. First, we observe that if both polynomials are bivariate forms in the same variables, say $F, G \in \mathbb{K}[x, y]$ (similarly if $F, G \in \mathbb{K}[x, z]$ or $F, G \in \mathbb{K}[y, z]$), then each curve is a finite union of lines passing through $O = (0 : 0 : 1)$. Hence, since the curves do not have common components, C and D intersect only at O. Note that, if $P \neq O$ is also a common point, then the line passing through P and O would be a common component of C and D. For instance, the curves of equations $x(x - y) = 0$ and $y(x + y) = 0$ only meet at O.

So now let us assume that at least one of the defining polynomials is not a bivariate form in x and y, say $F \notin \mathbb{K}[x, y]$ and that $(0 : 0 : 1)$ is neither on C nor on D; note that this requirement can always be achieved by means of a linear change of coordinates. Then, we consider the resultant $R(x, y)$ of F and G with respect to z. Since $\mathcal{C}$ and $\mathcal{D}$ do not have common components, and since $\deg_z(F) \geq 1$ and G is not constant, the resultant R is a non-constant bivariate homogeneous polynomial. Hence it factors as

$$R(x, y) = \prod_{i=1}^{s} (b_i x - a_i y)^{r_i}$$

for some $a_i, b_i \in \mathbb{K}$, and $r_i \in \mathbb{N}$. Then, the solutions of R provide the intersection points. Since $(0 : 0 : 0)$ is not a point of $\mathbb{P}^2(\mathbb{K})$, but it might be the formal result of extending the solution $(0, 0)$ of R, we check whether $(0 : 0 : 1)$ is an intersection point. The remaining intersection points are given by $(a_i : b_i : c_{i,j})$, where a_i, b_i are not simultaneously zero, and $c_{i,j}$ are the roots in $\mathbb{K}$ of $\gcd(F(a_i, b_i, z), G(a_i, b_i, z))$.

Once we know how to compute the intersection points of two curves we introduce the concept of multiplicity of intersection. Many of the ideas in the algorithms we will review are based on this notion that can be approached in different ways: axiomatically (see the book[30] by Fulton), computationally (see the book[14] by Brieskorn and Knörrer), *etc.* Here we present the computational approach. Let $\mathcal{C}$ and $\mathcal{D}$ be projective plane curves, without common components, such that $(0 : 0 : 1)$ is neither on $\mathcal{C}$ nor on $\mathcal{D}$ and such that it is not on any line connecting two intersection points of $\mathcal{C}$ and $\mathcal{D}$. Let $P = (a : b : c) \in \mathcal{C} \cap \mathcal{D}$, and let F and G be the defining forms of $\mathcal{C}$ and $\mathcal{D}$, respectively. Then, the *multiplicity of intersection of $\mathcal{C}$ and $\mathcal{D}$ at P* (we denote it by $\text{mult}_P(\mathcal{C}, \mathcal{D})$) is defined as the multiplicity of the factor $bx - ay$ in the resultant of F and G w.r.t. z. If $P \notin \mathcal{C} \cap \mathcal{D}$ then we define the multiplicity of intersection at P as 0. Also, observe that since the number of intersection points is finite, there always exist linear changes of coordinates satisfying the required conditions in the definition. Furthermore, one may prove that the concept does not depend on the coordinate system.

In addition, if $\mathcal{C}$ and $\mathcal{D}$ are two projective plane curves, without common components, and $P \in \mathbb{P}^2(\mathbb{K})$, it holds that $\text{mult}_P(\mathcal{C}, \mathcal{D}) \geq \text{mult}_P(\mathcal{C}) \cdot \text{mult}_P(\mathcal{D})$. Moreover, $\text{mult}_P(\mathcal{C}, \mathcal{D}) = \text{mult}_P(\mathcal{C}) \cdot \text{mult}_P(\mathcal{D})$ if and only if $\mathcal{C}$ and $\mathcal{D}$ intersect transversally at P (i.e., if the curves have no common tangents at P).

In this situation, one has the following theorem.

Theorem 4: (Bézout's theorem). Let $\mathcal{C}$ and $\mathcal{D}$ be two projective plane curves without common components and of degrees n and m, respectively.

Then

$$n \cdot m = \sum_{P \in \mathcal{C} \cap \mathcal{D}} \mathrm{mult}_P(\mathcal{C}, \mathcal{D}).$$

As a corollary, one knows that if $\mathcal{C}$ and $\mathcal{D}$ intersect at more than $\deg(\mathcal{C}) \cdot \deg(\mathcal{D})$ points, then they have a common component.

Example 5: We consider the projective cubics $\mathcal{C}$ and $\mathcal{D}$ (see Fig. 2) defined respectively by the polynomials

$$F(x,y,z) = \frac{516}{85}z^3 - \frac{352}{85}yz^2 - \frac{7}{17}y^2z + \frac{41}{85}y^3 + \frac{172}{85}xz^2 - \frac{88}{85}xyz + \frac{1}{85}y^2x$$
$$- 3x^2z + x^2y - x^3,$$
$$G(x,y,z) = -132z^3 + 128yz^2 - 29y^2z - y^3 + 28xz^2 - 76xyz + 31y^2x$$
$$+ 75x^2z - 41x^2y + 17x^3.$$

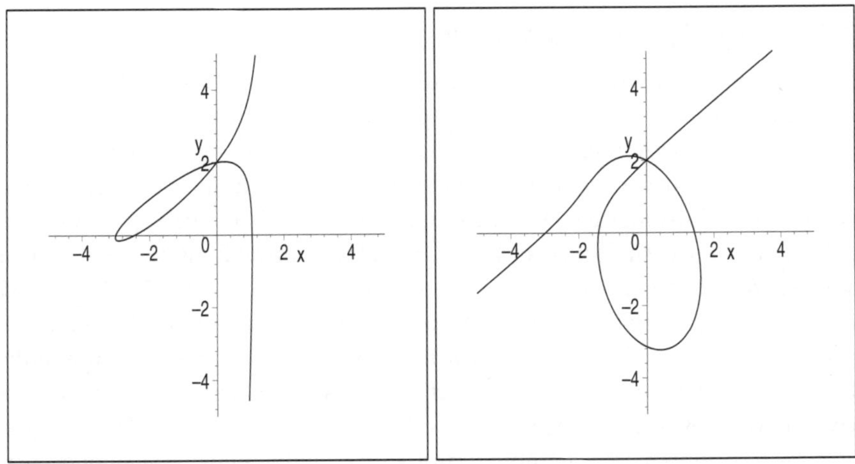

Fig. 2.   Real part of $\mathcal{C}$ (left) and real part of $\mathcal{D}$ (right)

Let us determine the intersection points of these two cubics and their corresponding multiplicities of intersection. For this purpose, we first compute the resultant

$$R(x,y) = \mathrm{Res}_z(F,G) = -\frac{5474304}{25}x^4\,y\,(3x+y)\,(x+2y)\,(x+y)\,(x-y).$$

For each factor $bx - ay$ of the resultant $R(x, y)$ we obtain the polynomial $D(z) = \gcd(F(a, b, z), G(a, b, z))$ in order to find the intersection points generated by this factor. The following table shows the results of this computation; note that $(0 : 0 : 1)$ is not on the cubics nor on any line connecting their intersection points.

factor	$D(z)$	intersection point	multipl. of intersection
x^4	$(2z - 1)^2$	$P_1 = (0 : 2 : 1)$	4
y	$z + 1/3$	$P_2 = (-3 : 0 : 1)$	1
$3x + y$	$z - 1$	$P_3 = (1 : -3 : 1)$	1
$x + 2y$	$z + 1$	$P_4 = (-2 : 1 : 1)$	1
$x + y$	$z + 1$	$P_5 = (-1 : 1 : 1)$	1
$x - y$	$z - 1$	$P_6 = (1 : 1 : 1)$	1

Note that P_1 is a double point on both cubics and they intersect transversally at P_1, and therefore the multiplicity of intersection is 4.

2.3. *Linear Systems of Curves*

Linear systems of curves (or higher dimensional objects) are a basic tool in algebraic geometry. The idea is to work with sets of curves of fixed degree that are related by means of some linear conditions, in particular, sets of curves of fixed degree that pass through some specific points with at least some fixed multiplicities. For this purpose, we will identify projective algebraic curves with forms in $\mathbb{K}[x, y, z]$. Thus, throughout this subsection, we consider that curves may have multiple components. So, in this subsection, curves are defined by arbitrary polynomials, not necessarily squarefree. More precisely, let $T_1, \ldots, T_n$ be a fixed ordering of the set of monomials in x, y, z of degree d, and $n = \frac{1}{2}(d + 1)(d + 2)$. Then, for every projective curve $\mathcal{C}$ of degree d there exists $(a_1 : \cdots : a_n) \in \mathbb{P}^{n-1}(\mathbb{K})$, such that $F = a_1 T_1 + \cdots + a_n T_n$ defines $\mathcal{C}$, and reciprocally. Thus, one may identify the set of all the curves of degree d with $\mathbb{P}^{n-1}(\mathbb{K})$. Now, if one introduces conditions on the curves, then one gets a subset of $\mathbb{P}^{n-1}(\mathbb{K})$. If this subset is a linear variety, then it is called a *linear system of curves*, and the dimension of the linear variety is called the *dimension* of the linear system. If the dimension is 1, then the linear system is called a *pencil*.

An interesting type of linear systems arises when we require that the curves pass through given points with given multiplicities. Let $P_1, \ldots, P_m \in \mathbb{P}^2(\mathbb{K})$, and $r_1, \ldots, r_m$ be non-negative integers. Then, we consider the subset of projective curves $\mathcal{C}$ of degree d passing through P_i and such that

$\mathrm{mult}_{P_i}(\mathcal{C}) \geq r_i$, $i = 1, \ldots, m$. Clearly, the required conditions are linear, and therefore one gets a linear system $\mathcal{S}$ of curves. The points P_i are called *base points* of multiplicity r_i of the system $\mathcal{S}$. In this case, $\mathcal{S}$ is called *the linear system of curves of degree d generated by the effective divisor $D = r_1 P_1 + \cdots + r_m P_m$* and we denote it by $\mathcal{H}(d, D)$ (for the notion of divisor we refer, for instance, to the book[30] by Fulton).

An important type of linear system of curves is the one formed by the adjoint curves. This notion will be studied in the next section.

2.4. *Local Parametrizations*

We will see in the next sections that not all irreducible algebraic curves can be parametrized by means of rational functions. However, one can also consider local parametrizations of the curve in a neighborhood of a point. Let $\mathcal{C}$ be an algebraic plane curve defined by $f \in \mathbb{K}[x, y]$, and let $\mathbb{K}((t))$ denote the field of formal Laurent series, that is, the quotient field of the domain of formal power series $\mathbb{K}[[t]]$. Then, (r_1, r_2) with $r_1, r_2 \in \mathbb{K}((t))$ is a *local parametrization* of $\mathcal{C}$ if $f(r_1(t), r_2(t)) = 0$, and r_1, r_2 are not both in $\mathbb{K}$. Now, since the field of formal Puiseux series is algebraically closed (see for instance the book[14] by Brieskorn and Knörrer, or the book[97] by Walker), one may always parametrize locally around any point of an irreducible curve.

2.5. *Space Curves*

In general one may introduce the notion of curve as a variety of dimension one, and use the term of *space curve* to emphasize that it is not necessarily a plane curve. The notions we have studied can be introduced similarly for space curves. The main result in this context, and for our purposes, is that any curve is birationally equivalent to a plane curve (see the book[30] by Fulton, or the book[97] by Walker). Thus, we may limit our study to plane curves.

3. Rational Plane Curves

Some plane algebraic curves can be expressed by means of rational parametrizations, i.e., pairs of univariate rational functions that represent all the points, with finitely many exceptions, on the curve. For instance, the parabola $y = x^2$ can also be described as $\{(t, t^2) \mid t \in \mathbb{K}\}$; in this case, all affine points on the parabola are given by the parametrization (t, t^2).

However, not all plane algebraic curves can be rationally parametrized. In this section we introduce the notion of rational or parametrizable curve and we study the main properties and characterizations of this type of curves. Afterwards we will show how to check the rationality by algorithmic methods and, in the next section, we will study how to actually compute rational parametrizations of algebraic curves.

Definition 6: An affine plane curve C over $\mathbb{K}$, defined by the squarefree polynomial $f(x, y)$, is *rational* (or *parametrizable*) if there is a $\mathcal{P}(t) \in \mathbb{K}(t)^2$ such that

(1) for almost all (i.e., for all but a finite number of exceptions) $t_0 \in \mathbb{K}$, $\mathcal{P}(t_0) \in C$,
(2) for almost every point $P \in C$ there is a $t_0 \in \mathbb{K}$ such that $P = \mathcal{P}(t_0)$.

In this case $\mathcal{P}(t)$ is called a (*rational affine*) *parametrization* of C. We say that $\mathcal{P}(t)$ is in *reduced form* if the rational functions in $\mathcal{P}(t)$ are in reduced form.

Definition 7: A projective plane curve C in $\mathbb{P}^2(\mathbb{K})$, defined by the square-free homogeneous polynomial $F(x, y, z)$, is *rational* (or *parametrizable*) if there is a $\mathcal{P}(t) = (\chi_1(t), \chi_2(t), \chi_3(t)) \in \mathbb{K}[t]^3$ with $\gcd(\chi_1, \chi_2, \chi_3) = 1$, such that

(1) for almost all $t_0 \in \mathbb{K}$, $\mathcal{P}(t_0) \in C$, and
(2) for almost every point $P \in C$ there is a $t_0 \in \mathbb{K}$ such that $P = \mathcal{P}(t_0)$.

In this case, $\mathcal{P}(t)$ is called a (*rational projective*) *parametrization* of C.

An important result on rational curves is the following theorem.

Theorem 8: Only irreducible curves can be rational.

The rationality of a curve does not depend on whether we embed it into an affine or projective plane. More precisely, an affine plane curve C is rational if and only if its associated projective curve C^* is rational. Furthermore, a parametrization of C can be computed from a parametrization of C^* by dehomogenizing and *vice versa*. So, in the sequel, we can choose freely between projective and affine situations, whatever we find more convenient.

Clearly the above definitions imply that associated with any rational plane curve there exists a pair of univariate rational functions over $\mathbb{K}$, not both simultaneously constant, which is a parametrization of the curve. The converse is also true. That is, associated with any pair of univariate rational functions over $\mathbb{K}$, not both simultaneously constant, there is a rational plane curve $\mathcal{C}$ such that the image of the parametrization is dense in $\mathcal{C}$. The implicit equation of this curve $\mathcal{C}$ is directly related to a resultant; in fact the resultant w.r.t. the parameter, of the two polynomials obtained by cleaning up denominators in the expression $(x, y) - \mathcal{P}(t)$, is a power of the defining polynomial of the curve (see the papers[49,93,94] for details).

Sometimes it is useful to apply equivalent characterizations of the concept of rationality. We recall some of them.

Theorem 9: An irreducible curve $\mathcal{C}$, defined by $f(x, y)$, is rational if and only if there exist rational functions $\chi_1(t), \chi_2(t) \in \mathbb{K}(t)$, not both constant, such that $f(\chi_1(t), \chi_2(t)) = 0$. In this case, $(\chi_1(t), \chi_2(t))$ is a rational parametrization of $\mathcal{C}$.

An alternative characterization of rationality in terms of field theory is given in the next theorem. For this purpose, one associates with an irreducible plane curve $\mathcal{C}$ the quotient field of the integral domain $\mathbb{K}[x, y]/(f(x, y))$, where $f(x, y)$ is the defining polynomial of $\mathcal{C}$. This field is called the *field of rational functions on* $\mathcal{C}$ and it is denoted by $\mathbb{K}(\mathcal{C})$.

Theorem 10: An irreducible affine curve $\mathcal{C}$ is rational if and only if $\mathbb{K}(\mathcal{C})$ is isomorphic to $\mathbb{K}(t)$ (where t is a transcendental element).

Rationality can also be established by means of rational maps.

Theorem 11: An affine algebraic curve $\mathcal{C}$ is rational if and only if it is birationally equivalent to $\mathbb{K}$.

Rationality can also be characterized by means of the notion of genus. To be more precise, consider a divisor (for the notion of divisor we refer, for instance, to the book[30] by Fulton)

$$D = \sum_{i=1}^{m} n_i P_i$$

on the curve $\mathcal{C}$, i.e., $P_i \in \mathcal{C}$ and $n_i \in \mathbb{Z}$. We consider rational functions in $\mathbb{K}(\mathcal{C})$ with poles only at the chosen points and order at these points no worse than n_i. So we consider the Riemann-Roch vector space by (for the notion of order we refer, for instance, to the book[30] by Fulton)

$$\mathcal{L}(D) = \{f \in \mathbb{K}(\mathcal{C}) \mid \mathrm{ord}_{P_i}(f) \geq -n_i \ \text{ for } \ 1 \leq i \leq m\}.$$

Let $\ell(D)$ be the vector space dimension of $\mathcal{L}(D)$. Then, the following theorem holds (see the book[30] by Fulton).

Theorem 12: (Riemann's theorem). Let C be an algebraic curve. There is a constant $g \in \mathbb{N}$ such that $\ell(D) \geq \deg(D) + 1 - g$ for all divisors D on C.

We define the *genus* of C, and we denote it by genus(C), as the least possible value of the constant g in Riemann's theorem. The genus of a curve C can also be introduced in different ways. For instance, we might view a complex curve as a surface in real 4-space (the *Riemann surface* of C), and define the genus of C as the number of topological handles of this surface (see Section 9.2 in Brieskorn and Knörrer's book[14]).

The following theorem states that rational curves are precisely those with genus zero.

Theorem 13: An algebraic curve C is rational if and only if genus(C) = 0.

In addition, it is important to mention that genus is a birational invariant of the curve, that is, it is invariant under birational transformations, i.e., under rational maps on the curve that are rationally invertible.

We have seen how the rationality can be characterized. However, we have not shown how to decide algorithmically whether a curve is rational or not. In order to do that we show how the genus can be computed and therefore in combination with Theorem 13 we will have a method to decide which curves are parametrizable.

For this purpose we will use the fact that the genus measures the difference between the maximum allowable limit of singularities and the actual number of singularities of the curve, counted *properly* with multiplicities. We have already mentioned that $(d-1)(d-2)$ bounds the complexity of the singularities of an irreducible projective curve of degree d. In the special case of irreducible projective curves C with only ordinary singularities this bound is actually sharp and can be used to compute the genus (see Fulton's book,[30] and Walker's book[97]).

Theorem 14: Let C be an irreducible projective curve with only ordinary singularities, and let d be the degree of C. Then

$$\text{genus}(C) = \frac{1}{2}\left[(d-1)(d-2) - \sum_{P \in \text{Sing}(C)} \text{mult}_P(C)(\text{mult}_P(C) - 1)\right].$$

From this result we can already deduce that lines, irreducible conics, and irreducible curves having a singularity of maximum multiplicity (i.e., a point of multiplicity $d-1$, where d is the degree of the curve), for instance cubics with a double point, are rational.

This formula can also be stated for irreducible curves with non-ordinary singularities, when multiplicities are counted properly. For this purpose, one may apply different approaches. Geometrically one introduces, by means of quadratic transformations, the notion of *neighboring points* and the idea of *blowing up* (see the textbooks[14,30,97]); algebraically, one uses the notion of *chain of critical pairs* of Puiseux expansions (see the books[1,14]); similarly, one may use arithmetic and topological approaches (see the book[1] by Abhyankar).

In the following, we briefly describe how to approach the problem by means of quadratic transformations. More precisely, the idea consists in observing that the genus is invariant under birational transformation, and therefore one may try to find a finite sequence of birational transformations which maps the original curve onto a new curve having only ordinary singularities.

The problem with non-ordinary singularities is that they have multiple tangents. We will resolve these multiple tangents by "blowing up" the singularity into a line. Then the tangents at the singularity correspond to points on this line. A multiple tangent will correspond to a multiple point on the blow-up. This point will also have to be properly counted in the genus formula. Now this multiple point, a "neighboring singularity", can be investigated further. If it is ordinary, then the process stops, and we have "resolved" the non-ordinariness of this singularity. Otherwise the process is continued with the next transformation. It can be shown that after finitely many such blow-ups every non-ordinary singularity can be resolved. We can achieve the blow-ups by the so-called *standard quadratic transformation* or *standard Cremona transformation*; i.e., transformations defined by $x' = yz$, $y' = xz$, $z' = xy$.

For the special points $(1 : 0 : 0)$, $(0 : 1 : 0)$ and $(0 : 0 : 1)$ the quadratic transformation is not defined. These points are called the *fundamental points* of the transformation. Every point lying on one of the lines $x = 0$, $y = 0$ or $z = 0$ is sent to the point $(1 : 0 : 0)$, $(0 : 1 : 0)$ or $(0 : 0 : 1)$, respectively. These lines are called the *irregular lines* of the transformation. One can easily prove that this transformation defines a one to one correspondence between points of $\mathbb{P}^2(\mathbb{K})$ not on irregular lines. Now we study the action of quadratic transformations on an irreducible projective curve. Let the projective curve $\mathcal{C}$ be defined by $F(x, y, z)$. Then the polynomial $G(x, y, z) = F(yz, xz, xy)$ is called the *algebraic transform* of F. However, although F is irreducible, G may have some irregular line as a factor. The *quadratic transform* of F is defined as the irreducible factor of G that is not an irregular line.

Now we could proceed in the following way for obtaining this sequence of quadratic transformations resolving the singularities of a given irreducible curve $\mathcal{C}$:

(1) Choose a non-ordinary singularity of $\mathcal{C}$ and apply a linear change of coordinates such that the singularity is moved to $(0:0:1)$, none of its tangents is an irregular line, and no other fundamental point is singular.

(2) Apply the standard quadratic transformation to $\mathcal{C}$ to get the transform curve $\mathcal{C}'$.

(3) Check whether there exists a non-fundamental intersection of $\mathcal{C}'$ and $z = 0$, being a non-ordinary singular point. If this is the case, apply (1) and (2) to $\mathcal{C}'$ and this non-ordinary singular intersection point. Otherwise, choose any other non-ordinary singularity and repeat the process, until there are no non-ordinary singularities left.

This method selects a coordinate system, and also the order in which the non-ordinary singularities of the curve are moved to the fundamental points. One can prove (see page 177 in Fulton's book[30]) that independent of these selections, the method always achieves an irreducible curve having only ordinary singularities in a finite number of steps.

For the purpose of describing this blowing-up process in more detail, we introduce the concept of neighboring points. Let $\mathcal{Q} = (\mathcal{Q}_1, \ldots, \mathcal{Q}_n)$ be a finite sequence of quadratic transformations constructed as it has been described above and reducing $\mathcal{C}$ to a curve which has only ordinary singularities. We adopt the convention that $\mathcal{Q}_i$ represents the composition of the quadratic transformation with a suitable change of the coordinate system that moves one of the singularities to a fundamental point. Let us also assume that $\mathcal{Q}$ generates the sequence of irreducible curves

$$\mathcal{C} = \mathcal{C}_0 \to^{\mathcal{Q}_1} \mathcal{C}_1 \to^{\mathcal{Q}_2} \cdots \to^{\mathcal{Q}_n} \mathcal{C}_n,$$

where $\mathcal{C}_{i+1}$ is the quadratic transform obtained from $\mathcal{C}_i$ by $\mathcal{Q}_{i+1}$, for $0 \leq i \leq n-1$. Given an r-fold point P on $\mathcal{C}$, suppose that during the process described by $\mathcal{Q}$ the point P has not been translated to a fundamental point till the action of the i-th quadratic transformation. Then the *first neighborhood* of P with respect to $\mathcal{Q}$ is defined as the set of all the non-fundamental intersections of the curve $\mathcal{C}_1$ with the irregular line $z = 0$, assuming that P was moved to $(0:0:1)$ by the according change of coordinates. Similarly, we take the non-fundamental intersections of $\mathcal{C}_1$ with $x = 0$ or $y = 0$ if P was translated to $(1:0:0)$ or $(0:1:0)$, respectively. The points in the first neighborhood of P with respect to Q are called the *neighboring points of P at its first neighborhood*. Using the fact that every neighboring point P' of P at its first neighborhood is a point on C_1, one defines the multiplicity and the character of P' as the multiplicity and character of P' as a point on C_1. Abusing of the notation, we represent by $\text{mult}_{P'}(C)$ the multiplicity of the neighboring point; that is $\text{mult}_{P'}(C) = \text{mult}_{P'}(C_1)$. Similarly, these notions are extended to neighborhoods of arbitrarily high order. The neighboring points of P with multiplicity higher than 1 will be called the *singular neighboring points* of P.

Now, the problem can be solved by local analysis of the curve at the non-ordinary singularities. Let $\{P_1, \dots, P_s\}$ be the set of all the non-ordinary singular points of C. It is clear that for every P_k there always exists a sequence of quadratic transformations $Q(P_k) = (Q_{1,k}, \dots, Q_{n_k,k})$ reducing C to a curve having only ordinary singularities and such that P_k is moved to a fundamental point by the action of $Q_{1,k}$. Then, for every P_k, we only compute the sequence $Q(P_k)$ till all the neighboring points of P_k w.r.t. $Q(P_k)$ have been determined, that is till another $P_{k'}$ is moved to a fundamental point. Let us say that this sequence is denoted by $Q^*(P_k)$. In this situation, Theorem 14 can be generalized as follows.

Theorem 15: Let $P_1, \dots, P_s$ be the singularities of the projective curve C of degree d. Let $S = \{P_1, \dots, P_s\} \cup N(P_1) \cup \dots \cup N(P_s)$, where $N(P_k)$ is the set of all the neighboring singularities of P_k w.r.t. $Q^*(P_k)$ as above. Then

$$\text{genus}(C) = \frac{1}{2}\left[(d-1)(d-2) - \sum_{P \in S} \text{mult}_P(C)(\text{mult}_P(C) - 1)\right].$$

Thus, the genus of an irreducible algebraic plane curve C can be determined computationally by analyzing the multiplicities of the singularities and neighboring singularities of C.

Example 16: We consider the tacnode curve C (see Fig. 3), that is the projective curve defined by the form

$$F(x, y, z) = 2x^4 - 3x^2 yz + y^2 z^2 - 2y^3 z + y^4.$$

Its singularities are $P_1 = (0:0:1)$ that is non-ordinary and $P_2 = (0:1:1)$ that is ordinary. Since the tangent to C at P_1 is $y = 0$, that is an irregular line, we transform C by means of a change of coordinates, for instance

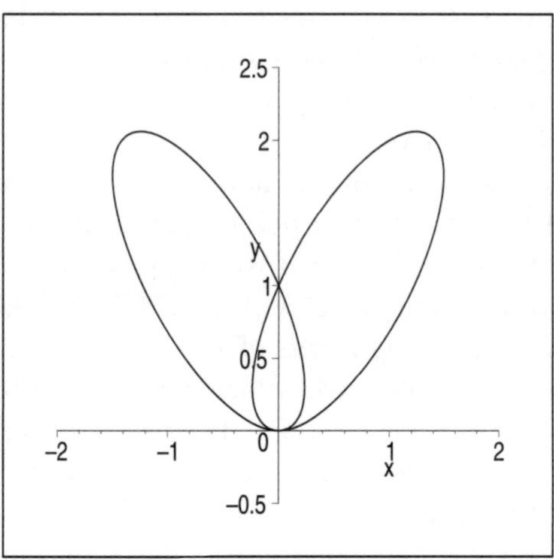

Fig. 3.   Tacnode curve

$\{x := x, y := x - y, z := z\}$. We obtain the curve $\overline{C}$ defined by

$$\overline{F} = 3x^4 + 4x^3y + 6x^2y^2 + 4xy^3 + y^4 - 5zx^3 - 9zx^2y - 6zxy^2 - 2zy^3$$
$$+ z^2x^2 + 2z^2xy + y^2z^2.$$

Now, we apply the Cremona transformation to get

$$G(x, y, z) = \frac{1}{z^2}\overline{F}(yz, xz, xy).$$

That is

$$G = 3z^2y^4 + 4z^2y^3x + 6z^2y^2x^2 + 4z^2yx^3 + z^2x^4 - 5zxy^4 - 9zx^2y^3$$
$$- 6zx^3y^2 - 2zx^4y + x^2y^4 + 2x^3y^3 + x^4y^2.$$

Thus the first neighborhood of P_1 is given by the non-fundamental intersections of $G(x, y, 0) = x^2y^2(x - y)^2$. Therefore, the first neighborhood of P_1 consists of the point $P_{1,1} = (1 : 1 : 0)$ that is an ordinary double point of G. Thus, the process finishes, and

$$\text{genus}(\overline{C}) = \frac{1}{2}((d - 1)(d - 2) - \sum_{i=1}^{2}\text{mult}_{P_i}(C)(\text{mult}_{P_i}(C) - 1)$$
$$- \text{mult}_{P_{1,1}}(C))(\text{mult}_{P_{1,1}}(C) - 1) = 0,$$

from which one deduces that C is rational.

4. Parametrization of Rational Plane Curves

In the previous section we have seen how to decide the rationality of a curve. This section is devoted to the actual computation of rational parametrizations of plane algebraic curves. Several authors have addressed this problem, and several algorithms for computing the genus and proper rational parametrizations of rational plane curves have been proposed.[2,41,42,73,89,90] Algorithms described in the papers[2,73,89,90] basically follow the classical algorithm scheme (see, e.g., the book[97] by Walker), while algorithmic methods presented in the papers[41,42] are based on integral basis computation and canonical divisors. In the paper[89] by Winkler and the author the symbolic difficulties of the classical method are analyzed and the notion of families of conjugate points on a curve is introduced. In addition, Schicho[73] presents an alternative approach by utilizing linear systems of curves of degree $\mathcal{O}(d^2)$, where d is the degree of the curve. The basic idea of Hoeij's approach[41] is to find a parameter p, that is, an element in $\mathbb{K}(\mathcal{C})$ (where $\mathcal{C}$ is the rational curve to be parametrized) that has precisely one pole of multiplicity one. Then expressing $x, y \in \mathbb{K}(\mathcal{C}) = \mathbb{K}(p)$ as rational functions in p, one gets a rational parametrization of $\mathcal{C}$. Subsequent algorithms presented by Hoeij,[42] and by Winkler and the author[90] are advanced and they deal with the problem of parametrizing curves over optimal field extensions. This type of problem will be analyzed in subsequent sections. For the case of space curves one may project the curve birationally onto a plane curve and then apply the above-mentioned algorithms. Parametrizations for space curves can be found in the papers.[3,12] In the following we focus our discussions on the geometric approach to parametrize plane curves.

4.1. *Parametrization by Lines*

In this subsection, we see how a certain type of curves can be parametrized by using a pencil of lines through a suitable point on the curve. First we analyze the simple case of rational conics (i.e., irreducible conics). Let $\mathcal{C}$ be an irreducible conic defined by the quadratic polynomial

$$f(x, y) = f_2(x, y) + f_1(x, y) + f_0(x, y)$$

where $f_i(x, y)$ is the homogeneous component of degree i. Let us assume without loss of generality that $\mathcal{C}$ passes through the origin, so $f_0(x, y) = 0$; otherwise one can always apply a suitable linear change of coordinates. Let $\mathcal{H}(t)$ be the linear system of lines through the origin, the elements of $\mathcal{H}(t)$ being parametrized by their slope t. So the defining polynomial of $\mathcal{H}(t)$ is

$h(x, y, t) = y - tx$. The intersection points of a generic element of $\mathcal{H}(t)$ and $\mathcal{C}$ are $P = (0, 0)$ and

$$Q = \left(-\frac{f_1(1, t)}{f_2(1, t)}, -\frac{t \cdot f_1(1, t)}{f_2(1, t)} \right)$$

that yields the desired parametrization of the conic. From these ideas we may derive the following algorithm for parametrizing conics. We assume that $F(x, y, z)$ is the defining polynomial of an irreducible projective conic $\mathcal{C}$. We will refer to it as **Algorithm 1.**

1. Compute the homogeneous components f_2, f_1, f_0 of $F(x, y, 1)$.
2. If $(0 : 0 : 1) \in \mathcal{C}$ then return $\mathcal{P}(t) = (-f_1(1, t), -tf_1(1, t), f_2(1, t))$.
3. Compute a point $(a : b : 1) \in \mathcal{C}$.
4. Set $g(x, y) = F(x + a, y + b, 1)$. Let $g_2(x, y)$ and $g_1(x, y)$ be the homogeneous components of $g(x, y)$ of degrees 2 and 1, respectively.
5. Return $\mathcal{P}(t) = (-g_1(1, t) + ag_2(1, t), -tg_1(1, t) + bg_2(1, t), g_2(1, t))$.

Example 17: Let $\mathcal{C}$ be the ellipse defined by $f(x, y) = x^2 + 2y^2 - z^2$. We apply Algorithm 1. It is clear that $\mathcal{C}$ does not pass through $(0 : 0 : 1)$. Thus, we take a point on $\mathcal{C}$, for instance $(1 : 0 : 1)$ (Step 3). Then, performing Step 4, one gets $g(x, y) = x^2 + 2x + y^2$. Thus, a parametrization of $\mathcal{C}$ is $\mathcal{P}(t) = (-1 + 2t^2, -2t, 1 + 2t^2)$.

This approach can be immediately generalized to the situation where we have an irreducible projective curve $\mathcal{C}$ of degree d with a $(d - 1)$-fold point P. Without loss of generality we consider $P = (0 : 0 : 1)$, so the defining polynomial of $\mathcal{C}$ is of the form

$$F(x, y, z) = f_d(x, y) + f_{d-1}(x, y)z$$

(where each f_i is a form of degree i). As above, we consider the linear system of lines $\mathcal{H}(t)$ through $(0 : 0 : 1)$. Intersecting $\mathcal{C}$ with an element of $\mathcal{H}(t)$ we get the origin as an intersection point of multiplicity at least $d - 1$. Reasoning as above, one sees that, since $\mathcal{C}$ is irreducible for all but finitely many values of t, P is an intersection point of multiplicity $d - 1$. Thus, by Bézout's theorem, we must get exactly one more intersection point Q depending rationally on the value of t. In fact,

$$Q = (-f_{d-1}(1, t) : -t \cdot f_{d-1}(1, t) : f_d(1, t)).$$

This is a rational parametrization of the curve $\mathcal{C}$. Applying this reasoning, one may derive an algorithm for parametrizing by lines. We assume that $F(x, y, z)$ is the defining polynomial of an irreducible projective curve $\mathcal{C}$ of degree $d > 1$, having a $(d-1)$-fold point. We will refer to this algorithm as **Algorithm 2.**

1. If $d = 2$, then apply Algorithm 1.
2. Compute the $(d-1)$-fold point P of $\mathcal{C}$.
3. If $P = (a : b : 1)$, then compute $g(x, y) = F(x + a, y + b, 1)$ and return $\mathcal{P}(t) = (-g_{d-1}(1, t) + ag_d(1, t), -tg_{d-1}(1, t) + bg_d(1, t), g_d(1, t))$, where $g_d(x, y)$ and $g_{d-1}(x, y)$ are the homogeneous components of $g(x, y)$ of degrees d and $d - 1$, respectively.
4. If $P = (a : b : 0)$, with $a \neq 0$, then compute $g(x, y) = F(a, y + b, x)$ and return $\mathcal{P}(t) = (-ag_d(1, t), tg_{d-1}(1, t) - bg_d(1, t), g_{d-1}(1, t))$, where $g_d(x, y)$ and $g_{d-1}(x, y)$ are the homogeneous components of $g(x, y)$ of degrees d and $d - 1$, respectively.
5. If $P = (0 : 1 : 0)$, then compute $g(x, y) = F(x, 1, y)$ and return $\mathcal{P}(t) = (g_{d-1}(1, t), -g_d(1, t), tg_{d-1}(1, t))$, where $g_d(x, y)$ and $g_{d-1}(x, y)$ are the homogeneous components of $g(x, y)$ of degrees d and $d-1$, respectively.

Example 18: Let $\mathcal{C}$ be the affine quartic curve (see Fig. 4 left) defined by

$$f(x, y) = 1 + x - 15\,x^2 - 29\,y^2 + 30\,y^3 - 25\,xy^2 + x^3y + 35\,xy + x^4$$
$$- 6\,y^4 + 6\,x^2y.$$

$\mathcal{C}$ has an affine triple point at $(1, 1)$. We apply Algorithm 2 to parametrize

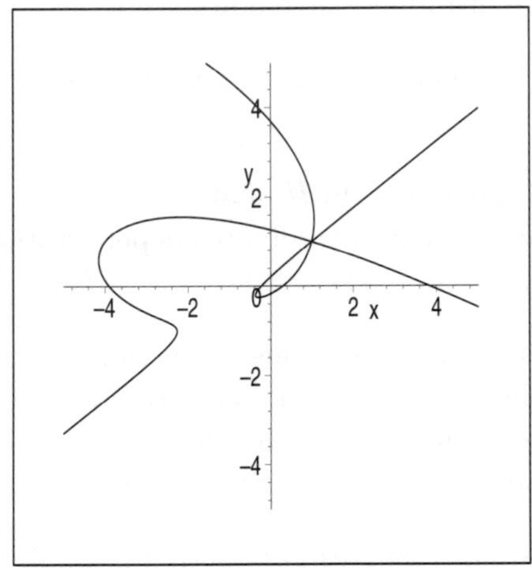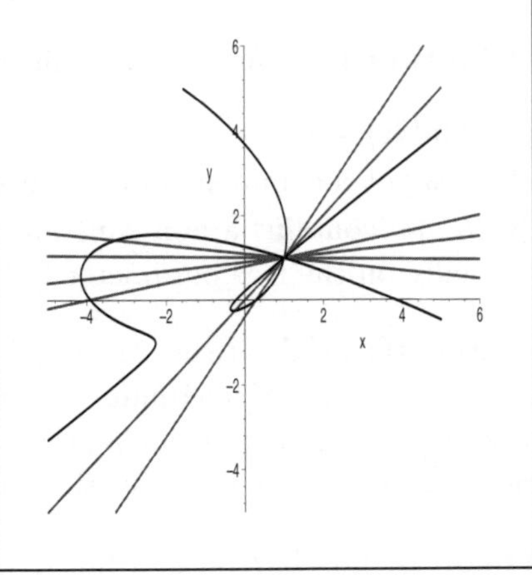

Fig. 4.   Quartic $\mathcal{C}$ (left), $\mathcal{C}$ and pencil of lines (right)

$\mathcal{C}$. In Step 3, we compute the polynomial

$$g(x, y) = 5\,x^3 + 6\,y^3 - 25\,xy^2 + x^3y + x^4 - 6\,y^4 + 9\,x^2y,$$

and determining the homogeneous forms of $g(x, y)$ we get the rational parametrization of $\mathcal{C}$

$$\mathcal{P}(t) = \left(\frac{4 + 6\,t^3 - 25\,t^2 + 8\,t + 6\,t^4}{-1 + 6\,t^4 - t}, \frac{4\,t + 12\,t^4 - 25\,t^3 + 9\,t^2 - 1}{-1 + 6\,t^4 - t} \right).$$

In Fig. 4 (right) one can see how the pencil of lines parametrizes $\mathcal{C}$.

4.2. *Parametrization by Adjoints*

The only curves that can be parametrized by lines are those having a singularity of maximum multiplicity. In order to treat the general case, we develop a method based on the notion of adjoint curve that, intuitively speaking, is a generalization of the idea underlining the method of parametrization by lines. The method described in this subsection follows basically Winkler and the author's approach.[89] There are alternative parametrization methods based on anticanonical divisors,[41] or on adjoints of high degree.[73]

Throughout this subsection, $\mathcal{C}$ will be an irreducible projective curve of degree $d > 2$. Note that this is not a loss of generality, because of the previous subsection.

Before showing how adjoints are defined and how they can be used to solve the parametrization problem, we introduce the following notion.

Definition 19: We say that a linear system $\mathcal{H}$ of curves *parametrizes* $\mathcal{C}$ if

(1) $\dim(\mathcal{H}) = 1$,
(2) $\mathcal{C}$ is not a common component of any curves in $\mathcal{H}$, and
(3) $\mathcal{H} \cap \mathcal{C}$ contains a non-constant point whose coordinates depend rationally on the free parameter in $\mathcal{H}$.

Note that if $\mathcal{C}$ satisfies the conditions of the previous subsection, i.e., it has a singularity of maximum multiplicity at P, then a pencil of lines with base point at P is a linear system parametrizing $\mathcal{C}$. Therefore, the notion introduced above generalizes the strategy of parametrizing by lines.

Theorem 20: If $\mathcal{H}(t)$ is a linear system of curves parametrizing $\mathcal{C}$, then there exists only one non-constant $\mathcal{P}(t) \in \mathcal{H}(t) \cap \mathcal{C}$ depending on t, and it is a parametrization of $\mathcal{C}$.

The following result shows how to actually compute a parametrization from a parametrizing linear system of curves. For this purpose, for a polynomial G in $\mathbb{K}[t][x, y, z]$ we use the notation $\mathrm{pp}_t(G)$ to denote the primitive part of G w.r.t. t.

Theorem 21: Let $F(x, y, z)$ and $H(t, x, y, z)$ be the defining polynomial of $\mathcal{C}$ and of a linear system $\mathcal{H}(t)$ parametrizing $\mathcal{C}$, respectively. Then, the parametrization generated by $\mathcal{H}(t)$ is the solution in $\mathbb{P}^2(\mathbb{K}(t))$ of the system of algebraic equations

$$\left. \begin{array}{l} \mathrm{pp}_t(\mathrm{Res}_y(F, H)) = 0 \\ \mathrm{pp}_t(\mathrm{Res}_x(F, H)) = 0 \end{array} \right\} .$$

The following theorem gives sufficient conditions on a linear system of curves to be a parametrizing system.

Theorem 22: Let $\mathcal{H}$ be a linear system of curves of degree k satisfying conditions (1) and (2) in Definition 19, and let $\mathcal{B}$ be the set of base points of $\mathcal{H}$. If for almost all curves $\mathcal{C}' \in \mathcal{H}$,

$$\sum_{P \in \mathcal{B}} \mathrm{mult}_P(\mathcal{C}, \mathcal{C}') = dk - 1$$

holds, then $\mathcal{H}$ parametrizes $\mathcal{C}$.

Now, a natural question is how to determine parametrizing linear systems of curves. We will show that adjoints provide an answer to this question. Adjoint curves can be defined for reducible curves. However, since our final goal is to work with rational curves, we only consider irreducible curves here. For the reducible case we refer to basic textbooks.[14,30,97]

Definition 23: We say that a projective curve $\mathcal{C}'$ is an *adjoint curve* of $\mathcal{C}$ if the following hold:

(1) if P is a singular point of $\mathcal{C}$, then $\mathrm{mult}_P(\mathcal{C}') \geq \mathrm{mult}_P(\mathcal{C}) - 1$,
(2) if P is a neighboring point of $\mathcal{C}$, then $\mathrm{mult}_P(\mathcal{Q}_P(\mathcal{C}')) \geq \mathrm{mult}_P(\mathcal{C}) - 1$, where $\mathcal{Q}_P$ is the finite sequence of quadratic transformations used to construct P.

All algebraic conditions required in the definition of adjoint curve are linear. Therefore, if one fixes the degree, the set of all adjoint curves of $\mathcal{C}$ is a linear system of curves. This remark motivates the following definition.

Definition 24: The set of all adjoints of $\mathcal{C}$ of degree k ($k \in \mathbb{N}$) is called the *system of adjoints* of $\mathcal{C}$ of degree k. We denote this system by $\mathcal{A}_k(\mathcal{C})$.

Theorem 25: If $\mathcal{C}$ is rational and $k \geq d - 2$, then

$$\dim(\mathcal{A}_k(\mathcal{C})) = \frac{k(k+3)}{2} - \frac{(d-1)(d-2)}{2}.$$

Now, we only need to introduce enough new base points in $\mathcal{A}_k(\mathcal{C})$ such that the condition in Theorem 22 is satisfied. This is done in the next two theorems by taking simple points on the curve.

Theorem 26: Let $k \in \{d-1, d-2\}$ and let $\mathcal{S} \subset [\mathcal{C} \setminus \mathrm{Sing}(\mathcal{C})]$ be such that $\mathrm{Card}(\mathcal{S}) = kd - (d-1)(d-2) - 1$. Then

$$\mathcal{A}_k(\mathcal{C}) \cap \mathcal{H}\left(k, \sum_{P \in \mathcal{S}} P\right)$$

parametrizes $\mathcal{C}$.

Theorem 27: Let $k \geq d$, let $Q \notin \mathcal{C}$, and let $\mathcal{S} \subset [\mathcal{C} \setminus \mathrm{Sing}(\mathcal{C})]$ be such that $\mathrm{Card}(\mathcal{S}) = kd - (d-1)(d-2) - 1$. Then

$$\mathcal{A}_k(\mathcal{C}) \cap \mathcal{H}\left(k, \sum_{P \in \mathcal{S}} P + (d-k+1)Q\right)$$

parametrizes $\mathcal{C}$.

These results provide a family of algorithms to parametrize any rational curve by means of adjoints. We assume that $F(x, y, z)$ is the defining polynomial of a rational projective curve $\mathcal{C}$ of degree d. The following algorithm will be referred to as **Algorithm 3.**

1. If $d \leq 3$ or $\mathrm{Sing}(\mathcal{C})$ consists of one point of multiplicity $d-1$, then apply Algorithm 2.
2. Choose $k \geq d - 2$ and compute the defining polynomial of $\mathcal{A}_k(\mathcal{C})$.
3. Choose a set $\mathcal{S} \subset (\mathcal{C} \setminus \mathrm{Sing}(\mathcal{C}))$ such that $\mathrm{Card}(\mathcal{S}) = kd - (d-1)(d-2) - 1$.
4. Compute the defining polynomial H of

$$\mathcal{H} = \mathcal{A}_k(\mathcal{C}) \cap \mathcal{H}\left(k, \sum_{P \in \mathcal{S}} P\right).$$

5. If $k \geq d$, then take $Q \notin \mathcal{C}$ and replace H by the defining polynomial of

$$\mathcal{H} \cap \mathcal{H}(k, (d-k+1)Q).$$

6. Return the solution of

$$\{\mathrm{pp}_t(\mathrm{Res}_y(F, H)) = 0, \mathrm{pp}_t(\mathrm{Res}_x(F, H)) = 0\}$$

in $\mathbb{P}^2(\mathbb{K}(t))$.

From the point of view of time efficiency one must choose $k = d - 2$ in Step 2, since then degrees of polynomials are the smallest. Nevertheless, the selection of $k = d$ can also be interesting in the sense that at most one algebraic number of degree d has to be introduced, and therefore it is a first fast approach to algebraic optimality in the output; see the paper[90] by Winkler and the author for more details. In the next subsection, we will briefly develop these ideas. But first, we illustrate the algorithm by an example.

Example 28: We consider the tacnode C analyzed in Example 3. There we have seen that it is rational, and that $P_1 = (0 : 0 : 1), P_2 = (0 : 1 : 1)$ were double points, and $P_{1,1} = (1 : 1 : 0)$ was a double neighboring point of P_1 constructed with the transformation

$$\mathcal{Q}_{P_1} = \{x := yz, y := xz, z = xy\} \circ \{x := x, y := x - y, z := z\}.$$

Now, we apply Algorithm 3 to parametrize C with $k = d - 2 = 2$. Thus, we

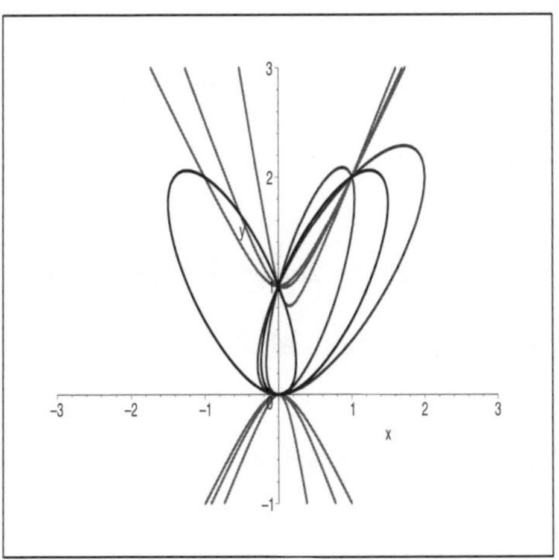

Fig. 5.   Tacnode C and conics adjoints

parametrize it with a linear system of conic adjoints. For this purpose, we consider a generic expression of a conic:

$$H(x, y, z) = a_0 x^2 + a_1 xy + a_2 y^2 + b_0 xz + b_1 yz + c_0 z^2.$$

In Step 3 we consider a set $\mathcal{S}$ of $kd - (d-1)(d-2) - 1$ simple points on C. That is, $\mathcal{S}$ consists of 1 simple point on C. We take $\mathcal{S} = \{P_3 := (1 : 2 : 1)\}$.

In Step 4, we must compute the defining polynomial of $\mathcal{A}_2(\mathcal{C}) \cap \mathcal{H}(2, P_3)$. The required conditions for $\mathcal{A}_2(\mathcal{C})$ related to P_1 and P_2 are

$$H(0,0,1) = c_0 = 0, \quad \text{and} \quad H(0,1,1) = a_2 + b_1 = 0.$$

Substituting $\{c_0 = 0, a_2 = -b_1\}$ in $H(x,y,z)$ we get

$$H(x,y,z) = a_0 x^2 + a_1 xy - b_1 y^2 + b_0 xz + b_1 yz.$$

Now we determine the condition on $P_{1,1}$. That is, we apply $\mathcal{Q}_{P_1}$ to the new H to get

$$\overline{H}(x,y,z) = za_0 y^2 + za_1 y^2 - za_1 yx - zb_1 y^2 + 2zb_1 yx - zb_1 x^2 + b_0 y^2 x$$
$$+ b_1 xy^2 - b_1 x^2 y.$$

Note that we have removed an irregular line factor, namely the factor z. In this situation, we ask $\overline{H}$ to vanish at $P_{1,1}$. This gives the additional condition: $\overline{H}(1,1,0) = b_0 = 0$. Substituting $b_0 = 0$ in $H(x,y,z)$ we get the defining polynomial of $\mathcal{A}_2(\mathcal{C})$:

$$H(x,y,z) = a_0 x^2 + a_1 xy - b_1 y^2 + b_1 yz.$$

Now we determine the conditions for $\mathcal{A}_2(\mathcal{C}) \cap \mathcal{H}(2, P_3)$. For this we impose $H(P_3) = 0$ to get

$$H(x,y,z) = (-2a_1 + 2b_1)x^2 + a_1 xy - b_1 y^2 + b_1 yz,$$

and therefore the defining polynomial of $\mathcal{A}_2(\mathcal{C}) \cap \mathcal{H}(2, P_3)$ can be expressed as

$$H(x,y,z,t) = (-2t + 2)x^2 + txy - y^2 + yz.$$

In Step 6, we consider

$$\mathrm{pp}_t(\mathrm{Res}_y(F,H)) = 18x + 64xt^2 - 48xt - 40t^3 x + 9t^4 x - 2t^4 z - 21tz$$
$$+ 7zt^3 + 18z = 0,$$
$$\mathrm{pp}_t(\mathrm{Res}_x(F,H)) = 18y + 64yt^2 - 48yt - 40t^3 y + 9yt^4 + 84tz + 28zt^3$$
$$- 4t^4 z - 36z - 73zt^2 = 0.$$

Taking $z = 1$, and solving w.r.t. $\{x,y\}$, we finally get the parametrization

$$\mathcal{P}(t) = \left(\frac{-7t^3 + 21t + 2t^4 - 18}{18 + 64t^2 - 48t - 40t^3 + 9t^4}, \frac{36 - 84t - 28t^3 + 4t^4 + 73t^2}{18 + 64t^2 - 48t - 40t^3 + 9t^4} \right).$$

4.3. *Advanced Parametrization Algorithms*

Rational parametrizations generated by most of the existing algorithmic methods[2,41,42,73,89,90] are optimal in the degree of the output; that is the output parametrization is proper (see the next section). However, these parametrization algorithms do not control the field extension to which the coefficients of the output belong. For instance (t, t^2) is a parametrization optimal in the degree of the parabola, but $(\sqrt{2}t, 2t^2)$ or $(it, -t^2)$ are also parametrizations, optimal in the degree, of the same curve, and they are expressed over the real extension $\mathbb{Q}(\sqrt{2})$ and over the complex extension $\mathbb{Q}(i)$, respectively.

The papers by Hoeij,[42] by Schicho,[73] and by Winkler and the author[90] address this problem of computing rational parametrizations with coefficients belonging to an optimal field extension of the ground field. In general, any rational plane curve can be parametrized over a field extension of the ground field of degree at most two. More precisely, throughout this section, let $\mathbb{F}$ be a computable subfield of $\mathbb{K}$, and let $\mathcal{C}$ be a rational projective plane curve over $\mathbb{K}$ of degree d with defining polynomial $F(x, y, z)$ over $\mathbb{F}$. Then, the following theorem holds.[39,59]

Theorem 29: (Hilbert-Hurwitz's theorem). If d is odd, then $\mathcal{C}$ can be parametrized over $\mathbb{F}$; otherwise $\mathcal{C}$ can be parametrized over an algebraic extension of $\mathbb{F}$ of degree at most two. We call such a parametrization an *algebraically optimal parametrization*.

Algorithms for computing such parametrizations can be found in the literature. In the paper by Hilbert and Hurwitz[39] the problem is solved by means of the recursive application of $\mathcal{O}(d)$ birational transformations over $\mathbb{F}$, that map the original curve onto a cubic or a conic, depending on whether d is odd or even. Thus, this approach involves in general $\mathcal{O}(d)$ resolutions of systems of algebraic equations in four variables. Winkler and the author[90] proposed an improved algorithmic version of Hilbert-Hurwitz's approach. This approach only needs one birational transformation to obtain an optimal parametrization in the even case, and no one in the odd case. Moreover, when the birational transformation is required, the image curve is computed by simply solving a linear system of five equations over $\mathbb{F}$. Schicho[73] presented an alternative different approach for the case of curves without neighboring singularities, that deals with linear systems of curves of $\mathcal{O}(d^2)$ degree; but Mňuk and others[58] showed that the degree of the linear system drastically affects the complexity of the processes presented by Winkler and the author,[89,90] and there are good reasons to expect that this will be similar in Schicho's approach. Applying similar ideas to his algorithm,[41] Hoeij[42] has also presented an optimal parametrization algorithm. The basic idea is to compute a basis (g_1, g_2, g_3) of the vector space $\mathcal{L}(D)$, where D is the anticanonical divisor, that defines a bijective morphism from the original curve on a conic. Then, parametrizing optimally the conic, and composing with the morphism one gets an optimal parametrization of the curve.

In the following, we briefly describe the algebraically optimal geometric approaches[39,90] based on adjoints. In the parametrization algorithm 3, the ground field could be extended only when we work either with the singularities or with the simple points. When we work with the singularities the ground field is not finally extended (see the papers[60,89] for details). Thus, the problem of computing algebraically optimal parametrizations reduces to the problem of computing simple points on the curve with coordinates over an optimal algebraic extension of $\mathbb{F}$, or equivalently, to solve Diophantine equations of genus zero.

In 1890, Hilbert and Hurwitz[39] introduced a method for dealing with this problem. Basically, their main result states that there exist adjoint curves $\Phi_1, \Phi_2, \Phi_3 \in \mathbb{F}[x, y, z]$ of degree $d - 2$ to $\mathcal{C}$ such that the restriction to $\mathcal{C}$ of the rational transformation

$$\{y_1 : y_2 : y_3 = \Phi_1 : \Phi_2 : \Phi_3\}$$

is over $\mathbb{F}$ and it is birational, and the transformed curve of $\mathcal{C}$ is of degree $d-2$. Furthermore, those adjoint curves not providing birational transformations satisfy certain algebraic conditions. Thus, the method consists in applying a birational transformation, defined by adjoint curves to $\mathcal{C}$ of degree $d - 2$, to map $\mathcal{C}$ onto a curve $\mathcal{C}'$ of degree $d - 2$. Then, since the transformation is birational and defined over $\mathbb{F}$, almost every *rational point* (i.e., a point with coordinates in $\mathbb{F}$) on $\mathcal{C}$ corresponds to a rational point on the curve defined by $\mathcal{C}$ and *vice versa*. Hence, the original curve is reduced to a rational plane curve, with defining polynomial over $\mathbb{F}$, of degree $d - 2$. This process is continued until one arrives at a curve of degree three or two, depending on whether the degree of the original curve is odd or even, respectively. Now, if d is odd, one can parametrize the cubic over $\mathbb{F}$ (note that any rational cubic with defining polynomial over $\mathbb{F}$ can be parametrized over $\mathbb{F}$ since no simple point is required in Algorithm 2), and obtain a parametrization of $\mathcal{C}$ over $\mathbb{F}$ using the birational transformations. Also, one can take rational points on the cubic and send them onto rational simple points on $\mathcal{C}$. On the other hand, if d is even, we observe that almost all optimal simple points on $\mathcal{C}$ (i.e., simple points with coordinates over the smallest algebraic extension of $\mathbb{F}$) are one-to-one related to almost all optimal simple points on an irreducible conic. Note that for conics, cutting with lines, one can always obtain simple points on algebraic extensions of degree at most two. Furthermore, over many interesting fields there are complete procedures[40,47] for computing optimal points on conics. Thus, either inverting an optimal parametrization of the conic or optimal simple points, one reaches an optimal parametrization of $\mathcal{C}$. The main difficulty of this approach is that, in general, $\mathcal{O}(d)$ birational transformations are required in order to reach a cubic, or a conic. This renders the method all but impossible in practical applications to curves whose degree is not extremely small.

To avoid this problem Winkler and the author[89,90] introduced the notion of families of conjugate points. Intuitively speaking, the basic idea is to collect points whose coordinates depend algebraically on all the conjugate roots of the same polynomial $m(t)$. This will imply that computations can be carried out by using the defining polynomial $m(t)$ of these algebraic numbers.

Definition 30: The set of projective points

$$\mathcal{F} = \{(p_1(\alpha) : p_2(\alpha) : p_3(\alpha)) \mid m(\alpha) = 0\}$$

is called a *family of s conjugate points over* $\mathbb{F}$ if the following conditions are satisfied:

(1) $p_1, p_2, p_3, m \in \mathbb{F}[t]$, and $\gcd(p_1, p_2, p_3) = 1$,
(2) m is squarefree and $\deg(m) = s$,
(3) $\deg(p_i) < \deg(m)$ for $i = 1, 2, 3$,
(4) $\mathcal{F}$ contains exactly s different points of $\mathbb{P}^2(\mathbb{K})$.

We denote such a family by

$$\{ (p_1(t) : p_2(t) : p_3(t)) \}_{m(t)},$$

and we refer to it as a family of conjugate points.

The basic idea in Winkler and the author's paper[90] is to decompose the $d - 3$ simple points needed in Algorithm 3, with $k = d - 2$, in families of conjugate points over $\mathbb{F}$. For instance, if $\mathcal{C}$ has a rational triple point, cutting with lines passing through it, one generates families with exactly $d - 3$ simple points over $\mathbb{F}$. Obviously, these special cases do not appear in general. Therefore, the idea is to find *optimal* families of conjugate simple points over $\mathbb{F}$ on $\mathcal{C}$ (i.e., families over $\mathbb{F}$ with minimal cardinality). Clearly, in general, it is not true that there always exist families with cardinality one, i.e., rational points. Thus, the best that one can try to get — in general — is families of pairs of points. For this purpose, two main results are presented. The first one generalizes Hilbert-Hurwitz's theorem, and shows how to control the dimension of subsystems of adjoints; while the second shows how adjoint curves can be applied to compute families of conjugate points. More precisely, Hilbert-Hurwitz's theorem is generalized as follows.

Theorem 31: Let $a \in \{d, d-1, d-2\}$, and $\mathcal{A}_a^s(\mathcal{C})$ be a linear subsystem of $\mathcal{A}_a(\mathcal{C})$ of dimension s with all its base points on $\mathcal{C}$ and being in conjugate families. Then, the following hold:

(1) if $\Phi_1, \Phi_2, \Phi_3 \in \mathcal{A}_a^s(\mathcal{C})$ are such that $\Phi_1 \cap \Phi_2 \cap \Phi_3 \cap \mathcal{C}$ is the set of base points of $\mathcal{A}_a^s(\mathcal{C})$, and such that the restriction of

$$\mathcal{T} = \{y_1 : y_2 : y_3 = \Phi_1 : \Phi_2 : \Phi_3\}$$

to $\mathcal{C}$ is a birational transformation, then $\mathcal{T}(\mathcal{C})$ is irreducible of degree s;

(2) those values of the parameters for which the restriction to $\mathcal{C}$ of the rational transformation $\mathcal{T}$ is not birational satisfy some algebraic conditions.

On the other hand, in the same paper[90] it is also proved constructively that any linear subsystem $\mathcal{A}_a^s(\mathcal{C})$ in the conditions of Theorem 31 provides curves that generate families of s conjugate simple points over $\mathbb{F}$ by intersection with $\mathcal{C}$. More precisely, one has the following process to compute families of s points (where $\mathcal{B}$ is the set of base points of $\mathcal{H}_a^s$):

1. Take $\mathcal{M} \in \mathcal{A}_a^s(\mathcal{C})$ such that for every $P \in \mathcal{B}$,

$$\text{mult}_P(\mathcal{M}, \mathcal{C}) = \text{mult}_P(\mathcal{M}) \, \text{mult}_P(\mathcal{C})$$

holds. This can always be achieved by analyzing the corresponding resultants.

2. Compute

$$\tilde{R}_1(x) := \text{Res}_y(M(x, y, 1), F(x, y, 1)),$$

and

$$\tilde{R}_2(y) := \text{Res}_x(M(x, y, 1), F(x, y, 1)),$$

where M is the defining polynomial of $\mathcal{M}$.

3. Cross out in $\tilde{R}_1$ (resp. $\tilde{R}_2$) the factors generated by $\mathcal{B}$ to obtain R_1 (resp. R_2).

4. Compute the first subresultant $q(y)x - p(y)$ of $F(x, y, 1)$ and $R_2(y)$ modulo $R_1(x)$.

5. Return the family $\{(q(t)\,t, p(t), q(t))\}_{R_1(t)}$.

Therefore, taking adjoints of degrees $d - 2, d - 1$, and d, one generates families of conjugate simple points over $\mathbb{F}$ with cardinalities $d - 2, 2d - 2$, and $2d - 3$, respectively. In this situation, one has the following process to find families of two conjugate points over $\mathbb{F}$.

1. Use $\mathcal{A}_{d-2}(\mathcal{C})$ to compute two families $\mathcal{F}_1, \mathcal{F}_2$ of $d - 2$ simple points over $\mathbb{F}$ on $\mathcal{C}$

2. Compute the subsystem $\mathcal{H}^\star_{d-1}$ by forcing $\mathcal{F}_1, \mathcal{F}_2$ to be simple base points on $\mathcal{A}_{d-1}(\mathcal{C})$.

3. Take curves in $\mathcal{H}^\star_{d-1}$ and generate families of two conjugate points over $\mathbb{F}$.

Now, using the previous results we can give the optimal parametrization algorithm. If d is odd, one can compute $\frac{d-3}{2}$ families of two points over $\mathbb{F}$ that can be used to construct a linear subsystem of $\mathcal{H}_{d-2}$ over $\mathbb{F}$ of dimension one. Therefore, a parametrization over the ground field can be determined. If d is even, one can compute $\frac{d-4}{2}$ families of two points over $\mathbb{F}$ that can be used to construct a linear subsystem of $\mathcal{H}_{d-2}$ over $\mathbb{F}$ of dimension two. Moreover, applying Theorem 31 to this subsystem one can always find a birational transformation, defined by elements of the linear subsystem, that maps $\mathcal{C}$ onto a conic. Hence, the optimality question is reduced to the existence and computation of optimal parametrizations of the corresponding conic. In fact, since one has a subsystem of dimension two, one only needs to lift a point on the conic with coordinates over an optimal field extension to obtain a new subsystem of dimension one, and therefore to parametrize $\mathcal{C}$ over an optimal extension. For further details on the computation of the birationally equivalent conic, and on the inversion of a rational point, when it exists, we refer to Winkler and the author's paper.[90]

5. Properness and Inversion

Although the implicit representation for a plane curve is unique, up to a constant, there exist infinitely many different parametrizations of the same rational curve. For instance, for every $i \in \mathbb{N}$, (t^i, t^{2i}) parametrizes the parabola $y = x^2$. Obviously (t, t^2) is the parametrization of lowest degree in this family. Such parametrizations are called proper parametrizations.

The parametrization algorithms presented in the previous section always output proper parametrizations. Furthermore, there are algorithms[33,63,81,93] for determining whether a given parametrization of a plane curve is proper, and if that is not the case, for transforming it to a proper one. In this section, we study the notion of proper parametrization as well as its inversion problem. For this purpose, in the following we assume that $\mathcal{C}$ is an affine rational plane curve, and

$$\mathcal{P}(t) = (\chi_1(t), \chi_2(t)) = \left(\frac{\chi_{1,1}(t)}{\chi_{1,2}(t)}, \frac{\chi_{2,1}(t)}{\chi_{2,2}(t)} \right)$$

is a rational affine parametrization of $\mathcal{C}$ in reduced form. In addition, we consider the polynomials

$$G_i^{\mathcal{P}}(s, t) = \chi_{i\,1}(s)\chi_{i\,2}(t) - \chi_{i\,2}(s)\chi_{i\,1}(t), \quad i = 1, 2,$$

as well as the polynomials

$$H_1^{\mathcal{P}}(t, x) = x\chi_{1\,2}(t) - \chi_{1\,1}(t), H_2^{\mathcal{P}}(t, y) = y\chi_{2\,2}(t) - \chi_{2\,1}(t).$$

5.1. *Properness*

We start with the notion of proper parametrization.

Definition 32: An affine parametrization $\mathcal{P}(t)$ of a rational curve $\mathcal{C}$ is *proper* if the map

$$\mathcal{P} : \mathbb{K} \longrightarrow \mathcal{C}; t \longmapsto \mathcal{P}(t)$$

is birational, or equivalently, if almost every point on $\mathcal{C}$ is generated by exactly one value of the parameter t.

Note that Theorem 11 implies that every rational curve can be properly parametrized.

Definition 33: We define the *inversion* of a proper parametrization $\mathcal{P}(t)$ as the inverse rational mapping of $\mathcal{P}$, and we denote it by $\mathcal{P}^{-1}$.

The notion of properness can also be stated algebraically in terms of fields of rational functions. In fact a rational parametrization $\mathcal{P}(t)$ is proper if and only if the induced monomorphism

$$\varphi_{\mathcal{P}} : \mathbb{K}(\mathcal{C}) \longrightarrow \mathbb{K}(t); R(x, y) \longmapsto R(\mathcal{P}(t))$$

is an isomorphism. Therefore, $\mathcal{P}(t)$ is proper if and only if the mapping $\varphi_{\mathcal{P}}$ is surjective, that is, if and only if $\varphi_{\mathcal{P}}(\mathbb{K}(\mathcal{C})) = \mathbb{K}(\mathcal{P}(t)) = \mathbb{K}(t)$. More precisely, $\mathcal{P}(t)$ is proper iff the monomorphism $\varphi_{\mathcal{P}}$ is an isomorphism iff $\mathbb{K}(\mathcal{P}(t)) = \mathbb{K}(t)$.

Now, we characterize proper parametrizations by means of the degree of the corresponding rational curve. To state this result, we define the *degree* of $\mathcal{P}(t)$ as the maximum of the degrees of its rational components. We start this study with the following result that shows how proper and improper parametrizations of a affine plane curve are related.

Theorem 34: Let $\mathcal{P}(t)$ be proper, and $\mathcal{P}'(t)$ be any rational parametrization of $\mathcal{C}$. Then

(1) there exists a rational function $R(t) \in \mathbb{K}(t) \setminus \mathbb{K}$ such that $\mathcal{P}'(t) = \mathcal{P}(R(t))$;
(2) $\mathcal{P}'(t)$ is proper iff there exists a linear $L(t) \in \mathbb{K}(t)$ such that $\mathcal{P}'(t) = \mathcal{P}(L(t))$.

This result seems to suggest that a parametrization of prime degree is proper. But in fact, this is not true, as can easily be seen from the parametrization (t^2, t^2) of a line. The next theorem[93] characterizes the properness of a parametrization by means of the degree of the implicit equation of the curve.

Theorem 35: Let $f(x,y) \in \mathbb{K}[x,y]$ be the defining polynomial of $\mathcal{C}$. Then $\mathcal{P}(t)$ is proper if and only if

$$\deg(\mathcal{P}(t)) = \max\{\deg_x(f), \deg_y(f)\}.$$

Furthermore, if $\mathcal{P}(t)$ is proper, then $\deg(\chi_1(t)) = \deg_y(f)$, and $\deg(\chi_2(t)) = \deg_x(f)$.

In order to apply Theorem 35 to check the properness one needs to know the implicit equation of the curve. The next result[93] shows how to do that without knowing $f(x,y)$.

Theorem 36: $\mathcal{P}(t)$ is proper if and only if $\deg_t(\gcd(G_1^{\mathcal{P}}, G_2^{\mathcal{P}})) = 1$.

Example 37: Consider the rational parametrization

$$\mathcal{P}(t) = \left(\frac{(t^2 - 1)\,t}{t^4 - t^2 + 1}, \frac{(t^2 - 1)\,t^2}{t^6 - 3\,t^4 + 3\,t^2 - 1 - 2\,t^3} \right).$$

We have

$$G_1^{\mathcal{P}} = s^3 t^4 - s^3 t^2 + s^3 - s t^4 + s t^2 - s - t^3 s^4 + s^2 t^3 - t^3 + t s^4 - t s^2 + t,$$

$$G_2^{\mathcal{P}} = s^4 t^6 - s^4 - 2\, t^3 s^4 - s^2 t^6 + s^2 + 2\, s^2 t^3 - t^4 s^6 + t^4 + 2\, s^3 t^4 + t^2 s^6$$
$$- t^2 - 2\, s^3 t^2;$$

their gcd is $G(s,t) = t - s + s t^2 - s^2 t$. Thus, the parametrization is not proper.

5.2. *Inversion of Proper Parametrizations*

We have deduced some algorithmic criteria for deciding the properness of a rational affine parametrization. Now, we show how to compute the inverse map of a proper rational affine parametrization. Let $\mathcal{P}(t)$ be a proper parametrization; then the inversion problem consists of computing the inverse rational mapping of the birational map $\mathcal{P}$ induced by the parametrization (see above). Note that, for almost all points $P \in \mathcal{C}$, the inverse will provide the parameter value t for which $\mathcal{P}(t) = P$. More precisely, we want to compute the rational map

$$\varphi = \mathcal{P}^{-1} : \mathcal{C} \longrightarrow \mathbb{K}; \, (x,y) \longmapsto \varphi(x,y)$$

satisfying

(1) $\varphi \circ \mathcal{P} = id_{\mathbb{K}}$; that is: $\varphi(\mathcal{P}(t)) = t$, and
(2) $\mathcal{P} \circ \varphi = id_{\mathcal{C}}$; that is: $\chi_{i2}(\varphi)x - \chi_{i1}(\varphi) = 0 \mod I(\mathcal{C})$, $i = 1, 2$.

So the inversion problem is essentially an elimination problem, and therefore elimination techniques such as Gröbner bases can be applied (see Schicho's paper[76]). Alternatively, Chionh and Goldman[18] approached the problem by using multiresultants. Here we give a different approach to the problem based on the computation of gcds over the function field of the curve. A generalization to surfaces of these ideas can be found in the paper by Pérez-Díaz and others.[63] A more general statement of the problem, namely the inversion of birational maps, has been treated by Schicho.[76]

In addition, in order to check whether a rational function is the inverse of a given parametrization, it is enough to test one of the two conditions given above (a proof of this fact, for the general case of hypersurfaces, can be found in the paper by Pérez-Díaz and others[63]). Thus, in the sequel, we will choose freely one of the conditions to check the rational invertibility of a parametrization.

First we observe that $\mathbb{K}(\mathcal{C})$ is a field, and hence $\mathbb{K}(\mathcal{C})[t]$ is a Euclidean domain. Furthermore, since we know how to computationally perform the arithmetic in the coordinate ring $\Gamma(\mathcal{C})$, we know how to compute gcds in $\mathbb{K}(\mathcal{C})[t]$. Moreover, since $I(\mathcal{C})$ is principal, all computations can be carried out by means of remainders. The main theorem is the following.

Theorem 38: Let $\mathcal{P}(t) = (\chi_1(t), \chi_2(t))$ be a proper parametrization not having constant components, and let $H_1^{\mathcal{P}}(t, x)$, and $H_2^{\mathcal{P}}(t, y)$ be considered as polynomials in $\mathbb{K}(\mathcal{C})[t]$. Then, the gcd in $\mathbb{K}(\mathcal{C})[t]$ of $H_1^{\mathcal{P}}, H_2^{\mathcal{P}}$ has only one root and this is the inverse of $\mathcal{P}$.

As we have mentioned above the gcd in $\mathbb{K}(\mathcal{C})[t]$ can be performed by means of the Euclidean algorithm. For this purpose, we need to computationally perform the arithmetic in the coordinate ring $\Gamma(\mathcal{C})$. In order to do that we may use the implicit equation of the curve. An alternative approach may be to use the parametrization $\mathcal{P}(t)$ to check whether a class in $\mathbb{K}(\mathcal{C})$ is zero. Of course, this second approach avoids the use of the implicit equation but representatives of the classes are not reduced. In addition, probabilistic approaches, by taking random points of $\mathcal{C}$ generated via the parametrization, can also be considered (for a more general treatment of this problem, and for empirical time analysis see Pérez-Díaz's Ph.D. thesis[62]).

Example 39: Let $\mathcal{C}$ be the plane curve over $\mathbb{C}$ defined by the rational parametrization

$$\mathcal{P}(t) = \left(\frac{t^3 + 1}{t^2 + 3}, \frac{t^3 + t + 1}{t^2 + 1} \right).$$

It is easy to check that $\mathcal{P}(t)$ is proper. We consider now the polynomials

$$H_1^{\mathcal{P}}(t, x) = xt^2 + 3\,x - t^3 - 1, \quad H_2^{\mathcal{P}}(t, y) = yt^2 + y - t^3 - t - 1$$

in $\mathbb{C}(\mathcal{C})[t]$. One gets

$$\gcd_{\mathbb{C}(\mathcal{C})[t]} (H_1^{\mathcal{P}}, H_2^{\mathcal{P}}) = \frac{\left(2\,x^2 - 3\,yx - 1 + y^2\right)}{(-x+y)^2} t + \frac{(-2\,y-1)x^2 + \left(2\,y^2 + 2\,y - 3\right)x - y^2 + y}{(-x+y)^2}.$$

Therefore, the inverse mapping is

$$\mathcal{P}^{-1}(x, y) = -\frac{-y^2 + 2\,y^2 x + 2\,yx - 3\,x - 2\,yx^2 - x^2 + y}{2\,x^2 - 3\,yx - 1 + y^2}.$$

6. Reparametrizations of Rational Plane Curves

In the previous sections we have studied different problems related to rational curves, assuming that the original curve was given implicitly. Now we consider again some of these problems but from another point of view, namely, we assume that the curve is given in parametric form. But, this parametric representation might not be optimal with respect to various criteria. For instance, it might have too high degree or the coefficients might not be optimal. So we want to transform this rational parametrization into a better one. This new statement of the problem is specially interesting in some practical applications in CAGD where objects are often given and manipulated parametrically.

A direct approach to these statements could consist in implicitizing the parametrization to apply afterwards algorithms developed in the previous sections to the implicit equation. This solution might be too time consuming, and we would like to approach the problem by means of rational *"reparametrizations"*. With rational reparametrization we basically mean without implicitizating, or more formally, by finding a non-constant rational change of parameter, if it exists, that transforms the input parametrization onto a new parametrization of the same curve that solves the problem. Note that any reparametrization of a rational parametrization is again a parametrization of the same curve.

6.1. *Proper Reparametrizations*

In the last section we have seen that any rational curve can be properly parametrized. Furthermore, we have also commented that the properness was characterized by means of the function field, and by means of the degree. Moreover, in Theorem 36 an algorithmic criterion, based on gcds, to decide the properness of a parametrization was given. An additional problem is to determine (reparametrizing) a proper parametrization of a rational curve given parametrically. There are many approaches to the problem, most of them based on constructive proofs of Lüroth's theorem, see for instance Sederberg's algorithm.[81] The development in this algorithm[81] is based on involutions to compute the rational function.

6.2. *Polynomial Reparametrizations*

Till now, we have been dealing with rational parametrizations. However, one may ask whether the curve accepts a polynomial parametrization, i.e., a rational parametrization where all components are polynomials. This type of representation is specially interesting for applications; for instance, if one is giving numerical values to the parameter, and the parametrization is not polynomial, one may have a numerically unstable behavior when getting close to the roots of a denominator.

Clear examples of curves having polynomial parametrizations are, for instance, curves defined by polynomials of the type $x - g(y)$, like the parabolas. This class of curves can be extended to a more general family, namely those affine rational curves having only one place at infinity (see the book[1] by Abhyankar).

In this section, we show how to decide whether a given parametrization can be reparametrized into a polynomial parametrization. Moreover, if this is the case, we explicitly compute the change of parameter to be performed. The theoretical development we present is done for plane algebraic curve; nevertheless, one may observe that it can be easily extended to space curves[56]. A similar analysis can be done for quasi-polynomial curves, i.e., rational affine curves that can be parametrized with a parametrization having at least one polynomial component, as for instance the hyperbola $yx - 1$. Here we do not consider this extension; for further details one may check the paper[88] by Villarino and the author.

Definition 40: A rational affine parametrization $\mathcal{P}(t)$ of a rational affine curve $\mathcal{C}$ is called a *polynomial parametrization* if all its components are polynomial. Furthermore, the affine curve $\mathcal{C}$ is called a *polynomial curve* if it is rational and can be parametrized by means of a polynomial parametrization.

We have introduced the notion of polynomial affine curve by asking the existence of a polynomial affine parametrization. However, we have not imposed to the polynomial parametrization the condition of being proper. One can easily prove that any polynomial curve can be properly and polynomially parametrized. In fact, the proper non-polynomial parametrizations of a polynomial curves can be characterized as follows.

Theorem 41: Any proper non-polynomial rational parametrization in reduced form of a polynomial curve is of the type

$$\left(\frac{\chi_{1,1}(t)}{(bt - a)^r}, \frac{\chi_{2,1}(t)}{(bt - a)^s} \right),$$

where $\deg(\chi_{1,1}) \leq r$ and $\deg(\chi_{2,1}) \leq s$. Furthermore, if $\mathcal{P}(t)$ has this form, then

$$\mathcal{P}\left(\frac{b + at}{bt} \right)$$

is polynomial.

Note that from these results one can easily derive an algorithm for polynomial reparametrization. Let us see an example.

Example 42: Let $\mathcal{C}$ be the rational affine curve properly parametrized as

$$\mathcal{P}(t) = \left(\frac{35\,t^3 + 66\,t^2 + 42\,t + 9}{27\,t^3 + 54\,t^2 + 36\,t + 8}, \frac{97\,t^4 + 248\,t^3 + 240\,t^2 + 104\,t + 17}{81\,t^4 + 216\,t^3 + 216\,t^2 + 96\,t + 16} \right).$$

The denominators of the parametrization are $(3t+2)^3$ and $(3t+2)^4$. Thus, since the condition on the degrees is satisfied, it follows from Theorem 41 that $\mathcal{C}$ is polynomial and

$$\mathcal{P}\left(\frac{3 - 2t}{3t} \right)$$

is a proper polynomial parametrization of $\mathcal{C}$. In fact, with this reparametrization, one gets the following new parametrization

$$\left(\frac{35}{27} - \frac{4}{27}\,t + \frac{2}{81}\,t^2 - \frac{1}{729}\,t^3, \frac{97}{81} - \frac{32}{243}\,t + \frac{8}{243}\,t^2 - \frac{8}{2187}\,t^3 + \frac{1}{6561}\,t^4 \right).$$

We also observe that the implicit equation of $\mathcal{C}$ is

$$f(x, y) = -2 + 4\,x + 3\,y - 6\,x^2 - 3\,y^2 + 4\,x^3 + y^3 - x^4.$$

Note that $\mathcal{C}$ has only one point at infinity, namely $(0 : 1 : 0)$, that is simple and consequently $\mathcal{C}$ has only one place at infinity.

6.3. *Normal Reparametrizations*

In the previous subsection we have studied the properness problem by analyzing under which conditions the natural map $\mathcal{P}$, induced by a parametrization $\mathcal{P}(t)$ of $\mathcal{C}$, is injective. A natural problem related to the injectivity is the computation of surjective parametrizations, i.e., normal parametrizations. The rational mapping $\mathcal{P}$ is dominant; i.e., $\mathcal{P}(\mathbb{K})$ is a non-empty Zariski subset of the curve. Thus, in general, the mapping might not be surjective (i.e., normal), and hence some points of the algebraic set are missed. This phenomenon may generate unexpected complications in applications; for instance in the problem of plotting of geometric objects in the screen of a computer. Therefore, the problem of deciding whether a rational parametrization is normal and if not computing a normal parametrization, if possible, arises.

This problem was approached by Chou and Gao[19] for the case of algebraic varieties of arbitrary dimension over algebraically closed field of characteristic zero. The method presented in Chou and Gao's paper[19] is based on Ritt-Wu's decomposition algorithm, and they provided normal parametrizations for conics and some quadrics. Bajaj and Royappa[11] have presented normal parametrizations for the remaining quadrics. Also, in this paper,[11] the authors provided a method to construct normal parametrizations over the field of real numbers for parametrizations where no real point on the variety corresponds only to complex parameter values. In the paper by the author[84] a complete analysis on the normality for algebraic plane curves over fields of characteristic zero, either algebraically closed or not, is presented. In the following, we briefly summarize the results in this paper[84] for the algebraically closed case.

For this purpose, in the following we assume that $\mathcal{C}$ is an affine rational plane curve, and

$$\mathcal{P}(t) = (\chi_1(t), \chi_2(t)) = \left(\frac{\chi_{1,1}(t)}{\chi_{1,2}(t)}, \frac{\chi_{2,1}(t)}{\chi_{2,2}(t)} \right)$$

is a rational affine parametrization of $\mathcal{C}$ in reduced form.

Definition 43: $\mathcal{P}(t)$ is *normal* if for all $P \in \mathcal{C}$ there exists a $t_0 \in \mathbb{K}$ such that $\mathcal{P}(t_0) = P$. If there exists a normal parametrization of $\mathcal{C}$, we say that $\mathcal{C}$ can be *normally parametrized*.

Chou and Gao[19] have given a sufficient condition for a rational parametrization to be normal.

Theorem 44: If $\deg_t(\chi_{i,1}(t)) > \deg_t(\chi_{i,2}(t))$ for some $i \in \{1, 2\}$, then $\mathcal{P}(t)$ is normal.

From this result one immediately gets the following corollary.

Corollary 45: *Any polynomial parametrization is normal.*

However, the above results do not characterize the normality. For instance, the parametrization

$$\mathcal{P}(t) = \left(\frac{t^2 - 1}{t^3}, \frac{t - 1}{t^2} \right)$$

of the plane cubic defined by the polynomial

$$f(x, y) = y^3 + 2y^2 - 3xy + x^2,$$

clearly, does not satisfy the condition in Theorem 44. Nevertheless, let us see that $\mathcal{P}(t)$ is normal. First of all, we observe that $\mathcal{P}(t)$ is a proper parametrization. Its inverse can be expressed as

$$\mathcal{P}^{-1}(t) = \frac{2y - x}{y^2}.$$

Thus, one deduces that for every $(a, b) \in C \setminus \{(0, 0)\}$,

$$(a, b) = \mathcal{P}\left(\frac{2b - a}{b^2}\right).$$

Furthermore, $\mathcal{P}(1) = (0, 0)$. Therefore, $\mathcal{P}(t)$ is normal.

For the case of algebraically closed fields, if $\mathcal{P}(t)$ is not normal, then it can be extended to a projective parametrization, that is surjective, by taking care of the point on C that is the image of the infinity of $\mathbb{K}$ (see Chapter I, Section 5, Theorem 2 in the book[95] by Shafarevich). Here we approach the problem of doing that algorithmically.

The next theorem gives a complete characterization of normal parametrizations. For this purpose, we use the following notation: if $p \in \mathbb{K}[t]$ and $k \in \mathbb{N}$, then $\mathrm{coeff}(p(t), t^k)$ denotes the coefficient of the term t^k in $p(t)$.

Theorem 46: Let $n = \deg(\chi_{1,1})$, $m = \deg(\chi_{1,2})$, $r = \deg(\chi_{2,1})$, $s = \deg(\chi_{2,2})$, and $a = \mathrm{coeff}(\chi_{1,1}, t^m)$, $b = \mathrm{coeff}(\chi_{1,2}, t^m)$, $c = \mathrm{coeff}(\chi_{2,1}, t^s)$, $d = \mathrm{coeff}(\chi_{2,2}, t^s)$. Then, the following hold:

(1) if $n > m$ or $r > s$, then $\mathcal{P}(t)$ is normal;
(2) if $n \leq m$ and $r \leq s$, then $\mathcal{P}(t)$ is normal if and only if

$$\gcd(aq_1(t) - bp_1(t), \quad cq_2(t) - dp_2(t)) \neq 1;$$

furthermore, if $\mathcal{P}(t)$ is not normal, then all points in C are generated by $\mathcal{P}(t)$ with the exception of

$$\left(\frac{a}{b}, \frac{c}{d}\right)$$

which is a point on C.

We have already approached the problem of deciding whether a given parametrization is normal. In the next theorem, due to Tomás Recio, we deal with the problem of computing normal reparametrizations. Geometrically, the idea is to take a projective parametrization that sends the infinity of $\mathbb{K}$ to a point of C at infinity.

Theorem 47: Every rational affine curve over $\mathbb{K}$ can be properly and normally parametrized.

Combining these ideas one can give the following algorithm to normally reparametrize a non-normal parametrization.

1. If $\chi_{1,2}(t)$ is not constant, then take $\alpha \in \mathbb{K}$ such that $\chi_{1,2}(\alpha) = 0$ but $\chi_{1,1}(\alpha) \neq 0$; else take $\alpha \in \mathbb{K}$ such that $\chi_{2,2}(\alpha) = 0$ but $\chi_{2,1}(\alpha) \neq 0$.

3. Return

$$\mathcal{P}\left(\frac{\alpha t + 1}{t}\right).$$

Note that in this algorithm one may extend the ground field in order to compute a normal parametrization, and therefore one may lose the algebraic optimality. In some cases this problem cannot be avoided. In the paper by the author[84] algorithmic criteria for checking this are given, and when possible the normality is achieved without extending the ground field.

6.4. *Advanced Reparametrization Algorithms*

In Section 4 we have seen how to obtain an algebraically optimal parametrization if the input curve is given implicitly. This problem can also be stated from a parametric point of view. There exist reparametrization algorithms for this purpose. We refer to the papers.[4,5,87,87] In the 1997 paper[4] by Andradas and others the problem is approached by means of anticanonical divisors, while in the 1999 paper[5] by Andradas and others the problem is solved using the Weil variety associated to the parametrization. In addition, in the papers[87,88] by Villarino and the author the problem is studied for the case of polynomial and quasi-polynomial parametrizations, showing that, in these cases, the Weil variety has to be a line.

7. Real Rational Curves

Let $\mathcal{C}$ be an irreducible affine plane curve over the field $\mathbb{C}$ of complex numbers defined by $f \in \mathbb{C}[x,y]$. Then we say that $\mathcal{C}$ is a *real curve* if the field $\mathbb{R}(\mathcal{C})$ of rational functions over $\mathbb{R}$ (where $\mathbb{R}$ denotes the field of real numbers) is orderable, or equivalently, if $\mathcal{C}$ has infinitely many real points. We observe that if $\mathcal{C}$ has infinitely many real points, then f is associated with a real polynomial. Indeed: let

$$f(x,y) = f_1(x,y) + i\, f_2(x,y)$$

with $f_1, f_2 \in \mathbb{R}[x,y]$. Since $\mathcal{C}$ has infinitely many real points, there exist infinitely many points $(a,b) \in \mathbb{R}^2$ such that

$$f_1(a,b) + i\, f_2(a,b) = 0;$$

hence $f_1(a,b) = f_2(a,b) = 0$. Therefore, by Bézout's theorem, $\gcd(f_1, f_2)$ is not constant. Thus, since f is irreducible, one deduces that either $f_1 = 0$ or $f_2 = 0$; that is, f is associated with a real polynomial. On the other hand, if C has infinitely many real points, then the irreducibility of $f(x, y)$ over $\mathbb{R}$ and $\mathbb{C}$ are equivalent (see for instance the book[100] by Winkler). Therefore, irreducible plane real curves correspond to irreducible polynomials in $\mathbb{R}[x, y]$ having infinitely many solutions in $\mathbb{R}^2$. In fact, using well-known results in real algebra that can be directly deduced from the theory of *cylindrical algebraic decomposition* one can deduce the following criterion for reality. We state it for irreducible curves, but it can be extended to curves defined by squarefree polynomials (see the papers[91,92] by Winkler and the author).

Theorem 48: Let $f \in \mathbb{R}[x, y]$ be an irreducible polynomial different from the polynomial ay. Let C be the affine plane curve defined by f over $\mathbb{C}$, and let $D(x)$ be the discriminant of f w.r.t. y. Then, the following hold.

(1) If $D(x)$ has no real root, then C is real iff $f(0, y)$ has real roots. Furthermore, if α is a real root of $f(0, y)$, then $(0, \alpha)$ is a real simple point of C.

(2) If $D(x)$ has real roots, let $b_0, \ldots, b_r \in \mathbb{R}$ be such that

$$-\infty = a_0 < b_0 < a_1 < b_1 < a_2 < \cdots < b_{r-1} < a_r < b_r < a_{r+1} = +\infty,$$

where $a_1, \ldots, a_r$ are the real roots of $D(x)$. Then, C is real iff there exists an $i \in \{0, \ldots, r\}$ such that $f(b_i, y)$ has real roots. Furthermore, if α is a real root of $f(b_i, y)$, then (b_i, α) is a real simple point of C.

Now, we assume that C is real and rational (i.e., C is parametrizable over $\mathbb{C}$); then a natural question is whether C is parametrizable over the reals. As we have already seen in Section 4, in Algorithm 3 the ground field is extended only when the simple points are introduced. However, since C is real, it has infinitely many real simple points. Therefore, the rationality over $\mathbb{C}$ implies the rationality over $\mathbb{R}$. A direct but non-constructive proof of this result can also be deduced from the ideas in the book[17] by Chevalley, and an elementary proof can be found in the paper[72] by Recio and the author. Consequently, an irreducible real plane curve is rational over $\mathbb{C}$ if and only if it is rational over $\mathbb{R}$. Furthermore, a rational plane curve over $\mathbb{C}$ can be parametrized over the reals if and only if it is a real curve. Then, the rationality over $\mathbb{R}$ can be algorithmically decided by applying over $\mathbb{C}$ the methods described previously. However, it is not obvious how to parametrize over the reals. In fact, the problem can be stated from two different points of view: implicitly or parametrically. In the sequel we briefly describe the approaches to these two problems presented in the references.[71,90,91]

7.1. *Real Parametrizations*

It is easy to achieve a real parametrization algorithm from the results in Section 4. Note that the problem can be stated in terms of field extensions. More precisely, let C be a rational projective plane curve over $\mathbb{C}$ defined by a homogeneous polynomial $F \in \mathbb{L}[x, y, z]$, where $\mathbb{L}$ is a computable subfield of $\mathbb{R}$. Then, we want to optimally parametrize C over $\mathbb{R}$; that is, to parametrize over the smallest possible real field extension of $\mathbb{L}$. For odd degree curves this can always be achieved. In fact, parametrizations over $\mathbb{L}$ can be computed. However, for even degree curves, the existence of parametrizations over $\mathbb{L}$ or over $\mathbb{R}$ depends on the existence of rational points (i.e., points over $\mathbb{L}$) or real points on a conic birationally equivalent to C, respectively. In fact, it is easy to prove[90] that C is parametrizable over $\mathbb{R}$ if and only if it is not birationally equivalent over $\mathbb{R}$ to the conic $x^2 + y^2 + z^2$. Therefore, the problem is computationally reduced to the well-known problem of deciding the existence of real points on conics.

In addition, if one does not worry about field extensions, one can proceed more directly, applying Algorithm 3 in combination with Theorem 48, to generate $d - 3$ simple real points on the curve.

7.2. *Real Reparametrizations*

In this subsection we assume that we are given a parametrization over $\mathbb{C}$, and we want to decide whether it can be reparametrized over the reals; and if so, we look for a real reparametrization of the input parametrization. This is done in the paper[71] by Recio and the author. The main idea is to associate with the original parametrization a plane curve that contains as points the complex values (taking the real and imaginary parts) of the parameter that the real points on the original curve generate, via the parametrization. Then the reality of the original curve is characterized by means of the reality of the associated curve, that is proved to be either a line or a circle. More precisely, let

$$\mathcal{P}(z) = (p_1(z), p_2(z)),$$

where

$$p_1(z) = \frac{q_1(z)}{h(z)}, \quad p_2(z) = \frac{q_2(z)}{h(z)},$$

and $\gcd(q_1, q_2, h) = 1$, be a proper complex parametrization of a rational plane curve C over $\mathbb{C}$. Then, we consider the formal change of variable

$z = x + iy$. That is:

$$\mathcal{P}(x + iy) = (p_1(x + iy), p_2(x + iy))$$

$$= \left(\frac{u_1(x,y) + i\,v_1(x,y)}{h_1(x,y)^2 + h_2(x,y)^2}, \frac{u_2(x,y) + i\,v_2(x,y)}{h_1(x,y)^2 + h_2(x,y)^2} \right),$$

where $h_1, h_2 \in \mathbb{R}[x,y]$, $u_1, v_1 \in \mathbb{R}[x,y]$ and $u_2, v_2 \in \mathbb{R}[x,y]$ are the real and imaginary parts of $h(x+i\,y)$, $q_1(x+i\,y) \cdot \bar{h}(x-i\,y)$ and $q_2(x+i\,y) \cdot \bar{h}(x-i\,y)$, respectively (here $\bar{h}$ denotes the conjugate of h). Then, it is proved[71] that the plane curve $\mathcal{C}$ is real iff $\gcd(v_1, v_2)$ is either a real line or a real circle. Furthermore, if the plane curve $\mathcal{C}$ is real, and $(m_1(z), m_2(z))$ is a real proper rational parametrization of $\gcd(v_1, v_2)$, then $\mathcal{P}(m_1(z) + i\,m_2(z))$ is now a real proper rational parametrization of $\mathcal{C}$.

Clearly, these two results provide an algorithm that decides the reality of the curves, and in the affirmative case, computes the linear change of parameter that reparametrizes the original complex proper parametrization on a real proper parametrization.

Example 49: Consider the proper complex parametrization

$$\mathcal{P}(z) = \left(\frac{q_1(z)}{q(z)}, \frac{q_2(z)}{q(z)} \right),$$

where

$$q_1(z) = 52\,z - 24\,z\,i - 20\,i + 16 - 30\,z^5 - 24\,z^5\,i - 8\,z^4 - 154\,z^4\,i$$
$$- 148\,z^3 - 184\,z^3\,i - 128\,z^2 - 4\,z^2\,i,$$
$$q_2(z) = -36\,z^5 + 4\,z^5\,i + 108\,z^4 - 176\,z^4\,i - 296\,z^3 - 368\,z^3\,i + 248\,z^2\,i$$
$$- 264\,z^2 + 230\,z + 20\,z\,i + 20 - 66\,i,$$
$$q(z) = 82\,z^5 + 240\,z^4 + 110\,z^4\,i - 60\,z^3 + 280\,z^3\,i + 300\,z^2\,i - 240\,z^2$$
$$+ 50\,z\,i - 40\,z - 18\,i - 2.$$

Let $\mathcal{C}$ be the affine plane curve defined by $\mathcal{P}(z)$. Then,

$$\gcd(v_1, v_2) = -1 - x + x^2 + y^2$$

that can be parametrized over the reals as:

$$\mathcal{M}(z) = (m_1(z), m_2(z)) = \left(-\frac{-1 + 2\,z}{z^2 + 1}, \frac{z^2 - 1 - z}{z^2 + 1} \right).$$

Thus, $\mathcal{C}$ has infinitely many real points, and a real parametrization of $\mathcal{C}$ is

$$\mathcal{P}(m_1(z) + im_2(z))$$

$$= \left(\frac{z^4 - 4\,z^3 + 6\,z^2 - 4\,z + 2}{z(z^4 - 5\,z^3 + 10\,z^2 - 10\,z + 5)}, \frac{z^4 - 4\,z^3 + 6\,z^2 - 2\,z + 3}{z(z^4 - 5\,z^3 + 10\,z^2 - 10\,z + 5)} \right).$$

8. Parametrization of Rational Surfaces

Till now we have been dealing only with algebraic curves. This section is devoted to the case of algebraic surfaces; i.e., to hypersurfaces in $\mathbb{K}^3$ or $\mathbb{P}^3(\mathbb{K})$. The notion of affine or projective surface as well as the concepts of defining polynomial, degree, irreducibility, singularities, tangent space, field of rational functions, *etc.*, can be introduced similarly as we did in Section 2 for the case of plane curves.

In the following we focus our discussions on the parametrization problem for surfaces. As in the curve case, not all algebraic surfaces can be parametrized. This leads again to the notion of unirational and rational surfaces. Let $\mathcal{V}$ be the surface defined by the polynomial $F(x,y,z) \in \mathbb{K}[x,y,z]$; then a triple $\mathcal{P}(t,h) \in \mathbb{K}(t,h)^3$ is called a *rational parametrization* of $\mathcal{V}$ if $F(\mathcal{P}(t,h)) = 0$ and the Jacobian matrix of $\mathcal{P}(t,h)$ has rank 2. Also, one may introduce the notion of *proper parametrization* by asking the rational map

$$\mathcal{P} : \mathbb{K}^2 \to \mathcal{V}; (t,h) \to \mathcal{P}(t,h)$$

to be birational. In this situation, we say that $\mathcal{V}$ is *unirational* if it has a rational parametrization, and *rational* if it has a proper rational parametrization. Over $\mathbb{C}$ both concepts, rationality and unirationality, are equivalent.[16,95]

In addition to purely parametrization algorithms, one needs a decision procedure for the rationality. A general criterion for rationality has been given by Castelnuovo.[16] Concerning parametrization there exist methods for particular types of surfaces such as irreducible quadrics,[32] cubic surfaces[82] or canal surfaces.[67] The first general algorithm that parametrizes any rational surface has been given by Schicho.[74] The main computational tool in Schicho's algorithm[74] is (as in the case of curves) adjunction, which has played a fundamental role in the surface theory of the Italian school.[24]

8.1. *Parametrization by Lines*

Let $\mathcal{V}$ be an irreducible quadric surface in $\mathbb{P}^3(\mathbb{K})$, and let $P \in \mathcal{V}$ be a nonsingular point. Let $E \subset \mathbb{P}^3(\mathbb{K})$ be a projective plane not containing P. Then the projection $\pi : \mathbb{P}^3(\mathbb{K}) \to E$ is a rational map defined everywhere outside P.

Each line L through P intersects $\mathcal{V}$ at one more point Q_L. Therefore, the restricted projection $\pi : \mathcal{V} \to E$ is birational. We can construct a parametrization by inverting π. This can be done, for instance, as follows.

Let $Q(t,h)$ be a generic point in E and let $\mathcal{H} = P + \lambda(Q(t,h) - P)$ be the pencil of lines. Then, computing the intersection of E and $\mathcal{H}$ one gets the parametrization. Therefore, if F is the defining polynomial of $\mathcal{V}$, from $F(\mathcal{H}) = 0$ one expresses rationally λ in terms of t, h. Finally, substituting in $\mathcal{H}$ one obtains the parametrization.

Note that the so-constructed parametrization is proper. In fact, the inversion formula is the stepping stone for computing the parametrization.

The same method can be applied when we have a surface $\mathcal{V}$ of degree d in $\mathbb{P}^3(\mathbb{K})$, and a point $P \in \mathcal{V}$ with multiplicity $d - 1$.

Example 50: We consider the irreducible quadric $\mathcal{V}$ defined by

$$F(x, y, z) = 97y + 50x^2 + 79xy + 56xz + 49yz + 63z^2.$$

We take the point $P = (0, 0, 0) \in [\mathcal{V} \setminus \mathrm{Sing}(\mathcal{V})]$, and the plane E defined by $z = 1$. Note that $P \notin E$. Then, $Q(t, h) = (t, h, 1)$ and $\mathcal{H} = (\lambda t, \lambda h, \lambda)$. Moreover,

$$F(\mathcal{H}) = \lambda(97h + 50\lambda t^2 + 79\lambda th + 56\lambda t + 49\lambda h + 63\lambda).$$

Thus, expressing λ in terms of t, h and substituting in $\mathcal{H}$ one gets the parametrization

$$\mathcal{P}(t, h) = \left(\frac{-97th}{m(t, h)}, \frac{-97h^2}{m(t)}, \frac{-97h}{m(t)} \right),$$

where $m(t, h) = 50\, t^2 + 79\, th + 56\, t + 49\, h + 63$.

8.2. *Parametrization of Surfaces with a Pencil of Rational Curves*

In this subsection we treat the parametrization problem for the class of surfaces having a pencil of rational curves. A *pencil of curves* on a surface $\mathcal{V}$ is a one-parameter family of curves on $\mathcal{V}$.

Now, let $\mathcal{V}$ be a surface having a pencil $\mathcal{C}_t$ of rational curves parametrized by another rational curve $\mathcal{T}$. Then the basic idea for trying to parametrize $\mathcal{V}$ consists of two steps. The first parameter, t, fixes a curve C_t in the pencil, then a second parameter, h, is used to parametrize rationally C_t. The problem is that although these functions depend rationally on h, it cannot be ensured so easily that they also depend rationally on t. To see this difficulty, one may treat the pencil $\mathcal{C}_t$ as a single curve defined over the algebraic closure of the function field $\mathbb{K}(t)$. We know that this curve is rational, but it is not known whether it has a parametrization with coefficients in $\mathbb{K}(t)$.

However, applying Theorem 29, and the ideas in Subsection 4.3, we know that: if the degree of C_t is odd, then C_t can be parametrized over $\mathbb{K}(t)$ and therefore $\mathcal{V}$ is rational; if the degree of C_t is even, then C_t is birationally equivalent to a conic over $\mathbb{K}(t)$ and therefore $\mathcal{V}$ is birationally equivalent to a surface of the form $A(t)x^2 + B(t)y^2 + C(t) = 0$, where $A, B, C \in \mathbb{K}[t]$. This type of surfaces is called pencil of conics or tubular surfaces.

To try to parametrize a tubular surface we see it again as a curve over the closure of $\mathbb{K}(t)$. Thus we have a conic over a complicated field. Then, in order to get a parametrization of it over $\mathbb{K}(t)$ we need to compute a point on the conic with coordinates in $\mathbb{K}(t)$. If this is achieved, then applying Algorithm 1 (see Section 4) one gets a parametrization of the tubular surface and, composing with the inverse of the birational map that sends $\mathcal{V}$ on the tubular surface, we get a parametrization of $\mathcal{V}$. Thus, the problem is reduced to the computation of a $\mathbb{K}(t)$-rational point, if it exists, on the conic. That is, we need to find a rational curve on the tubular surface with a parametrization of the form $(\chi_1(t), \chi_2(t), t)$, i.e., a *cross section*.

The existence of cross sections depends directly on the ground field. Over $\mathbb{C}$ every tubular surface has a cross section (see the paper by Noether[59] of 1870 or as a corollary of Tsen-Lang's theorem in Shavarevich's book[95]). For the actual computation of cross sections we refer to Schicho's paper[74] and the paper[40] by Hillgarter and Winkler. Thus as a consequence, if we work over $\mathbb{C}$, every surface with a pencil of rational curves can be parametrized and the ideas described before show how to compute a parametrization.

Example 51: Let $\mathcal{V}$ be the surface of equation $x^4 + z^4 + (xy + z^2)^3 = 0$. $\mathcal{V}$ has a pencil of cubic plane curves; namely $x - tz = (t^4 + 1)z + (ty + z)^3 = 0$. We analyze $C_t = (t^4 + 1)z + (ty + z)^3$ as a cubic over the closure of $\mathbb{C}(t)$. It has a double point at infinity; hence by the genus formula (see Theorem 14) it is rational. Now, we apply Algorithm 1 (see Section 4) to get the parametrization

$$\left(\frac{h^3 + ht^4 + h}{t^5 + t}, -\frac{h^3}{t^4 + 1} \right)$$

of C_t over $\mathbb{C}(t)$. Therefore, $\mathcal{V}$ can be parametrized as

$$\left(\frac{-h^3 t}{t^4 + 1}, \frac{h^3 + ht^4 + h}{t^5 + t}, \frac{-h^3}{t^4 + 1} \right).$$

8.3. *Checking Rationality*

In Section 3 we saw that the rationality of curves could be analyzed by means of the genus that is a birational invariant. In the case of surfaces the rationality is deduced from other invariants, namely the arithmetic genus p_a and the plurigenus P_m. More precisely, one has the following criterion.[16]

Theorem 52: (Castelnuovo's theorem). Let $\mathcal{V}$ be an algebraic surface over $\mathbb{C}$. Then $\mathcal{V}$ is unirational iff $\mathcal{V}$ is rational iff $p_a(\mathcal{V}) = P_2(\mathcal{V}) = 0$.

In order to have an algorithmic version of Theorem 52 we need to compute $p_a(\mathcal{V})$ and $P_2(\mathcal{V})$. For this purpose, we introduce the notion of adjoints. Let $\mathcal{V}$ be a surface with defining polynomial F. Then, we say that a polynomial is an m-*adjoint* of $\mathcal{V}$ iff it vanishes with order at least $m(r-1)$ at each r-fold singular curve, and it vanishes with order at least $m(r-2)$ at each r-fold singular point, where infinitely near singularities have to be taken into account (see the paper[74] by Schicho). We consider only polynomials that are reduced with respect to F and we compute orders modulo F.

For any two natural numbers n, m, we define the vector space $V_{n,m}$ as the space of all m-adjoints of $\mathcal{V}$ of degree at most $n + m(d-4)$, where d is the degree of the given surface $\mathcal{V}$. In this situation, the plurigenus $P_m(\mathcal{V})$ is nothing but $\dim(V_{0,m})$ and $p_a(\mathcal{V}) = d + 2\dim(V_{1,1}) - \dim(V_{2,1}) - 1$.

Adjoint computation, i.e., computation of a basis of the vector space $V_{n,m}$ for given F, n, m, is difficult because it requires a so-called "resolution of the singularities" of $\mathcal{V}$. For algorithms computing adjoints and resolving, we refer to the papers.[74,96,13,15]

8.4. *Parametrization of Surfaces: The General Case*

After analyzing how to decide the rationality of surfaces, at least over $\mathbb{C}$, and once we have studied parametrization algorithms for special types of surfaces, we approach the general case. Theoretically, the idea is based on the following theorem (see details in the references[23,53,54]) that reduces the parametrization problem to surfaces with a pencil of rational curves or to the so-called *Del Pezzo surfaces*.[22,55]

Theorem 53: (Enriques-Manin's theorem). A surface with $p_a = P_2 = 0$ has a pencil of rational curves or it is birationally equivalent to a *Del Pezzo surface*.

We have already seen how to parametrize surfaces with a pencil of rational curves. For parametrization methods for Del Pezzo surfaces we refer to the papers.[20,55] However, it still remains to make Enriques-Manin's statement algorithmic. This can be done with the method of adjoints. More precisely, if $V_{n,m}$ is not the zero space, then any basis $Q_0, \ldots, Q_\ell$,

$\ell := \dim(V_{n,m}) - 1$, defines a rational map

$$f_{n,m} : \mathcal{V} \to \mathbb{P}^{\ell}, p \mapsto (Q_0(p) : \cdots : Q_{\ell}(p)).$$

Schicho[74] shows that if $\mathcal{V}$ is rational, then there are integers n, m, such that $f_{n,m}$ is a birational map either to a plane, or to a surface with a pencil of lines, or to a surface with a pencil of conics, or to a Del Pezzo surface.

8.5. *Advanced Parametrization and Reparametrization Algorithms*

In general, Schicho's parametrization algorithm[74] computes a proper parametrization with complex coefficients. For the real case, several algorithms[66,75,78] have been found for special classes of surfaces. However, it is not known if all real algebraic surfaces with a complex parametrization also have a real parametrization. Concerning reparametrization algorithms there exist algorithms[79,63] for checking properness and for computing the inverse, but the problem of finding a proper parametrization from a given non-proper one is still open. Also, there exists a reparametrization algorithm[77,80] for simplifying the degree of the parametrization. Nevertheless, most of the optimality questions for surfaces, either implicitly or parametrically given, are still open.

9. Some Applications

As we have mentioned before, CAGD is a natural frame for applications[9,21,43,44,46,61] of algebraic curves and surfaces. A good example of that is the well-known theory of Bézier curves and surfaces. In this section we briefly discuss three of these applications, namely plotting of real curves, offsetting curves and surfaces, and blending of several surfaces. For further examples of applications and details we refer to Chapter 1 in this volume and to the paper.[37]

9.1. *Plotting of Real Plane Curves*

The plotting problem can be approached[57] either from the implicit equation or, in the rational case, from a parametrization. If one starts from a parametric representation the plotting is performed by giving values to the parameter. Note that for making this, available algorithms in Sections 4, 6 and 7 are required. However, if one starts from the implicit equation, the direct application of numerical techniques may lead to wrong answers

     Sendra

when getting close to the singularities of the curve. To illustrate this phenomenon, we consider the Tacnode curve (see Examples 3 and 6). For this curve, Maple 8 produces the pictures in Fig. 6. As one can check, the pic-

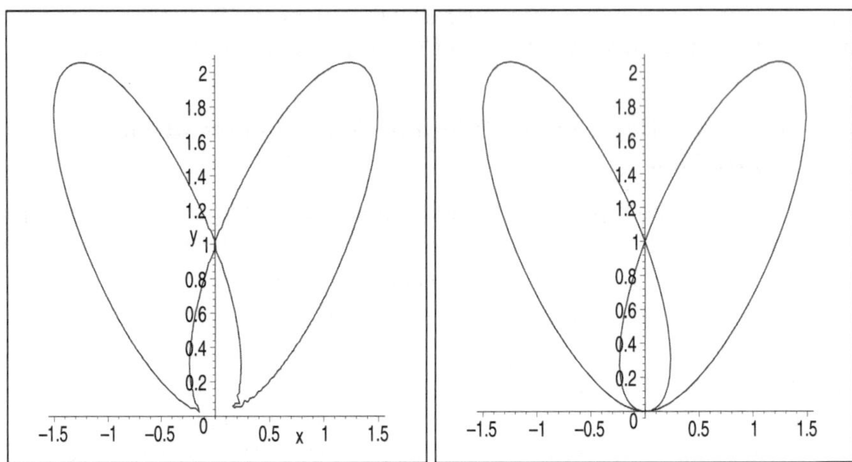

Fig. 6.   Plotting from implicit (left) and parametric (right) equations

ture generated from the implicit equation is not correct when getting close to the origin, that is a singularity of the curve.

To solve this problem one may get the topological graph of the curve. The problem of computing the topological graph of algebraic curves also plays an important role in other applications such as sectioning in computer aided geometric design (see the paper[10] by Bajaj and Hoffmann, and the paper[48] by Keyser and others). Many authors[6,31,35,34,45] have addressed the problem for the plane curve case, and in the paper[29] by Fortuna and others the computation of the topological type of a surface has been addressed for the non-singular case.

In the sequel, we briefly describe the standard strategy for computing the topological graph; for further computational and theoretical details we refer to the paper[35] by González-Vega and Necula and to Chapter 1[36] by González-Vega and others in this volume. Throughout this subsection, we assume that $\mathcal{H}$ is a real plane curve defined by a squarefree polynomial $h(x,y) \in \mathbb{R}[x,y]$. In this situation, one introduces the notion of critical points as follows. P is a *critical point* of $\mathcal{H}$ if h and its partial derivative w.r.t. y vanish at P. P is a *ramification point* of $\mathcal{H}$ if it is a non-singular critical point of $\mathcal{H}$. P is a *regular point* of $\mathcal{H}$ if $h(P) = 0$ and it is not critical. Then, the *graph associated to* $\mathcal{H}$, that we represent by $\mathrm{Graph}(\mathcal{H})$, is essentially introduced as the graph whose vertices are the real critical points and some additional real simple points on the curve, and where every edge of the graph corresponds to a branch of $\mathcal{H}$ joining two vertices.

In order to determine $\mathrm{Graph}(\mathcal{H})$, one assumes that the curve is in *planar general position*; i.e., no component of $\mathcal{H}$ is a real vertical line, $\mathcal{H}$ has no vertical asymptotes, and the x-coordinates of the real critical points of $\mathcal{H}$ are different. To ensure the first two conditions, one requires that the leading coefficient of $h(x,y)$ w.r.t. y has no real root. Also, note that almost all affine linear changes of variables transform $\mathcal{H}$ to a general position. Thus, one may always consider a random affine linear transformation or apply the deterministic algorithm described in the paper[27] by Farouki and Sakkalis.

The usual strategy for the computation of the graph of $\mathcal{H}$ is the following.

1. [Critical Points] Compute the discriminant of $h(x,y)$ w.r.t. y, and approximate its real roots, $\alpha_1 < \cdots < \alpha_r$ (i.e., the x-coordinates of the real critical points). For each α_i, compute the y-coordinates $\beta_{i,j}$ of the points of $\mathcal{H}$ lying on the line $x = \alpha_i$.
2. [In Out Edges] $\forall (\alpha_i, \beta_{i,j})$, compute the number of half-branches to the right and the left of the point $(\alpha_i, \beta_{i,j})$.
3. [Graph] Construct $\mathrm{Graph}(\mathcal{H})$ by appropriately joining the points in Step 1.

9.2. *Offsetting of Curves and Surfaces*

The notion of offset is directly related to the concept of envelope. More precisely, the offset hypersurface, at distance d, to an irreducible hypersurface $\mathcal{V}$ over $\mathbb{K}$ is "essentially" the envelope of the system of spheres centered at the points of $\mathcal{V}$ with fixed radius d (see Fig. 7 for the offset of a parabola and for the offset of an ellipsoid).

More formally, we define the *classical offset* to a hypersurface $\mathcal{V}$ over $\mathbb{K}$ at distance d as the Zariski closure in $\mathbb{K}^n$, of the constructible set $\mathcal{A}_d(\mathcal{V}_0)$ in $\mathbb{K}^n$ of the intersection points of the spheres of radius $d \in \mathbb{K}$ centered at each point $P \in \mathcal{V}_0$ and the normal line to $\mathcal{V}$ at P, where $\mathcal{V}_0 \subset \mathcal{V}$ is the set of all regular points of $\mathcal{V}$ having nonzero isotropic normal vectors to $\mathcal{V}$. Moreover, this notion can be generalized (see the 1997 paper[7] of Arrondo and others or Sendra's Ph.D. thesis[83]) by introducing the movement of the normal vector by means of a direct isometry.

This notion, for the case of plane curves, was already introduced by

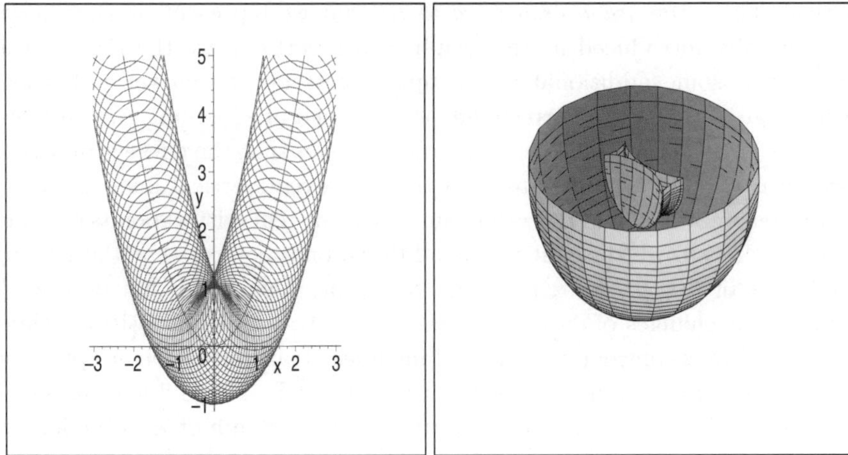

Fig. 7.   Offset to the parabola (left) and offset (half) to the ellipsoid (right)

Leibniz,[50] and in elementary texts on differential geometry and algebraic geometry some elementary aspects of offsets are studied. The CAGD community started, in the 1980s, to be interested in the topic, and problems related to "offsets" to curves and surfaces were addressed. The reason for this interest is that offsets play an important role in CAGD,[43,46] since they arise in practical applications such as tolerance analysis, geometric control, robot path-planning and numerical-control machining problems, like the description of the curve that a cylindrical tool executes when it moves through a prescribed path.

The study of offsets is an active research area (see for instance the references[7,8,25,26,43,44,46,51,52,66,67,68,69,85,86] and Chapter 5 in this volume). Indeed, as a consequence of this research, many interesting questions related to algebraic geometry, such as the study of the unirationality of the components of the offset to a given hypersurface, or the construction of rational parametrizations of the unirational components of an offset hypersurface, or the analysis of algebraic and geometric properties of the offset in terms of the corresponding properties of the initial variety (e.g., geometric genus offset curves), or the development of special implicitization techniques for offsets, have been treated.

9.3. *Blending of Surfaces*

Another interesting problem in CAGD is modeling objects.[43,46] Usually, one models the object as a collection of surfaces. However, in many cases, one wants this collection to form a composite object whose surface is smooth. This question leads to the blending problem. In fact, a blending surface is a surface that provides a smooth transition between distinct geometric features of an object. In Fig. 8 one can see a blending solution of a sphere and a cylinder.

Roughly speaking, if $V_1, \ldots, V_n$ (surfaces to be blended), and $U_1, \ldots, U_n$ (clipping surfaces) are given, the blending problem consists in finding an algebraic surface V such that $C_i = U_i \cap V_i \subset V$, and V meets each V_i at C_i with "certain" smooth conditions (G^k-continuity[98]).

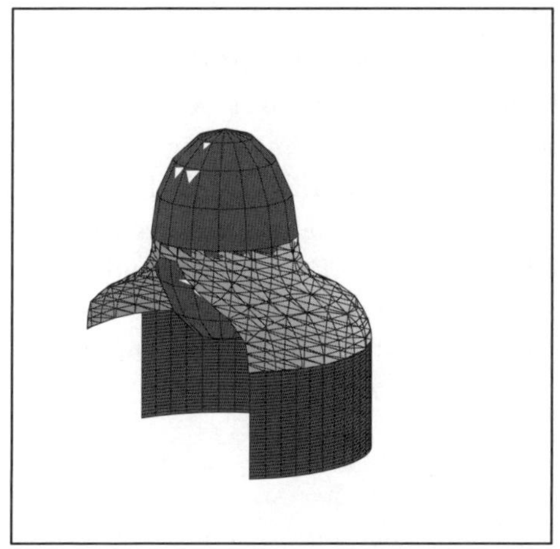

Fig. 8.   Blending of an sphere and a cylinder

The blending problem can be approached from two different points of view, namely, implicitly or parametrically. In the first case, one wants to compute an implicit expression of the solution while in the second parametric solutions are required. Some contributions[38,64,70] for the parametric case have been done, but most of the authors[28,99] have addressed the implicit version of the problem.

For implicit blending, the family of solutions is in the intersection of some polynomial ideals generated by the implicit equations of V_i, and powers of the equations of U_i, and therefore elimination techniques such as Gröbner bases can be applied (see Warren's Ph.D. thesis[98]). If the question is approached from the parametric point of view, one may ask whether there exist rational blending solutions of the problem, and if so, derive parametrizations of them. For this purpose, one may impose that V_i are rational, that parametrizations of them are known, and that the clipping surfaces U_i are taken such that the clipping curves C_i are also rational. In this situation, the set of all parametric solutions can be expressed as the addition of a parametric particular solution and a generic element of a free module of rank 3.[65] Since there exist algorithms[38,64,65] for computing particular parametric solutions and since a basis of the module is explicitly known, one has an algorithm for determining all the parametric solutions of the blending.

Acknowledgements

This work is partially supported by BMF2002-04402-C02-01 (*Curvas y Superficies: Fundamentos, Algoritmos y Aplicaciones*), Acción Integrada Hispano-Austriaca HU2001-0002 (*Computer Aided Geometric Design by Symbolic-Numerical Methods*), and GAIA II (IST-2002-35512).

Some of the material of this chapter has been taken from a manuscript jointly written with F. Winkler that corresponds to a joint project of a book on the topic that we are writing together. I thank F. Winkler for his permission to use the material. I also want to thank J. Schicho for his help and comments on the section of parametrization of surfaces.

References

1. Abhyankar S. S. (1990). *Algebraic Geometry for Scientists and Engineers.* Mathematical Surveys and Monographs vol. 35, AMS, Providence.
2. Abhyankar S. S., Bajaj C. L. (1988). *Automatic Parametrization of Rational Curves and Surfaces III: Algebraic Plane Curves.* Computer Aided Geometric Design vol. 5, pp. 390–321.
3. Abhyankar S. S., Bajaj C. L. (1989). *Automatic Rational Parametrization of Curves and Surfaces IV: Algebraic Space Curves.* Transactions on Graphics vol. 8, no. 4, pp. 325–334.
4. Andradas C., Recio T., Sendra J. R., (1997). *A Relatively Optimal Rational Space Curves Reparametrization Algorithm through Canonical Divisors.* Proc. ISSAC '97, Kchlin W. (ed.), pp. 349–356, ACM Press, New York.
5. Andradas C., Recio T., Sendra J. R. (1999). *Base Field Restriction Techniques for Parametric Curves.* Proc. ISSAC '99, Dooley S. (ed.), pp. 17–22, ACM Press, New York.
6. Arnon D., MacCallum S. (1988). *A Polynomial Time Algorithm for the Topology Type of a Real Algebraic Curve.* Journal of Symbolic Computation vol. 5, pp. 213–236.
7. Arrondo E., Sendra J., Sendra J. R. (1997). *Parametric Generalized Offsets to Hypersurfaces.* Journal of Symbolic Computation vol. 23, pp. 267–285.

8. Arrondo E., Sendra J., Sendra J. R. (1999). *Genus Formula for Generalized Offset Curves*. Journal of Pure and Applied Algebra vol. 136, no. 3, pp. 199–209.

9. Bajaj C. (ed.) (1994). *Algebraic Geometry and Its Applications*. Springer-Verlag, Berlin Heidelberg New York.

10. Bajaj C., Hoffmann C. M. (1988). *Tracing Surfaces Intersection*. Computer Aided Geometric Design vol. 5, pp. 285–307.

11. Bajaj C. L., Royappa A. V. (1995). *Finite Representation of Real Parametric Curves and Surfaces*. International Journal on Computational Geometry and Applications vol. 5, no. 3, pp. 313–326.

12. Berry T. G. (1997). *Parametrization of Algebraic Space Curves*. Journal of Pure and Applied Algebra vol. 117 & 118, pp. 81–95.

13. Bierstone E., Milman P. (1991). *A Simple Constructive Proof of Canonical Resolution of Singularities*. Effective Methods in Algebraic Geometry, Mora T., Traverso C. (eds.), pp. 11–30, Birkhäuser, Basel.

14. Brieskorn E., Knörrer H. (1986). *Plane Algebraic Curves*. Birkhäuser, Basel.

15. Bodnár G. Schicho J. (2000). *Automated resolution of Singularities for Hypersurfaces*. Journal of Symbolic Computation vol. 30, pp. 401–428.

16. Castelnuovo G. (1939). *Sulle Superficie di Genere Zero*. Memorie Scelte, Zanichelli, pp. 307–334.

17. Chevalley C. (1951). *Introduction to the Theory of Functions of One Variable*. Mathematical Surveys VI, AMS, Providence.

18. Chionh E. W., Goldman R. N. (1992). *Degree, Multiplicity and Inversion Formulas for Rational Surfaces Using u-Resultants*. Computer Aided Geometric Design vol. 9, no. 2, pp. 93–109.

19. Chou S. C., Gao. X. S. (1991). *On the Normal Parametrization of Curves and Surfaces*. International Journal on Computational Geometry and Applications vol. 1, no. 2, pp. 125–136.

20. Conforto F. (1939). *Le Superfici Razionali*. Zanichelli.

21. Cox D., Sturmfels B. (eds.) (1997). *Applications of Computational Algebraic Geometry*. Proc. of Symposia in Applied Mathematics vol. 53, AMS, Providence.

22. del Pezzo P. (1887). *On the Surfaces of Order n in Embedded in n-dimensional Space*. Rend. Mat. Palermo vol. 1, pp. 241–271.

23. Enriques F. (1895). *Sulle Irrazionalita da Cui Puo Farsi Dipendere la Risoluzione d'un Equazione f(xyz)=0 con Funzioni Razionali di due Parametri*. Math. Ann., pp. 1–23.

24. Enriques F. (1949). *Le Superfici Algebriche*. Zanichelli.

25. Farouki R. T., Neff C. A. (1990). *Analytic Properties of Plane Offset Curves*. Computer Aided Geometric Design vol. 7, pp. 83–99.

26. Farouki R. T., Neff C. A. (1990). *Algebraic Properties of Plane Offset Curves*. Computer Aided Geometric Design vol. 7, pp. 100–127.

27. Farouki R. T., Sakkalis T. (1990). *Singular Points on Algebraic Curves*. Journal of Symbolic Computation vol. 9, no. 4, pp. 405–421.

28. Feng Y., Chen F., Deng J., Chen C., Tang X. (2003). *Constructing Piecewise Algebraic Blending Surfaces*. Geometric Computation, Chen F., Wang D.

(eds.), pp. 34–64. World Scientific, Singapore New Jersey.

29. Fortuna E., Gianni P., Parenti P., Traverso C. (2002). *Computing the Topology of Real Algebraic Surfaces.* Proc. ISSAC 2002, Mora T. (ed.), pp. 92–100, ACM Press, New York.

30. Fulton W. (1989). *Algebraic Curves: An Introduction to Algebraic Geometry.* Addison Wesley Publishing Co., Inc.

31. Gianni P., Traverso C. (1983). *Shape Determination of Real Curves and Surfaces.* Ann. Univ. Ferrera Sez VII Sec. Math. XXIX, pp. 87–109.

32. Goldman R. N., Joe B., Wang W. (1997). *Rational Quadratic Parametrizations of Quadrics.* International Journal of Computational Geometry and Applications vol. 7, pp. 231–244.

33. Goldman R. N., Sederberg T. W., Anderson D. C. (1984). *Vector Elimination: A Technique for the Implicitization, Inversion, and a Intersection of Planar Parametric Rational Polynomial Curves.* Computer Aided Design vol. 1, pp. 337–356.

34. González-Vega L., El Kahoui M. (1996). *An Improved Upper Complexity Bound for the Topology Computation of a Real Algebraic Plane Curve.* Journal of Complexity vol. 12, pp. 527–544.

35. González-Vega L., Necula I. (2002). *Efficient Topology Determination of Implicitly Defined Algebraic Plane Curves.* Computer Aided Geometric Design vol. 19, pp. 719–743.

36. González-Vega L., Necula I., Pérez-Díaz S., Sendra J., Sendra J. R. (2003). *Algebraic Methods in Computer Aided Geometric Design: Theoretical and Practical Applications.* Geometric Computation, Chen F., Wang D. (eds.), pp. 1–33. World Scientific, Singapore New Jersey.

37. González-Vega L., Sendra J. R. (2001). *Algebraic-Geometric Methods for the Manipulation of Curves and Surfaces.* Actas del Congreso EACA 2001, Rubio J. (ed.), pp. 45–60. ORCCA Technical Report TR-01-07, 2001, Western Ontario University, Canada.

38. Hartmann E. (1995). *Blending an Implicit with a Parametric Surface.* Computer Aided Geometric Design vol. 12, pp. 825–835.

39. Hilbert D., Hurwitz A. (1890). *Über die Diophantischen Gleichungen vom Geschlecht Null.* Acta Math. vol. 14, pp. 217–224.

40. Hillgarter E., Winkler F. (1998). *Points on Algebraic Curves and the Parametrization Problem.* Automated Deduction in Geometry, Wang D. (ed.), pp. 185–203, Lecture Notes in Artificial Intelligence vol. 1360, Springer-Verlag, Berlin Heidelberg.

41. van Hoeij M. (1994). *Computing Parametrizations of Rational Algebraic Curves.* Proc. ISSAC '94, von zur Gathen J. (ed.), pp. 187–190, ACM Press, New York.

42. van Hoeij M. (1997). *Rational Parametrizations of Curves Using Canonical Divisors.* Journal of Symbolic Computation vol. 23, pp. 209–227.

43. Hoffmann C. M. (1993). *Geometric and Solid Modeling.* Morgan Kaufmann Publ. Inc.

44. Hoffmann C. M., Sendra J. R., Winkler F. (eds.) (1997). *Special Issue on Parametric Algebraic Curves and Applications.* Journal of Symbolic Compu-

tation vol. 23. Academic Press, London.

45. Hong H. (1996). *An Effective Method for Analyzing the Topology of Plane Real Algebraic Curves.* Math. Comput. Simulation vol. 42, pp. 571–582.

46. Hoschek J., Lasser D. (1993). *Fundamentals of Computer Aided Geometric Design.* A. K. Peters Wellesley MA. Ltd.

47. Ireland K., Rosen R. (1982). *A Classical Introduction to Modern Number Theory.* Graduate Texts in Mathematics, Springer-Verlag, New York.

48. Keyser J., Culver T., Manocha D., and Krishman S. (2000). *Efficient and Exact Manipulation of Algebraic Points and Curves.* Computer Aided Geometric Design vol. 32, no. 11, pp. 649–662.

49. Kotsireas I. S. (2003). *Panorama of Methods for Exact Implicitization of Algebraic Curves and Surfaces.* Geometric Computation, Chen F., Wang D. (eds.), pp. 126–155. World Scientific, Singapore New Jersey.

50. Leibniz G. W. (1692). *Generalia de Natura Linearum, Anguloque Contactus et Osculi Povocationibis Aliisque Cognatis et Eorum Usibus Nonnullis.* Acta Eruditorum.

51. Lü W. (1995). *Offset-Rational Parametric Plane Curves.* Computer Aided Geometric Design vol. 12, pp. 601–617.

52. Lü W. (1995). *Rational Parametrizations of Quadrics and Their Offsets.* Technical Report no. 24, Institut für Geometrie, Technische Universität Wien, Austria.

53. Manin Y. (1966). *Rational Surfaces over Perfect Fields I.* Inst. Hautes Et. Sci. Publ. Math. vol. 30, pp. 137–186.

54. Manin Y. (1967). *Rational Surfaces over Perfect Fields II.* Math. USSR Sb. vol. 1, pp. 141–168.

55. Manin Y. (1974). *Cubic Forms: Algebra, Geometry, Arithmetic.* North-Holland Publ. Co.

56. Manocha D., Canny J. F. (1991). *Rational Curves with Polynomial Parametrizations.* Computer Aided Design vol. 23, no. 9, pp. 645–652.

57. Mittermaier C., Schreiner W. and Winkler F. (2000). *Plotting Algebraic Space Curves by Cluster Computing.* Proc. ASCM 2000, Gao X. S., Wang D. (eds.), pp. 49–58, World Scientific, Singapore.

58. Mňuk M., Sendra J. R., Winkler F. (1997). *On the Complexity of Parametrizing Curves.* Beiträge zur Algebra und Geometrie vol. 37, no. 2, pp. 309–328.

59. Noether M. (1870). *Über Flächen, welche Scharen rationaler Kurven besitzen.* Math. Ann. vol. 3, pp. 161–227.

60. Noether M. (1883). *Rationale Ausführung der Operationen in der Theorie der Algebraischen Funktionen.* Math. Ann. vol. 23, pp. 311–358.

61. Patrikalakis N. M., Maekawa T. (2002). *Shape Interrogation for Computer Aided Design and Manufacturing.* Springer-Verlag, Berlin Heidelberg New York.

62. Pérez-Díaz S. (2003). *Variedades Paramétricas: Algoritmos y Aplicaciones en Blending Geométrico.* Ph.D. thesis, Universidad de Alcalá, Spain.

63. Pérez-Díaz S., Schicho J., Sendra J. R. (2002). *Properness and Inversion of Rational Parametrizations of Surfaces.* Applicable Algebra in Engineering, Communication and Computing vol. 13, pp. 29–51.

64. Pérez-Díaz S., Sendra J. R. (2001). *Parametric G^1 Blending of Several Surfaces.* Computer Algebra in Scientific Computing, pp 445–460, Springer-Verlag, Berlin Heidelberg New York.

65. Pérez-Díaz S., Sendra J. R. (2003). *Computing All Parametric Solutions for Blending Parametric Surfaces.* Journal of Symbolic Computation vol. 36, no. 6, pp. 925–964.

66. Peternell M. (1997). *Rational Parametrizations for Envelopes of Quadric Families.* Ph.D. thesis, Technische Universität Wien, Austria.

67. Peternell M., Pottmann H. (1998). *Applications of Laguerre Geometry in CAGD.* Computer Aided Geometric Design vol. 15, pp. 165–186.

68. Pottman H. (1995). *Rational Curves and Surfaces with Rational Offsets.* Computer Aided Geometric Design vol. 12, pp. 175–192.

69. Pottman H., Lü W., Ravani B. (1995). *Rational Ruled Surfaces and Their Offsets.* Technical Report no. 23, Institut für Geometrie, Technische Universität Wien, Austria.

70. Pottman H., Wallner J. (1997). *Rational Blending Surfaces between Quadrics.* Computer Aided Geometric Design vol. 14, pp. 407–419.

71. Recio T., Sendra J. R. (1997). *Real Reparametrizations of Real Curves.* Journal of Symbolic Computation vol. 23, pp. 241–254.

72. Recio T., Sendra J. R. (1997). *A Really Elementary Proof of Real Lüroth Theorem.* Revista Matemática de la Universidad Complutense de Madrid vol. 10, pp. 283–291.

73. Schicho J. (1992). *On the Choice of Pencils in the Parametrization of Curves.* Journal of Symbolic Computation vol. 14, pp. 557–576.

74. Schicho J. (1998). *Rational Parametrization of Surfaces.* Journal of Symbolic Computation vol. 26, pp. 1–9.

75. Schicho J. (1998). *Rational Parametrization of Real Algebraic Surfaces.* Proc. ISSAC '98, Gloor O. (ed), pp. 302–308, ACM Press, New York.

76. Schicho J. (1998). *Inversion of Birational Maps with Gröbner Basis.* Gröbner Basis and Applications, Buchberger B., Winkler F. (eds.), pp. 495–503, Lectures Notes Series 251, Cambridge University Press, Cambridge.

77. Schicho J. (1999). *A Degree Bound for the Parametrization of a Rational Surface.* Journal of Pure and Applied Algebra vol. 145, pp. 91–105.

78. Schicho J. (2000). *Proper Parametrization of Real Tubular Surfaces.* Journal of Symbolic Computation vol. 30, pp. 583–593.

79. Schicho J. (2000). *Proper Parametrization of Surfaces with a Rational Pencil.* Proc. ISSAC 2000, Traverso C. (ed.), pp. 292–299, ACM Press, New York.

80. Schicho J. (2002). *Symplification of Surface Parametrizations.* Proc. ISSAC 2002, Mora T. (ed.), pp. 229–237, ACM Press, New York.

81. Sederberg T.W. (1986). *Improperly Parametrized Rational Curves.* Computer Aided Geometric Design vol. 3, pp. 67–75.

82. Sederberg T. W., Snively J. P. (1987). *Parametrization of Cubic Algebraic Surfaces.* The Mathematics of Surfaces II, Martin R. R. (ed.), pp. 299–320, Oxford University Press, Oxford.

83. Sendra J. (1999). *Algoritmos Efectivos para la Manipulación de Offsets de Hipersuperficies.* Ph.D. thesis, Universidad Politécnica de Madrid, Spain.

84. Sendra J. R. (2002). *Normal Parametrizations of Algebraic Plane Curves.* Journal of Symbolic Computation vol. 33, pp. 863–885.
85. Sendra J., Sendra J. R. (1999). *Algebraic Analysis of Offsets to Hypersurfaces.* Mathematische Zeitschrift vol. 234, pp. 697–719.
86. Sendra J., Sendra J. R. (2000). *Rationality Analysis and Direct Parametrization of Generalized Offsets to Quadrics.* Applicable Algebra in Engineering, Communication and Computing vol. 11, no. 2, pp. 111–139.
87. Sendra J. R., Villarino C. (2001). *Optimal Reparametrization of Polynomial Algebraic Curves.* International Journal of Computational Geometry and Applications vol. 11, no. 4 pp. 439–453.
88. Sendra J. R., Villarino C. (2002). *Algebraically Optimal Reparametrizations of Quasi-Polynomial Algebraic Curves.* Journal of Algebra and Its Applications vol. 1, no. 1, pp. 51–74.
89. Sendra J. R., Winkler F. (1991). *Symbolic Parametrization of Curves.* Journal of Symbolic Computation vol. 12, no. 6, pp. 607–631.
90. Sendra J. R., Winkler F. (1997). *Parametrization of Algebraic Curves over Optimal Field Extensions.* Journal of Symbolic Computation vol. 23, pp. 191–207.
91. Sendra J. R., Winkler F. (1998). *Real Parametrization of Algebraic Plane Curves.* Lecture Notes in Artificial Intelligence vol. 1476, pp. 284–295, Springer-Verlag, Berlin Heidelberg New York.
92. Sendra J. R., Winkler F. (1999). *Algorithms for Rational Real Algebraic Curves.* Fundamenta Informaticae vol. 39, no. 1–2, pp. 211–228.
93. Sendra J. R., Winkler F. (2001). *Tracing Index of Rational Curve Parametrizations.* Computer Aided Geometric Design vol. 18, pp. 771–795.
94. Sendra J. R., Winkler F (2001). *Computation of the Degree of a Rational Map between Curves.* Proc. ISSAC '01, Mourrain B. (ed.), pp. 317–322, ACM Press, New York.
95. Shafarevich I. R. (1994). *Basic Algebraic Geometry,* vol. I, II. Springer-Verlag, Berlin Heidelberg New York.
96. Villamayor O (1991). *Introduction to the Algorithm of Resolution.* Algebraic Geometry and Singularities, La Rabida 1991, pp. 123–154, Birkhäuser, Basel.
97. Walker R. J. (1950). *Algebraic Curves.* Princeton University Press, Princeton.
98. Warren J. (1986). *On Algebraic Surfaces Meeting with Geometric Continuity.* Ph.D. thesis, Cornell University, USA.
99. Warren J. (1989). *Blending Algebraic Surfaces.* ACM Transactions on Graphics vol. 8, no. 4, pp. 263–278.
100. Winkler F. (1996). *Polynomial Algorithms in Computer Algebra.* Springer-Verlag, Wien New York.

CHAPTER 4

**PANORAMA OF METHODS FOR EXACT
IMPLICITIZATION OF ALGEBRAIC CURVES AND
SURFACES**

Ilias S. Kotsireas[a]

Wilfrid Laurier University
Computer Algebra Research Group, Department of Computing
Waterloo N2L 3C5, ON, Canada
E-mail: ikotsire@wlu.ca · http://www.cargo.wlu.ca
and
University of Western Ontario
Ontario Research Center for Computer Algebra
Computer Science Department
London N6A 5B7, ON, Canada
E-mail: ilias@orcca.on.ca · http://www.orcca.on.ca

This chapter is intended to present an overview of all major available Symbolic Computation methods for exact implicitization of algebraic curves and surfaces. The methods are discussed in a rigorous theoretical framework and the associated algorithms are illustrated with fully worked out examples in the Computer Algebra system Maple. Implicitization algorithms constitute an essential tool in the arsenal of available methods employed to tackle Geometric Computation problems, for instance, in Computer Aided Design and Computer Aided Geometric Design. An extensive bibliography on the subject of implicitization is included.

1. Introduction

Implicitization is a central topic in Computer Aided Geometric Design (CAGD) where one needs to manipulate large numbers of curves and surfaces in real time. Depending on the task at hand, parametric or implicit representations of these geometric objects may be more suitable. For instance, when we want to check whether a given point belongs to a certain

---

[a]This work is supported by a grant from the Natural Sciences and Engineering Research Council of Canada.

126

curve or surface, the implicit representation is advantageous. On the other hand, when we want to draw a given curve or surface, the parametric representation is usually better suited. Therefore we need to have efficient algorithms to convert parametric to implicit equations and vice-versa. The process of passing from the parametric equations of a curve or surface to the implicit equation is called implicitization. The dual process of passing from the implicit equation to a set of parametric equations is called parametrization.

The purpose of this chapter is to provide a hands-on introduction to the major available symbolic computation methods for exact implicitization of algebraic curves and surfaces. For a survey of parametrization methods, see Chapter 3 by Sendra[68] in this book.

The subject of implicitization has received attention in the Computational Algebra textbook[22] by Cox, Little and O'Shea and in the Computer Algebra textbook[69] by von zur Gathen and Gerhard. The book[1] on Gröbner bases by Adams and Loustaunau contains references to implicitization as well. A more extensive coverage of the subject is included in the computational algebraic geometry textbook[23] by Cox, Little and O'Shea. The book[34] by Gao and Wang contains a chapter on implicitization of rational parametric equations. The dissemination of implicitization methods developed within the symbolic computation community is unsatisfactory. This is exemplified by the descriptions of implicitization in the computer graphics books[74,40,3] by Angel, Hill and Watt. The second purpose of this chapter is to contribute to bridge this gap. The CAGD books[29,42] by Farin and Hoffmann contain algorithmic treatments of implicitization. The subject is touched upon from a computational as well as a theoretical perspective in the book[59] by Olver. The unique in its kind Computer Algebra Handbook[38] by Grabmeier, Kaltofen and Weispfenning contains an article in which implicitization is studied in the frame of Computer Aided Design (CAD) and Modeling algorithms. The extremely comprehensive CAGD handbook[28] by Farin, Hoschek and Kim contains a survey chapter[67] by Sederberg and Zheng on algebraic algorithms.

The reference books for the computer algebra systems Singular[39] and Magma[13] contain respectively code and examples for Gröbner-based implicitization methods, while the reference books[56,57] for the computer algebra system Maple 8 contain examples for the eigenvalue implicitization method. A general principle in symbolic computation is the exploitation of structure of the object of study. Following this principle, there are additional methods designed to solve the exact implicitization problem for particular classes of curves or surfaces, thus achieving greater levels of efficiency than the general-purpose methods. Important work has been done on many special types of curves and surfaces. See the papers[43,44] by Hong and Schicho on trigonometric curves and nested trigonometric curves, the paper[41] by Hobby on cubic curves, the paper[7] by Berry and Patterson on nonsingular cubic surfaces, the paper[63] by Sederberg, Anderson and Goldman on planar rational cubic curves, the paper[35] by Goldman on nonplanar, parametric, rational cubic curves, the papers[61,49] by Peternell, Pottmann, Landsmann, Schicho and Winkler on canal surfaces (parametrization), and the paper[62] by Schicho on tubular surfaces (parametrization).

Here we adopt purposedly an informal style of presentation (without sacrificing rigor and clarity) to make the material easily comprehensible and accessible to the non-specialist. An ample number of bibliographical references is included, for the interested reader who may want to delve further into the details of the various methods and learn of the latest research developments on the subject. A sufficient supply of fully worked out examples is included together with the associated ready-to-use code written in the widely used computer algebra system Maple. The examples and the code are meant to improve the understanding of the readers as well as their ability to apply quickly the methods to their own particular problems.

2. Exact Implicitization of Algebraic Curves

In this section we give a statement of the problem of exact implicitization for algebraic curves and algebraic surfaces. An important category of algebraic curves and surfaces that arise frequently in applications will be considered separately. These are the rational curves and surfaces. Finally we will mention briefly the implicitization methods described in the rest of this chapter.

2.1. *Algebraic Curves*

An affine algebraic curve is the set of zeros of a bivariate non-constant polynomial $p(x, y)$ whose coefficients belong to a field. Since we are interested in exact implicitization, we suppose that the field of coefficients is either the field of rational numbers or the field of algebraic numbers. A parametrization of an algebraic curve is given by equations of the form

$$x = f(t), \quad y = g(t) \tag{1}$$

where t is called the parameter of the parametrization. The functions f and g can be polynomial, rational, and trigonometric functions as well as functions involving square (or higher order) roots.

The exact implicitization problem for an algebraic curve given by (1) is to find the Cartesian implicit equation of the curve, that is a polynomial[b] $p(x,y)$ such that

$$p(f(t), g(t)) = 0$$

for all permissible values of the parameter t. The adjective *exact* refers to the fact that the coefficients appearing in the functions f, g and the polynomial $p(x,y)$ are integer, rational or algebraic numbers.

The implicitization problem for a curve is not always solvable. A simple example is the 2-parameter family of logarithmic spiral curves, whose parametric equations are

$$x = \alpha \cos \theta e^{\beta \theta}, \quad y = \alpha \sin \theta e^{\beta \theta}.$$

Here, θ is the parameter of the parametrization and the family is indexed by the two parameters α, β. For generic values of the parameters α, β this curve is not algebraic and therefore there is no polynomial equation $p_{\alpha,\beta}(\theta)$ that defines it.

2.2. *Algebraic Surfaces*

A parametrization of an algebraic surface is given by equations of the form

$$x = f(t,s), \quad y = g(t,s), \quad z = h(t,s) \tag{2}$$

where t, s are called the parameters of the parametrization. The functions f, g, h can be polynomial, rational, and trigonometric functions as well as functions involving square (or higher order) roots.

The exact implicitization problem for an algebraic surface given by (2) is to find the Cartesian implicit equation of the surface, that is a polynomial $p(x,y,z)$ such that

$$p(f(t,s), g(t,s), h(t,s)) = 0$$

for all permissible values of the parameters t,s. As above, the adjective *exact* refers to the fact that the coefficients appearing in the functions f, g, h and the polynomial $p(x,y,z)$ are integer, rational or algebraic numbers.

It is often the case that parametric equations of the form (2) represent a space curve and not a surface.

---

[b]When speaking about the implicit equation, we often write p instead of $p = 0$.

2.3. *Rational Curves and Surfaces*

When an algebraic curve or surface is given by parametric equations which are rational functions of the parameters, it is called a *rational* curve or surface. Rational curves and surfaces appear repeatedly in applications and their theory is understood better that the theory of curves and surfaces in general. An example is the following well-known result.

Theorem 1: An algebraic curve has a rational parametrization if and only if it is of genus 0.

The genus of an algebraic curve is an important invariant defined in terms of the degree of the curve and the multiplicities of the singular points of the curve. An algebraic curve has genus 1 if and only if it is birationally equivalent to a non-singular cubic. A classic book[31] on algebraic curves by Fulton explains in detail the notions of the genus of an algebraic curve and birational equivalence. An example of a plane algebraic curve of genus 1 is given by Neuberg's 21-point cubic defined by the determinantal equation[8,58]

$$\begin{vmatrix} 1 & a_1^2 + a_4^2 & a_1^2 a_4^2 \\ 1 & a_2^2 + a_5^2 & a_2^2 a_5^2 \\ 1 & a_3^2 + a_6^2 & a_3^2 a_6^2 \end{vmatrix} = 0.$$

In the above equation a_1, a_2, a_3 are the lengths of the sides of a triangle such that the side of length a_i is opposite from the vertex A_i of the triangle and a_4, a_5, a_6 are the distances of a point $P(x, y)$ in the plane from the vertices A_1, A_2, A_3 respectively. For generic triangles (i.e., non-equilateral) Neuberg's 21-point cubic is a non-singular cubic curve of genus 1.

A considerable amount of work in the exact implicitization problem has been devoted to rational curves and surfaces.

We will use the following notation for rational curves and surfaces in most of the rest of the chapter.

Parametric equations of a rational curve:

$$x = \frac{f(t)}{w(t)}, \quad y = \frac{g(t)}{w(t)}, \tag{3}$$

where f, g, w are univariate polynomials in the parameter t.

Parametric equations of a rational surface:

$$x = \frac{f(s, t)}{w(s, t)}, \quad y = \frac{g(s, t)}{w(s, t)}, \quad z = \frac{h(s, t)}{w(s, t)}, \tag{4}$$

where f, g, h, w are bivariate polynomials in the parameters s, t.

It is customary to suppose for simplicity that the denominators of the rational functions in parametric equations of rational curves (or surfaces) are equal. This assumption has its roots in the interplay between affine and projective space and it does not affect the validity of the algorithms.

2.4. *Methods for Exact Implicitization*

In the rest of this chapter we will present all major symbolic computation methods for exact implicitization of algebraic curves and surfaces. The methods can be categorized according to the basic underlying tools employed.

From an alternative viewpoint the implicitization problem can be interpreted as the elimination of the parameters $t_1, \ldots, t_k$ from the parametric equations. Therefore the classical (resultants) as well as the modern (Gröbner bases and characteristic sets) elimination methods yield corresponding implicitization methods.

Another wide family of methods is based on the concept of a moving line or in general of a moving algebraic curve. An important characteristic of these methods is that the implicit equation is expressed in a compact form as a determinant of a matrix.

Finally we will present implicitization methods based on perturbation arguments, multidimensional Newton formulae and the eigenvalue method. A simple method[73] based on undetermined coefficients to set up a sparse, partially triangular, system of linear equations has been developed recently by Wang. Another method[12] based on properties of approximation complexes and using a lot of machinery form algebraic geometry has been developed recently by Busé and Jouanolou. A method[60,2] for implicitization of a union of parametric varieties has been developed by Orecchia.

3. Resultants

Resultants are arguably the very first tool used for implicitization of rational curves and surfaces. Resultant-based implicitization methods have been studied extensively and continue to be a topic of active research mainly through the deep connections of resultants with more advanced concepts of algebraic geometry. A classical drawback of resultant-based methods for implicitization is the appearance of redundant factors, in the sense that the implicit equation is given as a factor of a higher degree polynomial.

Example 2: Consider the curve given by the polynomial parametric equations

$$x = t^5 - t^2 - 1, \quad y = t^4 - t^2 - 1.$$

The implicit equation of this curve may be computed in Maple with resultants as follows:

```
f:=t^5-t^2-1: g:=t^4-t^2-1: r:=sort(resultant(x-f,y-g,t),y);
```

$$r = y^5 + 5\,y^4 - 4\,xy^3 + 9\,y^3 + 5\,x^2y^2 + 4\,y^2 - 10\,xy^2 + 17\,x^2y + 3\,y + 6\,xy + 2\,x - 6\,x^3 - x^4 + 1$$

Example 3: Now consider a rational function parametrization of the unit sphere:

$$x = \frac{s^2 - t^2 - 1}{s^2 + t^2 + 1}, \quad y = \frac{2\,s}{s^2 + t^2 + 1}, \quad z = \frac{2\,s\,t}{s^2 + t^2 + 1}.$$

The implicit equation may be computed in Maple with resultants as follows:

```
r1:=factor(resultant(numer(x)-x*den,numer(y)-y*den,s));
```

$$4\,\left(t^2 + 1\right)\left(y^2t^2 + y^2 + x^2 - 1\right)$$

```
r2:=factor(resultant(numer(y)-y*den,numer(z)-z*den,s));
```

$$4\,\left(t^2 + 1\right)\left(-z + yt\right)^2$$

```
r:=factor(resultant(y^2*t^2+y^2+x^2-1,-z+y*t,t));
```

$$y^2\left(-1 + y^2 + x^2 + z^2\right)$$

We see that there is a redundant factor of y^2.

References for resultant implicitization[4,10,18,19,54,55]

4. Gröbner Bases

From a similar viewpoint the implicitization problem can be interpreted as the elimination of the parameter t for curves (respectively the parameters t, s for surfaces) from the parametric equations. Since Gröbner bases provide us with an algorithmic way to perform elimination of variables using the pure lexicographical ordering, it was realized very early on in the development of the theory of Gröbner bases that they could be used for implicitization.

We start with an example of Buchberger[9] in which the parametric equations are polynomial.

Example 4: Consider the algebraic surface given by the polynomial parametric equations

$$x = rt, \quad y = rt^2, \quad z = r^2.$$

The implicit equation can be computed in Maple as follows:

```
gbasis([x-r*t,y-r*t^2,z-r^2],plex(r,t,x,y,z));
```

which gives the result

$$\{-y^2z+x^4, -x^3+ytz, -y+tx, zt^2-x^2, -x^2+ry, -tz+xr, -x+rt, -z+r^2\}.$$

The first element $x^4 - y^2z$ of this Gröbner basis gives the implicit equation of the surface.

The next example is also due to Buchberger,[9] but now the parametric equations are rational functions. In this case we have to clear denominators before using Gröbner bases.

Example 5: Consider the rational function parametrization of the unit circle:

$$x = \frac{1-t^2}{1+t^2}, \quad y = \frac{2\,t}{1+t^2}.$$

The implicit equation can be computed in Maple as follows:

```
gbasis([x*(t^2+1)-1+t^2, y*(t^2+1)-2*t],plex(t,x,y));
```

which gives the result

$$\{y^2 + x^2 - 1, x - 1 + yt, tx - y + t\}.$$

The first element x^2+y^2-1 of this Gröbner basis gives the implicit equation of the unit circle.

In the following example the parametric equations are trigonometric and an additional preprocessing phase of polynomialization is required before using Gröbner bases.

Example 6: Consider the following trigonometric parametrization of a boomerang-shaped curve:

$$x = \cos\theta\sin\theta - \cos\theta, \quad y = \cos\theta\sin\theta - \sin\theta. \tag{5}$$

Define new variables $c = \cos\theta$ and $s = \sin\theta$ to represent the trigonometric functions. The new variables satisfy the polynomial equation

$$c^2 + s^2 = 1. \tag{6}$$

The polynomialization of equations (5) and (6) results in the following set of polynomials

$$\{x - cs + c, y - cs + s, c^2 + s^2 - 1\} \tag{7}$$

which is suitable for a Gröbner basis computation. We impose a lexicographical order on the variables with $s > c > x > y$ and compute the reduced lexicographical Gröbner basis as detailed below in Maple.

```
gb:=gbasis([x-c*s+c,y-c*s+s,c^2+s^2-1],plex(s,c,x,y)):
```

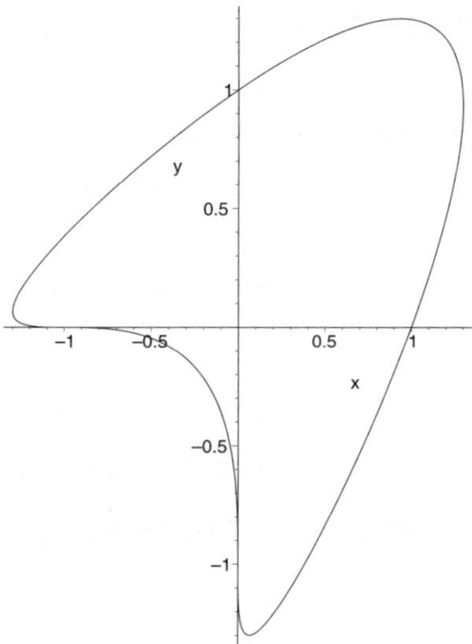

Fig. 1 Boomerang-shaped curve

The Gröbner basis is guaranteed to contain a polynomial in the variables x, y alone which will be the implicit equation of the Boomerang-shaped curve, that we give in the following semi-factored form:

$$(x - y)^4 + 2\,(x + y)\left((x - y)^2 - 1\right) + 4xy - 1 = 0. \tag{8}$$

Remark: Since the Boomerang-shaped curve is of genus 0, it has a rational parametrization. Typically a parametrization algorithm will produce a parametrization like

$$x = \frac{-8\,t\,(8\,t^3 - 12\,t^2 + 6\,t - 1)}{64\,t^4 - 64\,t^3 + 32\,t^2 - 8\,t + 1}, \quad y = \frac{1 - 4\,t}{64\,t^4 - 64\,t^3 + 32\,t^2 - 8\,t + 1},$$

with a non square-free denominator. This rational function parametrization seems more complicated than the trigonometric parametrization (5).

In this final example[53] we show how to deal with case where there are values of the parameter t (or parameters s, t for surfaces) such that $f(t) = g(t) = w(t) = 0$ (or $f(s, t) = g(s, t) = h(s, t) = w(s, t) = 0$ for surfaces).

Example 7: Consider the surface given by the parametric equations

$$x = \frac{st^2 - t}{st^2}, \quad y = \frac{st + s}{st^2}, \quad z = \frac{2s - 2t}{st^2}.$$

The point $(s, t) = (0, 0)$ annihilates all three numerators and the common denominator simultaneously. The usual Gröbner basis computation will not yield the implicit equation. However, if we supplement the equations with an equation of the form $wst^2 - 1$ (where w is a new indeterminate) to ensure that the denominator will be nonzero, then we obtain the implicit equation. In Maple we have:

```
eq:=[x*s*t^2-s*t^2+t,y*s*t^2-s*t-s,z*s*t^2-2*s+2*t,w*s*t^2-1];
gbasis(eq,plex(w,s,t,x,y,z));
```

The result of this Gröbner basis computation contains the implicit equation

$$z^2 - 4zx - 4zy + 4x^2 + 8xy + 4y^2 + 2z - 4x - 8y.$$

References for Gröbner basis implicitization[9,45,33,51,46,30,32]

5. Characteristic Sets

The elimination method of characteristic sets, developed by the Chinese mathematician Wen-tsün Wu, provides another device for implicitization. An elaborate presentation of the theory of characteristic sets is contained in the book[70] and the implementation paper[71] by Wang. Other relevant theories of triangular sets and the associated implementation issues are discussed in the two papers[5,6] by Aubry, Lazard and Moreno Maza.

Example 8: Refer to Examples 4–7 in the preceding section. The following computations using functions from Wang's Epsilon library[71] show that the implicit equations of the considered curves and surfaces may be obtained as the first elements of the corresponding characteristic sets:

```
charset([x-r*t,y-r*t^2,z-r^2],[z,y,x,t,r]);
```

$$[x^4 - y^2 z, -y + xt, -x^2 + yr]$$

```
CharSet([x*(t^2+1)-1+t^2, y*(t^2+1)-2*t],[y,x,t]);
```

$$[x^2 - 1 + y^2, -y + xt + t], \textit{factors removed} = \{y\}$$

```
CharSet([x-c*s+c,y-c*s+s,c^2+s^2-1],[y,x,c,s]);
```

$$[x^4 - 4\,x^3 y + 6\,x^2 y^2 - 4\,xy^3 + y^4 + 2\,x^3 - 2\,x^2 y - 2\,xy^2 + 2\,y^3 + 4\,xy$$
$$- 2\,x - 2\,y - 1, x^3 c - 3\,x^2 yc + 3\,xy^2 c - y^3 c - x^3 + 2\,x^2 y - x^2 c - xy^2$$
$$+ 4\,xyc - 3\,y^2 c - 2\,xy - xc - 3\,yc - x - c, -sc + x + c],$$
$$\textit{factors removed} = \{x\}$$

```
eq:=[x*s*t^2-s*t^2+t,y*s*t^2-s*t-s,z*s*t^2-2*s+2*t];
CharSet(eq,[z,y,x,t,s]);
```

$$[4\,x^2 + 8\,xy - 4\,xz + 4\,y^2 - 4\,yz + z^2 - 4\,x - 8\,y + 2\,z,$$
$$2\,tx - tz - 2\,t + 2\,x + 2\,y - z - 2, st^2 z - 2\,s + 2\,t],$$
$$\textit{factors removed} = \{t, y\}$$

We refer the reader to the extensive articles[32,72] by Gao and Wang, as well the older article[50] by Li, on the subject of implicitization via characteristic (or triangular) sets. Note that the curve or surface defined by the implicit equation may not be the same as that defined by the parametric equations. By means of computing regular systems[72] or characteristic sets with projection,[50] one can obtain implicit equations and inequations that define exactly the same parametric curve or surface.

6. Perturbations

Manocha and Canny[52,53] proposed an algorithm based on perturbation arguments to solve the exact implicitization problem for rational parametric surfaces. The algorithm can be used in conjunction with Gröbner bases as well as with resultants. Suppose that we are given rational parametric equations of an algebraic surface as in (4). The algorithm introduces a perturbation variable λ and an associated perturbation of the parametric equations given by

$$\begin{aligned}
G_1(s,t) &= x\,w(s,t) - f(s,t) + \lambda\,f_1(s,t), \\
G_2(s,t) &= y\,w(s,t) - g(s,t) + \lambda\,g_1(s,t), \\
G_3(s,t) &= z\,w(s,t) - h(s,t) + \lambda\,h_1(s,t),
\end{aligned} \tag{9}$$

where the bivariate polynomials f_1, g_1, h_1 are such that the perturbed system of equations (9) has no trivial solution. A random choice of f_1, g_1, h_1 is usually enough to guarantee this condition of solvability. The algorithm is based on the following theorem.[53]

Theorem 9: The implicit equation $p(x, y, z)$ of the rational surface is a factor of the coefficient of the lowest degree term in λ of the resultant of the perturbed equations (9).

The method can be used with resultants as well as with Gröbner bases. We illustrate the application of the method with an example of Manocha and Canny,[53] but we use a simpler and uniform perturbation.

Example 10: Consider a rational function parametrization of the unit sphere:

$$x = \frac{s^2 - t^2 - 1}{s^2 + t^2 + 1}, \quad y = \frac{2\,s}{s^2 + t^2 + 1}, \quad z = \frac{2\,s\,t}{s^2 + t^2 + 1}.$$

We choose the perturbation given by $f_1(s, t) = g_1(s, t) = h_1(s, t) = 1$. Using Maple, we compute the Gröbner basis of the perturbed equations with respect to a lexicographical ordering such that $z < y < x < \lambda < s < t$.

```
w:=s^2+t^2+1:
eqsp:=[x*w-s^2+1+t^2+lambda,y*w-2*s+lambda,z*w-2*s*t+lambda]:
gb:=gbasis(eqsp,plex(t,s,lambda,x,y,z)):
```

It turns out that the first element of the Gröbner basis is independent of s, t and we factorize the coefficient of its lowest degree term in λ:

```
factor(coeff(gb[1],lambda,1));
```

The result is

$$4\left(x^2 + y^2 + z^2 - 1\right)\left(2\,x^2 + 4\,x + 2 - 2\,xy - 2\,y + y^2 - 2\,zx - 2\,z + z^2\right)$$

and we see that the implicit equation $x^2 + y^2 + z^2 - 1$ of the unit sphere is indeed a factor of the coefficient of the lowest degree term.

7. Moving Lines, Moving Planes, Moving Curves, and Moving Surfaces

7.1. *Moving Lines*

Let a rational curve be given by the parametric equations

$$x = \frac{f(t)}{w(t)}, \quad y = \frac{g(t)}{w(t)}.$$

When $\deg f(t) = \deg g(t) = \deg w(t) = n$, this is called a degree n rational curve. It is also tacitly assumed that $\gcd(f(t), w(t)) = 1$ and

$\gcd(g(t), w(t)) = 1$. We begin by seeking all moving lines

$$(A_{n-1}x + B_{n-1}y + C_{n-1})t^{n-1} + \cdots + (A_1 x + B_1 y + C_1)t \\ + (A_0 x + B_0 y + C_0) = 0 \tag{10}$$

of degree $n - 1$ that follow the curve. Substituting into (10) the rational functions for x and y and clearing out denominators by multiplying by $h(t)$, we obtain the equation

$$(A_{n-1}x(t) + B_{n-1}y(t) + C_{n-1}h(t))t^{n-1} + \cdots + (A_0 x(t) \\ + B_0 y(t) + C_0 h(t)) = 0. \tag{11}$$

If (10) is a moving line that follows the degree n rational curve, then the polynomial (11) (in t) must be identically zero. Since $\deg f(t) = \deg g(t) = \deg h(t) = n$, this is a polynomial of degree $2n - 1$ in t. Setting all its coefficients to 0 gives rise to a homogeneous linear system of $2n$ equations in the $3n$ unknowns $A_{n-1}, B_{n-1}, C_{n-1}, \ldots, A_0, B_0, C_0$. Such a system has (at least) n linearly independent solutions that we denote by

$$p_1(t) = (A_{1,n-1}x + B_{1,n-1}y + C_{1,n-1})t^{n-1} + \cdots + A_{1,0}x + B_{1,0}y + C_{1,0}) = 0,$$
$$\vdots \qquad\qquad\qquad\qquad\qquad \vdots$$
$$p_n(t) = (A_{n,n-1}x + B_{n,n-1}y + C_{n,n-1})t^{n-1} + \cdots + A_{n,0}x + B_{n,0}y + C_{n,0}) = 0.$$

The implicit equation of the degree n curve is given by the determinant

$$\begin{vmatrix} A_{1,n-1}x + B_{1,n-1}y + C_{1,n-1} & \cdots & A_{1,0}x + B_{1,0}y + C_{1,0} \\ \vdots & & \vdots \\ A_{n,n-1}x + B_{n,n-1}y + C_{n,n-1} & \cdots & A_{n,0}x + B_{n,0}y + C_{n,0} \end{vmatrix}.$$

Example 11: Consider the degree $n = 5$ rational curve:

$$x = \frac{t^5 - t^2 + 1}{t^5 + t + 2}, \quad y = \frac{t^5 + t^4 + 1}{t^5 + t + 2}.$$

The generic moving line of degree $n - 1 = 4$ that follows this curve is defined in Maple by

```
ml:=(A4*x+B4*y+C4)*t^4+(A3*x+B3*y+C3)*t^3+(A2*x+B2*y+C2)*t^2+
(A1*x+B1*y+C1)*t+(A0*x+B0*y+C0);
```

The corresponding equation of degree $2n - 1 = 9$ is defined in Maple by

```
nml:=collect(simplify(ml*(t^5+t+2)),t);
```

and the result is

$$(A_4 + B_4 + C_4)\, t^9 + (C_3 + A_3 + B_4 + B_3)\, t^8 + (B_2 + B_3 + C_2 + A_2)\, t^7$$
$$+ (B_1 + C_1 + A_1 - A_4 + B_2)\, t^6 + (C_4 - A_3 + A0 + C_0 + B_1 + B_0)\, t^5$$
$$+ (B_4 + C_3 + A_4 + 2C_4 - A_2 + B_0)\, t^4 + (A_3 + B_3 + 2C_3 - A_1 + C_2)\, t^3$$
$$+ (2C_2 - A_0 + B_2 + C_1 + A_2)\, t^2 + (B_1 + 2C_1 + A_1 + C_0)\, t + B_0 + 2C_0 + A_0 = 0.$$

Equating all the coefficients to zero we get a homogeneous linear system of $2n = 10$ equations in the $3n = 15$ unknowns $A_4, B_4, C_4, \dots, A_0, B_0, C_0$. We solve this system in Maple and detect terms of the form `var = var` where `var` ranges in the set of the 15 unknowns. Thus we find that there are 5 such terms and therefore this linear system has at least 5 linearly independent solutions. We set particular values for these 5 (e.g., B_0, B_1, B_2, C_0, C_1) free unknowns (using random numbers) to find 5 specific linearly independent solutions that we place into a matrix:

$$\begin{bmatrix}
A_0 & B_0 & C_0 & A_1 & B_1 & C_1 & A_2 & B_2 & C_2 & A_3 & B_3 & C_3 & A_4 & B_4 & C_4 \\
11 & -1 & -5 & -3 & -4 & 6 & -7 & -4 & 8 & 4 & 3 & -9 & -5 & 2 & 3 \\
2 & -6 & 2 & 8 & -2 & -4 & -1 & -5 & 6 & 0 & 0 & 1 & -3 & -1 & 4 \\
-9 & 1 & 4 & -9 & -1 & 3 & 6 & 4 & -11 & -1 & 1 & 1 & -3 & -1 & 4 \\
-6 & 0 & 3 & -6 & 1 & 1 & 4 & -1 & -5 & 7 & 2 & -5 & -5 & -4 & 9 \\
-6 & 2 & 4 & -6 & 3 & 1 & 4 & -5 & -5 & 7 & 2 & -5 & -5 & -4 & 9
\end{bmatrix}$$

where the first row indicates the order of the unknowns that we introduced. We verify in Maple that the rank of this matrix (without the first row of unknowns of course) is equal to 5 and therefore we have found 5 linearly independent solutions. We view these solutions as polynomials in t (moving line formalism) and construct the corresponding determinant of linear forms

$$\begin{vmatrix}
11x - y - 5 & -3x - 4y + 6 & -7x - 4y + 8 & -5x + 2y + 3 & 4x + 3y - 9 \\
2x - 6y + 2 & 8x - 2y - 4 & -x - 5y + 6 & -3x - y + 4 & 1 \\
-9x + y + 4 & -9x - y + 3 & 6x + 4y - 11 & -3x - y + 4 & -x + y + 1 \\
-6x + 3 & -6x + y + 1 & 4x - y - 5 & -5x - 4y + 9 & 7x + 2y - 5 \\
-10x + 2y + 4 & -9x + 3y + 1 & 12x - 5y - 9 & -10x - 11y + 21 & 20x + 2y - 11
\end{vmatrix},$$

which is equal (up to a constant factor) to the implicit equation

$$-17x^5 + (-9y + 62)x^4 + (6y^2 - 82 + 12y)x^3 + (51 - 6y^3 + 2y^2 - 10y)x^2$$
$$+ (-39y^2 + 25y - 5y^4 - 19 + 28y^3)x + 32y^2 - y^5 + 8y^4 - 25y^3 - 18y + 5.$$

7.2. *Moving Curves and μ-bases*

Sederberg and others[64,66,65] introduced the method of moving curves. Cox, Sederberg and Chen[24] introduced the μ-bases method which provides a means of finding a suitable set of moving lines for a planar rational curve. An efficient algorithm to compute the μ-basis of a planar rational curve is given by Zheng and Sederberg.[76] The μ-bases method is extended to the case of a rational ruled surface by Chen, Zheng and Sederberg[17] and relevant further developments are established by Chen and Wang.[16] The moving curves method is applied to a planar rational curve with a high order singularity by Chen and Sederberg.[15] The method of moving planes[64,75] has been developed to implicitize rational surfaces.

7.3. *Moving Surfaces*

Consider a rational surface in homogeneous form:

$$S(s,t) = (x(s,t), y(s,t), z(s,t), w(s,t)).$$

This means that the Cartesian parametric equations of the surface S are

$$x_c = \frac{x(s,t)}{w(s,t)}, \quad y_c = \frac{y(s,t)}{w(s,t)}, \quad z_c = \frac{z(s,t)}{w(s,t)}.$$

A moving surface is defined as:

$$g(X, s, t) = \sum_{i=1}^{\sigma} h_i(X)\, \gamma_i(s,t) = 0 \tag{12}$$

where $h_i(X) = 0$, $i = 1, \ldots, \sigma$, is a collection of implicit surfaces. The bivariate polynomials $\gamma_i(s,t)$ are called *blending functions* for the moving surface. The moving surface g is said to follow the rational surface S if

$$g(S(s,t), s, t) = 0.$$

Let $g_j(X, s, t) = \sum_{i=1}^{\sigma} h_{ji}(X)\, \gamma_i(s,t) = 0$, $j = 1, \ldots, \sigma$, be a set of σ moving surfaces, each following the rational surface S. Define

$$f(X) = \begin{vmatrix} h_{11}(X) & \cdots & h_{1\sigma}(X) \\ \vdots & & \vdots \\ h_{\sigma 1}(X) & \cdots & h_{\sigma\sigma}(X) \end{vmatrix}.$$

If the degree of $f(X)$ is equal to the degree of the implicit equation of the rational surface S, then $f(X) = 0$ is the implicit equation of S. To obtain the implicit equation in x_c, y_c, z_c we have to dehomogenize (set $w = 1$) the equation $f(X) = 0$.

7.3.1. *Choice of the blending functions*

For two very wide (and commonly arising in practice) classes of rational parametric surfaces, there are explicit expressions for the blending functions $\gamma_i(s,t)$ appearing in (12).

- **Tensor product surface patches** are defined as

$$x(s,t) = \sum_{i=0}^{d_1}\sum_{j=0}^{d_2} x_{ij}s^i t^j, \quad y(s,t) = \sum_{i=0}^{d_1}\sum_{j=0}^{d_2} y_{ij}s^i t^j,$$

$$z(s,t) = \sum_{i=0}^{d_1}\sum_{j=0}^{d_2} z_{ij}s^i t^j, \quad w(s,t) = \sum_{i=0}^{d_1}\sum_{j=0}^{d_2} w_{ij}s^i t^j.$$

In this case the σ blending functions can be chosen as

$$\gamma_i(s,t) = s^j t^k, \quad j = 0,\dots,d_1, \ k = 0,\dots,d_2,$$

which also implies that $\sigma = (d_1 + 1)(d_2 + 2)$.

- **Triangular surface patches** are defined as

$$x(s,t) = \sum_{i+j\leq d} x_{ij}s^i t^j, \quad y(s,t) = \sum_{i+j\leq d} y_{ij}s^i t^j,$$

$$z(s,t) = \sum_{i+j\leq d} z_{ij}s^i t^j, \quad w(s,t) = \sum_{i+j\leq d} w_{ij}s^i t^j.$$

In this case the σ blending functions can be chosen as

$$\gamma_i(s,t) = s^j t^k, \quad j = 0,\dots,d-1, \ k = 0,\dots,d-j-1,$$

which also implies that $\sigma = d(d+1)/2$.

Example 12: For the cubic surface with

$$\begin{aligned}
x &= 2 + 2t^3 + s^2 + 4t^2 + 4ts + 2t + ts^2 + 3s,\\
y &= -2t^2s - ts - 2s^2 + s - s^3 - 2t + 2,\\
z &= -3t^2s + 2t^2 - 2ts^2 - 3ts - 2t - s^3 - 3s^2 - 2s,\\
w &= -t + ts^2 + s^2 - s + s^3 + t^3 - 1 + t^2,
\end{aligned}$$

the blending functions can be chosen as

$$\gamma_1(s,t) = s, \quad \gamma_2(s,t) = t, \quad \gamma_3(s,t) = 1.$$

We take $\sigma = 3$, and three moving surfaces are

$$\begin{aligned}
g_1(X,s,t) &= x\gamma_1(s,t) + y\gamma_2(s,t) + z\gamma_3(s,t),\\
g_2(X,s,t) &= (y + w)\gamma_1(s,t) + (2y - z)\gamma_2(s,t) + (y + 2w)\gamma_3(s,t),\\
g_3(X,s,t) &= (z - y)\gamma_1(s,t) + (-x + 2w)\gamma_2(s,t) + (x - y)\gamma_3(s,t).
\end{aligned}$$

A theorem tells us that the determinant of the matrix

$$\begin{bmatrix} x & y & z \\ y+w & 2y-z & y+2w \\ z-y & -x+2w & x-y \end{bmatrix}$$

is the implicit equation of the cubic surface (since it has the desired degree three). After dehomogenization (setting $w=1$) we obtain the implicit equation

$$z^3-3\,z^2y+3\,zy^2-zx^2-3\,y^2x+3\,yx^2+4\,zy-zx-y^2-3\,yx+2\,x^2+2\,z-4\,x=0.$$

Example 13: Now consider the Steiner surface with

$$x=2st, \quad y=2t, \quad z=2s, \quad w=s^2+t^2+1.$$

The blending functions can be chosen as $\gamma_1(s,t)=s$, $\gamma_2(s,t)=t$, $\gamma_3(s,t)=1$. We take $\sigma=3$, and three moving surfaces are

$$g_1(X,s,t)=y\gamma_1(s,t)-2z\gamma_2(s,t)+x\gamma_3(s,t),$$
$$g_2(X,s,t)=y\gamma_1(s,t)-z\gamma_2(s,t),$$
$$g_3(X,s,t)=xz\gamma_1(s,t)+(xy-xz-2zw)\gamma_2(s,t)+(x^2+yz)\gamma_3(s,t).$$

The above-mentioned theorem tells us that the determinant of the matrix

$$\begin{bmatrix} y & -2\,z & x \\ y & -z & 0 \\ zx & yx-zx-2\,zw & x^2+zy \end{bmatrix}$$

is the implicit equation of the Steiner surface, which, after dehomogenization, becomes

$$x^2y^2 + x^2z^2 + y^2z^2 - 2\,xyz = 0.$$

References for moving lines, planes, curves, or surfaces implicitization [64,65,24,75,21,25,11,75]

8. Multidimensional Newton Formulae and Symmetric Functions

González-Vega[37,36] introduced an implicitization method using multidimensional Newton formulae and symmetric functions. This methods works for rational curves and surfaces, and rational surfaces whose parametric equations exhibit a certain structure related to Pham systems. Often, it is possible to transform general rational parametric equations to ones that form a Pham system.

8.1. *Curves*

We mention the main theorem of González-Vega.[36]

Theorem 14: Let $\mathcal{C}$ be a plane algebraic curve given by polynomial parametric equations $x = f(t), y = g(t)$ with $n = \deg(g)$. Then the implicit equation of $\mathcal{C}$ is the squarefree part of the polynomial

$$\mathcal{H}_\mathcal{C}(x, y) = x^n + r_1(y) x^{n-1} + \cdots + r_n(y),$$

where

$$k\, r_k(y) = -S_k(y) - \left(\sum_{i=2}^{k} S_{k+1-i}(y)\, r_{i-1}(y) \right), \quad k = 1, \ldots, n,$$

and $S_i(y)$ is the coefficient of t^{n-1} in the remainder of the Euclidean division of

$$f(t)^i\, g'(t) \quad \text{by} \quad g(t) - y, \quad i = 1, \ldots, n.$$

The expression $g'(t)$ above denotes the usual derivative of $g(t)$ with respect to t. The theorem can be extended[36] to the general case of rational curves.

Example 15: Consider the curve given by the polynomial parametric equations

$$x = t^5 - t^2 - 1, \quad y = t^4 - t^2 - 1.$$

Since $n = \deg(g) = 4$, we have

$$\mathcal{H}_\mathcal{C}(x, y) = x^4 + r_1(y)\, x^3 + r_2(y)\, x^2 + r_3(y)\, x + r_4(y).$$

First we compute the Newton sums $S_1(y), S_2(y), S_3(y), S_4(y)$ on the values taken by $f(t) = t^5 - t^2 - 1$ over the roots of $g(t) - y$. In this case

$$S_i(y) = \text{coefficient of } t^3 \text{ in the remainder of } f(t)^i\, g'(t) \text{ by } g(t) - y,$$
$$i = 1, \ldots, 4.$$

They are computed in Maple as follows:

```
f:=t^5-t^2-1: g:=t^4-t^2-1: dg:=diff(g,t):
l:=[seq(coeff(rem(f^i*dg,g-y,t),t,3),i=1..4)];
```

The result is

$$l = [-6, 36 + 34y + 10y^2, -210 - 288y - 120y^2 - 12y^3,$$
$$70y^4 + 1554y^2 + 1252 + 2316y + 4y^5 + 472y^3].$$

Then we compute $r_1(y), r_2(y), r_3(y), r_4(y)$ recursively:

```
for i from 1 to 4 do S||i:=l[i]: od:
# give names to the Newton sums
r1:=-S1: r2:=(-S2-S1*r1)/2:
r3:=simplify((-S3-S2*r1-S1*r2)/3):
r4:=simplify((-S4-S3*r1-S2*r2-S1*r3)/4):
H:=sort(expand(x^4+r1*x^3+r2*x^2+r3*x+r4),y);
```

$$H := -y^5 - 5y^4 - 9y^3 + 4xy^3 - 4y^2 + 10xy^2 - 5x^2y^2 - 17x^2y \\ - 3y - 6xy + 6x^3 - 2x + x^4 - 1$$

Notice that $H = -r$, where r is the implicit equation computed with resultants in Section 3.

8.2. *Surfaces*

Theorem 16: Let S be a surface given by polynomial parametric equations $x = f(t, s)$, $y = g(t, s)$, $z = h(t, s)$ such that the bivariate polynomials g, h have the following structure: $g(t, s) = t^{n_1} + Q_1(t, s)$, $h(t, s) = s^{n_2} + Q_2(t, s)$ with $\deg(Q_1) < n_1$, $\deg(Q_2) < n_2$. Let $n = \deg(f)$ and $m = n_1 n_2$. Then the implicit equation of S is the squarefree part of the numerator of

$$\mathcal{H}_S(x, y, z) = x^m + r_1 \, x^{m-1} + \cdots + r_{m-1} \, x + r_m,$$

where

$$k \, r_k(y, z) = -S_k(y, z) - \left(\sum_{i=2}^{k} S_{k+1-i}(y, z) \, r_{i-1}(y, z) \right)$$

for $k = 1, \ldots, m$, every $S_j(y, z)$ is the coefficient of $t^{-1}s^{-1}$ in the Laurent polynomial

$$\frac{((f(t, s))^j \operatorname{Jac}(t, s))}{t^{n_1} s^{n_2}} \sum_{k=0}^{jn} (-1)^k \sum_{\alpha_1 + \alpha_2 = k} \left(\frac{Q_1(t, s) - y}{t^{n_1}} \right)^{\alpha_1} \left(\frac{Q_2(t, s) - z}{s^{n_2}} \right)^{\alpha_2},$$

$$(13)$$

and $\operatorname{Jac}(t, s)$ denotes the Jacobian determinant of $g(t, s)$, $h(t, s)$,

Example 17: Consider the surface given by the polynomial parametric equations

$$x = t^2 + s^2, \quad y = t^3 + s^2, \quad z = t^2 + s^3.$$

Since $n_1 = 3$, $n_2 = 3$, $m = 9$, the implicit equation has the form

$$\mathcal{H}_S(x, y, z) = x^9 + r_1(y, z) \, x^8 + \cdots + r_8(y, z) \, x + r_9(y, z).$$

The Jacobian determinant of g and h is equal to

$$\begin{vmatrix} \dfrac{\partial g}{\partial t} & \dfrac{\partial g}{\partial s} \\[2ex] \dfrac{\partial h}{\partial t} & \dfrac{\partial h}{\partial s} \end{vmatrix} = \begin{vmatrix} 3t^2 & 2s \\ 2t & 3s^2 \end{vmatrix} = ts\,(9\,ts - 4).$$

Calculating the Laurent polynomial (13), we see that $\mathcal{S}_1(y,z) = 0$, $\mathcal{S}_2(y,z) = 10$, and so on. Computing the coefficients $r_1(y,z), \ldots, r_9(y,z)$ as stipulated in the theorem, we obtain the implicit equation

$$\begin{aligned}
&x^9 - 5x^7 + (-3\,z^2 - 3\,y^2 + 14\,z + 14\,y)x^6 + (5 + 6\,y + 6\,z - 48\,zy - 9\,z^2 - 9\,y^2)x^5 \\
&+ (-24zy - 22y + 36yz^2 - 27z^2 - 22z - 2 + 36zy^2 - 27y^2)x^4 + (38z^3 + 38y^3 + 8z \\
&+ 38z^2 + 3z^4 + 60yz^2 + 60zy^2 - 21y^2z^2 + 76zy + 3y^4 + 38y^2 + 8y)x^3 + (-28y^3 \\
&- 54y^2z^2 - 18y^4 - 24zy - 60zy^3 - 60z^3y - 96zy^2 - 12z^2 - 18z^4 - 28z^3 - 96yz^2 - 12y^2)x^2 \\
&+ (8z^3 + 18z^4y + 24zy^2 + 8y^3 + 78y^2z^2 + 44z^3y + 18z^2y^3 + 44zy^3 + 5z^4 + 18y^2z^3 \\
&+ 18y^4z + 5y^4 + 24yz^2)x + 2y^5 - 12y^2z^2 - 2y^4z + 2z^5 - 3z^2y^4 - 16y^2z^3 - 8zy^3 \\
&- 2z^4y - 16z^2y^3 - 2z^4 - z^6 - 2y^4 - y^6 - 8z^3y - 3z^4y^2.
\end{aligned}$$

9. Eigenvalue Method

The eigenvalue method for implicitization is applicable to curves, surfaces and hypersurfaces given by very general classes of parametric equations. In addition, it can be used to implicitize multi-parametric families of such objects and thus it is suitable for generic implicitization. The implicitization problem is reduced to the computation of the basis of the nullspace of certain structured matrices, called *implicitization matrices*. Chen[14] used a similar method for approximate implicitization of rational curves.

9.1. *Curves*

Suppose that a curve is given by parametric equations

$$x = f(t), \quad y = g(t)$$

where f and g can be rational or trigonometric functions as well as functions involving square (and higher order) roots. Denote by m the (total) degree of the sought implicit equation. Reliable estimates for the value of m can be given using standard Algebraic Geometry arguments.[26,27] Then the algorithm proceeds by generating all the $\binom{2m+2}{2} = (2m+1)(m+1)$ monomials in the two variables x, y up to total degree $2m$:

$$\ell_{2m} = [\underbrace{1}_{\deg 0}, \underbrace{x, y}_{\deg 1}, \underbrace{x^2, xy, y^2}_{\deg 2}, \underbrace{x^3, \ldots, y^3}_{\deg 3}, \ldots, \underbrace{x^{2m}, x^{2m-1}y, \ldots, xy^{2m-1}, y^{2m}}_{\deg 2m}].$$

For each monomial $x^i y^j$ in ℓ_{2m} we need to compute the integral

$$\int_a^b x^i y^j \, dt = \int_a^b f(t)^i g(t)^j \, dt, \tag{14}$$

where the interval $[a, b]$ is chosen appropriately so as to avoid the singularities (if any) of f and g. Now we define the vector of monomials in x, y up to total degree m:

$$\ell_m = [1, x, y, x^2, xy, y^2, \ldots, x^m, x^{m-1}y, \ldots, xy^{m-1}, y^m]$$

and construct the matrix $\ell_m^t \ell_m$:

$$\begin{bmatrix} 1 \\ x \\ y \\ \vdots \\ x^m \\ \vdots \\ y^m \end{bmatrix} \cdot \begin{bmatrix} 1 \ x \ y \ \cdots \ x^m \ \cdots \ y^m \end{bmatrix} = \begin{bmatrix} 1 & x & y & \cdots & x^m & \cdots & y^m \\ x & x^2 & xy & \cdots & x^{m+1} & \cdots & xy^m \\ y & xy & y^2 & \cdots & x^m y & \cdots & y^{m+1} \\ \vdots & \vdots & \vdots & & \vdots & & \vdots \\ x^m & x^{m+1} & x^m y & \cdots & x^{2m} & \cdots & x^m y^m \\ \vdots & \vdots & \vdots & & \vdots & & \vdots \\ y^m & xy^m & y^{m+1} & \cdots & x^m y^m & \cdots & y^{2m} \end{bmatrix}.$$

$$(15)$$

The matrix (15) is symmetric of dimension $d_2 = \binom{m+2}{2}$, and contains $\binom{2m+2}{2}$ different elements. This is much less than the total number of elements which is equal to d_2^2. We construct a new matrix by replacing each entry $x^i y^j$ of the matrix (15) with the result of the corresponding integral (14). Thus we get an implicitization matrix with scalar elements and we compute a basis for its nullspace. If there is an implicit equation of degree m, then it will be given by taking the inner product of a nullvector of the implicitization matrix by the vector ℓ_m.

Example 18: Consider the following parametric equations of the unit circle involving square roots:

$$x = \frac{1}{\sqrt{t^2 + 1}}, \quad y = \frac{t}{\sqrt{t^2 + 1}}.$$

Take $m = 2$ and construct the vector $v = [1, x, y, x^2, xy, y^2]$ of all 6 ($= 1+2+3$) monomials in x, y up to total degree 2. Then compute the matrix $M = v^t \cdot v$:

$$\begin{bmatrix} 1 \\ x \\ y \\ x^2 \\ xy \\ y^2 \end{bmatrix} \cdot \begin{bmatrix} 1 \ x \ y \ x^2 \ xy \ y^2 \end{bmatrix} = \begin{bmatrix} 1 & x & y & x^2 & xy & y^2 \\ x & x^2 & xy & x^3 & x^2y & xy^2 \\ y & xy & y^2 & x^2y & xy^2 & y^3 \\ x^2 & x^3 & x^2y & x^4 & x^3y & x^2y^2 \\ xy & x^2y & xy^2 & x^3y & x^2y^2 & xy^3 \\ y^2 & xy^2 & y^3 & x^2y^2 & xy^3 & y^4 \end{bmatrix}.$$

This symmetric 6×6 matrix has 36 elements, out of which only $15 = \binom{2 \cdot 2 + 2}{2}$ are different. Performing the integrations for t from 0 to 1, we get a singular matrix of rank 5 which has $[-1, 0, 0, 1, 0, 1]$ as a basis of its nullspace. This gives directly the implicit equation of the unit circle:

$$-1 + x^2 + y^2 = 0.$$

The structure of the matrix G can be best seen by using the Maple Matrix Browser:

Fig. 2 Implicitization matrix for the unit circle

Example 19: (The Descartes folium[22]). Consider the following rational parametric equations for the plane algebraic curve known as the Descartes folium:

$$x = \frac{3t^2}{t^3 + 1}, \quad y = \frac{3t}{t^3 + 1}. \tag{16}$$

Take $m = 3$, construct the vector $v = [1, x, y, x^2, xy, y^2, x^3, x^2y, xy^2, y^3]$ and form the 10×10 matrix $M = v^t \cdot v$:

$$M = \begin{bmatrix} 1 & x & y & x^2 & xy & y^2 & x^3 & x^2y & xy^2 & y^3 \\ x & x^2 & xy & x^3 & x^2y & xy^2 & x^4 & x^3y & x^2y^2 & xy^3 \\ y & xy & y^2 & x^2y & xy^2 & y^3 & x^3y & x^2y^2 & xy^3 & y^4 \\ x^2 & x^3 & x^2y & x^4 & x^3y & x^2y^2 & x^5 & x^4y & x^3y^2 & x^2y^3 \\ xy & x^2y & xy^2 & x^3y & x^2y^2 & xy^3 & x^4y & x^3y^2 & x^2y^3 & xy^4 \\ y^2 & xy^2 & y^3 & x^2y^2 & xy^3 & y^4 & x^3y^2 & x^2y^3 & xy^4 & y^5 \\ x^3 & x^4 & x^3y & x^5 & x^4y & x^3y^2 & x^6 & x^5y & x^4y^2 & x^3y^3 \\ x^2y & x^3y & x^2y^2 & x^4y & x^3y^2 & x^2y^3 & x^5y & x^4y^2 & x^3y^3 & x^2y^4 \\ xy^2 & x^2y^2 & xy^3 & x^3y^2 & x^2y^3 & xy^4 & x^4y^2 & x^3y^3 & x^2y^4 & xy^5 \\ y^3 & xy^3 & y^4 & x^2y^3 & xy^4 & y^5 & x^3y^3 & x^2y^4 & xy^5 & y^6 \end{bmatrix}.$$

Perform the integrations with respect to t over the interval $[0, 2]$ to avoid the root $t = -1$ of the denominator of equations (16). The integrations can be performed symbolically or numerically. We prefer the numerical evaluation in this example, because the analytical expressions for the integrals yield a fairly complicated matrix. The difference in the computing times between calculating the nullvector for the analytical and the numerical matrix is dramatic. The numerical rank of the resulting matrix is 9, which means that its nullspace is of dimension 1 and thus generated by one nullvector. The Maple environment variable *Digits* is set to 15 in order to achieve a better accuracy. We compute the nullvector and multiply it by v, to obtain the equation

$$-0.9045\,xy + 0.3015\,x^3 + 0.3015\,y^3 = 0,$$

which shows that the implicit equation of the Descartes folium is

$$x^3 + y^3 - 3\,xy = 0. \tag{17}$$

The most time-consuming part of the computation (2.5 sec) is the numerical evaluation of the $\binom{2 \cdot 3 + 2}{2} = 28$ different definite integrals involved. The structure of the matrix M can be most conveniently seen with the following visual representations produced with the Maple 6 Matrix Browser:

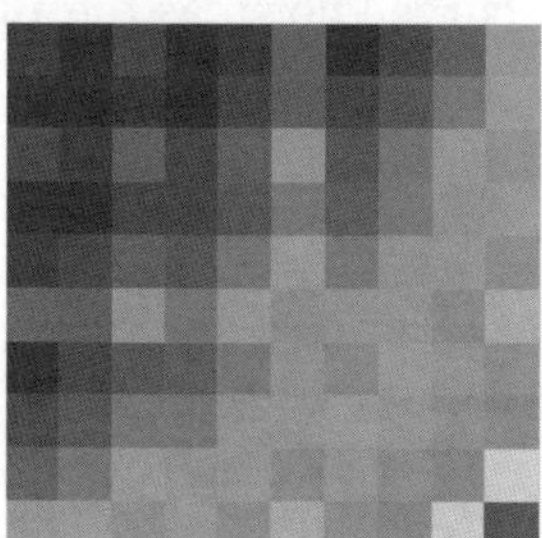 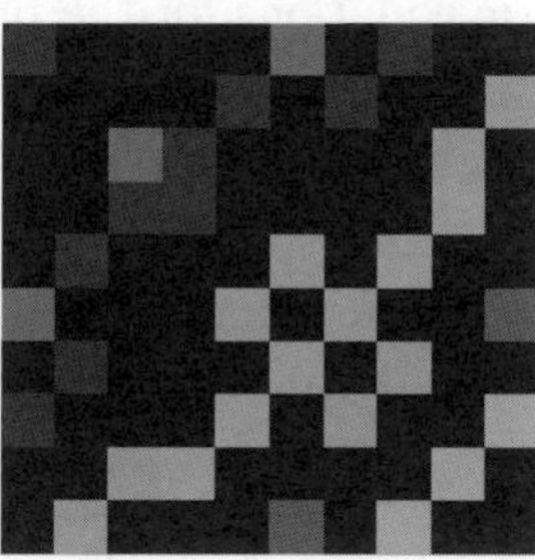

Fig. 3　Implicitization matrices for the folium of Descartes

9.2. *Surfaces*

Suppose that a surface is given by parametric equations

$$x = f(t), \quad y = g(t), \quad z = h(t)$$

where f, g, h can be very general functions as before. Denote by m the (total) degree of the sought implicit equation. Reliable estimates for the value of m can be given using Algebraic Geometry arguments as detailed for example in the references.[26,27] Then the algorithm proceeds by generating all the $\binom{2m+3}{3}$ monomials in the three variables x, y, z up to total degree $2m$:

$$\ell_{2m} = [\underbrace{1}_{\deg 0}, \underbrace{x, y, z}_{\deg 1}, \underbrace{x^2, xy, xz, yz, y^2, z^2}_{\deg 2}, \ldots, \underbrace{x^{2m}, x^{2m-1}y, x^{2m-2}yz \ldots, z^{2m}}_{\deg 2m}].$$

For each monomial $x^i y^j z^k$ in ℓ_{2m} we need to compute the triple integral

$$\int_a^b f(t)^i g(t)^j h(t)^k \, dt \tag{18}$$

where the interval $[a, b]$ is chosen appropriately so as to avoid the singularities (if any) of f, g, h. Now we define the vector of monomials in x, y, z up to total degree m:

$$\ell_m = [1, x, y, z, \ldots, x^m, \ldots, z^m]$$

and construct the matrix $\ell_m^t \ell_m$. This implicitization matrix is again symmetric of dimension $d_3 = \binom{m+3}{3}$, with $\binom{2m+3}{3}$ different elements, which is much less that d_3^2. Placing the results of the integrations in this matrix we obtain an implicitization matrix whose nullvector gives the implicit equation of degree m of the surface.

Example 20: This example is due to Buchberger.[9] Consider a surface given by the parametric equations

$$x = rt, \quad y = rt^2, \quad z = r^2. \tag{19}$$

In degree 4 and using for instance $[-2, 2]$ as the interval of integration for both parameters, we get a 35×35 matrix whose structure is shown in Fig. 4. The nullspace computation is almost instantaneous in Maple and we get the implicit equation $x^4 - zy^2 = 0$.

Note that using the sparse version[26,27] of the implicitization matrix, we would need a vector $v = [x^4, y^2 z]$ of only 2 elements and the corresponding 2×2 matrix

$$\begin{bmatrix} x^8 & x^4 y^2 z \\ x^4 y^2 z & y^4 z^2 \end{bmatrix}$$

to compute the implicit equation.

Fig. 4 Implicitization matrix for the Buchberger example

Example 21: Consider the two-parameter family of surfaces given by the polynomial parametric equations

$$x = \alpha\, r\, t + \beta, \quad y = r\, t^2, \quad z = r^2,$$

where α, β are parameters. Since there are no relations in degree 2 and 3, we need a 35×35 matrix. We integrate successively for t, r in $[0, 1]$, and obtain a matrix whose nullspace is generated by the vector

$$[\beta^4, -4\,\beta^3, 6\,\beta^2, -4\,\beta, 1, \overbrace{0, \ldots, 0}^{17\ 0\text{'s}}, -\alpha^4, \overbrace{0, \ldots, 0}^{12\ 0\text{'s}}].$$

This shows that an implicit equation for our two-parameter family of surfaces is

$$x^4 - 4\,\beta\, x^3 - \alpha^4 y^2 z + 6\,\beta^2 x^2 - 4\,\beta^3 x + \beta^4 = 0.$$

Example 22: Consider the four-parameter $(\alpha, \beta, \gamma, \delta)$ family of curves given by the following trigonometric parametric equations:

$$x = \alpha \cos\theta + \beta, \quad y = \gamma \sin\theta + \delta.$$

Setting $m = 2$ and integrating for θ in $[0, 8\,\pi]$, we obtain the implicit equation

$$x^2 + \frac{\alpha^2 y^2}{\gamma^2} - 2\,\beta\, x - 2\,\frac{\delta\,\alpha^2 y}{\gamma^2} - \frac{-\delta^2 \alpha^2 + \gamma^2 \alpha^2 - \beta^2 \gamma^2}{\gamma^2} = 0.$$

A discussion of special values for $\alpha, \beta, \gamma, \delta$ is necessary.

References for eigenvalue implicitization[20,26,27,47,48]

10. Conclusion

Implicitization of algebraic curves and surfaces is an important problem in geometric computation, computer graphics, CAD, CAGD and other areas. A wide spectrum of tools and concepts from computational algebra and algebraic geometry has been used to devise efficient algorithms for exact implicitization of algebraic curves and surfaces. We hope that this survey chapter will contribute in disseminating further the important algebraic ideas used in exact implicitization of algebraic curves and surfaces.

Acknowledgements

The author would like to thank Falai Chen and Dongming Wang for providing continuous encouragement, arduous support and valuable bibliographical references. The author would also like to thank the three anonymous referees for their detailed comments and observations.

References

1. W. W. Adams and P. Loustaunau. *An Introduction to Gröbner Bases*, volume 3 of *Graduate Studies in Mathematics*. American Mathematical Society, Providence, RI, 1994.
2. G. Albano, F. Cioffi, F. Orecchia, and I. Ramella. Minimally generating ideals of rational parametric curves in polynomial time. *Journal of Symbolic Computation*, 30(2): 137–149, 1999.
3. E. Angel. *Interactive Computer Graphics: A Top-down Approach with Open-GL* (3rd edn.). Addison-Wesley, 2003.
4. F. Aries and R. Senoussi. An implicitization algorithm for rational surfaces with no base points. *Journal of Symbolic Computation*, 31(4): 357–365, 2001.
5. P. Aubry, D. Lazard, and M. Moreno Maza. On the theories of triangular sets. *Journal of Symbolic Computation*, 28(1–2): 105–124, 1999. Special issue on Polynomial Elimination — Algorithms and Applications.
6. P. Aubry and M. Moreno Maza. Triangular sets for solving polynomial systems: A comparative implementation of four methods. *Journal of Symbolic Computation*, 28(1–2): 125–154, 1999. Special issue on Polynomial Elimination — Algorithms and Applications.
7. T. G. Berry and R. R. Patterson. Implicitization and parametrization of nonsingular cubic surfaces. *Computer Aided Geometric Design*, 18(8): 723–738, 2001.
8. B. H. Brown. The 21-point cubic. *American Mathematical Monthly*, 32(3): 110–115, 1925.

9. B. Buchberger. Applications of Gröbner bases in non-linear computational geometry. In J. R. Rice, editor, *Mathematical Aspects of Scientific Software*, volume 14 of *IMA Volumes in Mathematics and Its Applications*, pages 59–87. Springer-Verlag, New York, 1988.

10. L. Busé. Residual resultant over the projective plane and the implicitization problem. In B. Mourrain, editor, *Proceedings of ISSAC 2001*, London Ontario, pages 48–55. AMC Press, New York, 2001.

11. L. Busé, D. A. Cox, and C. D'Andrea. Implicitization of surfaces in $\mathbb{P}^3$ in the presence of base points. *J. Algebra Appl.*, 2(2): 189–214, 2003.

12. L. Busé and J.-P. Jouanolou. On the closed image of a rational map and the implicitization problem. *J. Algebra*, 265(1): 312–357, 2003.

13. J. Cannon and W. Bosma. *Handbook of Magma Functions*. Sydney, 2001. Version 2.8, Volume IV, Basic Rings and Commutative Algebra, available on-line.

14. F. Chen. Approximate implicitization of rational curves (in Chinese). *Chinese J. Computers*, 21(9): 855–859, 1998. Personal communication.

15. F. Chen and T. W. Sederberg. A new implicit representation of a planar rational curve with high order singularity. *Computer Aided Geometric Design*, 19(2): 151–167, 2002.

16. F. Chen and W. Wang. Revisiting the μ-basis of a rational ruled surface. *Journal of Symbolic Computation*, to appear.

17. F. Chen, J. Zheng, and T. W. Sederberg. The mu-basis of a rational ruled surface. *Computer Aided Geometric Design*, 18(1): 61–72, 2001.

18. E.-W. Chionh and R. N. Goldman. Degree, multiplicity, and inversion formulas for rational surfaces using u-resultants. *Computer Aided Geometric Design*, 9: 93–108, 1992.

19. E.-W. Chionh and R. N. Goldman. On the existence and the coefficients of the implicit equation of rational surfaces. *Graphical Models and Image Processing*, 56(1): 19–24, 1994.

20. R. M. Corless, M. W. Giesbrecht, I. S. Kotsireas, and S. M. Watt. Numerical implicitization of parametric hypersurfaces with linear algebra. In *Proceedings of AISC 2000*, Madrid, volume 1930 of *LNAI*, pages 174–183. Springer-Verlag, Berlin Heidelberg, 2000.

21. D. A. Cox, R. N. Goldman, and M. Zhang. On the validity of implicitization by moving quadrics for rational surfaces with no base points. *Journal of Symbolic Computation*, 29: 419–440, 2000.

22. D. A. Cox, J. Little, and D. O'Shea. *Ideals, Varieties, and Algorithms* (2nd edn.). Undergraduate Texts in Mathematics. Springer-Verlag, New York, 1997.

23. D. A. Cox, J. Little, and D. O'Shea. *Using Algebraic Geometry*, volume 185 of *Graduate Texts in Mathematics*. Springer-Verlag, New York, 1998.

24. D. A. Cox, T. W. Sederberg, and F. Chen. The moving line ideal basis of planar rational curves. *Computer Aided Geometric Design*, 15(8): 803–827, 1998.

25. C. D'Andrea. Resultants and moving surfaces. *Journal of Symbolic Computation*, 31(5): 585–602, 2001.

26. I. Z. Emiris and I. S. Kotsireas. On the support of the implicit equation of rational parametric hypersurfaces. Technical report, 2002. ORCCA TR-02-01, available on-line from http://www.orcca.on.ca.

27. I. Z. Emiris and I. S. Kotsireas. Implicit polynomial support optimized for sparseness. In V. Kumar et al., editors, *Proceedings of ICCSA 2003*, Montreal, volume 2669 of *LNCS*, pages 397–406. Springer-Verlag, Berlin Heidelberg, 2003.

28. G. E. Farin, J. Hoschek, and M.-S. Kim, editors. *Handbook of Computer Aided Geometric Design*. North-Holland, Amsterdam, 2002.

29. G. E. Farin. *Curves and Surfaces for CAGD: A Practical Guide* (5th edn.). Morgan Kaufmann, 2002.

30. G. Fix, C.-P. Hsu, and T. Luo. Implicitization of rational parametric surfaces. *Journal of Symbolic Computation*, 21: 329–336, 1996.

31. W. Fulton. *Algebraic Curves*. W. A. Benjamin, Inc., New York, 1969.

32. X.-S. Gao. Conversion between implicit and parametric representations of algebraic varieties. In X.-S. Gao and D. Wang, editors, *Mathematics Mechanization and Applications*, Chapter 14, pages 343–362. Academic Press, London, 2000.

33. X.-S. Gao and S.-C. Chou. Implicitization of rational parametric equations. *Journal of Symbolic Computation*, 14(5): 459–470, 1992.

34. X.-S. Gao and D. Wang, editors. *Mathematics Mechanization and Applications*. Academic Press, London, 2000.

35. R. N. Goldman. The method of resolvents: A technique for the implicitization, inversion, and intersection of nonplanar parametric, rational cubic curves. *Computer Aided Geometric Design*, 2(4): 237–255, 1985.

36. L. González-Vega. Implicitization of parametric curves and surfaces by using multidimensional Newton formulae. *Journal of Symbolic Computation*, 23(2–3): 137–151, 1997.

37. L. González-Vega and G. Trujillo. Implicitization of parametric curves and surfaces by using symmetric functions. In A. H. M. Levelt, editor, *Proceedings of ISSAC '95*, Montreal, pages 180–186. ACM Press, New York, 1995.

38. J. Grabmeier, E. Kaltofen, and V. Weispfenning. *Computer Algebra Handbook: Foundations, Applications, Systems*. Springer-Verlag, Berlin New York, 2003.

39. G.-M. Greuel and G. Pfister. *A Singular Introduction to Commutative Algebra*. Springer-Verlag, Berlin, 2002.

40. F. S. Hill. *Computer Graphics: Using OpenGL* (2nd edn.). Prentice Hall, Upper Saddle River, NJ, 2001.

41. J. D. Hobby. Numerically stable implicitization of cubic curves. *ACM Transactions on Graphics*, 10(3): 255–296, 1991.

42. C. M. Hoffmann. *Geometric and Solid Modeling: An Introduction*. Morgan Kaufmann, 1989.

43. H. Hong. Implicitization of nested circular curves. *Journal of Symbolic Computation*, 23: 177–189, 1997.

44. H. Hong and J. Schicho. Algorithms for trigonometric curves (simplification, implicitization, parameterization). *Journal of Symbolic Computation*,

26: 279–300, 1998.

45. M. Kalkbrener. Implicitization of rational parametric curves and surfaces. In S. Sakata, editor, *Proceedings of AAECC-8*, Tokyo, volume 508 of *LNCS*, pages 249–259. Springer-Verlag, Berlin Heidelberg, 1990.

46. M. Kalkbrener. Implicitization by Gröbner basis conversion. *Euromath Bull.*, 2(1): 197–204, 1996.

47. I. S. Kotsireas and E. Lau. Implicitization of polynomial curves. In Z. Li and W. Sit, editors, *Proceedings of ASCM 2003*, Beijing. World Scientific, Singapore New Jersey, 2003.

48. I. S. Kotsireas, E. Lau, and R. Voino. Implicitization of polynomial surfaces. In V. Ganzha et al., editors, *Proceedings of CASC 2003*, Passau, pages 241–247, 2003.

49. G. Landsmann, J. Schicho, and F. Winkler. The parametrization of canal surfaces and the decomposition of polynomials into a sum of two squares. *Journal of Symbolic Computation*, 32(1–2): 119–132, 2001. Special issue on Computer Algebra and Mechanized Reasoning (St. Andrews, 2000).

50. Z. Li. Automatic implicitization of parametric objects. *Mathematics-Mechanization Research Preprints*, 4: 54–62, 1989.

51. S. Licciardi and T. Mora. Implicitization of hypersurfaces and curves by the primbasissatz and basis conversion. In M. Giesbrecht and J. von zur Gathen, editors, *Proceedings of ISSAC '94*, Oxford, pages 191–196. ACM Press, New York, 1994.

52. D. Manocha and J. F. Canny. Algorithm for implicitizing rational parametric surfaces. *Computer Aided Geometric Design*, 9: 25–50, 1992.

53. D. Manocha and J. F. Canny. Implicit representation of rational parametric surfaces. *Journal of Symbolic Computation*, 13: 485–510, 1992.

54. A. Marco and J.-J. Martínez. Using polynomial interpolation for implicitizing algebraic curves. *Computer Aided Geometric Design*, 18(4): 309–319, 2001.

55. A. Marco and J.-J. Martínez. Implicitization of rational surfaces by means of polynomial interpolation. *Computer Aided Geometric Design*, 19(5): 327–344, 2002.

56. M. Monagan, K. O. Geddes, K. M. Heal, G. Labahn, S. M. Stefan, M. Vorkoetter, J. McCarron, and P. DeMarco. *Maple 8 Advanced Programming Guide*. Waterloo Maple Inc., 2002.

57. M. Monagan, K. O. Geddes, K. M. Heal, G. Labahn, S. M. Stefan, M. Vorkoetter, J. McCarron, and P. DeMarco. *Maple 8 Introductory Programming Guide*. Waterloo Maple Inc., 2002.

58. F. Morley. Note on Neuberg's cubic curve. *American Mathematical Monthly*, 32(8): 407–411, 1925.

59. P. J. Olver. *Applications of Lie Groups to Differential Equations* (2nd edn.), volume 107 of *Graduate Texts in Mathematics*. Springer-Verlag, Berlin Heidelberg, 1993.

60. F. Orecchia. Implicitization of a general union of parametric varieties. *Journal of Symbolic Computation*, 31(3): 343–356, 2001.

61. M. Peternell and H. Pottmann. Computing rational parametrizations of canal surfaces. *Journal of Symbolic Computation*, 23(2–3): 255–266, 1997. Special

issue on Parametric Algebraic Curves and Applications (Albuquerque, NM, 1995).

62. J. Schicho. Proper parametrization of real tubular surfaces. *Journal of Symbolic Computation*, 30: 583–593, 2000.

63. T. W. Sederberg, D. C. Anderson, and R. N. Goldman. Implicitization, inversion, and intersection of planar rational cubic curves. *Computer Vision, Graphics, and Image Processing*, 31: 89–102, 1985.

64. T. W. Sederberg and F. Chen. Implicitization using moving curves and surfaces. In *Proceedings of SIGGRAPH '95*, pages 301–308, 1995.

65. T. W. Sederberg, R. N. Goldman, and H. Du. Implicitizing rational curves by the method of moving algebraic curves. *Journal of Symbolic Computation*, 23(2–3): 153–175, 1997.

66. T. W. Sederberg, T. Saito, K. S. Qi, and D. Klimaszewski. Curve implicitization using moving lines. *Computer Aided Geometric Design*, 11(6): 687–706, 1994.

67. T. W. Sederberg and J. Zheng. Algebraic methods for computer aided geometric design. In *Handbook of Computer Aided Geometric Design*, pages 363–387. North-Holland, Amsterdam, 2002.

68. J. R. Sendra. Rational curves and surfaces: Algorithms and some applications. In F. Chen and D. Wang, editors, *Geometric Computation*, pages 65–125. World Scientific, Singapore New Jersey, 2003.

69. J. von zur Gathen and J. Gerhard. *Modern Computer Algebra*. Cambridge University Press, Cambridge, 1999.

70. D. Wang. *Elimination Methods*. Texts and Monographs in Symbolic Computation. Springer-Verlag, Wien New York, 2001.

71. D. Wang. Epsilon: A library of software tools for polynomial elimination. In A. Cohen, X.-S. Gao, and N. Takayama, editors, *Mathematical Software*, Beijing, pages 379–389. World Scientific, Singapore New Jersey, 2002.

72. D. Wang. Implicitization and offsetting via regular systems. In F. Chen and D. Wang, editors, *Geometric Computation*, pages 156–176. World Scientific, Singapore New Jersey, 2003.

73. D. Wang. A simple method for implicitizing rational curves and surfaces. Preprint, LIP6 – Université Paris VI, France, 2002.

74. A. H. Watt. *3D Computer Graphics* (3rd edn.). Addison-Wesley, 2000.

75. M. Zhang, R. N. Goldman, and E.-W. Chionh. Efficient implicitization of rational surfaces by moving planes. In X.-S. Gao and D. Wang, editors, *Computer Mathematics*, Chiang Mai, volume 8 of *Lecture Notes Series on Computing*, pages 142–151. World Scientific, Singapore New Jersey, 2000.

76. J. Zheng and T. W. Sederberg. A direct approach to computing the μ-basis of planar rational curves. *Journal of Symbolic Computation*, 31(5): 619–629, 2001.

CHAPTER 5

IMPLICITIZATION AND OFFSETTING VIA
REGULAR SYSTEMS

Dongming Wang

Laboratoire d'Informatique de Paris 6
Université Pierre et Marie Curie – CNRS
4 place Jussieu, 75252 Paris Cedex 05, France
E-mail: Dongming.Wang@lip6.fr

Given a geometric object defined by rational parametric equations, we show how to compute a disjunction of implicit equations and inequations that define exactly the same object by means of regular systems. The same technique is applied to the computation of quasi-offsets to algebraic curves and surfaces. Regular systems possess the projection property, are relatively easy to compute, and often have a compact form. Several examples are given to illustrate our approach based on the decomposition of polynomial systems into regular systems. A heuristic method is presented to simplify the output disjunction of polynomial equations and inequations.

1. Introduction

Computing the implicit equations of parametric curves and surfaces and of offsets to algebraic curves and surfaces is a classical problem in algebraic geometry that has applications in modern computer-aided geometric design and modeling. The implicitization of rational parametric curves and surfaces has been studied in a number of papers[2,3,4,6,7,11] after Sederberg.[10] We refer to the survey by Kotsireas[6] and references therein for the state of the art. Most of the effective algebraic methods proposed for the implicitization problem are based on the computation of resultants and Gröbner bases and the technique of moving curves and surfaces.[11,2] A simple method based on the principle of undetermined coefficients has been suggested recently by the author.[15] These methods are devised mainly to compute the implicit equations that define the Zariski closure of the parametrically defined geometric object.

156

As pointed out by Buchberger,[1] the geometric object defined by the implicit equation(s) may not be the same as that defined by the rational parametric equations. The former often contains some extraneous components of lower dimension that do not lie on the latter. It is Li[7] who first investigated this problem using Wu's method[17] of projection. We have observed that using Wu's or our method[12] of projection, the resulting sets of polynomial inequations (of the form $P \neq 0$) may be very complicated, and it is difficult to simplify them.

In this chapter we show how to compute the implicit equations ($=$) and inequations ($\neq$) that define exactly the same geometric object as that defined by the given rational parametric equations by means of regular systems. The same technique is applied to the computation of quasi-offsets to algebraic curves and surfaces. The concept of regular systems was introduced by the author;[13,14] we have also proposed an efficient algorithm for decomposing any polynomial system into finitely many regular systems. Regular systems enjoy many nice properties, are relatively easy to compute, and usually have a rather compact form. It is remarkable that regular systems possess the strong projection property. It is this property that enables us to compute the exact implicit equations and inequations of parametrically defined objects and of quasi-offsets to algebraic curves and surfaces. Our experiments show that using regular systems is a significant improvement over the use of projection in terms of computational efficiency and simplicity of output for implicitization and offsetting.

In the following section, we recall some basic concepts and notations in the theory of triangular sets. The strategy of eliminating inequations from a triangular system in order to obtain the projection property will be explained. In Sections 3 and 4, we apply our algorithm of decomposing polynomial systems into regular systems to the problems of implicitization and offsetting and give several illustrative examples. This application is quite straightforward, but the output disjunction of systems of polynomial equations and inequations is often complicated. Finally in Section 5 we present a heuristic method that allows us to simplify the disjunction in most cases.

2. Decomposition into Regular Systems

Let $\mathcal{K}$ be a computable field of characteristic 0, $\boldsymbol{x} = (x_1, \ldots, x_n)$ be n indeterminates ordered naturally as $x_1 \prec \cdots \prec x_n$, and $\mathcal{K}[\boldsymbol{x}]$ denote the ring of polynomials in $\boldsymbol{x}$ with coefficients in $\mathcal{K}$. A polynomial set is a finite set of nonzero polynomials in $\mathcal{K}[\boldsymbol{x}]$. For two polynomial sets $\mathbb{P}$ and $\mathbb{Q}$, $\mathrm{Zero}(\mathbb{P}/\mathbb{Q}) = \mathrm{Zero}([\mathbb{P}, \mathbb{Q}])$ denotes the set of all common zeros (in some extension field $\tilde{\mathcal{K}}$ of $\mathcal{K}$) of the polynomials in $\mathbb{P}$ which are not zeros of any polynomial in $\mathbb{Q}$. We write $\mathrm{Zero}(\mathbb{P})$ for $\mathrm{Zero}(\mathbb{P}/\mathbb{Q})$ when $\mathbb{Q} \subset \mathcal{K} \setminus \{0\}$. A *polynomial system* in $\mathcal{K}[\boldsymbol{x}]$ is a pair $[\mathbb{P}, \mathbb{Q}]$ of polynomial sets with which $\mathrm{Zero}(\mathbb{P}/\mathbb{Q})$ is of concern.

For any polynomial $P \in \mathcal{K}[\boldsymbol{x}]$ and variable x_k, denote by $\deg(P, x_k)$ the *degree* of P in x_k and by $\mathrm{lc}(P, x_k)$ the *leading coefficient* of P in x_k. When $P \notin \mathcal{K}$, the biggest index p such that $\deg(P, x_p) > 0$ is called the *class* of P, denoted by $\mathrm{cls}(P)$. For any $P \in \mathcal{K}$ and $P \neq 0$, the *class* of P is defined to be 0.

Let P be a polynomial of class $p > 0$; $\mathrm{lc}(P, x_p)$ is called the *initial* of P, denoted by $\mathrm{ini}(P)$. The *initial* of any $P \in \mathcal{K}$ is defined to be itself. For any polynomial set $\mathbb{P}$, we have

$$\mathrm{ini}(\mathbb{P}) := \{\mathrm{ini}(P) \mid P \in \mathbb{P}\}.$$

The *pseudo-remainder* and *pseudo-quotient* of Q divided by P $(\neq 0)$ with respect to x_k are denoted by $\mathrm{prem}(Q, P, x_k)$ and $\mathrm{pquo}(Q, P, x_k)$ respectively. Moreover, $\mathrm{prem}(Q, P)$ stands for $\mathrm{prem}(Q, P, x_p)$ and $\mathrm{prem}(\mathbb{Q}, P)$ for $\{\mathrm{prem}(Q, P) \mid Q \in \mathbb{Q}\}$, where $p = \mathrm{cls}(P) > 0$ and $\mathbb{Q}$ is an arbitrary polynomial set.

The number of elements of a finite set $\mathbb{T}$ is denoted by $|\mathbb{T}|$. An *ordered set* is written by enclosing its elements in a pair of square brackets.

Definition 1: A finite nonempty ordered set of polynomials in $\mathcal{K}[\boldsymbol{x}]$

$$\mathbb{T} = [T_1, T_2, \ldots, T_t]$$

is called a *triangular set* if $0 < \mathrm{cls}(T_1) < \mathrm{cls}(T_2) < \cdots < \mathrm{cls}(T_t)$.

Let $\mathbb{T}$ be a triangular set as in Definition 1 and P a polynomial. The *pseudo-remainder* of P with respect to $\mathbb{T}$ is

$$\mathrm{prem}(P, \mathbb{T}) := \mathrm{prem}(\cdots \mathrm{prem}(P, T_t), \ldots, T_1).$$

For any polynomial set $\mathbb{P}$, $\mathrm{prem}(\mathbb{P}, \mathbb{T})$ stands for $\{\mathrm{prem}(P, \mathbb{T}) \mid P \in \mathbb{P}\}$ and

$$\mathbb{P}^{(i)} := \mathbb{P} \cap \mathcal{K}[x_1, \ldots, x_i].$$

Similarly, for $\mathfrak{P} = [\mathbb{P}, \mathbb{Q}]$ we have $\mathfrak{P}^{(i)} = [\mathbb{P}^{(i)}, \mathbb{Q}^{(i)}]$.

Definition 2: A polynomial system $[\mathbb{T}, \mathbb{U}]$ in $\mathcal{K}[\boldsymbol{x}]$ is called a *triangular system* if $\mathbb{T}$ is a triangular set and $I(\bar{\boldsymbol{x}}) \neq 0$ for any $I \in \mathrm{ini}(\mathbb{T})$ and $\bar{\boldsymbol{x}} \in \mathrm{Zero}(\mathbb{T}^{(i)}/\mathbb{U})$, where $i = \mathrm{cls}(I)$.

A triangular system $[\mathbb{T}, \mathbb{U}]$ is said to be *fine* if $0 \notin \text{prem}(\mathbb{U}, \mathbb{T})$. A triangular set $\mathbb{T} \subset \mathcal{K}[\boldsymbol{x}]$ is said to be *fine* if $[\mathbb{T}, \text{ini}(\mathbb{T})]$ is fine.

For any given polynomial system $\mathfrak{P}$, one can compute finitely many fine triangular systems $\mathfrak{T}_1, \ldots, \mathfrak{T}_e$ such that

$$\text{Zero}(\mathfrak{P}) = \bigcup_{i=1}^{e} \text{Zero}(\mathfrak{T}_i). \tag{1}$$

There are several algorithms which may be used to compute such a zero decomposition. One of them is the well-known algorithm of Wu–Ritt based on characteristic sets. Two alternative algorithms are presented in the book[14] by the author.

Definition 3: A fine triangular set $\mathbb{T} = [T_1, \ldots, T_t] \subset \mathcal{K}[\boldsymbol{x}]$, with $\text{cls}(T_i) = p_i$, is said to be *irreducible* if there do not exist two polynomials F and G of class p_1 such that $T_1 = FG$, and for every $2 \leq i \leq t$ there do not exist two polynomials F and G of class p_i and a polynomial D of class $< p_i$ such that

$$\text{prem}(DT_i - FG, [T_1, \ldots, T_{i-1}]) = 0.$$

A fine triangular system $[\mathbb{T}, \mathbb{U}]$ is said to be *irreducible* if $\mathbb{T}$ is irreducible.

By means of polynomial factorization over successive algebraic extension fields, one can compute a zero decomposition of the form (1) with all triangular systems $\mathfrak{T}_i$ irreducible.

For any $1 \leq k \leq n$ we often write $\boldsymbol{x}_k$ for $x_1, \ldots, x_k$ or $(x_1, \ldots, x_k)$ with $\boldsymbol{x} = \boldsymbol{x}_n$, and similarly $\bar{\boldsymbol{x}}_k = (\bar{x}_1, \ldots, \bar{x}_k)$.

Definition 4: A triangular system $[\mathbb{T}, \mathbb{U}]$ in $\mathcal{K}[\boldsymbol{x}]$ is said to be *regular* or called a *regular system* if

(a) $\text{cls}(T) \neq \text{cls}(U)$ for any $T \in \mathbb{T}$ and $U \in \mathbb{U}$;
(b) $I(\bar{\boldsymbol{x}}_k) \neq 0$ for any $I \in \text{ini}(\mathbb{U})$, $\bar{\boldsymbol{x}}_k \in \text{Zero}(\mathbb{T}^{(k)}/\mathbb{U}^{(k)})$, and $1 \leq k = \text{cls}(I) \leq n - 1$.

A triangular set $\mathbb{T}$ is said to be *regular* or called a *regular set* if there exists a polynomial set $\mathbb{U}$ such that $[\mathbb{T}, \mathbb{U}]$ is a regular system.

Note that an irreducible triangular set must be a regular set, but an irreducible triangular system is not necessarily a regular system.

For any two polynomials of positive degree in $\mathcal{R}[x]$ (where $\mathcal{R}$ is a domain), one can compute their *subresultant chain* with respect to x using the standard algorithm[8,9] based on pseudo-division or the algorithm[5] using the Bézout matrix.

Definition 5: Let $S_{\mu+1}$ and S_μ be two polynomials in $\mathcal{R}[x]$ with $\deg(S_{\mu+1}, x) \geq \deg(S_\mu, x) > 0$ and

$$S_{\mu+1}, S_\mu, \ldots, S_0$$

be the subresultant chain of $S_{\mu+1}$ and S_μ with respect to x. Let $d_2, \ldots, d_r$ be a sequence of strictly decreasing nonnegative integers such that $\deg(S_{d_i}, x) = d_i$ for $2 \leq i \leq r$, and $\deg(S_j, x) < j$ for $0 \leq j \leq \mu$ and $j \notin \{d_2, \ldots, d_r\}$. The sequence of regular subresultants

$$S_{d_2}, \ldots, S_{d_r}$$

is called the *subresultant regular subchain (SRS)* of $S_{\mu+1}$ and S_μ with respect to x.

Lemma 6: *Let P_1, $P_2 \in \mathcal{K}[\boldsymbol{x}_k]$ be two polynomials with $\deg(P_1, x_k) \geq \deg(P_2, x_k) > 0$, $H_2, \ldots, H_r$ be the SRS of P_1 and P_2 with respect to x_k, and*

$$I = \mathrm{lc}(P_1, x_k), \qquad I_i = \mathrm{lc}(H_i, x_k), \quad 2 \leq i \leq r.$$

Let $\mathbb{P}, \mathbb{Q} \subset \mathcal{K}[\boldsymbol{x}_{k-1}]$ be two polynomial sets and assume that $I(\bar{\boldsymbol{x}}_{k-1}) \neq 0$ for any $\bar{\boldsymbol{x}}_{k-1} \in \mathrm{Zero}(\mathbb{P}/\mathbb{Q})$. Then

$$\mathrm{Zero}(\mathbb{P} \cup \{P_1\}/\mathbb{Q} \cup \{P_2\}) = \bigcup_{i=2}^{r} \mathrm{Zero}(\mathbb{P} \cup \mathbb{P}_i/\mathbb{Q} \cup \{P_2, I_i\}),$$

where $\mathbb{P}_i = \{\mathrm{pquo}(P_1, H_i, x_k), I_{i+1}, \ldots, I_r\}$ for each i. If $\mathrm{cls}(H_r) < k$, then $I_r = H_r$ and

$$\mathrm{Zero}(\mathbb{P} \cup \mathbb{P}_r/\mathbb{Q} \cup \{P_2, I_i\}) = \mathrm{Zero}(\mathbb{P} \cup \{P_1\}/\mathbb{Q} \cup \{I_r\}).$$

For a proof of this lemma, see Lemma 3.3.2, the proof of algorithm SimSer, and the remark following algorithm RegSer in the book.[14]

An algorithm has been devised[13,14] which can decompose any polynomial system into regular systems. To understand the strategy employed in the algorithm for eliminating inequations, we now explain briefly how to decompose a fine triangular system $[\mathbb{T}, \mathbb{U}]$ into regular systems. Let $\mathbb{T} = [T_1, \ldots, T_t]$, with $\mathrm{cls}(T_i) = p_i$ and $\deg(T_i, x_{p_i}) = m_i$ for $1 \leq i \leq t$.

To fulfill condition (a) in Definition 4, we need to eliminate all the polynomials of class p_i from $\mathbb{U}$ (if there is any) for each i. For this purpose, we perform top-down elimination for $i = t, \ldots, 1$.

If $\mathbb{U}$ does not contain any polynomial of class p_t, then proceed next for $i = t - 1$. Otherwise, let $U \in \mathbb{U}$ be a polynomial of class p_t. We assume that U is primitive with respect to x_{p_t} and $\deg(U, x_{p_t}) < m_t$ because, otherwise, U may be replaced by the content and primitive part of $\mathrm{prem}(U, T_t)$. As $[\mathbb{T}, \mathbb{U}]$ is a triangular system,

$$\mathrm{ini}(T_t)(\bar{x}) \neq 0 \ \text{ for any } \ \bar{x} \in \mathrm{Zero}([T_1, \dots, T_{t-1}]/\mathbb{U} \setminus \{U\}).$$

Now compute the SRS $H_2, \dots, H_r$ of T_t and U with respect to x_{p_t}, and let $I_i = \mathrm{lc}(H_i, x_{p_t})$ for $2 \leq i \leq r$. It follows from Lemma 6 that

$$\mathrm{Zero}(\mathbb{T}/\mathbb{U}) = \bigcup_{i=2}^{r} \mathrm{Zero}(\{T_1, \dots, T_{t-1}, Q_i, I_{i+1}, \dots, I_r\}/\mathbb{U} \cup \{I_i\}),$$

where $Q_i = \mathrm{pquo}(T_t, H_i, x_{p_t})$. When $\mathrm{cls}(H_i) = p_t$, $\deg(Q_i, x_{p_t}) < m_t$; it is always the case for $2 \leq i \leq r - 1$. If $\mathrm{cls}(H_r) < p_t$, then by Lemma 6 we have

$$\mathrm{Zero}([T_1, \dots, T_{t-1}, Q_r]/\mathbb{U} \cup \{I_r\}) = \mathrm{Zero}(\mathbb{T}/\mathbb{U} \setminus \{U\} \cup \{I_r\}).$$

In this case, U is eliminated from $\mathbb{U}$.

For the other polynomial systems $[\{T_1, \dots, T_{t-1}, Q_i, I_{i+1}, \dots, I_r\}, \mathbb{U} \cup \{I_i\}]$ with $\mathrm{cls}(H_i) = p_t$, one can use any algorithm to decompose them into fine triangular systems $[\mathbb{T}_j, \mathbb{U}_j]$. The last polynomial in each $\mathbb{T}_j$ will either have class $< p_t$ or have class p_t and degree $< m_t$ in x_{p_t}; in the latter case, we can use this polynomial of smaller degree to eliminate all the polynomials of class p_t from $\mathbb{U}_j$.

Therefore, repetition of the process will result in finitely many fine triangular systems $[\mathbb{T}_i^*, \mathbb{U}_i^*]$ such that one of $\mathbb{T}_i^*$ and $\mathbb{U}_i^*$ does not contain any polynomial of class p_t. For each $[\mathbb{T}_i^*, \mathbb{U}_i^*]$, we may continue the elimination process by considering the last polynomial of class $< p_t$ in each $\mathbb{T}_i^*$ (instead of T_t). In this way, $[\mathbb{T}, \mathbb{U}]$ will be decomposed into fine triangular systems satisfying the requirement (a) in Definition 4.

Condition (b) of Definition 4 may be easily fulfilled: for each polynomial $U \in \mathbb{U}$ of class q with $\mathrm{ini}(U) = I$ and $\deg(U, x_q) = m$, we can split $[\mathbb{T}, \mathbb{U}]$ into two triangular systems $[\mathbb{T}, \mathbb{U} \cup \{I\}]$ and $[\mathbb{T}, \mathbb{U} \setminus \{U\} \cup \{I, U - I x_q^m\}]$. Iterating this splitting process, all the obtained triangular systems will finally satisfy the condition (b).

The above informal discussions serve to illustrate the idea of how regular systems may be constructed from a fine triangular system by repeated computation of SRS. Combining different algorithms as necessary, one is able to decompose any given polynomial system $\mathfrak{P}$ into finitely many regular systems or even irreducible regular systems $\mathfrak{T}_1, \ldots , \mathfrak{T}_e$ such that (1) holds.

Definition 7: A finite set or sequence Ψ of (irreducible) triangular systems or regular systems $\mathfrak{T}_1, \ldots , \mathfrak{T}_e$ in $\mathcal{K}[\boldsymbol{x}]$ is called an *(irreducible) triangular series* or a *regular series* of a polynomial system $\mathfrak{P}$ in $\mathcal{K}[\boldsymbol{x}]$ if (1) holds.

When $\Psi = \emptyset$ or $e = 0$, it is understood that $\mathrm{Zero}(\mathfrak{P}) = \emptyset$.

Definition 8: For any polynomial system $\mathfrak{P}$ in $\mathcal{K}[\boldsymbol{x}]$ and $1 \le k \le n - 1$, the *projection* of $\mathrm{Zero}(\mathfrak{P})$ onto $\boldsymbol{x}_k$ is

$$\mathrm{Proj}_{\boldsymbol{x}_k} \mathrm{Zero}(\mathfrak{P}) := \left\{ \bar{\boldsymbol{x}}_k \in \tilde{\mathcal{K}}^{\,k} \,\middle|\, \exists\, \bar{x}_{k+1}, \ldots , \bar{x}_n \in \tilde{\mathcal{K}} \text{ such that } \bar{\boldsymbol{x}} \in \mathrm{Zero}(\mathfrak{P}) \right\}.$$

Moreover, we have

$$\mathrm{Proj}_{\boldsymbol{x}} \mathrm{Zero}(\mathfrak{P}) := \mathrm{Zero}(\mathfrak{P}), \quad \mathrm{Proj}\, \mathrm{Zero}(\mathfrak{P}) := \begin{cases} \emptyset & \text{if } \mathrm{Zero}(\mathfrak{P}) = \emptyset, \\ \{0\} & \text{otherwise} \end{cases}$$

for the two extreme cases $k = n$ and $k = 0$.

It is easy to see that $\mathrm{Proj}_{\boldsymbol{x}_k} \mathrm{Zero}(\mathfrak{P}) \ne \emptyset$ if and only if $\mathrm{Zero}(\mathfrak{P}) \ne \emptyset$.

Definition 9: A fine triangular system $\mathfrak{T}$ in $\mathcal{K}[\boldsymbol{x}]$ is said to possess the *strong projection property* if for all $0 \le k < n$

$$\mathrm{Zero}(\mathfrak{T}^{(k)}) \subset \mathrm{Proj}_{\boldsymbol{x}_k} \mathrm{Zero}(\mathfrak{T}).$$

Proposition 10: *Every regular system in $\mathcal{K}[\boldsymbol{x}]$ possesses the strong projection property.*

Proof: Let $[\mathbb{T}, \mathbb{U}]$ be a regular system in $\mathcal{K}[\boldsymbol{x}]$; then, for any $0 < k < n$ and $\bar{\boldsymbol{x}}_k \in \mathrm{Zero}(\mathbb{T}^{(k)} / \mathbb{U}^{(k)})$, the system acquired from

$$\left[\mathbb{T} \setminus \mathbb{T}^{(k)}, \mathbb{U} \setminus \mathbb{U}^{(k)} \right]$$

by substituting $\bar{\boldsymbol{x}}_k$ for $\boldsymbol{x}_k$ is a regular system in $\mathcal{K}(\bar{\boldsymbol{x}}_k)[x_{k+1}, \ldots , x_n]$. Thus, the conclusion follows from Definition 9 and the fact that every regular system has zeros in some extension field of $\mathcal{K}$ (see Theorem 5.1.12 in the book[14]). $\qquad\square$

The projection property of regular systems is of high interest because regular systems are relatively easy to compute. This property enables us to apply regular systems to several computational problems such as solving parametric polynomial systems and automated derivation of locus equations, in addition to the problems of implicitization and offsetting considered in this chapter.

3. Implicitization of Parametric Objects

Geometric objects like curves and surfaces may be represented algebraically by implicit equations or parametric equations. The advantage of each representation depends upon the type of problems to be solved. In geometric modeling, one often needs to convert one representation into the other. The rational parametrization of a geometric object in an n-dimensional affine space may be represented as

$$x_1 = \frac{P_1(\boldsymbol{y})}{Q_1(\boldsymbol{y})}, \dots, x_n = \frac{P_n(\boldsymbol{y})}{Q_n(\boldsymbol{y})},$$

where $\boldsymbol{y} = (y_1, \dots, y_m)$ are parametric variables. The problem of implicitization amounts to finding the implicit equations and inequations in $\boldsymbol{x}$ which define the same geometric object as the parametrized representation does. This can be done by using the following algorithm. The incorporation of projection into implicitization algorithms was suggested first by Li[7] (see also the paper[17] by Wu).

Algorithm I: Given two sets of polynomials $P_1, \dots, P_n$ and $Q_1, \dots, Q_n$ in $\mathcal{K}[\boldsymbol{y}]$, where $Q_1 \cdots Q_n \neq 0$ and $m \leq n$, this algorithm computes a finite set Ψ of polynomial systems $[\mathbb{P}_1, \mathbb{Q}_1], \dots, [\mathbb{P}_e, \mathbb{Q}_e]$ in $\mathcal{K}[\boldsymbol{x}]$ such that for any $\bar{\boldsymbol{x}} = (\bar{x}_1, \dots, \bar{x}_n) \in \tilde{\mathcal{K}}^n$,

$$\bar{\boldsymbol{x}} \in \bigcup_{i=1}^{e} \mathrm{Zero}(\mathbb{P}_i / \mathbb{Q}_i) \iff \begin{cases} \exists\, \bar{\boldsymbol{y}} \in \tilde{\mathcal{K}}^m \ \text{ such that} \\ \bar{x}_1 = \dfrac{P_1(\bar{\boldsymbol{y}})}{Q_1(\bar{\boldsymbol{y}})}, \dots, \bar{x}_n = \dfrac{P_n(\bar{\boldsymbol{y}})}{Q_n(\bar{\boldsymbol{y}})}. \end{cases}$$

I1. Let

$$\mathbb{P} := \{P_1 - x_1 Q_1, \dots, P_n - x_n Q_n\}, \quad \mathbb{Q} := \{Q_1, \dots, Q_n\}$$

and compute a regular series[a] Ψ of $[\mathbb{P}, \mathbb{Q}]$ with respect to the variable ordering $x_1 \prec \cdots \prec x_n \prec y_1 \prec \cdots \prec y_m$.

I2. Remove redundant sets from $\bigcup_{[\mathbb{T}, \mathbb{U}] \in \Psi} \mathrm{Zero}(\mathbb{T} \cap \mathcal{K}[\boldsymbol{x}] / \mathbb{U} \cap \mathcal{K}[\boldsymbol{x}])$, simplify it using the algorithm S described in Section 5, and let the obtained zero set be $\bigcup_{i=1}^{e} \mathrm{Zero}(\mathbb{P}_i / \mathbb{Q}_i)$. Then return

$$\Psi := \{[\mathbb{P}_1, \mathbb{Q}_1], \dots, [\mathbb{P}_e, \mathbb{Q}_e]\}.$$

Proof: The correctness of this algorithm follows from Definition 7 and Proposition 10. $\qquad\qquad\square$

---

[a] A function named **RegSer** is available in the Epsilon library (http://www-calfor.lip6.fr/~wang/epsilon) for computing regular series.

It is easier to compute the Zariski closure of the quasi-varieties $\mathrm{Zero}(\mathbb{P}_i/\mathbb{Q}_i)$ or the implicit ideal using other techniques without projection. For example, one can do so by means of Gröbner bases,[3] (multivariate) resultants, and the techniques of moving curves and surfaces[11] and undetermined coefficients.[15] However, without projection (and using inequations) the implicitly defined geometric object is not necessarily the same as the object defined by the parametric equations.[b]

Example 11: Consider the parametric surface defined by the equations

$$x = \frac{t^3}{2}, \quad y = \frac{(s^2 - 1)\,t^2}{s^2 + 1}, \quad z = \frac{2\,s\,t^2}{s^2 + 1} \tag{2}$$

in three-dimensional affine space. Let

$$\mathbb{P} = \{t^3 - 2\,x, (s^2 - 1)\,t^2 - y\,(s^2 + 1), 2\,s\,t^2 - z\,(s^2 + 1)\}, \quad \mathbb{Q} = \{s^2 + 1\}.$$

A regular series of $[\mathbb{P}, \mathbb{Q}]$ with respect to $x \prec y \prec z \prec s \prec t$ consists of five regular systems $[\mathbb{T}_1, \mathbb{U}_1], \dots, [\mathbb{T}_5, \mathbb{U}_5]$. Let $\mathfrak{T}_i = [\mathbb{T}_i \cap \mathcal{Q}[x, y, z], \mathbb{U}_i \cap \mathcal{Q}[x, y, z]]$ for $1 \le i \le 5$ (where $\mathcal{Q}$ denotes the field of rational numbers); then

$$\mathfrak{T}_1 = \left[[E], \{x, y^3 + 4\,x^2, y^3 - 4\,x^2\}\right],$$
$$\mathfrak{T}_2 = \left[[y^6 - 16\,x^4, z^4 + 3\,y^2 z^2 + 3\,y^4], \{x\}\right],$$
$$\mathfrak{T}_3 = \left[[y^3 + 4\,x^2, z], \{x\}\right],$$
$$\mathfrak{T}_4 = \mathfrak{T}_5 = [[x, y, z], \emptyset],$$

where

$$E = z^6 + 3\,y^2 z^4 + 3\,y^4 z^2 + y^6 - 16\,x^4.$$

It follows that

$$\bigcup_{i=1}^{5} \mathrm{Zero}(\mathfrak{T}_i) = \mathrm{Zero}(\mathfrak{T}_1) \cup \mathrm{Zero}(\mathfrak{T}_2) \cup \mathrm{Zero}([y^3 + 4\,x^2, z])$$

$$= \mathrm{Zero}([E]/\{x, y^3 - 4\,x^2\}) \cup \mathrm{Zero}([y^3 - 4\,x^2, z^4 + 3\,y^2 z^2 + 12\,x^2 y]).$$

This simplification has been done automatically by using the algorithm described in Section 5. Therefore, the desired implicit equations and inequations are

$$[E = 0 \wedge x(y^3 - 4\,x^2) \ne 0] \vee [y^3 - 4\,x^2 = 0 \wedge z^4 + 3\,y^2 z^2 + 12\,x^2 y = 0].$$

---

[b]If the rational parametric object and its Zariski closure are not the same, then the parametrization embedded in the projective parametric space has base points.

The implicit surface defined by $E = 0$ is the Zariski closure of the parametric surface defined by (2), but it is not the same as the parametric surface. For instance, $(x, y, z) = (4, 4, 0)$ satisfies the equation $E = 0$, but it is not on the parametric surface.[c]

Using our method[12] of 1993 with projection, we obtain

$$[[E], \mathbb{U}], \quad [[y^3 + 4\,x^2, z], \{x\}], \quad [[x, y, z], \emptyset],$$

where $\mathbb{U}$ contains a large polynomial of degree 4 in z which has 75 terms and is irreducible. Using Wu's method with projection, one may get an even larger polynomial with more computing time.

Example 12: The following parametric equations originate from the paper[2] by Busé and others:

$$x = P_x/Q, \quad y = P_y/Q, \quad z = P_z/Q,$$

where

$$\begin{aligned}
P_x &= s\,t^3 - s^4 - 2\,s^2 t^2 + s^2 t + 4\,s^3 t - 2\,t^3, \\
P_y &= s^2 t - s^3 t - 2\,s^3 + 3\,s\,t^2 - t^3, \\
P_z &= s^3 - s\,t^3 - 4\,s^2 t + 6\,t^3 - s\,t^2, \\
Q &= s^3 - 3\,s\,t^3 - 2\,s\,t^2 + 6\,s^2 t^2 + t^4 - ts^3.
\end{aligned}$$

These equations define a rational surface in three-dimensional affine space, whose implicit equation may be easily obtained by using the method[15] of undetermined coefficients. In order to see which points on the implicit surface are not defined by the parametric equations, we want to compute a regular series of $[\mathbb{P}, \mathbb{Q}]$, where $\mathbb{P} = \{P_x, P_y, P_z\}$ and $\mathbb{Q} = \{Q\}$. We have tried to compute such a series in Maple without success. By first computing a Gröbner basis using J.-C. Faugère's Gb package in C++ (see http://www-calfor.lip6.fr/~jcf/Software/Gb), we are able to obtain a regular series Ψ of $[\mathbb{P}, \mathbb{Q}]$ under $z \prec y \prec x \prec t \prec s$. Ψ consists of four regular systems $[\mathbb{T}_i, \mathbb{U}_i]$ with $\bar{\mathbb{T}}_i = \mathbb{T}_i \cap \mathcal{Q}[z, y, x]$ and $\bar{\mathbb{U}}_i = \mathbb{U}_i \cap \mathcal{Q}[z, y, x]$ as follows:

$$\bar{\mathbb{T}}_1 = [F], \qquad \bar{\mathbb{T}}_2 = [17\,z - 6, 17\,y + 1], \qquad \bar{\mathbb{T}}_3 = [z - 1, y + 2],$$

---

[c]Note that one of the motivations for implicitization comes from the fact that it is much easier to verify whether a given point lies on a curve or surface using its implicit equation than using its parametric equations!

$$\bar{\mathbb{T}}_4 = [\, 7\,z^5 + 52\,z^4 + 313\,z^3 + 100\,z^2 + 2\,z - 1,$$
$$692\,z^3y - 173\,z^2y + 187\,zy + 37\,y + 121\,z^4 + 1009\,z^3$$
$$- 163\,z^2 - 52\,z - 1, 17\,zx - 6\,x - 12\,y^2 - 23\,y + 6\,z^2 - 3\,z - 1\,];$$

$$\bar{\mathbb{U}}_1 = \{y + 3\,z - 1, -y^3 + 30\,zy^2 + 2\,y^2 + 3\,z^2y + 6\,zy - y + z^3, G,$$
$$2971\,y^5 - 9648\,zy^4 + 4279\,y^4 - 1975\,z^2y^3 - 876\,zy^3 + 658\,y^3$$
$$+ 3442\,z^3y^2 - 3993\,z^2y^2 + 1332\,zy^2 - 118\,y^2 + 284\,z^4y + 4\,z^3y$$
$$- 237\,z^2y + 108\,zy - 13\,y + 133\,z^5 - 218\,z^4 + 154\,z^3 - 59\,z^2$$
$$+ 12\,z - 1\},$$

$$\bar{\mathbb{U}}_2 = \{1734\,x^2 + 408\,x + 145, 17\,x^2 + 2\,x - 11, 1419857\,x^5 - 2839714\,x^4$$
$$- 938383\,x^3 + 1851045\,x^2 - 292043\,x + 100121\},$$

$$\bar{\mathbb{U}}_3 = \{x\}, \qquad \bar{\mathbb{U}}_4 = \emptyset,$$

where

$$F = yx + 3\,zx - x - 2\,y^2 - 4\,y + z^2 - z,$$
$$G = -12\,y^3 - 2\,zy^2 - 23\,y^2 + 6\,z^2y - 4\,zy - 2\,y + z^3 + 8\,z^2 - 6\,z + 1.$$

The first polynomial in $\bar{\mathbb{U}}_1$ may be removed by using algorithm S presented in Section 5. From the regular systems $[\bar{\mathbb{T}}_i, \bar{\mathbb{U}}_i]$, one can easily establish the exact implicit equations and inequations for the parametric surface. The zero set of the single polynomial F considered as an implicit surface contains several curves which do not lie on the parametrically defined surface. For example, the cubic curve defined by

$$2\,x^2y - y - x^3 + 3\,x^2 + x - 2 = 0, \quad z - 2\,xy + x^2 - 1 = 0$$

is an irreducible component of the reducible curve defined by $F = 0$ and $G = 0$. However, on this cubic there are only finitely many points (i.e., the zeros of $\bar{\mathbb{T}}_4$) which are on the parametric surface. The surface defined by $F = 0$ is the one in between shown in Fig. 2.

Example 13: Now we recall the surface of revolution studied in the paper[11] by Sederberg and Chen. This surface may be obtained by rotating around the z-axis the cubic polynomial Bézier curve with control points

$$(2, 0, 0.9), \quad (2, 0, 0.45), \quad (1.5, 0, 0.225), \quad (1.5, 0, 0.15)$$

and was used to model the lower body of a teapot. It is defined parametrically by

$$x = -\frac{(2\,s - 1)\,P}{2\,Q}, \quad y = -\frac{s\,(s - 1)\,P}{Q}, \quad z = -\frac{3\,(t^3 - 9\,t^2 + 18\,t - 12)}{40},$$

$$(3)$$

where

$$P = 2\,t^3 - 3\,t^2 + 4, \quad Q = 2\,s^2 - 2\,s + 1.$$

We wish to determine the implicit equations and inequations that define exactly the same surface as these parametric equations.

Let $\mathbb{P}$ denote the set of the three polynomials corresponding to (3) and $\mathbb{Q} = \{Q\}$. It is easy to compute an irreducible characteristic series Ψ of $[\mathbb{P}, \mathbb{Q}]$ with $x \prec y \prec z \prec t \prec s$; Ψ consists of four irreducible triangular sets $\mathbb{T}_1, \ldots, \mathbb{T}_4$ such that

$$\mathrm{Zero}(\mathbb{P}/\mathbb{Q}) = \bigcup_{i=1}^{4} \mathrm{Zero}(\mathbb{T}_i/\mathrm{ini}(\mathbb{T}_i) \cup \mathbb{Q}),$$

where

$$\begin{aligned}
\mathbb{T}_1 = {}& [E, (1280000\,z^3 + 10126800\,z^2 - 7200\,y^2 z - 7200\,x^2 z + 3407400\,z \\
& + 59319\,y^2 + 59319\,x^2 + 292626)\,t + 3\,(1984000\,z^3 - 766800\,z^2 \\
& + 24840 y^2 z + 24840 x^2 z - 402840 z - 128979 y^2 - 128979 x^2 - 36180), G], \\
\mathbb{T}_2 = {}& [4096\,y^6 + 12288\,x^2 y^4 + 127117107\,y^4 + 12288\,x^4 y^2 + 254234214\,x^2 y^2 \\
& + 98973163953\,y^2 + 4096\,x^6 + 127117107\,x^4 + 98973163953\,x^2 \\
& + 116700507, F, 545877552248991\,t^2 - 6\,(5746688\,y^4 + 11493376\,x^2 y^2 \\
& + 148682503809 y^2 + 5746688 x^4 + 148682503809 x^2 + 217869762017484)t \\
& - 2\,(69890048\,y^4 + 139780096\,x^2 y^2 + 2423086870725\,y^2 + 69890048\,x^4 \\
& + 2423086870725\,x^2 - 595618612975413), G], \\
\mathbb{T}_3 = {}& [x, y, 32000\,z^3 - 76500\,z^2 - 30240\,z - 2781, 200\,z t + 180\,z + 33\,t + 36], \\
\mathbb{T}_4 = {}& [15625\,y^2 + 15625\,x^2 - 49, F, 25\,t^2 - 60\,t + 54, G];
\end{aligned}$$

$$\begin{aligned}
E = {}& 324\,(y^2 + x^2)\,(1600\,z^2 + 6900\,z + 3\,y^2 + 3\,x^2 + 1197)^2 \\
& - (128000\,z^3 - 306000\,z^2 + 2160\,z y^2 + 2160\,z x^2 - 120960\,z \\
& - 11745\,y^2 - 11745\,x^2 - 11124)^2, \\
F = {}& 20\,(64000000\,y^4 + 128000000\,x^2 y^2 - 43555072953\,y^2 + 64000000\,x^4 \\
& - 43555072953\,x^2 + 265874801598)\,z - 9\,(872784000\,y^4 \\
& + 1745568000\,x^2 y^2 + 1643501398790\,y^2 + 872784000\,x^4
\end{aligned}$$

$$+ \, 1643501398790 \, x^2 - 105071597253),$$

$$G = 2 \left(2 \, t^3 - 3 \, t^2 + 2 \, y + 4\right) s - 2 \, t^3 + 3 \, t^2 - 2 \, y + 2 \, x - 4.$$

From these triangular sets we see that the surface of revolution may be defined by the implicit equation $E = 0$. In fact, the implicit polynomial E may also be computed easily by using other methods. However, the surface defined by $E = 0$ is not the same as the surface defined by the parametric equations (3); some points on the implicit surface do not lie on the parametric surface. In order to locate such points, we need to project the triangular sets onto x, y, z. For this purpose, we have tried to compute the regular series of $[\mathbb{T}_i, \mathrm{ini}(\mathbb{T}_i) \cup \mathbb{Q}]$. Unfortunately, the computation is very heavy and our program ran several days without completion (e.g., for $i = 1$). Therefore, we still do not know the exact implicit equations and inequations of the parametric surface.

Elimination methods may also be used to deal with other problems such as the independency of parameters, the propriety of parametrization, and the inversion problem which are related to the implicitization of parametric objects (see, e.g., the paper[3] by Gao and Chou).

4. Computation of Offsets

Let $F(x, y) = 0$ be the implicit equation of an algebraic curve $\mathfrak{C}$ in Euclidean plane. Roughly speaking, the r-offset to $\mathfrak{C}$ is the set of all the points that have the same perpendicular distance r to $\mathfrak{C}$. It is easy to prove that at every singular point (x_0, y_0) of $\mathfrak{C}$ all the points on the circle $(x - x_0)^2 + (y - y_0)^2 = r^2$ (called *extraneous circle*, as it may cause inconvenience for the study of algebraic properties such as rationality and irreducibility of the offset) are contained in the r-offset. We shall eliminate such known extraneous circles in our algebraic formulation.

Assume that the algebraic curve $\mathfrak{C}$ defined by $F(x, y) = 0$ is irreducible and r is a positive number. An algebraic formulation of the r-offset to the curve $\mathfrak{C}$ is given by the following equations:

$$\begin{cases} P_1 = F(u, v) = 0, \\ P_2 = (x - u)^2 + (y - v)^2 - r^2 = 0, \\ P_3 = F_v \, (x - u) - F_u \, (y - v) = 0, \\ P_4 = (F_u w - 1) \, (F_v w - 1) = 0, \end{cases} \tag{4}$$

where $F_u = \partial F(u, v)/\partial u$, $F_v = \partial F(u, v)/\partial v$, and u, v, w are new indeterminates. The meanings of the first two equations are obvious: the point

$\mathbf{q}(u, v)$ is on the generating curve $\mathfrak{C}$ and the distance between $\mathbf{q}$ and the point $\mathbf{p}(x, y)$ on the offset is r. The third equation means that the line $\mathbf{pq}$ is perpendicular to the tangent line of $\mathfrak{C}$ at $\mathbf{q}$. The last equation is added to rule out the case in which F_u and F_v vanish simultaneously (i.e., $\mathbf{q}$ is a singular point).

Let $\mathbb{P} = \{P_1, \dots, P_4\}$. We call the set of points

$$\mathrm{Proj}_{x,y}\mathrm{Zero}(\mathbb{P})$$

the *r-quasi-offset* to $\mathfrak{C}$. What is usually called the *r-offset* to $\mathfrak{C}$ is the Zariski closure of the r-quasi-offset to $\mathfrak{C}$. Here we are concerned mainly with the computation of algebraic equations and inequations for the r-quasi-offset $\mathrm{Proj}_{x,y}\mathrm{Zero}(\mathbb{P})$. This can be done by computing a regular series of $\mathbb{P}$. The algorithm is similar to and as simple as algorithm I, so we do not describe it formally. The reader will see from the examples given below how the algorithm works. Like the case of implicitization, a quasi-offset is expressed as a disjunction of systems of polynomial equations and inequations, and it is often necessary to simplify the disjunction. The equations for offsets may be obtained from the equations and inequations of quasi-offsets quite easily.

Similarly, for any algebraic surface $\mathfrak{S}$ defined by an implicit equation $F(x, y, z) = 0$ in three-dimensional Euclidean space, the r-offset to $\mathfrak{S}$ is the set of points that have the same perpendicular distance r to $\mathfrak{S}$. An algebraic formulation for it may be given by the following equations:[4]

$$
\begin{cases}
F(u, v, w) = 0, \\
(x - u)^2 + (y - v)^2 + (z - w)^2 - r^2 = 0, \\
F_v\,(x - u) - F_u\,(y - v) = 0, \\
F_w\,(y - v) - F_v\,(z - w) = 0, \\
F_u\,(z - w) - F_w\,(x - u) = 0, \\
(F_u\,t - 1)\,(F_v\,t - 1)\,(F_w\,t - 1) = 0,
\end{cases}
\tag{5}
$$

where u, v, w, t are new indeterminates. The projection of the algebraic variety defined by these equations onto x, y, z (which is a finite union of quasi-varieties) is defined to be the *r-quasi-offset* to $\mathfrak{S}$, and its Zariski closure is the commonly called *r-offset* to $\mathfrak{S}$.

Example 14: Consider the algebraic curve defined by $y^2 - x^3 = 0$ in Euclidean plane. The 1-offset to this curve may be formulated by the following equations:

$$\begin{cases} P_1 = (x - u)^2 + (y - v)^2 - 1 = 0, \\ P_2 = v^2 - u^3 = 0, \\ P_3 = 2\,v\,(x - u) + 3\,u^2\,(y - v) = 0, \\ P_4 = (3\,u^2 w - 1)\,(2\,vw - 1) = 0. \end{cases} \tag{6}$$

We want to determine the implicit equations and inequations (in x and y) of the quasi-offset. For this purpose, let $\mathbb{P} = \{P_1, \ldots, P_4\}$. Under $x \prec y \prec u \prec v \prec w$, $\mathbb{P}$ may be decomposed into six regular systems $[\mathbb{T}_1, \mathbb{U}_1], [\mathbb{T}_2, \emptyset], \ldots, [\mathbb{T}_6, \emptyset]$ such that

$$\mathrm{Zero}(\mathbb{P}) = \mathrm{Zero}(\mathbb{T}_1/\mathbb{U}_1) \cup \bigcup_{i=2}^{6} \mathrm{Zero}(\mathbb{T}_i),$$

where

$$\mathbb{T}_1 = [E, T_{12}, P_3, P_4], \qquad\qquad \mathbb{U}_1 = \{x, T_{21}, T_{41}\},$$
$$\mathbb{T}_2 = [T_{21}, T_{22}, T_{12}, P_3, P_4],$$
$$\mathbb{T}_3 = [T_{21}, T_{32}, T_{33}, P_3, P_4],$$
$$\mathbb{T}_4 = [T_{41}, T_{42}, T_{43}, P_3, P_4],$$
$$\mathbb{T}_5 = [T_{41}, y, 12\,xu + 2\,u - 9\,x^2 - 2\,x + 9, v^2 + u^2 - 2\,xu + x^2 - 1, P_4],$$
$$\mathbb{T}_6 = [x, 729\,y^4 - 956\,y^2 - 529, 85u - 81y^2 + 72, 6y^2 v + 23v + 12y^3 - 39\,y, P_4];$$

$$\begin{aligned} E ={}& 729\,x^8 + 216\,x^7 + 729\,x^6 y^2 - 2900\,x^6 - 1458\,x^5 y^2 - 2376\,x^5 \\ &- 2619\,x^4 y^2 + 3870\,x^4 - 1458\,x^3 y^4 - 4892\,x^3 y^2 + 4072\,x^3 \\ &+ 729\,x^2 y^4 - 297\,x^2 y^2 - 1188\,x^2 - 4158\,xy^4 + 5814\,xy^2 \\ &- 1656\,x + 427\,y^2 - 1685\,y^4 + 729\,y^6 + 529, \end{aligned}$$

$$\begin{aligned} T_{12} ={}& [2187\,y^4 - 6\,(729\,x^3 + 162\,x^2 + 2079\,x + 478)\,y^2 + 2187\,x^6 - 1944\,x^5 \\ &- 10125\,x^4 - 4800\,x^3 + 2501\,x^2 + 4968\,x - 1587]\,u \\ &+ 4\,x^2\,[27\,(18\,x - 1)\,y^2 + 243\,x^4 + 756\,x^3 - 270\,x^2 + 124\,x + 279], \end{aligned}$$

$$T_{21} = (81\,x^2 + 18\,x + 28)\,(729\,x^4 + 972\,x^3 - 1026\,x^2 + 1684\,x + 765),$$

$$\begin{aligned} T_{22} ={}& 729\,(30618\,x^5 + 38151\,x^4 + 8316\,x^3 + 2286\,x^2 + 59092\,x + 20664)\,y^2 \\ &+ 279686682\,x^5 - 194912487\,x^4 + 343568520\,x^3 + 126051867\,x^2 \\ &+ 74246894\,x + 30796164, \end{aligned}$$

$$\begin{aligned} T_{32} ={}& 6\,(18\,x - 1)\,(81\,x^2 + 81\,x + 83)\,y^2 - 2187\,x^6 + 7776\,x^5 + 18252\,x^4 \\ &- 4812\,x^3 - 4787\,x^2 + 540\,x + 2766, \end{aligned}$$

$$T_{33} = (243\,x^2 + 36\,x + 85)\,u^2 - (81\,y^2 + 162\,x^3 - 36\,x^2 - 154\,x - 72)\,u$$
$$- 72\,x^3 + 4\,x^2,$$
$$T_{41} = 27\,x^4 + 4\,x^3 - 54\,x^2 - 36\,x + 23,$$
$$T_{42} = 19683\,y^4 - 27\,(1458\,x^3 - 729\,x^2 + 4158\,x + 1685)y^2$$
$$- 64\,(2917\,x^3 + 2052\,x^2 - 2493\,x - 514),$$
$$T_{43} = 19683\,(13\,x^2 - 9)\,y^2 u - 864\,(1418\,x^3 + 129\,x^2 - 1692\,x - 59)\,u$$
$$- 8748\,(18\,x - 1)\,x^2 y^2 - 32\,(18952\,x^3 + 12663\,x^2 - 4734\,x - 943).$$

Thus the implicit equations and inequations of the quasi-offset are given as

$$(\mathbb{T}_1^{(2)} = 0 \wedge \mathbb{U}_1 \neq 0) \vee \bigvee_{i=2}^{6} \mathbb{T}_i^{(2)} = 0. \tag{7}$$

Using algorithm S, the above disjunction of polynomial equations and inequations is simplified to

$$E = 0, \quad x \neq 0 \tag{8}$$

or

$$x = 0, \quad 729\,y^4 - 956\,y^2 - 529 = 0. \tag{9}$$

These equations and inequations may also be derived by computing a characteristic or triangular series with projection. A characteristic set of $\mathbb{P}$ is easy to compute, but the computation of characteristic series may take much time. It takes only a few seconds to compute a triangular series of $\mathbb{P}$ with projection by using our method[12] of 1993, but the output is complicated.

The generating and offset curves are shown in Fig. 1. When $x = 0$, the first equation $E = 0$ in (8) becomes

$$(y^2 - 1)\,(729\,y^4 - 956\,y^2 - 529) = 0.$$

However, $(0, 1)$ and $(0, -1)$ satisfying $E = 0$ do not lie on the curve defined by (6) (i.e., there are no corresponding u, v and w such that the equations (6) are satisfied). This is why one needs (9) instead of (8) in the case $x = 0$. In summary, we have:

- any point (x, y) on the curve defined by (6) is a point on the curve defined by the equation $E = 0$;
- any point (x, y) other than $(0, 1)$ and $(0, -1)$ on the curve defined by $E = 0$ is a point on the curve defined by (6).

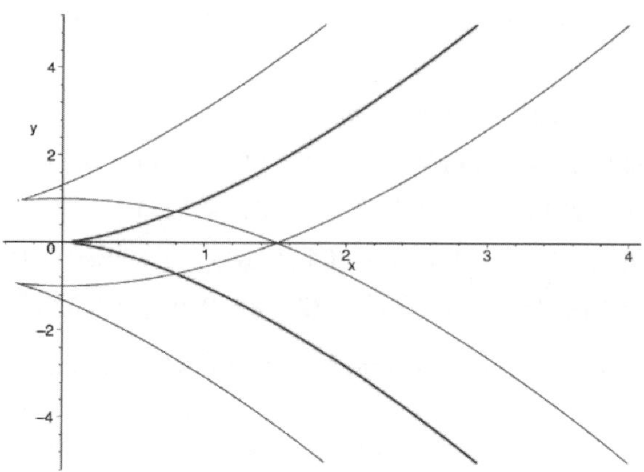

Fig. 1. Curve offsetting

Computing implicit equations and inequations for quasi-offsets is very expensive in general. If there is no need to exclude the extraneous components of lower dimension, one may consider offsets instead of quasi-offsets. More precisely, let $\mathfrak{I}$ be the ideal generated by the four polynomials $P_1, \ldots, P_4$ in (4) or by the six polynomials in (5). Then $\mathrm{Zero}(\mathfrak{I} \cap \mathcal{K}[x, y, z])$ is the Zariski closure of the quasi-offset, that is the offset to the generating curve or surface. Implicit equations of offsets may be more easily computed by using different elimination methods (e.g., Gröbner bases) without projection. It is clear that the Zariski closure of the point set determined by (7) is the algebraic curve defined by $E = 0$.

Example 15: Consider the implicit surface defined by

$$xy + 3\,xz - x - 2\,y^2 - 4\,y + z^2 - z = 0,$$

which has been derived in Example 12. To this quadratic surface the 1-offset may be formulated by the following equations:

$$
\begin{aligned}
P_1 &= F = uv + 3\,uw - u - 2\,v^2 - 4\,v + w^2 - w = 0, \\
P_2 &= (x - u)^2 + (y - v)^2 + (z - w)^2 - 1 = 0, \\
P_3 &= F_v\,(x - u) - F_u\,(y - v) = 0, \\
P_4 &= F_w\,(y - v) - F_v\,(z - w) = 0, \\
P_5 &= F_u\,(z - w) - F_w\,(x - u) = 0, \\
P_6 &= (F_u\,t - 1)\,(F_v\,t - 1)\,(F_w\,t - 1) = 0,
\end{aligned}
$$

where

$$F_u = v + 3\,w - 1, \quad F_v = u - 4\,v - 4, \quad F_w = 3\,u + 2\,w - 1.$$

We have tried to compute the polynomial equations and inequations for the quasi-offset without success. Computing the implicit equation of the offset is also not easy in Maple. Let $\mathbb{P} = \{P_1, \dots, P_5\}$. Using the Gb package of J.-C. Faugère, we are able to compute the Gröbner bases $\mathbb{G}_u, \mathbb{G}_v, \mathbb{G}_w$ of

$$\mathbb{P} \cup \{F_u\, t - 1\}, \quad \mathbb{P} \cup \{F_v\, t - 1\}, \quad \mathbb{P} \cup \{F_w\, t - 1\}$$

with respect to an elimination term order determined by $z \prec y \prec x \prec\!\!\prec w \prec v \prec u \prec t$. It is found that

$$\mathbb{G}_u \cap \mathcal{Q}[x, y, z] = \mathbb{G}_v \cap \mathcal{Q}[x, y, z] = \mathbb{G}_w \cap \mathcal{Q}[x, y, z] = [G],$$

where G is polynomial of total degree 12 in x, y, z, consisting of 451 terms. It follows that the 1-offset to the quadratic surface is given by $G = 0$. This offset surface and its generating surface are plotted in Fig. 2.

Fig. 2. Surface offsetting

In fact, the generating surface does not have any singular point, so the polynomial P_6 is not needed. Computing the Gröbner basis of $\mathbb{P}$ with Gb under the above-mentioned term order, one may get the same polynomial G for the 1-offset. However, we have not succeeded in computing a triangular or regular series of $\mathbb{P}$ in Maple 8.

5. Simplification of Equations and Inequations

The algorithms presented in the previous sections return as output a disjunction of systems of polynomial equations and inequations. The disjunction is complicated in most cases, and how to simplify it is a question that is difficult both to formulate and to answer.

Roughly speaking, we are given a finite sequence of polynomial systems $[\mathbb{P}_1, \mathbb{Q}_1], \ldots, [\mathbb{P}_s, \mathbb{Q}_s]$, and we need to determine finitely many other polynomial systems $[\mathbb{F}_1, \mathbb{G}_1], \ldots, [\mathbb{F}_t, \mathbb{G}_t]$ such that

$$\bigcup_{i=1}^{t} \mathrm{Zero}(\mathbb{F}_i/\mathbb{G}_i) = \bigcup_{j=1}^{s} \mathrm{Zero}(\mathbb{P}_j/\mathbb{Q}_j), \tag{10}$$

and in terms of polynomial representation of the zero set the left-hand side is *simpler* than the right-hand side of (10). The difficulty of the problem lies on how to measure the *simplicity*. One may consider that the left-hand side of (10) is simpler if $t < s$, or if $\mathbb{F}_i$ and $\mathbb{G}_i$ contain fewer polynomials, or these polynomials have fewer terms or take less space of computer memory, or they look simpler from a mathematical point of view. Which criterion to use depends on the form of the results desired, and it is thus difficult to give a general and satisfactory formulation for this simplification problem. Solving the problem with respect to a formulation may be even more difficult; it is much easier when all the $\mathbb{Q}_j$ are empty sets.

In our situation the polynomial systems $[\mathbb{P}_1, \mathbb{Q}_1], \ldots, [\mathbb{P}_s, \mathbb{Q}_s]$ are special: the polynomial sets $\mathbb{P}_j$ are triangular, not all but some of the $\mathbb{Q}_j$ are empty, and the dimensions of the $\mathbb{P}_j$ range over $0, 1, \ldots$. For these particular polynomial systems we present a heuristic method to deal with the simplification problem. As a criterion of simplicity we shall search for $[\mathbb{F}_1, \mathbb{G}_1], \ldots, [\mathbb{F}_t, \mathbb{G}_t]$ with t smaller and $\mathbb{F}_i$ and $\mathbb{G}_i$ containing fewer polynomials. Some concrete examples have been given in the previous sections to illustrate the effectiveness of such heuristic simplification.

Algorithm S: Given a finite set Ψ of polynomial systems in $\mathcal{K}[\boldsymbol{x}]$, this algorithm computes a set Φ of irreducible regular systems in $\mathcal{K}[\boldsymbol{x}]$ such that

$$\bigcup_{\mathfrak{P} \in \Psi} \mathrm{Zero}(\mathfrak{P}) = \bigcup_{\mathfrak{P} \in \Phi} \mathrm{Zero}(\mathfrak{P})$$

and, in case the polynomial systems in Ψ are triangular and irreducible, Φ is likely simpler than Ψ in terms of their size and the number of polynomials contained therein.

S1. Compute an irreducible regular series $\Omega_{\mathfrak{P}}$ of $\mathfrak{P}$ for each $\mathfrak{P} \in \Psi$, and let $\Omega := \bigcup_{\mathfrak{P} \in \Psi} \Omega_{\mathfrak{P}}$. For each $[\mathbb{T}, \mathbb{U}] \in \Omega$, let $\mathbb{U}$ be replaced by the set of all distinct irreducible factors of the polynomials in $\mathbb{U}$. Set $\Phi := \emptyset$.

S2. While $|\Omega| > 1$ do:

S2.1. Let $[\mathbb{T}, \mathbb{U}] \in \Omega$ with $|\mathbb{T}|$ the smallest possible, and set $\Omega := \Omega \setminus \{[\mathbb{T}, \mathbb{U}]\}$, $\mathbb{V} := \mathbb{U}$.

S2.2. For each $U \in \mathbb{V}$ do:

    S2.2.1. Compute an irreducible regular series $\tilde{\Omega}$ of $[\mathbb{T} \cup \{U\}, \mathbb{U} \setminus \{U\}]$ and set $\bar{\Omega} := \emptyset$.

    S2.2.2. While $\tilde{\Omega} \neq \emptyset$ and $\exists [\tilde{\mathbb{T}}, \tilde{\mathbb{U}}] \in \tilde{\Omega}$, $[\bar{\mathbb{T}}, \bar{\mathbb{U}}] \in \Omega$ such that $\mathrm{Zero}(\tilde{\mathbb{T}}/\tilde{\mathbb{U}}) = \mathrm{Zero}(\bar{\mathbb{T}}/\bar{\mathbb{U}})$ do: $\tilde{\Omega} := \tilde{\Omega} \setminus \{[\tilde{\mathbb{T}}, \tilde{\mathbb{U}}]\}$ and $\bar{\Omega} := \bar{\Omega} \cup \{[\bar{\mathbb{T}}, \bar{\mathbb{U}}]\}$.

    S2.2.3. If $\tilde{\Omega} = \emptyset$, then set $\mathbb{U} := \mathbb{U} \setminus \{U\}$, $\Omega := \Omega \setminus \bar{\Omega}$.

  S2.3. Set $\Phi := \Phi \cup \{[\mathbb{T}, \mathbb{U}]\}$.

S3. Set $\Phi := \Phi \cup \Omega$.

Proof: The algorithm terminates obviously, so we only need to show its correctness. In step S2.2.3, if $\tilde{\Omega} = \emptyset$, then either $\mathrm{Zero}(\mathbb{T} \cup \{U\}/\mathbb{U} \setminus \{U\}) = \emptyset$, or

$$\mathrm{Zero}(\mathbb{T} \cup \{U\}/\mathbb{U} \setminus \{U\}) = \bigcup_{[\bar{\mathbb{T}}, \bar{\mathbb{U}}] \in \bar{\Omega}} \mathrm{Zero}(\bar{\mathbb{T}}/\bar{\mathbb{U}}) \subset \bigcup_{[\bar{\mathbb{T}}, \bar{\mathbb{U}}] \in \Omega} \mathrm{Zero}(\bar{\mathbb{T}}/\bar{\mathbb{U}}).$$

In the former case, $\mathrm{Zero}(\mathbb{T}/\mathbb{U}) = \mathrm{Zero}(\mathbb{T}/\mathbb{U} \setminus \{U\})$ and thus U can be simply removed from $\mathbb{U}$. For the latter, one can remove U from $\mathbb{U}$ and the subset $\bar{\Omega}$ from Ω simultaneously. With these technical notes, the correctness of the algorithm now becomes evident.

In step S2.2.2, since both $[\tilde{\mathbb{T}}, \tilde{\mathbb{U}}]$ and $[\bar{\mathbb{T}}, \bar{\mathbb{U}}]$ are irreducible regular systems, whether $\mathrm{Zero}(\tilde{\mathbb{T}}/\tilde{\mathbb{U}}) = \mathrm{Zero}(\bar{\mathbb{T}}/\bar{\mathbb{U}})$ can be easily decided. $\qquad\square$

Some of the material presented in this chapter will also appear in the forthcoming book.[16]

Acknowledgments

This work is supported by the SPACES project (http://www.spaces-soft.org) and the Chinese national 973 project NKBRSF G19980306.

References

1. Buchberger, B.: Applications of Gröbner bases in non-linear computational geometry. In: *Mathematical Aspects of Scientific Software* (Rice, J. R., ed.), pp. 59–87. Springer, New York Berlin (1987).
2. Busé, L., Cox, D., D'Andrea, C.: Implicitization of surfaces in $\mathbb{P}^3$ in the presence of base points. Preprint, available from http://arxiv.org/abs/math.AG/0205251 (2002).

3. Gao, X.-S., Chou, S.-C.: Implicitization of rational parametric equations. *J. Symb. Comput.* **14**: 459–470 (1992).

4. Hoffmann, C. M.: Algebraic and numerical techniques for offsets and blends. In: *Computation of Curves and Surfaces* (Dahmen, W., Gasca, M., Micchelli, C. A., eds.), pp. 499–528. Kluwer Academic, Dordrecht (1990).

5. Hou, X., Wang, D.: Subresultants with the Bézout matrix. In: *Computer Mathematics — Proceedings of the Fourth Asian Symposium* (Gao, X.-S., Wang, D., eds.), pp. 19–28. World Scientific, Singapore New Jersey (2000).

6. Kotsireas, I. S.: Panorama of methods for exact implicitization of algebraic curves and surfaces. In: *Geometric Computation* (Chen, F., Wang, D., eds.), pp. 126–155. World Scientific, Singapore New Jersey (2003).

7. Li, Z.: Automatic implicitization of parametric objects. *Math. Mech. Res. Preprints* **4**: 54–62 (1989).

8. Loos, R.: Generalized polynomial remainder sequences. In: *Computer Algebra: Symbolic and Algebraic Computation* (Buchberger, B., Collins, G. E., Loos, R., eds.), pp. 115–137. Springer, Wien New York (1983).

9. Mishra, B.: *Algorithmic Algebra.* Springer, New York (1993).

10. Sederberg, T. W.: Implicit and parametric curves and surfaces for computer aided geometric design. Ph.D. thesis, Purdue University, USA (1983).

11. Sederberg, T. W., Chen, F.: Implicitization using moving curves and surfaces. In: *Proc. 22nd Ann. Conf. Comput. Graph. Interact. Tech.* (SIGGRAPH '95), pp. 301–308. ACM Press, New York (1995).

12. Wang, D.: An elimination method for polynomial systems. *J. Symb. Comput.* **16**: 83–114 (1993).

13. Wang, D.: Computing triangular systems and regular systems. *J. Symb. Comput.* **30**: 221–236 (2000).

14. Wang, D.: *Elimination Methods.* Springer, Wien New York (2001).

15. Wang, D.: A simple method for implicitizing rational curves and surfaces. Preprint, LIP6 – Université Paris VI, France (2002).

16. Wang, D.: *Elimination Practice: Software Tools and Applications.* Imperial College Press, London (2003).

17. Wu, W.-t.: On a projection theorem of quasi-varieties in elimination theory. *Chin. Ann. Math.* (Ser. B) **11**: 220–226 (1990).

CHAPTER 6

DETERMINING THE INTERSECTION CURVE OF TWO 3D IMPLICIT SURFACES BY USING DIFFERENTIAL GEOMETRY AND ALGEBRAIC TECHNIQUES

Laureano González-Vega[*], Ioana Necula[*], and Jaime Puig-Pey[†]

Universidad de Cantabria
Departamento de Matemáticas, Estadística y Computación[*]
Departamento de Matemática Aplicada y Ciencias de la Computación[†]
Avenida de los Castros, 39005 Santander, Spain
E-mail: {gonzalezl,neculai,puigpeyj}@unican.es

This chapter is devoted to showing how to solve the intersection problem for two algebraic surfaces presented implicitly by using algebraic techniques for manipulating polynomial systems of equations, the numerical solution of first order systems of differential equations and the properties of scalar and gradient vector fields.

1. Introduction

Geometric modeling by using implicit algebraic surfaces is becoming a very active research area in Computer Aided Geometric Design (CAGD): the simultaneous availability of the parametric and the implicit representations of a surface is extremely useful when we solve important problems such as intersection problems including sectioning and offsetting, ray tracing, extreme point location, convexity area detection and closest points computations.

In this work we formulate, in a purely geometric way, the above-mentioned intersection problems for two surfaces presented by their implicit equations resulting into a first order system of ordinary differential equations, whose solution curve will be determined either numerically or in terms of power series and whose parameter will be its arc length. When one of the considered surfaces is a plane (the sectioning problem), before solving the involved system of differential equations an algebraic/topological analysis of the considered curve is performed in order to determine the number of its connected components, to detect singularities, etc.

177

One critical problem for determining the intersection curve between two surfaces is the computation of one starting point. Interpreting scalar and vector fields will allow us to construct gradient curves on surfaces coming from the implicit equations of the considered surfaces and to design methods to compute starting points for intersection problems. Vector fields are used by Cheng[4] for obtaining the tracing direction at a tangential intersection point by analyzing the plane vector field function defined by the gradient of an oriented distance function of one surface from the other. In this chapter we use a 3D gradient vector field, which is projected on an implicit surface in order to construct a gradient curve on it.

For the surface intersection problem, several formulations are known.[7,16] Patrikalakis and Maekawa,[14] and Krishnan and Manocha[13] have presented several categories of methods for computing intersections. The analytic techniques allow one to obtain efficiently explicit representations of the intersection curve, but they can be applied only to particular cases of the intersection problem. The subdivision techniques decompose recursively the problem up to a certain level, in a convergent but possibly awkward way, generating pieces of intersection curves which have to be connected afterwards. The lattice evaluation methods transform the problem into problems of intersection of curves over a surface falling on the other, connecting afterwards the obtained discrete points. These methods are rather slow and lack robustness. The most used methods, consisting in marching over the intersection curve, are based on generating sequences of points which follow the intersection curve, starting from a given point on it. Finding starting points is an inherent problem for these methods. Patrikalakis and Maekawa,[14] and Abdel-Malek and Yeh[1] have proposed as starting points some special points like border points, turning points or singular points, which are obtained by solving non-linear equation systems. In the treatment of tracing and finding starting point problems, two approaches can be considered: an algebraic one, based on solving non-linear equation system, using for instance Newton techniques, and a differential one. Grandine and Klein[11,12] presented the intersection problem as an algebraic differential problem of second order, using techniques of solving non-linear equation systems for the starting point and specific techniques for the mentioned algebraic differential problem.

Garrity and Warren[15] proposed a specific data structure for representing the intersection curve. The method presented by Owen and Rockwood[16] uses space subdivision as a first step in the process of constructing the intersection curve.

The chapter is divided into five sections. In the next section the motivation for using implicitly represented curves and surfaces in CAGD is presented. In Section 3 the formulation of the intersection problem between two implicitly represented surfaces as a first order system of non-linear differential equations is presented together with a general solution, obtained using algebraic techniques, for the case when one of the surfaces is a plane. Section 4 is devoted to showing how to use scalar and vector fields to solve the problem of determining one starting point in the intersection curve of two implicitly represented surfaces. Finally, several examples are presented in the last section.

2. Implicit Curves and Surfaces

Using implicitly represented geometrical objects is a very interesting problem in CAGD. For curves in the plane, the situation is well understood and their manipulation is currently considered by any CAD system since it is a basic subtask for solving many geometrical problems: the computation of the intersection of a parametric surface with a plane in 3D space is reduced to the determination of the geometry of the implicit curve whose equation is obtained through the substitution of the parametric equations into the plane equation.

From the application and user point of view the best scenery is the one where both implicit and parametric representations for the considered curves and surfaces are available since, for example, drawing is considerably easier with the parametric representations while many intersection problems become easier if the implicit representations are available. This argument is well known and, from our point of view, the reason why implicit representations are not widely used in CAGD is due to the fact that computing the implicit equation is generally a very costly algebraic operation, requiring in most cases exact arithmetic. But the new algorithms introduced[5,6] for computing very accurate approximate implicit equations for parametric curves and surfaces motivate the real possibility of having both representations in many cases. The previous statements justify the investigation of algorithms allowing the manipulation of geometric entities defined by their implicit equations.

Another reason motivating the study of algorithms to deal with implicit curves and surfaces is the consideration of offsets, a fundamental geometrical operation in CAD. Offsets of rational curves or surfaces are not rational, in general, but they are algebraic: in order to manipulate the offset of a parametric object, first, it is approximated by another parametric object while it comes always equipped with an implicit equation since the offset is always an algebraic set.

3. Intersection Problems: Sectioning

In this section an algorithm is presented for computing the intersection curve between two implicitly represented surfaces. The main tool to be used is the following proposition, easy to prove, showing how to characterize the intersection curve, when the two surfaces are not tangent at the intersection curve, by means of a first order system of ordinary differential equations. It can be easily deduced by using two facts: first, the differential arc $dC = (dx, dy, dz)$ of the intersection curve is parallel to the cross product vector of the two normals to the intersecting surfaces and, second, the length of dC verifies $ds^2 = dx^2 + dy^2 + dz^2$.

Proposition 1: *Let f and g be two polynomials in $\mathbb{R}[x, y, z]$, S_f and S_g be the surfaces defined by f and g and $(x_0, y_0, z_0) \in S_f \cap S_g$. Then the solution curve of the first order system of ordinary differential equations*

$$\frac{dx}{ds} = \pm \frac{f_y g_z - f_z g_y}{\sqrt{(f_y g_z - f_z g_y)^2 + (f_x g_z - f_z g_x)^2 + (f_x g_y - f_y g_x)^2}},$$

$$\frac{dy}{ds} = \pm \frac{f_x g_z - f_z g_x}{\sqrt{(f_y g_z - f_z g_y)^2 + (f_x g_z - f_z g_x)^2 + (f_x g_y - f_y g_x)^2}}, \qquad (1)$$

$$\frac{dz}{ds} = \pm \frac{f_x g_y - f_y g_x}{\sqrt{(f_y g_z - f_z g_y)^2 + (f_x g_z - f_z g_x)^2 + (f_x g_y - f_y g_x)^2}}$$

with $x(0) = x_0, y(0) = y_0, z(0) = z_0$ is contained in $S_f \cap S_g$ (and arc-length parametrized).

The use of this formulation to compute the intersection of two implicitly represented surfaces presents several problems:

- computing the number of connected components of the intersection curve,
- computing the topological character of each connected component of the intersection curve: bounded or unbounded and with or without singular points,
- computing an initial point for each of the connected components of the intersection curve, and
- solving the corresponding initial value problem for each of the components of the intersection curve.

Next we describe how all these problems can be addressed in the particular case where one of the surfaces is a plane (i.e., the sectioning problem). Let S_f be the surface whose section by a plane is going to be computed. For simplicity (and after a change of coordinates), it can be assumed that the considered plane is horizontal and defined by equation $z = z_0$. In this way, the intersection curve is defined by the implicit equation $F(x,y) = f(x,y,z_0) = 0$ and the initial value problem in Proposition 1 is reduced to

$$\frac{dx}{ds} = \frac{\pm F_y}{\sqrt{F_x^2 + F_y^2}}, \quad \frac{dy}{ds} = \frac{\mp F_x}{\sqrt{F_x^2 + F_y^2}}. \tag{2}$$

Before presenting a way to determine the character of $F(x,y) = 0$, we recall the definition of subresultants.

Definition 2: Let P, Q be two polynomials in $\mathbb{R}[x]$ with $\deg(P) = p$, $\deg(Q) = q$ and

$$P = \sum_{k=0}^{p} a_k x^k, \quad Q = \sum_{k=0}^{q} b_k x^k.$$

If $i \in \{0, \ldots, \inf(p,q) - 1\}$, the subresultant of index i associated to P and Q is defined as follows:

$$\mathrm{Sres}_i(P,Q) = \sum_{j=0}^{i} M_j^i(P,Q) x^j,$$

where each $M_j^i(P,Q)$ is the determinant of the matrix constructed with the columns $1, 2, \ldots, p + q - 2i - 1$ and $p + q - i - j$ of the following matrix:

$$m_i(P,Q) = \overbrace{\begin{pmatrix} a_p & \cdots & a_0 & & \\ & \ddots & & \ddots & \\ & & a_p & \cdots & a_0 \\ b_q & \cdots & b_0 & & \\ & \ddots & & \ddots & \\ & & b_q & \cdots & b_0 \end{pmatrix}}^{p+q-i} \begin{matrix} \left.\vphantom{\begin{matrix}a\\b\\c\end{matrix}}\right\} q - i \\ \\ \left.\vphantom{\begin{matrix}a\\b\\c\end{matrix}}\right\} p - i \end{matrix}.$$

In order to determine the character of $F(x,y) = 0$ the following algebraic analysis is performed, under the initial assumption (always verified modulo a change of coordinates) that no couple of critical points (those points verifying simultaneously $F(x,y) = 0$ and $F_y(x,y) = 0$) has the same x-coordinates:

- The resultant $R(x)$ of $F(x,y) = 0$ and $F_y(x,y) = 0$ with respect to y (i.e., $\mathrm{Sres}_0(F, F_y)$) is computed. Its real roots provide the set of x-coordinates for the singular points or for those points with vertical tangent.

- The first subresultant of $F(x,y) = 0$ and $F_y(x,y) = 0$ with respect to y is computed, providing a polynomial $S(x,y) = u(x)y + v(x)$ which is a combination of $F(x,y) = 0$ and $F_y(x,y) = 0$. If $R(\alpha) = 0$ and $u(\alpha) \neq 0$ then

$$\left(\alpha, -\frac{v(\alpha)}{u(\alpha)}\right)$$

is the only critical point of the curve $F(x,y) = 0$ on the vertical line $x = \alpha$.

These computations (and others with higher order subresultants, required in case the polynomial $u(x)$ vanishes identically) produce a graph, as shown in Fig. 1 (left), indicating how many branches must be computed when solving numerically the differential equation producing the section $F(x,y) = 0$, plus the corresponding initial values for every branch to be determined. In this concrete case four branches are going to be computed by integrating the differential equation (2): those around the only singular point.

This algebraic formulation allows us to decide if the section curve has singular points or not, and provides, in the absence of singular points, the number of connected components and one point (or several) in each of these components. A more detailed explanation about the computation of the singular points, which is a meticulous task, together with several examples, concerning robustness issues, has been presented by González-Vega and Necula.[9]

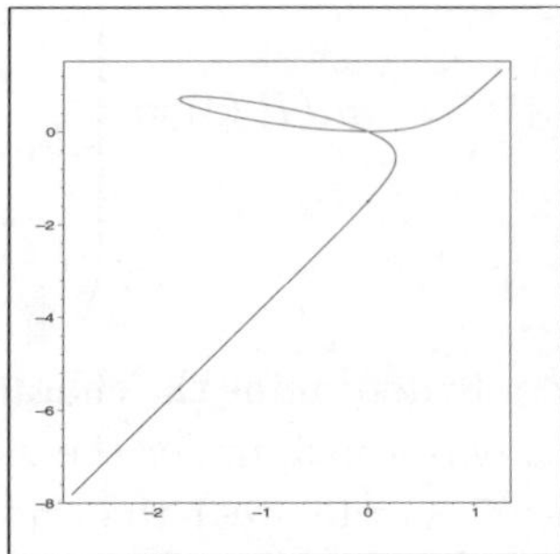

Fig. 1. $2y^3 - (3x - 3)y^2 - (3x^2 - 3x)y - x^3 = 0$

For the polynomial whose drawing appears in Fig. 1 (right) we have

$$R(x) = x^2(9x^4 - 18x^2 + 16x - 3)$$

with real roots $\alpha_1 = -1.764766900$, $\alpha_2 = 0$ and $\alpha_3 = 0.2621641473$. The first subresultant, in this case, is the polynomial

$$S(x,y) = (6x^2 - 8x + 2)y - 2x^2 + x + 3x^3$$

which allows us to determine the y-coordinates β_1, β_2 and β_3 of the critical points of $F(x,y) = 0$ by solving $S(\alpha_i, y) = 0$. Even in the case where higher order subresultants must be used the equation to be solved for determining the y-coordinates always has degree one.[8] In the usual case when the coefficients of $F(x,y) = 0$ are not rational numbers a matrix formulation can be used in order to replace this computation by a generalized eigenvalue problem. In this case, the main techniques are the reduction of the computation of the real roots of the discriminant of F to a sparse generalized eigenvalue problem and the use of the structure of the null space of Bezoutians of F and its derivatives.[13,10]

In the considered example we deduce that there are four branches to be computed having determined for each one, at least, one starting point and one end point. Some of the branches (two in our case) have some extra control points that are very helpful for solving the involved differential equation. For those branches starting and ending at a singular point, the initial point will be located in the middle of the branch; the nearness to these singular points will be used as a stopping criterion.

The initial value problem concerning the system of ordinary differential equations providing the desired curve is solved numerically by using any step-by-step ODE solver (the `Matlab ode45` routine in our experiments), with given absolute and relative tolerancies of the geometric error.

Another procedure can be based on the construction of a specially well suited power series approach around a chosen point providing a polynomial approximation to a piece of the solution curve within a given algebraic error. Since the ordinary differential equation is explicit, is very easy to generate a degree m power series approximation to the solution curve through the chosen starting point and decide up to which value of the parameter (arclength) this approximation fulfills the precision requirements: if $(x(s), y(s))$ denotes the power series approximation then solving the inequality

$$|F(x(s), y(s))| < \epsilon$$

around $s = 0$ (i.e., determining the smallest positive real root of the equation $|F(x(s), y(s))| = \epsilon$) provides a polynomial curve $(x(s), y(s))$ close up to ϵ of the corresponding branch of $F(x, y) = 0$. The resulting curve is projected onto the considered surface and the obtained end point is used as the starting point for the next integration step. The curve constructed in this way is just continuous.

Both ideas can be combined to obtain the power series approach of a piece of the intersection curve around a chosen point.

The approach introduced here is close to the one in the references:[11,12] the differences appear; firstly, for deciding the topological shape of the section, we use algebraic techniques such as subresultants (or its equivalent matrix formulation) and, secondly, we solve a first order initial value problem instead of a second order boundary algebraic-differential problem.

The general surface to surface intersection problem is more complicated from an algebraic point of view: one possibility to determine in advance the topology of the intersection curve is to project this space curve to the plane and then lift the result, but even this lifting is a complicated task. Anyway, in Subsection 4.2, an algorithm will be proposed to determine one point in the intersection curve where to start the numerical integration of the system of differential equations. Note that this procedure does not assure that all the different branches have been considered.

4. Gradient Problems

Associated to an implicit equation $f(x, y, z) = 0$ of a surface S some scalar and vector fields have particular interest.

The scalar field $f(x, y, z)$ establishes in most cases two disjoint regions in $\mathbb{R}^3$: one made of the points where $f(x, y, z) > 0$ and the other where $f(x, y, z) < 0$, separated by the set of points of the surface $f(x, y, z) = 0$ (there are special pathological cases where $f(x, y, z) \geq 0$ for any point $(x, y, z) \in \mathbb{R}^3$: for example $f(x, y, z) = x^2 + y^2 + z^2$). Traveling from one region to the other can be a way of obtaining a point on S, because when the travel path detects a change in sign of $f(x, y, z)$ it implies that the surface has been crossed. This could be considered as a "curved ray tracing" method for point location on S.

A constant direction D induces a vector field of constant value D at every point in $\mathbb{R}^3$. The gradient of $f(x, y, z)$, $\mathrm{grad}(f) = (f_x, f_y, f_z)$, can be considered as a vector field which associates the corresponding value $D(x, y, z) = \mathrm{grad}(f(x, y, z))$ to each point of $\mathbb{R}^3$.

Gradient curves on a surface (steepest curves with respect to a direction), that is, curves which are tangent to the projection on S of a direction vector, are associated with vector fields. For example, if the constant vector field $D = (0, 0, 1)$ is associated to a surface representing a terrain, the gradient curves are the lines followed by the water dropped on that terrain under the effect of gravity. For a non-constant vector field, let us consider two surfaces $f(x, y, z) = 0$, $g(x, y, z) = 0$. Traveling on $f(x, y, z) = 0$ along a gradient curve, which follows the vector field $\mathrm{grad}(g)$, is a method for detecting an intersection point between both surfaces.

4.1. *Differential Equation of a Gradient Curve*

Let $S : f(x, y, z) = 0$ be a surface, P a point on it, $N = (f_x, f_y, f_z)$ the normal vector to S at P, and $D(x, y, z)$ the vector value at P of a known vector field D, not necessarily constant, defined in $\mathbb{R}^3$. The vector $V = N \times D$ is orthogonal to N and D. The vector $T = N \times V$ has the direction of the orthogonal projection of D on the tangent plane to S at P (see Fig. 2 left).

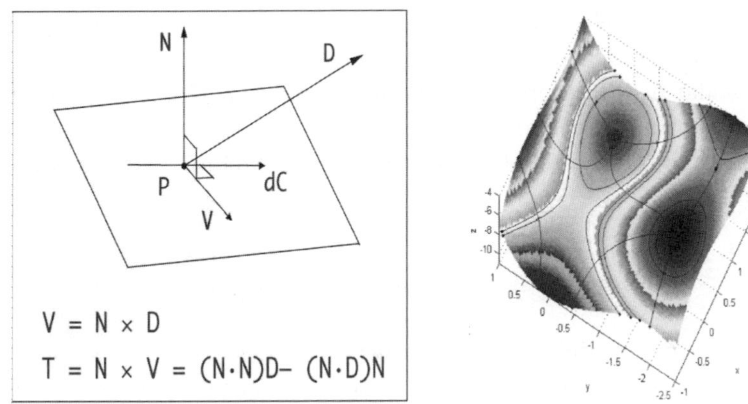

Fig. 2.   Gradient curves

The gradient curve C on S induced by D is tangent to the orthogonal projection of D on the tangent plane to S at the point P. The differential arc of C, $\mathrm{d}C = (\mathrm{d}x, \mathrm{d}y, \mathrm{d}z)$, follows the direction of vector $T = (T_1, T_2, T_3)$; therefore

$$\frac{\mathrm{d}x}{T_1} = \frac{\mathrm{d}y}{T_2} = \frac{\mathrm{d}z}{T_3}.$$

Combining these equations with the expression of the differential arc length of C, $\mathrm{d}s^2 = \mathrm{d}x^2 + \mathrm{d}y^2 + \mathrm{d}z^2$, the following first order, explicit system of differential equations is obtained:

$$\frac{\mathrm{d}x}{\mathrm{d}s} = \pm \frac{T_1}{\|T\|_2}, \quad \frac{\mathrm{d}y}{\mathrm{d}s} = \pm \frac{T_2}{\|T\|_2}, \quad \frac{\mathrm{d}z}{\mathrm{d}s} = \pm \frac{T_3}{\|T\|_2}.$$

After adding the initial conditions $x(0) = x_0$, $y(0) = y_0$, $z(0) = z_0$, which correspond to an initial point (x_0, y_0, z_0) for C, the gradient curve can be obtained by a standard numerical integration procedure.

The $\pm$ signs correspond to the two pieces of C joined at P. There are several special situations:

- Singularity at a point on S: N or D vanishes (and then T).
- N and D are parallel: one arrives at a maximum, minimum or saddle point on S with respect to the direction of the vector field D.

Observe that in the case of D being a constant vector field, the orthogonal trajectories to the gradient curves are the plane contour (constant level) curves on S with respect to the direction D. They are the sections of S by planes having D as their common normal vector. They are the equipotential lines on S of a scalar potential field with gradient vector D. A similar vector and scalar field interpretation can be made when D is not constant. Then the orthogonal curves to the gradient curves are not planar.

In Fig. 2 (right) the gradient curves and orthogonal lines (contour level) for the surface

$$x^3 + y^3 - 2x^2 + 3y^2 - z - 8 = 0,$$
$$x \in (-1, 2), \ y \in (-2, 3), \ D = (0, 0, 1),$$

associated with nine initial points are drawn on the surface.

As it can be seen in Fig. 2 (right) with the constant vector field D as reference, the availability of gradient curves and contour lines (plane sections) are very helpful for the location of maximum and minimum values and convexity areas on the surface, with respect to the given direction D. This is particularly interesting in the case of implicit surfaces, where the obtention of points on the surface is not as straightforward as in the parametric representation.

Determining the singularities must be made by an analysis of singular situations arising in the ODE system. The standard numerical procedures give information and protection with respect to the presence of singular points and there are specialized codes for stiff equations. The same remarks can be applied to the ODE system associated to the intersection problem.

4.2. *Computing the Starting Point for the Intersection Curve Between Two Surfaces*

Basic properties of scalar and vector fields are also useful for obtaining a point belonging to the intersection curve of two implicit surfaces[1] $f(x, y, z) = 0$, $g(x, y, z) = 0$. An algorithm for this process can be simply described as follows.

1. Take an "arbitrary" point P_I on the surface $f(x, y, z) = 0$.
2. Calculate the gradient vector function $D = \mathrm{grad}(g(x, y, z))$.

   (a) The gradient curve can be defined by $\pm\mathrm{grad}(g(x, y, z))$.
   (b) To choose the correct orientation, the value of the scalar field $g(x, y, z)$ at P_I is used: if $g(P_I) > 0$ (resp. < 0), then take $D = -\mathrm{grad}(g(x, y, z))$ (resp. $+\mathrm{grad}(g(x, y, z))$).

3. *Move* from P_I following the gradient curve lying on $f(x, y, z) = 0$ which has gradient vector D as guide *until* meeting $g(x, y, z) = 0$ (the gradient curve trajectory crosses then the 0 value for $g(P_0)$).

The integration process is stopped if the trajectory meets a singular point, exits from a box if this one has been chosen as a scenery, or when the zero value of $g(x, y, z)$ has been crossed.

Once a starting point is obtained, the differential equation providing the intersection curve between the two considered surfaces (see equation (1)) is solved by using the computed point as initial value.

Checking that $g(x, y, z)$ changes sign along the points of the gradient curve on f is a simple task to perform while obtaining progressively successive curve points. Systems like `Matlab` have parameters in the ODE integration routines to detect this kind of events. The roles of $f(x, y, z)$ and $g(x, y, z)$ can be reversed.

The method presented here allows one to obtain a starting point of the intersection curve but if it has several components, the user has to choose adequately starting points for the gradient curves in order to attain the different components of the curve. Only in the particular case of plane sections, as shown in Section 2, the algebraic techniques mentioned before provide all the components.

5. Examples

Figure 3 shows the computation of, first, a point on one of the intersection component curves between two ellipsoids and, second, the corresponding component curve. Let

$$E(a, b, c) = \frac{x^2}{a^2} + \frac{y^2}{b^2} + \frac{z^2}{c^2} - 1$$

and $f(x, y, z) = E(3.8, 2, 6) = 0$ and $g(x, y, z) = E(4, 1.5, 3) = 0$ be the considered ellipsoids. Both the gradient curve on f until the starting point and the intersection curve are shown. On a Pentium 4 (at 1.8 GHz) with `Matlab`, the calculation of 171 points of the approximation trajectory on the gradient curve takes 0.094 seconds, with 0.25 seconds for obtaining 481 points of the intersection curve. For the `ode45` routine in `Matlab` an absolute precision of 10^{-10} and a relative precision of 10^{-7} were used in the numerical integration process. The algebraic precision at the starting intersection point, measured by the evaluation of f and g, was $f(P_0) = 0.000000002073133$ and $g(P_0) = 0$.

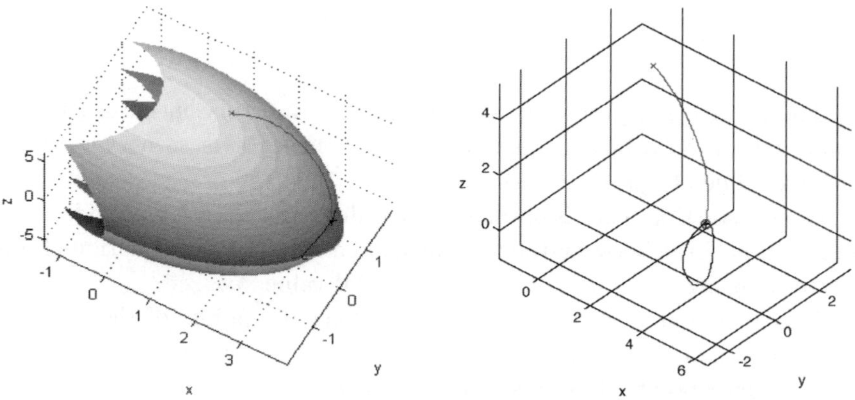

Fig. 3.   One component of the intersection of two ellipsoids

The complete intersection between two tangential ellipsoids is shown in Fig. 4. The intersection curve has two components and two singular points. The method described here does not produce the two components. They are computed in two separate processes, each one producing an initial point of intersection and one component. The two approximation trajectories for attaining the initial intersection points are also shown in Fig. 4. In each case, with an absolute tolerance of 10^{-10} and a relative tolerance of 10^{-7} in the integration routine `ode45` of `Matlab`, the path with 91 discretized points going to a starting point P_0 takes 0.062 seconds, and the intersection component, with 1431 points, takes 0.687 seconds. The algebraic precision at the starting intersection point, measured by the evaluation of f and g, was $f(P_0) = -0.0000000544608794$ and $g(P_0) = -0.0000000000000001$.

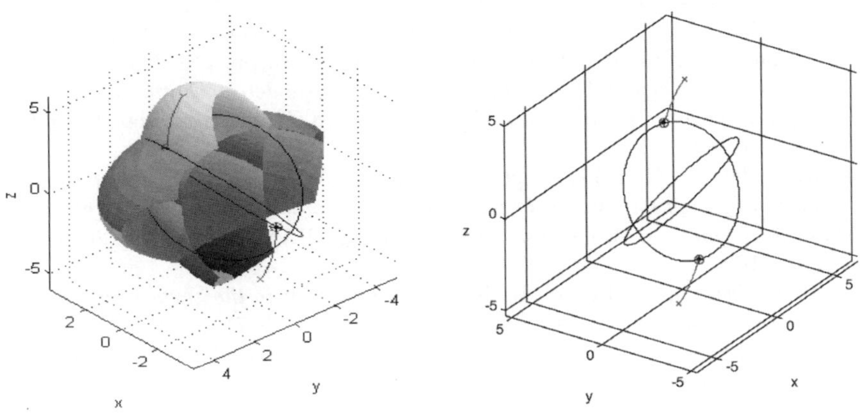

Fig. 4.   Intersection of two tangential ellipsoids

Acknowledgments

This work was supported by the projects DPI2001-1288 (the third author) and BFM2002-04402-C02-02 (the first and second authors), and by the EU project GAIA II (IST-2001-35512). The authors would like to thank the referees for their valuable comments and relevant suggestions on the originally submitted manuscript.

References

1. K. Abdel-Malek and H.-J. Yeh, *On the determination of starting points for parametric surface intersections*, Computer-Aided Design **28** (1997), pp. 21–35.
2. C. Asteasu, *Intersection of arbitrary surfaces*, Computer-Aided Design **20** (1988), pp. 533–538.
3. C. Bajaj, C. M. Hoffmann, J. E. H. Hopcroft and R. E. Lynch, *Tracing surface intersections*, Computer Aided Geometric Design **5** (1988), pp. 285–307.
4. K.-P. Cheng, *Using plane vector fields to obtain all the intersection curves of two general surfaces*, in *Theory and Practice of Geometric Modeling*, W. Strasser and H. Seidel (eds.), Springer-Verlag, New York (1989), pp. 187–204.
5. T. Dokken, *Approximate implicitization*, in *Mathematical Methods for Curves and Surfaces*, T. Lyche and L. L. Schumaker (eds.), Vanderbilt University, Nashville (2001), pp. 81–102.

6. T. Dokken, *Aspects of intersection algorithms and approximation*, Doctoral thesis, University of Oslo, Norway (1997).

7. G. Farin, *An SSI bibliography*, in *Geometry Processing for Design and Manufacturing*, R. Barnhill (ed.), SIAM, Philadelphia (1992), pp. 205–207.

8. R. T. Farouki, *The characterization of parametric surface sections*, Computer Vision, Graphics, and Image Processing **33** (1986), pp. 209–236.

9. L. González-Vega and I. Necula, *Efficient topology determination of implicitly defined algebraic plane curves*, Computer Aided Geometric Design **19** (2003), pp. 719–743.

10. R. Corless, L. González-Vega, I. Necula and A. Shakoori, *Topology determination of implicitly defined real algebraic plane curves*, Preprint (2003).

11. T. A. Grandine, *Applications of contouring*, SIAM Review **42** (2000), pp. 297–316.

12. T. A. Grandine and F. W. Klein, *A new approach to the surface intersection problem*, Computer Aided Geometric Design **14** (1997), pp. 111–134.

13. S. Krishnan and D. Manocha, *An efficient intersection algorithm based on lower dimensional formulation*, ACM Transactions on Computer Graphics **16** (1997), pp. 74–106.

14. M. P. Patrikalakis and T. Maekawa, *Shape Interrogation for Computer Aided Design and Manufacturing*, Springer-Verlag, New York (2002).

15. T. Garrity and J. Warren, *Geometric continuity*, Computer Aided Geometric Design **8** (1991), pp. 51–65.

16. J. Owen and A. Rockwood, *Intersection of general implicit surfaces*, in *Geometric Modeling: Algorithms and New Trends*, G. Farin (ed.), SIAM, Philadelphia (1987), pp. 335–345.

CHAPTER 7

ANALYTICAL PROPERTIES OF SEMI-STATIONARY SUBDIVISION SCHEMES

Hongxin Zhang and Guojin Wang

State Key Laboratory of CAD&CG, Zhejiang University, Hangzhou, China
E-mail: zhx@cad.zju.edu.cn

Based on the viewpoint of topological and geometrical operators, we propose a novel class of subdivision schemes named semi-stationary subdivision for freeform surface design. Compared with traditional stationary methods, their main advantage lies in the use of a parameter changing rule during the subdivision iterations. This facilitates shape control by the user. Local revolving surfaces, directional and bumpy effects can be generated. For practical and theoretical importance, we strictly analyze the convergence properties of cubic subdivision schemes by employing Discrete Fourier Transform and matrix computing techniques to deal with the dynamic subdivision matrix. Additionally, we generalize its basic algorithms by selecting multi-kernel functions. The resulting surfaces are similar to Catmull-Clark subdivision surfaces and have G^2 continuity except at irregular points. The simplicity in mathematical theory and practical implementation further enhance the usefulness of these schemes in computer aided design and computer graphics.

1. Introduction

In an earlier paper,[12] we presented a novel class of discrete curve/surface construction schemes as an extension of stationary subdivision methods.[2,4] In these new schemes, subdivision stencils are modified regularly during the subdivision operations to generate special surfaces. The main purposes of this chapter are to analyze the convergence properties of the derived high-order subdivision surfaces and to offer several practical extensions.

We will first describe the semi-stationary schemes in Section 2. Section 3 presents the convergence analysis of the basic algorithm. The algorithmic generalizations, and several typical examples are shown in Section 4. Finally, conclusions are offered in Section 5.

191

2. Semi-stationary Schemes

About twenty years ago, Catmull and Clark introduced the first subdivision surface method.[2] This method is applied on an arbitrary space polyhedron, also called *control mesh*, denoted by M^0. By splitting every face of the control mesh into a group of quadrilateral sub-faces, the first level mesh M^1 is obtained. Specifically, an n-side face is divided into n spatial quadrangles. The positions of the vertices on the mesh M^1 are computed by some weight-averaging method. This procedure is called subdivision. The subdivision procedure is repeated to obtain finer and finer meshes, and the *subdivision surface* is defined as the limit of the mesh sequence $M^0, M^1, M^2, \ldots$. With appropriate averaging method (or stencil, mask), the subdivision surface can achieve certain order of continuity. The early schemes[2,4,6] use the same mask in every subdivision step; thus they are called *stationary subdivision schemes*.

In one of our former papers,[12] we have presented a non-stationary scheme. The main idea is to decompose the subdivision procedure into a combination of basic subdivision operators and a subsequence of neighborhood convolutions. We first define some operations over a given mesh M.

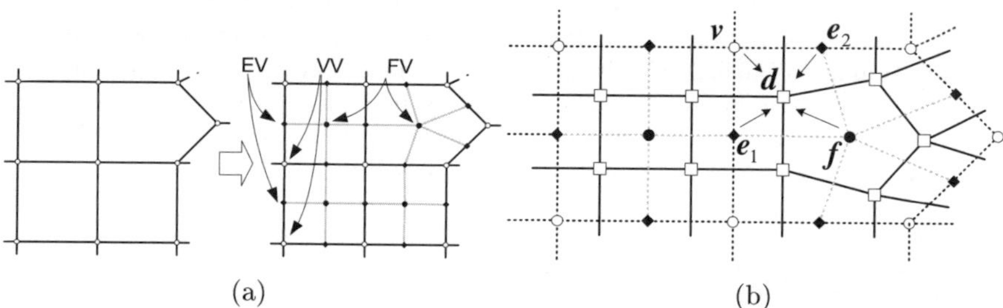

Fig. 1.   Operations over mesh: (a) is the up-sampling operation, and (b) is the dual convolution.

Definition 1: (Up-sampling). Let M be a mesh. For each edge E in M we insert an edge-vertex (abbreviate as EV):

$$\mathbf{e}' = \frac{1}{2}(\mathbf{v}_1 + \mathbf{v}_2),$$

where $\mathbf{v}_1$ and $\mathbf{v}_2$ are the two end points of edge E. For each face F in M, we create a new face-vertex (abbreviate as FV) on its central

$$\mathbf{f}' = \frac{1}{|F|} \sum_{\mathbf{v}_i \in F} \mathbf{v}_i.$$

Corresponding to each vertex v in M, we define $\mathbf{v}' = \mathbf{v}$ as the new vertex-vertex (abbreviated as VV). By connecting VV to EV and EV to FV, we obtain a new mesh M'. We denote this up-sampling operation as $M' = UM$.

Definition 2: (Dual convolution). Let M be a mesh generated by up-sampling operation. For each face in M, if it is a quadrangle, then create a dual point as follows:

$$\mathbf{d} = \frac{f(\alpha)^2 \mathbf{v} + f(\alpha)(\mathbf{e_1} + \mathbf{e_2}) + \mathbf{f}}{(1 + f(\alpha))^2}; \tag{1}$$

otherwise the dual point is defined by

$$\mathbf{d} = \frac{1}{|F|} \sum_{\mathbf{v}_i \in F} \mathbf{v}_i. \tag{2}$$

Here $f(\cdot)$ is the *kernel function* with parameter α. By connecting the dual points lying on adjacent faces, we obtain a dual mesh M' from the original mesh M. We denote this dual convolution operation as $M' = D(f, \alpha)M$.

Henceforth, we call a continuous function $f(\cdot)$ a *kernel function* if there exists a constant $c > 0$ such that

$$|f(\alpha) - f(\beta)| < c|\alpha - \beta|, \quad \forall \alpha, \beta \in [-\varepsilon, \varepsilon].$$

The simplest case is when $f(\cdot) \equiv 1$. In this case, equation (1) is equivalent to equation (2) with $n = 4$ and the dual convolution is just the dual averaging. Moreover, we do not need to know whether the vertices of the given input mesh are FV, EV or VV. Thus we denote $D(1, \cdot)$ as D_1 and relax the condition that the input mesh must be generated by up-sampling operation.

Definition 3: (Semi-stationary subdivision). The semi-stationary subdivision $S_n(f, \alpha)$ $(n \geq 2)$ is defined by

$$\begin{cases} S_2(f, \alpha) = D(f, \alpha)U, \\ S_n(f, \alpha) = D_1 S_{n-1}(f, \alpha) \quad (n > 2). \end{cases}$$

Thus we can obtain a generic class of subdivision algorithms by recursively applying $S_n(f, \alpha)$ over a mesh and letting $\alpha \leftarrow \alpha/2$ each time, i.e., $M^{j+1} = S_n(f, 2^{-j}\alpha)M^j$. Note that our schemes are equivalent to Zorin and Schröder's[13] when $f(\cdot) \equiv 1$. But in our basic subdivision operator S_2, the weights are dynamically modified due to the properties of the kernel function $f(\cdot)$. Hence we call the derived rules *semi-stationary subdivision schemes*.

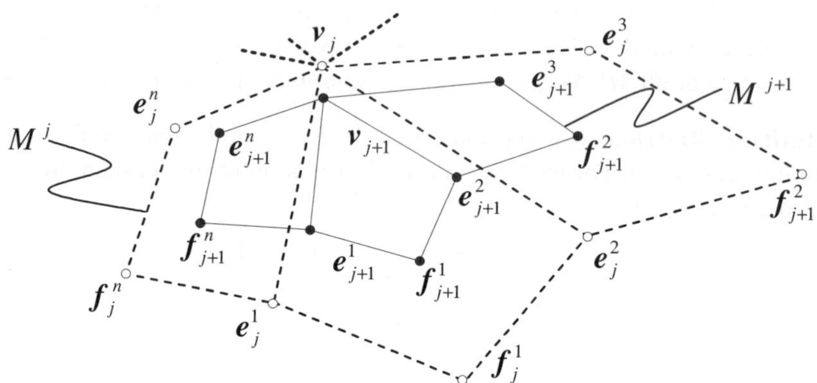

Fig. 2. Catmull-Clark subdivision: f, e and v are the face-vertices, edge-vertices and vertex-vertices respectively. The subscripts indicate the subdivision level, and the vertices around a vertex-vertex are marked with superscripts in counter-clockwise.

In a former work,[12] we have already defined and analyzed one special case $S_2(f,\alpha) = D(f,\alpha)U$. According to this framework, we can easily obtain an extended Catmull-Clark subdivision method by combining S_2 with one more step of dual convolution, i.e., $S_3(f,\alpha) = D_1S_2(f,\alpha)$, which is also reported by Warren and others[7] when $f(\cdot) = \cos(\cdot)$. We construct the averaging masks as follows. As mentioned before, every vertex on M^{j+1} corresponds to a topological element which may be a face, an edge or a vertex on M^j; thus they are called face-vertex, edge-vertex and vertex-vertex respectively. In Fig. 2, $\mathbf{f}^i_j, \mathbf{e}^i_j, \mathbf{v}^i_j$ are face-vertex, edge-vertex and vertex-vertex respectively, where the subscript j represents the subdivision mesh level. With simple computations, one can check that FV is the averaging of the corresponding face vertices, i.e.,

$$\mathbf{f}^i_{j+1} = (\mathbf{v}_j + \mathbf{e}^i_j + \mathbf{f}^i_j + \mathbf{e}^{i+1}_j)/4. \tag{3}$$

The equation of edge-vertex is

$$\mathbf{e}^i_{j+1} = \mu_j(\mathbf{v}_j + \mathbf{e}^i_j) + \nu_j(\mathbf{e}^{i-1}_j + \mathbf{f}^{i-1}_j + \mathbf{f}^i_j + \mathbf{e}^{i+1}_j), \tag{4}$$

where the superscript $i \in Z_n$, $Z_n := Z \bmod n$, and n is the vertex valence which is equal to the number of connected edges. The new vertex-vertex equation is

$$\mathbf{v}_{j+1} = (1 - \beta_j - \gamma_j)\mathbf{v}_j + \frac{\beta_j}{n}\sum \mathbf{e}_j^i + \frac{\gamma_j}{n}\sum \mathbf{f}_j^i.$$

Here the accessorial coefficients are

$$\begin{cases} f_j = f(2^{-j-1}\alpha), \\[2mm] \mu_j = \dfrac{2f_j + 1}{4f_j + 4}, \qquad \nu_j = \dfrac{1}{8f_j + 8}, \\[2mm] \eta_j = \dfrac{(2f_j + 1)^2}{(2f_j + 2)^2}, \quad \xi_j = \dfrac{4f_j + 2}{(4f_j + 4)^2}, \quad \zeta_j = \dfrac{1}{(4f_j + 4)^2}, \\[2mm] \beta_j = 4\xi_j, \qquad\qquad \gamma_j = 4\zeta_j. \end{cases} \qquad (5)$$

The vertices with valence 4 are called *regular vertices*, since its local area properties are the same as tensor product spline surface. Otherwise, they are *irregular vertices*.

3. Convergent and Continuity Analysis

In this section, we mainly discuss the convergence properties of the S_3 subdivision case around irregular vertices. This is because in the neighborhood of regular vertices, the generated surfaces by S_3 have similar properties as tensor product cubic spline. That is, the surface continuity in regular cases can be derived from the continuity of the corresponding curve subdivision method (please refer, e.g., to our former papers[11,12] for details). In an earlier work of Dyn and Levin,[5] they proved for curves that if a non-stationary scheme mask converges to the stationary mask sufficiently fast, then the non-stationary curve has the same continuity properties as the stationary scheme. Then applying Theorem 8 in their paper, our S_2 curve case is C^1 when the sufficient condition $f(0) > 1/2$ for the kernel function $f(.,.)$ is satisfied.[12] Since the subsequence subdivision curve scheme S_n is obtained by combining the convolution operator $n - 2$ times, they can achieve C^{n-1}. Thus, as a special case, the S_3 surface scheme is C^2 continuous except at irregular vertices.

3.1. *Local Subdivision Structure*

After one step of subdivision, all faces in the new mesh are quadrangles and the number of irregular vertices is fixed. If we subdivide the mesh further, irregular vertices will be isolated; in other words, each face contains at most one irregular vertex. In the following subdivision surface analysis, we shall assume that we have done sufficient steps of subdivision to generate the local subdivision structure shown in Fig. 3. The vertex marked as 0 is an irregular vertex with valence n. Its neighborhood is separated by incident edges into n sub-regions, which are called *segments* and are marked in counterclockwise order. In each segment, from center to outside, the control vertices are also numbered in counterclockwise order. After j times subdivision, we denote the vertex sequence around the irregular vertex as $\mathbf{P}_j := [\mathbf{P}_j^0; \mathbf{P}_j^1; \ldots ; \mathbf{P}_j^{n-1}]^{\mathrm{T}}$, where $\mathbf{P}_j^k := [\mathbf{P}_j^{k,0}, \mathbf{P}_j^{k,1}, \ldots, \mathbf{P}_j^{k,m-1}]^{\mathrm{T}}$ is the vertex sub-sequence in segment k with $m = L(L+1)+1$ for L-level neighborhood. For convenience, we also define $\mathbf{O}_j := \mathbf{P}_j^{0,0} = \mathbf{P}_j^{1,0} \cdots = \mathbf{P}_j^{n-1,0}$. To analyze the first order continuity, we consider the 3-level vertex neighborhood of the irregular vertex, i.e., $m = 13$.

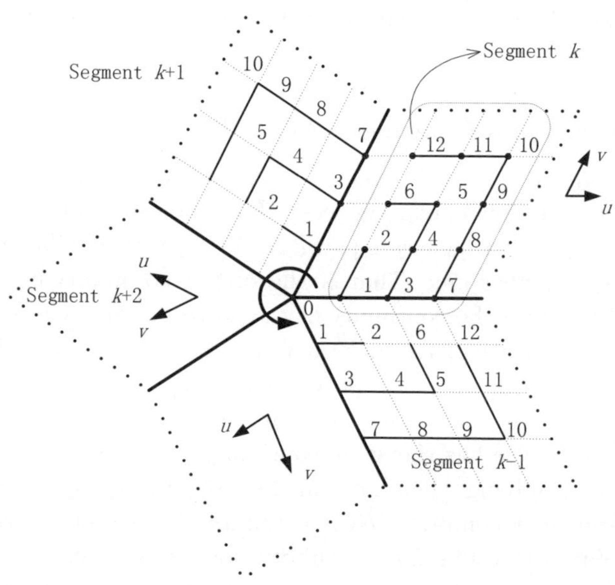

Fig. 3.   Local subdivision structure

3.2. *Subdivision Matrix*

Based on the subdivision schemes described in the last section, two successive vertex sequences have the following relationship

$$\mathbf{P}_j = \mathbf{S}_j \mathbf{P}_{j-1}.$$

Here $\mathbf{S}_j$ is an $mn \times mn$ matrix related to the subdivision level index j. Obeying the former segmented control vertices coding rules, the subdivision matrix $\mathbf{S}_j$ is made up of $n \times n$ matrix blocks $\mathbf{S}_j^{i,i'}$ whose size is $m \times m$. Thus we have

$$\mathbf{P}_j^k = \sum_{i=0}^{n-1} \mathbf{S}_j^{k,i} \mathbf{P}_{j-1}^i, \quad k \in Z_n. \tag{6}$$

The subdivision matrix has the following properties:

1. the sum of elements of each row is equal to 1;
2. the cyclic symmetry:

$$\mathbf{S}_j^i := \mathbf{S}_j^{i,0} = \mathbf{S}_j^{i+i',i'}, \quad i, i' \in Z_n.$$

By property 2, equation (6) can be re-written as

$$\mathbf{P}_j^k = \sum_{i=0}^{n-1} \mathbf{S}_j^{k-i} \mathbf{P}_{j-1}^i, \quad k \in Z_n.$$

Furthermore, noting property 2, we introduce the DFT (Discrete Fourier Transform):

$$\tilde{x}^k := \sum_{i=0}^{n-1} \omega_n^{-ik} x^i, \quad k \in Z_n.$$

Here $\omega_n := c_n + i s_n = \exp(2\pi i/n)$, and $x = (x^0, x^1, \ldots, x^{n-1})$ is an n-tuple whose elements can be scale value, vector or matrix. Applying DFT on both sides of equation (6), we obtain

$$\mathbf{S}_j = \mathbf{W} \operatorname{diag}(\tilde{\mathbf{S}}_j^0, \tilde{\mathbf{S}}_j^1, \ldots, \tilde{\mathbf{S}}_j^{n-1}) \mathbf{W}^{-1}, \tag{7}$$

with $\mathbf{W} = (\mathbf{W}_{ij})_{n \times n}$, $\mathbf{W}_{ij} = \omega_n^{ij} \mathbf{I}_{m \times m}$, $i, j \in \{0, 1, \ldots, n-1\}$. After several computations, one finds that the $m \times m$ matrix blocks $\tilde{\mathbf{S}}_j^k$ have the following structure

$$\tilde{\mathbf{S}}_j^k = \begin{pmatrix} \mathbf{A}_j^k & 0 & 0 \\ \mathbf{A}_{1,0}^k & \mathbf{B}_j^k & 0 \\ \mathbf{A}_{2,0}^k & \mathbf{A}_{2,1}^k & 0 \end{pmatrix},$$

where the sub-matrices in the diagonal line are

$$\mathbf{A}_j^k = \begin{pmatrix} (1 - \beta_j - \gamma_j)\delta_{k,0} & \beta_j & \gamma_j \\ \nu\delta_{k,0} & 2\mu_j c_n + \nu_j & \nu_j(1 + \bar{\omega}_n^k) \\ \frac{1}{4}\delta_{k,0} & \frac{1}{4}(1 + \omega_n^k) & \frac{1}{4} \end{pmatrix}$$

and

$$\mathbf{B}_j^k = \begin{pmatrix} \xi_j & \zeta_j & 0 & \zeta_j \bar{\omega}_n^k \\ \nu_j & \nu_j & 0 & 0 \\ \zeta_j(1+\omega_n^k) & \xi_j & \zeta_j & \xi_j \\ \nu_j \omega_n^k & 0 & 0 & \nu_j \end{pmatrix}.$$

In the last two equations, $\delta_{i,j}$ is the Kronecker delta. The eigenvalues of the sub-matrix $\mathbf{B}_j^k$ is

$$\left\{ \tau_j^{k,1}, \tau_j^{k,2}, \tau_j^{k,3}, \tau_j^{k,4} \right\} = \left\{ \frac{1}{16(1+f_j)^2}, \frac{f_j}{8(1+f_j)^2}, \frac{1}{8(1+f_j)}, \frac{1}{4(1+f_j)} \right\}.$$
$$(8)$$

When $f_j > 0$, the four eigenvalues are all less than $1/4$. For sub-matrix $\mathbf{A}_j^k$, if $k = 0$, and let $\sigma_j = 1 - \beta_j - \gamma_j$, its three eigenvalues are 1 and

$$\lambda_j^{0,i} = \frac{1}{8}\left(4\sigma_j - 1 \pm \sqrt{(4\sigma_j - 1)^2 + 8(2\beta_j - 1)\frac{f_j}{1+f_j}} \right), \quad i = 1, 2.$$

By equation (5), we can obtain $\lambda_j^{0,1} = f_j^2(2+2f_j)^{-2} < 1/4$ and $\lambda_j^{0,2} = f_j(2+2f_j)^{-1} < 1/2$. If $k \neq 0$, then the two none-zero eigenvalues are

$$\lambda_j^{k,i} = \frac{1}{8(1+f_j)}\left(c_{n,k} + 2 + 3f_j \pm \sqrt{c_{n,k}^2 + c_{n,k}(4+6f_j) + (2+f_j)^2} \right),$$
$$i = 1, 2,$$

with $c_{n,k} = \cos(2\pi k/n)$. Denote

$$\lambda_j := \lambda_j^{1,1} = \lambda_j^{n-1,1}$$

$$= \frac{1}{8(1+f_j)}\left(c_n + 2 + 3f_j + \sqrt{c_n^2 + c_n(4+6f_j) + (2+f_j)^2} \right);$$

we can get $1 > \lambda_j \geq 1/2 > \lambda_j^{k,2} > 0$ $(k = 1, 2, \ldots, n-1)$ and $\lambda_j > \lambda_j^{k,1} > 1/8$ $(k = 2, 3, \ldots, n-2)$ for every n.

3.3. *Convergence of Semi-stationary Subdivision Schemes*

We analyze the convergence of semi-stationary subdivision schemes in this subsection. Denote $\mathbf{T}_j = \mathbf{S}_j \mathbf{S}_{j-1} \cdots \mathbf{S}_1$ and $\tilde{\mathbf{T}}_j^k = \tilde{\mathbf{S}}_j^k \tilde{\mathbf{S}}_{j-1}^k \cdots \tilde{\mathbf{S}}_1^k$. By equation (7), we have

$$
\begin{aligned}
\mathbf{P}_j &= \mathbf{S}_j \mathbf{P}_{j-1} \\
&= \cdots \\
&= \mathbf{S}_j \mathbf{S}_{j-1} \cdots \mathbf{S}_1 \mathbf{P}_0 \\
&= \mathbf{T}_j \mathbf{P}_0 \\
&= \mathbf{W} \mathrm{diag}(\tilde{\mathbf{T}}_j^0, \tilde{\mathbf{T}}_j^1, \ldots \tilde{\mathbf{T}}_j^{n-1}) \mathbf{W}^{-1} \mathbf{P}_0 .
\end{aligned}
\tag{9}
$$

By induction, we can conclude that the sum of each row of $\mathbf{T}_j$ is equal to 1. Thus $(1, 1, \ldots, 1)^T$ must be its eigenvector corresponding to the largest eigenvalue 1. Thus, we obtain the following theorem.

Theorem 4: If $f_j > 0$ $(j = 1, 2, \ldots)$, the spectrum radius of matrix $\mathbf{T}_j$ is equal to the largest eigenvalue 1, and the other eigenvalues will be convergent to 0 when $j \to \infty$, then the subdivision schemes are convergent and continuous.

Proof: If $f_j > 0$ $(j = 1, 2, \ldots)$, then the elements of $\mathbf{T}_j$ are non-negative. In other words, the transpose of $\mathbf{T}_j$ is a stochastic matrix, so the spectrum radius of $\mathbf{T}_j$ is 1. By equation (9), the eigenvalues of $\mathbf{T}_j$ are the same as the blocked diagonal matrix $\mathrm{diag}(\tilde{\mathbf{T}}_j^0, \ldots, \tilde{\mathbf{T}}_j^{n-1})$. Based on the analysis in the last section, one can show that for every j, when $k \neq 0$, there exists a positive real number c such that the spectrum norm of $\tilde{\mathbf{S}}_j^k$ satisfies $\|\tilde{\mathbf{S}}_j^k\|_2 < c < 1$. By the matrix norm properties, we have

$$
\left\| \tilde{\mathbf{T}}_j^k \right\| \leq \left\| \tilde{\mathbf{S}}_j^k \right\| \left\| \tilde{\mathbf{S}}_{j-1}^k \right\| \cdots \left\| \tilde{\mathbf{S}}_1^k \right\| < c^j .
$$

So, when $j \to \infty$, $\|\tilde{\mathbf{T}}_j^k\| \to 0$. It follows that the eigenvalues of $\tilde{\mathbf{T}}_j^k$ $(k \neq 0)$ are all convergent to 0.

When $k = 0$, from the last section, we know that all eigenvalues of $\mathbf{B}_j^0$ are less than $1/4$. Similarly, one can verify that all eigenvalues of $\mathbf{B}_j^0 \mathbf{B}_{j-1}^0 \cdots \mathbf{B}_1^0$ are convergent to 0. For $\tilde{\mathbf{S}}_j^0$'s sub-block $\mathbf{A}_j^0$, its Jordan decomposition is $\mathbf{A}_j^0 = \mathbf{V}_j \mathrm{diag}(1, \lambda_1^0, \lambda_2^0) \mathbf{V}_j^{-1}$ with

$$
\mathbf{V}_j = \begin{pmatrix} 1 & (1+f_j)^{-2} & -(1+f_j)^{-1} \\ 1 & -(1+f_j)^{-1} & (2+2f_j)^{-1} \\ 1 & 1 & 1 \end{pmatrix},
$$

and

$$
\mathbf{V}_{j+1}^{-1}\mathbf{V}_j = \begin{pmatrix} 1 & \dfrac{(f_j - f_{j+1})^2}{(1+f_j)^2(2+f_{j+1})^2} & \dfrac{f_j - f_{j+1}}{(1+f_j)(2+f_{j+1})} \\[4mm] 0 & \dfrac{(2+f_j)^2(1+f_{j+1})^2}{(1+f_j)^2(2+f_{j+1})^2} & 0 \\[4mm] 0 & \dfrac{2(2+f_j)(f_j - f_{j+1})(1+f_{j+1})}{(1+f_j)^2(2+f_{j+1})^2} & \dfrac{(2+f_j)(1+f_{j+1})}{(1+f_j)(2+f_{j+1})} \end{pmatrix}.
$$

Thus, the eigenvalues of $\mathbf{A}_j^0 \mathbf{A}_{j-1}^0 \ldots \mathbf{A}_1^0$ are convergent to $(1,0,0)$ with $j \to \infty$. So there is a $\mathbf{T}_\infty$ which is the limit of $\mathbf{T}_j$ and whose eigenvalues are $(1,0,\ldots,0)$. Since $\mathbf{T}_\infty = \mathbf{R}_1 \operatorname{diag}(1,0,...,0)\mathbf{R}_2$, we have $\operatorname{rank}(\mathbf{T}_\infty) = 1$. Furthermore, it follows that there exists an $n \times m$-dimensional vector $\mathbf{a} = [a_1, a_2, \ldots, a_{mn}]$ such that $\mathbf{T}_\infty = [\mathbf{a}, \mathbf{a}, \ldots, \mathbf{a}]^{\mathrm{T}}$ and $\mathbf{P}_\infty = \mathbf{T}_\infty \mathbf{P}_0$. Hence the subdivision schemes are convergent. $\qquad\square$

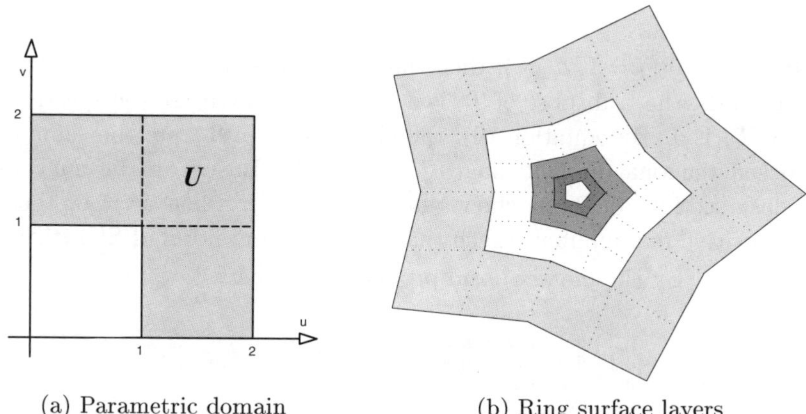

(a) Parametric domain　　　　　　　(b) Ring surface layers

Fig. 4.　The strict convergence definitions of subdivision surface

3.4. *Continuity of Semi-stationary Subdivision Surface*

In the continuity analysis of stationary subdivision surfaces,[1,9,8] the tangent plane continuity around an irregular vertex is defined by the limit of the tangent plane of the tensor product patch. Similarly, we strictly define the continuity of semi-stationary subdivision surfaces as follows. On a mesh, surrounding a single irregular vertex, the regular part of the control polygon corresponds to the tensor product surface $\mathbf{y}_j$ defined by the corresponding curve subdivision scheme.[12] By applying the subdivision operator, it produces an ascending surface sequence

$$\mathbf{y}_0 \subset \mathbf{y}_1 \subset \mathbf{y}_2 \subset \cdots$$

which converges to the limit surface $\mathbf{y} = \bigcup_{i=1}^{\infty} \mathbf{y}_i$. Then we introduce the ring surface layers

$$\mathbf{r}_j := \text{closure}(\mathbf{y}_{j+1} \setminus \mathbf{y}_j).$$

So we can define the limit surface as the union of non-intersected sets

$$\mathbf{y} = (\bigcup_{j \in N} \mathbf{r}_j) \cup \mathbf{y}_0.$$

Thus $\mathbf{r}_j$ are just defined on the parameter area $U \times Z_n$, with $U := [0,2]^2 \setminus [0,1]^2$. And every layer $\mathbf{r}_j$ can be represented as a linear combination of piecewise continuous functions N^k with control points $\mathbf{P}_j^k$, i.e.,

$$\mathbf{r}_j : \quad (u, v, k) \in U \times Z_n \mapsto \mathbf{r}_j^k(u, v) = \sum_{l=0}^{L} N^l(u, v, k)\mathbf{P}_j^l.$$

Furthermore, all the N^l can be represented as a row vector $\mathbf{N}$ and the control points $\mathbf{P}_j^k$ form a column vector $\mathbf{P}_j$. Then we have the following matrix form

$$\mathbf{r}_j(u, v, k) = \mathbf{r}_j^k(u, v) = \mathbf{N}(u, v, k)\mathbf{P}_j.$$

So we can more strictly give the convergence definition of subdivision surfaces (see Fig. 4).

Definition 5: A subdivision procedure S is *convergent*, if there exists a unique point $\mathbf{p}$ such that for any point sequence $\mathbf{p}_j \in \mathbf{r}_j$,

$$\lim_{j \to \infty} \mathbf{p}_j = \mathbf{p}.$$

Since $\mathbf{r}_j(u_0, v_0)$ is the convex linear combination of control points, the method we used to prove the control points convergent in Theorem 4 is equivalent to Definition 5. Note that the surface defined by Definition 5 is also continuous. We introduce the tangent plane continuity as follows.

Definition 6: A subdivision procedure S is *tangent plane continuous*, if S is convergent, and there exists a unique vector $\mathbf{n}(\mathbf{p})$ such that for any normal vector sequence $\mathbf{n}(\mathbf{p}_j)$, $\mathbf{p}_j \in \mathbf{r}_j$,

$$\lim_{j \to \infty} \mathbf{n}(\mathbf{p}_j) = \mathbf{n}(\mathbf{p}).$$

The vector $\mathbf{n}(\mathbf{p})$ is called the subdivision surface normal limit at $\mathbf{p}$.

Note that it is not necessary to be the true normal at $\mathbf{p}$, since it may not exist. Obeying the former definitions, we can prove the following theorem.

Theorem 7: If $f(0) \geq 1$, then the subdivision surfaces defined by scheme S_3 are tangent plane continuous.

Proof: By the definition, let $\mathbf{p}_j$ be an arbitrary point on the j-th layer ring surface with correspond parameters (u_0, v_0, k_0), and its normal vector is $\mathbf{n}(\mathbf{p}_j)$ which is paralleled to $\mathbf{r}_u^j \times \mathbf{r}_v^j \big|_{(u_0, v_0, k_0)}$. Obviously, there is an $mn \times mn$ matrix D_u^j such that $\mathbf{r}_x^j = \mathbf{D}_x^j \mathbf{P}_j = \mathbf{D}_x^j \mathbf{T}_j \mathbf{P}_0$ with $x \in \{u, v\}$. By the analyze in Subsections 3.2 and 3.3, $\mathbf{T}_j$ has the eigen-structure $(\mathbf{V}_j, \Delta_j)$ in the complex domain such that there exists a diagonal decomposition $\mathbf{T}_j = \mathbf{V}_j \Delta_j \mathbf{V}_j^{-1}$ with $\mathbf{V}_j = (\mathbf{v}_j^1, \mathbf{v}_j^2, \ldots, \mathbf{v}_j^{mn})$ and $\Delta_j = \mathrm{diag}(1, \delta_2^j, \ldots, \delta_{mn}^j)$. Here $\mathbf{v}_j^k$ are $m \times n$-dimension vectors, and we assume that

$$1 > \left|\delta_2^j\right| \geq \left|\delta_3^j\right| \geq \ldots \geq \left|\delta_{mn}^j\right|, \quad \mathbf{v}_j^1 = 1/\sqrt{mn}(1, 1, \ldots, 1).$$

Denote

$$\mathbf{Q}_j := \mathbf{V}_j^{-1} \mathbf{P}_0 := (\mathbf{Q}_j^1, \mathbf{Q}_j^2, \ldots, \mathbf{Q}_j^{mn});$$

we have

$$\mathbf{x}_u^j \times \mathbf{x}_v^j = \sum_{k=1}^{mn-1} \sum_{l=k+1}^{mn} \delta_j^k \delta_j^l \left[(\mathbf{D}_u^j \mathbf{v}_j^k)(\mathbf{D}_v^j \mathbf{v}_j^l) - (\mathbf{D}_u^j \mathbf{v}_j^l)(\mathbf{D}_v^j \mathbf{v}_j^k) \right] \mathbf{Q}_j^k \times \mathbf{Q}_j^l.$$

Note that the subdivision schemes we have defined are all linear precision. So, the sum of each row elements of D_x^x are 0 and $D_x^j \mathbf{v}_j^1 = 0$. From the last theorem and because of the symmetry properties of $\mathbf{T}_j$, diagonalizing it with DFT, we see that all eigenvalues of $\mathbf{T}_j$ except 1 are convergent to 0. But the convergent speeds of different eigenvalues are different. By Lemmas A.1 and A.2, δ_j^2 and δ_j^3 are generated from the matrix blocks $\mathbf{A}_j^1$ and $\mathbf{A}_j^{n-1}$, and

$$\lim_{j \to \infty} \delta_j^k / \delta_j^2 = \begin{cases} 0, & k \neq 3, \\ c, & k = 3. \end{cases}$$

Furthermore, the limits of $\mathbf{Q}_j^2$ and $\mathbf{Q}_j^3$ exist. It follows that

$$\lim_{j \to \infty} \mathbf{n}(\mathbf{p}_j) = \lim_{j \to \infty} \mathbf{x}_u^j \times \mathbf{x}_v^j / \left\| \mathbf{x}_u^j \times \mathbf{x}_v^j \right\| = \mathbf{Q}_\infty^2 \times \mathbf{Q}_\infty^3 / \left\| \mathbf{Q}_\infty^2 \times \mathbf{Q}_\infty^3 \right\|.$$

By the definition, the subdivision schemes can reach tangent plane continuity. $\quad\square$

Remark 8: Reif[9] pointed out that it is not enough to only check the normal vector convergence for tangent plane continuity. He proved that if the characteristic map of a given stationary subdivision scheme is regular and injective, then it is G^1 at an irregular vertex. However, it is impossible in our semi-stationary case to directly define a characteristic map via the dynamic subdivision matrices. Fortunately, in the proof of Theorem 7, $\mathbf{Q}^i_\infty$ ($i = 2, 3$) exist, which correspond to the eigenvectors in the stationary case to define the characteristic map. Note that $\mathbf{Q}^i_\infty$ can be viewed as continuous vector functions with subdivision parameter α, and $\alpha \equiv 0$ defines the stationary case, which is well researched by Reif[9] and Zorin.[13] So we conclude that at irregular vertices the S_3 scheme can achieve G^1.

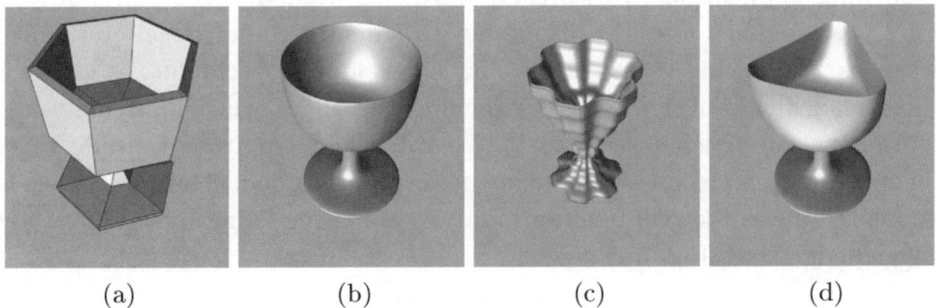

(a)   (b)   (c)   (d)

Fig. 5. Examples of semi-subdivision surfaces with local revolving part: (a) is the original control mesh; (b) shows revolving result created by typical settings with $f(\cdot) = \cos(\cdot), \alpha = 2\pi/6$; (c) produces special effect with $f(\cdot) = \cos(\cdot), \alpha = 10$; (d) is an example of applying non-uniform parameter selection over the vertices. All the examples are generated based on S_3 schemes.

4. Examples with Discussions

In this section, we give several examples of surfaces generated by our subdivision schemes.

Revolving surfaces are very important in CAD/CAM. In our algorithmic framework, it is very easy to create subdivision surfaces with local revolving part. We can simply select $S_3(\cos, \alpha)$ as the subdivision scheme. In the revolving part, we construct several regular n-sided planar polygons along an axis and set $\alpha = 2\pi/n$. The results demonstrate that our technique can be an alternative solution for representing circular shape exactly, though it is also possible to use non-uniform rational subdivision techniques.[10] In our framework, we can also change the value of α to modify the shape, which resembles rational-based techniques (see Fig. 5). To generate a complete surface of revolution, we apply the same method described by Morin and others[7] — use collapsed quads and alter the rules of linear subdivision $S_3(1,0)$ to generate exact surfaces of revolution. We wish to point out that it is not necessary for the whole mesh to use the same kernel function $f(\cdot)$ and parameter α. We have implemented a scheme with non-uniform parameters which can tag different α over a given mesh.

Some surfaces are anisotropic. For example, surfaces of revolution and sweeping can be viewed as a kind of anisotropic feature of surfaces. Furthermore, in the case of tensor product spline surfaces, one can choose different bases in different directions. However, traditional subdivision schemes are cyclic symmetric. Thus it is not powerful enough for certain geometric modelling applications. Researchers have employed the techniques of tagging special sharp features on meshes to enhance the classical stationary schemes.[3] Following these cues, we have developed a technique to create a directional fields over meshes by tagging the edges when applying semi-stationary subdivision schemes.[11] We call them longitude-latitude tags. Thus a new extension scheme can be easily obtained. The basic idea is to apply different kernel functions and α's along the longitude and latitude tagged edges (see Fig. 6).

5. Conclusion

We have presented a novel set of subdivision schemes in this chapter. Although they have dynamic subdivision matrices, we have shown that it is still possible to apply DFT-like techniques to analyze the geometric continuity properties. Compared with stationary schemes, our schemes are more flexible though less efficient. They can be used to create local revolving surfaces and anisotropic features. In the future, we will study the analytical properties of the anisotropic extended schemes.

Acknowledgements

We thank the reviewers for their comments which helped us to improve the content and the presentation of the chapter. Special thanks go to Professor Chiew-Lan Tai for her careful proof reading. This work is supported jointly by the National Natural Science Foundation of China (Grant No. 60173034), National Natural Science Foundation for Innovative Research Groups (No. 60021201) and the State Key Basic Research Project 973 (Grant No. 2002CB312101).

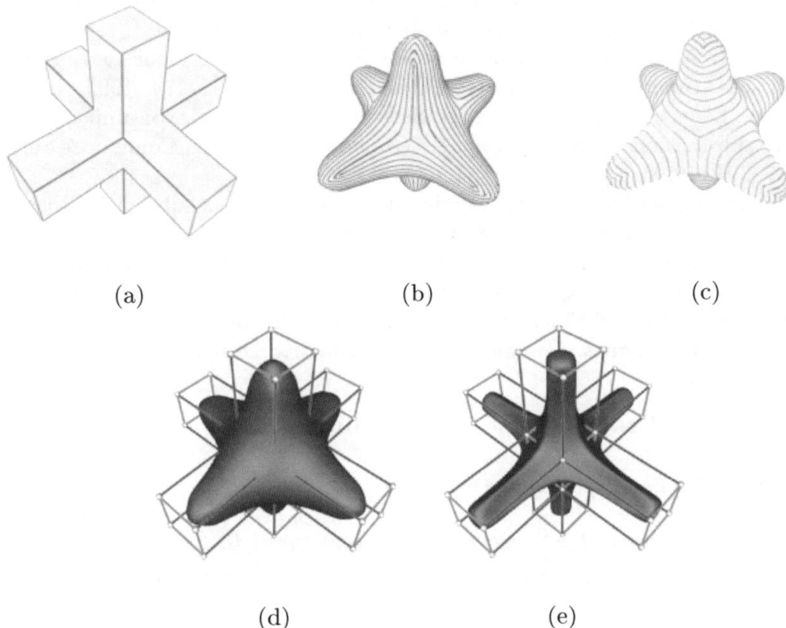

Fig. 6.　Example of subdivision surfaces with anisotropic feature: (a) is the original control mesh with tags; (b) and (c) are the latitude and longitude tags respectively after three subdivision steps; (d) and (e) are two resulting surfaces by applying different kennel functions. Both examples are based on the extended S_3 schemes.

References

1. A. A. Ball and D. J. Storry. Conditions for tangent plane continuity over recursively generated B-spline surfaces. *ACM Transactions on Graphics*, 7(2): 83–102, 1988.
2. E. Catmull and J. Clark. Recursively generated B-spline surfaces on arbitrary topological meshes. *Computer Aided Design*, 10(6): 350–355, 1978.
3. T. DeRose, M. Kass, and T. Truong. Subdivision surfaces in character animation. *Computer Graphics*, 32 (Annual Conference Series): 85–94, 1998.
4. D. Doo and M. Sabin. Behavior of recursive division surfaces near extraordinary points. *Computer Aided Design*, 10(6): 356–360, 1978.
5. N. Dyn and D. Levin. Analysis of asymptotically equivalent binary subdivision schemes. *Journal of Mathematical Analysis and Applications*, 193(2): 594–621, 1995.
6. N. Dyn, D. Levin, and J. Gregory. A butterfly subdivision scheme for surface interpolation with tension control. *ACM Transactions on Graphics*, 9(2): 160–169, 1990.
7. G. Morin, J. Warren, and H. Weimer. A subdivision scheme for surfaces of revolution. *Computer Aided Geometric Design*, 18: 483–502, 2001.

8. J. Peters and U. Reif. Analysis of algorithms generalizing B-spline subdivision. *SIAM Journal of Numerical Annual*, 35: 728–748, 1998.

9. U. Reif. A unified approach to subdivision algorithms near extraordinary vertices. *Computer Aided Geometric Design*, 12(2): 153–174, 1995.

10. T. W. Sederberg, J. M. Zheng, D. Sewell, and M. Sabin. Non-uniform recursive subdivision surfaces. *Computer Graphics*, 32 (Annual Conference Series): 387–394, 1998.

11. H. X. Zhang and G. J. Wang. Semi-stationary push-back subdivision schemes. *Journal of Software*, 13(9): 1830–1839, 2002.

12. H. X. Zhang and G. J. Wang. Semi-stationary subdivision operators in geometric modeling. *Progress in Natural Science*, 12(10): 772–776, 2002.

13. D. Zorin and P. Schröder. A unified framework for primal/dual quadrilateral subdivision schemes. *Computer Aided Geometric Design*, 18: 429–454, 2001.

Appendix A. Proofs of the Two Lemmas

Lemma A.1: *Let* $\mathbf{K}_j^k = \dfrac{\mathbf{A}_j^k}{\lambda_j}\dfrac{\mathbf{A}_{j-1}^k}{\lambda_{j-1}}\cdots\dfrac{\mathbf{A}_1^k}{\lambda_1}$; *then:*

(a) *The eigenvalues of* $\mathbf{K}_j^0$ *except 1 are convergent to 0, when* $j \to \infty$.

(b) *If* $k \neq 0, 1, n-1$, *then the eigenvalues of* $\mathbf{K}_j^k$ *convergent to 0, when* $j \to \infty$.

(c) *If* $k = 1, n-1$, *then the matrix limit* $\lim\limits_{j\to\infty} \mathbf{K}_j^k = \mathbf{K}_\infty^k$, *and* $\left\|\mathbf{K}_\infty^k\right\| > 0$ *when* $j \to \infty$. *In other words, they have a unique non-zero eigenvalue.*

Proof: Firstly, one can directly compute out all three eigenvalues of $\mathbf{K}_j^0$; they are

$$\left\{ 1, \frac{\lambda_j^{0,1}\lambda_{j-1}^{0,1}\cdots\lambda_1^{0,1}}{\lambda_j\lambda_{j-1}\cdots\lambda_1}, \frac{\lambda_j^{0,2}\lambda_{j-1}^{0,2}\cdots\lambda_1^{0,2}}{\lambda_j\lambda_{j-1}\cdots\lambda_1} \right\}.$$

This proves case (a).

When $k \neq 0, 1, n-1$, we have the following spectrum norm estimation

$$\left\|\mathbf{K}_j^k\right\| \leq \frac{\left\|\mathbf{A}_j^k\right\|\left\|\mathbf{A}_{j-1}^k\right\|\cdots\left\|\mathbf{A}_1^k\right\|}{\lambda_j\lambda_{j-1}\cdots\lambda_1} = \frac{\lambda_j^{k,1}\lambda_{j-1}^{k,1}\cdots\lambda_1^{k,1}}{\lambda_j\lambda_{j-1}\cdots\lambda_1}.$$

Then for a given scale M such that $\alpha \in [0, M)$, we have

$$\lim_{j\to\infty} \lambda_j^{k,1}/\lambda_j = \lambda_j^{k,1}(0)/\lambda_j(0) < 1,$$

where $\lambda_j^*(0)$ are the eigenvalues of $\mathbf{K}_j^k(0)$. It follows that $\left\|\mathbf{K}_j^k\right\| \to 0$ when $j \to \infty$. Thus case (b) is verified.

Note that $\mathbf{K}_j^k(\alpha)$ is determined by parameter α. When $k = 1$, we denote

$$\tilde{\mathbf{S}}_j^1(0) = \hat{\mathbf{S}}$$

and assume that the Jordan decomposition $\hat{\mathbf{S}} = \mathbf{Y}\Lambda\mathbf{Y}^{-1}$ exists. Consider

$$\Delta_j = \mathbf{V}^{-1}(\mathbf{S}_j^1(\alpha) - \mathbf{S}_j^1(0))\mathbf{V}.$$

When $\|\Delta_j\| \leq 2^{-j}C\alpha$, we have the following estimation

$$\left\|\hat{\mathbf{S}}^j - \mathbf{S}_j^1(\alpha)\mathbf{S}_{j-1}^1(\alpha)\cdots\mathbf{S}_1^1(\alpha)\right\|$$
$$= \left\|\mathbf{Y}[\Lambda^j - (\Lambda + \Delta_j)(\Lambda + \Delta_{j-1})\cdots(\Lambda + \Delta_1)]\mathbf{Y}^{-1}\right\|$$
$$\leq C_1\alpha.$$

Let $\lambda \stackrel{\Delta}{=} \lambda_j(0) = \cdots = \lambda_1(0)$; it follows that

$$\lim_{j\to\infty} \lambda_j^1\lambda_{j-1}^1 \cdots \lambda_1^1/\lambda^j = C_2 > 0.$$

So, there is a real number $C_3 > 0$ such that

$$\left\|\mathbf{K}_j^k(\alpha) - \mathbf{K}_j^k(0)\right\| \leq C_3\alpha.$$

Since the limit of sequence $\mathbf{K}_j^1(0) = \mathbf{Y}\mathrm{diag}(1, (\lambda_1^{1,2}(0)/\lambda)^j)\mathbf{Y}^{-1}$ is $\mathbf{K}_\infty^1(0)$, it follows that $\mathbf{K}_j^k(\alpha)$ is continuous near the zero point. Note that $\mathbf{K}_j^1(\alpha) = \mathbf{K}_{j-1}^1(\alpha/2)\tilde{\mathbf{S}}_1^1(\alpha)/\lambda_1(\alpha)$, so we can analyze the continuous property just in the neighborhood of the zero point. Furthermore, by the continuity, we have $\|\mathbf{K}_\infty^1(\alpha)\| \in (1-\varepsilon, 1+\varepsilon)$ with $\varepsilon > 0$, i.e., the largest eigenvalue is non-zero. For

$$\det(\mathbf{K}_j^1) = \det\left(\frac{\mathbf{S}_j^1\mathbf{S}_{j-1}^1\cdots\mathbf{S}_1^1}{\lambda_j\lambda_{j-1}\cdots\lambda_1}\right) = \frac{\lambda_j^{1,2}\lambda_{j-1}^{1,2}\cdots\lambda_1^{1,2}}{\lambda_j\lambda_{j-1}\cdots\lambda_1} \to 0$$

when $j \to \infty$, it is shown that other eigenvalues tend to zero. With a similar procedure, we can prove the case (c) when $k = n - 1$. $\qquad\square$

Lemma A.2: *Let* $\mathbf{L}_j^k = \dfrac{\mathbf{B}_j^k}{\lambda_j} \dfrac{\mathbf{B}_{j-1}^k}{\lambda_{j-1}} \cdots \dfrac{\mathbf{B}_1^k}{\lambda_1}$. *Then* $\mathbf{L}_j^k$ *tend to zero when* $j \to \infty$.

Proof: By direct calculation, one can verify that the eigen-vectors of $\mathbf{B}_j^k$ are

$$\begin{cases} \mathbf{b}_1 = \{0, 0, 1, 0\}, \\ \mathbf{b}_2 = \{-\frac{1}{\omega(1+f_j)}, \omega^{-1}, -\frac{(1+6f_j+4f_j^2)(1+\omega)}{(1-f_j-2f_j^2)\omega}, 1\}, \\ \mathbf{b}_3 = \{0, -\omega^{-1}, 2(1 - \omega^{-1}), 1\}, \\ \mathbf{b}_4 = \{\omega^{-1}, \omega^{-1}, 1 + \omega^{-1}, 1\}. \end{cases}$$

Denote $t_i = \tau_j^{k,i} \cdots \tau_1^{k,i}$ and $\mathbf{B}(j,k) = \mathbf{B}_j^k\mathbf{B}_{j-1}^k \cdots \mathbf{B}_1^k$, where $\tau_j^{k,i}$ ($i = 1, 2, 3, 4$) are defined by equation (8). Note that $\mathbf{b}_i$ ($i = 1, 3, 4$) are independent of f_j, so $\mathbf{B}(j,k)\mathbf{b}_i = t_i\mathbf{b}_i$ ($i = 1, 3, 4$). Let $\tilde{t}_2$ be the forth eigenvalue of $\mathbf{B}(j,k)$. Since

$$\det(\mathbf{B}(j,k)) = t_1 \tilde{t}_2 t_3 t_4$$

and

$$\det(\mathbf{B}(j,k)) = \det(\mathbf{B}_j^k) \cdots \det(\mathbf{B}_j^1) = t_1 t_2 t_3 t_4,$$

$\tilde{t}_2 = t_2$. Thus the eigenvalues of $\mathbf{B}_j^k \mathbf{B}_{j-1}^k \cdots \mathbf{B}_1^k$ are

$$\left\{ \tau_j^{k,1} \cdots \tau_1^{k,1}, \tau_j^{k,2} \cdots \tau_1^{k,2}, \tau_j^{k,3} \cdots \tau_1^{k,3}, \tau_j^{k,4} \cdots \tau_1^{k,4} \right\}.$$

Furthermore, since $\lim_{j \to \infty} \tau_j^{k,i}/\lambda_j \leq 1/2$, the eigenvalues of $\mathbf{L}_j^k$ are

$$\left\{ \frac{\tau_j^{k,1} \cdots \tau_1^{k,1}}{\lambda_j \lambda_{j-1} \cdots \lambda_1}, \frac{\tau_j^{k,2} \cdots \tau_1^{k,2}}{\lambda_j \lambda_{j-1} \cdots \lambda_1}, \frac{\tau_j^{k,3} \cdots \tau_1^{k,3}}{\lambda_j \lambda_{j-1} \cdots \lambda_1}, \frac{\tau_j^{k,4} \cdots \tau_1^{k,4}}{\lambda_j \lambda_{j-1} \cdots \lambda_1} \right\},$$

which tend to 0. $\qquad\square$

MESHLESS METHOD FOR NUMERICAL SOLUTION OF PDE USING HERMITIAN INTERPOLATION WITH RADIAL BASIS

Zongmin Wu

Shanghai Key Lab. for Contemporary Applied Mathematics
Department of Mathematics, Fudan University
Shanghai, China
E-mail: zmwu@fudan.edu.cn

Jianping Liu

Department of Mathematics
East China University of Science and Technology
Shanghai, China
E-mail: jpliu@yahoo.com

In CAGD, many curves and surfaces, which we want to design, are the solutions of some partial differential equations. The corresponding discrete equations often appear as Hermite-Birkhoff interpolations. Such equations are very difficult to solve in the function space of piecewise polynomials on mesh, since the solutions of the partial differential equations are very smooth even in C^∞. This chapter discusses a meshless method for numerical solution of PDE by using the Hermite-Birkhoff interpolation with radial basis, which is generalized from the thin plate spline. This method is a direct discretion of collocation type for ordinary and partial differential equations, with possibility of generalization to integral equations or even equations with time delays. If we adopt the results in the discussion of radial basis and the Hermite-Birkhoff interpolation, the solvability of the discrete system of equations can be proven on very weak assumptions. The order of the approximation of the scheme depends on the smoothness of the solution and the order of the differential equation.

1. Introduction

Most CAGD people use piecewise polynomials as their function space. Such function space possesses a lot of advantages, but it requires a partition or triangulation of the domain. The pre-process of triangulation is not very convenient for multivariate scattered data. In particular, the construction of the piecewise polynomial on a triangulation with high continuity is very difficult. In computer-aided design, many curves and surfaces, which we want to design, are the solutions of some partial differential equations. A typical example is the animation of fabric simulation. The discrete equation of such a problem often appears to be a Hermite-Birkhoff interpolation, so that we want to interpolate some of the functional data of the interpolated function. In this chapter we discuss a meshless method for solving partial differential equations (PDE) numerically by using the Hermite-Birkhoff interpolation with radial basis. Using standard multi-index notation, a boundary value problem (BVP) for a linear partial differential equation (PDE) on a domain $\Omega \subset I\!\!R^d$ can be written as

$$
\begin{aligned}
p(D)u(x) &= g(x), \quad x \in \Omega, \\
q(D)u(x) &= h(x), \quad x \in \partial\Omega,
\end{aligned}
\tag{1}
$$

where $D = (\frac{\partial}{\partial x_1}, \ldots, \frac{\partial}{\partial x_d})$ is the gradient operator. Here, p and q are polynomials in d variables with real function (in $C^l(R^d)$)–valued coefficients. Generalizations to linear systems of partial differential equations are possible, and we have not made any assumption about the type of differential equations (elliptical, etc.).

From another point of view, we can accept that $p(D)$ and $q(D)$ are differential operators applied to some function space defined on the domain Ω. We want to determine the solution $u(x)$ from the image $g(x), h(x)$ of the map $p(D), q(D)$.

Using the Riesz representation of the linear functional, the linear partial differential equation (operator) can be expressed in an integral form as

$$
\begin{aligned}
\int_\Omega P(x,y)u(y)dy &= g(x), \quad x \in \Omega, \\
\int_\Omega Q(x,y)u(y)dy &= h(x), \quad x \in \partial\Omega,
\end{aligned}
\tag{2}
$$

where $P(x,y)$ and $Q(x,y)$ are generalized functions in the dual space of $u(y)$ for fixed x. Here we use the low-case letter to denote the differential operator and the capital letter for its Riesz representation.

The numerical method for solving PDE is based on the numerical method to approximate the function. Recently a powerful method, which is called *radial basis approximation*, has become a topic in the study of multivariate scattered data approximation. The radial basis interpolation solves the interpolation problem in the function space generated by the radial basis $\{\phi(\|x - x_j\|)\}$, where $\phi : \mathbb{R}_+ \to \mathbb{R}$ is a univariate function. Essentially, the radial basis method uses a univariate function to solve a multivariate problem. For more details we recommend the papers[8,10,15] by Micchelli, Powell, Wu, Schaback and others. We want to adopt the interpolation method showed in the paper[14] by the first author, and develop it to solve the partial differential equation.

To discrete the equation (1), we assume that the function values $g(x_j)$ and $h(x_k)$ are known or can be measured at some points $\{x_j\}_{j=1}^n \in \Omega$ and $\{x_k\}_{k=n+1}^{n+m} \in \partial\Omega$. Then we get a system of discrete equations

$$\begin{aligned}
p(D)u(x_j) &= g(x_j), & x_j &\in \{x_j\}_{j=1}^n \subset \Omega; \\
q(D)u(x_k) &= h(x_k), & x_k &\in \{x_k\}_{n+9}^{n+m} \subset \partial\Omega.
\end{aligned} \tag{3}$$

It is clear that the values $g(x_j), h(x_k)$ are linear functional data of the function $u(x)$, if the differential operators $p(D)$ and $q(D)$ are linear.

Now the PDE problem (1) is turned to a Hermite-Birkhoff interpolation problem (3), and we can use the method presented in the paper[14] by the first author to get a solution of (3).

We would like to list at first some advantages of the scheme:

1. It is meshless: no partition (triangulation) of the domain as required in the finite elements method.

2. It is spatial dimension independent, compared with the difficulty of construction in the finite elements method for very high dimensional problems with high continuity.

3. This algorithm can be used for multiple boundary conditions, multiphases problems, integral equations and equations with time delays.

4. The solution can be represented by an explicit global function, which can be used for further analysis (e.g., wind tunnel test).

Then two problems must be discussed. The first is the solvability of the discrete equation. This problem will be discussed in Section 3 and the results are summarized here as a theorem.

Theorem 1: If the original equation (1) is uniquely solvable and well posed for any right-hand terms g and h, then the discrete equation or the radial basis interpolation of (3) is uniquely solvable too.

The second problem is the order of the approximation. In other words, we need to estimate the error of the discrete solution as an approximation to the real solution of the original equation. This will be discussed in Section 4 and we will get the following theorem.

Theorem 2: If the operators $p(D), q(D)$ map the function e^{ixw} to a C^L-continuous function, then the error of the solution of the discrete equation to the real solution of the original equation is of order $\mathcal{O}(h^{l+L})$, where h is the density of $\{x_j\}$ and l, L will be defined in the next section.

2. Preliminary

Now we discuss the problem in detail. For fixed x, $p(D)u(x) = g(x)$ and $q(D)u(x) = h(x)$ are linear functionals of the function u. Thus with the Riesz representation of the linear functional, the original equation (1) can be expressed in an integral form of (2), where $P(x,y), Q(x,y)$ are some generalized functions (delta distribution) for fixed x.

Example 3: Here is an example of the functions P, Q:

$$
\begin{aligned}
P(x,y) &= \sum c_\alpha(x) \frac{\partial^{|\alpha|} \delta(x - y - \bar{c}_\alpha)}{\partial y^\alpha} + p_1(x,y), \\
Q(x,y) &= \sum d_\alpha(x) \frac{\partial^{|\alpha|} \delta(x - y - \bar{d}_\alpha)}{\partial y^\alpha} + q_1(x,y),
\end{aligned}
\tag{4}
$$

which shows a partial differential and integral mixed equation with time delay. What we require is only the linearity of the operator.

To show our assertion in detail, we give at first some definitions.

Definition 4:

- The equation operator $\{p, q\}$ is of order l, if the generalized functions $P(x,y), Q(x,y)$ for every fixed x are in the dual space of $C^l(\Omega)$.
- We say that the equation operator $\{p, q\}$ is continuous of order L, if the operator maps the C^∞ continuous function to a C^L-function, i.e., $\{p, q\}(C^\infty) \subset (C^L(\Omega), C^L(\partial\Omega))$. This means that $P(x,y), Q(x,y)$ are C^L continuous functions with respect to the variable x.
- If the equation operator is of order l, then the function space S_l^p is defined by C^l continuous functions, whose S_l^p norm (the summation of p-norms of all derivatives, whose order does not exceeded l, $\|u\| = \sum_{|\alpha| \leq l} \|\frac{\partial^\alpha u}{\partial x^\alpha}\|_p$) is bounded.

In this chapter, we only use the space S_l^∞, so the notation is simplified to S_l. Then the equation operator maps a C^l function to a continuous function, and maps a C^∞ function to a C^L function:

$$\{p, q\}(S_l) \to C^0(\Omega) \times C^0(\partial\Omega),$$

$$\{p, q\}(S_l \cap C^\infty) \to C^L(\Omega) \times C^L(\partial\Omega).$$

Now we discrete the original equation as follows.

Take some pairwise distinct points $\{x_j\}_{j=1}^n \in \Omega$ and some pairwise distinct points $\{x_k\}_{k=n+1}^{n+m} \in \partial\Omega$.

Let $h = \max_{x\in\Omega, y\in\partial\Omega}\{\min_j \|x - x_j\|, \min_k \|y - x_k\|\}$ be the density of the points. Then

p applied to u and evaluated at x_j should be equal to $g(x_j)$;

q applied to u and evaluated at x_k should be equal to $h(x_k)$.

These can be represented as the following discrete equations:

$$\int_\Omega P(x_j, y)u(y)dy = L_j u = g(x_j), \qquad j = 1, \dots, n;$$

$$\int_\Omega Q(x_k, y)u(y)dy = L_k u = h(x_k), \qquad k = n+1, \dots, n+m, \tag{5}$$

where L_j are the corresponding linear functionals.

In order to solve the discrete equation, we will introduce radial basis interpolation for the Hermite-Birkhoff data (see the reference[14] for details).

The radial basis interpolation began with a univariate function $\phi : \mathbb{R}_+ \to \mathbb{R}$ and the radial function is defined to be $\Phi(x) = \phi(\|x\|)$. A function space is constructed by basis functions $\{L_{jy}^* \Phi(x - y) : j = 1, \dots, n+m\}$, where L_{jy}^* are the dual linear functionals of L_{jy} with respect to the variable y, if the functional $L_{jx}L_{ky}^*$ can be applied to the radial function $\Phi(x - y)$. The first author[14] has showed that the functions $\{L_{jy}^* \Phi(x - y) : j = 1, \dots, n+m\}$ are linearly independent if the linear functionals L_j are linearly independent and if the function Φ is positive definite. Now the method for solving PDE numerically by solving the linear system of (3) is a standard collocation method with the basis functions $\{L_{jy}^* \Phi(x - y) : j = 1, \dots, n+m)$ at the collocation points $y = x_j$ for the equation and $y = x_k$ for the boundary condition.

From the reference,[14] the solution of the discrete equation with radial basis interpolation can be written as a linear combination of the data $g(x_j), h(x_k)$:

$$u^*(x) = \sum_j \lambda_j L_j \Phi(x - x_j) + \sum_k \mu_k L_k \Phi(x - x_k),$$

where λ and μ satisfy the following linear system of equations:

$$\begin{pmatrix} A_{11} & A_{12} \\ A_{21} & A_{22} \end{pmatrix} \begin{pmatrix} \lambda_j \\ \mu_k \end{pmatrix} = \begin{pmatrix} g(x_j) \\ h(x_k) \end{pmatrix},$$

where

$$A_{11} = (\int \int P(x_{j1}, s) P^*(x_{j2}, t) \Phi(s - t) ds dt),$$

$$A_{12} = (\int \int P(x_{j1}, s) Q^*(x_{k2}, t) \Phi(s - t) ds dt),$$

$$A_{21} = (\int \int Q(x_{k1}, s) P^*(x_{j2}, t) \Phi(s - t) ds dt),$$

$$A_{22} = (\int \int Q(x_{k1}, s) Q^*(x_{k2}, t) \Phi(s - t) ds dt).$$

Then we get the solution

$$u^*(x) = (\cdots, P^*(D)\Phi(x - x_j), \cdots, Q^*(D)\Phi(x - x_k), \cdots) A^{-1} \begin{pmatrix} \vdots \\ g(x_j) \\ \vdots \\ h(x_k) \\ \vdots \end{pmatrix}. \tag{6}$$

We only need to solve one linear system of equations to get the solution. It is trivial to verify that the function $u^*(x)$ satisfies the discrete equation (5), if the matrix A is non-singular.

3. Solvability of the Discrete Equation

The scheme (6) for solving partial differential equations numerically, which we showed above, is now a linear system of equations. An important question is whether the linear system is uniquely solvable or whether the above coefficient matrix A is non-singular.

In order to show the non-singularity of the matrix A, we give a lemma first.

Lemma 5: *If the original equation is uniquely solvable for any given right-hand term ($g(x) \in C(\Omega)$, $h(x) \in C(\partial\Omega)$), then there exist unique general-*

ized functions $\Lambda(x,y)$ *and* $\Gamma(x,y)$ *such that the following equation holds:*

$$\int_\Omega (\int_\Omega \Lambda(x,y)P(y,s)e^{its}ds)dy + \int_{\partial\Omega}(\int_\Omega \Gamma(x,y)Q(y,s)e^{its}ds)dy = e^{itx}.$$

$$(7)$$

Proof: In fact, we can denote the inverse operator of $\{p,q\}$ by $\{\Lambda,\Gamma\}$ in the sense that

$$u(x) = \Lambda g + \Gamma h = \int_\Omega \Lambda(x,y)g(y)dy + \int_{\partial\Omega}\Gamma(x,y)h(y)dy$$

with the Riesz representation for the inverse operator, if the inverse operator exists. The equality (7) is thus derived from the existence of the inverse operator. $\square$

Based on the result of the above lemma, we can prove our first main theorem.

Theorem 6: If the original equation is uniquely solvable for any right-hand term $(g(x) \in C(\Omega), h(x) \in C(\partial\Omega))$, then the discrete equation is uniquely solvable too.

Proof: We only need to prove that the linear functionals L_j, $j = 1,\ldots,n+m$ are linearly independent or equivalently the generalized functions $\{P(x_j,s)\}, \{Q(x_k,s)\}$ are linearly independent, if the function Φ is a properly chosen positive definite radial function. Assume that the functions $\{P(x_j,s)\}, \{Q(x_k,s)\}$ are not linearly independent; then there exist non-trivial c_j, c_k, such that

$$\sum c_j P(x_j,s) + \sum c_k Q(x_k,s) = 0.$$

Thus

$$(\Lambda(x,y) + \sum c_j\delta(x_j,y), \Gamma(x,y) + \sum c_k\delta(x_k,y))$$

is another representation of the inverse operator, which contradicts Lemma 5. $\square$

4. The Order of the Approximation

The unique solvability of the discrete equation has already been showed above. Now we are interested if one can get a good approximation to the real solution via our scheme. From the reference,[15] we know that the solution of the radial basis interpolation minimizes the following Kriging-norm

$$\int \hat{\Phi}(w) I^2(w, x) dw, \tag{8}$$

where

$$I(w, x) := \int \left(\sum_j \lambda_j(x) P(x_j, s) + \sum_k \mu_k(x) Q(x_k, s) \right) e^{iws} ds - e^{iwx}. \tag{9}$$

Using Schwarz's inequality, the L_2 norm of the error $u^*(x) - u(x)$ is bounded by its Kriging-norm

$$\|u^* - u\|^2 = \| \int \hat{u}(w) I(w, x) dw \|^2$$

$$\leq \left(\int \frac{\hat{u}^2(w)}{\hat{\Phi}(w)} dw \right) \left(\int \hat{\Phi}(w) I^2(w, x) dw \right).$$

$\left(\int \frac{\hat{u}^2(w)}{\hat{\Phi}(w)} dw \right)$ is bounded, if the integral exists or the radial function is selected properly so that the function $u(x)$ is in the native space of the radial function Φ. So we only need to estimate the Kriging norm. If we choose Φ so that

$$\hat{\Phi}(w) \leq C(1 + \|w\|)^{-K}$$

with $K \geq 2l + d$, then we only need to estimate the minimal value of

$$\int (1 + \|w\|)^{-K} I^2(w, x) dw.$$

For a given yet fixed w, assume that $a(x), b(x)$ are the images of e^{ixw}:

$$a(x) = \int P(x, s) e^{isw} ds, \quad b(x) = \int Q(x, s) e^{isw} ds. \tag{10}$$

We approximate the functions $a(x), b(x)$ by $a^*(x), b^*(x)$ in the form

$$a^*(x) = \sum c_j(x) a(x_j), \quad b^*(x) = \sum d_j(x) b(x_j); \tag{11}$$

the existence of such approximation and the order of the approximation will be given in Theorem 8. Let

$$\lambda_j(x) = \int \Lambda(x, s) c_j(s) ds, \quad \mu_j(x) = \int \Gamma(x, s) d_j(s) ds.$$

Then

$$\{p, q\}(e^{ixw}) = (a, b),$$

$$\{p,q\}(\sum \lambda_j(x) \int P(x_j,s)e^{isw}ds + \sum \mu_k(x) \int Q(x_k,s)e^{isw}ds) = (a^*,b^*).$$

From this the following diagram is derived:

$$
\begin{array}{ccc}
e^{ixw} & \xrightarrow{\ \{P,Q\}\ } & (a,b) \\
\updownarrow \text{error} & & \updownarrow \text{approximation} \\
\cdot & \xleftarrow{\ \{P,Q\}^{-1}\ } & (a^*,b^*)
\end{array}
\qquad (12)
$$

The image of e^{ixw} is the function (a,b), the approximation of (a,b) is (a^*,b^*), and (a^*,b^*) is the image of the function which is denoted by a dot. The error, which we want to estimate, is $I(x,w) = \cdot - e^{ixw}$. The equation operator maps the error $I(x,w)$ to the error of the approximation (a^*,b^*) to the function (a,b). Thus we only need to prove that the inverse operator is bounded and to estimate the order of the approximation of (a^*,b^*) to the function (a,b).

We summarize the above discussion about the boundness of the inverse operator as the following theorem.

Theorem 7: The inverse operator $\{p,q\}^{-1} = \{\Lambda,\Gamma\}$ is bounded for the function in the function space $\{p,q\}(S_l \cap C^{l+1})$, if the equation is uniquely solvable and well posed for any right-hand term in $C(\Omega)$.

Proof: To show the boundness of the inverse operator, we prove that the operator itself is bounded, i.e., $\|\{p,q\}u\| > c\|u\|$ for $\|u\|_{S^l} = 1$ and the $(l+1)$-th derivative of the function is bounded. If the assumption is invalid, then there exists a u_n that $\|\{p,q\}u_n\| \to 0$, where $\|u_n\|_{S^l} = 1$ and $|u_n^{(l+1)}| < c$. This function series $\{u_n\}$ is uniformly continuous with respect to the S^l norm. Therefore, by the Arzelà-Ascoli theorem, there exists a function u such that a subseries of u_n (without loss of generality we still denote it u_n) is uniformly convergent to u in the S^l norm and $\|\{p,q\}u\| = 0$. However, from the unique solvability of the equation, we know that $u \neq 0$ since $\|u\|_{S^l} = 1$. Thus, we get a contradiction to the assertion of the unique solvability. $\square$

It is not a trivial problem to construct the approximation of (a^*,b^*) to (a,b) in the formula (11), because we should keep the inverse image of the approximation to be uniformly continuous and bounded in C^{l+1}.

We use the Shepard interpolation to interpolate the function e^{ixw}:

$$E(x) = \frac{\sum_{j=1}^{n+m}(\sum_{|\alpha|\leq l+L} \frac{(iw)^\alpha e^{ix_jw}}{\alpha!}(x-x_j)^\alpha)\prod_{k\neq j}\|x-x_k\|^{l+L+d+2}}{\sum_{j=1}^{n+m}\prod_{k\neq j}\|x-x_k\|^{l+L+d+2}},$$

$$(13)$$

where d is the space dimension and $(\sum_{|\alpha|\leq l+L}\frac{(iw)^\alpha}{\alpha!}(x-x_j)^\alpha)$ is the Taylor expansion of e^{ixw} at x_j.

This formula interpolates the data $(e^{ixw})^{(\alpha)}|_{x=x_j}$ for $j = 1,\ldots,n+m$, where $|\alpha| \leq l + L$. According to the paper[3] by Gordon and Wixson, if the domain Ω satisfies the regularity condition (e.g., convex) and the knots $\{x_j\}$ are distributed quasi-uniformly so that the number of the points $\{x_j\}\cap O(x,h)$ for $x \in \Omega$ is uniformly bounded, then the error can be estimated to be

$$\|e^{ixw} - E(x)\|_\infty \leq C\|w\|^{l+L}h^{l+L+1} \tag{14}$$

and furthermore

$$\|(e^{ixw} - E(x))^{(\alpha)}\|_\infty \leq C\|w\|^{l+L+|\alpha|}h^{l+L+1-|\alpha|}. \tag{15}$$

Thus the derivatives $E^{(\alpha)}(x)$ are bounded for $|\alpha| \leq l + L + 1$.

The image of the function $E(x)$ can be expressed in the form (11), since $E(x)$ is an interpolation. For example, if we define

$$a_j^*(x) = p(D)\frac{(\sum_{|\alpha|\leq l+L}\frac{(iw)^\alpha}{\alpha!}(x-x_j)^\alpha)\prod_{k\neq j}\|x-x_k\|^{l+L+d+2}}{\sum_{j=1}^{n+m}\prod_{k\neq j}\|x-x_k\|^{l+L+d+2}},$$

$$b_j^*(x) = q(D)\frac{(\sum_{|\alpha|\leq l+L}\frac{(iw)^\alpha}{\alpha!}(x-x_j)^\alpha)\prod_{k\neq j}\|x-x_k\|^{l+L+d+2}}{\sum_{j=1}^{n+m}\prod_{k\neq j}\|x-x_k\|^{l+L+d+2}},$$

then the functions satisfy the cardinal condition of

$$a_j^*(x_k) = \delta_{jk}a(x_j), \quad k = 1,\ldots,n,$$
$$b_j^*(x_k) = \delta_{jk}b(x_j), \quad k = n+1,\ldots,n+m$$

and thus $\{p(D)E(x), q(D)E(x)\}$ can be written in the form (11). We summarize the discussion as a theorem.

Theorem 8: If the equation operator is continuous of order L, the domain Ω and the distribution of the knots $\{x_j\}$ satisfy regular conditions as above, then we can get an approximation $\{a^*, b^*\}$ of $\{a, b\}$ such that the inverse image of $\{a^*, b^*\}$ are uniformly bounded in the norm S^{l+1}, and

$$|\{a^*, b^*\} - \{a, b\}| \leq \mathcal{O}(1 + \|w\|)^{l+L}h^{L+1}.$$

Our second main theorem can then be stated as follows.

Theorem 9: The error of the solution of the discrete equation to the real solution of the original equation depends on the order l and the order L of the continuity of the equation operator $\{p, q\}$. More clearly, if $u \in S^{K+l+2-d}$ ($|\hat{u}(w)| \leq C(1 + \|w\|)^{-(K+l+2)}$), then we can choose a positive definite function $\Phi \in S^{2(K+l+1)}$ ($|\hat{\Phi}(w)| \sim C(1 + \|w\|)^{-2(K+l+1)-d-\epsilon}$) such that $\|u - u^*\| \leq \mathcal{O}(h)^{K+l+1}$ for any $K \leq L$.

In particular, if we choose $K = d - 2$, then the following corollary is obtained.

Corollary 10: *If the order of the equation operator is l and the order L of the continuity of the equation operator is $\geq d - 2$, then $\|u - u^*\| \leq \mathcal{O}(h)^{d+l-1}$.*

5. Conclusion

The results of this chapter are obtained mainly from a theoretical consideration of the meshless method to solve PDE numerically by using the Hermite-Birkhoff interpolation. The error estimates show that for different problems we can find some suitable kernel function Φ to yield a good approximation order. Numerical tests are presented elsewhere, e.g., in the paper[4] by Hon and the author.

Acknowledgments

This work was supported by the National Science Foundation of China (project nos. 19971017 and 10125102). The first author would like to thank Professors Dongming Wang and Falai Chen from the University of Science and Technology of China, who invited him to the Seminar on Geometric Computation. Thanks to Professor Wang are also for his help on improving the English representation of this chapter. The authors would like to thank the referees, too, for their helpful comments and suggestions.

References

1. T. Belytschko, Y. Krongauz, D. Organ, M. Fleming, and P. Krysl, Meshless methods: An overview and recent developments. *Computer Methods in Applied Mechanics and Engineering* **139**: 3–47 (1996).
2. C. Franke and R. Schaback, Convergence order estimates of meshless collocation methods using radial basis functions. *Advances in Computational Mathematics* **8**: 381–399 (1998).

3. W. J. Gordon and J. A. Wixson, Shepard method of metric interpolation to bivariate and multivariate data. *Math. Comp.* **32**: 253–264 (1978).

4. Y. C. Hon and Z. Wu, A quasi-interpolation method for solving stiff ordinary differential equations. *International Journal for Numerical Methods in Engineering* **48**: 1187–1197 (2000).

5. E. J. Kansa, Multiquadrics — A scattered data approximation scheme with applications to computational fluid dynamics II. Solutions to parabolic, hyperbolic and elliptic partial differential equations. *CMA* **19**: 147–161 (1990).

6. W. A. Light, Some aspects of radial basis function approximation. *Approximation Theory, Spline Functions and Applications* (S. P. Singh, ed.), pp. 163–190. NATO Adv. Sci. Inst. Ser. C Math. Phys. Sci. 356, Kluwer Acad. Publ., Dordrecht (1992).

7. W. A. Madych and S. A. Nelson, Error bounds for multiquadric interpolation. *Approximation Theory VI*, vol. 2 (C. K. Chiu, L. L. Schumaker, and J. D. Ward, eds.), pp. 413–416. Academic Press, Boston, MA (1989).

8. C. A. Micchelli, Interpolation of scattered data: Distance matrix and conditionally positive definite functions. *Constructive Approximation* **2**: 11–22 (1986).

9. F. Oberhettinger, *Tables of Fourier Transforms and Fourier Transforms of Distributions.* Springer-Verlag, Berlin (1990).

10. M. J. D. Powell, Radial basis functions for multivariable interpolation: A review. *Numerical Analysis* (D. F. Griffiths and G. A. Watson, eds.), pp. 223–241. Longman Scientific & Technical, Harlow (1987).

11. I. J. Schoenberg, Metric space and completely monotone functions. *Ann. Math.* **39**: 811–841 (1938).

12. E. M. Stein and G. Weiss, *Introduction to Fourier Analysis on Euclidean Spaces*, Princeton University Press, Princeton (1971).

13. Z. Wu, *Die Kriging Methode zur Loesung mehrdimensionaler Interpolationsprobleme.* Ph. D. dissertation, Universität Göttingen, Göttingen (1986).

14. Z. Wu, Hermite-Birkhoff interpolation of scattered data by radial basis function. *Approx. Theory & Its Appl.* **8**: 1–10 (1992).

15. Z. Wu and R. Schaback, Local error estimates for radial basis function interpolation of scattered data. *IMA Journal of Numerical Analysis* **13**: 13–27 (1993).

16. Z. Wu, Multivariate compactly supported positive definite radial functions. *Advances in Computational Mathematics* **4**: 283–292 (1995).

CHAPTER 9

CLIFFORD ALGEBRAS IN GEOMETRIC COMPUTATION

Hongbo Li

Academy of Mathematics and System Sciences
Chinese Academy of Sciences
Beijing 100080, China
E-mail: hli@mmrc.iss.ac.cn

Clifford algebra is an important invariant algebra in geometric computing. In this chapter, we first introduce the background and the current status of Clifford algebra, then use five examples to illustrate how Clifford algebras are applied in geometric computation, and provide detailed explanations of the computation techniques. For a systematic study of the general techniques, we encourage further reading into the literature, for which a list is also provided.

1. Background

The following is a modern definition of Clifford algebra:[8]

Let $\mathcal{V}^n$ be an n-dimensional vector space over a field $\mathcal{K}$ whose characteristic $\neq 2$. Let Q be a quadratic form over $\mathcal{K}$ and defined in $\mathcal{V}^n$, i.e., $Q(\lambda\mathbf{x}) = \lambda^2 Q(\mathbf{x})$ for any $\lambda \in \mathcal{K}$ and $\mathbf{x} \in \mathcal{V}^n$. The *Clifford algebra* $\mathcal{CL}(\mathcal{V}^n, Q)$ generated by $\mathcal{V}^n$ and Q is the quotient of the tensor algebra generated by $\mathcal{V}^n$ modulo the two-sided ideal $I(Q)$ generated by elements of the form $x \otimes x - Q(x)$, where $x \in \mathcal{V}^n$:

$$\mathcal{CL}(\mathcal{V}^n, Q) = \frac{\bigotimes(\mathcal{V}^n)}{\{x \otimes x - Q(x), \ \forall x \in \mathcal{V}^n\}}.$$

The quotient of the tensor product is called the Clifford multiplication, or geometric product, and denoted by juxtaposition of elements. The geometric product is multilinear and associative, as a heritage of the tensor product. It is no longer commutative.

While the tensor product is clear enough, the reason why it should

221

be modulo the ideal $I(Q)$ is very confusing to most beginners of Clifford algebra. The following is a naive explanation.

In $\mathcal{R}^n$, a directed angle can be represented by two unit vectors $\mathbf{a}, \mathbf{b}$ as $\mathbf{ab}$: from $\mathbf{a}$ to $\mathbf{b}$. The angle has a supporting plane, an orientation and a scale of angle. It is allowed that the supporting plane can move anywhere in the space by translation, and the angle can move and rotate anywhere in the plane. Two such directed angles can be added up *only* through their geometric product, in which $\mathbf{bb}$ is replaced by 1:

$$(\mathbf{ab})(\mathbf{bc}) = \mathbf{a(bb)c} = \mathbf{ac}.$$

So this product realizes the summation of spatial angles, or in other words, the composition of rotations. From this explanation, there is no doubt that Clifford algebra will play an important role in problems related to spatial rotations.

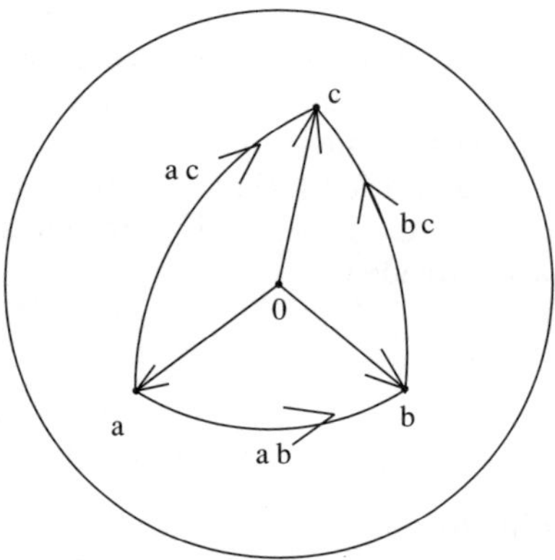

Fig. 1.   Directed angles

Clifford algebra has a history of about 150 years. It was first proposed in the form of "hypercomplex numbers", or high-dimensional numbers.

The algebraization of geometry started with Descartes' coordinates for analytic geometry. This is one of the biggest achievements in human history, in that it is a key step from qualitative description to quantitative analysis. On the other hand, it is the most preliminary algebraization of geometry. The great mathematician Leibniz once dreamed of having a geometric calculus dealing directly with geometric objects rather than with sequences of numbers. In the 2D case this can be realized by using complex numbers. How about higher dimensions?

In the 1840s, Grassmann proposed his extension theory of numbers, or "extended magnitudes", which were called "Grassmann numbers" for many years and are called vectors and multivectors nowadays. Grassmann is the first person who proposed the concept "n-dimensional vector space". His main contribution is the so-called outer (or exterior) product of vectors. This product is associative and graded anti-commutative, and can be understood as follows.

In $\mathcal{V}^n$, every vector represents a 1-dimensional direction. How about 2-dimensional directions? Such a direction should be generated by two vectors, say $\mathbf{a}, \mathbf{b}$, and if we reverse their order, the direction should be reversed. A 2D direction thus consists of a 2D vector space and an orientation of the 2D space. Such a direction can be represented by the product $\mathbf{a} \wedge \mathbf{b}$ of vectors $\mathbf{a}, \mathbf{b}$ by assuming that $\mathbf{b} \wedge \mathbf{a} = -\mathbf{a} \wedge \mathbf{b}$. If $\mathbf{a}, \mathbf{b}$ are collinear, then they do not generate a 2D direction, so their product $\mathbf{a} \wedge \mathbf{b} = 0$. Similarly, a 3D direction can be represented by the product $\mathbf{a} \wedge \mathbf{b} \wedge \mathbf{c}$ of three vectors $\mathbf{a}, \mathbf{b}, \mathbf{c}$ spanning the 3D space, by assuming that the product is associative. The outer product of i vectors is called an i-*blade*, and i is the *grade* of the element. All i-blades generate a vector space, called the i-*vector space*. The *Grassmann space* $\mathcal{G}(\mathcal{V}^n)$ is the vector space generated by all scalars in $\mathcal{K}$, all vectors of $\mathcal{V}^n$ and all the outer products. An i-vector for $i > n$ must be zero. So the Grassmann space is graded, and is the direct sum of i-vector spaces, where i ranges from 0 to n. The Grassmann space equipped with the outer product is called the *Grassmann algebra*.

Let $\mathbf{e}_1, \dots, \mathbf{e}_n$ be a basis of $\mathcal{V}^n$. They induce the following basis in the i-vector spaces for $0 \leq i \leq n$:

$$
\begin{aligned}
&i = 0: &&1; \\
&i = 1: &&\mathbf{e}_1, \dots, \mathbf{e}_n; \\
&i = 2: &&\mathbf{e}_{12} = \mathbf{e}_1\mathbf{e}_2, \dots, \mathbf{e}_{1n} = \mathbf{e}_1\mathbf{e}_n, \mathbf{e}_{23} = \mathbf{e}_2\mathbf{e}_3, \dots, \mathbf{e}_{(n-1)n} = \mathbf{e}_{n-1}\mathbf{e}_n; \\
&\ \ \vdots && \quad \ddots \\
&i = n: &&\mathbf{e}_{12\dots n} = \mathbf{e}_1\mathbf{e}_2 \cdots \mathbf{e}_n.
\end{aligned}
\tag{1}
$$

(1) is a basis of the whole Grassmann space. The multiplication table of the basis in Grassmann algebra is as follows:

- The product of 1 with any element X in (1) is X.
- The product of any non-unit element in (1) with itself is zero.
- If two elements from rows r_1, r_2, respectively, have common indices in their subscripts, then their product is zero, else their product is

the element in the row $r_1 + r_2$, whose index is a permutation of the union of the indices of the two elements, multiplied by the sign of the permutation.

Taken as numbers, the blades behave quite different from complex numbers. As real vector spaces, the set of complex numbers is isomorphic to the Grassmann algebra generated by a single vector $\mathbf{e}$. However, we have $\mathbf{e}^2 = -1$ versus $\mathbf{e}^2 = 0$. So as algebras they are different. This puzzled Grassmann himself greatly.

In the last days of Grassmann's life, he wrote down the following formula

$$\mathbf{ab} = \mathbf{a} \cdot \mathbf{b} + \mathbf{a} \wedge \mathbf{b},$$

where the dot is the inner product of the two vectors, and the juxtaposition is a new product. However, since Grassmann used $\mathbf{a} \wedge \mathbf{b}$ to represent the line passing through points $\mathbf{a}, \mathbf{b}$, he failed to identify the new product with that of the complex numbers.

The extension of complex numbers to higher dimensions was first achieved by Hamilton. His quaternions are 4D numbers. It took him 10 years to realize that there is no 3D numbers system at all. Hamilton's quaternions are defined as follows: Let $\mathbf{i}, \mathbf{j}, \mathbf{k}$ be three transcendental elements over the reals such that

$$\begin{aligned}
\mathbf{i}^2 = \mathbf{j}^2 &= \mathbf{k}^2 = -1, \\
\mathbf{ij} &= -\mathbf{ji} = \mathbf{k}, \\
\mathbf{jk} &= -\mathbf{kj} = \mathbf{i}, \\
\mathbf{ki} &= -\mathbf{ik} = \mathbf{j}.
\end{aligned} \tag{2}$$

Then $1, \mathbf{i}, \mathbf{j}, \mathbf{k}$ generate a real vector space equipped with a product defined by the multiplication table. Any element in the vector space is called a *quaternion*. Compared with the real and the complex numbers, the product of two quaternions is not commutative.

By a numbers system we mean an algebra with divisibility except for the zero element. After Hamilton's quaternions, great enthusiasm was inspired to look for numbers systems of higher dimensions, or *hypercomplex numbers*. Cayley came out with octonions which are 8D numbers, in which the associativity is lost, besides the loss of the commutativity. Then Frobenius proved that there are only four algebras having divisibility: the reals, complex numbers, quaternions and octonions. This is a very discouraging result.

In the 1870s, Clifford saved people's efforts by his *geometric algebra*, a genius hypercomplex numbers structure in the Grassmann space. His revision of Grassmann's multiplication table of (1) by (2) is pretty simple:

- The product of 1 with any X in (1) is X.
- The product of any element in the r-th row with itself is $(-1)^{\frac{r(r+1)}{2}}$.
- If two elements A_{r_1}, A_{r_2} from rows r_1, r_2, respectively, have s common indices in their subscripts, then their product is the element in the $(r_1 + r_2 - 2s)$-th row, whose subscript is the symmetric difference of the indices of the two elements, multiplied by a sign ϵ. If the two elements have no common indices, their product is the same as in the Grassmann algebra. The sign ϵ is computed as follows: Let $\sigma_s, \breve{\sigma}_s^i$ be a partition of the indices of A_{r_i} for $i = 1, 2$, where σ_s is the common indices in ascending order. Then

$$\epsilon = (-1)^{\frac{s(s+1)}{2}} \operatorname{sign}(\breve{\sigma}_s^1, \sigma_s) \operatorname{sign}(\sigma_s, \breve{\sigma}_s^2) \operatorname{sign}(\breve{\sigma}_s^1, \breve{\sigma}_s^2).$$

Clifford named his algebra "geometric algebra", with the implication that it is for high-dimensional geometric computation. There are three major forms of Clifford algebra nowadays.

1. **Hypercomplex numbers:** The original form. The complex analysis was extended to Clifford analysis in the 1970s in the hypercomplex numbers form.

2. **Matrices:** This form has its origin in Pauli's matrices, which are later found to be related to *spinors*, a fundamental physical quantity. The modern definition of spinors are that they are minimal left or right ideals of a Clifford algebra.

   Real and complex Clifford algebras are isomorphic to some matrix algebras, known as the periodicity theorem:

   Let $\mathcal{R}^{p,q}$ be the $(p+q)$-dimensional vector space equipped with the inner product matrix $\operatorname{diag}(1, \dots, 1, -1, \dots, -1)$, in which the numbers of 1 and -1 are p, q respectively. Let $M(\mathcal{R}), M(\mathcal{C}), M(\mathcal{H})$ be respectively the matrix algebras with real, complex and quaternion components of certain dimension. Let $^2M(\mathcal{R}), {}^2M(\mathcal{H})$ be respectively the direct sum of two identical matrix algebras. Then, when taken as real algebras,

$$\begin{aligned}
\mathcal{CL}(\mathcal{R}^{n+4m,n-4m}) &= M(\mathcal{R}), \quad \mathcal{CL}(\mathcal{R}^{n+4m+1,n-4m}) = {}^2M(\mathcal{R}), \\
\mathcal{CL}(\mathcal{R}^{n+4m+1,n-4m-1}) &= M(\mathcal{R}), \quad \mathcal{CL}(\mathcal{R}^{n+4m+2,n-4m-1}) = M(\mathcal{C}), \\
\mathcal{CL}(\mathcal{R}^{n+4m+2,n-4m-2}) &= M(\mathcal{H}), \quad \mathcal{CL}(\mathcal{R}^{n+4m+3,n-4m-2}) = {}^2M(\mathcal{H}), \\
\mathcal{CL}(\mathcal{R}^{n+4m+3,n-4m-3}) &= M(\mathcal{H}), \quad \mathcal{CL}(\mathcal{R}^{n+4m+4,n-4m-3}) = M(\mathcal{C}).
\end{aligned}$$

For complex algebras,

$$\mathcal{CL}(\mathcal{C}^{2k}) = M_{2^k}(\mathcal{C}), \quad \mathcal{CL}(\mathcal{C}^{2k+1}) = M_{2^k}(\mathcal{C}) \otimes M_{2^k}(\mathcal{C}).$$

The matrix form is used extensively in theoretical physics as a fundamental tool.

3. **Abstract symbols:** The definition is given at the beginning of this chapter. This form is convenient for symbolic computation in geometries to deduce formulas, find new conclusions, and find *all* solutions. The benefit is that some geometric meaning can be kept, and many algebraic computations can be simplified.

In this chapter, instead of providing detailed introductions of the operators and products of Clifford algebras and their properties, which generally give the beginners a lot of headache, we cut directly into the main application subject of Clifford algebra in its symbolic form — geometric computation. We analyze the applications in three geometries via five algebraic models, and in each model, we present one or two examples with details of how Clifford algebras are applied to simplify the representation and computation, thus making it easier and more interesting for the beginners to delve further into the subject by reading more material in the literature, for which a brief list is offered at the end of this chapter.

The geometries we are going to apply Clifford algebras are projective, affine and Euclidean geometries.

2. Two Examples in Projective Geometry

Example 1: (Pappus theorem). In the projective plane there are two lines **123** and **1'2'3'** each passing through three points. Then the intersections **12'** ∩ **1'2**, **13'** ∩ **1'3**, **23'** ∩ **2'3** are collinear.

2.1. *Algebraization*

An nD projective space is composed of the 1-spaces in an $(n+1)$D vector space. The Clifford algebra used in projective geometry can be identified with Grassmann-Cayley algebra. In this algebra, a projective point is represented by a nonzero vector in the corresponding 1-space. Line **12** is represented by the same symbol, with the juxtaposition of **1, 2** denoting the outer product of the two vectors. The intersection **12** ∩ **1'2'** is represented by **12** ∧ **1'2'**, where the wedge symbol no longer represents the outer product, but represents the *meet product*, the dual of the outer product. These

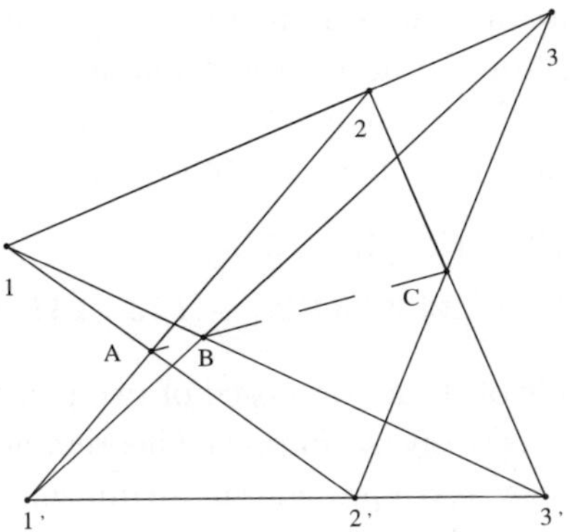

Fig. 2.   Pappus theorem

notations are used conventionally in the area of invariant theory instead
of Clifford algebra. We adopt them here by sacrificing the integrity of the
notations to save the effort of "language translation".

In projective plane geometry, the meet product of two 2-blades has two
kinds of expansions:

$$\mathbf{12} \wedge \mathbf{1'2'} = [\mathbf{11'2'}]\mathbf{2} - [\mathbf{21'2'}]\mathbf{1} = [\mathbf{122'}]\mathbf{1'} - [\mathbf{121'}]\mathbf{2'}. \tag{3}$$

Here the *bracket* $[\mathbf{121'}]$ denotes the determinant of the homogeneous coordinates of the three vectors $\mathbf{1}, \mathbf{2}, \mathbf{1'}$ in the 3D vector space. In some literature,
formula (3) is taken as the definition of the meet product.

The hypotheses of the theorem are

$$[\mathbf{123}] = [\mathbf{1'2'3'}] = 0, \tag{4}$$

i.e., three points are collinear if and only if their bracket is zero.

The conclusion is

$$[(\mathbf{12'} \wedge \mathbf{1'2})(\mathbf{13'} \wedge \mathbf{1'3})(\mathbf{23'} \wedge \mathbf{2'3})] = 0. \tag{5}$$

2.2. *Computation*

The proving of the conclusion is equivalent to reducing the left-hand side of
(5) to zero by the hypotheses (4), or in other words, changing the left-hand
side of (5) into a polynomial whose terms contain either $[\mathbf{123}]$ or $[\mathbf{1'2'3'}]$.
The computation has two steps: first, change the left-hand side of (5) into
a polynomial of brackets; second, replace the terms of the polynomial by
equivalent ones containing either $[\mathbf{123}]$ or $[\mathbf{1'2'3'}]$.

Changing an expression in Grassmann-Cayley algebra to an equivalent expression in the algebra of brackets (determinants) is called *Cayley expansion*. In this example, the left-hand side of (5) has no factored expansion. Its shortest expansion is binomial. The following is such an expansion:

$$[(\mathbf{12'} \wedge \mathbf{1'2})(\mathbf{13'} \wedge \mathbf{1'3})(\mathbf{23'} \wedge \mathbf{2'3})]$$
$$= -[\mathbf{123}][\mathbf{11'3'}][\mathbf{22'3'}][\mathbf{31'2'}] + [\mathbf{123'}][\mathbf{131'}][\mathbf{232'}][\mathbf{1'2'3'}]. \tag{6}$$

The right-hand side of (6) is composed of two terms containing brackets $[\mathbf{123}]$ and $[\mathbf{1'2'3'}]$ respectively, so Pappus Theorem is a direct consequence of the expansion. Moreover, (6) provides more information than the theorem itself, as it shows how the left-hand side depends on the two brackets.

The derivation of (6) is as follows:

$$[(\mathbf{12'} \wedge \mathbf{1'2})(\mathbf{13'} \wedge \mathbf{1'3})(\mathbf{23'} \wedge \mathbf{2'3})]$$
$$= \quad -[\mathbf{122'}][\mathbf{1'}(\mathbf{13'} \wedge \mathbf{1'3})(\mathbf{23'} \wedge \mathbf{2'3})] + [\mathbf{11'2'}][\mathbf{2}(\mathbf{13'} \wedge \mathbf{1'3})(\mathbf{23'} \wedge \mathbf{2'3})]$$
$$= \quad -[\mathbf{122'}][\mathbf{11'3'}][\mathbf{1'3}(\mathbf{23'} \wedge \mathbf{2'3})] - [\mathbf{11'2'}][\mathbf{232'}][\mathbf{2}(\mathbf{13'} \wedge \mathbf{1'3})\mathbf{3'}]$$
$$\overset{\text{form } p}{=} -[\mathbf{122'}][\mathbf{11'3'}][\mathbf{233'}][\mathbf{31'2'}] + [\mathbf{123'}][\mathbf{11'2'}][\mathbf{232'}][\mathbf{31'3'}]$$
$$\overset{\text{explode}}{=} -[\mathbf{123}][\mathbf{11'3'}][\mathbf{22'3'}][\mathbf{31'2'}] - \underline{[\mathbf{123'}][\mathbf{11'3'}][\mathbf{232'}][\mathbf{31'2'}]}$$
$$+ \underline{[\mathbf{123'}][\mathbf{11'2'}][\mathbf{232'}][\mathbf{31'3'}]}$$
$$\overset{\text{contract}}{=} -[\mathbf{123}][\mathbf{11'3'}][\mathbf{22'3'}][\mathbf{31'2'}] + [\mathbf{123'}][\mathbf{131'}][\mathbf{232'}][\mathbf{1'2'3'}].$$

By three steps of expansions using (3), we get a binomial form p, which has neither $[\mathbf{123}]$ nor $[\mathbf{1'2'3'}]$. This is the end of Cayley expansion.

We need to prove that form p is an element in the ideal generated by $[\mathbf{123}], [\mathbf{1'2'3'}]$ in the bracket ring. By definition, the *bracket algebra* generated by m symbols $\mathcal{M} = \{\mathbf{1}, \dots, \mathbf{m}\}$ in projective plane geometry over a field $\mathcal{K}$ with characteristic $\neq 2$ is the quotient of the polynomial ring $\mathcal{K}[\{[\mathbf{ijk}] \mid \mathbf{i}, \mathbf{j}, \mathbf{k} \in \mathcal{M}\}]$ modulo the ideal generated by the following three kinds of elements:

B1. $[\mathbf{ijk}]$ if two of the three components $\mathbf{i}, \mathbf{j}, \mathbf{k}$ are identical;

B2. $[\mathbf{ijk}] - \text{sign}(\sigma)[\sigma(\mathbf{i})\sigma(\mathbf{j})\sigma(\mathbf{k})]$ for any permutation σ of $\mathbf{i}, \mathbf{j}, \mathbf{k}$;

GP. (*Grassmann-Plücker polynomials*) for any elements $\mathbf{i}_1, \dots, \mathbf{i}_6$ in $\mathcal{M}$,

$$[\mathbf{i}_2\mathbf{i}_3\mathbf{i}_4][\mathbf{i}_1\mathbf{i}_5\mathbf{i}_6] - [\mathbf{i}_1\mathbf{i}_3\mathbf{i}_4][\mathbf{i}_2\mathbf{i}_5\mathbf{i}_6] + [\mathbf{i}_1\mathbf{i}_2\mathbf{i}_4][\mathbf{i}_3\mathbf{i}_5\mathbf{i}_6] - [\mathbf{i}_1\mathbf{i}_2\mathbf{i}_3][\mathbf{i}_4\mathbf{i}_5\mathbf{i}_6]. \tag{7}$$

Without loss of generality, let us first "divide" the first term of p by $[\mathbf{123}]$. The term has two brackets $[\mathbf{122'}], [\mathbf{233'}]$ each having two common vectors with $[\mathbf{123}]$, and according to (7), it is only possible to use them to generate $[\mathbf{123}]$. There is only one GP that realizes this:

$$[\mathbf{122'}][\mathbf{233'}] - [\mathbf{123}][\mathbf{22'3'}] - [\mathbf{123'}][\mathbf{232'}],$$

or in the form of an equality,

$$[\mathbf{122'}][\mathbf{233'}] = [\mathbf{123}][\mathbf{22'3'}] + [\mathbf{123'}][\mathbf{232'}]. \tag{8}$$

The transformation (8) is called *explosion*, as the number of terms is increased. Immediately after the transformation we need to do simplification to the "remainder of the division", which is

$$-\underline{[\mathbf{123'}]}[\mathbf{11'3'}]\underline{[\mathbf{232'}]}[\mathbf{31'2'}] + \underline{[\mathbf{123'}]}[\mathbf{11'2'}]\underline{[\mathbf{232'}]}[\mathbf{31'3'}],$$

where the common bracket factors are underlined. The simplification technique is to use GPs to factor or reduce the number of terms. Here there is only one GP that can reduce the number of terms:

$$[\mathbf{11'2'}][\mathbf{31'3'}] - [\mathbf{11'3'}][\mathbf{31'2'}] - [\mathbf{131'}][\mathbf{1'2'3'}],$$

or in the form of an equality,

$$[\mathbf{11'2'}][\mathbf{31'3'}] - [\mathbf{11'3'}][\mathbf{31'2'}] = [\mathbf{131'}][\mathbf{1'2'3'}]. \tag{9}$$

The transformation (9) is called *contraction*, as the number of terms is decreased. Its result contains the factor $[\mathbf{1'2'3'}]$. This finishes the computation.

In this example, two techniques are essential in carrying out the computation: (1) factored and binomial Cayley expansions; (2) explosions and contractions in bracket algebra. Some recent progress on the two topics can be found in the literature.[23]

Now let us proceed to the second example.

Example 2: (Desargues theorem). In the projective space there are two triangles $\mathbf{123}$ and $\mathbf{1'2'3'}$. If the three lines $\mathbf{11'}, \mathbf{22'}, \mathbf{33'}$ are concurrent, and the three pairs of lines $(\mathbf{12}, \mathbf{1'2'})$, $(\mathbf{13}, \mathbf{1'3'})$, $(\mathbf{23}, \mathbf{2'3'})$ are intersecting pairs of lines, then the three points of intersection are collinear.

2.3. *2D Desargues Theorem*

First let us consider the theorem in the projective plane. Three lines $\mathbf{11'}, \mathbf{22'}, \mathbf{33'}$ are concurrent if and only if their meet $\mathbf{11'} \wedge \mathbf{22'} \wedge \mathbf{33'}$ is zero. The meet has three different expansions:

$$\begin{aligned}
\mathbf{11'} \wedge \mathbf{22'} \wedge \mathbf{33'} &= [\mathbf{122'}][\mathbf{1'33'}] - [\mathbf{133'}][\mathbf{1'22'}] \\
&= [\mathbf{11'2'}][\mathbf{233'}] - [\mathbf{11'2}][\mathbf{2'33'}] \\
&= [\mathbf{11'3}][\mathbf{22'3'}] - [\mathbf{11'3'}][\mathbf{22'3}].
\end{aligned}$$

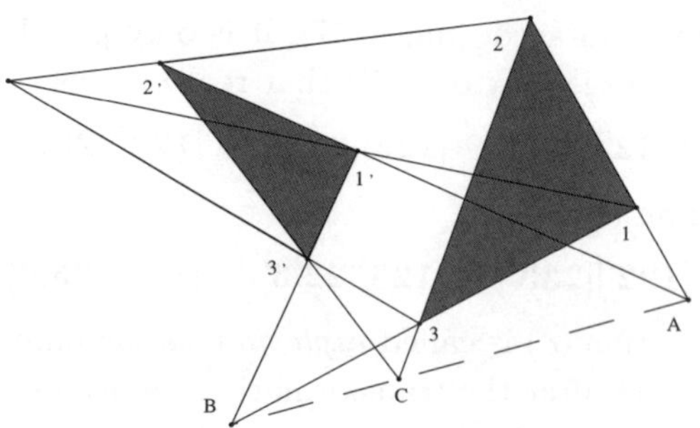

Fig. 3.   Desargues theorem

The hypothesis of the theorem is $\mathbf{11'} \wedge \mathbf{22'} \wedge \mathbf{33'} = 0$, and the conclusion is

$$[(\mathbf{12} \wedge \mathbf{1'2'})(\mathbf{13} \wedge \mathbf{1'3'})(\mathbf{23} \wedge \mathbf{2'3'})] = 0. \qquad (10)$$

The conclusion can be derived if there is an expansion of the left-hand side of (10) having $\mathbf{11'} \wedge \mathbf{22'} \wedge \mathbf{33'}$ as a factor. Indeed, the following is such a factored expansion:

$$[(\mathbf{12} \wedge \mathbf{1'2'})(\mathbf{13} \wedge \mathbf{1'3'})(\mathbf{23} \wedge \mathbf{2'3'})] = -[\mathbf{123}][\mathbf{1'2'3'}]\mathbf{11'} \wedge \mathbf{22'} \wedge \mathbf{33'}. \qquad (11)$$

Formula (11) can be derived by direct Cayley expansions and a Cayley factorization:

$$
\begin{aligned}
&[(\mathbf{12} \wedge \mathbf{1'2'})(\mathbf{13} \wedge \mathbf{1'3'})(\mathbf{23} \wedge \mathbf{2'3'})] \\
&= \ [\mathbf{11'2'}][\mathbf{2}(\mathbf{13} \wedge \mathbf{1'3'})(\mathbf{23} \wedge \mathbf{2'3'})] - [\mathbf{21'2'}][\mathbf{1}(\mathbf{13} \wedge \mathbf{1'3'})(\mathbf{23} \wedge \mathbf{2'3'})] \\
&= \ [\mathbf{11'2'}][\mathbf{22'3'}][\mathbf{2}(\mathbf{13} \wedge \mathbf{1'3'})\mathbf{3}] - [\mathbf{21'2'}][\mathbf{11'3'}][\mathbf{13}(\mathbf{23} \wedge \mathbf{2'3'})] \\
&= \ [\mathbf{11'2'}][\mathbf{22'3'}][\mathbf{31'3'}]\underline{[\mathbf{123}]} - [\mathbf{21'2'}][\mathbf{11'3'}][\mathbf{32'3'}]\underline{[\mathbf{123}]} \\
&\overset{\text{factor}}{=} -[\mathbf{123}][\mathbf{1'2'3'}]\mathbf{11'} \wedge \mathbf{22'} \wedge \mathbf{33'}.
\end{aligned}
$$

The first three steps are expansions using (3). The last step is a transform from a bracket polynomial to a Cayley expression, called *Cayley factorization*.

The multilinear case of Cayley expansion is solved by White.[33] The factorization in this example follows from a formula developed by Li.[23]

2.4. *nD Desargues Theorem*

Formula (11) remains valid in nD projective space where $n \geq 3$; hence the theorem is true not only in 2D but also in nD, and in particular, in 3D.

In the Grassmann-Cayley algebra generated by $(n+1)$D vector space, the symbols in (11) are explained in a different manner. The bracket $[\mathbf{123}]$ is now *Mourrain bracket*, i.e., an abbreviation of

$$[\mathbf{U}_1\mathbf{U}_2\cdots\mathbf{U}_{n-2}\mathbf{123}],$$

where the $\mathbf{U}$'s are dummy vectors in the vector space. The meet product $\mathbf{12}\wedge\mathbf{1'2'}$ is an abbreviation of

$$\mathbf{U}_1\mathbf{U}_2\cdots\mathbf{U}_{n-2}\mathbf{12}\wedge\mathbf{1'2'},$$

and the meet product $\mathbf{11'}\wedge\mathbf{22'}\wedge\mathbf{33'}$ is an abbreviation of

$$\mathbf{U}_1\mathbf{U}_2\cdots\mathbf{U}_{n-2}\mathbf{11'}\wedge\mathbf{U}_1\mathbf{U}_2\cdots\mathbf{U}_{n-2}\mathbf{22'}\wedge\mathbf{33'}.$$

Let $u = \mathbf{U}_1\mathbf{U}_2\cdots\mathbf{U}_{n-2}$. Then (11) becomes

$$[u(u\mathbf{12}\wedge\mathbf{1'2'})(u\mathbf{13}\wedge\mathbf{1'3'})(u\mathbf{23}\wedge\mathbf{2'3'})] = -[u\mathbf{123}][u\mathbf{1'2'3'}]u\mathbf{11'}\wedge u\mathbf{22'}\wedge\mathbf{33'},$$

whose proof is the same as in the 2D case.

2.5. *Short Summary*

Using Clifford algebra, the representations of not only the geometric entities and constraints but also the geometric theorems are very succinct. A geometric theorem is often the result of an algebraic identity, and the identity tells more than the theorem. This algebraization is of a higher level than the coordinates.

3. An Example in Affine Geometry

Example 3: Let there be a hyperbola whose two asymptotes are l_1, l_2 and whose center is $\mathbf{0}$. Let $\mathbf{1}, \mathbf{2}, \mathbf{3}$ be any three points on the hyperbola. Let $\mathbf{6} = \mathbf{12}\cap l_1$, and let $\mathbf{7}$ be the intersection of the parallel line of l_1 through $\mathbf{3}$ and the parallel line of l_2 through $\mathbf{1}$. Then $\mathbf{23}$ and $\mathbf{67}$ are parallel.

3.1. *Algebraization*

The affine plane is a subset of the projective plane: it is composed of all the points not lying on a fixed line of the plane. In Clifford algebra, the line can be represented by a fixed 2-blade I. A point $\mathbf{a}$ is in the affine plane if and only if $[\mathbf{a}I] \neq 0$. Points on line I are *at infinity*. In affine geometry, the Mourrain bracket of a vector will never occur, and it is safe to use the abbreviation

$$[\mathbf{a}] = [\mathbf{a}I].$$

The geometric configuration of the example is constructed as follows:

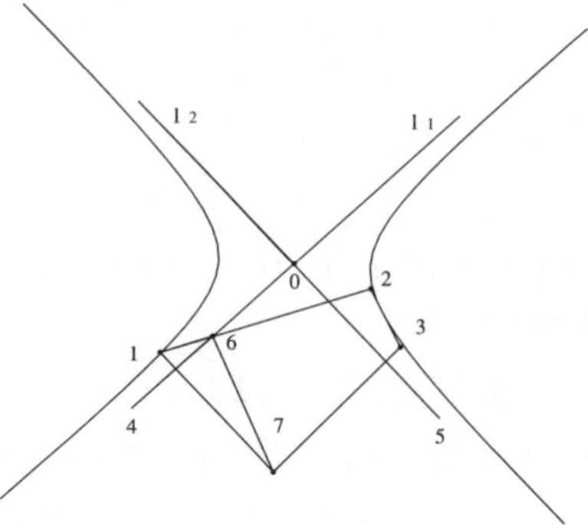

Fig. 4.   Example 3

Free points: **1, 2, 3**.

Free points at infinity: **4, 5**.

Pole: $\mathbf{0} = \mathrm{pole}_{\mathbf{45}}(\mathbf{12345})$, i.e., **0** is the intersection of the two tangents (asymptotes) at **4** and **5** of the projective conic passing through **1, 2, 3, 4, 5**.

Intersections: $\mathbf{6} = \mathbf{12} \cap \mathbf{04}$, $\mathbf{7} = \mathbf{34} \cap \mathbf{15}$.

The conclusion is $[\mathbf{23} \wedge \mathbf{67}] = 0$, i.e., the lines **23, 67** intersect at a point at infinity.

3.2. *Proof of the Conclusion*

The conclusion can be proved only after the constrained points **6, 7, 0** are eliminated from the expression $[\mathbf{23} \wedge \mathbf{67}]$.

$$[\mathbf{23} \wedge \mathbf{67}] = [\mathbf{3}][\mathbf{267}] - [\mathbf{2}][\mathbf{367}]$$

$$\boxed{\begin{array}{l}[\mathbf{2}(\mathbf{12}\wedge\mathbf{04})(\mathbf{34}\wedge\mathbf{15})] = [\mathbf{125}][\mathbf{134}][\mathbf{240}] \\[4pt] [\mathbf{3}(\mathbf{12}\wedge\mathbf{04})(\mathbf{34}\wedge\mathbf{15})] = [\mathbf{124}][\mathbf{135}][\mathbf{340}]\end{array}}$$

$$\overset{6,7}{=} \begin{array}{l}[\mathbf{3}][\mathbf{125}][\mathbf{134}][\mathbf{240}] \\[4pt] -[\mathbf{2}][\mathbf{124}][\mathbf{135}][\mathbf{340}]\end{array}$$

$$= \begin{array}{l}[\mathbf{3}][\mathbf{125}][\mathbf{134}][\mathbf{240}_{45,231}] \\[4pt] -[\mathbf{2}][\mathbf{124}][\mathbf{135}][\mathbf{340}_{45,312}]\end{array}$$

$$\boxed{\begin{array}{l}\mathbf{0}_{45,231} = [\mathbf{125}][\mathbf{134}][\mathbf{235}]\mathbf{4} \\[2pt] \qquad +[\mathbf{124}][\mathbf{135}][\mathbf{234}]\mathbf{5}-[\mathbf{123}][\mathbf{145}][\mathbf{345}]\mathbf{2} \\[4pt] \mathbf{0}_{45,312} = [\mathbf{124}][\mathbf{135}][\mathbf{235}]\mathbf{4} \\[2pt] \qquad +[\mathbf{125}][\mathbf{134}][\mathbf{234}]\mathbf{5}-[\mathbf{123}][\mathbf{145}][\mathbf{245}]\mathbf{3}\end{array}}$$

$$= \begin{array}{l}[\mathbf{124}][\mathbf{125}][\mathbf{134}][\mathbf{135}][\mathbf{234}] \\[4pt] ([\mathbf{3}][\mathbf{245}] - [\mathbf{2}][\mathbf{345}])\end{array}$$

$$= 0.$$

The first step is to expand $[\mathbf{23} \wedge \mathbf{67}]$ into a bracket binomial. There are two different expansions:

$$[\mathbf{23} \wedge \mathbf{67}] = [\mathbf{3}][\mathbf{267}] - [\mathbf{2}][\mathbf{367}] = [\mathbf{6}][\mathbf{237}] - [\mathbf{7}][\mathbf{236}].$$

The second expansion in fact leads to a slightly simpler proof.

The second step is to eliminate $\mathbf{6}$, $\mathbf{7}$ at the same time. The reason for this batch elimination is that $\mathbf{6}$, $\mathbf{7}$ are both at the end of the sequence of constructions:

$$1, 2, 3, 4, 5 \prec \begin{cases} \mathbf{0} \prec \mathbf{6}; \\ \mathbf{7}; \end{cases}$$

and both are intersections of lines. After the elimination, the brackets $[\mathbf{267}]$ and $[\mathbf{367}]$ are expanded into monomials.

The third step is to choose representations for $\mathbf{0}$ before its elimination. This is the highlight of the method: *No* other algebraic method has ever considered using different algebraic representations for the same geometric entity in the same algebraic expression.

The pole of line $\mathbf{12}$ with respect to conic($\mathbf{12345}$) is:[23]

$$\mathrm{pole}_{\mathbf{12},\mathbf{345}} = [\mathbf{145}][\mathbf{234}][\mathbf{235}]\mathbf{1} + [\mathbf{134}][\mathbf{135}][\mathbf{245}]\mathbf{2} - [\mathbf{124}][\mathbf{125}][\mathbf{345}]\mathbf{3}. \tag{12}$$

The representation is symmetric with respect to $\mathbf{1}, \mathbf{2}$ but antisymmetric with respect to $\mathbf{3}, \mathbf{4}, \mathbf{5}$.

By (12), $\mathbf{0}$ is a linear combination of $\mathbf{4}, \mathbf{5}$ and another conic point $\mathbf{X}$, so it has two *essential points* $\mathbf{4}, \mathbf{5}$, which occur in every representation of $\mathbf{0}$. It is the point $\mathbf{X}$ that is to be chosen within each bracket containing $\mathbf{0}$. In $[\mathbf{240}]$, $\mathbf{2}$ is chosen as $\mathbf{X}$, while in $[\mathbf{340}]$, $\mathbf{3}$ is chosen as $\mathbf{X}$. The result is that both brackets have monomial expansions after the elimination of $\mathbf{0}$.

The last step is a contraction. It is based on the following *affine GP relation*

$$[\mathbf{3}][\mathbf{245}] - [\mathbf{2}][\mathbf{345}] = [\mathbf{4}][\mathbf{235}] - [\mathbf{5}][\mathbf{234}],$$

and the bracket computation rules $[\mathbf{4}] = [\mathbf{5}] = 0$.

3.3. *Short Summary*

The elimination procedure is a sequence of loops of batch elimination according to the order of construction. Each loop has three steps: (1) choose algebraic representations for the geometric entity before its elimination; (2) expand the result of the substitution, which is usually a Cayley expansion; (3) simplify the result of the expansion in the bracket ring.

4. First Example in Euclidean Geometry

Example 4: Let a_i, b_i, c_i, d_i, e_i for $i = 1, 2, 3$ be variables such that $a_i^2 + b_i^2 + c_i^2 = 1$. Let x_i, y_i, z_i for $i = 1, 2, 3$ be unknowns. Let i, j, k be any permutation of $1, 2, 3$. Solve the equations

$$a_i x_i + b_i y_i + c_i z_i - d_i = 0,$$
$$x_i^2 + y_i^2 + z_i^2 = 1, \tag{13}$$
$$x_i x_j + y_i y_j + z_i z_j = e_k.$$

The geometric origin of the example is as follows: let

$$\mathbf{n}_i = (a_i, b_i, c_i),$$
$$\mathbf{i} = (x_i, y_i, z_i).$$

Then (13) can be written as

$$\mathbf{n}_i \cdot \mathbf{i} = d_i,$$
$$\mathbf{i} \cdot \mathbf{j} = e_k,$$
$$\mathbf{i}^2 = 1, \tag{14}$$
$$\mathbf{n}_i^2 = 1.$$

The geometric translation is that given three planes $(\mathbf{n}_i, d_i)$ for $i = 1, 2, 3$ whose equations are

$$\mathbf{n}_i \cdot \mathbf{x} = d_i, \quad \text{for } \mathbf{x} = (x, y, z)^T,$$

find three points $\mathbf{1}, \mathbf{2}, \mathbf{3}$ on the three planes respectively, such that they form a spherical triangle on the unit sphere with given spherical distance e_1, e_2, e_3.

Below we use the vectorial equation-solving method[21] to solve (14), with $\mathbf{n}$, e and d as parameters and with $\mathbf{1}, \mathbf{2}, \mathbf{3}$ as unknown vector variables.

Set the order of the unknowns as $\mathbf{3} \prec \mathbf{2} \prec \mathbf{1}$. We need to find a vectorial triangular form

$$\mathbf{1} = \mathbf{1}(\mathbf{2}, \mathbf{3}, u), \quad \mathbf{2} = \mathbf{2}(\mathbf{3}, u), \quad \mathbf{3} = \mathbf{3}(u),$$

in which the u are given and unknown parameters.

4.1. *Step 1*

Vector $\mathbf{1}$ satisfies three linear equations:

$$\mathbf{1} \cdot \mathbf{2} = e_3,$$
$$\mathbf{1} \cdot \mathbf{3} = e_2,$$
$$\mathbf{1} \cdot \mathbf{n}_1 = d_1.$$

So

$$\mathbf{1} \cdot (\mathbf{n}_1 \wedge \mathbf{2} \wedge \mathbf{3}) = (\mathbf{1} \cdot \mathbf{n}_1)\mathbf{2} \wedge \mathbf{3} - (\mathbf{1} \cdot \mathbf{2})\mathbf{n}_1 \wedge \mathbf{3} + (\mathbf{1} \cdot \mathbf{3})\mathbf{n}_1 \wedge \mathbf{2} \tag{15}$$
$$= d_1 \mathbf{2} \wedge \mathbf{3} - e_3 \mathbf{n}_1 \wedge \mathbf{3} + e_2 \mathbf{n}_1 \wedge \mathbf{2}.$$

The wedge here denotes the outer product. The first equality is the expansion formula of the inner product.

Now square both sides of (15). The easiest way is to do inner product of each side with its *reverse* — the product in the reverse order. For example, the reverse of $\mathbf{1} \cdot (\mathbf{n}_1 \wedge \mathbf{2} \wedge \mathbf{3})$ is $(\mathbf{3} \wedge \mathbf{2} \wedge \mathbf{n}_1) \cdot \mathbf{1}$, and the reverse of $\mathbf{2} \wedge \mathbf{3}$ is $\mathbf{3} \wedge \mathbf{2}$. Expanding the inner products of blades into the inner products of vectors, we get

$$\mathbf{1}^2 \begin{vmatrix} \mathbf{n}_1 \cdot \mathbf{n}_1 & \mathbf{n}_1 \cdot \mathbf{2} & \mathbf{n}_1 \cdot \mathbf{3} \\ \mathbf{2} \cdot \mathbf{n}_1 & \mathbf{2} \cdot \mathbf{2} & \mathbf{2} \cdot \mathbf{3} \\ \mathbf{3} \cdot \mathbf{n}_1 & \mathbf{3} \cdot \mathbf{2} & \mathbf{3} \cdot \mathbf{3} \end{vmatrix}$$

$$= d_1^2 \left(\mathbf{2}^2 \mathbf{3}^2 - (\mathbf{2} \cdot \mathbf{3})^2 \right) + e_3^2 \left(\mathbf{n}_1^2 \mathbf{3}^2 - (\mathbf{n}_1 \cdot \mathbf{3})^2 \right) + e_2^2 \left(\mathbf{n}_1^2 \mathbf{2}^2 - (\mathbf{n}_1 \cdot \mathbf{2})^2 \right)$$
$$- 2d_1 e_3 \left(\mathbf{3}^2 \, \mathbf{n}_1 \cdot \mathbf{2} - \mathbf{n}_1 \cdot \mathbf{3} \, \mathbf{2} \cdot \mathbf{3} \right)$$
$$+ 2d_1 e_2 \left(\mathbf{n}_1 \cdot \mathbf{2} \, \mathbf{2} \cdot \mathbf{3} - \mathbf{2}^2 \, \mathbf{n}_1 \cdot \mathbf{3} \right)$$
$$- 2e_2 e_3 \left(\mathbf{n}_1^2 \, \mathbf{2} \cdot \mathbf{3} - \mathbf{n}_1 \cdot \mathbf{2} \, \mathbf{n}_1 \cdot \mathbf{3} \right).$$

Using $\mathbf{i}^2 = \mathbf{n}_i^2 = 1$ and $\mathbf{2} \cdot \mathbf{3} = e_1$, we can simplify the above result as follows:

$$(1 - e_2^2)(\mathbf{2} \cdot \mathbf{n}_1)^2 + (1 - e_3^2)(\mathbf{3} \cdot \mathbf{n}_1)^2 + 2(e_2 e_3 - e_1)\, \mathbf{2} \cdot \mathbf{n}_1 \, \mathbf{3} \cdot \mathbf{n}_1$$
$$+ 2d_1(e_1 e_2 - e_3)\, \mathbf{2} \cdot \mathbf{n}_1 + 2d_1(e_1 e_3 - e_2)\, \mathbf{3} \cdot \mathbf{n}_1 \tag{16}$$
$$+ d_1^2 - d_1^2 e_1^2 + e_1^2 + e_2^2 + e_3^2 - 2e_1 e_2 e_3 - 1 = 0.$$

4.2. *Step 2*

Vector $\mathbf{3}$ satisfies only one linear equation $\mathbf{3} \cdot \mathbf{n}_3 = d_3$, so

$$\mathbf{3} \cdot (\mathbf{n}_1 \wedge \mathbf{n}_2 \wedge \mathbf{n}_3) = \mathbf{3} \cdot \mathbf{n}_1 \, \mathbf{n}_2 \wedge \mathbf{n}_3 - \mathbf{3} \cdot \mathbf{n}_2 \, \mathbf{n}_1 \wedge \mathbf{n}_3 + \mathbf{3} \cdot \mathbf{n}_3 \, \mathbf{n}_1 \wedge \mathbf{n}_2 \tag{17}$$
$$= \mathbf{3} \cdot \mathbf{n}_1 \, \mathbf{n}_2 \wedge \mathbf{n}_3 - \mathbf{3} \cdot \mathbf{n}_2 \, \mathbf{n}_1 \wedge \mathbf{n}_3 + d_3 \mathbf{n}_1 \wedge \mathbf{n}_2.$$

Squaring both sides, using $\mathbf{3}^2 = \mathbf{n}_i^2 = 1$ and setting $\mathbf{n}_i \cdot \mathbf{n}_j = f_k$ for any permutation i, j, k of $1, 2, 3$, we get

$$(1 - f_1^2)(\mathbf{3} \cdot \mathbf{n}_1)^2 + (1 - f_2^2)(\mathbf{3} \cdot \mathbf{n}_2)^2 + 2(f_1 f_2 - f_3)\, \mathbf{3} \cdot \mathbf{n}_1 \, \mathbf{3} \cdot \mathbf{n}_2$$
$$+ 2d_3(f_1 f_3 - f_2)\, \mathbf{3} \cdot \mathbf{n}_1 + 2d_3(f_2 f_3 - f_1)\, \mathbf{3} \cdot \mathbf{n}_2 \tag{18}$$
$$+ d_3^2 - d_3^2 f_3^2 + f_1^2 + f_2^2 + f_3^2 - 2f_1 f_2 f_3 - 1 = 0.$$

4.3. *Step 3*

Vector $\mathbf{2}$ satisfies $\mathbf{2} \cdot \mathbf{3} = e_1$ and $\mathbf{2} \cdot \mathbf{n}_2 = d_2$, so

$$\begin{aligned}
\mathbf{2} \cdot (\mathbf{n}_1 \wedge \mathbf{n}_2 \wedge \mathbf{3}) &= \mathbf{2} \cdot \mathbf{n}_1\, \mathbf{n}_2 \wedge \mathbf{3} - \mathbf{2} \cdot \mathbf{n}_2\, \mathbf{n}_1 \wedge \mathbf{3} + \mathbf{2} \cdot \mathbf{3}\, \mathbf{n}_1 \wedge \mathbf{n}_2 \\
&= \mathbf{2} \cdot \mathbf{n}_1\, \mathbf{n}_2 \wedge \mathbf{3} - d_2 \mathbf{n}_1 \wedge \mathbf{3} + e_1 \mathbf{n}_1 \wedge \mathbf{n}_2 .
\end{aligned} \tag{19}$$

Squaring both sides, using $\mathbf{2}^2 = \mathbf{3}^2 = \mathbf{n}_i^2 = 1$ and $\mathbf{n}_1 \cdot \mathbf{n}_2 = f_3$, we get

$$-(\mathbf{2} \cdot \mathbf{n}_1)^2 (\mathbf{3} \cdot \mathbf{n}_2)^2 + (\mathbf{2} \cdot \mathbf{n}_1)^2 + (\mathbf{3} \cdot \mathbf{n}_2)^2 + 2(d_2\, \mathbf{3} \cdot \mathbf{n}_1 + e_1 f_3)\, \mathbf{3} \cdot \mathbf{n}_2\, \mathbf{2} \cdot \mathbf{n}_1$$

$$-2(e_1\, \mathbf{3} \cdot \mathbf{n}_1 + d_2 f_3)\, \mathbf{2} \cdot \mathbf{n}_1 - 2(f_3\, \mathbf{3} \cdot \mathbf{n}_1 + d_2 e_1)\, \mathbf{3} \cdot \mathbf{n}_2$$

$$+(1 - d_2^2)\,(\mathbf{3} \cdot \mathbf{n}_1)^2 + 2 d_2 e_1 f_3\, \mathbf{3} \cdot \mathbf{n}_1 + d_2^2 + e_1^2 + f_3^2 - e_1^2 f_3^2 - 1 = 0.$$

$$\tag{20}$$

4.4. *Step 4*

By now we have three equations (16), (18), (20) with three unknowns $\mathbf{3} \cdot \mathbf{n}_1 \prec \mathbf{3} \cdot \mathbf{n}_2 \prec \mathbf{2} \cdot \mathbf{n}_1$. Denote the unknowns by u_3, u_2, u_1 respectively, and eliminate u_1^2, u_2^2 from (20) using (16), (18). The result is an equation of the form

$$\lambda_0 u_1 u_2 + \lambda_1 u_1 + \lambda_2 u_2 + \lambda_3 = 0, \tag{21}$$

where the λ's are polynomials in u_3 of degree $2, 3, 3, 4$ respectively.

(16) and (18) can be written as

$$\begin{aligned}
\mu_0 u_1^2 + \mu_1 u_1 + \mu_2 &= 0, \\
\nu_0 u_2^2 + \nu_1 u_2 + \nu_2 &= 0,
\end{aligned} \tag{22}$$

where the μ's (and the ν's) are polynomials in u_3 of degree $0, 1, 2$ respectively.

Doing pseudodivision of the first equation of (22) by (21) with respect to u_1, we get

$$\begin{aligned}
&(\lambda_0^2 \mu_2 - \lambda_0 \lambda_2 \mu_1 + \lambda_2^2 \mu_0)\, u_2^2 \\
&+(2\lambda_0 \lambda_1 \mu_2 + 2\lambda_2 \lambda_3 \mu_0 - \lambda_0 \lambda_3 \mu_1 - \lambda_1 \lambda_2 \mu_1)\, u_2 \\
&+(\lambda_1^2 \mu_2 + \lambda_3^2 \mu_0 - \lambda_1 \lambda_3 \mu_1) = 0.
\end{aligned} \tag{23}$$

Eliminating u_2^2 from (23) by (22), we get

$$\begin{aligned}
&(2\lambda_0 \lambda_1 \mu_2 \nu_0 + 2\lambda_2 \lambda_3 \mu_0 \nu_0 - \lambda_0 \lambda_3 \mu_1 \nu_0 - \lambda_1 \lambda_2 \mu_1 \nu_0 \\
&\qquad\qquad\qquad -\lambda_0^2 \mu_2 \nu_1 + \lambda_0 \lambda_2 \mu_1 \nu_1 - \lambda_2^2 \mu_0 \nu_1)\, u_2 \\
&+(\lambda_1^2 \mu_2 \nu_0^2 + \lambda_3^2 \mu_0 \nu_0^2 - \lambda_1 \lambda_3 \mu_1 \nu_0^2 - \lambda_0^2 \mu_2 \nu_2 + \lambda_0 \lambda_2 \mu_1 \nu_2 - \lambda_2^2 \mu_0 \nu_2) = 0,
\end{aligned} \tag{24}$$

which can be written as $\alpha_0 u_2 + \alpha_1 = 0$, where the α's are polynomials in u_3 of degree $7, 8$ respectively.

Substituting (24) into the second equation of (22), we get

$$\nu_0 \alpha_1^2 + \nu_2 \alpha_0^2 - \nu_1 \alpha_0 \alpha_1 = 0, \tag{25}$$

which is a polynomial of degree 16 in u_3.

4.5. *Short Summary*

The usage of Clifford algebra in this example is very preliminary: only the inner product and the outer product, but not the geometric product, are used. When the outer product of two vectors is replaced by the cross product in vector algebra, the computation is much the same.

The vectorial equation-solving method is essentially a moving frame method.

5. Second Example in Euclidean Geometry

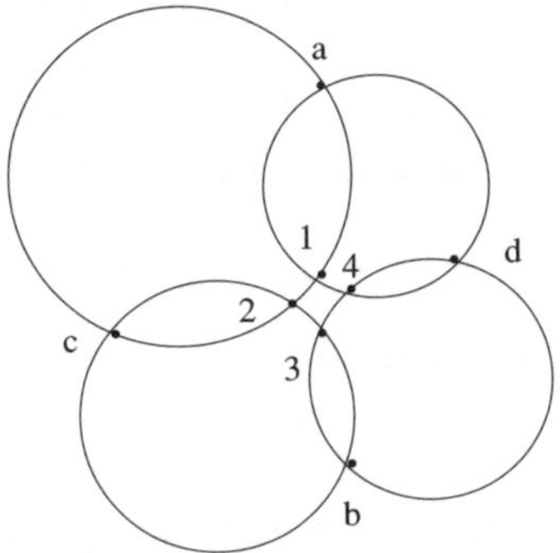

Fig. 5.   Miquel theorem

Example 5: (Miquel theorem). In the plane there are four circles intersecting as in Fig. 5. If points $1, 2, 3, 4$ are co-circular, so are points a, b, c, d.

5.1. *Algebraization*

A very efficient algebraic model for Euclidean geometry is the *homogeneous model*. It is a realization of Euclidean geometry in non-Euclidean space in a nonlinear manner, and it can *simplify* geometric computation. The history of the model goes back to the discoverers of non-Euclidean geometry. The following is a modern explanation.

We embed $\mathcal{R}^n$ into a Minkowski space $\mathcal{R}^{n+1,1}$ as a subspace. The orthogonal supplement of $\mathcal{R}^n$ is a Minkowski plane which has two null 1-spaces, i.e., 1-spaces in which the inner product is degenerate. Let $\mathbf{e}, \mathbf{e}_0$ be null vectors in the 1-spaces respectively. Rescale them to make $\mathbf{e} \cdot \mathbf{e}_0 = -1$. Define

$$c \mapsto \mathbf{c} = \mathbf{e}_0 + c + \frac{c^2}{2}\mathbf{e}, \quad \text{for } c \in \mathcal{R}^n. \tag{26}$$

The range of the mapping is

$$\mathcal{N}_{\mathbf{e}}^n = \{\mathbf{x} \in \mathcal{R}^{n+1,1} \mid \mathbf{x}^2 = 0, \mathbf{x} \cdot \mathbf{e} = -1\}. \tag{27}$$

This mapping is an isometry:

$$|\mathbf{c} - \mathbf{d}| = |c - d|. \tag{28}$$

The *homogeneous model* of nD Euclidean geometry[19,22] refers to the pair $(\mathbf{e}, \mathcal{N}_{\mathbf{e}}^n)$, where $\mathbf{e}$ is a null vector in $\mathcal{R}^{n+1,1}$, $\mathcal{N}_{\mathbf{e}}^n$ is a parabolic section of the null cone of $\mathcal{R}^{n+1,1}$. In this model,

- any element in $\mathcal{N}_{\mathbf{e}}^n$ is called a *Euclidean point*. $\mathbf{e}$ is the unique point at infinity.
- The distance between two Euclidean points is induced from the metric of $\mathcal{R}^{n+1,1}$. Let $\mathbf{c}, \mathbf{d}$ be two points. Then

  $$\mathbf{c} \cdot \mathbf{d} = -\frac{|c - d|^2}{2},$$

  where c, d are the projections of vectors $\mathbf{c}, \mathbf{d}$ into any Euclidean n-space of $\mathcal{R}^{n+1,1}$ orthogonal to $\mathbf{e}$.
- An r-blade $B_{r-1,1}$ with Minkowski signature represents an $(r-2)$-sphere or plane: a Euclidean point $\mathbf{a}$ is on the sphere or plane $B_{r-1,1}$ if and only if $\mathbf{a} \wedge B_{r-1,1} = 0$. Blade $B_{r-1,1}$ represents a plane if and only if $\mathbf{e} \wedge B_{r-1,1} = 0$.
- The r-sphere passing through $r + 2$ generic points $\mathbf{a}_1, \ldots, \mathbf{a}_{r+2}$ is represented by $\mathbf{a}_1 \wedge \mathbf{a}_2 \wedge \cdots \wedge \mathbf{a}_{r+2}$. The r-plane passing through $r+1$ generic points $\mathbf{a}_1, \ldots, \mathbf{a}_{r+1}$ is represented by $\mathbf{e} \wedge \mathbf{a}_1 \wedge \cdots \wedge \mathbf{a}_{r+1}$.

We come back to Miquel Theorem. The hypotheses are:

$$a, b, 1, 2, 3, 4 \text{ are free points in the plane,}$$
$$c = 12a \cap 23b, \quad d = 14a \cap 34b,$$
$$[\mathbf{1234}] = 0 \text{ (points } \mathbf{1}, \mathbf{2}, \mathbf{3}, \mathbf{4} \text{ are co-circular).}$$

The conclusion is $[\mathbf{abcd}] = 0$.

5.2. *Computation*

The conclusion can be derived if after the batch elimination of $\mathbf{c}, \mathbf{d}$ from $[\mathbf{abcd}]$, the result has a factor $[\mathbf{1234}]$.

For the elimination purpose we need the formula on the *second point of intersection* of two circles $\mathbf{012}$ and $\mathbf{01'2'}$. The other point of intersection is obviously $\mathbf{0}$. Denote the second point of intersection by $\mathbf{012} \cap \mathbf{01'2'}$. We have

$$
\begin{aligned}
\mathbf{012} &\cap \mathbf{01'2'} \\
&= 1 \cdot 2[011'2'][021'2']0 + [12; 1'2']_0([021'2']1 - [011'2']2) \qquad (29) \\
&= 1' \cdot 2'[0121'][0122']0 - [12; 1'2']_0([0122']1' - [0121']2'),
\end{aligned}
$$

where

$$
[12; 1'2']_0 = 0 \cdot 1\,[021'2'] - 0 \cdot 2\,[011'2'] = 0 \cdot 2'\,[0121'] - 0 \cdot 1'\,[0122'].
\tag{30}
$$

Substituting

$$
\begin{aligned}
\mathbf{c} &= 1 \cdot \mathbf{a}\,[23\mathbf{b}1][23\mathbf{b}\mathbf{a}]\,2 + [1\mathbf{a}; 3\mathbf{b}]_2([23\mathbf{b}\mathbf{a}]\,1 - [23\mathbf{b}1]\,\mathbf{a}), \\
\mathbf{d} &= 1 \cdot \mathbf{a}\,[43\mathbf{b}1][43\mathbf{b}\mathbf{a}]\,4 + [1\mathbf{a}; 3\mathbf{b}]_4([43\mathbf{b}\mathbf{a}]\,1 - [43\mathbf{b}1]\,\mathbf{a})
\end{aligned}
\tag{31}
$$

into $[\mathbf{abcd}]$, we get

$$
\begin{aligned}
[\mathbf{abcd}] \overset{\mathbf{c},\mathbf{d}}{=}\ & 1 \cdot \mathbf{a}\,[23\mathbf{b}\mathbf{a}][43\mathbf{b}\mathbf{a}]\{1 \cdot \mathbf{a}\,[\mathbf{ab}24][23\mathbf{b}1][43\mathbf{b}1] \\
& [\mathbf{ab}41][43\mathbf{b}1][1\mathbf{a}; 3\mathbf{b}]_2 - [\mathbf{ab}21][23\mathbf{b}1][1\mathbf{a}; 3\mathbf{b}]_4\} \\[6pt]
\overset{\text{expand}}{=}\ & -1 \cdot \mathbf{a}\,[23\mathbf{ab}][34\mathbf{ab}]\,\{-1 \cdot \mathbf{a}\,\underline{[123\mathbf{b}][134\mathbf{b}]}[24\mathbf{ab}] \\
& + 1 \cdot 4\,[12\mathbf{ab}][123\mathbf{b}][34\mathbf{ab}] - 4 \cdot \mathbf{a}\,[12\mathbf{ab}]\underline{[123\mathbf{b}][134\mathbf{b}]} \\
& - 1 \cdot 2\,[134\mathbf{b}][14\mathbf{ab}][23\mathbf{ab}] + 2 \cdot \mathbf{a}\,\underline{[123\mathbf{b}][134\mathbf{b}]}[14\mathbf{ab}]\} \\[6pt]
\overset{\text{contract}}{=}\ & -1 \cdot \mathbf{a}\,[23\mathbf{ab}][34\mathbf{ab}]\,\{\mathbf{a} \cdot \mathbf{b}\,[124\mathbf{a}][123\mathbf{b}][134\mathbf{b}] \\
& + 1 \cdot 4\,[123\mathbf{b}][12\mathbf{ab}][34\mathbf{ab}] - 1 \cdot 2\,[134\mathbf{b}][14\mathbf{ab}][23\mathbf{ab}]\} \\[6pt]
\overset{\text{factor}}{=}\ & -1 \cdot \mathbf{a}\,[14\mathbf{ab}][23\mathbf{ab}][34\mathbf{ab}] \\
& (\tfrac{1}{2}[123\mathbf{b}][12\mathbf{ab}34] - 1 \cdot 2\,[134\mathbf{b}][23\mathbf{ab}]) \\[6pt]
\overset{\text{contract}}{=}\ & -(1 \cdot \mathbf{a})(3 \cdot \mathbf{b})[1234][12\mathbf{ab}][14\mathbf{ab}][23\mathbf{ab}][34\mathbf{ab}].
\end{aligned}
\tag{32}
$$

5.3. *Explanation of the Elimination*

Recall that an elimination loop has three steps: (1) choose algebraic representations for the geometric entity before its elimination; (2) expand the result of the substitution; (3) simplify the result of the expansion in the bracket ring.

In Clifford algebra, the criteria for a good representation are that it should lead to (1) a factored expression, when this is impossible then (2) an expression with minimal number of terms, and when neither is possible then (3) a contractible expression. By (29), $\mathbf{c}, \mathbf{d}$ each have two representations. The representations in (31) lead to an expression with three monomial factors $\mathbf{1} \cdot \mathbf{a}\,[\mathbf{23ba}][\mathbf{43ba}]$, and are thus optimal.

After the elimination, $[\mathbf{1a}; \mathbf{3b}]_2$ and $[\mathbf{1a}; \mathbf{3b}]_4$ each have two different expansions, and the criteria for a good expansion are the same as those for a good representation. In this example, no expansions can lead to either a factored expression or an expression less than five terms. The expansions used in the proof lead to a contractible polynomial, and are optimal.

The contraction is based on the following *generalized GP relation*:

$$-1 \cdot \mathbf{a}\,[\mathbf{24ab}] + 2 \cdot \mathbf{a}\,[\mathbf{14ab}] - 4 \cdot \mathbf{a}\,[\mathbf{12ab}] = \mathbf{a} \cdot \mathbf{b}\,[\mathbf{124a}]. \tag{33}$$

Definition 6: (Inner-product bracket algebra). Let $\mathcal{K}$ be a field of characteristic $\neq 2$. Let $n \leq m$ be two positive integers, and let ι be a fixed element in $\mathcal{K} - \{0\}$. The n-dimensional *inner-product bracket algebra* generated by m symbols $\mathbf{a}_1, \ldots, \mathbf{a}_m$ is the quotient of the polynomial ring over $\mathcal{K}$ whose indeterminates are elements of $\{\mathbf{a}_i \cdot \mathbf{a}_j, [\mathbf{a}_{i_1} \ldots \mathbf{a}_{i_n}] \mid 1 \leq i, j, i_1, \ldots, i_n \leq m\}$, modulo the two-sided ideal generated by the following 5 types of elements:

B1. $[\mathbf{a}_{i_1} \ldots \mathbf{a}_{i_n}]$ if $i_j = i_k$ for some $j \neq k$;

B2. $[\mathbf{a}_{i_1} \ldots \mathbf{a}_{i_n}] - \mathrm{sign}(\sigma)[\mathbf{a}_{i_{\sigma 1}} \ldots \mathbf{a}_{i_{\sigma n}}]$ for any permutation σ of $1, \ldots, n$;

B3. $\mathbf{a}_i \cdot \mathbf{a}_j - \mathbf{a}_j \cdot \mathbf{a}_i$ for $i \neq j$;

GP1. $\displaystyle\sum_{k=1}^{n+1}(-1)^{k+1}\mathbf{a}_j \cdot \mathbf{a}_{i_k}\,[\mathbf{a}_{i_1} \ldots \breve{\mathbf{a}}_{i_k} \ldots \mathbf{a}_{i_{n+1}}]$;

GP2. $[\mathbf{a}_{i_1} \ldots \mathbf{a}_{i_n}][\mathbf{a}_{j_1} \ldots \mathbf{a}_{j_n}] = \iota \det(\mathbf{a}_{i_k} \cdot \mathbf{a}_{j_l})_{k,l=1,\ldots,n}$.

In this example, (33) is a GP1 relation.

5.4. *Explanation of the Factorization*

By now the elimination procedure of $\mathbf{c}, \mathbf{d}$ has finished, and we are still far away from obtaining a factored form of

$$p = \mathbf{a} \cdot \mathbf{b}\,[\mathbf{124a}][\mathbf{123b}][\mathbf{134b}] + 1 \cdot 4\,[\mathbf{123b}][\mathbf{12ab}][\mathbf{34ab}]$$
$$-1 \cdot 2\,[\mathbf{134b}][\mathbf{14ab}][\mathbf{23ab}] \qquad (34)$$

containing factor [**1234**]. The factorization succeeding the elimination in the proof highlights the unique role of Clifford algebra in Euclidean geometry. Before this step, only the inner and outer products occur in the representation and computation. Without the geometric product, it is extremely difficult to do the factorization. The geometric product introduces a new kind of invariant — the dual of the pseudoscalar part (in this example, the 4-graded part) of the geometric product of six vectors, denoted by [**12ab34**]. It changes its sign by a left shift, a right shift or a reversion of its elements, and has the following *rational binomial expansion*:

$$[\mathbf{12ab34}] = 2\,\frac{\mathbf{a} \cdot \mathbf{b}\,[\mathbf{124a}][\mathbf{134b}] + 1 \cdot 4\,[\mathbf{12ab}][\mathbf{34ab}]}{[\mathbf{14ab}]}. \qquad (35)$$

Definition 7: (Clifford bracket ring). Let $\mathcal{K}$ be a field of characteristic $\neq 2$. Let $n \leq m$ be two positive integers, and let ι be a fixed element in $\mathcal{K} - \{0\}$. The n-dimensional *Clifford bracket algebra* generated by symbols $\mathbf{a}_1, \ldots, \mathbf{a}_m$ is the quotient of the polynomial ring over $\mathcal{K}$ whose indeterminates are elements of $\{\langle \mathbf{a}_{i_1} \ldots \mathbf{a}_{i_{2p}} \rangle, [\mathbf{a}_{j_1} \ldots \mathbf{a}_{j_{n+2q-2}}] \mid p, q \geq 1;\ 1 \leq i_1, \ldots, i_{2p}, j_1, \ldots, j_{n+2q-2} \leq m\}$, modulo the two-sided ideal generated by the following 7 types of elements: **B1, B2, B3** in which $\mathbf{a}_i \cdot \mathbf{a}_j$ is replaced by $\langle \mathbf{a}_i \mathbf{a}_j \rangle$, **GP1, GP2**, and

DF1. $\langle \mathbf{a}_{i_1} \cdots \mathbf{a}_{i_{2l}} \rangle - \displaystyle\sum_{j=2}^{2l} (-1)^j \langle \mathbf{a}_{i_1} \mathbf{a}_{i_j} \rangle \langle \mathbf{a}_{i_2} \cdots \breve{\mathbf{a}}_{i_j} \cdots \mathbf{a}_{i_{2l}} \rangle,$

DF2. $[\mathbf{a}_{i_1} \cdots \mathbf{a}_{i_{n+2l-2}}] - \displaystyle\sum_{1 \leq \sigma_{2l} \leq n+2l-2} \mathrm{sign}(\sigma_{2l}, \breve{\sigma}_{2l}) \langle \sigma_{2l}(\mathbf{a}_i) \rangle\,[\breve{\sigma}_{2l}(\mathbf{a}_i)],$

where $\sigma_{2l}, \breve{\sigma}_{2l}$ is a partition of $1, 2, \ldots, n + 2l - 2$ into two subsequences of length $2l$ and $n - 2$ respectively.

In this example, the new invariant [**12ab34**] is defined by the following DF2 relation:

$$\begin{aligned}
[\mathbf{12ab34}] \\
=\ & 1 \cdot 2[\mathbf{ab34}] - 1 \cdot \mathbf{a}[\mathbf{2b34}] + 1 \cdot \mathbf{b}[\mathbf{2a34}] - 1 \cdot 3[\mathbf{2ab4}] + 1 \cdot 4[\mathbf{2ab3}] \\
& + 2 \cdot \mathbf{a}[\mathbf{1b34}] - 2 \cdot \mathbf{b}[\mathbf{1a34}] + 2 \cdot 3[\mathbf{1ab4}] - 2 \cdot 4[\mathbf{1ab3}] \\
& + \mathbf{a} \cdot \mathbf{b}[\mathbf{1234}] - \mathbf{a} \cdot 3[\mathbf{12b4}] + \mathbf{a} \cdot 4[\mathbf{12b3}] \\
& + \mathbf{b} \cdot 3[\mathbf{12a4}] - \mathbf{b} \cdot 4[\mathbf{12a3}] \\
& + 3 \cdot 4[\mathbf{12ab}].
\end{aligned}$$

The factorization of p in this example relies completely on the expansion (35). Notice that the first two terms of p are in the following form:

$$[\mathbf{123b}](\mathbf{a}\cdot\mathbf{b}\,[\mathbf{124a}][\mathbf{134b}] + \mathbf{1}\cdot\mathbf{4}\,[\mathbf{12ab}][\mathbf{34ab}]). \qquad (36)$$

The first and third terms are in a similar form:

$$[\mathbf{134b}](\mathbf{a}\cdot\mathbf{b}\,[\mathbf{124a}][\mathbf{123b}] - \mathbf{1}\cdot\mathbf{2}\,[\mathbf{14ab}][\mathbf{23ab}]). \qquad (37)$$

Applying (35) to (36), we get $[\mathbf{123b}][\mathbf{14ab}][\mathbf{12ab34}]/2$, so

$$p = [\mathbf{14ab}](\frac{1}{2}[\mathbf{123b}][\mathbf{12ab34}] - \mathbf{1}\cdot\mathbf{2}\,[\mathbf{134b}][\mathbf{23ab}]). \qquad (38)$$

This finishes the first stage of the factorization. Now apply (35) once again to (38); by the unique correspondence

$$\mathbf{1}\leftrightarrow\mathbf{b}, \quad \mathbf{2}\leftrightarrow\mathbf{a}, \quad \mathbf{3}\leftrightarrow\mathbf{4},$$

we get the second factorization:

$$p = -[\mathbf{14ab}]\mathbf{3}\cdot\mathbf{b}\,[\mathbf{a21b}][\mathbf{2143}] = \mathbf{3}\cdot\mathbf{b}\,[\mathbf{1234}][\mathbf{12ab}][\mathbf{14ab}].$$

5.5. *Generalized Miquel Theorem*

Miquel Theorem is a direct consequence of (32), and the identity says more than the theorem. However, (32) is not an identity, because it changes when the vectors are rescaled. The two sides of (32) are equal only up to a nonzero scale.

To change (32) into an identity, we compute $\mathbf{a}\cdot\mathbf{c}$, $\mathbf{b}\cdot\mathbf{d}$ and then divide both sides by their product. Using the first equality in (31), we get

$$\mathbf{a}\cdot\mathbf{c} = (\mathbf{1}\cdot\mathbf{2})(\mathbf{1}\cdot\mathbf{a})[\mathbf{23ab}]^2.$$

Using the following representation of $\mathbf{d}$ from (29):

$$\mathbf{d} = \mathbf{3}\cdot\mathbf{b}[\mathbf{41a3}][\mathbf{41ab}]\mathbf{4} - [\mathbf{1a;3b}]_4([\mathbf{41ab}]\mathbf{3} - [\mathbf{41a3}]\mathbf{b}),$$

we get

$$\mathbf{b}\cdot\mathbf{d} = (\mathbf{3}\cdot\mathbf{4})(\mathbf{3}\cdot\mathbf{b})[\mathbf{14ab}]^2.$$

Generalized Miquel Theorem: For 6 generalized points $a, b, 1, 2, 3, 4$ in the plane, let $c = 12a \cap 23b$, $d = 14a \cap 34b$; then

$$\frac{[\mathbf{abcd}]}{\mathbf{a}\cdot\mathbf{c}\,\mathbf{b}\cdot\mathbf{d}} = -\frac{[\mathbf{1234}]}{\mathbf{1}\cdot\mathbf{2}\,\mathbf{3}\cdot\mathbf{4}}\frac{[\mathbf{12ab}][\mathbf{34ab}]}{[\mathbf{14ab}][\mathbf{23ab}]}.$$

5.6. *Short Summary*

The elimination procedure in Euclidean geometric computing with Clifford algebra is much the same as that in projective and affine geometry except for the set of generalized GPs. However, the factorization procedure is completely different. The proof of Miquel Theorem shows that the geometric product, and hence Clifford algebra, is the unique structure in the construction of invariants.

6. Third Example in Euclidean Geometry

Example 8: Find the condition for the existence of an inscribed sphere in a five-faced convex polytope.

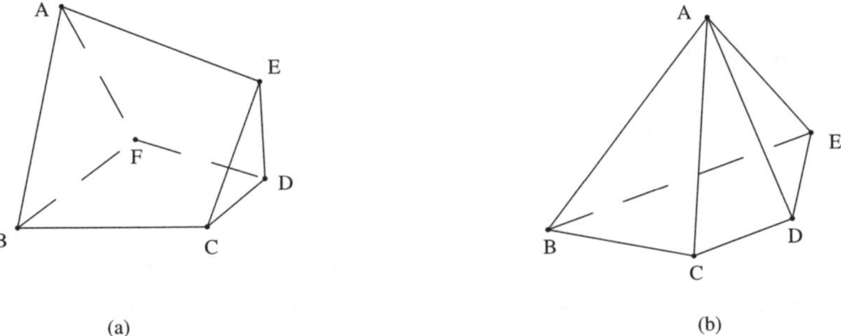

Fig. 6.   Five-faced convex polytope

6.1. *Algebraization*

In the homogeneous model of Euclidean 3-space, spheres and planes can be represented by 4-graded blades of Minkowski signature. The dual of such a blade in the Clifford algebra $\mathcal{CL}(\mathcal{R}^{4,1})$ is a vector of positive signature, and when the blade is of unit magnitude, the vector has unit square. Thus we can also use positive unit vectors to represent spheres and planes in the Euclidean space. A vector $\mathbf{s}$ satisfying $\mathbf{s}^2 = 1$ represents a plane if and only if $\mathbf{e} \cdot \mathbf{s} = 0$.

In the dual representation, a sphere with center $\mathbf{o}$ and passing through point $\mathbf{a}$ is represented by $(\mathbf{e} \wedge \mathbf{c}) \cdot \mathbf{a}$. A plane with normal $\mathbf{n}$ and passing through point $\mathbf{a}$ is represented by $(\mathbf{e} \wedge \mathbf{n}) \cdot \mathbf{a}$.

To represent the geometric relation that two spheres or planes are in *oriented contact*, i.e., they are tangent to each other and at the point of tangency they have the same tangent vector, we need one more dimension to represent the orientation.[4,20] The corresponding algebraic model is called the *Lie model*.

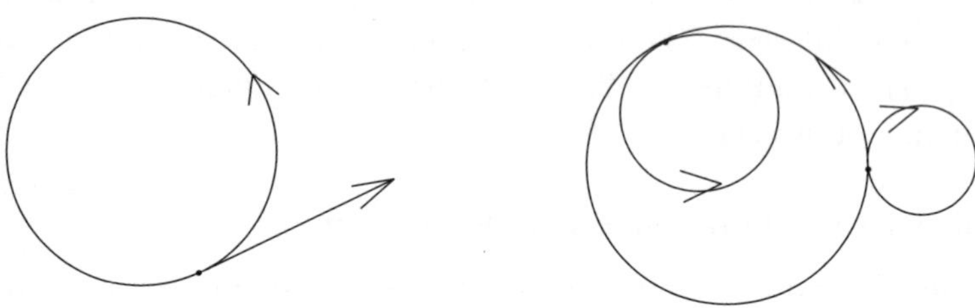

Fig. 7.   Oriented contact

Theorem 9: (S. Lie). A *Lie sphere* in nD Euclidean space is one of the following objects: (1) a point; (2) an oriented hyperplane; (3) an oriented hypersphere; (4) the point at infinity.

Any null vector in $\mathcal{R}^{n+1,2}$ represents a Lie sphere in nD Euclidean space, and any Lie sphere can be represented in this way. A point represented by a null vector $\mathbf{x}$ is on the Lie sphere represented by a null vector $\mathbf{s}$ if and only if $\mathbf{x} \cdot \mathbf{s} = 0$. The representation is unique up to a nonzero scale.

Fix a negative unit vector $\mathbf{e}_{-1}$ and a null vector $\mathbf{e}$ orthogonal to $\mathbf{e}_{-1}$. Then a null vector $\mathbf{s}$ of $\mathcal{R}^{n+1,2}$ represents

(1) the point at infinity if $\mathbf{s} \cdot \mathbf{e} = \mathbf{s} \cdot \mathbf{e}_{-1} = 0$;
(2) a point if $\mathbf{s} \cdot \mathbf{e}_{-1} = 0$ but $\mathbf{s} \cdot \mathbf{e} \neq 0$;
(3) an oriented hyperplane if $\mathbf{s} \cdot \mathbf{e} = 0$ but $\mathbf{s} \cdot \mathbf{e}_{-1} \neq 0$;
(4) an oriented hypersphere otherwise.

Conversely,

(1) the point at infinity is represented by $\mathbf{e}$.
(2) A point c is represented by $\mathbf{c}$ as in the homogeneous model.
(3) The oriented hyperplane with unit normal $\mathbf{n}$ and passing through point a is represented by $\mathbf{n} + (\mathbf{a} \cdot \mathbf{n})\mathbf{e} + \mathbf{e}_{-1}$.
(4) The sphere with center c and radius ρ, whose orientation is outward, is represented by $\mathbf{c} - \rho^2 \mathbf{e}/2 + \rho \mathbf{e}_{-1}$. The sphere with opposite orientation is represented by $\mathbf{c} - \rho^2 \mathbf{e}/2 - \rho \mathbf{e}_{-1}$.

We come back to Example 5. The vector space is $\mathcal{R}^{4,2}$. In $\mathcal{R}^3$, let the unit outward normal vectors of the five faces be $\mathbf{n}_i$ for $1 \leq i \leq 5$. Let A be the intersection of the three faces with normals $\mathbf{n}_1$, $\mathbf{n}_2$, $\mathbf{n}_3$ respectively, and let δ_4, δ_5 be the distances from A to the faces with normals $\mathbf{n}_4$, $\mathbf{n}_5$ respectively.

Choose A as the origin of $\mathcal{R}^3$. Then in Lie's model, the five faces are represented by

$$\begin{cases} \mathbf{s}_1 = \mathbf{n}_1 + \mathbf{e}_{-1}, \\ \mathbf{s}_2 = \mathbf{n}_2 + \mathbf{e}_{-1}, \\ \mathbf{s}_3 = \mathbf{n}_3 + \mathbf{e}_{-1}, \\ \mathbf{s}_4 = \mathbf{n}_4 + \delta_4\mathbf{e} + \mathbf{e}_{-1}, \\ \mathbf{s}_5 = \mathbf{n}_5 + \delta_5\mathbf{e} + \mathbf{e}_{-1}. \end{cases} \tag{39}$$

6.2. *Computation*

The five planes share a common oriented contact sphere if and only if[20]

$$\mathbf{s}_1 \wedge \mathbf{s}_2 \wedge \mathbf{s}_3 \wedge \mathbf{s}_4 \wedge \mathbf{s}_5 = 0.$$

Substituting (39) into it, and after some easy computation, we get

$$\frac{\delta_4}{\delta_5} = \frac{\partial(\mathbf{n}_1 \wedge \mathbf{n}_2 \wedge \mathbf{n}_3 \wedge \mathbf{n}_4)}{\partial(\mathbf{n}_1 \wedge \mathbf{n}_2 \wedge \mathbf{n}_3 \wedge \mathbf{n}_5)}. \tag{40}$$

So the polytope has an inscribed sphere if and only if for any vertex A (or equivalently, for some vertex A), the relation (40) holds. On the right-hand side of (40), $\partial(\mathbf{n}_1 \wedge \mathbf{n}_2 \wedge \mathbf{n}_3 \wedge \mathbf{n}_4)$ is six times the signed volume of the tetrahedron with vertices $\mathbf{n}_1, \mathbf{n}_2, \mathbf{n}_3, \mathbf{n}_4$, the vectors being understood to start from the origin and thus represent points on the unit sphere of $\mathcal{R}^3$.

7. Further Reading

From the previous sections, we see that Clifford algebra is an effective symbolic algebra for geometric representation and computation. However, a lot of stuff on this algebra has been completely omitted in this chapter, including the versor and spinor groups, the representation of spinors, the Dirac differentiation and integration theory, the generalization of harmonic and analytic functions, to name a few. For further reading, except for the references listed at the end, the following are some public resources available on the internet:

http://modelingnts.la.asu.edu
http://www.mrao.cam.ac.uk/~clifford
http://carol.wins.uva.nl/~leo
http://cage.rug.ac.be/~fb/crg

References

1. M. Barnabei, A. Brini and G.-C. Rota. On the exterior calculus of invariant theory. *J. Algebra* **96**: 120–160, 1985.
2. J. Bokowski and B. Sturmfels. *Computational Synthetic Geometry*. LNM **1355**, Springer, Berlin Heidelberg, 1989.
3. T. Boy de la Tour, S. Fèvre and D. Wang. Clifford term rewriting for geometric reasoning in 3D. In: *Proc. ADG '98*, X.-S. Gao, D. Wang and L. Yang (eds.), LNAI **1669**, Springer, Berlin Heidelberg, pp. 130–155, 1999.
4. T. E. Cecil. *Lie Sphere Geometry*. Springer, New York, 1992.
5. S.-C. Chou, X.-S. Gao and J.-Z. Zhang. *Machine Proofs in Geometry — Automated Production of Readable Proofs for Geometric Theorems*. World Scientific, Singapore, 1994.
6. E. B. Corrochano and G. Sobczyk (eds.). *Geometric Algebra with Applications in Science and Engineering*. Birkhäuser, Boston, 2001.
7. H. Crapo and J. Richter-Gebert. Automatic proving of geometric theorems. In: *Invariant Methods in Discrete and Computational Geometry*, N. White (ed.), Kluwer, Dordrecht, pp. 107–139, 1994.
8. A. Crumeyrolle. *Orthogonal and Symplectic Clifford Algebras*. Kluwer, Dordrecht, 1990.
9. L. Dorst, C. Doran and J. Lasenby (eds.). *Applications of Geometric Algebra in Computer Science and Engineering*. Birkhäuser, Boston, 2002.
10. P. Doubilet, G.-C. Rota and J. Stein. On the foundations of combinatorial theory IX: Combinatorial methods in invariant theory. *Stud. Appl. Math.* **57**: 185–216, 1974.
11. S. Fèvre and D. Wang. Proving geometric theorems using Clifford algebra and rewrite rules. In: *Proc. CADE-15*, C. Kirchner and H. Kirchner (eds.), LNAI **1421**, Springer, Berlin Heidelberg, pp. 17–32, 1998.
12. S. Fèvre and D. Wang. Combining Clifford algebraic computing and term-rewriting for geometric theorem proving. *Fundamenta Informaticae* **39**: 85–104, 1999.
13. X.-S. Gao and D. Wang (eds.). *Mathematics Mechanization and Applications*. Academic Press, London, 2000.
14. D. Hestenes. *Space Time Algebra*. Gordon & Breach, New York, 1966.
15. D. Hestenes and G. Sobczyk. *Clifford Algebra to Geometric Calculus*. Kluwer, Dordrecht, 1984.
16. D. Hestenes. *New Foundations for Classical Mechanics*. Kluwer, Dordrecht, 1987.
17. D. Hestenes and R. Ziegler. Projective geometry with Clifford algebra. *Acta Appl. Math.* **23**: 25–63, 1991.
18. W. V. D. Hodge and D. Pedoe. *Methods of Algebraic Geometry*. Cambridge University Press, Cambridge, 1953.
19. H. Li. Some applications of Clifford algebras to geometries. In: *Proc. ADG '98*, X.-S. Gao, D. Wang and L. Yang (eds.), LNAI **1669**, Springer, Berlin Heidelberg, pp. 156–179, 1999.
20. H. Li. The Lie model for Euclidean geometry. In: *Proc. AFPAC 2000*, G.

Sommer and Y. Zeevi (eds.), LNCS **1888**, Springer, Berlin Heidelberg, pp. 115–133, 2000.

21. H. Li. Vectorial equation-solving for mechanical geometry theorem proving. *J. Automated Reasoning* **25**: 83–121, 2001.

22. H. Li, D. Hestenes and A. Rockwood. Generalized homogeneous coordinates for computational geometry. In: *Geometric Computing with Clifford Algebras*, G. Sommer (*ed.*), Springer, Heidelberg, pp. 27–60, 2001.

23. H. Li and Y. Wu. Automated short proof generation for projective geometric theorems with Cayley and bracket algebras I. Incidence geometry. Accepted by *J. Symbolic Computation*. Also available at http://www.mmrc.iss. ac.cn/pub/li1.ps.

24. H. Li and Y. Wu. Automated short proof generation for projective geometric theorems with Cayley and bracket algebras II. Conic geometry. Accepted by *J. Symbolic Computation*. Also available at http://www.mmrc.iss. ac.cn/pub/li2.ps.

25. H. Li. Expansions and summations in Clifford algebra. *Mathematics Mechanization Research Preprint* **21**, 2002. Available at http://www.mmrc.iss.ac. cn/pub/li1.pdf.

26. P. Lounesto. *Clifford Algebras and Spinors*. Cambridge University Press, Cambridge, 1997.

27. B. Mourrain. New aspects of geometrical calculus with invariants. *Advances in Mathematics*, to appear. Also in *MEGA 91*, 1991.

28. J. Richter-Gebert. Mechanical theorem proving in projective geometry. *Annals of Math. and Artificial Intelligence* **13**: 159–171, 1995.

29. G. Sommer (ed.). *Geometric Computing with Clifford Algebras — Theoretical Foundations and Applications in Computer Vision and Robotics*. Springer, Berlin Heidelberg, 2001.

30. B. Sturmfels. *Algorithms in Invariant Theory*. Springer, New York, 1993.

31. D. Wang. *Clifford algebraic calculus for geometric reasoning with application to computer vision*. In: *Proc. ADG' 96*, D. Wang (ed.), LNAI **1360**, Springer, Berlin Heidelberg, pp. 115–140, 1997.

32. N. White. The bracket ring of combinatorial geometry I. *Trans. Amer. Math. Soc.* **202**: 79–103, 1975.

33. N. White. Multilinear Cayley factorization. *J. Symbolic Computation* **11**: 421–438, 1991.

34. W.-T. Wu. *Mathematics Mechanization*. Science Press and Kluwer Academic, Beijing, 2000.

35. I. Yaglom. *Felix Klein and Sophus Lie*. Birkhäuser, Boston Basel, 1988.

CHAPTER 10

AUTOMATED DEDUCTION IN REAL GEOMETRY

Lu Yang

Chengdu Institute of Computer Applications
Chinese Academy of Sciences, Chengdu 610041 and
Guangzhou University, Guangzhou 510405, China
E-mail: cdluyang@mail.sc.cninfo.net

Bican Xia

School of Mathematical Sciences
Peking University
Beijing 100871, China
E-mail: xbc@math.pku.edu.cn

Including three aspects: problem solving, theorem proving and theorem discovering, automated deduction in real geometry depends essentially upon semi-algebraic system solving. A *semi-algebraic system* is a system consisting of polynomial equations, polynomial inequations and polynomial inequalities, where all the polynomials are of integer coefficients. We give three practical algorithms respectively for the three kinds of problems mentioned above. A package based on these algorithms for *solving* semi-algebraic systems at the three levels has been implemented as Maple programs. The performance of the package on many famous examples is reported.

1. Introduction

A semi-algebraic system is a system of polynomial equations, inequalities and inequations. More precisely, we call

$$\begin{cases} p_1(x_1,\ldots,x_n) = 0,\ldots,p_s(x_1,\ldots,x_n) = 0, \\ g_1(x_1,\ldots,x_n) \geq 0,\ldots,g_r(x_1,\ldots,x_n) \geq 0, \\ g_{r+1}(x_1,\ldots,x_n) > 0,\ldots,g_t(x_1,\ldots,x_n) > 0, \\ h_1(x_1,\ldots,x_n) \neq 0,\ldots,h_m(x_1,\ldots,x_n) \neq 0 \end{cases} \qquad (1)$$

248

a *semi-algebraic system* (SAS for short), where $n, s \geq 1$, $r, t, m \geq 0$ and p_i, g_j, h_k are all polynomials in $x_1, \ldots, x_n$ with integer coefficients.

Many problems in both practice and theory can be reduced to problems of solving SAS. For example, we may mention some special cases of the "p-3-p" problem[15] which originates from computer vision, the problem of constructing limit cycles for plane differential systems[26] and the problem of automated discovering and proving for geometric inequalities.[49,48] Moreover, many problems in geometry, topology and differential dynamical systems are expected to be solved by translating them into certain semi-algebraic systems.

There are two classical methods, Tarski's method[32] and the cylindrical algebraic decomposition (CAD) method proposed by Collins,[10] for solving semi-algebraic systems and numerous improvements and progresses[11,7,14,3] have been made since then. But this problem is well known to have for the general case double exponential complexity in the number of variables.[13] Therefore, the best way to attack quantifier elimination may be to classify the problems and to offer practical algorithms for some special cases from various applications.[36,37,38,19,16,48,49,52]

Two classes of SAS with strong geometric backgrounds are discussed in this chapter. A SAS is called a *constant-coefficient* SAS if $n = s$ and $\{p_1, \ldots, p_s\}$ is assumed to have only a finite number of common zeros, while a SAS is called a *parametric* SAS if $s < n$ (s indeterminates are viewed as variables and the other $n - s$ indeterminates as parameters) and $\{p_1, \ldots, p_s\}$ is assumed to have only a finite number of common zeros on all the possible values of the parameters. A very recent algorithm to solve general SAS (where the ideal generated by the polynomials may be of positive dimension) appears in the paper[2] by Aubry and others.

For a constant-coefficient SAS, counting and isolating real solutions are two key problems in the study of the real solutions of the system from the viewpoint of symbolic computation. And algorithms for this kind of problems often form the base of some other algorithms for solving parametric SAS. Becker and Weispfenning[4] presented an algorithm for isolating the real zeros of a system of polynomial equations by Gröbner bases computing and Sturm theorem. Some effective methods for counting real solutions of SAS are those using trace forms or the rational univariate representation[28,29,17] and the algorithm proposed by Xia and Hou.[44] Usually, these methods may suggest some algorithms for isolating real solutions of SAS. In Section 2, we present an algorithm[45] for isolating the real solutions of constant-coefficient SAS, which, in some sense, can be viewed as a generalization of the Uspensky algorithm.[12] Lu and others[25] proposed a different algorithm for isolating the real solutions of polynomial equations. Recently, Xia and Zhang[46] presented a new and faster algorithm for isolating the real zeros of polynomial equations based on interval arithmetic.

Sections 3 and 4 are devoted to algorithms for "solving" parametric SAS. Automated theorem proving and discovering on inequalities are always considered as difficult topics in the area of automated reasoning. To prove or disprove a geometric inequality, it is often required to decide whether a parametric SAS has any real solutions or not. A so-called "dimension-decreasing" algorithm[52,51] is very fast for this kind of problems and is sketched in Section 3. To discover inequality-type theorems automatically, it is often required to find conditions on the parameters of a parametric SAS such that the system has a specified number of real solutions. A complete and practical algorithm for this kind of problems is described in Section 4.

2. Find Real Solutions of Geometric Problems

In this section we discuss an algorithm for isolating the real solutions of a constant-coefficient SAS and its application to finding real solutions of geometric problems.

2.1. *Basic Definitions*

For any polynomial P of positive degree, the *leading variable x_l* of P is the one with greatest index l that effectively appears in P. A *triangular set* is a set of polynomials $\{f_i(x_1,\dots,x_i), f_{i+1}(x_1,\dots,x_{i+1}),\dots,f_l(x_1,\dots,x_l)\}$ in which the leading variable of f_j is x_j. If the ideal generated by $p_1,\dots,p_n$ is zero-dimensional, then it is well known that the Ritt-Wu method, Gröbner basis methods or subresultant methods can be used to transform the system of equations into one or more systems in triangular form.[41,8,33,1,54] Therefore, in this section, we only consider triangular sets and the problem we discuss is to isolate the real solutions of the following system

$$\begin{cases} f_1(x_1) = 0, \\ f_2(x_1, x_2) = 0, \\ \quad \dots\dots \\ f_s(x_1, x_2, \dots, x_s) = 0, \\ g_1(x_1, x_2, \dots, x_s) \geq 0, \dots, g_r(x_1, x_2, \dots, x_s) \geq 0, \\ g_{r+1}(x_1, x_2, \dots, x_s) > 0, \dots, g_t(x_1, x_2, \dots, x_s) > 0, \\ h_1(x_1, x_2, \dots, x_s) \neq 0, \dots, h_m(x_1, x_2, \dots, x_s) \neq 0, \end{cases} \tag{2}$$

where $s \geq 1$, $r, t, m \geq 0$ and $\{f_1, f_2, \ldots, f_s\}$ is a normal ascending chain[54] (see also Definition 1 in this section). We call a system in this form a *triangular semi-algebraic system* (TSA for short).

Given a polynomial $g(x)$, let resultant(g, g'_x, x) be the Sylvester resultant of g and g'_x with respect to x, where g'_x means the derivative of $g(x)$ with respect to x. We call it the *discriminant* of g with respect to x and denote it by $\mathrm{dis}(g, x)$ or simply by $\mathrm{dis}(g)$ if its meaning is clear.

Given a polynomial g and a triangular set $\{f_1, f_2, \ldots, f_s\}$, let

$$r_s := g, \quad r_{s-i} := \mathrm{resultant}(r_{s-i+1}, f_{s-i+1}, x_{s-i+1}), \quad i = 1, 2, \ldots, s;$$

$$q_s := g, \quad q_{s-i} := \mathrm{prem}(q_{s-i+1}, f_{s-i+1}, x_{s-i+1}), \quad i = 1, 2, \ldots, s,$$

where resultant(p, q, x) means the Sylvester resultant of p and q with respect to x and prem(p, q, x) means the pseudo-remainder of p divided by q with respect to x.

We denote r_{i-1} and q_{i-1} $(1 \leq i \leq s)$ by $\mathrm{res}(g, f_s, \ldots, f_i)$ and $\mathrm{prem}(g, f_s, \ldots, f_i)$ and call them the *resultant* and *pseudo-remainder* of g with respect to the triangular set $\{f_i, f_{i+1}, \ldots, f_s\}$, respectively.

Definition 1: Given a triangular set $\{f_1, f_2, \ldots, f_s\}$, denote by I_i the leading coefficient of f_i in x_i $(i = 1, \ldots, s)$. The triangular set $\{f_1, f_2, \ldots, f_s\}$ is called a *normal ascending chain* if $\mathrm{res}(I_i, f_{i-1}, \ldots, f_1) \neq 0$ for $i = 2, \ldots, s$. Note that $I_1 \neq 0$ follows from the definition of a triangular set.

Remark 2: A normal ascending chain is also called a *regular chain* by Kalkbrener[21] and a *regular set* by Wang,[34] and was called a *proper ascending chain* by Yang and Zhang.[53]

Definition 3: Let a TSA be given as defined in (2), called T. For every f_i $(i \geq 1)$, let $\mathrm{CP}_{f_i} = \mathrm{dis}(f_i, x_i)$ $(i \leq 2)$ and

$$\mathrm{CP}_{f_i} = \mathrm{res}\left(\mathrm{dis}(f_i, x_i), f_{i-1}, f_{i-2}, \ldots, f_2\right), \quad i > 2.$$

For any $q \in \{g_j \mid 1 \leq j \leq t\} \bigcup \{h_k \mid 1 \leq k \leq m\}$, let

$$\mathrm{CP}_q = \begin{cases} \mathrm{res}\left(q, f_s, f_{s-1}, \ldots, f_2\right), & \text{if } s > 1, \\ q, & \text{if } s = 1. \end{cases}$$

We define

$$\mathrm{CP}_T(x_1) = \prod_{1 \leq i \leq s} \mathrm{CP}_{f_i} \cdot \prod_{1 \leq j \leq t} \mathrm{CP}_{g_j} \cdot \prod_{1 \leq k \leq m} \mathrm{CP}_{h_k},$$

and call it the *critical polynomial* of the system T with respect to x_1. We also denote $\mathrm{CP}_T(x_1)$ by CP or $\mathrm{CP}(x_1)$ if its meaning is clear.

Remark 4: Let a TSA T be given and denote by T_1 the system formed by deleting $f_1(x_1)$ from T. In T_1, we view x_1 as a parameter and let it vary continuously on the real number axis. From Theorem 7 below, we know that the number of distinct real solutions of T_1 will remain fixed, provided that x_1 varies on an interval in which there are no real zeros of $\mathrm{CP}_T(x_1)$. That is why $\mathrm{CP}_T(x_1)$ is called the *critical polynomial* of the system T.

Definition 5: A TSA is *regular* if $\mathrm{resultant}(f_1(x_1), \mathrm{CP}(x_1), x_1) \neq 0$.

Remark 6: According to Definition 5, for a regular TSA no CP_{h_k} ($1 \leq k \leq m$) has common zeros with $f_1(x_1)$, which implies that every solution of $\{f_1 = 0, \ldots, f_s = 0\}$ satisfies $h_k \neq 0$ ($1 \leq k \leq m$). Thus if a TSA is regular we can omit the h_k's in it without loss of generality. Similarly, every solution of $\{f_1 = 0, \ldots, f_s = 0\}$ satisfies $g_j \neq 0$ ($1 \leq j \leq t$). That is to say, each of the inequalities $g_j \geq 0$ ($1 \leq j \leq r$) in a regular TSA can be treated as $g_j > 0$.

2.2. *The Algorithm*

Given two polynomials $p(x)$, $q(x) \in \mathbb{Z}[x]$, suppose that $p(x)$ and $q(x)$ have no common zeros, i.e., $\mathrm{resultant}(p, q, x) \neq 0$, and $\alpha_1 < \alpha_2 < \cdots < \alpha_n$ are all distinct real zeros of $p(x)$. By the modified Uspensky algorithm,[12,30] we can obtain a sequence of intervals $[a_1, b_1], \ldots, [a_n, b_n]$ satisfying

(1) $\alpha_i \in [a_i, b_i]$ for $i = 1, \ldots, n$,
(2) $[a_i, b_i] \bigcap [a_j, b_j] = \emptyset$ for $i \neq j$,
(3) a_i, b_i ($1 \leq i \leq n$) are all rational numbers, and
(4) the maximal size of each isolating interval can be less than any positive number given in advance.

Because $p(x)$ and $q(x)$ have no common zeros, the intervals can also satisfy

(5) no zeros of $q(x)$ are in any $[a_i, b_i]$.

In the following we denote an algorithm to do this by $\mathtt{nearzero}(p, q, x)$, or $\mathtt{nearzero}(p, q, x, \epsilon)$ if the maximal size of the isolating intervals is specified to be not greater than a positive number ϵ.

Theorem 7: Let a regular TSA be given. Suppose that $f_1(x_1)$ has n distinct real zeros; then, by calling $\mathtt{nearzero}(f_1, \mathrm{CP}(x_1), x_1)$ we can obtain a sequence of intervals $[a_1, b_1], \ldots, [a_n, b_n]$ satisfying: for any $[a_i, b_i]$ ($1 \leq i \leq n$) and any $\beta, \gamma \in [a_i, b_i]$,

(1) if $s > 1$, then the system

$$\begin{cases} f_2(\beta, x_2) = 0, \dots, f_s(\beta, x_2, \dots, x_s) = 0, \\ g_1(\beta, x_2, \dots, x_s) > 0, \dots, g_t(\beta, x_2, \dots, x_s) > 0 \end{cases}$$

and the system

$$\begin{cases} f_2(\gamma, x_2) = 0, \dots, f_s(\gamma, x_2, \dots, x_s) = 0, \\ g_1(\gamma, x_2, \dots, x_s) > 0, \dots, g_t(\gamma, x_2, \dots, x_s) > 0 \end{cases}$$

have the same number of distinct real solutions, and
(2) if $s = 1$, then for any g_j $(1 \le j \le t)$, $\operatorname{sign}(g_j(\beta)) = \operatorname{sign}(g_j(\gamma))$, where $\operatorname{sign}(x)$ is 1 if $x > 0$, -1 if $x < 0$, and 0 if $x = 0$.

Theorem 8:[45] For an irregular TSA T, there is an algorithm which can decompose T into regular systems T_i. Let all the distinct real solutions of a given system be denoted by $\operatorname{Rzero}(\cdot)$; then this decomposition satisfies $\operatorname{Rzero}(T) = \bigcup \operatorname{Rzero}(T_i)$.

By Theorem 8, we only need to consider regular TSAs. Given a regular TSA T, for $2 \le i \le s$, $1 \le j < i$, let

$$U_{ij} = \begin{cases} \operatorname{res}\left(\dfrac{\partial f_i}{\partial x_j}, f_i, f_{i-1}, \dots, f_{j+1}\right), & \text{if } \dfrac{\partial f_i}{\partial x_j} \not\equiv 0, \\[2em] 1, & \text{if } \dfrac{\partial f_i}{\partial x_j} \equiv 0, \end{cases}$$

$$\operatorname{MP}_T(x_j) = \prod_{j \le k < i \le s} U_{ik}, \quad (1 \le j \le s - 1).$$

Algorithm: REALZERO
Input: A regular TSA $T^{(1)}$ and an optional parameter, w, indicating the maximal sizes of the output intervals on $x_1, \dots, x_s$;
Output: Isolating intervals of real solutions of $T^{(1)}$ or reports fail.
Step 1. Set $i \leftarrow 1$ and compute $\operatorname{resultant}(f_i(x_i), \operatorname{MP}_{T^{(i)}}(x_i), x_i)$. If it is zero, then return "fail" and stop. Otherwise,

$$S^{(i)} \leftarrow \texttt{nearzero}(f_i(x_i), \operatorname{CP}_{T^{(i)}} \cdot \operatorname{MP}_{T^{(i)}}, x_i).$$

Step 2. For each i-dimensional cube I in $S^{(i)}$:

Step 2a. Let V_I be the set of the vertices of the i-dimensional cube I.
Step 2b. For each vertex $(v_j^{(1)}, \dots, v_j^{(i)})$ in V_I, substitute $x_1 = v_j^{(1)}$, $\dots, x_i = v_j^{(i)}$ into $T^{(1)}$ and delete the first i equations (denote the

other equations still by f_l $(i + 1 \le l \le s)$ and the new system by $T_j^{(i+1)}$). Compute

$$\text{resultant}(f_{i+1}(x_{i+1}), \text{MP}_{T_j^{(i+1)}}(x_{i+1}), x_{i+1}).$$

If it is zero, then return "fail" and stop. Otherwise,

$$R_j^{(i+1)} \leftarrow \texttt{nearzero}(f_{i+1}(x_{i+1}), \text{CP}_{T_j^{(i+1)}} \cdot \text{MP}_{T_j^{(i+1)}}, x_{i+1}).$$

Step 2c. Merge all $R_j^{(i+1)}$ into one list of intervals, denoted by $R^{(i+1)}$. If any two intervals in $R^{(i+1)}$ intersect or the maximal size of these intervals is greater than w, shrink I by the sub-algorithm $\texttt{SHR}(I)$ given below and go back to Step 2a. Otherwise,

$$S_I^{(i+1)} \leftarrow I \times R^{(i+1)}.$$

Step 3. Set $S^{(i+1)} \leftarrow \bigcup_{I \in S^{(i)}} S_I^{(i+1)}$, $i \leftarrow i + 1$; If $i < s$, then go to Step 2.

Step 4. For each s-dimensional cube I, check the sign of each g_j $(1 \le j \le t)$ on I and determine the output.

Sub-algorithm: SHR

Input: A k-dimensional cube I_0 in $S^{(k)}$;

Output: A k-dimensional cube $I \subset I_0$.

Step 0. Suppose that $I_0 = [a_1, b_1] \times \cdots \times [a_k, b_k]$ and x_1^0 is the unique zero of $f_1(x_1)$ in $[a_1, b_1]$. By the intermediate value theorem, we can get an interval $[a_1', b_1'] \subset [a_1, b_1]$ with $x_1^0 \in [a_1', b_1']$ and $b_1' - a_1' = (b_1 - a_1)/8$.

Step 1. Set $i \leftarrow 1$, $I \leftarrow [a_1', b_1']$.

Step 2. Let V_I be the set of the vertices of the i-dimensional cube I. For each $(v_j^{(1)}, \ldots, v_j^{(i)})$ in V_I, substitute $x_1 = v_j^{(1)}, \ldots, x_i = v_j^{(i)}$ into $T^{(1)}$ and delete the first i equations of it (denote the new system by $T_j^{(i+1)}$). Compute

$$Q_j^{i+1} \leftarrow \texttt{nearzero}\,(f_{i+1}(x_{i+1}), \text{CP}_{T_j^{(i+1)}} \cdot \text{MP}_{T_j^{(i+1)}}, x_{i+1}).$$

When $\texttt{nearzero}$ is called to compute Q_j^{i+1}, let the maximal size of the intervals be $\dfrac{1}{8}$ of that we used to compute R_j^{i+1} in $\texttt{REALZERO}$.

Step 3. Merge $Q_j^{(i+1)}$ into one sequence $Q^{(i+1)}$. Of course, we know to which interval in $Q^{(i+1)}$ $[a_{i+1}, b_{i+1}]$ should correspond. Denote the interval by $[a_{i+1}', b_{i+1}']$.

Step 4. Set $I \leftarrow I \times [a_{i+1}', b_{i+1}']$, $i \leftarrow i + 1$. If $i = k$, then output I and stop; otherwise, go to Step 2.

Remark 9: In the steps of REALZERO, calling $\texttt{nearzero}(f_i(x_i), \text{CP}\cdot\text{MP}, x_i)$ aims at getting the isolating intervals of $f_i(x_i)$ that have the following two properties: (1) the property stated in Theorem 7; (2) every x_j $(j > i)$, when viewed as a function of x_i implicitly defined by f_j, is monotonic on each isolating interval. The first property is guaranteed by Theorem 7 because the TSA is regular, but the second one is not guaranteed. So, in some cases (for example, when some zero of $f_1(x_1)$ is an extreme point of x_2 that is viewed as a function of x_1 implicitly defined by f_2) the algorithm does not work.

We illustrate the algorithm REALZERO in detail by the following simple example which we encountered while solving a geometric constraint problem.

Example 10: Given a regular TSA

$$
T^{(1)} : \quad \begin{cases} f_1 = 10x^2 - 1 = 0, \\ f_2 = -5y^2 + 5xy + 1 = 0, \\ f_3 = 30z^2 - 20(y + x)z + 10xy - 11 = 0, \\ x \geq 0,\ y \geq 0, \end{cases}
$$

by REALZERO, we take the following steps to get the isolating intervals.

Step 1. $\text{MP}_{T^{(1)}}(x) = (5x^2 + 22)(110x^2 + 529)$ and $\text{CP}_{T^{(1)}}(x) = x(4 + 5x^2)(7 + 2x^2)$ up to some non-zero constants. Because

$$
\text{resultant}(f_1(x), \text{MP}_{T^{(1)}}(x), x) \neq 0,
$$

we get

$$
S^{(1)} = \texttt{nearzero}(f_1(x), \text{CP}_{T^{(1)}} \cdot \text{MP}_{T^{(1)}}, x)
$$

$$
= \left[\left[\frac{-3}{8}, \frac{-5}{16} \right], \left[\frac{5}{16}, \frac{3}{8} \right] \right].
$$

Obviously, the first interval need not be considered in the following. So

$$
S^{(1)} = \left[\frac{5}{16}, \frac{3}{8} \right].
$$

Step 2. $S^{(1)}$ has only one interval $I = \left[\frac{5}{16}, \frac{3}{8} \right]$.

Step 2a. $V_I = \left\{ v_1^{(1)} = \frac{5}{16},\ v_2^{(1)} = \frac{3}{8} \right\}.$

Step 2b. Substituting $x = v_1^{(1)} = \dfrac{5}{16}$ into $T^{(1)}$ and deleting f_1 from it, we get

$$T_1^{(2)} : \begin{cases} f_2 = 1 + \dfrac{25}{16}y - 5y^2 = 0, \\[2mm] f_3 = 30z^2 - (20y + \dfrac{25}{4})z + \dfrac{25}{8}y - 11 = 0, \\[2mm] y \geq 0. \end{cases}$$

Now $\mathrm{MP}_{T_1^{(2)}}(y) = -1$ and $\mathrm{CP}_{T_1^{(2)}}(y) = (\dfrac{4349}{1280} - \dfrac{5}{16}y + y^2)y$; by

$$\mathtt{nearzero}(f_2(y), \mathrm{CP}_{T_1^{(2)}} \cdot \mathrm{MP}_{T_1^{(2)}}, y),$$

we get $R_1^{(2)} = \left[\left[\dfrac{-3}{8}, \dfrac{-5}{16} \right], \left[\dfrac{5}{8}, \dfrac{11}{16} \right] \right]$. Obviously, the first interval

need not to be considered in the following, so $R_1^{(2)} = \left[\dfrac{5}{8}, \dfrac{11}{16} \right]$.

Similarly, by substituting $x = v_2^{(1)} = \dfrac{3}{8}$ into $T^{(1)}$, we get $R_2^{(2)} = \left[\dfrac{5}{8}, \dfrac{11}{16} \right]$.

Step 2c. Merge $R_1^{(2)}$ and $R_2^{(2)}$ into $R^{(2)} : \left[\dfrac{5}{8}, \dfrac{11}{16} \right]$ and let $S_I^{(2)} = I \times R^{(2)}$.

Step 3. Because $S^{(1)}$ has only one interval, we have

$$S^{(2)} = S_I^{(2)} = \left[\dfrac{5}{16}, \dfrac{3}{8} \right] \times \left[\dfrac{5}{8}, \dfrac{11}{16} \right].$$

Now $i = 2 < s = 3$, so repeat Step 2 for $S^{(2)}$.

Step 2a. $S^{(2)}$ has only one element $I = \left[\dfrac{5}{16}, \dfrac{3}{8} \right] \times \left[\dfrac{5}{8}, \dfrac{11}{16} \right]$ and

$$V_I = \left\{ (v_1^{(1)}, v_1^{(2)}) = \left(\dfrac{5}{16}, \dfrac{5}{8} \right), \ (v_2^{(1)}, v_2^{(2)}) = \left(\dfrac{5}{16}, \dfrac{11}{16} \right), \right.$$
$$\left. (v_3^{(1)}, v_3^{(2)}) = \left(\dfrac{3}{8}, \dfrac{5}{8} \right), \ (v_4^{(1)}, v_4^{(2)}) = \left(\dfrac{3}{8}, \dfrac{11}{16} \right) \right\}.$$

Step 2b. Substituting $x = v_1^{(1)} = \dfrac{5}{16}$, $y = v_1^{(2)} = \dfrac{5}{8}$ into $T^{(1)}$ and deleting f_1, f_2 from it, we get $T_1^{(3)} : \{ f_3 = 640z^2 - 400z - 193 = 0 \}$. Because this is the last equation in the ascending chain, we let $\mathrm{CP}_{T_1^{(3)}} \cdot \mathrm{MP}_{T_1^{(3)}} = 1$ and, by $\mathtt{nearzero}(f_3(z), 1, z)$, get

$R_1^{(3)} = [[-1, 0], [0, 1]]$. Similarly, we have $R_2^{(3)} = R_3^{(3)} = R_4^{(3)} = [[-1, 0], [0, 1]]$.

Step 2c. Merge $R_1^{(3)}, R_2^{(3)}, R_3^{(3)}$ and $R_4^{(3)}$ into $R^{(3)} : [[-1, 0], [0, 1]]$ and let $S_I^{(3)} = I \times R^{(3)}$.

Because $S^{(2)}$ has only one element, we have

$$S^{(3)} = S_I^{(3)} = \left[\left[\frac{5}{16}, \frac{3}{8} \right] \times \left[\frac{5}{8}, \frac{11}{16} \right] \times [-1, 0], \right.$$
$$\left. \left[\frac{5}{16}, \frac{3}{8} \right] \times \left[\frac{5}{8}, \frac{11}{16} \right] \times [0, 1] \right].$$

Now $i = 3 = s$, so go to Step 4 and output

$$\left[\left[\left[\frac{5}{16}, \frac{3}{8} \right], \left[\frac{5}{8}, \frac{11}{16} \right], [-1, 0] \right], \left[\left[\frac{5}{16}, \frac{3}{8} \right], \left[\frac{5}{8}, \frac{11}{16} \right], [0, 1] \right] \right].$$

2.3. *Realzero* **and Examples**

Our method has been implemented as a Maple program `realzero`. In general, for a SAS the computation of `realzero` consists of three main steps. First, by the Ritt-Wu method, the system of equations is transformed into one or more systems in triangular form. In our implementation, we use `wsolve`,[35] a program which realizes Wu's method in Maple. The second step is to check whether each component is a regular TSA and, if not, transform it into regular TSAs by Theorem 8. In the third step, REALZERO is applied to each resulting regular TSA.

There are three basic kinds of calling sequences for a constant-coefficient SAS:

```
realzero([p₁,...,pₙ],[q₁,...,qᵣ],[g₁,...,gₜ],[h₁,...,hₘ],[x₁,...,xₛ]);
realzero([p₁,...,pₙ],[q₁,...,qᵣ],[g₁,...,gₜ],[h₁,...,hₘ],[x₁,...,xₛ],width);
realzero([p₁,...,pₙ],[q₁,...,qᵣ],[g₁,...,gₜ],[h₁,...,hₘ],[x₁,...,xₛ],
        [w₁,...,wₛ]);
```

The command `realzero` returns a list of isolating intervals for all real solutions of the input system or reports that the method does not work on some components. If the 6th parameter "width", a positive number, is given, then the maximal size of the output intervals is less than or equal to this number. If the 6th parameter is a list $[w_1, \ldots, w_s]$ of positive numbers, then the maximal sizes of the output intervals on $x_1, \ldots, x_s$ are less than or equal to $w_1, \ldots, w_s$, respectively. If the 6th parameter is omitted, then the most convenient width is used for each interval returned. That is to say, the isolating intervals for certain x_i are returned, provided that they do not intersect with each other.

Example 11: This is a problem of solving geometric constraints: Are we able to construct a triangle with elements $a = 1, R = 1$ and $h_a = 1/10$, where a, h_a and R denote the side-length, altitude, and circumradius, respectively?

A result given by Mitrinovic and others[27] says that there exists a triangle with elements a, R, h_a if and only if $R_1 = 2R - a \geq 0$ and $R_2 = 8Rh_a - 4h_a^2 - a^2 \geq 0$. From our study[49] (see also Section 4 in this chapter for details), we know that the result is incorrect. We can also see this from the following computations. For $a = 1, R = 1, h_a = 1/10$, we have $R_1 > 0, R_2 < 0$ and

$$\begin{cases} f_1 = 1/100 - 4s(s-1)(s-b)(s-c) = 0, \\ f_2 = 1/5 - bc = 0, \\ f_3 = 2s - 1 - b - c = 0, \\ b > 0, c > 0, b + c - 1 > 0, 1 + c - b > 0, 1 + b - c > 0, \end{cases}$$

where s is the half perimeter and b, c are the lengths of the other two sides, respectively. Calling

$$\texttt{realzero}\,([f_1, f_2, f_3], [\,], [b, c, b + c - 1, 1 + c - b, 1 + b - c], [\,], [s, b, c]);$$

we get

$$\left[\left[\left[\frac{259}{256}, \frac{519}{512}\right], \left[\frac{33}{128}, \frac{17}{64}\right], \left[\frac{97}{128}, \frac{197}{256}\right]\right], \left[\left[\frac{259}{256}, \frac{519}{512}\right], \left[\frac{97}{128}, \frac{99}{128}\right], \left[\frac{1}{4}, \frac{69}{256}\right]\right],\right.$$

$$\left.\left[\left[\frac{297}{256}, \frac{595}{512}\right], \left[\frac{11}{64}, \frac{23}{128}\right], \left[\frac{73}{64}, \frac{295}{256}\right]\right], \left[\left[\frac{297}{256}, \frac{595}{512}\right], \left[\frac{73}{64}, \frac{37}{32}\right], \left[\frac{21}{128}, \frac{47}{256}\right]\right]\right],$$

which means that there are two different triangles with elements $a = 1, R = 1$ and $h_a = 10^{-1}$ since b and c are symmetric in the system. The time spent for the computation on a PC (Pentium IV/2.8G) with Maple 8 is 0.2 s. Furthermore, setting $width = 10^{-6}$ in the calling sequence:

$$\texttt{realzero}\,([f_1, f_2, f_3], [\,], [b, c, b + c - 1, 1 + c - b, 1 + b - c], [\,], [s, b, c], 10^{-6});$$

we obtain a much more accurate result:

$$\left[\left[\left[\frac{10624409}{10485760}, \frac{1062441}{1048576}\right], \left[\frac{4386135}{16777216}, \frac{4386137}{16777216}\right], \left[\frac{64173779}{83886080}, \frac{12834761}{16777216}\right]\right],\right.$$

$$\left[\left[\frac{10624409}{10485760}, \frac{1062441}{1048576}\right], \left[\frac{3208689}{4194304}, \frac{12834761}{16777216}\right], \left[\frac{21930659}{83886080}, \frac{1096535}{4194304}\right]\right],$$

$$\left[\left[\left[\frac{152143}{131072}, \frac{12171441}{10485760}\right], \left[\frac{731239}{4194304}, \frac{1462479}{8388608}\right], \left[\frac{9623217}{8388608}, \frac{24058049}{20971520}\right]\right],\right.$$

$$\left.\left[\left[\frac{152143}{131072}, \frac{12171441}{10485760}\right], \left[\frac{9623217}{8388608}, \frac{19246439}{16777216}\right], \left[\frac{2924953}{16777216}, \frac{7312403}{41943040}\right]\right]\right].$$

The time spent is 0.3 s.

Example 12:[15] Which triangles can occur as sections of a regular tetrahedron by planes which separate one vertex from the other three? In fact, this is one of the special cases of the p-3-p problem which originates from camera calibration. Making use of another program called DISCOVERER,[49] we will get the so-called complete solution classification of this problem in Section 4.

Now, let $1, a, b$ be the lengths of the three sides of the triangle (assume that $b \geq a \geq 1$), and x, y, z the distances from the vertex to the three vertexes of the triangle respectively and suppose that (a, b) is the real roots of

$$\{a^2 - 1 + b - b^2 = 0, 3b^6 + 56b^4 - 122b^3 + 56b^2 + 3 = 0\}.$$

We want to find x, y and z. Thus, the system is

$$\begin{cases} h_1 = x^2 + y^2 - xy - 1 = 0, \\ h_2 = y^2 + z^2 - yz - a^2 = 0, \\ h_3 = z^2 + x^2 - zx - b^2 = 0, \\ h_4 = a^2 - 1 + b - b^2 = 0, \\ h_5 = 3b^6 + 56b^4 - 122b^3 + 56b^2 + 3 = 0, \\ x > 0, y > 0, z > 0, a - 1 \geq 0, b - a \geq 0, a + 1 - b > 0. \end{cases}$$

Call

`realzero`$([h_1, h_2, h_3, h_4, h_5], [b - a, a - 1], [x, y, z, a + 1 - b], [\,], [b, a, x, y, z])$;

the output is

$$\left[\left[\left[\frac{162993}{131072}, \frac{81497}{65536}\right], \left[\frac{73}{64}, \frac{147}{128}\right], \left[\frac{1181}{1024}, \frac{2363}{2048}\right], \left[\frac{1349206836}{2188300897}, \frac{348432792}{556866289}\right],\right.\right.$$

$$\left.\left.\left[\frac{3247431090114025}{2465566125550592}, \frac{202944373270641}{154042321050112}\right]\right]\right].$$

The time spent is 15.02 s. Setting $width = 10^{-6}$ in the calling sequence:

$$\texttt{realzero}([h_1, h_2, h_3, h_4, h_5], [b - a, a - 1], [x, y, z, a + 1 - b], [\,],$$
$$[b, a, x, y, z], 10^{-6});$$

we obtain a much more accurate result:

$$\left[\left[\left[\frac{162993137}{131072000}, \frac{1303945097}{1048576000}\right], \left[\frac{1225595355}{1073741824}, \frac{1225595357}{1073741824}\right], \left[\frac{77410187}{67108864}, \frac{154820375}{134217728}\right],\right.\right.$$

$$\left[\frac{560741379519956970719218 75}{9010681213432120850199 3472}, \frac{1057264334012463994320375}{169894178757541867867 3408}\right],$$

$$\left.\left.\left[\frac{3526190623631913263644638012202592 11}{267676127050613514331758788608000 000}, \frac{5571405430451419205920677477912 3}{42293011923906715097526960128000}\right]\right]\right].$$

The time spent is $19.95\,$s.

3. Prove or Disprove Propositions

Let Φ be a semi-algebraic system and Φ_0 a polynomial equation, inequation or inequality. Prove or disprove that $\Phi \Rightarrow \Phi_0$. Obviously, the statement is true if and only if the system $\Phi \wedge \neg\Phi_0$ is inconsistent, where $\neg\Phi_0$ stands for the negative statement of Φ_0.

Automated theorem proving in real algebra and real geometry is always considered a difficult topic in the area of automated reasoning. A universal algorithm (such as methods for real quantifier elimination) would be of very high complexity (double exponential complexity in the number of variables for the general case). Fortunately, the problem is easier for the so-called constructive geometry which, roughly speaking, deals with a class of problems where the geometric elements (points, lines and circles) are constructed step by step with rulers and compasses from the ones previously constructed.

An inequality of constructive geometry can be converted to an inequality of polynomial/radicals in independent parameters, with some inequality constraints. Let us see the following example:

Given real numbers $x, y, z, u_1, u_2, u_3, u_4, u_5, u_6$ satisfying the following 15 conditions

$$\begin{cases}
(xy + yz + xz)^2 u_1^2 - x^3(y + z)(xy + xz + 4\,yz) = 0, \\
(xy + yz + xz)^2 u_2^2 - y^3(x + z)(xy + yz + 4\,xz) = 0, \\
(xy + yz + xz)^2 u_3^2 - z^3(x + y)(yz + xz + 4\,xy) = 0, \\
(x + y + z)(u_4^2 - x^2) - xyz = 0, \\
(x + y + z)(u_5^2 - y^2) - xyz = 0, \\
(x + y + z)(u_6^2 - z^2) - xyz = 0, \\
x > 0, \ y > 0, \ z > 0, \\
u_1 > 0, \ u_2 > 0, \ u_3 > 0, \ u_4 > 0, \ u_5 > 0, \ u_6 > 0,
\end{cases} \tag{3}$$

prove that $u_1 + u_2 + u_3 \leq u_4 + u_5 + u_6$.

Eliminating $u_1, \ldots, u_6$ from (3) by solving the 6 equations, we convert the proposition to the following inequality which appeared as a conjecture in the book[31] by Shan.

Example 13: Show that

$$\frac{\sqrt{x^3(y+z)(xy+xz+4yz)}}{xy+yz+xz} + \frac{\sqrt{y^3(x+z)(xy+yz+4xz)}}{xy+yz+xz}$$

$$+ \frac{\sqrt{z^3(x+y)(yz+xz+4xy)}}{xy+yz+xz}$$

$$\leq \sqrt{x^2 + \frac{xyz}{x+y+z}} + \sqrt{y^2 + \frac{xyz}{x+y+z}} + \sqrt{z^2 + \frac{xyz}{x+y+z}}, \quad (4)$$

where $x > 0$, $y > 0$, $z > 0$.

This includes 3 variables but 6 radicals, while (3) includes 9 variables. A dimension-decreasing algorithm introduced by the first author can efficiently treat parametric radicals and maximize reduction of the dimensions. Based on this algorithm, a generic program called BOTTEMA has been implemented on a PC computer. Thousands of algebraic and geometric inequalities including hundreds of open problems have been proved or disproved in this way.[23] The total CPU time spent for proving 100 basic inequalities, which include some classical results such as Euler's inequality, Finsler-Hadwiger's inequality, and Gerretsen's inequality, from Bottema *et al.*'s monograph[6] on a PC (Pentium IV/2.8G) was less than 3 s. It can be seen later that the inequality class, to which our algorithm is applicable, is very inclusive.

In this section, we deal with a class of propositions which take the following form (though the algorithm is applicable to a more extensive class):

$$\Phi_1 \wedge \Phi_2 \wedge \cdots \wedge \Phi_s \Rightarrow \Phi_0, \quad (5)$$

where $\Phi_0, \Phi_1, \ldots, \Phi_s$ are *algebraic inequalities* (see Definition 14) in $x, y, z, \ldots$ and the hypothesis $\Phi_1 \wedge \Phi_2 \wedge \cdots \wedge \Phi_s$ defines either an open set (possibly disconnected) or an open set with the whole/partial boundary.

Example 13 may be written as $(x > 0) \wedge (y > 0) \wedge (z > 0) \Rightarrow$ (4), where the hypothesis $(x > 0) \wedge (y > 0) \wedge (z > 0)$ defines an open set in the parametric space $\mathbb{R}^3$, so it belongs to the class we described. This class covers most of the inequalities in the books[6,27] by Bottema, Mitrinovic and others.

3.1. *Basic Definitions*

Before we sketch the so-called dimension-decreasing algorithm, some definitions should be introduced and illustrated.

Definition 14: Assume that $l(x, y, z, \dots)$ and $r(x, y, z, \dots)$ are continuous algebraic functions of $x, y, z, \dots$. We call

$$l(x, y, z, \dots) \leq r(x, y, z, \dots) \quad \text{or} \quad l(x, y, z, \dots) < r(x, y, z, \dots)$$

an *algebraic inequality* in $x, y, z \dots$, and $l(x, y, z, \dots) = r(x, y, z, \dots)$ an *algebraic equality* in $x, y, z, \dots$.

Definition 15: Assume that Φ is an algebraic inequality (or equality) in $x, y, z, \dots$. $L(T)$ is called a *left polynomial* of Φ if

- $L(T)$ is a polynomial in T and its coefficients are polynomials in $x, y, z, \dots$ with rational coefficients;
- the left-hand side of Φ is a zero of $L(T)$.

The following condition is unnecessary for this definition, but it may help to reduce the computational complexity in the process later.

- *Amongst all the polynomials satisfying the two conditions above, $L(T)$ is the one that has the lowest degree in T.*

According to this definition, $L(T) = T$ if the left-hand side of Φ is 0. The *right polynomial* of Φ, namely $R(T)$, can be defined analogously.

Definition 16: Assume that Φ is an algebraic inequality (or equality) in $x, y, \dots$, and $L(T)$ and $R(T)$ are the left and right polynomials of Φ, respectively. Denote by $P(x, y, \dots)$ the resultant of $L(T)$ and $R(T)$ with respect to T, and call it the *border polynomial* of Φ, and the surface defined by $P(x, y, \dots) = 0$ the *border surface* of Φ, respectively.

The notions of left and right polynomials are needed in practice for computing the border surface more efficiently. In Example 13, we set

$$
\begin{aligned}
f_1 &= (xy + yz + xz)^2 u_1^2 - x^3(y + z)(xy + xz + 4yz), \\
f_2 &= (xy + yz + xz)^2 u_2^2 - y^3(x + z)(xy + yz + 4xz), \\
f_3 &= (xy + yz + xz)^2 u_3^2 - z^3(x + y)(yz + xz + 4xy), \\
f_4 &= (x + y + z)(u_4^2 - x^2) - xyz, \\
f_5 &= (x + y + z)(u_5^2 - y^2) - xyz, \\
f_6 &= (x + y + z)(u_6^2 - z^2) - xyz,
\end{aligned}
$$

then the left and right polynomials of (4) can be found by successive resultant computation:

$$
\text{resultant}(\text{resultant}(\text{resultant}(u_1 + u_2 + u_3 - T, f_1, u_1), f_2, u_2), f_3, u_3),
$$
$$
\text{resultant}(\text{resultant}(\text{resultant}(u_4 + u_5 + u_6 - T, f_4, u_4), f_5, u_5), f_6, u_6).
$$

Removing the factors that do not involve T, we have

$$
\begin{aligned}
L(T) = {}& (xy + xz + yz)^8 T^8 - 4(x^4 y^2 + 2x^4 yz + x^4 z^2 + 4x^3 y^2 z \\
& + 4x^3 yz^2 + x^2 y^4 + 4x^2 y^3 z + 4x^2 yz^3 + x^2 z^4 + 2xy^4 z + 4xy^3 z^2 \\
& + 4xy^2 z^3 + 2xyz^4 + y^4 z^2 + y^2 z^4)(xy + xz + yz)^6 T^6 + \cdots,
\end{aligned}
$$

$$
\begin{aligned}
R(T) = {}& (x + y + z)^4 T^8 - 4(x^3 + x^2 y + x^2 z + xy^2 + 3xyz + xz^2 + y^3 + y^2 z \\
& + yz^2 + z^3)(x + y + z)^3 T^6 + 2(16xyz^4 + 14xy^2 z^3 + 14xy^3 z^2 + 16xy^4 z \\
& + 14x^2 yz^3 + 14x^2 y^3 z + 14x^3 yz^2 + 14x^3 y^2 z + 16x^4 yz + 3x^6 + 5x^4 y^2 \\
& + 5x^4 z^2 + 5x^2 y^4 + 5x^2 z^4 + 5y^4 z^2 + 5y^2 z^4 + 21x^2 y^2 z^2 + 3y^6 + 3z^6 \\
& + 6x^5 y + 6x^5 z + 4x^3 y^3 + 4x^3 z^3 + 6xy^5 + 6xz^5 + 6y^5 z + 4y^3 z^3 + 6yz^5) \\
& \cdot (x + y + z)^2 T^4 \\
& - 4(x + y + z)(x^6 - x^4 y^2 - x^4 z^2 + 2x^3 y^2 z + 2x^3 yz^2 - x^2 y^4 + 2x^2 y^3 z \\
& + 7x^2 y^2 z^2 + 2x^2 yz^3 - x^2 z^4 + 2xy^3 z^2 + 2xy^2 z^3 + y^6 - y^4 z^2 - y^2 z^4 + z^6) \\
& \cdot (x^3 + 3x^2 y + 3x^2 z + 3xy^2 + 7xyz + 3xz^2 + y^3 + 3y^2 z + 3yz^2 + z^3)T^2 \\
& + (-6xy^2 z^3 - 6xy^3 z^2 - 6x^2 yz^3 - 6x^2 y^3 z - 6x^3 yz^2 - 6x^3 y^2 z + x^6 \\
& - x^4 y^2 - x^4 z^2 - x^2 y^4 - x^2 z^4 - y^4 z^2 - y^2 z^4 - 9x^2 y^2 z^2 + y^6 + z^6 + 2x^5 y \\
& + 2x^5 z - 4x^3 y^3 - 4x^3 z^3 + 2xy^5 + 2xz^5 + 2y^5 z - 4y^3 z^3 + 2yz^5)^2.
\end{aligned}
$$

The successive resultant computation for $L(T)$ and $R(T)$ took 0.13 s and 0.03 s of CPU time, respectively, on a PC (Pentium IV/2.8G) with Maple 8. It then took 33.05 s to obtain the border polynomial of degree 100 with 2691 terms.

We may of course reform (4) to an equivalent inequality, e.g.,

$$\frac{\sqrt{x^3(y+z)(xy+xz+4\,yz)}}{xy+yz+xz} + \frac{\sqrt{y^3(x+z)(xy+yz+4\,xz)}}{xy+yz+xz}$$

$$+\frac{\sqrt{z^3(x+y)(yz+xz+4\,xy)}}{xy+yz+xz} - \sqrt{x^2+\frac{xyz}{x+y+z}} - \sqrt{y^2+\frac{xyz}{x+y+z}}$$

$$\leq \sqrt{z^2+\frac{xyz}{x+y+z}} \tag{6}$$

by transposition of terms. However, the left polynomial of (6) cannot be found on the same computer (with 256 Mb of memory)by a Maple procedure as we did for (4):

```
f:=u1+u2+u3-u4-u5-T;
for i to 5 do f:=resultant(f,f.i,u.i) od;
```

This procedure did not terminate within 5 hours.

One might try to compute the border polynomial directly without employing left and right polynomials, that is, using the procedure

```
f:=u1+u2+u3-u4-u5-u6;
for i to 6 do f:=resultant(f,f.i,u.i) od;
```

but the situation is not better. The procedure did not terminate within 5 hours either.

Example 17: Given an algebraic inequality in x, y, z:

$$m_a + m_b + m_c \leq 2\,s, \tag{7}$$

where

$$m_a = \frac{1}{2}\sqrt{2\,(x+y)^2 + 2\,(x+z)^2 - (y+z)^2},$$

$$m_b = \frac{1}{2}\sqrt{2\,(y+z)^2 + 2\,(x+y)^2 - (x+z)^2},$$

$$m_c = \frac{1}{2}\sqrt{2\,(x+z)^2 + 2\,(y+z)^2 - (x+y)^2},$$

$$s = x+y+z$$

with $x > 0$, $y > 0$, $z > 0$, compute the left, right and border polynomials.

Let

$$f_1 = 4\,m_a^2 + (y+z)^2 - 2\,(x+y)^2 - 2\,(x+z)^2,$$

$$f_2 = 4\,m_b^2 + (x+z)^2 - 2\,(y+z)^2 - 2\,(x+y)^2,$$

$$f_3 = 4\,m_c^2 + (x+y)^2 - 2\,(x+z)^2 - 2\,(y+z)^2$$

and do successive resultant computation

resultant(resultant(resultant($m_a + m_b + m_c - T, f_1, m_a), f_2, m_b), f_3, m_c$);

we obtain a left polynomial of (7):

$$\begin{aligned}
T^8 &- 6(x^2 + y^2 + z^2 + xy + yz + zx)T^6 + 9(x^4 + 2xyz^2 + y^4 + 2xz^3 \\
&+ 2x^3y + z^4 + 3y^2z^2 + 2y^2zx + 2y^3z + 2yz^3 + 3x^2z^2 + 2x^3z + 2x^2yz \\
&+ 2xy^3 + 3x^2y^2)T^4 - (72x^4yz + 78x^3yz^2 + 4x^6 + 4y^6 + 4z^6 + 12xy^5 \\
&- 3x^4y^2 - 3x^2z^4 - 3x^2y^4 - 3y^4z^2 - 3y^2z^4 - 3x^4z^2 - 26x^3y^3 - 26x^3z^3 \\
&- 26y^3z^3 + 12xz^5 + 12y^5z + 12yz^5 + 12x^5z + 12x^5y + 84x^2y^2z^2 \\
&+ 72xyz^4 + 72xy^4z + 78xy^3z^2 + 78xy^2z^3 + 78x^2yz^3 + 78x^3y^2z \\
&+ 78x^2y^3z)T^2 + 81x^2y^2z^2(x + y + z)^2.
\end{aligned} \tag{8}$$

It is trivial to find a right polynomial for this inequality because the right-hand side contains no radicals. We simply take

$$T - 2(x + y + z). \tag{9}$$

Computing the resultant of (8) and (9) with respect to T, we have

$$\begin{aligned}
(144x^5y &+ 144x^5z + 780x^4y^2 + 1056x^4yz + 780x^4z^2 + 1288x^3y^3 \\
&+ 3048x^3y^2z + 3048x^3yz^2 + 1288x^3z^3 + 780x^2y^4 + 3048x^2y^3z \\
&+ 5073x^2y^2z^2 + 3048x^2yz^3 + 780x^2z^4 + 144xy^5 + 1056xy^4z \\
&+ 3048xy^3z^2 + 3048xy^2z^3 + 1056xyz^4 + 144xz^5 + 144y^5z \\
&+ 780y^4z^2 + 1288y^3z^3 + 780y^2z^4 + 144yz^5)(x + y + z)^2.
\end{aligned}$$

Removing the non-vanishing factor $(x+y+z)^2$, we obtain the border surface

$$\begin{aligned}
144x^5y &+ 144x^5z + 780x^4y^2 + 1056x^4yz + 780x^4z^2 + 1288x^3y^3 \\
&+ 3048x^3y^2z + 3048x^3yz^2 + 1288x^3z^3 + 780x^2y^4 + 3048x^2y^3z \\
&+ 5073x^2y^2z^2 + 3048x^2yz^3 + 780x^2z^4 + 144xy^5 + 1056xy^4z \\
&+ 3048xy^3z^2 + 3048xy^2z^3 + 1056xyz^4 + 144xz^5 + 144y^5z \\
&+ 780y^4z^2 + 1288y^3z^3 + 780y^2z^4 + 144yz^5 = 0.
\end{aligned} \tag{10}$$

3.2. *The Dimension-Decreasing Algorithm*

We take the following steps when the conclusion Φ_0 in (5) is of type $\leq$. (As for Φ_0 of type $<$, what we need to do in addition is to verify if the equation $l_0(x, y, \dots) - r_0(x, y, \dots) = 0$ has no real solutions under the hypothesis, where $l_0(x, y, \dots)$ and $r_0(x, y, \dots)$ denote the left- and right-hand sides of Φ_0, respectively.)

Step 1. Find the border surfaces of the inequalities Φ_0, Φ_1, ... , Φ_s.

Step 2. These border surfaces decompose the parametric space into a finite number of cells. Among them we just take all the connected open sets $D_1, D_2, \ldots, D_k$ and discard the lower dimensional cells. Choose at least one test point in every connected open set, say $(x_\nu, y_\nu, \ldots) \in D_\nu$, $\nu = 0, 1, \ldots, k$. This step can be done by an incomplete cylindrical algebraic decomposition which is much easier than the complete one since all the lower dimensional cells were discarded. Furthermore, we can make every test point a rational point because it is chosen in an open set.

Step 3. We only need to check the proposition for such a finite number of test points $(x_1, y_1, \ldots), \ldots, (x_k, y_k, \ldots)$. The statement is true if and only if it holds over these test values.

The proof of the correctness of the method is sketched as follows.

Denote the left- and right-hand sides and border surface of Φ_μ by $l_\mu(x, y, \ldots)$, $r_\mu(x, y, \ldots)$ and $P_\mu(x, y, \ldots) = 0$, respectively, and

$$\delta_\mu(x, y, \ldots) \overset{\text{def}}{=} l_\mu(x, y, \ldots) - r_\mu(x, y, \ldots)$$

for $\mu = 0, \ldots, s$.

The set of real zeros of all the $\delta_\mu(x, y, \ldots)$ is a closed set, so its complementary set, say Δ, is an open set. On the other hand, the set

$$D \overset{\text{def}}{=} D_1 \cup \cdots \cup D_k$$

is exactly the complementary set of real zeros of all the $P_\mu(x, y, \ldots)$.

We have $D \subset \Delta$ since any zero of $\delta_\mu(x, y, \ldots)$ must be a zero of $P_\mu(x, y, \ldots)$. Denote by $\Delta_1, \ldots, \Delta_t$ all the connected components of Δ, so each one is a connected open set. Every Δ_λ must contain a point of D for an open set cannot be filled with the real zeros of all the $P_\mu(x, y, \ldots)$. Assume that Δ_λ contains a point of D_i, some connected component of D. Then, $D_i \subset \Delta_\lambda$ because it is impossible that two different components of Δ both intersect D_i. By Step 2, D_i contains a test point $(x_i, y_i, \ldots)$. So, every Δ_λ contains at least one test point obtained from Step 2.

Thus, $\delta_\mu(x, y, \ldots)$ keeps the same sign over Δ_λ as that of $\delta_\mu(x_{i_\lambda}, y_{i_\lambda}, \ldots)$, where $(x_{i_\lambda}, y_{i_\lambda} \ldots)$ is a test point in Δ_λ for $\lambda = 1, \ldots, t$; $\mu = 0, \ldots, s$. Otherwise, if there is some point $(x', y', \ldots) \in \Delta_\lambda$ such that $\delta_\mu(x', y', \ldots)$ has the opposite sign to $\delta_\mu(x_{i_\lambda}, y_{i_\lambda}, \ldots)$, connecting the two points $(x', y', \ldots)$ and $(x_{i_\lambda}, y_{i_\lambda}, \ldots)$ with a path Γ, and $\Gamma \subset \Delta_\lambda$, then there is a point $(\bar{x}, \bar{y}, \ldots) \in \Gamma$ such that $\delta_\mu(\bar{x}, \bar{y}, \ldots) = 0$, a contradiction!

Denote by $A \cup B$ the set defined by the hypothesis, where A is an open set defined by

$$(\delta_1(x, y, \dots) < 0) \wedge \cdots \wedge (\delta_s(x, y, \dots) < 0),$$

that consists of a number of connected components of Δ and some real zeros of $\delta_0(x, y, \dots)$, namely $A = Q \cup S$, where $Q = \Delta_1 \cup \cdots \cup \Delta_j$ and S is a set of some real zeros of $\delta_0(x, y, \dots)$. And B is the whole or partial boundary of A, that consists of some real zeros of $\delta_\mu(x, y, \dots)$ for $\mu = 1, \dots, s$.

Now, let us verify whether $\delta_0 < 0$ holds for all the test points in A, one by one. If there is a test point whereat $\delta_0 > 0$, then the proposition is false. Otherwise, $\delta_0 < 0$ holds over Q because every connected component of Q contains a test point and δ_0 keeps the same sign over each component Δ_λ; hence $\delta_0 \leq 0$ holds over A by continuity, so it also holds over $A \cup B$, i.e., the proposition is true.

The above procedure sometimes may be simplified. When the conclusion Φ_0 belongs to an inequality class called "class CGR", what we need to do in Step 3 is to compare the greatest roots of the left and right polynomials of Φ_0 over the test values.

Definition 18: An algebraic inequality is said to belong to *class CGR* if its left-hand side is the greatest (real) root of the left polynomial $L(T)$, and its right-hand side is the greatest (real) root of the right polynomial $R(T)$.

It is obvious in Example 13 that the left- and right-hand sides of the inequality (4) are the greatest roots of $L(T)$ and $R(T)$, respectively, because all the radicals have got positive signs. Thus, the inequality belongs to class CGR. What we need to do is to verify whether the greatest root of $L(T)$ is less than or equal to that of $R(T)$, that is much easier than determining which one between two complicated radicals is greater, in the sense of accurate computation.

If an inequality involves only mono-layer radicals, then it can always be transformed into an equivalent one which belongs to class CGR by transposition of terms. Actually, most of the inequalities in the books[6,27] by Bottema, Mitrinovic and others, including most of the examples in this section, belong to the class CGR. For some more material, see the paper[47] by the first author.

3.3. *Inequalities on Triangles*

An absolute majority of the hundred inequalities discussed in the book[6] by Bottema and others are on triangles, and so are the thousands appeared in various publications since then.

For geometric inequalities on a single triangle, usually the geometric invariants are used as global variables instead of Cartesian coordinates. Denote by a, b, c the side-lengths and by s the half perimeter, i.e., $s = (a + b + c)/2$, and let $x = s - a$, $y = s - b$, $z = s - c$, as people used to do. In addition, denote by A, B, C the interior angles, S the area, R the circumradius, r the inradius, r_a, r_b, r_c the radii of escribed circles, h_a, h_b, h_c the altitudes, m_a, m_b, m_c the lengths of medians, w_a, w_b, w_c the lengths of interior angular bisectors of the triangle, and so on.

People used to choose x, y, z as independent variables and others as dependents. Sometimes, another choice is better for decreasing the degrees of polynomials occurring in the process.

An algebraic inequality $\Phi(x, y, z)$ can be regarded as a geometric inequality on a triangle if

- $x > 0$, $y > 0$, $z > 0$;
- the left- and right-hand sides of Φ, namely $l(x, y, z)$ and $r(x, y, z)$, are both homogeneous;
- $l(x, y, z)$ and $r(x, y, z)$ have the same degree.

The first condition means that the sum of two edges of a triangle is greater than the third edge. The second and third conditions mean that a similar transformation does not change the truth of the proposition. For example, (7) is such an inequality for its left- and right-hand sides, $m_a + m_b + m_c$ and $2\,s$, are both homogeneous functions of degree 1 (in x, y, z).

In addition, assume that the left- and right-hand sides of $\Phi(x, y, z)$, namely, $l(x, y, z)$ and $r(x, y, z)$, are both symmetric functions of x, y, z. It does not change the truth of the proposition to replace x, y, z in $l(x, y, z)$ and $r(x, y, z)$ by x', y', z', where $x' = \rho x$, $y' = \rho y$, $z' = \rho z$ and $\rho > 0$.

Clearly, the left and right polynomials $L(T, x', y', z')$ and $R(T, x', y', z')$ of $\Phi(x', y', z')$ are both symmetric with respect to x', y', z', so they can be re-coded in the elementary symmetric functions of x', y', z', say

$$H_l(T, \sigma_1, \sigma_2, \sigma_3) = L(T, x', y', z'), \quad H_r(T, \sigma_1, \sigma_2, \sigma_3) = R(T, x', y', z'),$$

where $\sigma_1 = x' + y' + z'$, $\sigma_2 = x'y' + y'z' + z'x'$, $\sigma_3 = x'y'z'$.

Setting $\rho = \sqrt{(x + y + z)/(xyz)}$, we have $x'y'z' = x' + y' + z'$, i.e., $\sigma_3 = \sigma_1$. Further letting

$$s = \sigma_1 \ (= \sigma_3), \quad p = \sigma_2 - 9,$$

we can transform $L(T, x', y', z')$ and $R(T, x', y', z')$ into polynomials, say

$F(T, p, s)$ and $G(T, p, s)$, in T, p, s. Especially, if both F and G have only even-degree terms in s, then they can be transformed into polynomials in T, p and q, where $q = s^2 - 4p - 27$. Usually the degrees and the numbers of terms of the latter are much less than those of $L(T, x, y, z)$ and $R(T, x, y, z)$. We thus construct the border surface encoded in p, s or p, q, and do the decomposition described in the last section on the (p, s)-plane or (p, q)-plane instead of $\mathbb{R}^3$. This may reduce the computational complexity considerably for a large class of geometric inequalities. The following example is taken from the book[6] by Bottema and others.

Example 19: Denote by w_a, w_b, w_c and s the interior angular bisectors and half the perimeter of a triangle, respectively. Prove that

$$w_b w_c + w_c w_a + w_a w_b \le s^2.$$

It is well known that

$$w_a = 2 \, \frac{\sqrt{x\,(x+y)(x+z)(x+y+z)}}{2\,x+y+z},$$

$$w_b = 2 \, \frac{\sqrt{y\,(x+y)(y+z)(x+y+z)}}{2\,y+x+z},$$

$$w_c = 2 \, \frac{\sqrt{z\,(x+z)(y+z)(x+y+z)}}{2\,z+x+y},$$

and $s = x + y + z$. By successive resultant computation as above, we get a left polynomial which is of degree 20 and has 557 terms, while the right polynomial $T - (x + y + z)^2$ is very simple, and the border polynomial $P(x, y, z)$ is of degree 15 and has 136 terms.

However, if the left and right polynomials are encoded in p, q, we get

$$(9p + 2q + 64)^4 T^4 - 32$$

$$\cdot (4p + q + 27)(p + 8)(4p^2 + pq + 69p + 10q + 288)(9p + 2q + 64)^2 T^2$$

$$- 512(4p + q + 27)^2 (p + 8)^2 (9p + 2q + 64)^2 T + 256(4p + q + 27)^3$$

$$\cdot (p + 8)^2 (-1024 - 64p + 39p^2 - 128q - 12pq - 4q^2 + 4p^3 + p^2 q)$$

and $T - 4p - q - 27$, respectively, and hence the border polynomial

$$Q(p, q) = 5600256p^2 q + 50331648p + 33554432q + 5532160p^3$$

$$+ 27246592p^2 + 3604480q^2 + 22872064pq + 499291p^4 + 16900p^5$$

$$+ 2480q^4 + 16q^5 + 143360q^3 + 1628160pq^2 + 22945p^4 q$$

$$+ 591704p^3 q + 11944p^3 q^2 + 2968p^2 q^3 + 242568p^2 q^2 + 41312pq^3$$

$$+ 352pq^4,$$

which is of degree 5 and has 20 terms only. The whole proving process in this way takes about 0.03 s on the same machine.

3.4. *BOTTEMA and Examples*

As a prover, the whole program BOTTEMA is written in Maple including the cell decomposition, without external packages employed.

On verifying an inequality with BOTTEMA, we only need to type in a proving command; then the machine will do everything else. If the statement is true, then the computer screen will show *"The inequality holds"*; otherwise, it will show *"The inequality does not hold"* with a counterexample. There are three kinds of proving commands: *prove, xprove* and *yprove*.

prove — prove a geometric inequality on a triangle, or an equivalent algebraic inequality.

Calling Sequence:

> prove(ineq);
> prove(ineq, ineqs);

Parameters:

ineq — an inequality to be proven, which is encoded in the geometric invariants listed later;

ineqs — a list of inequalities as the hypothesis, which is encoded as well in the geometric invariants listed later.

Examples:

```
> read bottema;
> prove(a^2+b^2+c^2>=4*sqrt(3)*S+(b-c)^2+(c-a)^2+(a-b)^2);
```

The theorem holds

```
> prove(cos(A)>=cos(B),[a<=b]);
```

The theorem holds

xprove — prove an algebraic inequality with positive variables.

Calling Sequence:

> xprove(ineq);
> xprove(ineq, ineqs);

Parameters:

ineq — an algebraic inequality to be proven, with positive variables;

ineqs — a list of algebraic inequalities as the hypothesis, with positive variables.

Examples:

```
> read bottema;
> xprove(sqrt(u^2+v^2)+sqrt((1-u)^2+(1-v)^2)>=sqrt(2),
  [u<=1,v<=1]);
```

The theorem holds

```
> f:=(x+1)^(1/3)+sqrt(y-1)+x*y+1/x+1/y^2:
> xprove(f>=42496/10000,[y>1]);
```

The theorem holds

```
> xprove(f>=42497/10000,[y>1]);
```

with a counter example

$$\left[x = \frac{29}{32},\ y = \frac{294117648}{294117647} \right]$$

The theorem does not hold

yprove — prove an algebraic inequality in general.

Calling Sequence:

yprove(ineq);

yprove(ineq, ineqs);

Parameters:

ineq — an algebraic inequality to be proven;

ineqs — a list of algebraic inequalities as the hypothesis.

Examples:

```
> read bottema;
> f:=x^6*y^6+6*x^6*y^5-6*x^5*y^6+15*x^6*y^4-36*x^5*y^5+15*x^4*y^6
    +20*x^6*y^3-90*x^5*y^4+90*x^4*y^5-20*x^3*y^6+15*x^6*y^2
    -120*x^5*y^3+225*x^4*y^4-120*x^3*y^5+15*x^2*y^6+6*x^6*y
    -90*x^5*y^2+300*x^4*y^3-300*x^3*y^4+90*x^2*y^5-6*x*y^6+x^6
    -36*x^5*y+225*x^4*y^2-400*x^3*y^3+225*x^2*y^4-36*x*y^5+y^6
    -6*x^5+90*x^4*y-300*x^3*y^2+300*x^2*y^3-90*x*y^4+6*y^5+15*x^4
    -120*x^3*y+225*x^2*y^2-120*x*y^3+15*y^4-20*x^3+90*x^2*y
    -90*x*y^2+20*y^3+16*x^2-36*x*y+16*y^2-6*x+6*y+1:
> yprove(f>=0);
```

The theorem holds

3.5. *More Examples*

All the examples in this subsection are computed by BOTTEMA on a PC (Pentium IV/2.8G) with Maple 8.

The following example is the well-known Janous inequality[20] which was proposed as an open problem in 1986 and solved in 1988.

Example 20: Denote the three medians and perimeter of a triangle by m_a, m_b, m_c and $2\,s$. Show that

$$\frac{1}{m_a} + \frac{1}{m_b} + \frac{1}{m_c} \geq \frac{5}{s}.$$

The left-hand side of the inequality implicitly contains three radicals. BOTTEMA automatically interprets the geometric proposition as an algebraic one before proving it. The total CPU time spent for this example is 3.58 s.

The next example was proposed as an open problem, E. 3146*, in the *Amer. Math. Monthly* **93**: 299 (1986).

Example 21: Denote the side-lengths and half perimeter of a triangle by a, b, c and s, respectively. Prove or disprove that

$$2\,s(\sqrt{s-a}+\sqrt{s-b}+\sqrt{s-c}) \leq 3\left(\sqrt{bc(s-a)}+\sqrt{ca(s-b)}+\sqrt{ab(s-c)}\right).$$

The proof took 9.91 s on the same machine.

The following open problem appeared as Problem 169 in *Mathematical Communications* (in Chinese).

Example 22: Denote the radii of the escribed circles and the interior angular bisectors of a triangle by r_a, r_b, r_c and w_a, w_b, w_c, respectively. Prove or disprove that

$$\sqrt[3]{r_a r_b r_c} \leq \frac{1}{3}(w_a + w_b + w_c).$$

In other words, *the geometric average of r_a, r_b, r_c is less than or equal to the arithmetic average of w_a, w_b, w_c.*

The right-hand side of the inequality implicitly contains 3 radicals. BOTTEMA proved this conjecture with 96.60 s of CPU time. Another conjecture proposed by J. Liu[31] and stated in the following example was proven on the same machine with 52.36 s of CPU time.

Example 23: Denote the side lengths, medians and interior angular bisectors of a triangle by a, b, c, m_a, m_b, m_c and w_a, w_b, w_c, respectively. Prove or disprove that

$$a\, m_a + b\, m_b + c\, m_c \leq \frac{2}{\sqrt{3}} \left(w_a^2 + w_b^2 + w_c^2 \right).$$

The following conjecture was proposed first by J. Garfunkel in *Crux Math.* in 1985 and then twice by Mitrinovic *et al.*[27] and Kuang.[22]

Example 24: Denote the three angles of a triangle by A, B, C. Prove or disprove that

$$\cos\frac{B-C}{2} + \cos\frac{C-A}{2} + \cos\frac{A-B}{2}$$
$$\leq \frac{1}{\sqrt{3}} \left(\cos\frac{A}{2} + \cos\frac{B}{2} + \cos\frac{C}{2} + \sin A + \sin B + \sin C \right).$$

It was proven by BOTTEMA with 21.75 s of CPU time.

A. Oppenheim studied the following inequality[27] in order to answer a question asked by P. Erdös.

Example 25: Let a, b, c and m_a, m_b, m_c be the side-lengths and medians of a triangle, respectively. If $c = \min\{a, b, c\}$, then

$$2\, m_a + 2\, m_b + 2\, m_c \leq 2\, a + 2\, b + (3\sqrt{3} - 4)\, c.$$

The hypothesis includes one more condition $c = \min\{a, b, c\}$, so we type in

```
prove(2*ma+2*mb+2*mc<=2*a+2*b+(3*sqrt(3)-4)*c, [c<=a,c<=b]);
```

This took 262.50 s. If we type in

```
prove(2*ma+2*mb+2*mc<=2*a+2*b+(3*sqrt(3)-4)*c);
```

without the additional condition, then the screen will show "*The inequality does not hold*" with a counter-example, $[a = 203, b = 706, c = 505]$.

The following problem of positive semi-definite decision originated from one of the conjectures proposed by Liu.[23]

Example 26: Assume that $x > 0$, $y > 0$, $z > 0$. Prove that

$$2187(y^4 z^4 (y + z)^4 (2x + y + z)^8 + x^4 z^4 (x + z)^4 (x + 2y + z)^8$$
$$+ x^4 y^4 (x + y)^4 (x + y + 2z)^8)$$
$$- 256(x + y + z)^8 (x + y)^4 (x + z)^4 (y + z)^4 \geq 0.$$

The polynomial after being expanded is of 201 terms with the largest coefficient (absolute value) 181394432. Usually it is non-trivial to decide a polynomial to be positive semi-definite or not, but this one took only $0.58\,$s of CPU time, because of the homogeneity and symmetry which can help decrease the dimension and degree concerned.

There are two well-known geometric inequalities: one is the so-called *Euler inequality* $R \geq 2r$, and another is $m_a \geq w_a$. They are often cited in the illustration of various algorithms[9,42,43] for inequality proving. The following example makes a comparison between the two differences $R - 2r$ and $m_a - w_a$.

Example 27: Denote the circumradius and inradius of a triangle by R, r, and the median and the interior angular bisector on a certain side by m_a, w_a; prove that

$$m_a - w_a \leq R - 2r.$$

The proof using BOTTEMA took $2.86\,$s.

The geometric inequalities which can be verified by the program, of course, are not limited to those on triangles. To prove the so-called *Ptolemy inequality*, we will use Cartesian coordinates instead of geometric invariants.

Example 28: Given four points A, B, C, D on a plane, denote the distances between the points by AB, AC, AD, BC, BD, CD, respectively. Prove that

$$AB \cdot CD + BC \cdot AD \geq AC \cdot BD. \tag{11}$$

Put $A = (-1/2, 0)$, $B = (x, y)$, $C = (1/2, 0)$, $D = (u, v)$, and convert (11) to

$$\sqrt{(-\tfrac{1}{2} - x)^2 + y^2} \sqrt{(\tfrac{1}{2} - u)^2 + v^2} + \sqrt{(x - \tfrac{1}{2})^2 + y^2} \sqrt{(-\tfrac{1}{2} - u)^2 + v^2}$$
$$\geq \sqrt{(x - u)^2 + (y - v)^2}. \tag{12}$$

We only need to type in "yprove(%)" where % stands for inequality (12). The screen shows "The inequality holds" after the program runs $3.83\,$s.

According to our record, the CPU time spent (with Maple 8 on a Pentium IV/2.8G) and the numbers of the test points for above examples are listed as follows:

Example	13	92.44 s	23 test points
Example	17	0.02 s	1 test point
Example	19	0.03 s	1 test point
Example	20	3.58 s	12 test points
Example	21	9.91 s	135 test points
Example	22	9.28 s	4 test points
Example	23	52.36 s	3 test points
Example	24	21.75 s	121 test points
Example	25	262.50 s	287 test points
Example	26	0.58 s	2 test points
Example	27	2.86 s	22 test points
Example	28	3.83 s	48 test points

The times listed above include those spent for all steps: finding the left, right and border polynomials, cell decomposition, and one-by-one sample point test, etc.

Remark 29: We have the following conclusions about our algorithm and program.

- The program is applicable to any inequality-type theorem whose hypothesis and thesis are both inequalities in rational functions or radicals, but the thesis is of type "$\leq$" or "$\geq$", and the hypothesis defines either an open set or an open set with the whole/partial boundary.
- It is beyond the capacity of this program to deal with algebraic functions other than the rational ones and radicals.
- It runs in a completely automatic mode, without human intervention.
- It is especially efficient for geometric inequalities on triangles. The input, in this case, is encoded in geometric invariants.

The program BOTTEMA can be used in global optimization to find the optimal values of polynomial/radical functions. See the papers[47,50] by the authors for details.

4. Discover Inequality-Type Theorems

In this section, we solve another problem about a parametric SAS: Give the necessary and sufficient conditions on the parameters of a parametric

SAS for the system to have a given number of distinct real solutions. Based on the idea in Section 2 and a partial cylindrical algebraic decomposition, we introduce a practical algorithm for the problem, which can discover new inequalities automatically, without requiring us to put forward any conjectures beforehand. The algorithm is complete for an extensive class of inequality-type theorems. It is also applied to the classification of the real solutions of geometric constraint problems.

4.1. *Basic Definitions*

As discussed at the beginning of Section 2, a parametric SAS can be transformed into one or more systems in the following form

$$
\begin{cases}
f_1(U, x_1) = 0, \\
f_2(U, x_1, x_2) = 0, \\
\quad \cdots \cdots \\
f_s(U, x_1, x_2, \ldots, x_s) = 0, \\
g_1(U, x_1, \ldots, x_s) \geq 0, \ldots, g_r(U, x_1, \ldots, x_s) \geq 0, \\
g_{r+1}(U, x_1, \ldots, x_s) > 0, \ldots, g_t(U, x_1, \ldots, x_s) > 0, \\
h_1(U, x_1, \ldots, x_s) \neq 0, \ldots, h_m(U, x_1, \ldots, x_s) \neq 0,
\end{cases}
\tag{13}
$$

where $U = (x_{s+1}, \ldots, x_n)$ are viewed as parameters, usually denoted by $U = (u_1, \ldots, u_d)$. We call a system in this form a *parametric* TSA.

All the definitions for a TSA are valid for a parametric TSA.

Definition 30: Given a parametric TSA T, let $\mathrm{BP}_{f_1} = \mathrm{CP}_{f_1}$ and

$$
\mathrm{BP}_q = \mathrm{resultant}(\mathrm{CP}_q, f_1, x_1),
$$
$$
q \in \{f_i, g_j, h_k \mid 1 < i \leq s, 1 \leq j \leq t, 1 \leq k \leq m\}.
$$

We define

$$
\mathrm{BP}_T(U) = \prod_{1 \leq i \leq s} \mathrm{BP}_{f_i} \cdot \prod_{1 \leq j \leq t} \mathrm{BP}_{g_j} \cdot \prod_{1 \leq k \leq m} \mathrm{BP}_{h_k}
$$

and call it the *boundary polynomial* of T. It is also denoted by BP.

Then, a regular parametric TSA can be defined by $\mathrm{BP} \neq 0$. As remarked in Section 2, if a parametric TSA is regular, we can omit the h_k's in it without loss of generality and each of the inequalities $g_j \geq 0$ $(1 \leq j \leq r)$ in the system can be treated as $g_j > 0$.

Definition 31: Given a polynomial $f(x) = a_0 x^n + a_1 x^{n-1} + \cdots + a_n$ with real symbolic coefficients, the following $2n \times 2n$ matrix in terms of the coefficients of $f(x)$

$$\begin{bmatrix} a_0 & a_1 & a_2 & \cdots & a_n & & & & \\ 0 & na_0 & (n-1)a_1 & \cdots & a_{n-1} & & & & \\ & a_0 & a_1 & \cdots & a_{n-1} & a_n & & & \\ & 0 & na_0 & \cdots & 2a_{n-2} & a_{n-1} & & & \\ & & \cdots & \cdots & & & & & \\ & & \cdots & \cdots & & & & & \\ & & & a_0 & a_1 & a_2 & \cdots & a_n \\ & & & 0 & na_0 & (n-1)a_1 & \cdots & a_{n-1} \end{bmatrix}$$

is called the *discrimination matrix* of $f(x)$, and denoted by $\mathrm{Discr}\,(f)$. Denote by d_k the determinant of the submatrix of $\mathrm{Discr}\,(f)$, formed by the first k rows and the first k columns for $k = 1, 2, \ldots, 2n$.

Definition 32: Let $D_0 = 1$ and $D_k = d_{2k}$, $k = 1, \ldots, n$. We call the $(n+1)$-tuple $[D_0, D_1, D_2, \ldots, D_n]$ the *discriminant sequence* of $f(x)$, and denote it by $\mathrm{DiscrList}\,(f)$. Obviously, the last term D_n is $\mathrm{dis}(f, x)$.

Definition 33: We call the list

$$[\mathrm{sign}(A_0), \mathrm{sign}(A_1), \mathrm{sign}(A_2), \ldots, \mathrm{sign}(A_n)]$$

the *sign list* of a given sequence $A_0, A_1, \ldots, A_n$.

Definition 34: Given a sign list $[s_1, s_2, \ldots, s_n]$, we construct a new list

$$[t_1, t_2, \ldots, t_n]$$

(which is called the *revised sign list*) as follows:

- If $[s_i, s_{i+1}, \ldots, s_{i+j}]$ is a section of the given list, where

$$s_i \neq 0, \; s_{i+1} = \cdots = s_{i+j-1} = 0, \; s_{i+j} \neq 0,$$

  then we replace the subsection

$$[s_{i+1}, \ldots, s_{i+j-1}]$$

  by the first $j - 1$ terms of $[-s_i, -s_i, s_i, s_i, -s_i, -s_i, s_i, s_i, \ldots]$, that is, let

$$t_{i+r} = (-1)^{[(r+1)/2]} \cdot s_i, \quad r = 1, 2, \ldots, j - 1.$$

- Otherwise, let $t_k = s_k$, i.e., no change for other terms.

Theorem 35: Given a polynomial

$$f(x) = a_0 x^n + a_1 x^{n-1} + \cdots + a_n$$

with real coefficients, if the number of sign changes of the revised sign list of

$$[D_0, D_1(f), D_2(f), \ldots, D_n(f)]$$

is ν, then the number of distinct pairs of conjugate imaginary roots of $f(x)$ is equal to ν. Furthermore, if the number of non-vanishing members of the revised sign list is l, then the number of distinct real roots of $f(x)$ is equal to $l - 1 - 2\nu$.

Definition 36: Given two polynomials $g(x)$ and

$$f(x) = a_0 x^n + a_1 x^{n-1} + \cdots + a_n,$$

let

$$r(x) = \mathrm{rem}(f'g, f, x) = b_0 x^{n-1} + b_1 x^{n-2} + \cdots + b_{n-1}.$$

The following $2n \times 2n$ matrix

$$\begin{bmatrix}
a_0 & a_1 & a_2 & \cdots & & a_n & & & \\
0 & b_0 & b_1 & \cdots & & b_{n-1} & & & \\
& & a_0 & a_1 & \cdots & a_{n-1} & a_n & & \\
& & 0 & b_0 & \cdots & b_{n-2} & b_{n-1} & & \\
& & & \cdots & \cdots & & & & \\
& & & \cdots & \cdots & & & & \\
& & & & a_0 & a_1 & a_2 & \cdots & a_n \\
& & & & 0 & b_0 & b_1 & \cdots & b_{n-1}
\end{bmatrix}$$

is called the *generalized discrimination matrix* of $f(x)$ with respect to $g(x)$, and denoted by $\mathrm{Discr}\,(f, g)$.

Definition 37: Given two polynomials $f(x)$ and $g(x)$, let $D_0 = 1$ and denote by

$$D_1(f, g), D_2(f, g), \ldots, D_n(f, g)$$

the even order principal minors of $\mathrm{Discr}\,(f, g)$. We call

$$[D_0, D_1(f, g), D_2(f, g), \ldots, D_n(f, g)]$$

the *generalized discriminant sequence* of $f(x)$ with respect to $g(x)$, and denote it by $\mathrm{GDL}(f, g)$. Clearly, $\mathrm{GDL}(f, 1) = \mathrm{DiscrList}\,(f)$.

Theorem 38: Given two polynomials $f(x)$ and $g(x)$, if the number of sign changes of the revised sign list of $\mathrm{GDL}(f,g)$ is ν, and the number of non-vanishing members of the revised sign list is l, then

$$l - 1 - 2\nu = c(f, g_+) - c(f, g_-),$$

where

$$c(f, g_+) = \mathrm{card}(\{x \in R | f(x) = 0, g(x) > 0\}),$$
$$c(f, g_-) = \mathrm{card}(\{x \in R | f(x) = 0, g(x) < 0\}).$$

Definition 39: A normal ascending chain $\{f_1, \dots, f_s\}$ is said to be *simplicial* with respect to a polynomial g if either $\mathrm{prem}(g, f_s, \dots, f_1) = 0$ or $\mathrm{res}(g, f_s, \dots, f_1) \neq 0$.

Theorem 40:[54] For a triangular set $AS = \{f_1, \dots, f_s\}$ and a polynomial g, there is an algorithm which can decompose AS into some normal ascending chains $AS_i = \{f_{i1}, f_{i2}, \dots, f_{is}\}$ $(1 \leq i \leq n)$, such that every chain AS_i is simplicial with respect to g and $\mathrm{Zero}(AS) = \bigcup_{1 \leq i \leq n} \mathrm{Zero}(AS_i)$, where $\mathrm{Zero}(\cdot)$ means the set of zeros of a given system.

Remark 41: We call this decomposition the RSD decomposition of AS with respect to g and the algorithm the RSD algorithm. The decomposition and the algorithm were called WR decomposition and WR algorithm respectively by Yang and others.[54] Wang[34] proposed a similar decomposition algorithm. By Theorem 40, we always consider the triangular set $\{f_1, f_2, \dots, f_s\}$ appearing in a TSA as a normal ascending chain, without loss of generality.

Definition 42:[24] Let D_k^t be the submatrix of $\mathrm{Discr}\,(f)$, formed by the first $2n - 2k$ rows, the first $2n - 2k - 1$ columns and the $(2n - 2k + t)$th column, where $0 \leq k \leq n - 1$, $0 \leq t \leq 2k$. Let $|D_k^t| = \det(D_k^t)$. We call $|D_k^0|$ $(0 \leq k \leq n - 1)$ the kth *principal subresultant* of $f(x)$. Obviously, $|D_k^0| = D_{n-k}$ $(0 \leq k \leq n - 1)$.

Definition 43:[24] Let $Q_{n+1}(f, x) = f(x)$, $Q_n(f, x) = f'(x)$, and

$$Q_k(f, x) = \sum_{t=0}^{k} |D_k^t| x^{k-t} = |D_k^0| x^k + |D_k^1| x^{k-1} + \cdots + |D_k^k|$$

for $k = 0, 1, \dots, n - 1$. We call $\{Q_0(f, x), \dots, Q_{n+1}(f, x)\}$ the *subresultant polynomial chain* of $f(x)$.

Theorem 44:[55] Suppose that $\{f_1, f_2, \ldots, f_j\}$ is a normal ascending chain, where K is a field and $f_i \in K[x_1, \ldots, x_i]$ $(i = 1, 2, \ldots, j)$, and $f(x) = a_0 x^n + a_1 x^{n-1} + \cdots + a_{n-1} x + a_n$ is a polynomial in $K[x_1, \ldots, x_i][x]$. Let

$$PD_k = \mathrm{prem}(|D_k^0|, f_j, \ldots, f_1) = \mathrm{prem}(D_{n-k}, f_j, \ldots, f_1), \quad 0 \le k < n.$$

If, for some $k_0 \ge 0$,

$$\mathrm{res}(a_0, f_j, \ldots, f_1) \ne 0,$$
$$PD_0 = \cdots = PD_{k_0-1} = 0,$$
$$\mathrm{res}(|D_{k_0}^0|, f_j, \ldots, f_1) \ne 0,$$

then we have $\gcd(f, f_x') = Q_{k_0}(f, x)$ in $K[x_1, \ldots, x_j]/(f_1, \ldots, f_j)$.

Theorem 45: For an irregular parametric TSA T, there is an algorithm which can decompose T into regular systems T_i. Let all the distinct real solutions of a given system be denoted by $\mathrm{Rzero}(\cdot)$; then this decomposition satisfies $\mathrm{Rzero}(T) = \bigcup_i \mathrm{Rzero}(T_i)$.

Proof: For T, BP= $\mathrm{resultant}(f_1, \mathrm{CP}, x_1) = 0$.

- If there is some CP_{h_k} such that $\mathrm{resultant}(f_1, \mathrm{CP}_{h_k}, x_1) = 0$, then do the RSD decomposition of $\{f_1, \ldots, f_s\}$ with respect to h_k and suppose, without loss of generality, that we get two new chains $\{A_1, \ldots, A_s\}$ and $\{B_1, \ldots, B_s\}$, for which $\mathrm{prem}(h_k, A_s, \ldots, A_1) = 0$ but $\mathrm{res}(h_k, B_s, \ldots, B_1) \ne 0$. If we replace $\{f_1, \ldots, f_s\}$ by $\{B_1, \ldots, B_s\}$ in T, then the new system is regular and has the same real solutions as those of the original system. Obviously, another system obtained by replacing $\{f_1, \ldots, f_s\}$ with $\{A_1, \ldots, A_s\}$ in T has no real solutions.
- If there is some CP_{g_j} such that $\mathrm{resultant}(f_1, \mathrm{CP}_{g_j}, x_1) = 0$, then do the RSD decomposition of $\{f_1, \ldots, f_s\}$ with respect to g_j and suppose that we get $\{A_1, \ldots, A_s\}$ and $\{B_1, \ldots, B_s\}$, for which $\mathrm{prem}(g_j, A_s, \ldots, A_1) = 0$ but $\mathrm{res}(g_j, B_s \ldots, B_1) \ne 0$. Now, if $g_j > 0$ in T, we simply replace $\{f_1, \ldots, f_s\}$ by $\{B_1, \ldots, B_s\}$. The new system is regular and has the same real solutions as those of the original system. If $g_j \ge 0$ in T, we first get a new system T_1 by replacing $\{f_1, \ldots, f_s\}$ with $\{B_1, \ldots, B_s\}$ and then get another new system T_2 by replacing $\{f_1, \ldots, f_s\}$ with $\{A_1, \ldots, A_s\}$ and deleting g_j from it. These two systems are both regular and we have $\mathrm{Rzero}(T) = \mathrm{Rzero}(T_1) \bigcup \mathrm{Rzero}(T_2)$.
- If there is some CP_{f_i} such that $\mathrm{resultant}(f_1, \mathrm{CP}_{f_i}, x_1) = 0$, then let $[D_1, \ldots, D_{n_i}]$ be the discriminant sequence of f_i with respect to x_i. First of all, we do the RSD decomposition of $\{f_1, \ldots, f_{i-1}\}$ with respect

to D_{n_i} and suppose that we get $\{A_1, \dots, A_{i-1}\}$ and $\{B_1, \dots, B_{i-1}\}$, for which $\operatorname{prem}(f_i, A_{i-1}, \dots, A_1) = 0$ but $\operatorname{res}(f_i, B_{i-1}, \dots, B_1) \neq 0$. Step 1: replacing $\{f_1, \dots, f_{i-1}\}$ by $\{B_1, \dots, B_{i-1}\}$, we will get a regular system. Step 2: let us consider the system obtained by replacing $\{f_1, \dots, f_{i-1}\}$ with $\{A_1, \dots, A_{i-1}\}$ which is still irregular. Consider D_{n_i-1}, the next term in $[D_1, \dots, D_{n_i}]$. If $\operatorname{res}(D_{n_i-1}, A_{i-1}, \dots, A_1) = 0$, then do the RSD decomposition of $\{A_1, \dots, A_{i-1}\}$ with respect to D_{n_i-1}. Keep repeating the same procedure until we have, for certain D_{i_0} and $\{\bar{A}_1, \dots, \bar{A}_{i-1}\}$, $\operatorname{res}(D_{i_0}, \bar{A}_{i-1}, \dots, \bar{A}_1) \neq 0$ and $\operatorname{prem}(D_j, \bar{A}_{i-1}, \dots, \bar{A}_1) = 0$ for all j $(i_0 < j \leq n_i)$. Note that this procedure must terminate because $\{f_1, \dots, f_s\}$ being a normal ascending chain implies that $\operatorname{res}(I_i, f_{i-1}, \dots, f_1) \neq 0$ and $D_1 = n_i I_i^2$ implies that $\operatorname{res}(D_1, f_{i-1}, \dots, f_1) \neq 0$. By Theorem 2.3, $\gcd(f_i, f_i') = Q_{n_i - i_0}(f_i, x_i)$ in $K[x_1, \dots, x_{i-1}]/(\bar{A}_1, \dots, \bar{A}_{i-1})$. Now, let $\bar{f}_i$ be the pseudo-quotient of f_i divided by $\gcd(f_i, f_i')$ and replace $\{f_1, \dots, f_{i-1}, f_i\}$ by $\{\bar{A}_1, \dots, \bar{A}_{i-1}, \bar{f}_i\}$; the new system will be regular. If the new regular systems are T_j $(1 \leq j \leq j_i)$, then it is easy to see that $\operatorname{Rzero}(T) = \bigcup_{1 \leq j \leq j_i} \operatorname{Rzero}(T_j)$. $\square$

By Theorem 45, every parametric TSA in the rest of this section can be treated as a regular one.

4.2. *The Algorithm*

Let $ps = \{p_i \mid 1 \leq j \leq n\}$ be a non-empty, finite set of polynomials. We define

$$\operatorname{mset}(ps) = \{1\} \cup \{p_{i_1} p_{i_2} \cdots p_{i_k} \mid 1 \leq k \leq n, 1 \leq i_1 < i_2 < \cdots < i_k \leq n\}.$$

Given a parametric TSA T, we define

$$P_{s+1} = \{g_1, g_2, \dots, g_t\};$$
$$U_i = \bigcup_{q \in \operatorname{mset}(P_{i+1})} \operatorname{GDL}(f_i, q),$$
$$P_i = \{h(u, x_1, \dots, x_{i-1}) \mid h \in U_i\}, \quad i = s, s-1, \dots, 2;$$
$$P_1(g_1, g_2, \dots, g_t) = \{h(u) \mid h \in U_1\},$$

where U_i means the set consisting of all the polynomials in each $\operatorname{GDL}(f_i, q)$, where q belongs to $\operatorname{mset}(P_{i+1})$. Analogously, we can define $P_1(g_1, \dots, g_j)$ $(1 \leq j \leq t)$. It is clear that all the factors of the boundary polynomial BP of T are included in $P_1(g_1, g_2, \dots, g_t)$. With a little abuse of notations, we write $\operatorname{BP} \subseteq P_1(g_1, g_2, \dots, g_t)$.

Theorem 46: The necessary and sufficient condition for a parametric TSA T to have a given number of distinct real solutions can be expressed in terms of the signs of the polynomials in $P_1(g_1, g_2, \dots, g_t)$.

Proof: First of all, we regard f_s and every g_i as polynomials in x_s. From Theorems 35 and 38 we know that under the constraints $\{g_i \geq 0 \mid 1 \leq i \leq t\}$, the number of distinct real solutions of $f_s = 0$ can be determined by the signs of the polynomials in P_s. Let h_j $(1 \leq j \leq l)$ be the polynomials in P_s; then we regard h_j and f_{s-1} as polynomials in x_{s-1}. Repeating the same argument as that for f_s and g_i's, we see that, under the constraints $\{g_i \geq 0 \mid 1 \leq i \leq t\}$, the number of distinct real solutions of $f_s = 0, f_{s-1} = 0$ can be determined by the signs of the polynomials in P_{s-1}. Continuing in this way until $P_1(g_1, g_2, \dots, g_t)$ is employed, we will prove the theorem because the conditions obtained in each step are necessary and sufficient. $\square$

Remark 47: Ben-Or and others[5] gave a different way to define a smaller set of polynomials in the parameters for a parametric TSA which can determines the sign assignments to the g_j at roots of $\{f_1, \dots, f_s\}$.

Now, theoretically speaking, we can obtain the necessary and sufficient condition for a parametric TSA T to have (exactly N distinct) real solutions as follows:

Step 1. Compute $P_1(g_1, g_2, \dots, g_t)$, the set of polynomials in the parameters, for T.

Step 2. By the algorithm of PCAD,[10,7] we can obtain a P_1-*invariant cad D* of the parameter space $\mathbb{R}^d$ and its *cylindrical algebraic sample* (cas) S.[40] Roughly speaking, D is a finite set of cells such that each polynomial of P_1 keeps its sign in each cell; and S is a finite set of points obtained by taking from each cell one point at least, which is called the sample point of the cell.

Step 3. For each cell c in D and its sample point $s_c \in S$, substitute s_c into T and denote it by $T(s_c)$. Compute the number of distinct real solutions of the system $T(s_c)$, in which polynomials all have constant coefficients now. At the same time, compute the signs of the polynomials in $P_1(g_1, g_2, \dots, g_t)$ on this cell by substituting s_c into them respectively. Record the signs of the polynomials in $P_1(g_1, g_2, \dots, g_t)$ when the number of distinct real solutions of the system $T(s_c)$ is equal to the required number N (or when the number is > 0, if we are asked to find the condition for T to have real solutions). Obviously, the signs of the polynomials in $P_1(g_1, g_2, \ldots, g_t)$ on cell c form a first order formula, denoted by Φ_c.

Step 4. If, in Step 3, all we have recorded are $\Phi_{c_1}, \ldots, \Phi_{c_k}$, then $\Phi = \Phi_{c_1} \vee \cdots \vee \Phi_{c_k}$ is what we want.

The above algorithm is not practical in many cases since $P_1(g_1, \ldots, g_t)$ usually has too many polynomials and a complete cylindrical algebraic decomposition is usually inefficient. So, in order to make our algorithm practical, we take the following strategies. First, we give an effective algorithm to choose those polynomials which are necessary for expressing the condition from $P_1(g_1, \ldots, g_t)$. Second, we always omit the "boundaries" when using PCAD and the incompleteness caused by this omission will be fixed up later.

Theorem 48: Let a parametric TSA T be given. If PS is a finite set of polynomials in the parameters U, e.g.,

$$PS = \{q_i(U) \in \mathbb{Z}[u_1, \ldots, u_d] \mid 1 \leq i \leq k\},$$

then by the algorithm of PCAD we can get a PS-invariant cad D of the parameter space $\mathbb{R}^d$ and its cas. If PS satisfies that

(1) the number of distinct real solutions of the system T is invariant in the same cell, and

(2) the numbers of distinct real solutions of the system T in two distinct cells C_1 and C_2 are the same if PS has the same sign in C_1 and C_2,

then the necessary and sufficient conditions for T to have exactly N distinct real solutions can be expressed by the signs of the polynomials in PS. If PS satisfies condition (1) only, then some necessary conditions for T to have exactly N distinct real solutions can be expressed by the signs of the polynomials in PS.

Proof: We replace the parameters U in T by each sample point respectively. Because D is PS-invariant and PS satisfies condition (1), we can record the signs of the polynomials in PS and the number of distinct real solutions of T on each cell respectively. Choose all those cells on which T has N distinct real solutions. The signs of the polynomials in PS on those cells form a first order formula, say

$$\Phi = \Phi_1 \vee \Phi_2 \vee \cdots \vee \Phi_l,$$

where each Φ_i represents the signs of the polynomials in *PS* on a certain cell on which T has N distinct real solutions. We show that Φ is the condition we want.

Given a d-tuple $a = (a_1, \dots, a_d)$ of parametric values, if $T(a)$ has N distinct real solutions, then a must belong to a cell on which T has N distinct real solutions, i.e., a must satisfy a certain formula Φ_i. On the contrary, if a satisfies a certain formula Φ_i, because T has N distinct real solutions on the cell represented by Φ_i and *PS* satisfies condition (2), we then know that T must have N distinct real solutions on the cell to which a belongs. $\qquad\square$

Theorem 49: Let T be a regular parametric TSA, i.e., BP $\neq 0$. If we consider only those cells which are homeomorphic to $\mathbb{R}^d$ but not the cells that are homeomorphic to $\mathbb{R}^k$ $(k < d)$ when using PCAD, then BP satisfies condition (1) in Theorem 48, so a necessary condition (if we omit the parameters on those cells homeomorphic to $\mathbb{R}^k$ with $k < d$) for system T to have N distinct real solutions can be expressed by the sign of BP or the signs of the factors of BP.

Proof: By PCAD, we can get a BP-invariant cad of $\mathbb{R}^d$ and its cas. Because we only consider those cells which are homeomorphic to $\mathbb{R}^d$, the signs of BP_{f_i} and BP_{g_j} on a given cell C are invariant and not equal to 0.

First of all, by the definition of BP_{f_1}, that the sign of BP_{f_1} on C is invariant implies that the number of real solutions of $f_1(U, x_1)$ is invariant on C. We regard $f_2(U, x_1, x_2)$ as a polynomial in x_2, because on C,

$$f_1(U, x_1) = 0 \quad \text{and} \quad \mathrm{BP}_{f_2} = \mathrm{res}(\mathrm{dis}(f_2, x_2), f_1, x_1) \neq 0,$$

we have $\mathrm{dis}(f_2, x_2) \neq 0$ on C. Thus, if we replace x_1 in f_2 by the roots of f_1, the number of real solutions of f_2 is invariant. That is to say, the signs of BP_{f_1} and BP_{f_2} being invariant on C implies that the number of real solutions of $f_1 = 0, f_2 = 0$ is invariant on C; now, it is easy to see that the signs of $\mathrm{BP}_{f_1}, \dots, \mathrm{BP}_{f_s}$ being invariant on C implies that the number of real solutions of $f_1 = 0, \dots, f_s = 0$ is invariant on C.

Secondly, by the definition of BP_{g_j}, $\mathrm{BP}_{g_j} \neq 0$ implies that the sign of g_j is invariant on C if we replace $x_1, \dots, x_s$ in g_j by the roots of $f_1 = 0, \dots, f_s = 0$. This completes the proof. $\qquad\square$

By Theorem 49, for a regular parametric TSA T, we can start our algorithm from BP as follows.

Algorithm: `tofind`

Input: A regular parametric TSA T and an integer N;

Output: The necessary and sufficient condition on the parameters for T to have exactly N distinct real solutions, provided that the parameter are not on some "boundaries".

Step 1. Let $PS = \mathrm{BP}$, $i = 1$.

Step 2. By the algorithm of PCAD, compute a PS-invariant cad D of the parameter space $\mathbb{R}^d$ and its cylindrical algebraic sample (cas) S. In this step, we consider only the cells homeomorphic to $\mathbb{R}^d$ but not the cells homeomorphic to $\mathbb{R}^k$ $(k < d)$; thus all the cells in D are homeomorphic to $\mathbb{R}^d$ and all sample points in S are taken from the cells in D.

Step 3. For each cell c in D and its sample point $s_c \in S$, substitute s_c into T and denote it by $T(s_c)$. Compute the number of distinct real solutions of the system $T(s_c)$, in which polynomials all have constant coefficients now. At the same time, compute the signs of the polynomials in PS on this cell by substituting s_c into them respectively. Obviously, the signs of the polynomials in PS on cell c form a first order formula, denoted by Φ_c. When all the $T(s_c)$'s are computed, let

$$set_1 = \{\Phi_c \mid T \text{ has } N \text{ distinct real solutions on } c\},$$

$$set_0 = \{\Phi_c \mid T \text{ does not have } N \text{ distinct real solutions on } c\}.$$

Step 4. Decide whether all the recorded Φ_c's can form a necessary and sufficient condition or not by verifying whether $set_1 \cap set_0$ is empty or not (because of Theorems 48 and 49). If $set_1 \cap set_0 = \emptyset$, then go to Step 5; If $set_1 \cap set_0 \neq \emptyset$, then let

$$PS = PS \cup P_1(g_1, \ldots, g_i), \quad i = i + 1,$$

and go back to Step 2.

Step 5. If $set_1 = \{\Phi_{c_1}, \ldots, \Phi_{c_m}\}$, then $\Phi = \Phi_{c_1} \vee \cdots \vee \Phi_{c_m}$ is what we want.

Remark 50: The termination of this algorithm is guaranteed by Theorem 46.

Remark 51: In order to make our algorithm practical, we do not consider the "boundaries" when using PCAD. So, the condition obtained by this algorithm is a necessary and sufficient one if we omit the situation on the "boundaries".

Actually, in many cases the condition obtained by `tofind` is satisfactory enough because we do not lose too much information though it is not a necessary and sufficient one. In the following, we give a complementary algorithm which deals with the situation where the parameters are on the "boundaries" and thus makes the practical algorithm to be a complete one.

Given a parametric TSA T, let $R(u_1, \ldots, u_d)$ be one of the polynomials in the parameters to express the condition for T to have N distinct real solutions, which is obtained by tofind. Now, we need to determine the condition for T to have N distinct real solutions when the parameters are on $R = 0$. We take the following steps.

Algorithm: Tofind

Input: A regular parametric TSA T, a boundary $R = 0$ and an integer N;

Output: The necessary and sufficient condition for T to have exactly N distinct real solutions when the parameter are on $R = 0$.

Step 1. Let TR be the new system obtained by adding $R = 0$ to T. Now, we regard (u_1, X) as variables and $(u_2, \ldots, u_d)$ as parameters, where $X = (x_1, \ldots, x_s)$. Then, TR is of the same type as T. If TR is not regular, by Theorem 45, we can decompose it into regular ones. So, for concision, we regard TR as a regular system.

Step 2. Let $PS = \mathrm{BP}_{TR}$, $i = 1$.

Step 3. By the algorithm of PCAD, compute a PS-invariant cad D of the parameter space $\mathbb{R}^{d-1}$ and its cylindrical algebraic sample (cas) S.

Step 4. Let $S' = \emptyset$. For every sample point $s_c \in S$, substitute s_c into $R = 0$. If the distinct real solutions of $R(s_c) = 0$ are $a_1 < \cdots < a_k$, then put every (a_i, s_c) $(1 \leq i \leq k)$ into S'.

Step 5. For every sample point $(a_j, s_c) \in S'$, substitute it into T and the obtained new system is denoted by $T(a_j, s_c)$. Compute the number of distinct real solutions of the system $T(a_j, s_c)$. At the same time, compute the signs of the polynomials in PS at s_c. Obviously, the signs of the polynomials in PS at s_c form a first order formula, denoted by Φ_c. For (a_j, s_c), we replace Φ_c by (Φ_c, j). Then, let

$$set_1 = \{(\Phi_c, j) \mid T \text{ has the required real solutions at } (a_j, s_c)\},$$

$$set_0 = \{(\Phi_c, j) \mid T \text{ does not have the required real solutions}$$
$$\text{at } (a_j, s_c)\}.$$

Step 6. Decide whether set_1 can form a necessary and sufficient condition or not by verifying whether $set_1 \cap set_0$ is empty or not. If $set_1 \cap set_0 = \emptyset$, then go to Step 7; If $set_1 \cap set_0 \neq \emptyset$, then let

$$PS = PS \cup P_1(g_1, \ldots, g_i), \quad i = i + 1,$$

and go back to Step 3, where $P_1(g_1, \ldots, g_i)$ is defined with respect to TR.

Step 7. If $set_1 = \{(\Phi_{c_1}, j_1), \ldots, (\Phi_{c_m}, j_m)\}$, then $\Phi = (\Phi_{c_1}, j_1) \vee \cdots \vee (\Phi_{c_m}, j_m)$ is what we want, where (Φ_{c_i}, j_i) means that the parameters $(u_1, \ldots, u_d)$ should satisfy Φ_{c_i} and u_1 is the j_ith real root of $R = 0$ when $(u_2, \ldots, u_d)$ is fixed.

Remark 52: In Step 3 of `Tofind`, as in `tofind`, we consider only the cells homeomorphic to $\mathbb{R}^{d-1}$ but not those homeomorphic to $\mathbb{R}^k$ ($k < d - 1$). Therefore, if $S(u_2, \ldots, u_d)$ is a member of the final PS and further results in the case where the parameters are on both $R = 0$ and $S = 0$ are needed, we just put $S = 0$ into TR and apply the above algorithm again.

4.3. *DISCOVERER and Examples*

The algorithms described in the last subsection have been implemented as a Maple program DISCOVERER. It has two main functions `tofind` and `Tofind`. They are applicable to those problems which can be formulated into a parametric SAS. Usually, we call `tofind` first to find a satisfactory condition (see Remark 51) and then, if necessary, call `Tofind` to find further results when the parameters are on some boundaries.

The calling sequence in DISCOVERER for a parametric SAS T is:

$$\text{tofind} ([p_1, \ldots, p_s], [g_1, \ldots, g_r], [g_{r+1}, \ldots, g_t], [h_1, \ldots, h_m],$$
$$[x_1, \ldots, x_s], [u_1, \ldots, u_d], \alpha);$$

where α has the following three kinds of choices:

- a non-negative integer b which means the condition for T to have exactly b distinct real solutions;
- a range $b..c$ (where b, c are non-negative integers and $b < c$) which means the condition for T to have b or $b + 1$ or $\ldots$ or c distinct real solutions;
- a range $b..w$ (where b is a non-negative integer and w a name) which means the condition for T to have b or more distinct real solutions.

Similarly, the calling sequence of `Tofind` for T and some "boundaries" $R_1 = 0, \ldots, R_l = 0$ is:

$$\text{Tofind} ([p_1, \ldots, p_s, R_1, \ldots, R_l], [g_1, \ldots, g_r], [g_{r+1}, \ldots, g_t],$$
$$[h_1, \ldots, h_m], [x_1, \ldots, x_s], [u_1, \ldots, u_d], \alpha);$$

where each R_i is a "boundary" which can be a polynomial obtained by `tofind` or a constraint polynomial in the parameters.

Example 53:[15] Which triangles can occur as sections of a regular tetrahedron by planes which separate one vertex from the other three?

If we let $1, a, b$ (assume that $b \geq a \geq 1$) be the lengths of the three sides of the triangle, and x, y, z the distances from the vertex to the three vertexes of the triangle respectively, then, what we need is to find the necessary and sufficient condition that a, b should satisfy for the following system to have real solutions:

$$\begin{cases} h_1 = x^2 + y^2 - xy - 1 = 0, \\ h_2 = y^2 + z^2 - yz - a^2 = 0, \\ h_3 = z^2 + x^2 - zx - b^2 = 0, \\ x > 0, y > 0, z > 0, a - 1 \geq 0, b - a \geq 0, a + 1 - b > 0. \end{cases}$$

Using our program DISCOVERER, we attack this problem according to the following two steps. First of all, we type in:

tofind $([h_1, h_2, h_3], [a - 1, b - a], [x, y, z, a + 1 - b], [\ ], [x, y, z], [a, b], 1..n)$;

After running $3\,\mathrm{s}$ on a PC (Pentium IV/2.8G) with Maple 8, DISCOVERER outputs the following.

FINAL RESULT :

The system has required real solutions IF AND ONLY IF

$$[0 < R_1, 0 < R_2]$$

or

$$[0 < R_1, R_2 < 0, 0 < R_3]$$

where

$$R_1 = a^2 + a + 1 - b^2$$

$$R_2 = a^2 - 1 + b - b^2$$

$$\begin{aligned} R_3 = {} & 1 - \frac{8}{3}a^2 - \frac{8}{3}b^2 + \frac{16}{9}a^8 - \frac{68}{27}b^6 a^2 + \frac{241}{81}b^4 a^4 - \frac{68}{27}b^2 a^6 \\ & - \frac{68}{27}b^4 a^2 - \frac{68}{27}b^2 a^4 - \frac{2}{9}b^6 + \frac{16}{9}b^8 - \frac{2}{9}a^6 + \frac{46}{9}b^2 a^2 \\ & + \frac{16}{9}b^4 + \frac{16}{9}a^4 + \frac{46}{9}b^2 a^8 + \frac{46}{9}b^8 a^2 - \frac{68}{27}b^6 a^4 - \frac{68}{27}b^4 a^6 \\ & + \frac{16}{9}b^4 a^8 - \frac{8}{3}b^{10} a^2 + \frac{16}{9}b^8 a^4 - \frac{2}{9}b^6 a^6 - \frac{8}{3}b^2 a^{10} - \frac{8}{3}b^{10} \\ & + b^{12} - \frac{8}{3}a^{10} + a^{12} \end{aligned}$$

PROVIDED THAT :

$$-b + a \neq 0$$
$$a - 1 \neq 0$$
$$b - 1 \neq 0$$
$$a^2 - 1 + b - b^2 \neq 0$$
$$a^2 - 1 - b - b^2 \neq 0$$
$$a^2 - a + 1 - b^2 \neq 0$$
$$a^2 + a + 1 - b^2 \neq 0$$
$$a^2 - 1 - ab + b^2 \neq 0$$
$$a^2 - 1 + ab + b^2 \neq 0$$
$$R_3 \neq 0$$

Folke[15] gave a sufficient condition that any triangle with two angles $> 60°$ is a possible section. It is easy to see that this condition is equivalent to $[R_1 > 0, R_2 > 0]$.

Now, if the parameters a, b are not on the boundaries (that is, $R_1 = 0$, $R_2 = 0$, $R_3 = 0$, $a - 1 = 0$, $b - a = 0, \dots$), the condition obtained above is already a necessary and sufficient one. But, strictly speaking, to get a necessary and sufficient condition, we have to give the result when a, b are on the boundaries. Thus, we take the second step. If we want to know the result when a, b are on a certain boundary, say R_2, we only need to type in

Tofind $([h_1, h_2, h_3, R_2], [a - 1, b - a], [x, y, z, a + 1 - b], [\,], [x, y, z], [a, b], 1..n)$;

DISCOVERER outputs the following (in 0.44 s).

FINAL RESULT:

The system has required real solutions IF AND ONLY IF

$$[S_1 < 0, (2)R_2]$$

where

$$S_1 = b^6 + \frac{56}{3}b^4 - \frac{122}{3}b^3 + \frac{56}{3}b^2 + 1$$

PROVIDED THAT :

$$b - 1 \neq 0$$
$$S_1 \neq 0$$

$[S_1 < 0, (2)R_2]$ in the output means that a point (a_0, b_0) in the parametric plane should satisfy that $S_1 < 0$ and a_0 is the second root (from the smallest one up) of $R_2(a, b_0) = 0$. Furthermore, the situation when (a, b) is on $R_2 = 0 \wedge b - 1 = 0$ or $R_2 = 0 \wedge S_1 = 0$ can be determined by typing in

Tofind $([h_1, h_2, h_3, R_2, b - 1], [a - 1, b - a], [x, y, z, a + 1 - b], [\ ], [x, y, z],$
$\qquad [b, a], 1..n)$;

Tofind $([h_1, h_2, h_3, R_2, S_1], [a - 1, b - a], [x, y, z, a + 1 - b], [\ ], [x, y, z],$
$\qquad [b, a], 1..n)$;

respectively. In both cases the output is:

The system has 1 real solution!

The timings of the computations are 1.13 and 1.44ś, respectively.

In this way, together with some interactive computations, we finally get the condition for the system to have real solutions:

$$[0 < R_1, 0 < R_2, R_3 \le 0, 0 < a - 1, 0 \le b - a, 0 < a + 1 - b]$$

or

$$[0 < R_1, 0 \le R_3, 0 \le a - 1, 0 \le b - a, 0 < a + 1 - b].$$

Actually, by our algorithm and program, we can do more than the request to this problem. If we type in

tofind $([h_1, h_2, h_3], [a - 1, b - a], [x, y, z, a + 1 - b], [\ ], [x, y, z], [a, b], 1)$;

tofind $([h_1, h_2, h_3], [a - 1, b - a], [x, y, z, a + 1 - b], [\ ], [x, y, z], [a, b], 2)$;

tofind $([h_1, h_2, h_3], [a - 1, b - a], [x, y, z, a + 1 - b], [\ ], [x, y, z], [a, b], 3)$;

respectively, we will get the condition for the above system to have exactly 1, 2, or 3 real solutions respectively. In this way, we obtain the so-called complete solution classification of this problem, as indicated in Fig. 1. The number (0, 1, 2 or 3) in a certain region indicates the number of distinct real solutions of the system when the parameters a, b are in the region.

Example 54: It is well known that for a triangle there are four tritangent circles (i.e., one inscribed circle and three escribed circles) and a Feuerbach circle (i.e., the nine-point circle) whose radius is equal to half the circumradius. Given a triangle ABC whose vertices $B(1, 0)$ and $C(-1, 0)$ are fixed and the vertex $A(u_1, u_2)$ depends on two parameters, we want to find the conditions on u_1, u_2 such that there are four, three, two, one, or none of the tritangent circles whose radii are smaller than that of the Feuerbach circle, respectively.

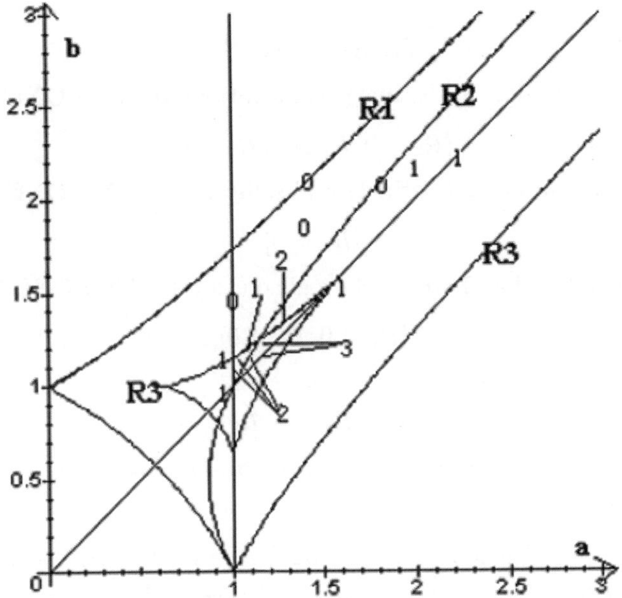

Fig. 1.   The complete solution classification of Example 53

By a routine computation, the system to be dealt with becomes

$$\begin{cases} f = 16x^2u_2^2 - (u_1^2 + 2u_1 + 1 + u_2^2)(1 - 2u_1 + u_1^2 + u_2^2) = 0, \\ i = y^4u_2 + (2 - 2u_2^2 - 2u_1^2)y^3 + u_2(u_1^2 - 5 + u_2^2)y^2 + 4u_2^2y - u_2^3 = 0, \\ x > 0, \ x^2 - y^2 > 0, \end{cases}$$

where x is the radius of the Feuerbach circle and $|y|$ is the radii of the four tritangent circles.

We type in

$$\text{tofind}([f, i], [\ ], [x, x^2 - y^2], [\ ], [x, y], [u_1, u_2], 4);$$

$$\text{tofind}([f, i], [\ ], [x, x^2 - y^2], [\ ], [x, y], [u_1, u_2], 3);$$

$$\text{tofind}([f, i], [\ ], [x, x^2 - y^2], [\ ], [x, y], [u_1, u_2], 2);$$

$$\text{tofind}([f, i], [\ ], [x, x^2 - y^2], [\ ], [x, y], [u_1, u_2], 1);$$

$$\text{tofind}([f, i], [\ ], [x, x^2 - y^2], [\ ], [x, y], [u_1, u_2], 0);$$

respectively and get the following results (for concision, the outputs are rearranged in a simpler form).

                                     Yang and Xia

FINAL RESULT :

The system has 3 (distinct) real solutions IF AND ONLY IF

$$[R_1 < 0, R_2 > 0, R_3 < 0]$$

The system has 2 (distinct) real solutions IF AND ONLY IF

$$[R_1 > 0]$$

The system has 1 (distinct) real solution IF AND ONLY IF

$$[R_1 < 0, R_2 < 0]$$

or

$$[R_1 < 0, R_2 > 0, R_3 > 0]$$

The system does not have 0 or 4 real solutions

where

$$R_1 = -7 + 20u_2^6 u_1^2 + 20u_2^2 + 28u_1^2 - 52u_1^2 u_2^2 - 42u_1^4 + 70u_2^4 - 204u_2^6$$
$$+ 68u_2^4 u_1^2 + 9u_2^8 + 6u_2^4 u_1^4 + 28u_1^6 - 7u_1^8 + 44u_1^4 u_2^2 - 12u_2^2 u_1^6,$$

$$R_2 = 189 + 189u_1^{12} + 720u_2^2 - 1134u_1^2 - 1977u_2^8 + 2835u_1^4 - 1235u_2^4$$
$$- 3560u_2^6 - 3780u_1^6 + 2835u_1^8 - 8088u_2^6 u_1^2 - 1968u_1^2 u_2^2 + 2332u_2^4 u_1^2$$
$$+ 558u_2^4 u_1^4 + 672u_1^4 u_2^2 + 2592u_2^2 u_1^6 + 984u_2^6 u_1^6 - 1566u_2^8 u_1^2 - 40u_2^{10} u_1^2$$
$$+ 135u_2^8 u_1^4 - 2776u_2^6 u_1^4 - 3172u_2^4 u_1^6 - 2928u_1^8 u_2^2 + 1517u_1^8 u_2^4$$
$$+ 912u_2^2 u_1^{10} + 15u_2^{12} - 168u_2^{10} - 1134u_1^{10},$$

$$R_3 = -63 + 225u_2^{14} u_1^2 - 63u_1^{16} + 4284u_1^{12} - 345u_2^2 - 504u_1^2 + 515u_2^8$$
$$+ 4284u_1^4 + 485u_2^4 + 3347u_2^6 - 11592u_1^6 + 15750u_1^8 + 73991u_2^6 u_1^2$$
$$- 2851u_1^2 u_2^2 + 23658u_2^4 u_1^2 - 29957u_2^4 u_1^4 + 9791u_1^4 u_2^2 - 4163u_2^2 u_1^6$$
$$+ 69174u_2^6 u_1^6 - 125788u_2^8 u_1^2 - 48997u_2^{10} u_1^2 + 274u_2^8 u_1^4 + 89942u_2^6 u_1^4$$
$$- 22516u_2^4 u_1^6 - 12163u_1^8 u_2^2 + 36971u_1^8 u_2^4 + 13567u_2^2 u_1^{10} + 1031u_2^{12} u_1^4$$
$$- 1974u2^{12} u_1^2 - 2245u_2^{10} u_1^4 + 1717u_2^{10} u_1^6 - 5609u_2^6 u_1^8 - 1052u_2^8 u_1^6$$
$$+ 995u_2^8 u_1^8 - 7766u_2^4 u_1^{10} - 875u_2^4 u_1^{12} - 3427u_1^{12} u_2^2 - 445u_2^6 u_1^{10}$$
$$- 409u_1^{14} u_2^2 + 407u_2^{12} - 1643u_2^{10} - 11592u_1^{10} - 15u_2^{14} - 504u_1^{14};$$

PROVIDED THAT :

$$u_1 \neq 0,$$
$$u_2 \neq 0,$$
$$(u_1 + 1)^2 + u_2^2 \neq 0,$$
$$(u_1 - 1)^2 + u_2^2 \neq 0,$$

$$L(u_1, u_2) = 9 + 84u_2^6 u_1^2 + 84u_2^2 - 36u_1^2 - 116u_1^2 u_2^2 + 54u_1^4 + 166u_2^4 - 140u_2^6$$
$$+ 132u_2^4 u_1^2 + 25u_2^8 + 102u_2^4 u_1^4 - 36u_1^6 + 9u_1^8 - 20u_1^4 u_2^2 + 52u_2^2 u_1^6 \neq 0,$$
$$R_1 \neq 0.$$

The total time for executing the five instructions is 87.69 s.

The non-degenerate condition $u_2 \neq 0$ is a premise because otherwise the vertices A, B, C are on a line. Thus $(u_1 + 1)^2 + u_2^2 \neq 0$ and $(u_1 - 1)^2 + u_2^2 \neq 0$ are verified. Furthermore, it can be easily shown (by DISCOVERER, say) that $L(u_1, u_2)$ is positive if $u_1 \neq 0$ and $u_2 \neq 0$. Because we are concerned with the complement of the algebraic curve $R_1 = 0$, the only "non-degenerate" condition we need to consider is $u_1 \neq 0$.

As we did in the preceding example, by typing in

$$\text{Tofind}([R_2, f, i], [\ ], [-R_1, x, x^2 - y^2], [u_1, u_2], [x, y], [u_1, u_2], 1);$$

$$\text{Tofind}([R_2, f, i], [\ ], [-R_1, x, x^2 - y^2], [u_1, u_2], [x, y], [u_1, u_2], 3);$$

we get the situation when (u_1, u_2) is on $R_2 = 0$. Finally, we obtain the following results.

(1) If $u_1 \neq 0$,

The system has 3 (distinct) real solutions IF AND ONLY IF

$$[R_1 < 0, R_2 > 0, R_3 < 0]$$

The system has 2 (distinct) real solutions IF AND ONLY IF

$$[R_1 > 0]$$

The system has 1 (distinct) real solution IF AND ONLY IF

$$[R_1 < 0, R_2 \leq 0]$$

or

$$[R_1 < 0, R_2 > 0, R_3 > 0]$$

The system does not have 0 or 4 real solutions.

(2) If $u_1 = 0$ (in the case ABC is an isosceles triangle),

The system has 2 (distinct) real solutions IF AND ONLY IF

$$[S_1 \cdot S_2 \geq 0]$$

The system has 1 (distinct) real solution IF AND ONLY IF

$$[S_1 < 0, S_2 > 0]$$

The system does not have 0 or 3 or 4 real solutions

where $S_1 = u_2^4 - 22u_2^2 - 7$, $S_2 = u_2^2 - 1/3$.

Note that if $u_1 = 0$ and the system has two distinct real solutions, then one of the solutions is of multiplicity 2 and thus the system has three real solutions indeed.

This example was studied in a different way by Guergueb and others.[18] They did not give any quantifier-free formulas but illustrated the situation with a sketch figure.

Example 55: Give the necessary and sufficient condition for the existence of a triangle with elements a, h_a, R, where a, h_a, R means the side-length, altitude, and circumradius, respectively.

Clearly, we need to find the necessary and sufficient condition for the following system to have real solutions:

$$\begin{cases} f_1 = a^2 h_a^2 - 4s(s-a)(s-b)(s-c) = 0, \\ f_2 = 2Rh_a - bc = 0, \\ f_3 = 2s - a - b - c = 0, \\ a > 0, b > 0, c > 0, a + b - c > 0, b + c - a > 0, \\ c + a - b > 0, R > 0, h_a > 0. \end{cases}$$

In the same way as in the preceding examples, we obtain the following result.

The system has real solutions IF AND ONLY IF

$$[0 \leq R_1, 0 \leq R_3]$$

or

$$[0 \leq R_1, R_2 \leq 0, R_3 \leq 0]$$

where

$$R_1 = R - \frac{1}{2}a$$

$$R_2 = Rh_a - \frac{1}{4}a^2$$

$$R_3 = -\frac{1}{2}h_a^2 + Rh_a - \frac{1}{8}a^2.$$

The time spent is $0.61\,\text{s}$.

The condition given by Mitrinovic and others[27] is $R_1 \geq 0 \wedge R_3 \geq 0$. Now, we know that their condition is wrong and it is only a sufficient condition.

Our program DISCOVERER is very efficient for solving this kind of problems. By DISCOVERER, we have discovered or rediscovered about 70 such conditions for the existence of a triangle, and found three mistakes in the book[27] by Mitrinovic and others.

Acknowledgments

The authors acknowledge the support provided by NKBRSF (G199803-0600).

References

1. Aubry, P., Lazard, D., Moreno Maza, M., On the theories of triangular sets, *J. Symb. Comput.*, **28**, 105–124, 1999.
2. Aubry, P., Rouillier, F., Safey El Din, M., Real solving for positive dimensional systems, *J. Symb. Comput.*, **34**, 543–560, 2002.
3. Basu, S., Pollack, R., Roy, M.-F., *Algorithms in Real Algebraic Geometry*, Algorithms and Computation in Mathematics 10, Springer-Verlag, Berlin Heidelberg, 2003.
4. Becker, T., Weispfenning, V., *Gröbner Bases*, Springer-Verlag, New York, 1993.
5. Ben-Or, M., Kozen, D., Reif, J., The complexity of elementary algebra and geometry, *J. Computer and System Sciences*, **32**, 251–264, 1986.
6. Bottema, O., Dordevic, R. Z., Janic, R. R., Mitrinovic, D. S., Vasic, P. M., *Geometric Inequalities*, Wolters-Noordhoff Publ., Groningen, The Netherlands, 1969.
7. Brown, C. W., Simple CAD construction and its applications, *J. Symb. Comput.*, **31**, 521–547, 2001.
8. Buchberger, B., Gröbner bases: An algorithmic method in polynomial ideal theory, in *Multidimensional Systems Theory* (Bose, N. K., ed.), Reidel, Dordrecht, pp. 184–232, 1985.
9. Chou, S.-C., Gao, X.-S., Arnon, D. S., On the mechanical proof of geometry theorems involving inequalities, in *Advances in Computing Research*, **6**, JAI Press Inc., pp. 139–181, 1992.
10. Collins, G. E., Quantifier elimination for real closed fields by cylindrical algebraic decomposition, in *Lecture Notes in Computer Science* **33**, Springer-Verlag, Berlin Heidelberg, pp. 134–165, 1975.
11. Collins, G. E., Hong, H., Partial cylindrical algebraic decomposition for quantifier elimination, *J. Symb. Comput.*, **12**, 299–328, 1991.
12. Collins, G. E., Loos, R., Real zeros of polynomials, in *Computer Algebra: Symbolic and Algebraic Computation* (Buchberger, B., Collins, G. E., Loos, R., eds.), Springer-Verlag, Wien New York, pp. 83–94, 1983.
13. Davenport, J. H., Heintz, J., Real quantifier elimination is doubly exponential, *J. Symb. Comput.*, **5**(1–2), 29–35, 1988.
14. Dolzmann, A., Sturm, T., Weispfenning, V., Real quantifier elimination in practice, in *Algorithmic Algebra and Number Theory* (Matzat, B. H., Greuel, G.-M., Hiss, G., eds.), Springer-Verlag, Berlin Heidelberg, pp. 221–247, 1998.

15. Folke, E., Which triangles are plane sections of regular tetrahedra? *American Mathematical Monthly*, **101**(10), pp. 788–789, 1994.

16. Gonzalez-Vega, L., A combinatorial algorithm solving some quantifier elimination problems, in *Quantifier Elimination and Cylindrical Algebraic Decomposition* (Caviness, B. F., Johnson, J. R., eds.), Springer-Verlag, Wien New York, pp. 365–375, 1998.

17. Gonzalez-Vega, L., Rouillier, F., Roy, M.-F., Trujillo, G., Symbolic recipes for real solutions, in *Some Tapas of Computer Algebra* (Cohen, A. M., Cuypers, H., Sterk, H., eds.), Springer-Verlag, Berlin Heidelberg, 1999.

18. Guergueb, A., Mainguené, J., Roy, M-F., Examples of automatic theorem proving in real geometry, in *Proceedings of ISSAC '94*, ACM Press, New York, pp. 20–24, 1994.

19. Hong, H., Quantifier elimination for formulas constrained by quadratic equations, in *Proceedings of ISSAC '93* (Bronstein, M., ed.), ACM Press, New York, pp. 264–274, 1993.

20. Janous, W., Problem 1137, *Crux Math.*, **12**, 79, 177, 1986.

21. Kalkbrener, M., A generalized Euclidean algorithm for computing triangular representations of algebraic varieties, *J. Symb. Comput.*, **15**, 143–167, 1993.

22. Kuang, J. C., *Applied Inequalities* (2nd edn., in Chinese), Hunan Edu. Publ. House, China, 1993.

23. Liu, B., *BOTTEMA, What we see* (in Chinese), Tibet People's Publ. House, Lhasa, 2003.

24. Loos, R., Generalized polynomial remainder sequences, in *Computer Algebra: Symbolic and Algebraic Computation* (Buchberger, B., Collins, G. E., Loos, R., eds.), Springer-Verlag, Wien New York, pp. 115–137, 1983.

25. Lu, Z., He, B., Luo, Y., Pan, L., An algorithm of real root isolation for polynomial systems, *MM Research Preprints*, No. 20, 187–198. MMRC AMSS, Academia Sinica, Beijing, 2001.

26. Ma, S., Zheng, Z., On a cubic system with eight small-amplitude limit cycles, *Appl. Math. Lett.*, **7**, 23–27, 1994.

27. Mitrinovic, D. S., Pecaric, J. E., Volenec, V., *Recent Advances in Geometric Inequalities*, Kluwer Academic Publ., Dordrecht, 1989.

28. Pedersen, P., Roy, M.-F., Szpirglas, A., Counting real zeros in the multivariate case, in *Computational Algebraic Geometry* (Eyssette, F., Galligo, A., eds.), Birkhäuser, Boston, 1993.

29. Rouillier, F., Solving zero-dimensional systems through the rational univariate representation, *Appl. Algebra Engrg. Comm. Comput.*, **9**, 433–461, 1999.

30. Rouillier, F., Zimmermann, P., Efficient isolation of a polynomial real roots, Technical Report RR-4113, INRIA, 2001.

31. Shan, Z. (ed.), *Geometric Inequality in China* (in Chinese), Jiangsu Edu. Publ. House, China, 1996.

32. Tarski, A., *A Decision Method for Elementary Algebra and Geometry*, University of California Press, Berkeley, 1951.

33. Wang, D., Decomposing polynomial systems into simple systems, *J. Symb. Comput.*, **25**, 295–314, 1998.

34. Wang, D., Computing triangular systems and regular systems, *J. Symb. Com-*

put., **30**, 221–236, 2000.

35. Wang, D. K., Zero decomposition algorithms for systems of polynomial equations, in *Proceedings of ASCM 2000* (Gao, X.-S., Wang, D., eds.), World Scientific, Singapore New Jersey, pp. 67–70, 2000.

36. Weispfenning, V., The complexity of linear problems in fields, *J. Symb. Comput.*, **5**(1–2), 3–27, 1988.

37. Weispfenning, V., Quantifier elimination for real algebra — The cubic case, in *Proceedings of ISSAC '94*, ACM Press, New York, pp. 258–263, 1994.

38. Weispfenning, V., Quantifier elimination for real algebra — The quadratic case and beyond, *Appl. Algebra Engrg. Comm. Comput.*, **8**, 85–101, 1997.

39. Weispfenning, V., A new approach to quantifier elimination for real algebra, in *Quantifier Elimination and Cylindrical Algebraic Decomposition* (Caviness, B. F., Johnson, J. R., eds.), Springer-Verlag, Wien New York, pp. 376–392, 1998.

40. Winkler, F., *Polynomial Algorithms in Computer Algebra*, Springer-Verlag, Wien New York, 1996.

41. Wu, W.-T., On zeros of algebraic equations — An application of Ritt principle, *Kexue Tongbao*, **31**, 1–5, 1986.

42. Wu, W.-T., On a finiteness theorem about problem involving inequalities, *Sys. Sci. & Math. Scis.*, **7**, 193–200, 1994.

43. Wu, W.-T., On global-optimization problems, in *Proceedings of ASCM '98*, Lanzhou University Press, Lanzhou, pp. 135–138, 1998.

44. Xia, B., Hou, X., A complete algorithm for counting real solutions of polynomial systems of equations and inequalities, *Computers & Mathematics with Applications*, **44**, 633–642, 2002.

45. Xia, B., Yang, L., An algorithm for isolating the real solutions of semi-algebraic systems, *J. Symb. Comput.*, **34**, 461–477, 2002.

46. Xia, B., Zhang, T., Real root isolation based on interval arithmetic, Preprint, 2003.

47. Yang, L., Recent advances in automated theorem proving on inequalities, *J. Comput. Sci. & Tech.*, **14**(5), 434–446, 1999.

48. Yang, L., Hou, X., Xia, B., Automated discovering and proving for geometric inequalities, in *Automated Deduction in Geometry* (Gao, X.-S., Wang, D., Yang, L., eds.), LNAI **1669**, Springer-Verlag, Berlin Heidelberg, pp. 30–46, 1999.

49. Yang, L., Hou, X., Xia, B., A complete algorithm for automated discovering of a class of inequality-type theorems, *Science in China* (Ser. F), **44**, 33–49, 2001.

50. Yang, L., Xia, S., An inequality-proving program applied to global optimization, in Proceedings of ATCM 2000 (Yang, W.-C. *et al.*, eds.), ATCM, Inc., Blacksburg, pp. 40–51, 2000.

51. Yang, L., Xia, S., Automated proving for a class of constructive geometric inequalities (in Chinese), *Chinese J. Comput.*, **26**(7), 769–778, 2003.

52. Yang, L., Zhang, J., A practical program of automated proving for a class of geometric inequalities, in *Automated Deduction in Geometry* (Richter-Gebert, J., Wang, D., eds.), LNAI **2061**, Springer-Verlag, Berlin Heidelberg,

pp. 41–57, 2001.

53. Yang, L., Zhang, J.-Z., Searching dependency between algebraic equations: An algorithm applied to automated reasoning, Technical Report IC/91/6, International Centre for Theoretical Physics, Trieste, 1991.

54. Yang, L., Zhang, J.-Z., Hou, X., An efficient decomposition algorithm for geometry theorem proving without factorization, in *Proceedings of ASCM '95* (Shi, H., Kobayashi, H., eds.), Scientists Inc., Tokyo, pp. 33–41, 1995.

55. Yang, L., Zhang, J.-Z., Hou, X., *Nonlinear Algebraic Equation System and Automated Theorem Proving* (in Chinese), Shanghai Sci. and Tech. Edu. Publ. House, Shanghai, 1996.

CHAPTER 11

AUTOMATED DERIVATION OF UNKNOWN RELATIONS AND DETERMINATION OF GEOMETRIC LOCI

Yong-Bin Li

Institute of Mathematics, Shantou University
Shantou, Guangdong 515063, P. R. China and
Sichuan Vocational and Technical College of Communication
Chengdu, Sichuan 610013, P. R. China
E-mail: yongbinli@hotmail.com

This chapter introduces the concept of strong regular sets and presents some of their properties. Three algorithms for zero decomposition of polynomial systems are fully described. Based on two of them, we propose two alternative methods for automated derivation of unknown relations and automated determination of geometric loci. Some well-known examples are also discussed.

1. Introduction

Let $\mathbf{K}$ be a computable field of characteristic 0 and $\mathbf{K}[x_1, \ldots, x_n]$ (or $\mathbf{K}[\mathbf{x}]$ for short) the ring of polynomials in the variables $(x_1, \ldots, x_n)$ with coefficients in $\mathbf{K}$. By a *polynomial set* we mean a finite set of nonzero polynomials in $\mathbf{K}[\mathbf{x}]$. In what follows, the number of elements of a finite set $\mathbb{P}$ is denoted $|\mathbb{P}|$; it is also called the *length* of $\mathbb{P}$. An *ordered set* is written by enclosing its elements in a pair of square brackets. Given any nonzero polynomial $P \notin \mathbf{K}$, the biggest index p such that $\deg(P, x_p) > 0$ is called the *class*, x_p the *leading variable*, and $\deg(P, x_p)$ the *leading degree* of P, denoted by $\mathrm{cls}(P)$, $\mathrm{lv}(P)$ and $\mathrm{ldeg}(P)$, respectively. A finite nonempty ordered set $\mathbb{T} = [f_1, \ldots, f_s]$ of polynomials in $\mathbf{K}[\mathbf{x}] \setminus \mathbf{K}$ is called a *triangular set* if $\mathrm{cls}(f_1) < \cdots < \mathrm{cls}(f_s)$.

Any triangular set $\mathbb{T}$ can be written in the following form

$$\mathbb{T} = [f_1(u_1, \ldots, u_r, y_1), \ldots, f_s(u_1, \ldots, u_r, y_1, \ldots, y_s)], \tag{1}$$

where $(u_1, \ldots, u_r, y_1, \ldots, y_s)$ is a permutation of $(x_1, \ldots, x_n)$. We call $u_1, \ldots, u_r$ (abbreviated to $\mathbf{u}$) the *parameters* and $y_1, \ldots, y_s$ the *dependents*

299

of $\mathbb{T}$. $\mathbb{C}_{f_i}$ denotes the set of all the nonzero coefficients of f_i in y_i, I_i denotes the leading coefficient of f_i in y_i for each i, and $\mathrm{ini}(\mathbb{T})$ stands for the set of all I_i.

The extension field $\tilde{\mathbf{K}}$ of $\mathbf{K}$ considered in this chapter is an algebraically closed field. While speaking about a *polynomial system*, we refer to a pair $[\mathbb{P}, \mathbb{Q}]$ of polynomial sets. The set of all zeros of $[\mathbb{P}, \mathbb{Q}]$ is defined as

$$\mathrm{Zero}(\mathbb{P}/\mathbb{Q}) \triangleq \{\mathbf{z} \in \tilde{\mathbf{K}}^n : P(\mathbf{z}) = 0, Q(\mathbf{z}) \neq 0, \forall P \in \mathbb{P}, Q \in \mathbb{Q}\}.$$

Let $\mathbb{T}$ be a triangular set as in (1) and P any polynomial. The polynomial

$$\mathrm{prem}(\cdots \mathrm{prem}(P, f_s, y_s), \cdots, f_1, y_1),$$

denoted simply by $\mathrm{prem}(P, \mathbb{T})$, is called the *pseudo-remainder* of P with respect to $\mathbb{T}$. It is easy to deduce the following *pseudo-remainder formula*

$$(\prod_{i=1}^{s} I_i^{c_i})P = \sum_{i=1}^{s} q_i f_i + \mathrm{prem}(P, \mathbb{T}), \tag{2}$$

where each c_i is a nonnegative integer and $q_i \in \mathbf{K}[\mathbf{x}]$ for all i. Similarly, the polynomial

$$\mathrm{res}(\cdots \mathrm{res}(P, f_s, y_s), \cdots, f_1, y_1),$$

denoted simply by $\mathrm{res}(P, \mathbb{T})$, is called the *resultant* of P with respect to $\mathbb{T}$. If $P \in \mathbf{K}[\mathbf{u}, y_1, \ldots, y_s] \setminus \mathbf{K}[\mathbf{u}]$, the index k with $\mathrm{lv}(P) = y_k$ is called the *class* of P with respect to $\mathbb{T}$, denoted by $\mathrm{cls}(P, \mathbb{T})$.

Given a nonempty polynomial set $\mathbb{P}$, using Wu method,[19] one can obtain a zero decomposition of the form

$$\mathrm{Zero}(\mathbb{P}) = \bigcup_i \mathrm{Zero}(\mathbb{T}_i/\mathrm{ini}(\mathbb{T}_i)),$$

in which each $\mathbb{T}_i$ is an *ascending set*[19] $\mathbb{P}$.

A triangular set $\mathbb{T} = [f_1, \ldots, f_s]$ is called a *regular set*, if $I_1 \neq 0$ and $\mathrm{res}(I_j, \mathbb{T}) \neq 0$ for $j = 2, \cdots, s$. The ideal $\mathrm{Ideal}(\mathbb{T}) : J^{\infty}$ is called the *saturation* of $\mathbb{T}$, denoted by $\mathrm{sat}(\mathbb{T})$, where $J = \prod_{j=1}^{s} I_j$. The concept of regular sets was introduced by Yang and Zhang[24] under a different name. Independently, it was also introduced by Kalkbrener.[6]

Theorem 1: There exist two algorithms, by which one can decompose any polynomial set $\mathbb{P}$ into finitely many regular sets $\mathbb{T}_i$ such that

$$\mathrm{Zero}(\mathbb{P}) = \bigcup_{i=1}^{e} \mathrm{Zero}(\mathbb{T}_i/\mathrm{ini}(\mathbb{T}_i)) = \bigcup_{i=1}^{e} \mathrm{Zero}(\mathrm{sat}(\mathbb{T}_i));$$

the set $\{\mathbb{T}_1, \ldots, \mathbb{T}_e\}$, denoted by $\mathrm{Reg}(\mathbb{P})$, is called a *regular series* of $\mathbb{P}$.

Remark 2: One of the algorithms mentioned in the above theorem is presented by Kalkbrener,[6] and the other is a simple application of the algorithm RegSer proposed by Wang.[16,17] RegSer may be used to compute a *regular series*[17] of any polynomial system. It is also very efficient for computing regular sets from nonempty polynomial sets.

For any $\bar{\mathbf{z}} = (\bar{z}_1, \ldots, \bar{z}_n) = (\bar{\mathbf{u}}, \bar{y}_1, \ldots, \bar{y}_s) \in \mathrm{Zero}(\mathbb{T})$, we write $\bar{\mathbf{z}}^{\{i\}}$ for $\bar{\mathbf{u}}, \bar{y}_1, \ldots, \bar{y}_i$ or $(\bar{\mathbf{u}}, \bar{y}_1, \ldots, \bar{y}_i)$ with $\bar{\mathbf{z}} = \bar{\mathbf{z}}^{\{s\}}$ and $\bar{\mathbf{u}} = \bar{\mathbf{z}}^{\{0\}}$. $\bar{\mathbf{z}}$ is said to be *regular* if either $\bar{z}_i = x_i$ or x_i is a dependent of $\mathbb{T}$ for any $1 \leq i \leq n$. The set of all regular zeros of $\mathbb{T}$ is denoted by $\mathrm{RegZero}(\mathbb{T})$.

The following result given in the paper[1] by Aubry and others (see also Theorem 6.2.4 in the book[17] by Wang) is very useful.

Theorem 3: A triangular set $\mathbb{T} = [f_1, \ldots, f_s]$ is a regular set if and only if $\mathrm{sat}(\mathbb{T}) = \{P \in \mathbf{K}[\mathbf{x}] : \mathrm{prem}(P, \mathbb{T}) = 0\}$.

In Section 2, we present the theory of *weakly nondegenerate conditions* of regular sets introduced by Zhang, Yang and Hou.[27] The concept of *strong regular sets* will also be introduced. Such sets have some useful properties. For instance, when $\mathbb{T}$ is a strong regular set, we have $\mathrm{Zero}(\mathrm{sat}(\mathbb{T})) = \mathrm{Zero}(\mathbb{T})$.

Section 3 focuses mainly on the description of three algorithms SReg, RSplit and SRD*. The algorithm SRD* may decompose any polynomial system into strong regular sets in $\mathbf{K}[\mathbf{x}, t]$, where t is a new variable. It is developed and improved from the algorithm Dec presented in the paper[11] by Zhang, Yang, and the author.

In Section 4, we present two alternative methods for automated derivation of unknown relations and determination of geometric loci using SRD* and RSplit. Some well-known examples show that our methods have certain advantages.

2. The Theory of Weakly Nondegenerate Conditions and Strong Regular Sets

Let $\mathbb{T} = [f_1, \ldots, f_s]$; a zero $\mathbf{z}_0 \in \mathrm{Zero}(\mathbb{T})$ is called a *quasi-normal zero*, or in other words, it satisfies the *weakly nondegenerate condition*, if $\mathbf{z}_0^{\{i\}} \notin \mathrm{Zero}(\mathbb{C}_{f_i})$ for any $1 \leq i \leq s$. The theory of weakly nondegenerate conditions of regular sets in $\mathbf{K}[\mathbf{x}]$ was established by Zhang, Yang and Hou[27] using the analytic method.

For any regular set $\mathbb{T}$ and polynomial P, if there exists a nonnegative integer d such that $\mathrm{prem}(P^d, \mathbb{T}) = 0$, then it follows from the pseudo-remainder formula (2) that $\mathrm{Zero}(\{P\}) \supseteq \mathrm{Zero}(\mathbb{T}/\mathrm{ini}(\mathbb{T}))$. The following theorem given in the papers[9,11] by Zhang, Yang, and the author shows that, if $\mathbf{z}_0$ is a quasi-normal zero of $\mathbb{T}$, then $\mathbf{z}_0 \in \mathrm{Zero}(\{P\})$, no matter whether $\prod_{i=1}^{s} I_i$ vanishes at $\mathbf{z}_0$ or not.

Theorem 4: Let $\mathbb{T}$ be a regular set and P a polynomial. If there exists an integer $d > 0$ such that $\mathrm{prem}(P^d, \mathbb{T}) = 0$, then every quasi-normal zero of $\mathbb{T}$ is also a zero of P.

Corollary 5: *Let $\mathbb{P}$ be a polynomial set in $\mathbf{K}[\mathbf{x}]$ and $\mathrm{Reg}(\mathbb{P}) = \{\mathbb{T}_1, \dots, \mathbb{T}_e\}$ with $\mathbb{T}_i = [f_{i,1}, \dots, f_{i,s_i}]$ for $1 \le i \le e$. Then*

$$\mathrm{Zero}(\mathbb{P}) = \bigcup_{i=1}^{e} \mathrm{Zero}(\mathbb{T}_i/\mathbb{U}_i),$$

where

$$\mathbb{U}_i = \{\mathrm{ini}(f_{i,j}) : \ \mathrm{Zero}(\mathbb{T}_i^{\{j\}} \cup \mathbb{C}_{f_{i,j}}) \ne \emptyset, \ 1 \le j \le s_i\}$$

for $1 \le i \le e$.

Proof: From Theorem 1, we know that

$$\mathrm{Zero}(\mathbb{P}) = \bigcup_{i=1}^{e} \mathrm{Zero}(\mathrm{sat}(\mathbb{T}_i)) = \bigcup_{i=1}^{e} \mathrm{Zero}(\mathbb{T}_i/\mathrm{ini}(\mathbb{T}_i)).$$

It is obvious that $\mathrm{Zero}(\mathbb{T}_i/\mathrm{ini}(\mathbb{T}_i)) \subseteq \mathrm{Zero}(\mathbb{T}_i/\mathbb{U}_i)$ by the construction of $\mathbb{U}_i$ for each i. Thus

$$\mathrm{Zero}(\mathbb{P}) \subseteq \bigcup_{i=1}^{e} \mathrm{Zero}(\mathbb{T}_i/\mathbb{U}_i).$$

On the other hand, it is easy to see that any $\mathbf{z} \in \mathrm{Zero}(\mathbb{T}_i/\mathbb{U}_i)$ is also a quasi-normal zero of $\mathbb{T}_i$. As $\{\mathbb{T}_1, \dots, \mathbb{T}_e\}$ is a regular series of $\mathbb{P}$, there exists an integer $d^* > 0$ such that $\mathrm{prem}(P^{d^*}, \mathbb{T}_i) = 0$ for each $P \in \mathbb{P}$ and $1 \le i \le e$. It follows from Theorem 4 that $\mathrm{Zero}(\mathbb{P}) \supseteq \mathrm{Zero}(\mathbb{T}_i/\mathbb{U}_i)$ for each i. This implies that

$$\mathrm{Zero}(\mathbb{P}) \supseteq \bigcup_{i=1}^{e} \mathrm{Zero}(\mathbb{T}_i/\mathbb{U}_i).$$

Therefore,

$$\mathrm{Zero}(\mathbb{P}) = \bigcup_{i=1}^{e} \mathrm{Zero}(\mathrm{sat}(\mathbb{T}_i)) = \bigcup_{i=1}^{e} \mathrm{Zero}(\mathbb{T}_i/\mathrm{ini}(\mathbb{T}_i)) = \bigcup_{i=1}^{e} \mathrm{Zero}(\mathbb{T}_i/\mathbb{U}_i).$$

$\square$

For any triangular set $\mathbb{T}$, we denote $\mathrm{ldeg}(\mathbb{T}) \triangleq \prod_{f \in \mathbb{T}} \mathrm{ldeg}(f)$. The next assertion is taken from the paper[10] by the author.

Theorem 6: Let $\mathbb{T} = [f_1, \ldots, f_s]$ be a regular set and P a polynomial in $\mathbf{K}[\mathbf{x}]$. Then the following properties are equivalent:

a. $\mathrm{Zero}(\mathbb{T}/\mathrm{ini}(\mathbb{T})) \subset \mathrm{Zero}(\{P\})$;

b. For any quasi-normal zero z_0 of $\mathbb{T}$, $z_0 \in \mathrm{Zero}(\{P\})$;

c. There exists an integer $0 < d \leq \mathrm{ldeg}(\mathbb{T})$ such that $\mathrm{prem}(P^d, \mathbb{T}) = 0$.

Proof:

c $\Longrightarrow$ b: Theorem 4.

b $\Longrightarrow$ a: It is obvious.

a $\Longrightarrow$ c: Write $\mathbb{T} = [f_1, \ldots, f_s]$ in the form (1) with $\mathrm{ini}(f_i) = I_i$, $\mathrm{ldeg}(f_i) = d_i$ for $1 \leq i \leq s$, and $\mathrm{ldeg}(\mathbb{T}) = d = d_1 \ldots d_s$. It follows that $I \in \mathbf{K}[\mathbf{u}] \setminus \{0\}$ with $I = \prod_{i=1}^{s} \mathrm{res}(I_i, \mathbb{T})$. Therefore,

$$\mathrm{Zero}(\mathbb{T}/\{I\}) \subseteq \mathrm{Zero}(\mathbb{T}/\mathrm{ini}(\mathbb{T})) \subseteq \mathrm{Zero}(\{P\}).$$

Consider first the case $s = 1$ and let

$$R = \mathrm{prem}(P^{d_1}, \mathbb{T}) = \mathrm{prem}(P^{d_1}, f_1, y_1).$$

We have the pseudo-remainder formula

$$I_1^{q_1} P^{d_1} = Q f_1 + R$$

for some integer $q_1 \geq 0$ and $Q, R \in \mathbf{K}[\mathbf{u}, y_1]$. Denote all the nonzero coefficients of R in y_1 by $R_1, \ldots, R_m$; then $I_1, R_i \in \mathbf{K}(\mathbf{u})$ for all i, where $\mathbf{K}(\mathbf{u})$ denotes the transcendental-extension field of $\mathbf{K}$ acquired by adjoining $u_1, \ldots, u_r$. Suppose there exists $1 \leq i_0 \leq m$ such that $R_{i_0}(\mathbf{u}) \neq 0$; then f_1 contains a factor $f_1^* \in \mathbf{K}(\mathbf{u})[y_1]$ not occurring in P according to the above pseudo-remainder formula. There exists a $\bar{y}_1$ in some algebraic-extension field of $\mathbf{K}(\mathbf{u})$ such that $f_1^*(\bar{y}_1) = 0$ and $P(\bar{y}_1) \neq 0$. This contradicts the fact that $\mathrm{Zero}(\mathbb{T}/\mathrm{ini}(\mathbb{T})) = \mathrm{Zero}(\{f_1\}/\{I_1\}) \subset \mathrm{Zero}(\{P\})$. Thus $R_i \equiv 0$ in $\mathbf{K}(\mathbf{u})$ for all i, so $R \equiv 0$.

Now suppose that the assertion holds for any regular set $\mathbb{T}$ with $|\mathbb{T}| < s$, and we proceed to prove it for $|\mathbb{T}| = s$. Let $J_{s-1} = I_1 \ldots I_{s-1}$ and $R = \mathrm{prem}(P^{d_s}, f_s, y_s)$. Similarly, we have the following pseudo-remainder formula

$$I_s^{q_s} P^{d_s} = Q f_s + R$$

for some integer $q_s \geq 0$ and Q, $R \in \mathbf{K}[\mathbf{u}, y_1, \ldots, y_s]$. Denote all the nonzero coefficients of R in y_s by $R_1, \ldots, R_m$, and let $\mathbb{T}^* = [f_1, \ldots, f_{s-1}]$. For any

$$\mathbf{w}_0 = (\bar{\mathbf{u}}_0, \bar{y}_1, \ldots, \bar{y}_{s-1}) \in \mathrm{Zero}(\mathbb{T}^*/\mathrm{ini}(\mathbb{T}^*) \cup \{I\}) = \mathrm{Zero}(\mathbb{T}^*/\{I\})$$

considered in $\mathbf{K}[\mathbf{u}, y_1, \ldots, y_{s-1}]$, plunging $\mathbf{w}_0$ in the two sides of the above pseudo-remainder formula, we obtain the following formula

$$I_s^{q_s}(\mathbf{w}_0) P^{d_s}(\mathbf{w}_0, y_s) = Q(\mathbf{w}_0, y_s) f_s(\mathbf{w}_0, y_s) + R(\mathbf{w}_0, y_s).$$

It is obvious that $I_s^{q_s}(\mathbf{w}_0) \neq 0$. We shall prove that $R_i(\mathbf{w}_0) = 0$ for all i.

Suppose there exists some $1 \leq i_0 \leq m$ such that $R_{i_0}(\mathbf{w}_0) \neq 0$; then f_s contains a factor $f_s^* \in \tilde{\mathbf{K}}[y_s]$ not occurring in $P(\mathbf{w}_0, y_s) \in \tilde{\mathbf{K}}[y_s]$ according to the above pseudo-remainder formula. So there exists a $\bar{y}_s$ in $\tilde{\mathbf{K}}$ such that $f_s^*(\bar{y}_s) = 0$ and $P(\mathbf{w}_0, \bar{y}_s) \neq 0$. This contradicts the fact that $\mathrm{Zero}(\mathbb{T}/\mathrm{ini}(\mathbb{T})) \subset \mathrm{Zero}(\{P\})$. Thus $R_i(\mathbf{w}_0) = 0$ for all i. Namely,

$$\mathrm{Zero}(\mathbb{T}^*/\mathrm{ini}(\mathbb{T}^*) \cup \{I\}) \subseteq \mathrm{Zero}(\{R_i\})$$

for any $1 \leq i \leq m$. Now let $\bar{\mathbb{T}}^* = [If_1, f_2, \ldots, f_{s-1}]$. It is easy to see that $\bar{\mathbb{T}}^*$ is a regular set in $\mathbf{K}[\mathbf{u}, y_1, \ldots, y_{s-1}]$. The above zero relation becomes

$$\mathrm{Zero}(\bar{\mathbb{T}}^*/\mathrm{ini}(\bar{\mathbb{T}}^*)) \subseteq \mathrm{Zero}(\{R_i\})$$

for any $1 \leq i \leq m$. By the induction hypothesis, we have $\mathrm{prem}(R_i^{d^*}, \bar{\mathbb{T}}^*) = 0$ for each i, where $d^* = \mathrm{ldeg}(\bar{\mathbb{T}}^*) = \mathrm{ldeg}(\mathbb{T}^*)$. Thus there exists an integer $q > 0$ such that

$$I^q J_{s-1}^q R_i^{d^*} \in \mathrm{Ideal}(\bar{\mathbb{T}}^*) \subset \mathrm{Ideal}(\mathbb{T}^*), \quad 1 \leq i \leq m.$$

It follows that $I^q J_{s-1}^q R^{d^*} \in \mathrm{Ideal}(\mathbb{T}^*)$. Hence

$$I^q J_{s-1}^q I_s^{d^* q_s} P^{d^* d_s} = I^q J_{s-1}^q R^{d^*} + I^q J_{s-1}^q (I_s^{q_s} P^{d_s} - R)$$
$$[(I_s^{q_s} P^{d_s})^{d^*-1} + \cdots + R^{d^*-1}] \in \mathrm{Ideal}(\mathbb{T}).$$

Let $d = \mathrm{ldeg}(\mathbb{T}) = d^* d_s$. Then $I^q P^d \in \mathrm{sat}(\mathbb{T})$, so $\mathrm{prem}(I^q P^d, \mathbb{T}) = 0$ by Theorem 3. One can easily see that $\mathrm{prem}(P^d, \mathbb{T}) = 0$. $\square$

Remark 7: The idea of proof of the part a $\Longrightarrow$ c is analogous to the proof of Theorem 5.1.9 in the book[17] by Wang.

The following concept is introduced in the papers[9,11] by Zhang, Yang, and the author.

Definition 8: A regular set $\mathbb{T}$ is called a *strong regular set* if every zero of $\mathbb{T}$ is also a quasi-normal zero.

At times, one can simply determine that a regular set $\mathbb{T}$ is a strong regular set if $\mathbb{C}_f \cap \mathbf{K} \neq \emptyset$ for each $f \in \mathbb{T}$. The following criterion given in the paper[11] by Zhang, Yang, and the author is generally used.

Proposition 9: *Let $\mathbb{T} = [f_1, \ldots, f_s]$ be a regular set with the above notation. If $\mathrm{Zero}(\mathbb{C}_{f_i}) = \emptyset$ or $\mathrm{Zero}(\bar{\mathbb{C}}_{f_i}) = \emptyset$ for any $1 \leq i \leq s$, where $\bar{\mathbb{C}}_{f_i} = \{\mathrm{res}(c, \mathbb{T}) : \forall\, c \in \mathbb{C}_{f_i}\}$, then $\mathbb{T}$ is a strong regular set.*

The next theorem taken from the papers[9,11] Zhang, Yang, and the author is very useful.

Theorem 10: Let $\mathbb{T}$ be a strong regular set and P a polynomial. If there exists an integer $d > 0$ such that $\mathrm{prem}(P^d, \mathbb{T}) = 0$, then every zero of $\mathbb{T}$ is also a zero of P. Moreover, $\mathrm{Zero}(\mathrm{sat}(\mathbb{T})) = \mathrm{Zero}(\mathbb{T})$.

If every regular set $\mathbb{T}_i$ in Theorem 1 is a strong regular set for $1 \leq i \leq e$, then it follows from Theorem 10 that $\mathrm{Zero}(\mathbb{P}) = \bigcup_{i=1}^{e} \mathrm{Zero}(\mathbb{T}_i)$.

Example 11: Refer to Example 7.1.1 in the book[17] by Wang. We have $\mathrm{Reg}(\mathbb{P}) = \{\mathbb{T}_1, \mathbb{T}_2\}$, where

$$\mathbb{T}_1 = [b^3 + 4, x_1^3 + 1, x_1 x_2 - 1, bx_3 - 2], \quad \mathbb{T}_2 = [b, x_1^3 - 1, x_1 x_2 - 1, x_3].$$

It is easy to see that both $\mathbb{T}_1$ and $\mathbb{T}_2$ are strong regular sets. Thus $\mathrm{Zero}(\mathbb{P}) = \mathrm{Zero}(\mathbb{T}_1) \cup \mathrm{Zero}(\mathbb{T}_2)$.

Example 12: Refer to Example 2.4.3 in the book[17] by Wang, which has been considered by several researchers. We know that $\mathbb{P}$ can be decomposed into 7 *fine triangular systems*[17] $[\mathbb{T}_1, \mathbb{U}_1], \ldots, [\mathbb{T}_7, \mathbb{U}_7]$. It is easy to see that $\mathbb{T}_i$ is a strong regular set for each $i \neq 2$. Thus, we have

$$\mathrm{Zero}(\mathbb{P}) = \bigcup_{\substack{i = 1 \\ i \neq 2}}^{7} \mathrm{Zero}(\mathbb{T}_i) \cup \mathrm{Zero}(\mathbb{T}_2/\mathbb{U}_2)$$

by Theorem 10. In fact $\mathbb{T}_6$ and $\mathbb{T}_7$ can be removed according to the result presented by Chou and Gao.[4]

Example 13: Refer to Example 6.2.1 in the book[17] by Wang. As $\mathbb{T}_2$ therein is a strong regular set, we know immediately from Theorem 10 that $\mathrm{Zero}(\mathrm{sat}(\mathbb{T}_2)) = \mathrm{Zero}(\mathbb{T}_2)$. It is not necessary to compute a Gröbner basis of $\mathbb{T}_2 \cup \{x_2 z - 1\}$.

3. Decomposing Polynomial Systems into Strong Regular Sets

In this section, we present three algorithms SReg, RSplit and SRD* for the decomposition of polynomial sets and systems into strong regular sets. Most of the following description is reproduced from the paper[10] by the author.

3.1. *Decomposing Polynomial Sets into Strong Regular Sets*

For any polynomial set $\mathbb{P} \subset \mathbf{K}[\mathbf{x}]$, one cannot guarantee that every regular set of $\mathrm{Reg}(\mathbb{P})$ is a strong regular set even though most of the regular sets are indeed so in practical computation. In order to obtain a *strong regular series* of $\mathbb{P}$, we add a new variable t (with variable ordering $x_1 \prec \cdots \prec x_n \prec t$) and decompose $\mathbb{P}$ in $\mathbf{K}[x_1, \ldots, x_n, t]$ (or $\mathbf{K}[\mathbf{x}, t]$). By the following result, one can compute a *strong regular series* of not only a polynomial set $\mathbb{P}$ in $\mathbf{K}[\mathbf{x}]$, but also some special polynomial set in $\mathbf{K}[\mathbf{x}, t]$.

Hereinafter, only a special class of polynomial sets in $\mathbf{K}[\mathbf{x}, t]$ is considered: for each polynomial set $\mathbb{P}$ in the class, either $\mathbb{P} \subset \mathbf{K}[\mathbf{x}]$ or $\mathbb{P} = \mathbb{P}_0 \cup \{\mu t - 1\} \subset \mathbf{K}[\mathbf{x}, t]$ with $\mathbb{P}_0 \cup \{\mu\} \subset \mathbf{K}[\mathbf{x}]$. Any triangular set $\mathbb{T}$ in $\mathbf{K}[\mathbf{x}, t]$ implies that $\mathbb{T} = [f_1, \ldots, f_s]$ or $\mathbb{T} = [f_1, \ldots, f_s, \mu_0 t - 1]$, where $f_i, \mu_0 \in \mathbf{K}[\mathbf{x}]$ and $[f_1, \ldots, f_s]$ is a triangular set in $\mathbf{K}[\mathbf{x}]$.

For any polynomial set $\mathbb{P}$ in $\mathbf{K}[\mathbf{x}, t]$, $\mathrm{Proj}_{\mathbf{x}} \mathrm{Zero}(\mathbb{P})$ denotes the projection of $\mathrm{Zero}(\mathbb{P})$ onto $\mathbf{x} = (x_1, \ldots, x_n)$.

Theorem 14: Let $\mathbb{P}$ be a polynomial set in $\mathbf{K}[\mathbf{x}, t]$. Then one can obtain a finite set Ψ, denoted by $\mathrm{SReg}(\mathbb{P})$, of strong regular sets in $\mathbf{K}[\mathbf{x}, t]$ such that

$$\mathrm{Proj}_{\mathbf{x}} \mathrm{Zero}(\mathbb{P}) = \bigcup_{\mathbb{T}^* \in \Psi} \mathrm{Proj}_{\mathbf{x}} \mathrm{Zero}(\mathbb{T}^*);$$

the set Ψ is called a *strong regular series* of $\mathbb{P}$.

Proof: Consider first the case $\mathbb{P} \subset \mathbf{K}[\mathbf{x}]$ and compute $\mathrm{Reg}(\mathbb{P}) = \{\mathbb{T}_1, \ldots, \mathbb{T}_e\}$. With the notation introduced in Corollary 5, one can obtain $\mathbb{U}_i$ for $1 \leq i \leq e$ such that

$$\mathrm{Zero}(\mathbb{P}) = \bigcup_{i=1}^{e} \mathrm{Zero}(\mathbb{T}_i / \mathbb{U}_i).$$

Set $\mathbb{T}_i^* = \mathbb{T}_i$ if $\mathbb{U}_i = \emptyset$; otherwise, set

$$\mathbb{T}_i^* = \mathbb{T}_i \cup [(\prod_{c \in \mathbb{U}_i} c) t - 1]$$

for $1 \le i \le e$. Then Theorem 14 holds true with $\Psi = \{\mathbb{T}_1^*, \ldots, \mathbb{T}_e^*\}$.

Next consider the case $\mathbb{P} = \mathbb{P}_0 \cup \{\mu t - 1\} \subset \mathbf{K}[\mathbf{x}, t]$ with $\mathbb{P}_0 \cup \{\mu\} \subset \mathbf{K}[\mathbf{x}]$. Compute similarly $\mathrm{Reg}(\mathbb{P}) = \{\bar{\mathbb{T}}_1, \ldots, \bar{\mathbb{T}}_{\bar{e}}\}$ with

$$\bar{\mathbb{T}}_i = [\bar{f}_{i,1}, \ldots, \bar{f}_{i,\bar{s}_i}, \bar{\mu}_{i,0} t - 1]$$

for $1 \le i \le \bar{e}$. It follows from Corollary 5 that

$$\mathrm{Zero}(\mathbb{P}) = \bigcup_{i=1}^{\bar{e}} \mathrm{Zero}(\bar{\mathbb{T}}_i / \bar{\mathbb{U}}_i),$$

where $\bar{\mathbb{U}}_i = \{\mathrm{ini}(\bar{f}_{i,j}) : \mathrm{Zero}(\bar{\mathbb{T}}_i^{\{j\}} \cup \mathbb{C}_{\bar{f}_{i,j}}) \ne \emptyset, 1 \le j \le \bar{s}_i\}$. Set

$$\bar{\mathbb{T}}_i^* = [\bar{f}_{i,1}, \ldots, \bar{f}_{i,\bar{s}_i}, (\prod_{c \in \bar{\mathbb{U}}_i} c) \bar{\mu}_{i,0} t - 1].$$

It is easy to see that

$$\mathrm{Proj}_{\mathbf{x}} \mathrm{Zero}(\mathbb{P}) = \bigcup_{\mathbb{T}^* \in \Psi} \mathrm{Proj}_{\mathbf{x}} \mathrm{Zero}(\mathbb{T}^*),$$

where $\Psi = \{\bar{\mathbb{T}}_1^*, \ldots, \bar{\mathbb{T}}_{\bar{e}}^*\}$. $\qquad\square$

3.2. *Algorithms RSplit and SRD**

Expanding pseudo-remainder of a polynomial with respect to a triangular set, introduced by the author[8,9], will play a crucial role in the algorithms presented below. Some improvement will be made along with the description.

Definition 15: Let $\mathbb{T} = [f_1, \ldots, f_s, \mu_0 t - 1]$ or $[f_1, \ldots, f_s]$ be a triangular set in $\mathbf{K}[\mathbf{x}, t]$ and P any nonzero polynomial in $\mathbf{K}[\mathbf{x}]$. One can form a sequence of nonzero polynomials

$$P_{-1}, P_0, P_1, \ldots, P_{m-1}, P_m,$$

with $P_{-1} = P$ and $P_0 = \mathrm{prem}(P_{-1}, \mathbb{T})$, such that

$$P_i = \mathrm{prem}(\mathrm{prem}(f_{\mathrm{cls}(P_{i-1}, \mathbb{T})}, P_{i-1}, y_{\mathrm{cls}(P_{i-1}, \mathbb{T})}), \mathbb{T}), \quad i = 1, \cdots, m,$$

and either $P_m \in \mathbf{K}[\mathbf{u}] \setminus \{0\}$ or

$$\mathrm{prem}(\mathrm{prem}(f_{\mathrm{cls}(P_m, \mathbb{T})}, P_m, y_{\mathrm{cls}(P_m, \mathbb{T})}), \mathbb{T}) = 0.$$

P_m is called the *expanding pseudo-remainder* of P with respect to $\mathbb{T}$, denoted simply by $\mathrm{Eprem}(P, \mathbb{T})$.

For any triangular set $\mathbb{T}$ in $\mathbf{K}[\mathbf{x}, t]$ and polynomial P in $\mathbf{K}[\mathbf{x}]$, $\mathbb{T}$ is said to be *strongly independent*[8,9] of P if $\mathrm{Zero}(\mathbb{T} \cup \{P\}) = \emptyset$, or $\mathrm{Proj}_{\mathbf{x}}\mathrm{Zero}(\mathbb{T} \cup \{P\}) = \emptyset$. By the following proposition, one can easily determine whether $\mathbb{T}$ is strongly independent of P.

Proposition 16: *Let* $\mathbb{T} = [f_1, \ldots, f_s]$ *or* $\mathbb{T} = [f_1, \ldots, f_s, \mu_0 t - 1]$ *be a triangular set in* $\mathbf{K}[\mathbf{x}, t]$ *and* P *any polynomial in* $\mathbf{K}[\mathbf{x}]$. *If* $\mathrm{Eprem}(P, \mathbb{T}) \in \mathbf{K} \setminus \{0\}$ *or* $\mathrm{Eprem}(P, \mathbb{T})$ *divides* $\mathrm{Eprem}(\mu_0, \mathbb{T})$, *then* $\mathbb{T}$ *is strongly independent of* P.

Remark 17: $\mathrm{Eprem}(P, \mathbb{T})$ is different from $\mathrm{res}(P, \mathbb{T})$. P in Definition 15 must be a nonzero polynomial, and $\mathrm{Eprem}(P, \mathbb{T})$ is also a nonzero polynomial at all times. On the other hand, $\mathrm{Eprem}(P, \mathbb{T})$ is simpler than $\mathrm{res}(P, \mathbb{T})$ when $\mathrm{res}(P, \mathbb{T}) \neq 0$. In fact, we are mainly concerned with the case $\mathrm{res}(P, \mathbb{T}) = 0$, because $\mathrm{Zero}(\{P\} \cup \mathbb{T}) \neq \emptyset$. We are ready to split strong regular set $\mathbb{T}$ with respect to P by dint of $\mathrm{Eprem}(P, \mathbb{T})$ in the following theorems.

Theorem 18: Let $\mathbb{T}$ be a strong regular set such that $\mathbb{T} \in \mathrm{SReg}(\mathbb{P}_0)$, where $\mathbb{P}_0$ is a polynomial set in $\mathbf{K}[\mathbf{x}, t]$ and P any polynomial in $\mathbf{K}[\mathbf{x}] \setminus \mathbf{K}[\mathbf{u}]$. If $\mathrm{cls}(P^*, \mathbb{T}) = k$ $(1 \leq k \leq s)$ with $P^* = \mathrm{Eprem}(P, \mathbb{T})$ and $\mathbb{T}$ is strongly independent of $\mathrm{ini}(P^*)$, then $\mathbb{T}$ can be split up into two strong regular sets $\mathbb{T}_1$ and $\mathbb{T}_2$ in $\mathbf{K}[\mathbf{x}, t]$ with respect to P such that

$$\mathrm{Zero}(\mathbb{T}) = \mathrm{Zero}(\mathbb{T}_1) \cup \mathrm{Zero}(\mathbb{T}_2).$$

Proof: Consider the case in which $\mathbb{T} = [f_1, \ldots, f_s, \mu_0 t - 1]$ with the above notation. It follows from Definition 15 that

$$I_0^{q_0} f_k = f_{k,1} f_{k,2} + R, \quad \mathrm{prem}(R, [f_1, \ldots, f_{k-1}]) = 0, \tag{3}$$

where $f_{k,1} = P^*$, $I_0 = \mathrm{ini}(f_{k,1})$, $f_{k,2}, R \in \mathbf{K}[\mathbf{u}, y_1, \ldots, y_k]$ and q_0 is some nonnegative integer. One can obtain two triangular sets $\mathbb{T}_1$ and $\mathbb{T}_2$ by substituting f_k in $\mathbb{T}$ for $f_{k,1}$ and $f_{k,2}$ respectively.

For any $\bar{\mathbf{z}} = (\bar{\mathbf{u}}, \bar{y}_1, \ldots, \bar{y}_s, \bar{t}) \in \mathrm{Zero}(\mathbb{T})$, as $\mathbb{T}$ is a strong regular set, it is easy to see that $\bar{\mathbf{z}}^{\{k-1\}} = (\bar{\mathbf{u}}, \bar{y}_1, \ldots, \bar{y}_{k-1})$ is also a quasi-normal zero of $[f_1, \ldots, f_{k-1}]$ in $\mathbf{K}[\mathbf{u}, y_1, \ldots, y_{k-1}]$, which is a regular set. Thereby, we have $R(\bar{\mathbf{z}}) = 0$. It follows from (3) that $f_{k,1}(\bar{\mathbf{z}}) f_{k,2}(\bar{\mathbf{z}}) = 0$. Thus we have $\mathrm{Zero}(\mathbb{T}) \subseteq \mathrm{Zero}(\mathbb{T}_1) \cup \mathrm{Zero}(\mathbb{T}_2)$.

Consider any $\mathbf{z_0} \in \mathrm{Zero}(\mathbb{T}_1) \cup \mathrm{Zero}(\mathbb{T}_2)$. As $\mathbb{T} \in \mathrm{SReg}(\mathbb{P}_0)$, $\mathbf{z_0}^{\{k-1\}}$ is a quasi-normal zero of the regular set $[f_1, \ldots, f_{k-1}]$ by the construction of $\mathrm{SReg}(\mathbb{P}_0)$ in Theorem 14. This implies $R(\mathbf{z_0}) = 0$. Note that $\mathbb{T}$ is strongly independent of I_0, so $I_0(\mathbf{z_0}) = I_0(\mathbf{z}_0^{\{k-1\}}) \neq 0$. It follows from (3) that $f_k(\mathbf{z_0}) = 0$. Thus $\mathrm{Zero}(\mathbb{T}) \supseteq \mathrm{Zero}(\mathbb{T}_1) \cup \mathrm{Zero}(\mathbb{T}_2)$. Therefore

$$\mathrm{Zero}(\mathbb{T}) = \mathrm{Zero}(\mathbb{T}_1) \cup \mathrm{Zero}(\mathbb{T}_2).$$

We shall show that $\mathbb{T}_1$ and $\mathbb{T}_2$ are both regular sets. The fact that $\mathrm{res}(I_0, \mathbb{T}) \neq 0$ implies that $[f_1, \ldots, f_{k-1}, f_{k,1}]$ is a regular set. As

$$\mathrm{ini}(f_{k,1})\mathrm{ini}(f_{k,2}) = I_0^{q_0}\mathrm{ini}(f_k),$$

one can easily see that $\mathrm{res}(\mathrm{ini}(f_{k,2}), \mathbb{T}^{\{k-1\}}) \neq 0$. Thus $[f_1, \ldots, f_{k-1}, f_{k,2}]$ is also a regular set. If $k = s$, then $\mathbb{T}_1$ and $\mathbb{T}_2$ are both regular sets. Now consider the case $k < s$: for any

$$\mathbf{z}^{\{k\}} = (\mathbf{u}, \eta_1, \ldots, \eta_k) \in \bigcup_{i=1}^{2} \mathrm{RegZero}([f_1, \ldots, f_{k-1}, f_{k,i}]),$$

it is easy to see that

$$R(\mathbf{z}^{\{k\}}, y_k) = R(\mathbf{z}^{\{k-1\}}, y_k) \equiv 0, \quad I_0(\mathbf{z}^{\{k\}}) = I_0(\mathbf{z}^{\{k-1\}}) \neq 0$$

by Proposition 5.1.4 in the book[17] by Wang. Hence

$$\mathrm{RegZero}([f_1, \ldots, f_{k-1}, f_k]) \supseteq \bigcup_{i=1}^{2} \mathrm{RegZero}([f_1, \ldots, f_{k-1}, f_{k,i}]).$$

We proceed to show that $[f_1, \ldots, f_{k-1}, f_{k,i}, f_{k+1}]$ is a regular set for each $i = 1, 2$. Suppose that

$$\mathrm{res}(\mathrm{ini}(f_{k+1}), [f_1, \ldots, f_{k-1}, f_{k,i}]) = 0$$

for some i. By Proposition 5.1.5 in the book[17] by Wang, $\mathrm{ini}(f_{k+1})(\mathbf{z}^{\{k\}}) = 0$ for some

$$\mathbf{z}^{\{k\}} \in \mathrm{RegZero}([f_1, \ldots, f_{k-1}, f_{k,i}]).$$

This contradicts the fact that $[f_1, \ldots, f_{k-1}, f_k, f_{k+1}]$ is a regular set. Thus,

$$[f_1, \ldots, f_{k-1}, f_{k,i}, f_{k+1}]$$

is a regular set for each $i = 1, 2$. By induction, we can see that $\mathbb{T}_1$ and $\mathbb{T}_2$ are both regular sets.

At last, we are ready to show that $\mathbb{T}_1$ and $\mathbb{T}_2$ are both strong regular sets in $\mathbf{K}[\mathbf{x}, t]$. It is easy to see that $\mathbb{T}_1$ is a strong regular set. We shall prove that $\mathbb{T}_2$ is also a strong regular set. For any $\mathbf{z} \in \mathrm{Zero}(\mathbb{T}_2)$, it follows from the above result that $\mathbf{z}$ is also a quasi-normal zero of $\mathbb{T}$. Suppose that

$\mathbf{z}$ is not a quasi-normal zero of $\mathbb{T}_2$; this induces that $\mathbf{z}^{\{k-1\}} \in \mathrm{Zero}(\mathbb{C}_{f_{k,2}})$. Plunging $\mathbf{z}^{\{k-1\}}$ into (3), we get

$$I_0^{q_0}(\mathbf{z}^{\{k-1\}})f_k(\mathbf{z}^{\{k-1\}}, y_k) = f_{k,1}(\mathbf{z}^{\{k-1\}}, y_k)f_{k,2}(\mathbf{z}^{\{k-1\}}, y_k) + R(\mathbf{z}^{\{k-1\}}, y_k).$$

Since $I_0^{q_0}(\mathbf{z}^{\{k-1\}}) \neq 0$, we have $f_k(\mathbf{z}^{\{k-1\}}, y_k) \equiv 0$, i.e., $\mathbf{z}$ is not a quasi-normal zero of $\mathbb{T}$. This is impossible; hence $\mathbb{T}_2$ is a strong regular set.

The case in which $\mathbb{T} = [f_1, \ldots, f_s]$ may be proved similarly, and we omit the details. $\qquad\square$

Remark 19: In most cases, we have $\mathrm{prem}(P^d, \mathbb{T}_1) = 0$ with $d = \mathrm{ldeg}(\mathbb{T}_1)$, and $\mathbb{T}_2$ is usually strongly independent of P in Theorem 18.

Theorem 20: Let $\mathbb{T}$ be a strong regular set in $\mathbf{K}[\mathbf{x}, t]$ and P any polynomial in $\mathbf{K}[\mathbf{x}]$ such that $\mathrm{prem}(P, \mathbb{T}) \neq 0$. If $P^* \in \mathbf{K}[\mathbf{u}] \setminus \mathbf{K}$, or $\mathrm{Zero}(\mathbb{T} \cup \{\mathrm{ini}(P^*)\}) \neq \emptyset$ and $\mathrm{cls}(P^*, \mathbb{T}) = k$ $(1 \leq k \leq s)$ with $P^* = \mathrm{Eprem}(P, \mathbb{T})$, then $\mathbb{T}$ can be split up into a set $\Psi_{\mathbb{T}}$ of strong regular sets in $\mathbf{K}[\mathbf{x}, t]$ with respect to P such that

$$\mathrm{Proj}_{\mathbf{x}}\mathrm{Zero}(\mathbb{T}) = \bigcup_{\mathbb{T}^* \in \Psi_{\mathbb{T}}} \mathrm{Proj}_{\mathbf{x}}\mathrm{Zero}(\mathbb{T}^*).$$

Proof: We first consider the case with $P^* \in \mathbf{K}[\mathbf{u}] \setminus \mathbf{K}$, or $\mathrm{ini}(P^*) \in \mathbf{K}[\mathbf{u}] \setminus \mathbf{K}$ and $\mathrm{cls}(P^*, \mathbb{T}) = k$ $(1 \leq k \leq s)$.

Set $c_0 = P^*$ if $P^* \in \mathbf{K}[\mathbf{u}] \setminus \mathbf{K}$, or $c_0 = \mathrm{ini}(P^*)$ otherwise. Put

$$\mathbb{T}_1 = \begin{cases} [f_1, \ldots, f_s, c_0 t - 1] & \text{if } \mathbb{T} = [f_1, \ldots, f_s], \\ [f_1, \ldots, f_s, c_0 \mu_0 t - 1] & \text{if } \mathbb{T} = [f_1, \ldots, f_s, \mu_0 t - 1] \end{cases}$$

and

$$\mathbb{T}_2 = \begin{cases} \{c_0, f_1, \ldots, f_s\} & \text{if } \mathbb{T} = [f_1, \ldots, f_s], \\ \{c_0, f_1, \ldots, f_s, \mu_0 t - 1\} & \text{if } \mathbb{T} = [f_1, \ldots, f_s, \mu_0 t - 1]. \end{cases}$$

$\mathbb{T}_1$ is obviously a strong regular set in $\mathbf{K}[\mathbf{x}, t]$, but $\mathbb{T}_2$ is not necessarily a regular set. By Theorem 14, one can compute $\mathrm{SReg}(\mathbb{T}_2)$ such that

$$\mathrm{Proj}_{\mathbf{x}}\mathrm{Zero}(\mathbb{T}_2) = \bigcup_{\mathbb{T}^* \in \mathrm{SReg}(\mathbb{T}_2)} \mathrm{Proj}_{\mathbf{x}}\mathrm{Zero}(\mathbb{T}^*).$$

Set $\Psi_{\mathbb{T}} \leftarrow \{\mathbb{T}_1\} \cup \mathrm{SReg}(\mathbb{T}_2)$. This implies that

$$\mathrm{Proj}_{\mathbf{x}}\mathrm{Zero}(\mathbb{T}) = \mathrm{Proj}_{\mathbf{x}}\mathrm{Zero}(\mathbb{T}_1) \cup \mathrm{Proj}_{\mathbf{x}}\mathrm{Zero}(\mathbb{T}_2) = \bigcup_{\mathbb{T}^* \in \Psi_{\mathbb{T}}} \mathrm{Proj}_{\mathbf{x}}\mathrm{Zero}(\mathbb{T}^*).$$

Now, we consider the case with $\mathrm{ini}(P^*) \notin \mathbf{K}[\mathbf{u}] \setminus \mathbf{K}$ and $\mathrm{cls}(P^*, \mathbb{T}) = k$ $(1 \leq k \leq s)$.

Set $c_0 = \mathrm{ini}(P^*)$. $\mathbb{T}_1$ and $\mathbb{T}_2$ are similarly defined as above. Note that $\mathbb{T}_1$ is not necessarily a triangular set at all. By Theorem 14, one can compute $\mathrm{SReg}(\mathbb{T}_1)$ and $\mathrm{SReg}(\mathbb{T}_2)$ respectively, such that

$$\mathrm{Proj}_{\mathbf{x}}\mathrm{Zero}(\mathbb{T}_i) = \bigcup_{\mathbb{T}^* \in \mathrm{SReg}(\mathbb{T}_i)} \mathrm{Proj}_{\mathbf{x}}\mathrm{Zero}(\mathbb{T}^*),$$

for $i = 1, 2$. Now set $\Psi_{\mathbb{T}} \leftarrow \mathrm{SReg}(\mathbb{T}_1) \cup \mathrm{SReg}(\mathbb{T}_2)$. It follows that

$$\mathrm{Proj}_{\mathbf{x}}\mathrm{Zero}(\mathbb{T}) = \mathrm{Proj}_{\mathbf{x}}\mathrm{Zero}(\mathbb{T}_1) \cup \mathrm{Proj}_{\mathbf{x}}\mathrm{Zero}(\mathbb{T}_2) = \bigcup_{\mathbb{T}^* \in \Psi_{\mathbb{T}}} \mathrm{Proj}_{\mathbf{x}}\mathrm{Zero}(\mathbb{T}^*). \qquad \square$$

Algorithm RSplit: $[\Phi_1, \Phi_2] \leftarrow \mathrm{RSplit}(\mathbb{P}_0, P)$. Given a polynomial set $\mathbb{P}_0$ in the above-mentioned class in $\mathbf{K}[\mathbf{x}, t]$ and any polynomial P in $\mathbf{K}[\mathbf{x}]$, this algorithm computes two sets Φ_1 and Φ_2 of strong regular sets in $\mathbf{K}[\mathbf{x}, t]$ such that

$$\mathrm{Proj}_{\mathbf{x}}\mathrm{Zero}(\mathbb{P}_0) = \bigcup_{\mathbb{T}^* \in \Phi_1 \cup \Phi_2} \mathrm{Proj}_{\mathbf{x}}\mathrm{Zero}(\mathbb{T}^*),$$

there exists an integer $d > 0$ such that $\mathrm{prem}(P^d, \mathbb{T}^*) = 0$ for any $\mathbb{T}^* \in \Phi_1$, and $\mathbb{T}^*$ is strongly independent of P for any $\mathbb{T}^* \in \Phi_2$.

SP1. Compute $\mathrm{SReg}(\mathbb{P}_0)$ according to Theorem 14 and set $\Phi_1 \leftarrow \emptyset$, $\Phi_2 \leftarrow \emptyset$ and $\Psi \leftarrow \mathrm{SReg}(\mathbb{P}_0)$.

SP2. While $\Psi \neq \emptyset$, do:

SP2.1. Let $\mathbb{T}$ be an element of Ψ and set $\Psi \leftarrow \Psi \setminus \{\mathbb{T}\}$. If $\mathrm{prem}(P^d, \mathbb{T}) = 0$, where $d = \mathrm{ldeg}(\mathbb{T})$, then set $\Phi_1 \leftarrow \Phi_1 \cup \{\mathbb{T}\}$ and go to SP2.

SP2.2. If $\mathbb{T}$ is strongly independent of P by Proposition 16, then set $\Phi_2 \leftarrow \Phi_2 \cup \{\mathbb{T}\}$ and go to SP2.

SP2.3. If the condition of Theorem 18 holds, then $\mathbb{T}$ can be split up into two strong regular sets $\mathbb{T}_1$ and $\mathbb{T}_2$ with respect to P by Theorem 18, and in this case set $\Psi \leftarrow \Psi \cup \{\mathbb{T}_1, \mathbb{T}_2\}$ and go to SP2.

SP2.4. Now the condition of Theorem 18 does not hold and $\mathbb{T}$ can be split up into a set $\Psi_{\mathbb{T}}$ of strong regular sets with respect to P by Theorem 20. Set $\Psi \leftarrow \Psi \cup \Psi_{\mathbb{T}}$.

Remark 21: Algorithm RSplit here is better than its previous version presented in the paper[11] by Zhang, Yang, and the author. Now we can split any polynomial set $\mathbb{P}_0$ into two sets Φ_1 and Φ_2 of strong regular sets in $\mathbf{K}[\mathbf{x}, t]$ with respect to any polynomial P such that

$$\mathrm{Zero}(\mathbb{P}_0) = \bigcup_{\mathbb{T}^* \in \Phi_1 \cup \Phi_2} \mathrm{Proj}_{\mathbf{x}}\mathrm{Zero}(\mathbb{T}^*)$$

and

$$\mathrm{Zero}(\{P\}) \supseteq \bigcup_{\mathbb{T}^* \in \Phi_1} \mathrm{Proj}_{\mathbf{x}} \mathrm{Zero}(\mathbb{T}^*), \quad \mathrm{Zero}(\{P\}) \cap \bigcup_{\mathbb{T}^* \in \Phi_2} \mathrm{Proj}_{\mathbf{x}} \mathrm{Zero}(\mathbb{T}^*) = \emptyset.$$

3.3. *Algorithm SRD**

Algorithm SRD*: $\Phi \leftarrow \mathrm{SRD}^*(\mathbb{P}, \mathbb{Q})$. Given a polynomial system $[\mathbb{P}, \mathbb{Q}]$ in $\mathbf{K}[\mathbf{x}]$, this algorithm computes a finite set Φ of strong regular sets in $\mathbf{K}[\mathbf{x}, t]$ such that

$$\mathrm{Zero}(\mathbb{P}/\mathbb{Q}) = \bigcup_{\mathbb{T} \in \Phi} \mathrm{Proj}_{\mathbf{x}} \mathrm{Zero}(\mathbb{T}),$$

for any $\mathbb{T} \in \Phi$, $P \in \mathbb{P}$ and $Q \in \mathbb{Q}$, there exists an integer $d > 0$ such that $\mathrm{prem}(P^d, \mathbb{T}) = 0$, and $\mathbb{T}$ is strongly independent of Q. Φ is called a *strong regular series* of polynomial system $[\mathbb{P}, \mathbb{Q}]$.

D1. Compute $\mathrm{SReg}(\mathbb{P})$ according to Theorem 14 and set $\Phi \leftarrow \emptyset$, $\Psi \leftarrow \mathrm{SReg}(\mathbb{P})$.

D2. While $\Psi \neq \emptyset$, do:

D2.1. Let $\mathbb{T}$ be an element of Ψ and set $\Psi \leftarrow \Psi \setminus \{\mathbb{T}\}$.

D2.2. For $Q \in \mathbb{Q}$ do:

D2.1.1. If $\mathrm{prem}(Q^d, \mathbb{T}) = 0$ with $d = \mathrm{ldeg}(\mathbb{T})$, then go to D2.

D2.1.2. If $\mathrm{prem}(Q, \mathbb{T}) \neq 0$ but $\mathbb{T}$ is not strongly independent of Q, then compute $[\Phi_1, \Phi_2] \leftarrow \mathrm{RSplit}(\mathbb{T}, Q)$, set $\Psi \leftarrow \Psi \cup \Phi_2$, and go to D2.

D2.3. Set $\Phi \leftarrow \Phi \cup \{\mathbb{T}\}$.

Remark 22: Algorithm SRD* has the same advantages as the algorithm Dec presented in the paper[11] by Zhang, Yang, and the author (see Remark 3.3 therein for details). These algorithms have some disadvantages. For example, we need to add a new variable t to obtain a strong regular series of $[\mathbb{P}, \mathbb{Q}]$. Their efficiency depends heavily upon the algorithm for Reg. In practical computation, we recommend one to compute $\mathrm{Reg}(\mathbb{P})$ through $\mathrm{RegSer}(\mathbb{P}, \emptyset)$.

4. Automated Derivation of Unknown Relations and Determination of Geometric Loci

Since the pioneering work of Wu,[19,20,22] automated theorem proving in geometry has been an active area of research. Most of the successful methods for proving geometric theorems have been implemented by different researchers (including Chou,[2] Kapur,[5] Ko and Hussain,[7] Wang and Gao,[18] Zhang, Yang and Hou,[26,28,29] and Wang[12,14,17]). A large number of geometric theorems (including Steiner's theorems,[14] Morley's theorem, and Thébault-Taylor's theorem) have also been proved by using different implementations.[8,25]

In the book[17] by Wang, several successful methods for automatically deriving unknown algebraic relations among geometric entities are proposed and have been implemented. In this section we present two alternative algorithms based on algorithms SRD* and RSplit. Because the polynomial equations expressing geometric hypotheses are divided in advance, our new methods have certain advantages.

4.1. *Geometric Formulas*

With the same notation used by Wang,[17] we suppose that a set *HYP* of geometric hypotheses is expressed as a system of polynomial equations and inequations

$$\mathbb{P} = \{P_1(\mathbf{u}, \mathbf{v}, \mathbf{y}), \dots, P_s(\mathbf{u}, \mathbf{v}, \mathbf{y})\} = 0,$$
$$\mathbb{Q} = \{Q_1(\mathbf{u}, \mathbf{v}, \mathbf{y}), \dots, Q_t(\mathbf{u}, \mathbf{v}, \mathbf{y})\} \neq 0$$

in three sets of geometric entities

$$\mathbf{u} = (u_1, \dots, u_r), \quad \mathbf{v} = (v_1, \dots, v_m), \quad \mathbf{y} = (y_1, \dots, y_k)$$

with coefficients in the field $\mathbf{K}$ and $(u_1, \dots, u_r; v_1, \dots, v_m; y_1, \dots, y_k)$ is a permutation of $(x_1, \dots, x_n)$. In the following algorithm, we assume that $s > 1$ and $m = 1$.

Algorithm DeriverA: *HC, NO*, or $R \leftarrow$ DeriverA$(\mathbb{P}, \mathbb{Q})$. Given a set *HYP* of geometric hypotheses expressed as $\mathbb{P} = 0$ and $\mathbb{Q} \neq 0$ as above, this algorithm either reports *HC(HYP)* or determines whether there exists a polynomial relation $R(\mathbf{u}, \mathbf{v}) = 0$ between $\mathbf{u}$ and $\mathbf{v}$ such that Zero$(\mathbb{P}/\mathbb{Q}) \subset$ Zero$(\{R\})$, and if so, finds such a $R(\mathbf{u}, \mathbf{v})$; otherwise, the algorithm reports *NO*.

D1. Choose a polynomial H from $\mathbb{P}$ with $\deg(H, v_1) > 0$. Under the variable ordering $u_1 \prec \cdots \prec u_r \prec v_1 \prec y_1 \prec \cdots \prec y_k$, compute $\Phi \leftarrow$ SRD*$(\mathbb{P} \setminus \{H\}, \mathbb{Q})$. If $\Phi = \emptyset$, then report *HC(HYP)* and the algorithm terminates.

D2. Compute $R_{\mathbb{T}} \leftarrow \mathrm{Eprem}(H, \mathbb{T})$ for every $\mathbb{T} \in \Phi$, and remove redundant divisor F of $R_{\mathbb{T}}$ with $R_{\mathbb{T}} = FR_{\mathbb{T}}^*$, if one of the following two cases holds true:

    a. $\mathbb{T}$ is strongly independent of F by Proposition 16;

    b. $\Phi_1 = \emptyset$ and $\Phi_2 \neq \emptyset$, where $[\Phi_1, \Phi_2] = \mathrm{RSplit}(\mathbb{T} \cup \{F, H\}, R_{\mathbb{T}}^*)$.

Suppose that $R_{\mathbb{T}}$ has been simplified for every $\mathbb{T} \in \Phi$.

D3. Remove any redundant polynomial $R_{\mathbb{T}^*}$ if there exists another $\mathbb{T}^{**} \in \Phi$ such that $R_{\mathbb{T}^*}$ divides $\mathrm{Eprem}(R_{\mathbb{T}^{**}}, \mathbb{T}^*)$. Denote all the remaining polynomials by $R_1, \ldots, R_e$ and set

$$\Psi \leftarrow \{R_i : \ \deg(R_i, v_1) > 0, \ i = 1, \ldots, e\}.$$

If $\Psi \neq \emptyset$, then return $R \leftarrow \prod_{R^* \in \Psi} R^*$; else return *NO*.

Remark 23: The algorithm DeriverA is still valid when $\mathrm{Eprem}(H, \mathbb{T})$ is replaced by $\mathrm{res}(H, \mathbb{T})$.

Example 24: (Qin-Heron formula considered by Wu,[21] Chou and Gao,[3] and Wang[13]). Refer to Example 7.3.1 in the book[17] by Wang. We take $H = H_4$ because $\deg(H_4, \triangle) > 0$. Compute

$$\{\mathbb{T}_1\} = \mathrm{SRD}^*(\{H_1, H_2, H_3\}, \mathbb{Q}) = \{[x_1^2 - c^2, 2x_1 x_2 - c^2 + b^2 - a^2, x_2^2 + x_3^2 - a^2]\},$$

where $\mathbb{Q} = \{abc, x_1 x_2 x_3\}$. Now

$$\begin{aligned}
R_1 &= \mathrm{Eprem}(H, \mathbb{T}_1) \\
&= -16 c^2 \triangle^2 - c^6 + 2c^4 b^2 + 2c^4 a^2 - b^4 c^2 + 2b^2 a^2 c^2 - c^2 a^4,
\end{aligned}$$

so $R_1 = 0$ gives the algebraic relation we wanted to derive. Let $p = (a + b + c)/2$, one obtains the well-known Qin-Heron formula

$$\triangle^2 = p(p - a)(p - b)(p - c).$$

Example 25: (Brahmagupta formula investigated by Chou and Gao,[3] and Wang[13]). Referring to Example 7.3.2 in the book[17] by Wang, we set $H = H_5$. One can compute a strong regular series $\Phi = \{\mathbb{T}_1, \ldots, \mathbb{T}_8\}$ of $[\{H_1, \ldots, H_4\}, \mathbb{Q}]$ by algorithm SRD^*, where $\mathbb{Q} = \{abcd, x_2 x_4\}$.

Computing $\mathrm{Eprem}(H, \mathbb{T}_i) = R_i$, we obtain

$$R_1 = 16b^2(-bc + da)^4(ab - cd)^4(R_0 + 8bacd),$$
$$R_2 = 16\Theta^2 - 2c^2a^2 + c^4 + a^4 - 4b^2a^2 + 8ab^2c - 4c^2b^2,$$
$$R_3 = (da - b^2)^4(a^4 - 4a^2b^2 - 2d^2a^2 + 8dab^2 + d^4 - 4b^2d^2 + 16\Theta^2),$$
$$R_4 = 16\Theta^2 + a^4 - 6b^2a^2 + 8b^3a - 3b^4,$$
$$R_5 = 16(da + bc)^4b^2(cd + ab)^4(R_0 - 8bacd),$$
$$R_6 = 16\Theta^2 - 2a^2c^2 + c^4 + a^4 - 4b^2a^2 - 8acb^2 - 4c^2b^2,$$
$$R_7 = (da + b^2)^4(a^4 - 2d^2a^2 - 4a^2b^2 - 8dab^2 + d^4 - 4b^2d^2 + 16\Theta^2),$$
$$R_8 = 16\Theta^2 - 6d^2a^2 + a^4 - 8ad^3 - 3d^4,$$
$$R_0 = 16\Theta^2 + d^4 - 2(c^2 + b^2 + a^2)d^2 + c^4 - 2(b^2 + a^2)c^2 + (b^2 - a^2)^2.$$

According to step D2 of algorithm DeriverA, we simplify each R_i. The divisors b^2, $(-bc + da)^4$, $(ab - cd)^4$ of R_1 can be removed. By analogy, the divisor $(da - b^2)^4$ of R_3 can also be removed; and R_5, R_7 can be simplified as $R_0 - 8bacd$, $a^4 - 2d^2a^2 - 4a^2b^2 - 8dab^2 + d^4 - 4b^2d^2 + 16\Theta^2$ respectively as $a > 0$, $b > 0$, $c > 0$, $d > 0$.

At the same time, we have

$$\mathrm{Eprem}(R_1, \mathbb{T}_2) = R_2^2, \quad \mathrm{Eprem}(R_1, \mathbb{T}_3) = R_3^2,$$
$$\mathrm{Eprem}(R_1, \mathbb{T}_4) = R_4^2, \quad \mathrm{Eprem}(R_5, \mathbb{T}_6) = R_6^2,$$
$$\mathrm{Eprem}(R_5, \mathbb{T}_7) = R_7^2, \quad \mathrm{Eprem}(R_5, \mathbb{T}_8) = R_8^2.$$

According to step D3 of algorithm DeriverA, $R_2, R_3, R_4, R_6, R_7, R_8$ can all be removed. Setting

$$R = R_{11}R_{21} = (R_0 - 8bacd)(R_0 + 8bacd),$$

we get the algebraic relation $R = 0$.

Example 26: (Gauss pentagon theorem). Refer to Example 1.3 in Chap. 8 of the book[23] by Wu. Now let $\mathbb{P} = \{h_1, \ldots, h_5\}$, $H = h_6$, $Q_1 = x_1 \cdots x_{12}$ and the variables be ordered as $x_1 \prec \cdots \prec x_{12}$. Computation shows that $\mathrm{SRD}^*(\mathbb{P}, \{Q_1\}) = \{\mathbb{T}_1, \mathbb{T}_2\}$, where

$$\mathbb{T}_1 = [-x_5^2x_8^2 - (x_5x_7x_3 - x_7x_5^2 - x_7x_4x_5 - x_7x_5x_2 + x_7x_5x_1)x_8 - x_7^2x_4x_5$$
$$+x_7^2x_4x_1 + x_5x_7^2x_3, -2x_1 + x_7x_9, x_7x_4 - x_5x_{10}, (-x_5x_8 + x_5x_7)x_{11}$$
$$+2x_5(x_2 - x_1) + 2x_4x_1, x_7x_{12} - 2x_5, (x_4x_1 + x_5x_2 - x_5x_1)(x_7 - x_8),$$
$$Q_1t - 1],$$

$$\mathbb{T}_2 = [(x_2 - x_1)x_5 + x_4 x_1, -x_8 + x_7, x_7 x_9 - 2x_1, x_1 x_{10} + x_7 x_2 - x_7 x_1,$$
$$(x_2 - x_1)x_1 x_7^3 x_{11} - 2x_1 x_7^2 x_2 x_3 + 2x_7^2 x_1^2 x_3 - 4x_7^2 x_2 x_1^2 + 2x_7^2 x_1^3$$
$$+2x_1 x_4 x_7^2 x_2 + 2x_1 x_7^2 x_2^2, x_7 x_2 x_{12} - x_7 x_1 x_{12} + 2x_4 x_1, Q_1 t - 1].$$

Computing $\mathrm{Eprem}(h_6, \mathbb{T}_i) = R_i$, we find that

$$R_1 = 4x_5^4 x_7^4 (x_2 x_5 - x_1 x_5 + x_4 x_1)R_0,$$
$$R_2 = -2x_5^4 x_7^4 ((x_1 - x_2)x_6 + x_1 x_2 - x_4 x_1 + x_3 x_2 - x_1^2 - x_3 x_1),$$
$$R_0 = x_6^2 - (x_1 + x_2 + x_3 + x_4 + x_5)x_6 + (x_4 + x_1)x_5 + x_3 x_4 + x_1 x_2 + x_3 x_2.$$

According to step D2 of algorithm DeriverA, the divisor $4x_5^4 x_7^4 (x_2 x_5 - x_1 x_5 + x_4 x_1)$ of R_1 and the divisor $-2x_5^4 x_7^4$ of R_2 can be removed.

One can compute $\mathrm{Eprem}(R_1, \mathbb{T}_2) = R_2$. By step D3 of algorithm DeriverA, R_2 can be removed. Setting

$$R = R_0 = x_6^2 - (x_1 + x_2 + x_3 + x_4 + x_5)x_6 + x_5 x_4 + x_3 x_4 + x_1 x_2 + x_1 x_5 + x_3 x_2,$$

we get the algebraic relation $R = 0$.

4.2. *Locus Equations*

Given a set *HYP* of geometric hypotheses expressed as a system of polynomial equations and inequations

$$\mathbb{P} = \{P_1(\mathbf{u}, \mathbf{v}, \mathbf{y}), \dots, P_s(\mathbf{u}, \mathbf{v}, \mathbf{y})\} = 0,$$
$$\mathbb{Q} = \{Q_1(\mathbf{u}, \mathbf{v}, \mathbf{y}), \dots, Q_t(\mathbf{u}, \mathbf{v}, \mathbf{y})\} \neq 0$$

in three sets of geometric entities $\mathbf{u} = (u_1, \dots, u_r)$, $\mathbf{v} = (v_1, \dots, v_m)$ and $\mathbf{y} = (y_1, \dots, y_k)$ with coefficients in the field $\mathbf{K}$ and

$$(u_1, \dots, u_r; v_1, \dots, v_m; y_1, \dots, y_k)$$

is a permutation of $(x_1, \dots, x_n)$.

Algorithm DeriverB: $\Psi \leftarrow \mathrm{DeriverB}(\mathbb{P}, \mathbb{Q})$. Given a set *HYP* of geometric hypotheses expressed as $\mathbb{P} = 0$ and $\mathbb{Q} \neq 0$ as above, this algorithm computes a polynomial system $[\mathbb{P}_0, \mathbb{Q}_0]$ in $\mathbf{K}[\mathbf{u}, \mathbf{v}]$ such that

    a. for any $(\bar{\mathbf{u}}, \bar{\mathbf{v}}, \bar{\mathbf{y}}) \in \mathrm{Zero}(\mathbb{P}/\mathbb{Q})$, $(\bar{\mathbf{u}}, \bar{\mathbf{v}}) \in \mathrm{Zero}(\mathbb{P}_0/\mathbb{Q}_0)$;

    b. for $(\bar{\mathbf{u}}, \bar{\mathbf{v}}) \in \mathrm{Zero}(\mathbb{P}_0/\mathbb{Q}_0)$, there exists a $\bar{\mathbf{y}} \in \tilde{\mathbf{K}}^k$ such that $(\bar{\mathbf{u}}, \bar{\mathbf{v}}, \bar{\mathbf{y}}) \in \mathrm{Zero}(\mathbb{P}/\mathbb{Q})$.

The disjunction $\mathbb{P}_0 = 0 \wedge \mathbb{Q}_0 \neq 0$ is called the *locus equations* of point $\mathbf{v}$ (in terms of $\mathbf{u}$).

D1. Choose a subset $\mathbb{H}$ of $\mathbb{P}$ satisfying the condition that there exists $1 \leq i \leq k$ such that $\deg(H, y_i) > 0$ for every $H \in \mathbb{H}$. Compute $\Phi \leftarrow \mathrm{SRD}^*(\mathbb{P} \setminus \mathbb{H}, \mathbb{Q})$. If $\Phi = \emptyset$, then report $HC(HYP)$ and the algorithm terminates.

D2. Compute $\mathrm{Eprem}(H, \mathbb{T}) = R_{<H,\mathbb{T}>}$ for all $H \in \mathbb{H}$ and $\mathbb{T} \in \Phi$, and remove any redundant divisor F of $R_{<H,\mathbb{T}>}$ with $R_{<H,\mathbb{T}>} = F R^*_{<H,\mathbb{T}>}$, if one of two following cases holds true:

    a. $\mathbb{T}$ is strongly independent of F by Proposition 16;

    b. $\Phi_1 = \emptyset$ and $\Phi_2 \neq \emptyset$, where $[\Phi_1, \Phi_2] = \mathrm{RSplit}(\mathbb{T} \cup \{F, H\}, R^*_{<H,\mathbb{T}>})$.

Suppose that each $R_{<H,\mathbb{T}>}$ has been simplified for $H \in \mathbb{H}$ and $\mathbb{T} \in \Phi$.

D3. Remove every polynomial $R_{<H,\mathbb{T}^*>}$, if there exists another $\mathbb{T}^{**} \in \Phi$ such that $R_{<H,\mathbb{T}^*>}$ divides $\mathrm{Eprem}(R_{<H,\mathbb{T}^{**}>}, \mathbb{T}^*)$.

D4. Denote those remaining polynomials as $R_{<H_1^*,\mathbb{T}_1^*>}, \ldots, R_{<H_e^*,\mathbb{T}_e^*>}$ for which there exists $1 \leq j \leq m$ such that $\deg(R_{<H_i^*,\mathbb{T}_i^*>}, v_j) > 0$ for each i. Set

$$\mathbb{P}_0 \leftarrow \{R_{<H_1^*,\mathbb{T}_1^*>}, \ldots, R_{<H_e^*,\mathbb{T}_e^*>}\},$$
$$\mathbb{Q}_0 \leftarrow \{\mathrm{res}(\mu_i^*, \mathbb{T}_i^*) : \mathbb{T}_i^* = [f_1^\star, \ldots, f_s^\star, \mu_i^* t - 1], \ 1 \leq i \leq e\}.$$

Remark 27: Algorithm DeriverB remains valid when $\mathrm{res}(H, \mathbb{T})$ is replaced by $\mathrm{Eprem}(H, \mathbb{T})$. For the sake of efficiency, one usually chooses the subset $\mathbb{H}$ in step D1 such that $|\mathbb{P} \setminus \mathbb{H}| \geq k$.

Example 28: Referring to Example 7.3.3 in the book[17] by Wang, we set $\mathbb{H} = \{H_{10}, H_{11}\}$, $Q_1 = u_1 u_6$ and order the variables as $u_1 \prec \cdots \prec u_6 \prec X \prec Y \prec Z \prec y_1 \prec \cdots \prec y_9$. Computation shows that $\mathrm{SRD}^*(\mathbb{P} \setminus \mathbb{H}, \{Q_1\}) = \{\mathbb{T}_1, \mathbb{T}_2\}$, where

$$\mathbb{T}_1 = [-Dy_1 + u_4 u_1 - 2u_1 X, -Dy_2 - 2u_2 X + u_2 u_4, -Dy_3 - 2u_3 X + u_3 u_4,$$
$$-Dy_4 + 2u_4 X - 2u_2 X - u_4 u_1, -Dy_5 - u_2 u_5 - u_1 u_5 - 2u_3 X + u_3 u_4$$
$$+2u_5 X, -Dy_6 - u_2 u_6 + 2u_6 X - u_1 u_6, Dy_7 + u_2 u_4 - 2u_4 X + 2u_1 X,$$
$$Dy_8 + u_2 u_5 + u_1 u_5 - 2u_5 X, Dy_9 + u_2 u_6 - 2u_6 X + u_1 u_6, Q_1 Dt - 1],$$

$$\mathbb{T}_2 = [D, u_2 + u_1 - 2X, -u_1 y_2 + y_1 u_2, u_1 y_3 - y_1 u_3, -y_4 - y_1 + u_2 + u_1,$$
$$-y_5 u_1 - y_1 u_5 + y_1 u_3 + u_1 u_5, y_6 u_1 + u_6 y_1 - u_1 u_6, -u_1 y_7 + u_2 u_1$$
$$+u_1^2 - y_1 u_2, -u_1 y_8 + u_1 u_5 - y_1 u_5, -u_1 y_9 - u_6 y_1 + u_1 u_6, Q_1 t - 1],$$

$$D = u_4 - u_1 - u_2.$$

Computing $\mathrm{Eprem}(H_j, \mathbb{T}_i) = R_{<H_j,\mathbb{T}_i>}$ for $i = 1, 2$ and $j = 10, 11$, we find that

$$R_{<H_{10},\mathbb{T}_1>} = 2(u_3 - u_5)X - 2(u_1 + u_2 - u_4)Y + u_1u_5 + u_2u_5 - u_3u_4,$$
$$R_{<H_{11},\mathbb{T}_1>} = -2u_6X - 2(u_1 + u_2 - u_4)Z + (u_1 + u_2)u_6,$$
$$R_{<H_{10},\mathbb{T}_2>} = y_1u_3 + (u_1 - y_1)u_5 - 2u_1Y,$$
$$R_{<H_{11},\mathbb{T}_2>} = 2u_1Z + (y_1 - u_1)u_6.$$

It is easy to verify that

$$\mathrm{Eprem}(R_{<H_{10},\mathbb{T}_1>}, \mathbb{T}_2) = \mathrm{Eprem}(R_{<H_{11},\mathbb{T}_1>}, \mathbb{T}_2) = 0.$$

Thus one can remove $R_{<H_{10},\mathbb{T}_2>}$ and $R_{<H_{11},\mathbb{T}_2>}$ according to step D3 of DeriverB. Therefore, the locus equations are

$$R_{<H_{10},\mathbb{T}_1>} = 0 \wedge R_{<H_{11},\mathbb{T}_1>} = 0.$$

Example 29: (Biarcs[13]). Refer to Example 7.3.4 in the book[17] by Wang. Let $\mathbb{H} = \{H_1\}$, $\mathbb{Q} = \emptyset$ and the variables be ordered as $u_1 \prec u_2 \prec u_3 \prec X \prec Y \prec x_1 \prec x_2 \prec x_3$. We can compute a strong regular series $\{\mathbb{T}_1, \dots, \mathbb{T}_{15}\}$ of $[\mathbb{P} \setminus \mathbb{H}, \mathbb{Q}]$ by algorithm SRD*.

Computing $\mathrm{Eprem}(H_1, \mathbb{T}_i) = R_i$, we obtain

$$R_1 = (Y^3 + X^2Y - 2u_2XY + u_3X^2 - u_3Y^2)R_0,$$
$$R_2 = (-Y + u_3)(-u_3Y^2 + u_3u_2^2 + 2u_2^2Y - 2u_1u_2Y),$$
$$R_3 = R_5 = (u_1 - u_2)(-x_2 + u_2),$$
$$R_4 = R_{11} = 0,$$
$$R_6 = -u_2(2u_2Y - 2u_1Y - Y^2 + u_2^2),$$
$$R_7 = u_3(u_3 - Y),$$
$$R_8 = 2u_1x_2 + u_3^2,$$
$$R_9 = u_3^2,$$
$$R_{10} = 2u_3(u_2 - X)(-2u_2X + 2u_1X - X^2 + u_3^2),$$
$$R_{12} = u_3(u_2^2 + 2u_1x_2 - 2u_1u_2 + u_3^2),$$
$$R_{13} = u_2^2(u_2 - u_1),$$
$$R_{14} = -u_1x_2,$$
$$R_{15} = u_3(2u_1x_2 + u_3^2),$$

where

$$R_0 = u_3(X^2 + Y^2)^2 - 2u_1u_3X(X^2 + Y^2) + 2(u_1u_2 - u_2^2 - u_3^2)(X^2 + Y^2)Y$$
$$+ (2u_1u_2 - u_2^2 - u_3^2)u_3(X^2 - Y^2) + 2(u_2^3 - u_1u_2^2 + u_2u_3^2 + u_1u_3^2)XY.$$

By step D2 of DeriverB, the divisor $Y^3 + X^2Y - 2u_2XY + u_3X^2 - u_3Y^2$ of R_1 can be removed. Further computation shows that

$$\mathrm{Eprem}(R_1, \mathbb{T}_2) = R_2,$$
$$\mathrm{Eprem}(R_1, \mathbb{T}_3) = \mathrm{Eprem}(R_1, \mathbb{T}_4) = \mathrm{Eprem}(R_1, \mathbb{T}_5) = 0,$$
$$\mathrm{Eprem}(R_1, \mathbb{T}_6) = (u_2 - Y)^2 R_6,$$
$$\mathrm{Eprem}(R_1, \mathbb{T}_7) = Y(-Y + u_3)R_7,$$
$$\mathrm{Eprem}(R_1, \mathbb{T}_8) = \mathrm{Eprem}(R_1, \mathbb{T}_9) = 0,$$
$$\mathrm{Eprem}(R_1, \mathbb{T}_{10}) = -1/2R_{10},$$
$$\mathrm{Eprem}(R_1, \mathbb{T}_{11}) = \mathrm{Eprem}(R_1, \mathbb{T}_{12}) = \mathrm{Eprem}(R_1, \mathbb{T}_{13}) = 0,$$
$$\mathrm{Eprem}(R_1, \mathbb{T}_{14}) = \mathrm{Eprem}(R_1, \mathbb{T}_{15}) = 0.$$

Thus $R_2, \dots, R_{15}$ can be removed, and $R_1 = R_0 = 0$ is the locus equation that we wanted to derive.

Remark 30: Compared to other methods for automated derivation of unknown algebraic relations among geometric entities, DeriverA and DeriverB are more efficient in most cases because direct computation of $\mathrm{SRD}^*(\mathbb{P}, \mathbb{Q})$, which is difficult at times, is not necessary. However, the operation Eprem and algorithm RSplit are frequently used, and the choice of the polynomial H or polynomial subset $\mathbb{H}$ determines the efficiency of our methods. In fact, the algorithms DeriverA and DeriverB remain valid when algorithm SRD^* is replaced by RegSer or SimSer proposed by Wang,[15] but a slight modification is needed.

Acknowledgments

The author is grateful to Dr. Dongming Wang for his helpful comments and suggestions, and to the referees for several suggestions and corrections.

References

1. Aubry, P., Lazard, D., Moreno Maza, M., On the theories of triangular sets. *J. Symb. Comput.* 28, 1999, 105–124.
2. Chou, S.-C., An introduction to Wu's method for mechanical theorem proving in geometry. *J. Automat. Reason.* 4, 1988, 237–267.
3. Chou, S.-C., Gao, X.-S., Mechanical formula derivation in elementary geometries. In: *Proceedings ISSAC '90* (Tokyo, August 20–24), 1990, pp. 265–270. Association for Computing Machinery, New York.
4. Chou, S.-C., Gao, X.-S., Ritt-Wu's decomposition algorithm and geometry theorem proving. In: Stickel, M. E. (ed.): *10th International Conference on*

Automated Deduction, 1990, pp. 207–220. Springer, Berlin Heidelberg New York Tokyo [LNCS 449].

5. Kapur, D., Automated geometric reasoning: Dixon resultants, Gröner bases, and characteristic sets. In: Wang, D. (ed.): *Automated Deduction in Geometry*, 1997, pp. 1–36. Springer, Berlin Heidelberg New York Tokyo [LNAI 1360].

6. Kalkbrener, M., A generalized Euclidean algorithm for computing triangular representations of algebraic varieties. *J. Symb. Comput.* 15, 1993, 143–167.

7. Ko, H.-P., Hussain, M. A., ALGE-prover: An algebraic geometry theorem proving software. Tech. Rep. 85CRD139, General Electric Co., Schenectady, N.Y., 1985.

8. Li, Y.-B., The expanding WE algorithm of mechanical geometry theorem proving. *J. Sichuan University* (Nat. Sci. Edn.) 37(3), 2000, 331–335 [in Chinese].

9. Li, Y.-B., *The Expanding WE Algorithm and the Approach of Strong Regular Decomposition on Nonlinear Algebraic Equation Systems*. Ph.D. thesis, Mathematical College, Sichuan University, Chengdu, China, 2001 [in Chinese].

10. Li, Y.-B., Applications of the theory of weakly nondegenerate conditions to zero decomposition for polynomial systems (submitted for publication), 2002.

11. Li, Y.-B., Zhang, J.-Z., Yang, L., Decomposing polynomial systems into strong regular sets. In: Cohen, A. M., Gao, X.-S., Takayama, N. (eds.): *Mathematical Software*, 2002, pp. 360–371. World Scientific, Singapore.

12. Wang, D., Algebraic factoring and geometry theorem proving. In: Bundy, A. (ed.): *Automated Deduction — CADE-12*, 1994, pp. 386–400. Springer, Berlin Heidelberg [LNAI 814].

13. Wang, D., Reasoning about geometric problems using an elimination method. In: Pfalzgraf, J., Wang, D. (eds.): *Automated Practical Reasoning: Algebraic Approaches*, 1995, pp. 147–185. Springer, Wien New York.

14. Wang, D., Elimination procedures for mechanical theorem proving in geometry. *Ann. Math. Artif. Intell.* 13, 1995, 1–24.

15. Wang, D., Decomposing triangular systems into simple systems. *J. Symb. Comput.* 25, 1998, 295–314.

16. Wang, D., Computing triangular systems and regular systems. *J. Symb. Comput.* 30, 2000, 221–236.

17. Wang, D., *Elimination Methods*. Springer, Wien New York, 2001.

18. Wang, D., Gao, X.-S., Geometry theorems proved mechanically using Wu's method — Part on Euclidean geometry. *Math. Mech. Res. Preprints* 2, 1987, 75–106.

19. Wu, W.-T., On the decision problem and the mechanization of theorem-proving in elementary geometry. *Scientia Sinica* 21, 1978, 159–172.

20. Wu, W.-T., Basic principles of mechanical theorem proving in elementary geometries. *J. Syst. Sci. Math. Sci.* 4, 1984, 207–235. Also in *J. Automat. Reason* 2, 1986, 221–252.

21. Wu, W.-T., A mechanization method of geometry and its applications I: distances, areas, and volumes. *J. Syst. Sci. Math. Sci.* 6, 1986, 204–216.

22. Wu, W.-T., *Mechanical Theorem Proving in Geometries: Basic Principles*. Springer, Wien New York, 1994 [translated from the Chinese by X. Jin and D. Wang].
23. Wu, W.-T., *Mathematics Mechanization*. Science Press/Kluwer Academic Publishers, 2000.
24. Yang, L., Zhang J.-Z., Search dependency between algebraic equations: An algorithm applied to automated reasoning. Technical Report IC/91/6, International Atomic Energy, Miramare, Trieste, 1991.
25. Yang, L., Zhang J.-Z., Hou X.-R., An efficient decomposition algorithm for geometry theorem proving without factorization. *Math. Mech. Res. Preprints* 9, 1993, 115–131.
26. Yang L., Zhang J.-Z., Hou X.-R., *Non-linear Equation Systems and Automated Theorem Proving*. Shanghai Sci. Tech. Education Publ., Shanghai, 1996 [in Chinese].
27. Zhang, J.-Z., Yang, L., Hou, X.-R., A note on Wu Wen-Tsün's nondegenerate condition. Technical Report IC/91/160, International Atomic Energy, Miramare, Trieste, 1991. Also in *Chinese Science Bulletin* 38(1), 1993, 86–87.
28. Zhang, J.-Z., Yang, L., Hou, X.-R., A criterion for dependency of algebraic equations with applications to automated theorem proving. *Sci. China* (Ser. A) 37, 1994, 547–554.
29. Zhang, J.-Z., Yang, L., Hou, X.-R., The WE complete algorithm for automated theorem proving in geometry. *J. Syst. Sci. Math. Sci.* 15, 1995, 200–207 [in Chinese].

CHAPTER 12

ON GUARANTEED ACCURACY COMPUTATION

Chee K. Yap[a]

Department of Computer Science
Courant Institute of Mathematical Sciences
New York University
251 Mercer Street, New York
NY 10012, USA
E-mail: yap@cs.nyu.edu

The concept of *guaranteed accuracy computation* is a natural one: the user could specify any *á priori* relative or absolute precision bound on the numerical values which are to be computed in an algorithm. It is a generalization of *guaranteed sign computation*, a concept originally proposed to solve the ubiquitous problem of non-robustness in geometric algorithms. In this chapter, we investigate some basic properties of such computational mode. We formulate a theory of real computation and approximation to capture guaranteed accuracy computation. We also introduce an algebraic and a numerical model of computation based on Schönhage's pointer machines.

1. Introduction

Numerical non-robustness of computer programs is a ubiquitous phenomenon: it is experienced as program failures (crashes) that inevitably happen when the program is run on certain combinations of logically valid inputs. One approach to solving such problems is to compute "exactly", but only in the geometric sense.[55] This is called *Exact Geometric Computation* (EGC, for short). The basic idea of EGC is to ensure that each

---

[a]The work is supported by NSF/ITR Grant #CCR-0082056. This chapter is an expansion of two keynote talks with the same title, at the National Computer Theory Conference of China, Changsha, China, October 13–18, 2002, and at the International Conference on Computational Science and its Applications (ICCSA 2003), Montreal, Canada, May 18–21, 2003.

322

computed real number $\widetilde{x}$ has the same sign as the exact value x for which $\widetilde{x}$ is an approximation. In particular, if $x = 0$ then $\widetilde{x} = 0$. We may call this *guaranteed sign computation*. Within the last 10 years, the EGC approach has emerged as the most successful approach to numerical non-robustness. Unlike many approaches that require a case-by-case application of some general principle, the EGC solution to non-robustness can be provided through the use of a general number library. Such a library provides *EGC numbers*, a designation that means the numbers support guaranteed sign computation. Two such number libraries are currently available: `LEDA Real`[12,35] and `Core Library`.[30] Using such libraries, programmers can routinely implement robust programs by using standard algorithms (not specially crafted "robust" algorithms). A large collection of such robust algorithms have been implemented in the major software libraries `CGAL`[20,27] and `LEDA`.[35,14,28] Many novel computing techniques to support EGC have been developed in the last decade, including new efficient guaranteed sign algorithms,[10] floating point filters and its generalizations[9,23] and constructive zero bounds.[13,44]

In this chapter, we investigate a generalization of guaranteed sign: we want to *guarantee numerical accuracy*. This means that we want to be able to specify *á priori* any number of correct bits in each computed numerical quantity $\widetilde{x}$. This ability is desirable in various applications. One example comes from numerical statistical computations.[34] McCullough[17] described the problem of evaluating the accuracy of statistical packages. One basic task here is to pre-compute model answers for standardized test suites. We need a certain guaranteed numerical precision in the model answers in order to evaluate the answers produced by commercial statistical packages. At the National Institute of Standards and Technology (NIST), such model answers must have 15 digits of accuracy, and these are generated by running the program at 500 bits of accuracy. It is by no means clear that 500 bits are sufficient; it is also possible that 500 bits are sometimes more than is strictly necessary. What we would like is software that automatically computes to the accuracy that is sufficient to guarantee the final 15 digits. Dhiflaoui and others[18] addressed the problem of guaranteeing the results from linear programming software. Frommer,[22] Tulone and others[50] provided examples of applications in proving mathematical conjectures such as the resolution of the Kepler conjecture.

Guaranteed accuracy is closely related to several important topics in numerical computing. The first is *arbitrary precision computation*. This is often associated with the well-known concept of Big Numbers.[56] The main guarantee of such number types is that the ring operations $(+, -, \times)$ are exact: these operations will not overflow or underflow, provided that computer memory is available and that the result is representable in the number type. In the presence of errors, we may add an additional capability: the iteration of a sub-computation at increasing precision. In the programming language `Numerical Turing`,[26] this is encoded as a "precision block" (syntactically, it resembles the begin-end block of conventional programming languages). Perhaps guaranteed accuracy is most similar to *interval analysis* or more generally, *enclosure methods*.[39,41,33] As a computational mode, it is often known as[b] *certified accuracy computation*. One form of certified accuracy is *significance arithmetic*[36] where we automatically track the "significance" of the bits in numerical approximations. Such capabilities are found in, e.g., the `BigFloat` class in `Real/Expr`[56] and in the `PRECISE` package.[32]

There are three common misconceptions about guaranteed accuracy computation. First is the distinction between guaranteed accuracy and certified accuracy. Consider the problem of computing the determinant of a numerical matrix M. A certified accuracy computation of $\det(M)$ might return with the answer: "the determinant is 12.34 ± 0.02". It certifies the bound $12.32 \leq \det(M) \leq 12.36$. More to the point, the error bound 0.02 is *á posteriori*, and deduced automatically by the computation. It depends not only on the determinant algorithm but also on some implicit accuracy for the basic arithmetic operations. In contrast, in a guaranteed computation of $\det(M)$, the input is a pair (M, θ) where θ is any desired error bound (say $\theta = 0.02$). The computation may return with "the determinant is $12.32 \pm \theta$". As before, this answer is certified. The difference is that the bound θ was given *á priori*.

The second misconception is to think of guaranteed accuracy as simply "iterated certified accuracy", that is, guaranteed accuracy can be achieved simply by repeating a computation with higher and higher certified accuracy. To see that this may not succeed, consider the special case of guaranteed sign where we want to discover the sign of a real quantity x. If x_i is an approximation for x in the ith iteration, then clearly $x_i \to x$ as $i \to \infty$. Certified accuracy will further furnish us with a bound $\varepsilon_i > 0$ such that $|x - x_i| \leq \varepsilon_i$. In case $x = 0$, the pair (x_i, ε_i) is consistent with the conclusion that x has any sign $(0, \pm)$. Hence the sign determination algorithm

---

[b]Or *validated*, or *verified*, or *reliable accuracy*. It is sometimes known as "guaranteed accuracy", but this terminology is less established. In this chapter, we reserve the guaranteed terminology for our special usage.

cannot stop in the ith iteration. Intuitively, *the gap between guaranteed accuracy and certified accuracy is analogous to the gap between total recursiveness and partial recursiveness* (see Section 3). This problem can be located in the so-called *Zero Problem*,[45] which we shall treat in its several forms. Richardson,[45] one of the pioneers in this area, puts it this way: "most people do not even see this as a problem at all".

Third, it is even less appreciated that there is a non-trivial gap between guaranteed accuracy of individual functions, and their composition. It is well known that there are algorithms, even efficient ones, to compute most of the well-known mathematical functions (elementary functions, hypergeometric functions, etc.) to any guaranteed accuracy. But it is not obvious how the guaranteed accuracy computation of two functions $f, g : \mathbb{R} \to \mathbb{R}$ implies that $f \circ g : \mathbb{R} \to \mathbb{R}$ can also be computed with guaranteed accuracy. This issue is captured in the problem of *expression evaluation*, another theme of this chapter.

We hope to outline the basic features of a theory of guaranteed accuracy computation. But this presupposes a theory of real computation. A widely used approach here, following Weihrauch, is the *Type II Theory of Effectivity* (TTE).[51,31] Weihrauch [Chapter 9][51] surveys several other approaches to computing with real numbers. Another rival approach is the algebraic theory of Blum, Shub and Smale (BSS, 1989).[6] Neither approaches are suitable for us. For instance, approaches to real computing such as TTE concede the key property of guaranteed accuracy computation (namely, equality tests) from the start. Hence our approach cannot be equivalent to such approaches. On the other hand, the BSS theory does not address issues of numerical approximation which is central in real world computation. Interestingly, one of the aims of the BSS theory [BCSS, Section 1.6][6] is to address complexity issues in numerical analysis.

The starting point of our approach to real computation is the following idea: all numerical inputs as well as intermediate results must be "representable". We axiomatically introduce a set $\mathbb{F} \subseteq \mathbb{R}$ of *representable reals*. For instance, $\mathbb{F}$ is countable but dense in $\mathbb{R}$, and is a ring extension of the integers $\mathbb{Z}$. The role of $\mathbb{F}$ mirrors that of floating point numbers in the world of numerical computing. We initially use the Turing model of computation to study guaranteed accuracy computation based on $\mathbb{F}$. Algebraic operators in our theory are replaced by approximate operators.

Next we introduce a model of numerical computation that lies between the Turing model and the algebraic models. To motivate this, note that the numerical computation of a function f in the "real world" might be construed in two steps: (A) First find an algebraic algorithm A which computes f in an ideal error-free setting. This algorithm assumes some *basis set* Ω of algebraic operators (such as $\pm, \times$) as primitives. (B) Next, construct a numerical algorithm B that is modeled after A. But B takes into account numerical representation, and accuracy of implementing the primitives of Ω. Algorithm A might be regarded as a program in a suitable algebraic model (e.g., BSS Model, but we will propose another one). But algorithm B does not seem to have a natural theoretical model (the Turing model notwithstanding). We propose to fill this gap by introducing the *Numerical Pointer Model* based on Schönhage's elegant pointer machines.[47] We choose pointer machines to avoid artificial (Gödel) encoding of "semi-numerical" problems. Our main result here answers the following question: *when is a function F that is algebraically computable (over a basis Ω) also numerically approximable?* We give a sufficient condition on Ω.

Overview of the Chapter

Section 2 reviews the place of guaranteed precision computation in the landscape of numerical computing. A brief description of the `Core Library` implementation of guaranteed accuracy is also given. Section 3 proposes a new approach to computing with real numbers, and gives its main features using Turing computability. The key concept is relative approximability of functions. Section 4 examines in detail the approximability of standard algebraic operators such as $\pm, \times, \div, \sqrt{\ }$. Section 5 considers the relative approximability of a composition of such algebraic operators (the expression evaluation problem). The role of constructive zero bounds is emphasized. Section 6 describes the Algebraic Pointer Model based on Schönhage's pointer machines. This model is suitable for capturing the algebraic complexity of semi-numerical problems. Section 7 introduces the Numerical Pointer Model, and proves the basic transfer theorem relating algebraic computability with numerical computability. Section 8 closes with some open problems.

Preliminaries: Precision Bounds

We use $\mathbb{N} \subseteq \mathbb{Z} \subseteq \mathbb{Q} \subseteq \mathbb{R} \subseteq \mathbb{C}$ for the sets of natural numbers, integers, rationals, reals and complex numbers. Let $x, \tilde{x} \in \mathbb{C}$. If $\tilde{x}$ is an approximation to x, the *error* in $\tilde{x}$ is $|x - \tilde{x}|$. There are two standard ways to quantify error, relative and absolute. Let $a, r \in \mathbb{R} \cup \{+\infty\}$. We say that $\tilde{x}$ has a *absolute bits* of precision if $|\tilde{x} - x| \leq 2^{-a}$, and write

$$\tilde{x} \in x[a]. \tag{1}$$

Thus the expression "$x[a]$" denotes the interval $x \pm 2^{-a}$. If $a = \infty$ then $\tilde{x} = x$. Similarly, we say that $\tilde{x}$ has r *relative bits* of precision if $|(\tilde{x}-x)/x| \leq 2^{-r}$, and write

$$\tilde{x} \in x\langle r \rangle. \tag{2}$$

We can combine them[56] and say that $\tilde{x}$ *approximates* x *to composite precision* $[a, r]$, written

$$\tilde{x} \in x[a, r], \tag{3}$$

if $\tilde{x} \in x[a]$ or $\tilde{x} \in x\langle r \rangle$. Our terminology allows fractional number of bits. But when a, r are input arguments in a computation, we normally restrict a to $\mathbb{Z}_\infty := \mathbb{Z} \cup \{\infty\}$, and restrict r to $\mathbb{N}_\infty := \mathbb{N} \cup \{\infty\}$. To see why we may restrict r to non-negative values, note that when $r < 0$, $0 \in x\langle r \rangle$ is always true. The composite precision $[a, r] = [\infty, \infty]$ amounts to asking for an exact answer which may not exist in our computational approach (Section 3).

Note on terminology: in this chapter, we do not distinguish between "accuracy" and "precision" (but see a distinction made by Higham[25]). Our definitions use "precision", leaving the term "accuracy" for informal usage. A related term is "error". But we regard precision and error as complementary views[c] of the same phenomenon.

2. Modes of Numerical Accuracy and the Core Library

In this section, we give an overview of how guaranteed accuracy computation fits into the world of numerical computation. Although the rest of this chapter will focus on the theory of guaranteed accuracy, this section overviews a specific system, the Core Library.[30] Of course, big number package can also offer guaranteed accuracy as long as the computed numbers remain rational: but our main interest is in systems that admit irrational numbers (in particular square roots and more generally algebraic numbers). Currently, there is one[d] other general implementation of guaranteed accuracy, the LEDA Real number type.[12,35]

---

[c]Just as "half-full" (precision or optimistic) and "half-empty" (error or pessimistic) both describe the state of a glass of milk.

[d]It should be noted that LEDA Real is part of a much more ambitious system called LEDA that provides efficient data structures and algorithms for many standard problems.

Numerical computing involves numbers. Depending on the nature of the problem, the number domain may be $\mathbb{N}$ as in number theory; finite fields as in algebraic coding; $\mathbb{R}$ or $\mathbb{C}$ as in most scientific and engineering computations. Computer algebra deals with more abstract algebraic structures but numerically, the underlying domain is often the algebraic numbers $\overline{\mathbb{Q}}$ (algebraic closure of $\mathbb{Q}$). Because of the diversity of these applications, the field of numerical computing has evolved several "modes" of numerical computation:

- The *symbolic mode* is best represented by computer algebra systems such as `Macsyma`, `Maple` or `Mathematica`. A number such as $\sqrt{2}$ is represented "symbolically" and exactly.

- The *FP mode* is by far the most important mode[e] in numerical computing today. Here numbers are represented by fixed precision numbers, typically machine numbers. In modern hardware, machine numbers have converged to the IEEE Standard.[49] This mode is very fast, and is the "gold standard" whereby other numerical modes are measured against. The main goal of numerical algorithm design in the FP mode is to achieve high numerical accuracy possible within the applicable constraints. The term "fixed precision" needs some clarification since it is clear that the precision θ can be introduced as a parameter in FP algorithms, where $0 \leq \theta < 1$. The algorithms will converge to the exact answer as $\theta \to 0$. See, e.g., page 9 of the book[15] by Chaitin-Chatelin and Fraysse. Nevertheless, most FP algorithms are *precision oblivious* in the sense that their operations do not adapt to the θ parameter.

- The *arbitrary precision mode* is characterized by its use of multi-precision such as in Big Number Packages. One survey has been given by Gowland and Lester,[24] and another by Dubé and the author[56]. Well-known examples include the `MP` Multiprecision Package of Brent,[8] and the `MPFun` Library of Bailey.[2] The `iRRAM` Package of Müller[40] has the interesting ability to compute limits of its functions. The ability to reiterate an arbitrary precision computation can be codified into suitable programming constructs, as in the `Numerical Turing` language.[29] Another variant exploits the fact that arbitrary precision arithmetic need not be viewed as monolithic operations, but can be performed incrementally. This gives

---

[e]FP stands for "floating point" or "fixed precision", both of which seem to be characteristic of this mode.

rise to the *lazy evaluation mode*.[37,3]

- Of growing importance are various *enclosure modes* such as those represented by the use of interval arithmetic. Enclosure methods can be introduced in the FP mode or in the arbitrary precision mode.

- The *guaranteed precision mode* is increasingly used in computational geometry community, at least in the simplest form, of guaranteed sign mode. This mode is the norm in the libraries LEDA and CGAL. Conceptually, every computational problem is modified for this mode so that, in addition to the usual inputs, one is also given a precision bound. Thus, a function $f(x)$ is replaced by $f(x, \theta)$ where θ is some precision bound. In contrast to the oblivious algorithms in the FP mode, guaranteed precision algorithms will actively adjust its computation to according to θ.

The above modes can overlap, though each mode has typical areas of application and also its own "cultural" practices. Hence it is not easy to fully characterize these modes. But by focusing on their numerical accuracies, we can capture the main features of some of these modes under a common framework. Following our previous work,[52] we note three "prototype" numerical accuracies which we call *Level I, II* and *III accuracies*. These correspond roughly to the FP Mode, the Arbitrary Accuracy Mode and the Guaranteed Accuracy Mode, respectively. In this framework, there is the possibility to combine all three modes within a computation: this we call *Level IV*. Briefly:

Level I or FP Accuracy. For practical purposes, it is identified with the IEEE standard.

Level II or Arbitrary Accuracy. No overflow or underflow occurs in our number representation until some user-specified accuracy (say 2000 bits) is exceeded. Thus $\sqrt{2}$ will initially be approximated to 2000 bits.

Level III or Guaranteed Accuracy. The computed value of variable is guaranteed to user-specified accuracy, in absolute or relative terms. To guarantee sign of x, we need to compute x to 1 relative bit of accuracy.

Level IV or Mixed Accuracy. Each numerical variable in a computation is given one of the previous three levels of accuracy. This gives the user better control of computational efficiency.

The Core Library

The integration of these levels of accuracy within a single programming framework is one of the main design goals[52] of the `Core Library`,[30] a system implemented in C++. Providing all 4 accuracy levels in a single programming environment can be achieved by asking programmers to explicitly specify the accuracy level for each variable in their programs. This is essentially Level IV accuracy. But to make this framework widely usable, we want a little more. We would like to execute *any* program (either a standard C++ program or one that is explicitly written using the `Core Library` constructs) at any Level Accuracy, just by a simple recompilation. For instance, taking an existing C++ program, we would like to add a simple preamble in order to compile it into a Level X executable (X=I, II, III):

```
#define CORE_LEVEL N          /* N=1,2,3 or 4 */
#include "CORE.h"
// ... STANDARD C++ PROGRAM FOLLOWS ...
```

Thus a single program P can be executed in any of the four levels of accuracy. One then has the potential to trade-off the strengths and weaknesses of the different levels: clearly, Level I is faster than Level II, which is in turn faster than Level III. The robustness of the levels goes in the opposite direction: Level III is fully robust while Level I is the most error-prone.

How can this be achieved? We exploit the operator overloading capability of C++, of course. To see the `Core Library` solution, we first identify the *native number types* of each level: Level I inherits from C++ the four machine number types: `int`, `long`, `float`, `double`. Level II has the usual number types found in Big Number packages: `BigInt`, `BigRat`, `BigFloat`. In `Core Library` we define a class `Real` that includes all the Level I and II number as subclasses. Level III has only one number type, called `Expr`. This number type is basically structured as a dag (directed acyclic graph) to maintain information about its defining expression. Both `Real` and `Expr` were originally introduced in the `Real/Expr Package`.[56]

Let us define a *Level X program* (X=I, II, III) to be one that contains a Level X number type, but no number types at level greater than X. For instance, a *Level I program* is synonymous with a "standard C++ program". To allow such a Level I program to access Level III accuracy, we introduce a *type promotion/demotion* mechanism. This mechanism is triggered by the "Compilation Level" (i.e., the `CORE_LEVEL` defined in the preamble above):

- At Level I Compilation, `BigInt` demotes to `long`, while `BigRat`, `BigFloat`, and `Expr` demote to `double`.
- At Level II Compilation, `long` promotes to `BigInt`, `double` promotes to `BigFloat`, while `Expr` demotes to `BigFloat`.
- At Level III Compilation, `long`, `double`, `BigInt`, `BigRat` and `BigFloat` are all promoted to `Expr`.
- At Level IV Compilation, no promotion or demotion occurs.

Note that `int` and `float` remain at machine precision at all compilation levels. Hence every compilation level can access Level I variables in the form of `int` and `float`; these are useful for numerical quantities with low accuracy requirements (e.g., `int` variables for indexing arrays). Our approach has two major benefits. First, it reduces the effort necessary to convert existing libraries and application programs into fully robust programs. These programs are Level I programs, and we would like to make them fully robust just by recompiling them at Level III, say. Second, it does not automatically (a) force programmers to design new algorithms, nor (b) require the programmer to use new programming constructs.

Although our approach essentially allows the logic of a program to be left intact, some amount of adjustments may still be necessary for two reasons: (i) Issues of numerical input/output. This is inevitable because[53] numerical precision at different levels will lead to different input/output behavior. (ii) Efficiency issues. Level III computation can be extremely slow. We generally expect there to be opportunity for optimization. Innocuous decisions in Level I programs can be unnecessarily inefficient when run as a Level III program. A major challenge is to automatically detect such inefficiencies and to replace them by optimized constructs. Techniques similar to those in optimization compilers may ultimately be crucial.[52] For more details about such issues in Level III programming, see the Core Tutorial.[53]

There is considerable research still to be done within the preceding framework. Nevertheless much has been achieved: first and foremost, non-robustness is no longer seen as the intractable problem of the early 1990s. After a decade of research, for a large class of computational problems, the speed of Level III programs can be brought down to within a factor of 3–10 of a corresponding Level I computation on typical input data. This can be automatically achieved with general software tools, not hand-crafted code. Such results are deemed a suitable trade-off between speed and robustness for many applications.[56] The critical technique here is the idea of *floating point filters*,[9] originally pioneered by Fortune and van Wyk.[21] A

major direction in current efforts aims at extending the domain of successful
practical applications to nonlinear domains.[4]

3. Theory of Real Computation and Approximation

This section introduces a new approach to computing with real numbers.
We will treat two aspects of guaranteed accuracy computation. This section,
based on Turing computability, treats one aspect. Sections 6 and 7 will
develop the algebraic and numerical models of computability.

In the approximation of real numbers, there are two basic decision[f]
problems: deciding if a real number is zero and determining its sign. These
issues are best approached from the view point of function evaluation. Let

$$f : \mathbb{R}^m \to \mathbb{R} \tag{4}$$

be a partial function and $\mathbf{x} \in \mathbb{R}^m$. If $f(\mathbf{x})$ is undefined, we write $f(\mathbf{x}) \uparrow$ and
call $\mathbf{x}$ an *invalid input*. Otherwise, $f(\mathbf{x})$ is defined, written $f(\mathbf{x}) \downarrow$; then we
say that $\mathbf{x}$ is *valid*. We will associate five computational problems with f.
But first we briefly review the computational model.

3.1. *Turing Computability*

The standard Turing model[43,54] of computation will be used in this section.
We assume deterministic machines, and focus our attention only on time
complexity. In the Turing model, all objects must be represented as strings
or words over some alphabet Σ. Let

$$g : \Sigma^* \to \Sigma^* \tag{5}$$

be a partial function. We recognize three notions of what it means to compute g.

- We say that g is *conditionally computable* if there is a Turing machine M such that for all $w \in \Sigma^*$, if $g(w) \downarrow$ then M on input w will
  halt and output $g(w)$. We make no assumption about the behavior
  of M in case $g(w) \uparrow$. In particular, M may or may not halt.
- We say that g is *unconditionally computable* if it is conditionally
  computable by a Turing machine M as before, but in case $g(w) \uparrow$,

---

[f]In the theory of computation, decision problems have two possible outputs: 0/1 or
yes/no or true/false. In geometric computation, it seems more natural to regard decision
problems as any function with a finite range. For example, most geometric predicates
have three outputs: $-1/0/+1$ or in/on/out.

M must halt and enter a special state $q_\uparrow$. This state will never be entered on other inputs. Thus M can recognize invalid inputs and always halt.

- Finally, we say that g is *partially computable* if it is conditionally computable by a Turing machine M as before, but in case $g(w) \uparrow$, M must *loop* (i.e., not halt). Note that partial computability is the standard definition of what it means to compute a partial function in computability theory.[46]

The three definitions coincide when g is a total function. We call g a *decision problem* if g is total and has finite range. In general, we have:

$$g \text{ is unconditionally computable} \implies g \text{ is partially computable}$$

$$\implies g \text{ is conditionally computable.}$$

We will simply say "computability" for unconditional computability, as this will be the main concept we use. We can further introduce complexity considerations to the above, e.g., "polynomial-time unconditional computability" is just unconditional computability in which the Turing machine halts after a polynomial number of steps.

Representation and encodings. Let D be an algebraic domain with a partial function $\omega : D^m \to D$. In this chapter, D will always be a subset of $\mathbb{C}$. We often call such a partial function an *operator*. To discuss computation over D we need to represent its elements as strings. A *representation* of D is any partial onto function $\rho : \Sigma^* \to D$. If $\rho(w) \uparrow$, then w is said to be *ill-formed*; otherwise it is *well-formed* and *represents* the element $\rho(w) \in D$. Since ρ is onto, every element in D has a representation. Relative to ρ, a partial function

$$f : (\Sigma^*)^m \to \Sigma^* \tag{6}$$

is an *implementation* of ω if

(i) for all well-formed $w_1, \ldots, w_m$, if $\omega(\rho(w_1), \ldots, \rho(w_m)) \downarrow$ then

$$\rho(f(w_1, \ldots, w_m)) = \omega(\rho(w_1), \ldots, \rho(w_m)); \tag{7}$$

(ii) if any w_i is ill-formed, or if $\omega(\rho(w_1), \ldots, \rho(w_m)) \uparrow$ then

$$f(w_1, \ldots, w_m) \uparrow .$$

Relative to ρ, we say that ω is *(polynomial-time) computable* if it has an implementation (6) that is (polynomial-time) computable. Note that "polynomial-time" in computing $f(w_1, \ldots, w_m)$ is with respect to the *representation size* $n = |w_1| + |w_2| + \cdots + |w_m|$.

Two basic decision problems arise with any representation ρ. The *parsing problem* wants to know from any given $w \in \Sigma^*$, whether $\rho(w) \downarrow$. The *isomorphism problem* wants to know, for any given $v, w \in \Sigma^*$, whether $\rho(v) = \rho(w)$. In our applications, both problems will be easily (polynomial-time) solvable.

3.2. *Representable Real Numbers*

Since $\mathbb{R}$ is uncountable, no representation of $\mathbb{R}$ is possible. In this chapter, we propose to treat real computation through the following device: we postulate a set $\mathbb{F}$ called the *representable real numbers*. This set satisfies the following axioms.

- $(\mathbb{F}, +, -, \times, 0, 1)$ is a ring that extends the integer ring, $\mathbb{Z} \subseteq \mathbb{F}$.
- If $x \in \mathbb{F}$ then $x/2 \in \mathbb{F}$. Hence $\mathbb{F}$ is dense in the reals.
- $\mathbb{F}$ is countable and hence it has a representation $\rho : \Sigma^* \to \mathbb{F}$ such that $\lg |\rho(w)| \leq |w|$ whenever w is well-formed. The parsing problem and the isomorphism problem for ρ are both polynomial-time decidable.
- Relative to ρ, there are polynomial-time implementations of the operations of $+, -, \times, \mathrm{div}_2$ and the comparison of representable numbers. Here, $\mathrm{div}_2(x)$ denote the function $x \mapsto x/2$.

This approach is natural and conforms fairly closely to numerical computation found in practice: typically, $\mathbb{F}$ is the set of floating point numbers in a fixed base $B \geq 2$. In practice, there may be limits on the precision in the floating point representation, but these will be removed for our purposes. The set of *base B floating point numbers* is given by $\{mB^e : m \in \mathbb{Z}, e \in \mathbb{Z}\}$. The standard representation of mB^e is given by a pair of binary integers (m, e). The *size* of mB^e is simply $1 + \lceil \lg |m| \rceil + \lceil \lg |e| \rceil$. A possible alternative to floating point numbers is the choice $\mathbb{F} = \mathbb{Q}$, the field of rational numbers.

Once $\mathbb{F}$ and its representation $\rho : \mathbb{F} \to \Sigma^*$ are fixed, whenever we speak of "computing f", it is understood that our algorithms will be Turing machines that accept an arbitrary string $w \in \Sigma^*$ as input. In particular, ill-formed inputs may be fed to our machine, but our axioms about ρ assure us that we can readily recognize these inputs (and enter the state $q_\uparrow$). But another situation arises: we are often interested in functions $f : R^m \to R$ where R is a proper subset of $\mathbb{F}$. In this case, the Turing machine for f must recognize inputs that do not represent elements of R. This is polynomial-time computable when $R = \mathbb{Z}$ or $R = \mathbb{N}$. This is shown in the following fact.

Lemma 1: *The following total functions are polynomial-time computable:*

(i) $\lceil \lg |x| \rceil$ *and* $\lfloor \lg |x| \rfloor$;

(ii) $\lceil x \rceil$ *and* $\lfloor x \rfloor$;

(iii) *the function* $f : \mathbb{F} \to \{0,1\}$ *where* $f(x) = 1$ *iff* $x \in \mathbb{Z}$.

Proof: Fix any $x \in \mathbb{F}$.

(i) We can determine in $O(\lg |x|)$ steps the smallest $k \in \mathbb{N}$ such that $2^k \geq |x|$. This k is $\lceil \lg |x| \rceil$. This is polynomial-time since every representation w of x satisfies $|w| \geq \lg |x|$ (see the axioms for $\mathbb{F}$). Similarly, we can compute $\lfloor \lg |x| \rfloor$ in polynomial time. Note that we can even do this in $O(\lg \lg |x|)$ time.

(ii) Using $\lceil \lg |x| \rceil$ from part (i), we can next compute the value $\lceil |x| \rceil$ in $O(\lg |x|)$ steps. The algorithm amounts to determining each bit in the binary representation of $\lceil |x| \rceil$. Similarly for $\lfloor |x| \rfloor$.

(iii) Using part (ii), we can compare x with $\lceil x \rceil$. Note that $x = \lceil x \rceil$ iff $x \in \mathbb{Z}$. $\hfill\square$

It is interesting to see in this proof that (i) is the prerequisite to (ii). We will see this phenomenon again.

Decision problems associated with a function. Associated to the function (4), we have three natural decision problems.

- The *validity problem*, denoted VALID(f), is to decide for any $x \in \mathbb{F}$, whether $f(x) \uparrow$. Recall that by our general conventions, a Turing machine for deciding validity actually accepts strings $w \in \Sigma^*$. If w is ill-formed, by assumption, we can detect whether w is ill-formed or not in polynomial time. Assuming w is well-formed, our Turing machine must then decide whether $f(\rho(w)) \uparrow$. In the following discussion, we do not distinguish between an ill-formed w or a well-formed w such that $f(\rho(w)) \uparrow$. Both are simply considered invalid. Hence, the VALID(f) problem has 2 possible outputs: invalid, valid.
- The *zero problem*, denoted ZERO(f), is to decide for any $x \in \mathbb{F}$ whether $f(x) \downarrow$ and if so, whether $f(x) = 0$. This problem has 3 possible outputs: invalid, zero, non-zero.

- The *sign problem*, denoted $\texttt{SIGN}(f)$, is to determine for any $x \in \mathbb{F}$, whether $f(x)$ is valid and if so determine the sign of $f(x)$ (this is $0, \pm 1$). This problem has 4 possible outputs: invalid, zero, positive, negative.

Although the sign problem is more important for practical applications, the zero problem is more general since it is meaningful in unordered domains such as $\mathbb{C}$. To investigate the decidability (i.e., computability) of these problems, the concept of reducibility is useful. We say that f is *reducible* to g if there are total computable functions s, t such that for all $x \in \mathbb{F}$, $f(x) = s(g(t(x)))$. Also, f, g are *recursively equivalent* if f is reducible to g and vice-versa. It is immediate that if f is reducible to g and g is computable, then f is computable. So an uncomputable f is not reducible to a computable g.

Lemma 2: *For any f:*

(i) $\texttt{VALID}(f)$ *is reducible to* $\texttt{ZERO}(f)$, *but there is an* f_0 *such that* $\texttt{VALID}(f_0)$ *is decidable and* $\texttt{ZERO}(f_0)$ *is undecidable;*

(ii) $\texttt{ZERO}(f)$ *is reducible to* $\texttt{SIGN}(f)$, *but there is an* f_1 *such that* $\texttt{ZERO}(f_1)$ *is decidable and* $\texttt{SIGN}(f_1)$ *is undecidable.*

Proof: The reducibility of $\texttt{VALID}(f)$ to $\texttt{ZERO}(f)$, and $\texttt{ZERO}(f)$ to $\texttt{SIGN}(f)$ is immediate from the definition. To see f_0, we just define $f_0 : \mathbb{N} \to \{0, 1\}$ such that $f_0(i) = 1$ iff the ith Turing machine on i halts. The function f_1 is a simple variant, $f_1 : \mathbb{N} \to \{-1, 1\}$ such that $f_1(i) = 1$ iff the ith Turing machine on i halts. $\qquad\square$

For many problems (in particular, the evaluation problems in Section 5), $\texttt{VALID}(f)$ and $\texttt{ZERO}(f)$ are basically the same problem. On the other hand, there is a potentially exponential gap between $\texttt{ZERO}(f)$ and $\texttt{SIGN}(f)$ in the well-known problem of *sum of square-roots*. More precisely, define the function S that, on any input sequence of integers $a_1, \ldots, a_n$, computes the sum

$$S(a_1, \ldots, a_n) = \sum_{i=1}^{n} \texttt{sign}(a_i) \sqrt{|a_i|}.$$

This is the famous sum of square-roots problem. An observation of the author[5] is that $\texttt{ZERO}(S)$ is polynomial-time. On the other hand, the best current algorithms for $\texttt{SIGN}(S)$ require exponential time. Another important problem where there seems to be a complexity gap is $\texttt{ZERO}(det)$ and $\texttt{SIGN}(det)$ where det is the problem of computing the determinant of a square integer matrix. Since *det* can be solved in $O_L(n^3 M(n \lg n + L))$ time for n square matrices with L-bit entries and $M(L)$ is the complexity of L-bit integer multiplication, this gap (if it exists) is at most a factor of n^2 (ignoring logarithmic terms).

Exact and approximate computability. The function f in (4) is said to be *exactly computable* if (i) $f(\mathbf{x}) \in \mathbb{F}$ for all valid $\mathbf{x} \in \mathbb{F}^m$, and (ii) f is unconditionally computable. For instance, if f is a ring operation $(+, -, \times)$ or div_2, then f is exactly computable, by our assumptions about $\mathbb{F}$. But when f does not satisfy (i), we next introduce weaker notions of computing f, based on approximation. Indeed, even when f satisfies (i), we may still want to compute it approximately.

A partial function

$$\widetilde{f} : \mathbb{F}^m \times \mathbb{Z} \to \mathbb{F} \tag{8}$$

is an *absolute approximation* function of f if for all $\mathbf{x} \in \mathbb{F}^m, a \in \mathbb{Z}$, we have $\widetilde{f}(\mathbf{x}, a) \in f(\mathbf{x})[a]$. By definition, this means that $\widetilde{f}(\mathbf{x}, a)$ is undefined iff $f(\mathbf{x})$ is undefined. Similarly a partial function

$$\widetilde{f} : \mathbb{F}^m \times \mathbb{N} \to \mathbb{F} \tag{9}$$

is a *relative approximation* of f if for all $\mathbf{x} \in \mathbb{F}^m, r \in \mathbb{N}$, we have $\widetilde{f}(\mathbf{x}, r) \in f(\mathbf{x})\langle r \rangle$. Again, $\widetilde{f}(\mathbf{x}, r) \uparrow$ iff $\widetilde{f}(\mathbf{x}) \uparrow$.

Notation: we will add a "colon flourish" and write "$f(x : a)$" to denote an absolute approximation $\widetilde{f}(x, a)$. Similarly, we add a "semicolon flourish" and write "$f(x; r)$" to denote a relative approximation $\widetilde{f}(x, r)$.

The outputs of approximation functions (as in (8) and (9)) are restricted to $\mathbb{F}$. We say that f is *absolutely approximable* if it has an approximation function (8) that is unconditionally computable. Similarly, f is *relatively approximable* if it has an approximation function (9) that is unconditionally computable. We also say that f has *guaranteed accuracy* if it is relatively approximable. It follows from these definitions that if f is absolutely or relatively approximable, then $\mathtt{VALID}(f)$ is decidable.

3.3. *Basic Relations*

The next theorem shows that guaranteed relative precision is a generalization of guaranteed sign computation.

Theorem 3: For all $x \in \mathbb{F}$, we have $\mathtt{sign}(f(x)) = \mathtt{sign}(f(x; 1))$.

Proof: We have

$$|f(x) - f(x; 1)| \leq |f(x)|/2. \tag{10}$$

If $f(x) = 0$ then $f(x; 1)$ must also be 0. Conversely, if $f(x; 1) = 0$ then $f(x)$ is also 0. Hence, assume that $f(x)f(x; 1) \neq 0$. If $f(x)f(x; 1) > 0$, the result is also true. It remains to consider the case $f(x)f(x; 1) < 0$. In this case, we have

$$|f(x) - f(x; 1)| = |f(x)| + |f(x; 1)| \geq |f(x)|. \tag{11}$$

But (10) and (11) imply $f(x) = 0$, contradicting $f(x)f(x; 1) < 0$. $\square$

Corollary 4: *The problem* SIGN(f) *is reducible to the relative approximability of* f.

Theorem 5: The following are equivalent:

(i) the function f is relatively approximable;
(ii) the function f is absolutely approximable and ZERO(f) is decidable.

Proof: In the first direction, assume that f is relatively approximable. By the previous lemma, ZERO(f) is decidable. So it is sufficient to show how to approximate f absolutely. First compute $x' = f(x; 1)$ that approximates x to one relative bit. Thus $|x'| \geq |f(x)|/2$. Using Lemma 1, we compute $r = a + 1 + \lceil \lg |x'| \rceil$. Finally compute $x'' = f(x; r)$. We have $|x'' - f(x)| \leq 2^{-r}|f(x)|$, i.e.,

$$\lg |x'' - f(x)| \leq -r + \lg |f(x)| \leq -r + 1 + \lg |x'| = -a.$$

Hence we can output x'' as $f(x : a)$.

In the other direction, suppose that f is absolutely approximable and ZERO(f) is decidable. To compute $f(x; r)$, we first check if $f(x) = 0$, and if so, we output 0. Otherwise we perform the following code:

$$\boxed{\begin{aligned}
&a \leftarrow 1; \\
&\text{While } |f(x : a)| < 2^{-a+1} \\
&\quad \text{Do } a \leftarrow a + 1.
\end{aligned}}$$

Since $f(x) \neq 0$, this while-loop will terminate. Upon loop termination, $|f(x : a)| \geq 2^{-a+1}$. Since $|f(x)| + 2^{-a} \geq |f(x : a)|$, we deduce that $|f(x)| \geq 2^{-a+1} - 2^{-a} = 2^{-a}$. If we choose $a' = r + a$, then

$$|f(x : a') - f(x)| \leq 2^{-a'} = 2^{-r-a} \leq 2^{-r}|f(x)|.$$

Thus $f(x : a')$ approximates $f(x)$ with r relative bits of precision. $\qquad\square$

Theorem 5 suggests that absolute precision may be a weaker concept than relative precision. The next result confirms this.

Theorem 6: There is a function $f_K : \mathbb{F} \to \mathbb{F}$ that is absolutely approximable in polynomial time but f is not relatively approximable.

Proof: Let $M_0, M_1, M_2, \ldots$ be a standard enumeration of Turing machines restricted to binary input strings. By introducing a bijection between binary strings and $\mathbb{N}$ (e.g., the dyadic notation), we can view the input set for each M_i to be $\mathbb{N}$. Let $K : \mathbb{N} \to \{0, 1\}$ be the diagonal function where $K(i) = 0$ if M_i does not halt on input i and $K(i) = 1$ otherwise. It is well known that K is not computable. Consider the function $f_K : \mathbb{N} \to \mathbb{F}$ defined as follows:

$$f_K(i) = \begin{cases} 0 & \text{if } M_i \text{ on input } i \text{ does not halt,} \\ 2^{-k} & \text{if } M_i \text{ on input } i \text{ halts in exactly } k \text{ steps.} \end{cases}$$

The theorem follows from two facts:

(a) f_K is not relatively approximable. For $i \in \mathbb{N}$, clearly $f_K(i; 1) = 0$ iff $K(i) = 0$. Hence if f_K were relatively approximable, then K would be computable, contradiction.

(b) f_K is absolutely approximable. It is sufficient to show how, given $(i, j) \in \mathbb{N} \times \mathbb{Z}$, we may compute an absolute approximation $f_K(i : j)$. If $j \leq 0$, we can just output 1. Hence assume $j > 0$. We first simulate M_i on i for j steps. If M_i halts in some $k \leq j$ steps, then we output 2^{-k}. Otherwise, we output 2^{-j}.

We show that this algorithm is correct. Consider two possibilities: (i) Suppose $f_K(i) = 0$. In case $j \leq 0$, $|f_K(i) - f_K(i : j)| = 1 \leq 2^{-j}$. So assume $j > 0$. Since M_i on i does not halt, we will output 2^{-j} as the value of $f_K(i : j)$. This output is correct since $|f_K(i) - f_K(i : j)| = |f_K(i : j)| = 2^{-j}$. (ii) Suppose $f_K(i) \neq 0$. Assume that M_i on i halts in $k \geq 0$ steps. In case $j \leq 0$, $|f_K(i) - f_K(i : j)| = |1 - 2^{-k}| \leq 2^{-j}$. Otherwise, we will output 2^{-m} as the value of $f_K(i : j)$, where $m = \min\{j, k\}$. This output is correct since $|f_K(i : j) - f_K(i)| = |2^{-m} - 2^{-k}| < 2^{-m} \leq 2^{-j}$.

Finally, is this algorithm polynomial-time? To simulate M_i on i for j steps takes $O(\log(i)j)$ time. Since the input size is $\Theta(\log(i) + \log(j))$, this is exponential time. To fix this, we can modify the function f_K so that instead of $f_K(i) = 2^{-k}$, we have $f_K(i) = 2^{\mathtt{msb}(k)}$, where $\mathtt{msb}(k) = \lfloor \lg |k| \rfloor$. But $\mathtt{msb}(k)$, and hence $2^{\mathtt{msb}(k)}$, can be computed in polynomial time, by Lemma 1. $\qquad\square$

In the next section, we will address the problems of zero determination and sign determination, using more efficient and practical algorithms than those implied by the above generic proofs.

4. Guaranteed Accuracy for Basic Operators

The previous section gives an abstract treatment of the approximability of partial functions $f : \mathbb{R}^m \to \mathbb{R}$. This section examines in the main operators in practice: rational operators ($\pm, \times, \div$), square root ($\sqrt{\cdot}$), exponential and logarithm operators ($\exp(\cdot), \ln(\cdot)$). We will assume the availability of algorithms that can implement these operations to any specified accuracy. Such algorithms may be found in the paper[8] by Brent (see the paper[19] by Du and others for hypergeometric functions). Our main concern is how to propagate precision bounds.

Such algorithms were first given in detail and analyzed by Ouchi[42] for the rational operators and square root. These were implemented in the `Real/Expr` package,[56] and incorporated into the original `Core Library`.[30] The algorithms were based on propagating composite precision bounds. What is new in this section is to revisit these questions, but here we propagate either absolute or relative precision bounds, but not both. This is simpler and more intuitive.

In the following, whenever we guarantee "k relative bits", it is implicit that $k \geq 0$. But when we guarantee "k absolute bits", k may be negative.

The role of the most significant bit position. The proofs of Lemma 1 (and Theorem 5) indicate the usefulness of approximating $\lg |x|$. Another use is for transforming any precision bound, from an absolute bound to a relative one or vice-versa. To facilitate such transformations, we use the function $\mu(x) := \lg |x|$. In implementations, we prefer to work with the related *msb function*, defined by $\mathtt{msb}(x) = \lfloor \lg |x| \rfloor$. By definition, $\mu(0) = \mathtt{msb}(0) = -\infty$. By Lemma 1, the function $\mathtt{msb}(x)$ is computable. Thus

$$2^{\mathtt{msb}(x)} \leq |x| < 2^{1+\mathtt{msb}(x)}.$$

If the binary notation for x is $\cdots b_2 b_1 b_0 . b_{-1} b_{-2} \cdots$ ($b_i = 0, 1$) then $\mathtt{msb}(x) = t$ iff $b_t = 1$ and for all $i > t$, $b_i = 0$. When x is a general expression, it may be difficult[g] to determine $\mathtt{msb}(x)$ exactly: let $\mu^+(x)$ and $\mu^-(x)$ denote any

---

[g]This remark does not contradict Lemma 1, which assumes that x is explicitly given as an element of $\mathbb{F}$.

upper and lower bounds on $\mu(x)$:

$$\mu^-(x) \leq \mu(x) \leq \mu^+(x).$$

Here, $\mu^+(x), \mu^-(x)$ are not functional notations, as the actual values of $\mu^+(x), \mu^-(x)$ will depend on the context. The choices $\mu^-(x) = -\infty$ and $\mu^+(x) = \infty$ are trivial bounds. Non-trivial bounds on $\mu(x)$ may not be hard to obtain; usually, $\mu^-(x)$ is harder than $\mu^+(x)$.

Lemma 7: *Let $x \in \mathbb{R}$ and $a, r \in \mathbb{R}$.*

(i) $x[a] \supseteq x\langle a + \mu^+(x)\rangle$.
(ii) $x\langle r\rangle \supseteq x[r - \mu^-(x)]$.
(iii) $x[a, r] \supseteq x\langle \min\{r, a + \mu^+(x)\}\rangle$.
(iv) $x[a, r] \supseteq x[\min\{a, r - \mu^-(x)\}]$.

This lemma is just another way of writing the following inequalities:

(i, iii) $2^{-a} \geq |x| 2^{-a-\mu^+(x)}$,
(ii, iv) $|x| 2^{-r} \geq 2^{-r+\mu^-(x)}$.

The four cases in the lemma should be viewed as rules for converting precision bounds. Thus, (i) says that if we want to guarantee a absolute bits in x, it is enough to guarantee $a + \mu^+(x)$ relative bits in x. Since $\mu^-(x)$ is generally harder to come by than $\mu^+(x)$, it is preferable to assume absolute bounds at the start to the propagation, and to convert such bounds into relative bounds as needed. In short, rules (i) and (iii) are generally preferable over the rules (ii) and (iv).

Guaranteeing 5 bits in multiplication. To understand the difference between relative and absolute precision, consider how to guarantee that a value x has 5 relative bits precision. Assume $x = y \cdot z$. Suppose that we wish to compute $\tilde{x} = x(1 + \rho_x)$ as an approximation to x. Moreover, we want to compute $\tilde{x}$ as the product $\tilde{y}\tilde{z}$, where $\tilde{y} = y(1 + \rho_y)$ and $\tilde{z} = z(1 + \rho_z)$ are approximations to y, z. This gives

$$x(1 + \rho_x) = yz(1 + \rho_y)(1 + \rho_z) = yz(1 + \rho_y + \rho_z + \rho_y \rho_z).$$

Ignoring the second order term $\rho_y \rho_z$, we conclude that $\rho_x = \rho_y + \rho_z$. Thus, if $|\rho_y|$ and $|\rho_z|$ are at most 2^{-6}, then $|\rho_x| \leq 2^{-5}$. In other words, we only need to guarantee 6 relative bits in y and z, respectively. If we wish to take the second order effects into account, it is sufficient to guarantee an extra bit in either y or z.

Next, consider how to guarantee 5 absolute bits in $x = yz$. Now we need upper bounds on the sizes of y and z. Let us write $\widetilde{y} = y + \delta_y$, $\widetilde{z} = z + \delta_z$, and

$$x + \delta_x = (y + \delta_y)(z + \delta_z) \tag{12}$$

$$= yz + y\delta_z + z\delta_y + \delta_y\delta_z. \tag{13}$$

Ignoring the second order term again, we have $\delta_x = y\delta_z + z\delta_y$. Hence, if $|\delta_y| \leq 2^{-6-\mu^+(z)}$ and $|\delta_z| \leq 2^{-6-\mu^+(y)}$, then we would have $|\delta_x| \leq 2^{-6} + 2^{-6} = 2^{-5}$. Thus it is sufficient to guarantee $6 + \mu^+(z)$ absolute bits for y, and $6 + \mu^+(y)$ absolute bits for z. We now account for the omission of the second order term: First, if $\mu(x) \geq -5$, then $|\delta_z\delta_y| \leq 2^{-12-\mu^+(x)} \leq 2^{-7}$ and so it is enough to guarantee an extra bit in either y or z. But what if $\mu(x) < -5$? Choose a_y and a_z such that $a_y + a_z = 7$ (for instance $a_y = 3, a_z = 4$). Then it suffices to require $\max\{a_y, 7 + \mu^+(z)\}$ and $\max\{a_z, 6 + \mu^+(y)\}$ absolute bits from y and z (respectively). Then $|y\delta_z| + |z\delta_y| \leq 2^{-6} + 2^{-7}$, as before. Moreover, $|\delta_y\delta_z| \leq 2^{-a_y-a_z} \leq 2^{-7}$, and hence $|\delta_x| \leq 2^{-5}$, as desired.

We may represent the flow of information in the guaranteed precision multiplication operator as in Fig. 1. This is typical of the other operators as well. Basically, in computing an approximate value for x, we see a downward flow of precision bounds $[a, r]$, and an upward flow of approximation values $\widetilde{x}$. In general, we will need to iterate this downward-upward cycle of computation.

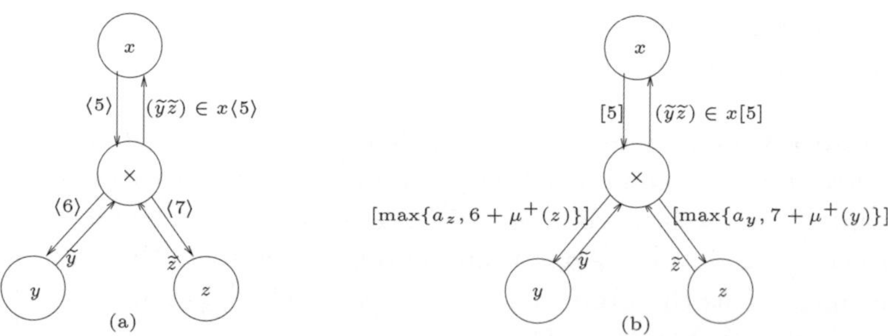

Fig. 1. Propagation rules: (a) Relative precision multiplication; (b) Absolute precision multiplication

The above analysis is completely general: to guarantee k bits in x, we just replace the constants "$5, 6, 7$" in the preceding arguments by "$k, k + 1, k + 2$" (respectively). Thus we have proved the following lemma.

Lemma 8: *Let $x = yz$. We want to compute an approximate value $\widetilde{x}$ as*

$\widetilde{y}\widetilde{z}$, *where* $\widetilde{y}, \widetilde{z}$ *are approximate values for* y, z. *Assume that we can multiply approximate values without error.*

(i) *To guarantee* k *relative bits in* x, *it is sufficient to guarantee* $k+1$ *bits in* y *and* $k+2$ *bits in* z.

(ii) *Let* $a_y + a_z = k+2$. *To guarantee* k *absolute bits in* x, *it is sufficient to guarantee* $\max\{a_y, k+1+\mu^+(z)\}$ *absolute bits for* y *and* $\max\{a_z, k+1+\mu^+(y)\}$ *absolute bits for* z.

In the absence of other information, we propagate precision bounds to y and z symmetrically. When there is asymmetry in our treatment of y and z, it is clear that we reverse the roles of y and z. The optimal allocation of bits to y and z is an interesting problem that we will not treat in the present chapter. This calls for a sensitivity analysis of the underlying expression and a reasonable cost model. In the example of multiplication, absolute precision is harder to guarantee than relative precision. We next see that the reverse is true for addition, but in a more profound way.

Can we guarantee relative precision in addition? It is trivial to guarantee absolute precision in addition. For instance, to guarantee 5 absolute bits of precision for $x = y + z$, it is enough to guarantee 6 absolute bits for y and for z. Then we have $|\delta x| \leq |\delta y| + |\delta z| \leq 2^{-6} + 2^{-6} = 2^{-5}$.

What about relative bits? If we guarantee 5 relative bits from y and z, then $x(1 + \rho_x) = y(1 + \rho_y) + z(1 + \rho_z)$ and so

$$|x\rho_x| = |y\rho_y + z\rho_z| \leq |y|2^{-5} + |z|2^{-5}.$$

In case $yz \geq 0$, the last expression is equal to $|y + z|2^{-5} = |x|2^{-5}$, as desired. But if $yz < 0$ then we get nothing of the sort when catastrophic cancellation takes place. Indeed, when $y = -z$, $x = 0$ and it is impossible to write a bound of the form $|x\rho_x| \leq |x|C$ for any finite value of C. This is the first indication that guaranteeing the relative precision of addition can be non-trivial.

But suppose that we have some lower bound on $|x|$, say, in the form $\mu^-(x)$. Let $k' = 1 + k - \mu^-(x)$. Then we can compute $\widetilde{y} = y(1 + \rho_y)$ and $\widetilde{z} = z(1 + \rho_z)$ such that $\lg|\rho_y| \leq -k'$ and $\lg|\rho_z| \leq -k'$. Then

$$|\widetilde{x} - x| = |y\rho_y + z\rho_z| \leq 2^{-k+\mu^-(x)} \leq |x|2^{-k},$$

thus ensuring k relative bits of precision. Note that in case $x = 0$, $\mu^-(x) = -\infty$. In summary, we have the following.

Lemma 9: *Let $x = y + z$.*

(i) *To guarantee k absolute bits in x, it suffices to guarantee $k + 1$ bits in y and z.*

(ii) *To guarantee k-relative bits in x, it suffices to guarantee $k + 1 - \mu^-(x)$ relative bits in y and z.*

Note that part (ii) cannot be used in a recursive evaluation method since what we need is an estimate of $\mu(x)$, not an estimate of $\mu(y)$ or $\mu(z)$. We shall see that $\mu^-(x)$ can be replaced by a weaker concept, namely *conditional lower bound* $\beta(x)$. Such a lower bound has the property that, in case $x \neq 0$, $\beta(x) \leq \mu(x)$. We return to this issue in the next section.

Guaranteeing division. Next consider the problem of guaranteeing k relative bits in the division $x = y/z$, assuming $z \neq 0$. Let $\widetilde{y} = y(1 + \rho_y)$ and $\widetilde{z} = z(1 + \rho_z)$. A new phenomenon arises: the division, $\widetilde{y}/\widetilde{z}$, cannot be computed without error for number representations such as Big Floats. For addition and multiplication, we had assumed that $\widetilde{y} + \widetilde{z}$ and $\widetilde{y}\widetilde{z}$ can be computed exactly (this agrees with our axioms for the representable reals $\mathbb{F}$). For division, we need to specify a precision bound for this operation: assume a relative error of $\rho_{\div}$. Then we may write

$$
\begin{aligned}
x(1 + \rho_x) = \widetilde{x} \\
= \frac{\widetilde{y}}{\widetilde{z}}(1 + \rho_{\div}) \\
= \frac{y(1 + \rho_y)}{z(1 - \rho_z)}(1 + \rho_{\div}) \\
= x(1 + \rho_y + \rho_{\div} + \rho_y\rho_{\div})\left(1 + \rho_z + \rho_z^2\frac{1}{1 - \rho_z}\right).
\end{aligned}
$$

To first order terms, $\rho_x = \rho_y + \rho_{\div} + \rho_z$. Therefore, if $|\rho_y|, |\rho_{\div}|, |\rho_z|$ were at most 2^{-k-2}, then we have $|\rho_x| \leq 2^{-k}$. The neglected nonlinear terms are in

$$
D = \rho_z(\rho_y + \rho_{\div}) + \frac{\rho_z^2}{1 - \rho_z} + \frac{\rho_y\rho_{\div}}{1 - \rho_z} + (\rho_y + \rho_{\div})\frac{\rho_z^2}{1 - \rho_z}.
$$

Assuming $\max\{|\rho_y|, |\rho_z|, |\rho_{\div}|\} \leq 2^{-k-2}$, we have

$$
|D| \leq 2 \cdot 2^{-2k-4} + 2 \cdot 2^{-2k-4} + 2 \cdot 2^{-2k-4} + 4 \cdot 2^{2k-4} \leq 5 \cdot 2^{-2k-3}.
$$

The total absolute error is therefore at most

$$
3 \cdot 2^{-k-2} + 5 \cdot 2^{-2k-3} \leq 2^{-k}
$$

(assuming $k \geq 2$). This proves the following lemma.

Lemma 10: *Let $x = y/z$ and $z \neq 0$. We want to compute the approximate value $\widetilde{x}$ as $\widetilde{y}/\widetilde{z}$, where $\widetilde{y}, \widetilde{z}$ are approximate values for y, z Assume that we can divide approximate values with relative error $\rho_{\div}$. To guarantee $k \geq 2$ relative bits in x, it is sufficient to guarantee $k+2$ bits in both y and z, and to perform division with relative precision $k + 2$.*

Next consider the propagation of absolute precision: instead of writing $\widetilde{y} = y + \delta_y$, we write $\widetilde{y} = y(1 + \delta'_y)$ where $\delta'_y = \delta_y/y$. Similarly, write $\widetilde{z} = z(1 - \delta'_z)$ where $\delta'_z = \delta_z/z$. Then

$$x + \delta_x = \widetilde{x}$$
$$= \frac{\widetilde{y}}{\widetilde{z}} + \delta_{\div}$$
$$= \frac{y(1 + \delta'_y)}{z(1 - \delta'_z)} + \delta_{\div}.$$

Assuming $|\delta'_z| \leq 1/2$, we see that $(1 - \delta'_z)^{-1} = 1 + C\delta'_z$ for some $|C| \leq 2$ or

$$\delta_x = x(\delta'_y + C\delta'_z + C\delta'_y\delta'_z) = \frac{\delta_y}{z} + \frac{C\delta_z y}{z^2} + \frac{C\delta_y\delta'_z}{z} = \frac{C'\delta_y}{z} + \frac{Cy\delta_z}{z^2}$$

for some $|C'| = 1 + |C\delta'_z| \leq 2$. Thus we have the following.

Lemma 11: *With the notations of Lemma 10, to guarantee k absolute bits from $x = y/z$, it is sufficient to guarantee $k+1$ absolute bits in the division operation, and to guarantee k_y and k_z absolute bits from y and z, where*

$$k_y \geq k + 2 - \mu^-(z),$$
$$k_z \geq \max\{1 - \mu^-(z), k + 2 - 2\mu^-(z) + \mu^+(y)\}.$$

If $\mu(z) = -\infty$ (i.e., $z = 0$) then the operation is invalid. But even when the operation is valid, we cannot propagate absolute precision bounds without knowing effective lower bounds on $\mu(z)$ or upper bounds on $\mu(y)$.

Guaranteeing square roots. Let $x = \sqrt{y}$, assuming $y > 0$. As in division, computing the square root of an approximate value is generally inexact, and we assume that the relative error is $\rho_{\sqrt{}}$. Hence, if $\widetilde{x} = x(1 + \rho_x)$

and $\widetilde{y} = y(1 + \rho_y)$, then we have

$$
\begin{aligned}
x(1 + \rho_x) &= \sqrt{\widetilde{y}}(1 + \rho_{\sqrt{}}) \\
&= \sqrt{y(1 + \rho_y)}(1 + \rho_{\sqrt{}}) \\
&= \sqrt{y}(1 + \rho_y)^{1/2}(1 + \rho_{\sqrt{}}),
\end{aligned}
$$

$$
\begin{aligned}
(1 + \rho)^{1/2} &= 1 + \frac{\rho}{2} + \frac{(1/2)(-1/2)}{2!}\rho^2 + \frac{(1/2)(-1/2)(-3/2)}{3!}\rho^3 + \cdots \\
&= 1 + \sum_{k \geq 1}(-1)^{k+1}\frac{(2k - 3)!!}{2^k k!}\rho^k \\
&= 1 + \frac{\rho}{2} - \sum_{k \geq 1}\rho^{2k}\frac{(4k - 3)!!}{4^k(2k)!}\left(1 - \rho\frac{4k - 1}{4k + 2}\right).
\end{aligned}
$$

Here $n!!$ is the double factorial given by the recursive formula $n!! = (n-2)!! \cdot n$ when $n \geq 1$, with base case $(-1)!! = 0!! = 1$. To first order, we see that $x(1 + \rho_x) = \sqrt{y}(1 + \frac{1}{2}\rho_y + \rho_{\sqrt{}})$ or $\rho_x = \frac{1}{2}\rho_y + \rho_{\sqrt{}}$. To bound the nonlinear terms, let us simply write ρ for ρ_y. Also let $(1 + \rho)^{1/2} = 1 + \frac{1}{2}\rho + K\rho^2$ for some K. We will further assume $\max\{|\rho|, |\rho_{\sqrt{}}|\} \leq 1/2$. The following shows that $|K| < 5/24$:

$$
\begin{aligned}
\left|(1 + \rho)^{1/2} - (1 + \frac{1}{2}\rho)\right| &< \sum_{k \geq 1}\rho^{2k}\frac{1}{8}\left(1 + \frac{1}{4}\right) \\
&= \frac{\rho^2}{1 - \rho^2}\frac{5}{32} \\
&\leq \frac{5\rho^2}{24}.
\end{aligned}
$$

The neglected nonlinear terms in $x(1 + \rho_x) = \sqrt{y}(1 + \frac{1}{2}\rho + K\rho^2)(1 + \rho_{\sqrt{}})$ is bounded by

$$
\left|K\rho^2 + \frac{1}{2}\rho\rho_{\sqrt{}} + K\rho^2\rho_{\sqrt{}}\right| < \rho\left(\frac{|K|}{2} + \frac{1}{4} + \frac{|K|}{4}\right) < \rho/6.
$$

Summarizing, we have

$$
|\rho_x| < \frac{1}{2}|\rho_y| + |\rho_{\sqrt{}}| + \frac{1}{6}|\rho_y|. \tag{14}
$$

We can similarly guarantee absolute precision by propagating absolute precision bounds. Writing δ'_y for $\delta_y/\sqrt{y}$, we have:

$$
\begin{aligned}
x + \delta_x &= \sqrt{y + \delta_y} + \delta_{\sqrt{}} \\
&= \sqrt{y}\sqrt{1 + \delta'_y} + \delta_{\sqrt{}} \\
&= \sqrt{y}\left(1 + \frac{1}{2}\delta'_y + K\delta'^2_y\right) + \delta_{\sqrt{}}.
\end{aligned}
$$

To first order, we have $\delta_x = \sqrt{y}(\delta'_y/2) + \delta_{\sqrt{}} = \frac{1}{2}\delta_y + \delta_{\sqrt{}}$. The neglected term is $\sqrt{y}K\delta'^2_y = \delta_y(K\delta'_y)$. Assuming $|\delta'_y| \leq 1/2$, we get the bound $|K\delta'_y| < 5|\delta'_y|/24 < 5/48$. Summarizing, we have

$$
|\delta_x| \leq |\delta_y|\left(\frac{1}{2} + \frac{5}{48}\right) + |\delta_{\sqrt{}}|. \tag{15}
$$

Lemma 12: *Let* $x = \sqrt{y}$.

(i) *To guarantee* $k \geq 0$ *relative bits in* $\widetilde{x}$*, it suffices to ensure* $k+1$ *relative bits in* $\widetilde{y}$ *and* $k+1$ *relative bits in the approximate square root extraction.*

(ii) *To guarantee* k *absolute bits in* $\widetilde{x}$*, it suffices to ensure* $k_y = \max\{k + 1, 1 - \mu^-(y)/2\}$ *absolute bits in* $\widetilde{y}$ *and* $k+1$ *absolute bits in the approximate square root extraction.*

Proof: (i) If $|\rho_y| \leq 2^{-k-1}$ and $|\rho_{\sqrt{}}| \leq 2^{-k-1}$, then we conclude from (14) that $|\rho_x| \leq 2^{-k}$. Note that requirement $\max\{|\rho_y|, |\rho_{\sqrt{}}|\} \leq 1/2$ is satisfied since $k \geq 0$.

(ii) If $|\delta_y| \leq 2^{-k_y} \leq 2^{-k-1}$ and $|\delta_{\sqrt{}}| \leq 2^{-k-1}$, then we conclude from (15) that $|\delta_x| \leq 2^{-k}$. But our derivation also requires $|\delta'_y| \leq 1/2$ or $|\delta_y| \leq \sqrt{y}/2$. This follows if we ensure that $|\delta_y| \leq 2^{-k_y} \leq 2^{-1+(\mu^-(y))/2}$. $\qquad\square$

Like propagating absolute precision for division, propagating relative precision for square roots requires a lower bound on y.

Exponential function. Let $x = \exp(y)$. Suppose that we want to guarantee k absolute bits in the approximate value $\widetilde{x}$.

Lemma 13: *Let* $k_y \geq \max\{1, k + 2 + 2^{\mu^+(y)+1}\}$. *If* $\widetilde{y}$ *has* k_y *absolute bits of precision and* $\widetilde{x} = \exp(\widetilde{y}, k + 1)$ *(i.e.,* $\exp(\widetilde{y})$ *is computed to* $k + 1$ *absolute bits), then* $\widetilde{x}$ *will have* k *absolute bits of precision.*

Proof: Now $\widetilde{y} = y + \delta_y$ where $|\delta_y| \leq 2^{-k_y}$. It is sufficient to show that $|x - \exp(\widetilde{y})| \leq 2^{-k-1}$. The lemma now follows from:

$$
\begin{aligned}
|\exp(\widetilde{y}) - x| &= |\exp(y + \delta_y) - \exp(y)| \\
&= \exp(y)\,|\exp(\delta_y) - 1| \\
&< \exp(y)\,|2\delta_y| \qquad\qquad (|\delta_y| \leq 1/2) \\
&\leq \exp(y)2^{-k_y+1} \\
&\leq \exp(y)2^{-k-1-2^{\mu^+(y)+1}} \\
&\leq 2^{-k-1}. \qquad\qquad\qquad\quad \square
\end{aligned}
$$

Next, suppose that we want to compute $x = \exp(y)$ to $k \geq 0$ relative bits. Let $\widetilde{y} = y(1 + \rho_y)$ where $|\rho_y| \leq 2^{-k_y}$ for some k_y, and assume that an approximate $\widetilde{x}$ is $\exp(\widetilde{y})$ computed to k_e relative bits.

Lemma 14: *If $k_y \geq k + 2 + \mu^+(y)$ and $k_e \geq k + 2$, then $\widetilde{x}$ has at least k relative bits.*

Proof: We have

$$
\begin{aligned}
\widetilde{x} &= \exp(\widetilde{y})(1 + \rho_e) \qquad\qquad\quad (\lg|\rho_e| \leq -k_e) \\
&= \exp(y)\exp(y\rho_y)(1 + \rho_e), \qquad (\lg|\rho_y| \leq -k_y) \\
|x - \widetilde{x}| &= \exp(y) \cdot |1 - \exp(y\rho_y)(1 + \rho_e)|.
\end{aligned}
$$

So we need

$$
|1 - \exp(y\rho_y)(1 + \rho_e)| \leq 2^{-k}
$$

or

$$
1 - 2^{-k} \leq \exp(y\rho_y)(1 + \rho_e) \leq 1 + 2^{-k}. \tag{16}
$$

Since $|\rho_e| \leq 2^{-k-2}$, (16) will be satisfied if $\exp(y\rho_y) = (1 + \rho')$ with $|\rho'| \leq 2^{-k-1}$. Note that $|y\rho_y| < 1/2$ because $|y\rho_y| \leq |y|2^{-k_y} \leq 2^{-2-k}$. From the fact that $|\exp(z) - (1 + z)| \leq |z|$ for $|z| \leq 1/2$, we get $\exp(z) = 1 + \rho'$ with $|\rho'| \leq 2|z|$. Hence $\exp(y\rho_y) = 1 + \rho'$ with

$$
|\rho'| \leq 2|y\rho_y| \leq 2|y|2^{-2-k-\mu^+(y)} \leq 2^{-k-1}
$$

as desired. $\qquad\qquad\qquad\qquad\qquad\qquad\qquad\qquad\qquad\qquad\qquad\qquad\quad \square$

Logarithm function. Let $x = \ln(y)$. This is only defined when $y > 0$, which we will assume. First consider the problem of guaranteeing k absolute bits in $\widetilde{x}$ as an approximation of x.

Lemma 15: *Let $k_y \geq \max\{1 - \mu^-(y), k + 2 - \mu^-(y)\}$. If $\widetilde{y}$ has k_y absolute bits as an approximation of y, and $\widetilde{x} = \ln(\widetilde{y}, k+1)$ (i.e., $\widetilde{x}$ is $\ln(\widetilde{y})$ computed to $k + 1$ absolute bits), then $\widetilde{x}$ has k absolute bits of precision.*

Proof: It is enough to show that $|\ln(\widetilde{y}) - \ln(y)| \leq 2^{-k-1}$. Let $\widetilde{y} = y + \delta_y$, $\lg|\delta_y| \leq -k_y$. Since $k_y \geq 1 - \mu^-(y)$, we have $|\delta_y|/y \leq 1/2$. Then

$$
\begin{aligned}
|\ln(y + \delta_y) - \ln(y)| &= |\ln(y(1 + \delta_y')) - \ln(y)| && (\delta_y' = \delta_y/y) \\
&= |\ln(1 + \delta_y')| \\
&\leq 2|\delta_y'| && (|\delta_y'| \leq 1/2) \\
&\leq 2^{-k_y+1}/y \\
&\leq 2^{-k-1+\mu^-(y)}/y \\
&\leq 2^{-k-1}. && \square
\end{aligned}
$$

Unfortunately, guaranteeing k *relative* bits using our usual framework of propagating relative precision bounds does not seem to work here. Intuitively, the reason is that $\ln(y)$ vanishes at $y = 1$.

Remarks. 1. The analysis shows that propagating absolute precision is easier ("more natural") for addition and logarithms. Similarly, relative precision is more natural for multiplication, division and square roots. Exponentiation seems not to have any preference.

2. More importantly, in case of $x = y \pm z$ and $x = \ln y$, we could not propagate relative precision from x to its children without knowledge of $\mu^-(x)$ (i.e., lower bounds size on $|x|$). Similarly, in case of $x = \sqrt{y}$, we could not propagate absolute precision without knowledge of $\mu^-(x)$. We consider these cases difficult, because lower bounds are not easy to compute in general.

3. In the above analysis, we were either propagating absolute bits into absolute bits or propagating relative bits into relative bits. One could also propagate absolute bits into relative bits, or vice-versa. For instance, to compute $x = yz$ to k absolute bits, let k_y, k_z be the *relative* bits required for y or z. Then it is sufficient to choose

$$
k_y = \max\{a + 1 + \mu^+(x), r_y\}, \quad k_z = \max\{a + 2 + \mu^+(x), r_z\}
$$

where $r_y + r_z = k + 2$.

5. Expression Evaluation and Constructive Zero Bounds

Until now, we examine the approximability of individual functions. We now examine the approximability of composition of functions. This turns out to be a key problem in guaranteed accuracy computation.

Suppose that e is an algebraic expression involving the operators $\pm$, $\times, \div, \sqrt{\ }$ with constants $\mathbb{Z}$. We want to approximately compute the value of e (if e is valid). The considerations in the previous section show that, in the presence of $\pm$ operators, we could not guarantee relative precision in evaluating e. At least, it is not clear how to do this using only the elementary considerations of that section. Similarly, in the presence of division, we could not guarantee absolute precision. Some new idea is needed: this is the concept of constructive zero bounds to be introduced. The problem of approximate expression evaluation was first treated by Dubé and the author.[56]

Let Ω be any set of partial real functions. Each $\omega \in \Omega$ is called an *operator*. Let $\Omega^{(m)}$ denote all the operators of arity m in Ω. In particular, the operators in $\Omega^{(0)}$ are the constant operators, and these are identified with elements of $\mathbb{R}$. We call Ω a *computational basis* if $\Omega_0 \subseteq \Omega$ where $\Omega_0 = \{+, -, \times\} \cup \mathbb{Z}$. If, in addition, each operator in Ω is absolutely (resp., relatively) approximable, then we call Ω a *absolute basis* (resp., *relative basis*).

The evaluation problem. Let $\text{Expr}(\Omega)$ be the set[h] of *expressions* over Ω. We view expressions in $\text{Expr}(\Omega)$ as a rooted dags (directed acyclic graphs), where each node of out-degree m is labeled by operators in $\Omega^{(m)}$. So the leaves are labeled by the constant operators. The dag is ordered in the sense that the outgoing edges from each node have a total order (so that we can speak of the first outgoing edge, second outgoing edge, etc.). There is a natural *evaluation function*, denoted Val_Ω (or simply Val),

$$\text{Val}_\Omega : \text{Expr}(\Omega) \to \mathbb{R}$$

which is also a partial function. The value $\text{Val}(e)$ is defined recursively, by applying the operators at each node of e to their arguments. For instance, if the root of e has the operator $\div$ and its first child is e' and second child is e'' then $\text{Val}(e) = \text{Val}(e')/\text{Val}(e'')$. We have the standard rule that

---

[h]For emphasis, we may call these *constant expressions* to contrast them to the more general notion of expressions which allow free variables. For example, $x^2 + 3y - 1$ where x, y are free variables.

$\omega(x_1, \ldots, x_m)$ is undefined if any x_i is undefined. We say that e is *valid* if Val$(e) \downarrow$, and *invalid* otherwise. Unlike some contexts (e.g., IEEE arithmetic), we do not distinguish among the invalid values. Thus $\pm 1/0 = \pm\infty$ as well as $0/0 = \mathtt{NaN}$ are equally invalid.

The *evaluation problem for* Ω amounts to computing the function Val$_\Omega$. In general, we want to approximately evaluate this function.

Approximate numerical and semi-numerical problems. The problem of approximating Val$_\Omega$ is slightly different from the kinds of functions discussed in Section 3. There, we defined approximability of "purely" numerical problems, of the form $f : \mathbb{R}^m \to \mathbb{R}$ where m is fixed. One immediate generalization we need is to allow m to vary and to become unbounded. For instance, if f is the problem of computing a determinant, then m ranges over the set $\{n^2 : n \in \mathbb{N}\}$. Hence a "purely numerical problem" is now a partial function of the form $f : \mathbb{R}^* \to \mathbb{R}^*$, where $\mathbb{R}^* = \cup_{m \geq 0}\mathbb{R}^m$.

But the problem of computing Val$_\Omega$ is not purely numerical because its domain is Expr(Ω) and not $\mathbb{R}^*$. So the input to Val$_\Omega$ has combinatorial data (namely, a dag with internal operator labels) as well as numerical data (real numbers at leaves). Following Knuth, we call such problems *semi-numerical*. Traditionally, one can continue to pretend that a semi-numerical problem is purely numerical by encoding its domain in $\mathbb{R}^*$. This is plausible for simple problems, but we will be granted that trying to encode Expr(Ω) in $\mathbb{R}^*$ is not a satisfactory solution. In general, the output is also semi-numerical (e.g., in convex hulls). The author[55] argued that the semi-numerical data arising in geometry can generally be modeled as digraphs whose nodes and edges are labeled with tuples of numbers. The digraphs comprise the *combinatorial data* and the numerical labels comprise the *numerical data*. In the following, we will assume that all semi-numerical data are of this sort. We now extend our definition of approximability of numerical problems to approximability of semi-numerical problems as follows.

- As usual, the input is augmented with a composite precision bound $[a, r]$.
- The combinatorial data remain exact, for the input as well as output.
- The numerical data in the input and output are restricted to $\mathbb{F}$.
- The numerical output satisfies the given precision bound $[a, r]$.

This definition of *approximate semi-numerical problem* is consistent with the Exact Geometric Computation paradigm, which stipulates that output combinatorial data must be exact.[55]

The question of approximating Val_Ω (relative or absolute) amounts to this: does the approximability of individual operators in Ω translate into the approximability of expressions over Ω? The significance of this will become clear in Section 8. As noted in the introduction, it may not be obvious that there is an issue here. Consider the composition of two functions, $f(g(x))$. The input x in our framework is restricted to representable reals, but the input to f is now $g(x)$ and this may not be representable. Hence, the approximability of f and g may not necessarily imply the approximability of $f(g(x))$.

Before we go further into the approximability question, let us consider the associated decision problems $\mathrm{VALID}(\mathrm{Val}_\Omega)$, $\mathrm{ZERO}(\mathrm{Val}_\Omega)$ and $\mathrm{SIGN}(\mathrm{Val}_\Omega)$, which may simply be denoted by

$$\mathrm{VALID}(\Omega), \quad \mathrm{ZERO}(\Omega), \quad \mathrm{SIGN}(\Omega).$$

They are the "fundamental problems" of guaranteed accuracy computation over Ω. In Section 3, we have shown that $\mathrm{VALID}(f), \mathrm{ZERO}(f), \mathrm{SIGN}(f)$ may not be recursively equivalent. But when $f = \mathrm{Val}_\Omega$, these problems are often recursively equivalent.

Lemma 16: *Let Ω be a basis.*

(i) *If $\div \in \Omega$ then $\mathrm{VALID}(\Omega)$ and $\mathrm{ZERO}(\Omega)$ are recursively equivalent.*
(ii) *If $\sqrt{\cdot} \in \Omega$ then $\mathrm{VALID}(\Omega)$ and $\mathrm{SIGN}(\Omega)$ are recursively equivalent.*

Proof: (i) It suffices to reduce $\mathrm{ZERO}(\Omega)$ to $\mathrm{VALID}(\Omega)$: given an expression e, $\mathrm{Val}(e) = 0$ iff e is valid and $1/e$ is invalid.

(ii) Similarly, to reduce $\mathrm{SIGN}(\Omega)$ to $\mathrm{VALID}(\Omega)$, note that $\mathrm{Val}(e) \geq 0$ iff e and $\sqrt{e}$ are both valid. $\square$

A hierarchy of computational bases. We first describe a hierarchy of bases that are important in practice.

- $\Omega_0 = \{+, -, \times\} \cup \mathbb{Z}$. The expressions over Ω_0 are the set of constant integral polynomials. Expressions such as determinants are found here. By definition, Ω_0 is the smallest basis. A useful extension of Ω_0 is $\Omega_0^+ = \Omega_0 \cup \mathbb{Q}$ (see the paper[44] by Pion and the author).
- $\Omega_1 = \Omega_0 \cup \{\div\}$. The expressions over Ω_1 are the set of constant[i] rational

---

[i]It is paradoxical to call a constant expression a "rational function" or an "integral polynomial". To justify such a view, think of a constant expression as a functional expression *together with* input constants. Our approximation algorithms take this viewpoint, and evaluate constant expressions as functional expressions with perturbed input numbers.

functions.

- $\Omega_2 = \Omega_1 \cup \{\sqrt{\cdot}\}$. The expressions over Ω_2 are called *constructible expressions*, as they evaluate to the so-call constructible reals. The majority of problems in computational geometry are computable over this basis. We may extend Ω_2 to Ω_2^+ if we add $\sqrt[k]{}$ for each $k > 2$. This basis defines the *radical expressions*.

- $\Omega_3 = \Omega_2 \cup \{\mathrm{RootOf}(P, i) : P \in \mathbb{Z}[X], i \in \mathbb{Z}\}$. If $i > 0$, $\mathrm{RootOf}(P, i)$ denotes the ith largest real root of $P(X)$. For example, $i = 1$ refers to the largest real root. If $i < 0$, we refer to the $|i|$th smallest real root of $P(X)$. If $i = 0$, we refer to the smallest positive root of $P(X)$, and we may also write $\mathrm{RootOf}(P)$ instead of $\mathrm{RootOf}(P, 0)$. Note that $\mathrm{RootOf}(P, i)$ is considered a constant (0-ary) operator. We could also allow the coefficients of $P(X)$ to be expressions, so that $\mathrm{RootOf}(P, i)$ is a $(d+1)$-ary operator that takes $d+1$ expressions as the coefficients of $P(X)$; this more general operator is denoted $\diamond(E_0, E_1, \ldots, E_d, i)$ in the paper[13] by Burnikel and others. Let Ω_3^+ be the extension of Ω_3 when we allow the $\diamond$-operators (diamond-operators).

- $\Omega_4 = \Omega_3 \cup \{\exp(\cdot), \ln(\cdot)\}$. This gives us the class of constant elementary expressions.[16]

- $\Omega_5 = \Omega_3 \cup \mathcal{H}$ where $\mathcal{H}$ is the set of real hypergeometric functions. The hypergeometric parameters in $_pF_q(\mathbf{a}, \mathbf{b}; x) \in \mathcal{H}$ are assumed to be in $\mathbb{F}$. Now, $\mathrm{Expr}(\Omega_5)$ contains the trigonometric and inverse trigonometric functions.

Lemma 17: *Assume that $\mathbb{F}$ is the set of floating point numbers over some base B, with the standard representation.*

(i) *The basis Ω_i ($i = 0, \ldots, 4$) is a relative basis.*
(ii) *The basis Ω_5 is an absolute basis.*

Proof: (i) It is sufficient to show that Ω_4 is a relative basis. It is well known that each operator $\omega \in \Omega_4$ is absolutely approximable. If $\mathbf{x} \in \mathbb{F}^m$ and ω has arity m, we can also determine if $\omega(\mathbf{x})$ is defined or not, and whether $\omega(\mathbf{x}) = 0$. It follows that ω is relatively approximable.

(ii) To evaluate $_pF_q(\mathbf{a}, \mathbf{b}; x)$ with absolute error bound of ε, it is sufficient to determine an $n = n(\mathbf{a}, \mathbf{b}, x)$ such that, if we ignore terms beyond the nth term, the absolute value of the sum of the neglected terms is at most $\varepsilon/2$. This was shown in the paper[19] by Du and others. Then it is sufficient to evaluate the sum of the first n terms with error $\varepsilon/2$, which we can easily do. $\qquad\square$

Remarks: On page 7 of his book,[41] Neumaier described a slightly different class of "elementary operators" that are important in interval analysis. The $\mathrm{RootOf}(P, i)$ operator can be replaced by $\mathrm{RootOf}(P, I)$ where I is an isolating interval whose endpoints can be specified by other expressions. If i is out of bounds, or if I is not isolating interval, then $\mathrm{RootOf}(P, i)$ and $\mathrm{RootOf}(P, I)$ are invalid. We could generalize much of this discussion by viewing the operators of Ω to be partial functions over $\mathbb{C}$, or some even more general algebraic structure. When viewed as complex operators, the trigonometric functions already appear in $\mathrm{Expr}(\Omega_4)$. In the presence of trigonometric functions, it is natural to admit π as a constant operator of Ω.

Computable zero bounds. According to Theorem 5, we could achieve relative approximability by absolute approximability plus a decision procedure for zero. For example, for the class Ω_2, one could use a direct method for deciding zero (indeed, the sign) of expressions, by repeated squaring. In practice, such an approach is not used. The most effective method for this seems to be the use of constructive zero bounds. Mignotte[38] was the first to use this, for testing the equality of two algebraic numbers. In the context of EGC, it was first introduced in the `Real/Expr` package.[56] We call[j] a function

$$B : \mathrm{Expr}(\Omega) \to \mathbb{R}_{>0}$$

a *zero bound function* for Ω if for all $e \in \mathrm{Expr}(\Omega)$, whenever e is valid and $\mathrm{Val}(e) \neq 0$,

$$|\mathrm{Val}(e)| \geq B(e).$$

Such bounds are always "conditional bounds" since it is a bound only when e is valid and non-zero. A simple example of zero bound function is $B(e) = |\mathrm{Val}(e)|$ (when e is invalid, $B(e)$ can be arbitrary). This is not a useful choice for B since its main purpose is to help us approximate the value $\mathrm{Val}(e)$. What we need are "easily" computable zero bound functions. If B is a zero bound function, the function $\beta : \mathrm{Expr}(\Omega) \to \mathbb{R}$ where $\beta(e) := -\lg B(e)$ is called a *zero bit-bound function* for Ω. We use B or β interchangeably.

Several such constructive zero bounds are known.[44] It is not easy to compare these zero bounds because they depend on different parameters.

---

[j]These have also been called "root bounds".

One of the most effective bounds currently available is the so-called BFMSS Bound.[13]

The result of Section 3 shows that Val_Ω can be relatively approximated by combining an absolute approximation algorithm, with a decision procedure for $\mathrm{ZERO}(\Omega)$. We now give an alternative and more practical approach based on zero bounds.

In general, we are interested in subsets $E \subseteq \mathrm{Expr}(\Omega)$. Given $e \in E$ and $a \in \mathbb{Z}$, consider three related problems:

- $\mathrm{Val}(e : a)$ computes an absolute approximation to $\mathrm{Val}(e)$ with a absolute bits;
- $\mu^+(e)$: to compute an upper bound on $\lg(|\mathrm{Val}(e)|)$;
- $\mathtt{sign}(e)$: to determine the sign of $\mathrm{Val}(e)$.

These problems are intertwined: from $\mathrm{Val}(e : a)$, we can obtain $\mu^+(e)$ and sometimes deduce $\mathtt{sign}(e)$. But to compute $\mathrm{Val}(e : a)$, we may need first determine $\mathtt{sign}(e')$ or $\mu^+(e')$ where e' is a child of e. If e is invalid, then all three values $\mathrm{Val}(e, a), \mu^+(e), \mathtt{sign}(e)$ are undefined.

Let $\mathrm{Val}_E : \mathrm{Expr}(\Omega) \to \mathbb{R}$ be the problem of evaluating expressions $e \in E$, with $\mathrm{Val}_E(e) \uparrow$ when $e \notin E$. We need some restrictions on E. In general, for sets $X \subseteq Y$, we call X *a decidable subset of* Y if there is a Turing machine which, given $y \in Y$, will return 1 or 0, depending on whether $y \in X$ or not. A set $E \subseteq \mathrm{Expr}(\Omega)$ is said to be *admissible* if (1) $\mathrm{Expr}(\Omega_0) \subseteq E$, (2) E is a decidable subset of $\mathrm{Expr}(\Omega)$, and (3) E is closed under subexpressions, i.e., if $e \in E$ and e' is a subexpression of e then $e' \in E$.

Theorem 18: Let $E \subseteq \mathrm{Expr}(\Omega_4)$ be admissible. If $\beta : E \to \mathbb{F}_{\geq 0}$ is a computable zero bound function, then $\mathrm{Val}(e : a), \mu^+(e)$ and $\mathtt{sign}(e)$ are computable for $e \in E$.

Proof: Let $\beta : E \to \mathbb{F}_{\geq 0}$ be a computable zero bit-bound function. The following proof gives a single algorithm to compute all three functions simultaneously. Given an expression e, we consider the "type" of e:

$e \in \Omega^{(0)}$:

    (1) $b \leftarrow \max\{a, \beta(e) + 2\}$, and $v \leftarrow \mathrm{Val}(e : b)$. By assumption, we can compute such a v. Note that the $\mathrm{RootOf}(P, i)$ operator falls under this case.

    (2) $\mu^+(e) \leftarrow \lceil \lg |v| + 1 \rceil$.

    (3) If $v \leq 2^{-\beta(e)-1}$, then $\mathrm{return}(\mathrm{ZERO})$; else $\mathtt{sign}(e) \leftarrow \mathtt{sign}(v)$.

$e = e_1 \pm e_2$:

    (1) $\mu^+(e) \leftarrow 1 + \max\{\mu^+(e_1), \mu^+(e_2)\}$.

    (2) $v \leftarrow \text{Val}(e_1 : b) \pm \text{Val}(e_2 : b)$, where $b \leftarrow \max\{a + 1, \beta(e) + 2\}$.

    (3) If $v \leq 2^{-\beta(e)-1}$, then return(ZERO); else $\text{sign}(e) \leftarrow \text{sign}(v)$.

$e = e_1 e_2$:

    (1) $\text{sign}(e) \leftarrow \text{sign}(e_1)\text{sign}(e_2)$. If $\text{sign}(e) = 0$, then return(ZERO).

    (2) $\mu^+(e) \leftarrow \mu^+(e_1) + \mu^+(e_2)$.

    (3) $v_i \leftarrow \text{Val}(e_i : a + 1 + \mu^+(e_{3-i})$ and $v \leftarrow v_1 v_2$. [cf. Lemma 8]

$e = e_1 / e_2$:

    (1) If $\text{sign}(e_2) = 0$, then return(INVALID). If $\text{sign}(e_1) = 0$, then return(ZERO); else $\text{sign}(e) \leftarrow \text{sign}(e_1)\text{sign}(e_2)$.

    (2) $\mu^+(e) \leftarrow \mu^+(e_1) - \beta(e_2)$.

    (3) $v_1 \leftarrow \text{Val}(e_1 : a + 2 - \beta(e_2)$ and $v_2 \leftarrow \text{Val}(e_2 : \max\{1 - \beta(e_2), k + 4 - 2\beta(e_2) + \mu + (e_1)\})$. Finally, $v \leftarrow v_1 / v_2 [a + 1]$ (approximate to $a + 1$ absolute bits). [cf. Lemma 11]

$e = \sqrt{e_1}$:

    (1) If $\text{sign}(e_1) < 1$, then return(INVALID). If $\text{sign}(e_1) = 0$, then return(ZERO); else $\text{sign}(e) \leftarrow 1$.

    (2) $\mu^+(e) \leftarrow \mu^+(e_1)/2$.

    (3) $v_1 \leftarrow \text{Val}(e_1 : \max\{a + 1, 1 - \beta(e_1)/2\})$ and compute v as an $a + 1$ absolute bit approximation to $\sqrt{v_1}$. [cf. Lemma 12]

$e = \exp(e_1)$:

    (1) $\text{sign}(e) \leftarrow 1$.

    (2) $\mu^+(e) \leftarrow 4^{\mu^+(e_1)}$.

    (3) $v_1 \leftarrow \text{Val}(e_1 : a + 2 + 2^{\mu^+(y)+1})$ and $v \leftarrow \exp(v_1 : a + 1)$. [cf. Lemma 13]

$e = \ln(e_1)$:

    (1) If $\text{sign}(e_1) \leq 0$, then return(INVALID).

    (2) $\mu^+(e) \leftarrow \lceil \lg(\mu^+(e_1)) \rceil$.

    (3) $b_0 \leftarrow \beta(e_1 - 1)$, and $v_1 \leftarrow \text{Val}(e_1 : b_0 + 1)$. Note that $e_1 - 1$ is a new expression whose conditional zero bound is needed.

    (4) If $|v_1 - 1| < 2^b$, then return(ZERO); else $\text{sign}(e) \leftarrow \text{sign}(v_1 - 1)$.

    (5) $b_1 \leftarrow \max\{1 + \beta(e_1), a + 2 + \beta(e_1)\}$ and $v \leftarrow \text{Val}(e_1 : b_1)$. [cf. Lemma 15]

Normally, the values returned are $v = \text{Val}(e : a)$, $\mu^+(e)$ and $\text{sign}(e)$. But there are two special return statements: INVALID and ZERO, in which cases these values are determined.

The justification of the various cases comes from the propagation bounds we derived in the previous section. We just cover the details of the last case, for logarithms. After checking validity of the expression (Step 1), we can bound $\mu^+(e)$ as in Step 2. Determining the sign of $\mathrm{Val}(e)$ is trickier, since it amounts to comparing $\mathrm{Val}(e_1)$ to 1. Hence we need to determine a zero bound $b_0 = \beta(e_1 - 1)$ for a new expression "$e_1 - 1$". With this in hand, we evaluate $\mathrm{Val}(e_1)$ to $b_0 + 1$ absolute bits. This approximation can then tell us whether $\mathrm{Val}(e_1)$ is equal to, less than, or greater than 1 (Step 4). This is the information needed to determine $\mathrm{sign}(e)$. Finally in Step 5, we approximate $\mathrm{Val}(e)$ to a absolute bits, following Lemma 15. We could have combined Steps 3 and 5 for efficiency. $\qquad\square$

The algorithm in the proof aims at simplicity. In practice, it would be more efficient to separate the algorithm into three mutually recursive algorithms. Furthermore, the zero bound β should not be used directly, but to control an adaptive algorithm.

Corollary 19: *Let $E \subseteq \mathrm{Expr}(\Omega_4)$ be admissible. Then E has a computable zero bound function iff Val_E is relatively approximable.*

Proof: ($\Rightarrow$) If $\beta : E \to \mathbb{R}_{\geq 0}$ is a computable zero bit-bound function, then by the preceding theorem, Val_E is absolutely approximable and $\mathrm{SIGN}(E)$ is computable. By Theorem 5, Val_E is relatively approximable.

($\Leftarrow$) If Val_E is relatively approximable, then a zero bit-bound for $e \in E$ can be computed as

$$\beta(e) \leftarrow 1 - \lg |\mathrm{Val}(e; 1)|.$$

If $\mathrm{Val}(e) = 0$, we may set $\beta(e) = 0$ (or any other value we like). $\qquad\square$

Algebraic expressions and beyond. The strongest positive result about the guaranteed accuracy evaluation of expressions from our hierarchy is the following.

Theorem 20: The function $\mathrm{Val}_{\Omega_3^+}$ is relatively approximable.

One way to show this result is to invoke a decision procedure for Tarski's language of real closed fields. A weaker version of this theorem says that Val_{Ω_3} is relatively approximable: this follows from Corollary 19, and the fact[13] that $\mathrm{Expr}(\Omega_3)$ has a computable zero bound function.

It is a major open question whether $\mathrm{ZERO}(\Omega_4)$ is decidable. This question is closely related to undecidable questions (by introducing variables into these expressions). Put another way, it is unknown whether we can compute with guaranteed precision over the basis Ω_4. The main result in this direction is from Richardson.[45] It seems to imply the following claim: $\text{ZERO}(\Omega_4)$ *is decidable if Schanuel's conjecture is true.*

Here, *Schanuel's conjecture* says if $x_1, \ldots, x_n \in \mathbb{C}$ are linearly independent over $\mathbb{Q}$ then the transcendence degree of $x_1, \ldots, x_n, e^{x_1}, \ldots, e^{x_n}$ is at least n. This assertion is highly non-trivial because it implies many known but deep results in transcendental number theory. Richardson's result does not directly this claim. The reason we do not have an immediate result is because Richardson has a different framework than us. First, he treats the more general complex case. But he uses a concept of "expressions", which is captured as follows. Let $\Omega_4^- := \Omega_4 \setminus \{\div, \ln(\cdot)\}$. His expressions are systems of equations (involving free variables) over the operators of Ω_4^-, together with some additional side restrictions in order to ensure that such a system determines a unique number. The advantage of Ω_4^- is that one can compute absolute approximations for its expressions *without zero bounds*. Richardson's algorithm for deciding zero uses two non-trivial algorithms, lattice reduction and Wu's algorithm.

6. The Algebraic Computational Model

Standard complexity theory, based on the Turing model, requires all inputs to be encoded as strings. This is unsuitable for some problems in algebraic computing. An example is the Mandelbrot set comprising those $z \in \mathbb{C}$ such that the infinite sequence $T(0), T^2(0), T^3(0), \ldots$ is bounded where $T(w) = w^2 + z$. Is this set computable? This question is not meaningful in the standard theory (see discussions in [BCSS, Section 1.2.1][6]). The most direct way to attack this problem is to consider algebraic models of computation.[7,11] In the algebraic model, we postulate an algebraic set D together with a set Ω of operators on D. For our purposes, we take $D = \mathbb{R}$.

The simplest algebraic model is the *straightline program*.[7] By allowing decision nodes, we get *algebraic decision trees*. Such models are finite or non-uniform. The uniform version of such models was first studied by Blum, Shub and Smale.[6] The Mandelbrot decision problem above turns out to be undecidable. The BSS model achieves uniformity by introducing a bi-infinite array, indexed by the integers, $i \in \mathbb{Z}$. Each machine instruction transforms the contents of the cell at position 0. To bring other cells into the 0 position, we use the left- and right-shift operators. Let $f : \mathbb{R}^* \to \mathbb{R}$ be a *numerical problem*; an input $w = (w_1, \ldots, w_n) \in \mathbb{R}^*$ is placed into the array so that w_i is in position i ($i = 1, \ldots, n$). To indicate the number n of arguments, we may place the number n in position 0. Finally, the output can be placed in position 0.

This model is awkward for modeling semi-numerical problems. Our evaluation problem Val_Ω is such an example. The BSS model would require encoding the input expressions as a linear sequence of array values. To overcome this, we introduce an algebraic model which supports semi-numerical objects more naturally. We based it on the elegant Storage Modification Machines, or *Pointer Machines*, of Schönhage.[47] Similar models were earlier proposed by Kolmogorov and Uspenskiĭ, and by Barzdin and Kalnin'sh.

Pointer structures. Like Turing's model, pointer machines use finite state control to determine the step-by-step execution of instructions. What is interesting is that pointer machines manipulate data structures with changeable neighborhoods, unlike the fixed neighborhoods of Turing machine tapes. Let Δ be an arbitrary finite set of symbols; each $a \in \Delta$ is called a *color*. Consider the class of finite, directed graphs with out-degree $|\Delta|$ but arbitrary in-degree. Let G be a member of this class. The edges of G are called *pointers*, and each edge is labeled ("colored") by some $a \in \Delta$. The outgoing edges from a node have distinct colors. Thus, for each color a and each node u, there is a unique *a-pointer* coming out of u. One of the nodes is designated the *origin*. Call G a Δ-*structure* or *pointer structure*. Each word $w \in \Delta^*$ is said to *access* the unique node obtained by following the sequence of pointers labeled by colors in w, starting from the origin. Let this node be denoted $[w]_G$ (or simply $[w]$ when G is understood). The *empty word* ϵ accesses the origin, denoted $[\epsilon]$. In general, there will be inaccessible nodes. For any node $u \in G$, let $G|u$ denote *u-accessible structure*, namely, the Δ-structure with origin u and comprising all nodes accessible from u. If $w \in \Delta^*$ then we write $G|w$ instead of $G|[w]$.

Let $\mathcal{G}_\Delta$ denote the class of all Δ-structures, and $\mathcal{G}$ denote the union of $\mathcal{G}_\Delta$ over all Δ. Notice that if $\Delta \subseteq \Delta'$ then there is a natural embedding of $\mathcal{G}_\Delta$ in $\mathcal{G}_{\Delta'}$. For simplicity, we shall just treat $\mathcal{G}_\Delta$ as a subset of $\mathcal{G}_{\Delta'}$.

As directed labeled graph, each Δ-structure has a standard graphical representation. This is illustrated in Fig. 2. The origin (node 1) is indicated by an unlabeled arrow from nowhere. Node 4 can be accessed by $w = aabb$ as well as $w' = bab$. So $4 = [w] = [w']$. We use two conventions to reduce clutter: (1) If a pointer is a self-loop (i.e., its target and source are the same), it is omitted in the diagram. For instance, the self-loop at node 1 can be omitted. Node 6 has a self-loop with color b that has already been omitted. (2) If two or more pointers share the same source and target, then

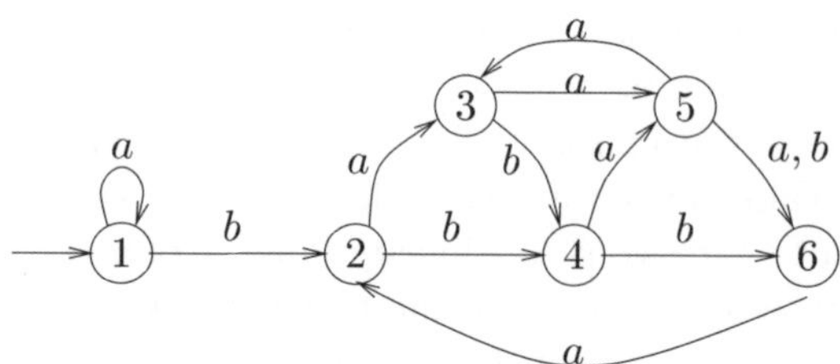

Fig. 2.   Pointer machine Δ-structure ($\Delta = \{a, b\}$)

we only draw one arrow and label them with a list of colors for this arrow. Thus, the two pointers out of node 5 have already been collapsed into one using this convention.

We define a *pointer machine* (for any color set Δ) as a finite sequence of instructions of the following four types:

Type	Name	Instruction	Meaning
(i)	Node Assignment	$w \leftarrow w'$	$[w]_{G'} = [w']_G$
(ii)	Node Creation	$w \leftarrow \mathbf{new}$	$[w]_{G'}$ is new
(iii)	Node Comparison	**if** $w \equiv w'$ **goto** L	$G' = G$
(iv)	Halt and Output	$\mathbf{HALT}(w)$	Output $G|w$

In this table, $w, w' \in \Delta^*$ and L is a natural number viewed as the label of instructions. The instructions of the pointer machines are implicitly labeled by the numbers $1, 2, 3, \ldots$ in sequential order. Normally, instruction $i+1$ is executed after instruction i unless we branch to an instruction after a type (iii) instruction. Let us explain the last column of this table (the meaning of the instructions). Let G be the Δ-structure before executing an instruction; it is transformed by the instruction to G'.

(i) If w' accesses the node v in G then after executing this assignment, both w and w' access v in G'. In symbols, $[w]_{G'} = [w']_G \ (= [w']_{G'})$. This is achieved by modifying a single pointer in G. If $w = u.a$ where $u \in \Delta^*$ and $a \in \Delta$, then this instruction makes the a-pointer issuing from $[u]$ to next point to $[w']_G$. There is a special case, when $w = \epsilon$. In this case, no pointer is modified, but the new origin is $[w']_G$.

(ii) We add a "brand new" node v to G to form G', and w now accesses v. Furthermore, each pointer from v points back to itself. As in (i), the transformation $G \to G'$ is achieved by modifying a single pointer in G.

(iii) If $[w']_G = [w]_G$ then we branch to the Lth statement; otherwise we execute the next instruction in the normal fashion. The Δ-graph is unchanged: $G = G'$.

(iv) The machine halts and outputs the Δ-structure $G|w$. We also allow a variant of halt with *no* output (i.e., w is unspecified). This is analogous to a Turing machine halting in state $q_\uparrow$.

Computation and I/O conventions. Each pointer machine M computes a partial function

$$f_M : \mathcal{G}_\Delta \to \mathcal{G}_\Delta$$

for some color set Δ: on input $G \in \mathcal{G}_\Delta$, the machine will transform G according to the instruction it is executing. At each step, it is executing some instruction (numbered) L. At the next step, it normally executes instruction $L + 1$ unless a type (iii) instruction succeeds in transferring it to some other instruction L'. The machine *halts* iff it executes a type (iv) instruction. When it halts, it either produces an output $f(G) \in \mathcal{G}_\Delta$, or has no output (equivalent to entering state $q_\uparrow$). It may not halt for one of two reasons: it executes infinitely many instructions of non-type (iv), or it tries to execute a non-existent instruction. If it does not halt or halts with no output, then $f(G)$ is undefined. It is then clear what it means for M to *unconditionally* (resp., *partially, conditionally*) *compute* a function $f : \mathcal{G}_\Delta \to \mathcal{G}_\Delta$.

An arbitrary Turing machine M can be simulated by a pointer machine P: Suppose that M has k work tapes and the set of tape symbols is Σ. Then we let $\Delta = \Sigma \cup \{S, L, R, C_1, \ldots, C_k\}$, where C_i will indicate the current position of the ith tape head. The colors L, R are used to from a tape cell u to its left (L) or its right (R) neighbor. The cell u is said to store the symbol $\sigma \in \Sigma$ if $[u.\sigma] \neq [u]$ (we must make sure that there is exactly one such σ). The states of M will be directly remembered in the states of P (identified with the instruction numbers of P). Each step of M will only require $O(1)$ steps of P. We leave the detailed simulation to the reader. When we use a Turing machine to compute a function f, we have some input/output convention. This convention is easily transformed into our I/O convention for pointer machines. In particular, if M enters the special state $q_\uparrow$, we can also ensure that P enters a corresponding special state (still denoted $q_\uparrow$). If the output size is k, our pointer machine will take $O(k)$ steps to produce an output. This extra time does not change the overall time complexity. The following lemma record these observations.

Theorem 21: A partial function $f : \Sigma^k \to \Sigma$ is unconditionally (partially, conditionally) computed by a Turing machine in time $T(n)$ iff it is unconditionally (partially, conditionally) computed by a Pointer machine in time $O(T(n))$.

In other words, the concept of computability is invariant whether we use Turing machines or Pointer machines (again confirming Church's thesis).

Algebraic pointer machines. We now augment the Pointer machines to support algebraic computation. Let R be any ring and Ω be a set of operators (i.e., partial functions of various arity) over R. Such machines compute over the set of *algebraic pointer structures*: these are just pointer structures in which each node u can hold an arbitrary value of R or may be undefined. Let $\mathcal{G}_\Delta(R)$ denote the set of pointer structures with color set Δ and values taken from R. For $G \in \mathcal{G}_\Delta(R)$ and $w \in \Delta^*$, write $\mathrm{Val}_G(w)$ for the value stored at $[w]_G$. Let

$$\mathcal{G}(R) = \bigcup_\Delta \mathcal{G}_\Delta(R)$$

where Δ ranges over all color sets.

We add two new types of instructions:

Type	Name	Instruction
(v)	Value Comparison	**if** $(w \circ w')$ **goto** L where $\circ \in \{=, <, \le\}$
(vi)	Value Assignment	$w := f(w_1, \dots, w_m)$ where $f \in \Omega$ and $w, w_i \in \Delta^*$

Let us discuss the meaning of the new instruction types. A type (v) instruction causes a branch to instruction L if the predicate $\mathrm{Val}_G(w) \circ \mathrm{Val}_G(w')$ is true, but does not change the pointer structure: $G = G'$. The comparison $\circ$ would be restricted to "$=$" when R is not ordered. A type (vi) instruction changes G to G' so that $\mathrm{Val}_{G'}(w) = f(\mathrm{Val}_G(w_1), \dots, \mathrm{Val}_G(w_m))$. The values of other nodes are unchanged. The pointers in G and G' are unchanged.

The treatment of undefined values in type (vi) instructions is standard — they are propagated by assignment. But in the case of type (v) instructions, there is no standard treatment. We adopt the following convention: viewing the undefined value $\uparrow$ as a special symbol, we assume that the undefined value is equal only to another undefined value but to no other values. This implies that we can test for the undefined value. Also the predicate "$\uparrow \le x$" holds iff x is undefined, and the predicate "$\uparrow < x$" never holds.

Observe[k] that types (i) and (vi) are analogous: we use $w \leftarrow \ldots$ to denote pointer assignment, while $w := \ldots$ denotes assigning $f(\mathrm{Val}(w_1), \ldots, \mathrm{Val}(w_m))$ to $\mathrm{Val}(w)$. Similarly, (iii) and (v) are analogous: $w \equiv w'$ compares the nodes $[w]$ and $[w']$, while $w \circ w'$ compares their *values* $\mathrm{Val}(w)$ and $\mathrm{Val}(w')$.

An *algebraic pointer machine over basis* Ω (or simply, *algebraic* Ω-*machine*) is a finite sequence of instructions of types (i)–(vi). Computation by algebraic pointer machines follows exactly the same conventions as given by the regular pointer machines. So an algebraic machine M computes a partial function

$$f_M : \mathcal{G}_\Delta(R) \to \mathcal{G}_\Delta(R). \tag{17}$$

Given another partial function

$$F : \mathcal{G}_\Delta(R) \to \mathcal{G}_\Delta(R), \tag{18}$$

we say M to *unconditionally compute* F if (i) M halts on all inputs and (ii) F and f_M are identical as partial functions. We then say that F is *algebraically computable* or Ω-*computable*. Note that in "algebraically computability", there is always a computational basis Ω which may be implicit.

Remark: In any programming model, we expect the identity assignment. In our notation, this amounts to the instruction "$w := v$" where $w, v \in \Delta^*$. This amounts to assuming that the basis Ω has the identity function. This assumption is harmless: since R is a ring and Ω contains Ω_0, the identity assignment may be simulated by two instructions "$w := v + v_0$; $w := w - v_0$" where $[v_0]$ is any node with a defined value.

Real pointer machines. Let us now specialize R to the reals $\mathbb{R}$. Then algebraic pointer machines will be called *real pointer machines* and these, operates on *real pointer structures*, $\mathcal{G}(\mathbb{R})$. Such machines compute partial functions of the form

$$F : \mathcal{G}(\mathbb{R}) \to \mathcal{G}(\mathbb{R}).$$

Other semi-numerical structures can easily be embedded in $\mathcal{G}(\mathbb{R})$ as in the next two examples.

---

[k]Here is a mnemonic device to differentiate "$\leftarrow$" from "$:=$", and "$\equiv$" from "$=$". The arrow in "$\leftarrow$" suggests a pointer link, and hence refers to pointer assignment; in contrast, the symbol $:=$ recalls the "$=$" in comparing algebraic values. Similarly, the symbol $\equiv$ suggests symbolic identity (as in polynomial identity), and hence refers to equality of nodes; in contrast, the symbol $=$ suggests equality of values in the mathematical domain.

Example 1. Assume some fixed encoding of $\mathbb{R}^*$ in $\mathcal{G}_{\Delta_0}(\mathbb{R})$ where Δ_0 is a suitable color set. Then we may speak of a purely numerical problem $F : \mathbb{R}^* \to \mathbb{R}^*$ as being Ω-computed by real pointer machines using any color set $\Delta \supseteq \Delta_0$ (recall our subset embedding convention $\mathcal{G}_{\Delta_0}(\mathbb{R}) \subseteq \mathcal{G}_\Delta(\mathbb{R})$).

Example 2. Consider the problem of evaluation of expressions over Ω. We assume that $\Omega^{(0)} \subseteq \mathbb{R}$ and $\Omega \setminus \Omega^{(0)}$ is a finite set. Let Δ contain a color $op(\omega)$ for each $\omega \in \Omega \setminus \Omega^{(0)}$, and the integers $1, \ldots, m^*$ where m^* is the maximum arity in Ω. We describe the encoding $e \in \text{Expr}(\Omega)$ as a Δ-structure $G(e)$. If we restrict $G(e)$ to the pointers colored by numbers $(1, \ldots, m^*)$ and which are not self-loops, then G is isomorphic to the DAG of e. The i-pointer $(i = 1, \ldots, m^*)$ leads to the ith argument of a node. If node u in e is an operator $\omega \in \Omega^{(m)}$, $m \geq 1$, then the $op(\omega)$-pointer of u points to the origin; all other operator pointers are self-loops. Finally, if u is a leaf, then all i-pointers are self-loops and $\text{Val}_G(u)$ stores a valie $\Omega^{(0)}$. Given such $G(e)$, an algebraic Ω-machine computes $\text{Val}_\Omega(e)$ in the obvious way: it amounts to a bottom-up evaluation of the nodes of the DAG. Finally we return the value at the root of the DAG.

Remarks: In terms of computability, the Algebraic Pointer Model is equivalent to the BSS model. The Algebraic Pointer Model is clearly an elegant basis for algebraic computation involving combinatorial structures. But the fundamental reason for preferring the Algebraic Pointer Model is a complexity-theoretic one: the BSS model can distort the complexity of problems with low complexity. This has two causes: first, the BSS model does not encode combinatorial structures easily (it requires the analogue of Gödel numberings in recursive function theory). Second, BSS machines are too slow in accessing new array elements with its shift operator. One possible solution is to augment the BSS model by introducing special "index variables" which are restricted to values in $\mathbb{Z}$ and can be added and subtracted (or even multiplied). Index variables are to be used as arguments to the shift operators. In pointer machines, no such facility is needed: the standard technique of "pointer doubling" can achieve the same effect of rapid access. Like the Turing model, point machines are capable of many interesting variations. It is easy to expand the repertoire of instructions in non-essential ways (e.g., allowing the ability to branch on a general Boolean combination of equality tests). We may assume these without much warning.

7. Numerical Model of Computation

The algebraic model is natural and useful for investigating many algebraic complexity questions. But it is far removed from the real world "computation modes" described in Section 2. For instance, it does not address two known criticisms [Weihrauch,[51] Chapter 9] of non-effectiveness in real algebraic models: (I) Arbitrarily numbers as objects that are directly manipulated. Such numbers might be uncomputable reals. In the real world, we need to represent numerical quantities with non-trivial description sizes. (II) The operators in Ω as perfect oracles. Since the operators can be applied to values with non-trivial complexity, even "simple" operators such as $+$ are highly non-trivial.

This section introduces a numerical model of computation which lies intermediate[1] between the algebraic model (which is too abstract) and the Turing model (which is too concrete). Our model restricts numerical inputs to some representable set $\mathbb{F} \subseteq \mathbb{R}$. Second, we consider "approximate operators" that accept an auxiliary "precision" parameter $p \geq 0$. These steps remove the above objections (I) and (II).

Numerical pointer machines. These are essentially a special kind of real pointer machines. Let Ω be a basis of real operators. We need three changes: First, the value set R is now the set $\mathbb{F}$ of representable reals introduced in Section 3. The new computational structures $\mathcal{G}(\mathbb{F})$ are called *numerical pointer structures*. Second, each $f \in \Omega^{(m)}$ is replaced by a relative approximation function $f(x_1, \ldots, x_m; p)$. Third, the instructions of type (vi) are replaced by the following type (vii) instructions:

Type	Name	Instruction
(vii)	Approximate Assignment	$w := f(w_1, \ldots, w_m; v)$ where $f \in \Omega$

Here, $w_1, \ldots, w_m, v \in \Delta^*$. The semantics is evident: $\mathrm{Val}_{G'}(w)$ will be assigned a relative approximate value $f(\mathrm{Val}_G(w_1), \ldots, \mathrm{Val}_G(w_m); \mathrm{Val}(v))$. In practice $\mathrm{Val}(v)$ will be non-negative and even integers, but there is no harm allowing it to be unrestricted for this definition.

---

[1]We are aware that the BSS model *formally* incorporates the Turing model as a special case, when $R = \mathbb{Z}_2$. But it is clear that the development of the BSS theory is novel only when R is an infinite ring like $R = \mathbb{R}$. It seems more useful for our purposes to view these as two distinct theories.

This modification has one interesting consequence: even constants $\omega \in \Omega^{(0)}$ can become non-trivial functions that takes a precision parameter. For instance, if $\pi \in \Omega^{(0)}$ then the numerical model must provide an operator $\pi(r)$ to produce arbitrarily precise approximations to π.

Approximating semi-numerical functions. A sequence of instructions of types (i)–(v) and type (vii) will be called a *numerical Ω-machine* (or *numerical pointer machine*). Let N be such a machine. Clearly, N computes a partial function similar to (17), but with $R = \mathbb{F}$. But we want to view N as *approximating* some semi-numerical function. We proceed as follows: fix some standard embedding of $\mathcal{G}_\Delta(\mathbb{F}) \times \mathbb{F}$ into $\mathcal{G}_\Delta(\mathbb{F})$. Then we can re-interpret N as computing the following partial function

$$f_N : \mathcal{G}_\Delta(\mathbb{F}) \times \mathbb{F} \to \mathcal{G}_\Delta(\mathbb{F}), \tag{19}$$

with an extra precision parameter.

We have already clarified what it means to approximate semi-numerical data (Section 5). Applied to $G \in \mathcal{G}(\mathbb{R})$, let

$$G\langle p \rangle$$

denote the set of $G' \in \mathcal{G}(\mathbb{R})$ that approximates G with relative precision p: this means that the underlying pointer structures of G and G' agree, but at each node $u \in G$, we have $|\mathrm{Val}_{G'}(u) - \mathrm{Val}_G(u)| \leq 2^{-p}|\mathrm{Val}_G(u)|$. Similarly, $G[p]$ denotes the approximations to G to absolute precision p.

If

$$F : \mathcal{G}_\Delta(\mathbb{R}) \to \mathcal{G}_\Delta(\mathbb{R})$$

is any partial function, we shall say that the machine N *relatively approximates* F if for all $(G, p) \in \mathcal{G}_\Delta(\mathbb{F}) \times \mathbb{F}$, if $F(G)$ is defined then

$$f_N(G, p) \in F(G)\langle p \rangle,$$

and if $F(G)$ is undefined then N halts with no output. We say that the function F is *numerically approximable* if F is relatively approximated by some numerical pointer machine. Note that for a function F to be "numerically approximable", there is an implicit basis Ω. So we say that F is *Ω-approximable* to make this basis explicit.

It is not hard to see that the results of Section 5 about "relative approximability" can now be restated as results about "numerical approximability". For instance, Theorem 18 and its corollary translate into the following result.

Theorem 22: Let $E \subseteq \mathrm{Expr}(\Omega_4)$ be admissible. Then E has a computable zero bound iff Val_E is numerically Ω_4-approximable.

Main result. We give a sufficient condition for when algebraic computability implies numerical approximability. More precisely, we want conditions on Ω such that an (algebraic) Ω-computable function is (numerically) Ω-approximable. For this we need to make the assumption that

$$\Omega \setminus \mathbb{F} \tag{20}$$

is a finite set. This is because each operator in this set requires an approximation operator, and our model allows only a finite number of them.

Theorem 23: Let the function $F : \mathcal{G}(\mathbb{R}) \to \mathcal{G}(\mathbb{R})$ be Ω-computable. If Val_Ω is Ω-approximable then F is Ω-approximable.

Proof: Let A be an algebraic pointer machine that computes F. We must describe a numerical pointer machine N to numerically approximate F. Assume that the color set of A is Δ; the color set of N will be some superset Δ' of Δ. The valid inputs[m] for N has the form pair $(G_0, p) \in \mathcal{G}_\Delta(\mathbb{F}) \times \mathbb{F}$. Our goal is to simulate the computation of A on the input G_0, and ultimately produce an output in $F(G_0)\langle p \rangle$.

The machine N simulates A step-by-step. Suppose at some step that the algebraic Δ-structure of A is G. Then for machine N, we maintain a corresponding numerical Δ'-structure G'. Basically G' is G with extra embellishments. In particular, for each node $u \in G$ the corresponding node in G' (still denoted u) has an associated expression that can be accessed as $u.\mathtt{Expr}$. Here $\mathtt{Expr} \in \Delta'$ is a special color for accessing expressions associated with nodes.

We encode expressions over Ω as in Example 2 (Section 6). For each $f \in \Omega \setminus \mathbb{F}$, we have the color $op(f) \in \Delta'$ to represent this operator in expressions. Consider the various types of instructions:

- For instructions of types (i)–(iii), N will execute exactly the same instructions as A. These instructions manipulate purely combinatorial data.
- For type (iv) instruction, we halt with output. N must go over the output Δ'-structure, and for each node u, to evaluate the expression

---

[m]In particular, if $G_0 \in \mathcal{G}_{\Delta'}(\mathbb{F}) \setminus \mathcal{G}_\Delta(\mathbb{F})$ then N can halt with no output. Recall our convention that $\mathcal{G}_\Delta(\mathbb{F}) \subseteq \mathcal{G}_{\Delta'}(\mathbb{F})$.

u.**Expr** to precision required by the input specification. By assumption, this is possible.

- Consider a type (vi) instruction of the form "$w := f(w_1, w_2)$". We assume that f is binary here, but it clearly generalizes to any m-ary f. We execute the following sequence of instructions:

$$
\begin{aligned}
&w.\textbf{Expr} := \textbf{new}; \\
&w.\textbf{Expr}.op(f) := \epsilon; \\
&w.\textbf{Expr}.1 := w_1.\textbf{Expr}; \\
&w.\textbf{Expr}.2 := w_2.\textbf{Expr};
\end{aligned}
$$

Thus, we simply construct the corresponding expression for the desired value.

- Consider a type (v) instruction of the form "**if** $(w \circ w')$ **goto** L". Although N has type (v) instructions like A, their semantics are not the same. In A, when we ask for the comparison $w \circ w'$ where $w, w' \in \Delta^*$, we are comparing the values $\mathrm{Val}_G(w), \mathrm{Val}_G(w') \in \mathbb{R}$. In N, we can only approximate these values. We execute the following sequence of instructions to construct a temporary expression corresponding to $[w].\textbf{Expr} - [w'].\textbf{Expr}$:

$$
\begin{aligned}
&\texttt{tmp}.\textbf{Expr} := \textbf{new}; \\
&\texttt{tmp}.\textbf{Expr}.op(-) := \epsilon; \\
&\texttt{tmp}.\textbf{Expr}.1 := w.\textbf{Expr}; \\
&\texttt{tmp}.\textbf{Expr}.2 := w'.\textbf{Expr}; \\
&\textbf{goto}\ \mathrm{L}_{tmp};
\end{aligned}
$$

where $\texttt{tmp} \in \Delta'$ is just another color and L_{tmp} is the beginning of instructions to evaluate the temporary expression just constructed. We invoke the relative approximability of Val_Ω to achieve this, and this implies that we can get the correct sign and hence jump to the correct "next instruction" of A. For simplicity, we assume that N has a special location L_{tmp} for each branch instruction of A. Then this segment of code knows the correct next instruction. Clearly, more general programming techniques can reduce this code bloat in N. $\square$

If we wish to compute F according to the principles of EGC (see introduction), then we can relax the conditions of this theorem: in that case, the Ω-approximability of Val_Ω can be replaced by the Ω-computability of $\mathrm{SIGN}(\Omega)$.

8. Conclusion

This chapter outlines a theory of real approximation and introduces a model of numerical computation. Together, they capture the main features of "guaranteed precision mode of computation" which is being developed in the software libraries **LEDA Real** and **Core Library**. The practical deployment of this computational mode will open up many new applications, from the verification of conjectures to the advancement of reliable computing. We pose several open problems in this context.

- Guaranteed precision is a very strong requirement, not known to be possible outside of the algebraic realm. The main open question revolves around the decidability of the fundamental problems $\mathrm{ZERO}(\Omega)$ where Ω is a basis containing non-algebraic operators.
- We focused our study on the computability of approximation, to outline the main features of this theory. Clearly, the complexity-theoretic aspects ought to be developed. Another extension is to develop non-determinism and give yet another form of NP-completeness (this is expected to be different from the known theories).
- The expression evaluation problem is central. There are several open problems here: generalize the Ω-results of this chapter by requiring only general conditions on Ω (e.g., conditions on the derivatives). Even simpler: when is $f(g(x))$ approximable? Another problem is to give provably optimal algorithms for approximating Val_Ω or for $\mathrm{SIGN}(\Omega)$. We want here some "precision sensitive"[48,1] concept of optimality. This is unclear even for $\Omega = \Omega_0$.
- In constructive zero bounds, an open question is whether there is a zero bound for $\mathrm{Expr}(\Omega_2)$ whose zero bit-bound is linear in the degree. There remains the practical need for stronger and more adaptive zero bounds. For instance, approximating expressions over Ω_3^+ is currently impractical with known zero bounds.
- Section 2 suggests a programming environment (or language) where different numerical accuracy requirements can co-exist and interplay. This presents many practical as well as theoretical challenges. Programming environments of the future ought to support such paradigms. For instance, Moore's law predicts an inexorable increase of machine speed. Such an environment can exploit this, to achieve a trade-off between

speed and accuracy (or "robustness").

- Section 7 gives us a condition when an abstract algebraic algorithm A can be implemented as a numerical algorithm B. Such A-to-B type results can provide some theoretical foundation for numerical analysis (as sought by the BCSS theory[6]). Clearly, there are other A-to-B type results.

Acknowledgments

I am grateful for the support of Kurt Mehlhorn and the facilities of the Max-Planck Institute of Computer Science in Saarbrücken where this chapter was completed. Thanks are due to Susanne Schmitt for her careful reading of the manuscript and comments.

References

1. T. Asano, D. Kirkpatrick, and C. Yap. Pseudo approximation algorithms, with applications to optimal motion planning. In *ACM Symp. on Computational Geometry*, volume 18, pages 170–178. ACM Press, New York, 2002. To appear in Special Conference Issue of J. Discrete & Comp. Geom.
2. D. H. Bailey. Multiprecision translation and execution of Fortran programs. *ACM Trans. on Math. Software*, 19(3): 288–319, 1993.
3. M. Benouamer, D. Michelucci, and B. Péroche. Boundary evaluation using a lazy rational arithmetic. In *Proc. 2nd ACM/IEEE Symposium on Solid Modeling and Applications*, pages 115–126. ACM Press, New York, 1993.
4. E. Berberich, A. Eigenwillig, M. Hemmer, S. Hert, K. Mehlhorn, and E. Schömer. A computational basis for conic arcs and boolean operations on conic polygons. In *Proc. 10th European Symp. on Algorithms* (ESA '02), pages 174–186. Lecture Notes in Computer Science, volume 2461. Springer, Berlin Heidelberg, 2002.
5. J. Blömer. *Simplifying Expressions Involving Radicals*. Ph.D. thesis, Department of Mathematics, Free University Berlin, October 1992.
6. L. Blum, F. Cucker, M. Shub, and S. Smale. *Complexity and Real Computation*. Springer, New York, 1997.
7. A. Borodin and I. Munro. *The Computational Complexity of Algebraic and Numeric Problems*. American Elsevier Publishing Company, Inc., New York, 1975.
8. R. P. Brent. A Fortran multiple-precision arithmetic package. *ACM Trans. on Math. Software*, 4: 57–70, 1978.
9. H. Brönnimann, C. Burnikel, and S. Pion. Interval arithmetic yields efficient dynamic filters for computational geometry. *Discrete Applied Mathematics*, 109(1–2): 25–47, 2001.
10. H. Brönnimann and M. Yvinec. Efficient exact evaluation of signs of determinants. *Algorithmica*, 27: 21–56, 2000.

11. P. Bürgisser, M. Clausen, and M. A. Shokrollahi. *Algebraic Complexity theory*. Series of Comprehensive Studies in Mathematics, volume 315. Springer, Berlin, 1997.

12. C. Burnikel, R. Fleischer, K. Mehlhorn, and S. Schirra. Exact geometric computation made easy. In *Proc. 15th ACM Symp. Comp. Geom.*, pages 341–450. ACM Press, New York, 1999.

13. C. Burnikel, S. Funke, K. Mehlhorn, S. Schirra, and S. Schmitt. A separation bound for real algebraic expressions. In *Lecture Notes in Computer Science*, pages 254–265. Springer, Berlin Heidelberg, 2001. To appear in Algorithmica.

14. C. Burnikel, J. Könnemann, K. Mehlhorn, S. Näher, S. Schirra, and C. Uhrig. Exact geometric computation in LEDA. In *Proc. 11th ACM Symp. Comp. Geom.*, pages C18–C19, 1995.

15. F. Chaitin-Chatelin and V. Fraysse. *Lectures on Finite Precision Computations*. Society for Industrial and Applied Mathematics, Philadelphia, 1996.

16. T. Y. Chow. What is a closed-form number? *Amer. Math. Monthly*, 106(5): 440–448, 1999.

17. B. M. Cullough. Assessing the reliability of statistical software: Part II. *The American Statistician*, 53: 149–159, 1999.

18. M. Dhiflaoui, S. Funke, C. Kwappik, K. Mehlhorn, M. Seel, E. Schmer, R. Schulte, and D. Weber. Certifying and repairing solutions to large lps, how good are lp-solvers? In *Proc. SODA 2003*, to appear.

19. Z. Du, M. Eleftheriou, J. Moreira, and C. Yap. Hypergeometric functions in exact geometric computation. In V. Brattka, M. Schoeder, and K. Weihrauch, editors, *Proc. 5th Workshop on Computability and Complexity in Analysis*, pages 55–66. Malaga, Spain, July 12-13, 2002. In Electronic Notes in Theoretical Computer Science, 66: 1 (2002), `http://www.elsevier.nl/locate/entcs/volume66.html`. Also available as "Computability and Complexity in Analysis", Informatik Berichte No. 294-6/2002, Fern University, Hagen, Germany.

20. A. Fabri, G.-J. Giezeman, L. Kettner, S. Schirra, and S. Schoenherr. The CGAL kernel: A basis for geometric computation. In M. C. Lin and D. Manocha, editors, *Applied Computational Geometry: Towards Geometric Engineering*, pages 191–202. Lecture Notes in Computer Science, volume 1148. Springer, Berlin, 1996. Proc. 1st ACM Workshop on Applied Computational Geometry (WACG), Federated Computing Research Conference 1996, Philadelphia, USA.

21. S. J. Fortune and C. J. van Wyk. Static analysis yields efficient exact integer arithmetic for computational geometry. *ACM Transactions on Graphics*, 15(3): 223–248, 1996.

22. A. Frommer. Proving conjectures by use of interval arithmetic. In U. Kulisch, R. Lohner, and A. Facius, editors, *Perspectives on Enclosure Methods*. Springer, Vienna, 2001.

23. S. Funke, K. Mehlhorn, and S. Näher. Structural filtering: A paradigm for efficient and exact geometric programs. In *Proc. 11th Canadian Conference on Computational Geometry*, 1999.

24. P. Gowland and D. Lester. A survey of exact arithmetic implementations. In

J. Blank, V. Brattka, and P. Hertling, editors, *Computability and Complexity in Analysis*. Lecture Notes in Computer Science, volume 2064. Springer, Berlin Heidelberg, 2000. 4th International Workshop, CCA 2000, Swansea, UK, September 17–19, 2000, Selected Papers.

25. N. J. Higham. *Accuracy and Stability of Numerical Algorithms*. Society for Industrial and Applied Mathematics, Philadelphia, 1996.

26. Holt, Matthews, Rosselet, and Cordy. *The Turing Programming Language*. Prentice-Hall, Englewood Cliffs, NJ, 1988.

27. CGAL Homepage, 1998. Computational Geometry Algorithms Library (CGAL) Project. A 7-institution European Community effort. See URL `http://www.cgal.org/`.

28. LEDA Homepage, 1998. Library of Efficient Data Structures and Algorithms (LEDA) Project. From the Max Planck Institute of Computer Science. See URL `http://www.mpi-sb.mpg.de/LEDA/`.

29. T. Hull, M. Cohen, J. Sawchuk, and D. Wortman. Exception handling in scientific computing. *ACM Trans. on Math. Software*, 14(3): 201–217, 1988.

30. V. Karamcheti, C. Li, I. Pechtchanski, and C. Yap. A Core library for robust numerical and geometric libraries. In *15th ACM Symp. Computational Geometry*, pages 351–359, 1999.

31. K.-I. Ko. *Complexity Theory of Real Functions*. Progress in Theoretical Computer Science. Birkhäuser, Boston, 1991.

32. S. Krishnan, M. Foskey, T. Culver, J. Keyser, and D. Manocha. PRECISE: Efficient multiprecision evaluation of algebraic roots and predicates for reliable geometric computation. In *ACM Symp. on Computational Geometry*, volume 17, pages 274–283, 2001.

33. U. Kulisch, R. Lohner, and A. Facius, editors. *Perspectives on Enclosure Methods*. Springer, Vienna, 2001.

34. K. Lange. *Numerical Analysis for Statisticians*. Springer, New York, 1999.

35. K. Mehlhorn and S. Schirra. Exact computation with `leda_real` — Theory and geometric application. In G. Alefeld, J. Rohn, S. Rump, and T. Yamamoto, editors, *Symbolic Algebraic Methods and Verification Methods*, volume 379, pages 163–172. Springer, Vienna, 2001.

36. N. Metropolis. Methods of significance arithmetic. In D. A. H. Jacobs, editor, *The State of the Art in Numerical Analysis*, pages 179–192. Academic Press, London, 1977.

37. D. Michelucci and J.-M. Moreau. Lazy arithmetic. *IEEE Transactions on Computers*, 46(9): 961–975, 1997.

38. M. Mignotte. Identification of algebraic numbers. *J. of Algorithms*, 3: 197–204, 1982.

39. R. E. Moore. *Interval Analysis*. Series in Automatic Computation. Prentice-Hall, Englewood Cliffs, NJ, 1966.

40. N. T. Müller. The iRRAM: Exact arithmetic in C++. In J. Blank, V. Brattka, and P. Hertling, editors, *Computability and Complexity in Analysis*. Lecture Notes in Computer Science, volume 2064. Springer, Berlin Heidelberg, 2000. 4th International Workshop, CCA 2000, Swansea, UK, September 17–19, 2000, Selected Papers.

41. A. Neumaier. *Interval Methods for Systems of Equations*. Cambridge University Press, Cambridge, 1990.

42. K. Ouchi. Real/Expr: Implementation of an exact computation package. Master thesis, Department of Computer Science, Courant Institute, New York University, January 1997. Download from `http://cs.nyu.edu/exact/doc/`.

43. C. H. Papadimitriou. *Computational Complexity*. Addison-Wesley, Reading, Massachusetts, 1994.

44. S. Pion and C. Yap. Constructive root bound method for k-ary rational input numbers. In *Proc. 19th ACM Symp. on Comp. Geom.*, pages 256–263. ACM Press, New York, 2003.

45. D. Richardson. How to recognize zero. *J. of Symbolic Computation*, 24: 627–645, 1997.

46. H. Rogers. *Theory of Recursive Functions and Effective Computability*. McGraw-Hill, New York, 1967.

47. A. Schönhage. Storage modification machines. *SIAM J. Computing*, 9: 490–508, 1980.

48. J. Sellen, J. Choi, and C. Yap. Precision-sensitive Euclidean shortest path in 3-space. *SIAM J. Computing*, 29(5): 1577–1595, 2000. Also in *11th ACM Symp. on Comp. Geom.*, pages 350–359, 1995.

49. The Institute of Electrical and Electronic Engineers, Inc. IEEE Standard 754-1985 for binary floating-point arithmetic, 1985. ANSI/IEEE Std 754-1985. Reprinted in SIGPLAN 22(2): 9–25.

50. D. Tulone, C. Yap, and C. Li. Randomized zero testing of radical expressions and elementary geometry theorem proving. In J. Richter-Gebert and D. Wang, editors, *Proc. 3rd Int'l. Workshop on Automated Deduction in Geometry* (ADG '00), pages 58–82. Lecture Notes in Artificial Intelligence, volume 2061. Springer, Berlin Heidelberg, 2001.

51. K. Weihrauch. *Computable Analysis*. Springer, Berlin, 2000.

52. C. Yap. A new number core for robust numerical and geometric libraries. In *3rd CGC Workshop on Geometric Computing*, 1998. Invited talk at Brown University, October 11–12, 1998. Abstracts available from `http://www.cs.brown.edu/cgc/cgc98/home.html`.

53. C. Yap, C. Li, and S. Pion. Core Library Tutorial: A library for robust geometric computation, 1999. Released with the Core Library software package, 1999–2003. Download from `http://cs.nyu.edu/exact/core/`.

54. C. K. Yap. Introduction to the theory of complexity classes, 1987. Book manuscript. Preliminary version, URL `ftp://cs.nyu.edu/pub/local/yap/complexity-bk`.

55. C. K. Yap. Robust geometric computation. In J. E. Goodman and J. O'Rourke, editors, *Handbook of Discrete and Computational Geometry*, 2nd (revised, expanded) edition, chapter 41. CRC Press LLC, Boca Raton, FL, 2003, to appear.

56. C. K. Yap and T. Dubé. The exact computation paradigm. In D.-Z. Du and F. K. Hwang, editors, *Computing in Euclidean Geometry*, 2nd edition, pages 452–486. World Scientific, Singapore, 1995.

CHAPTER 13

DIXON $\mathcal{A}$-RESULTANT QUOTIENTS FOR
6-POINT ISOSCELES TRIANGULAR CORNER CUTTING

Mao-Ching Foo and Eng-Wee Chionh

School of Computing
National University of Singapore
Singapore 117543
E-mail: {foomaoch, chionhew} @comp.nus.edu.sg

The Dixon formulation for three bivariate polynomials produces explicit pure bracket sparse resultant expressions for several classes of unmixed monomial supports. When the monomial support is a complete rectangle or a corner-cut rectangle, the sparse resultant is the Dixon determinant; when the monomial support is a complete rectangle with corner edge cutting or a corner-cut rectangle with corner point pasting, the sparse resultant is the Dixon determinant divided by a priori known brackets. But the Dixon determinant vanishes with isosceles triangular corner cutting when the isosceles triangle has six or more points. However, if the isosceles triangle consists of exactly six points, we are able to identify all the maximal minors with corresponding brackets such that each maximal minor divided by the product of these corresponding brackets is the sparse resultant. Our approach is interesting because it extends the applicability of the well-known Dixon method and it produces a much smaller determinant than that of other determinantal methods. All proofs are constructive. One of the proofs is done mechanically by a Maple program with the "assume" facility which allows properties of and relationships among symbols to be specified.

1. Introduction

Resultants are an important computational tool in solving polynomial systems [Cox *et al.*[7], Wang[20]]. In computer aided geometric design, the resultant has the additional advantage of producing the implicit equation of a parametric rational surface. Furthermore, the implicit equation is a compact determinant form whenever the resultant for three bivariate polynomials can be expressed in determinants. There has been much research

374

in finding and understanding the resultant for an arbitrary monomial support $\mathcal{A}$ for three bivariate polynomials [Aries & Senoussi[1], Busé[2], Chionh[5], Chtcherba & Kapur[6], D'Andrea & Emiris[8], Khetan[17], Zhang & Goldman[21]] and general polynomial systems [D'Andrea[9], Jouanolou[16]]. These custom made resultants are known as sparse resultants or $\mathcal{A}$-resultants. In this chapter we will simply refer to them as resultants.

Our interest is in finding pure bracket (a bracket is a 3×3 determinant) expressions for an unmixed monomial support. Compared to Sylvester-style Macaulay and hybrid resultants, a pure bracket resultant expression involves much smaller determinants. Dixon[10] gave a Bezout-style pure bracket determinant as the resultant for an unmixed monomial support which is a complete rectangle. The second author[5] showed that the Dixon formulation still applies when the unmixed monomial support is a corner-cut rectangle (that is, a complete rectangle with sub-rectangles removed at one or more corners). But when the unmixed monomial support is a complete rectangle with corner edge cutting [Foo & Chionh[13]] or a corner-cut rectangle with point pasting [Foo & Chionh[14]], the Dixon determinant is a multiple of the resultant with a priori known brackets as extraneous factors. In other words, for the two latter monomial supports, the resultant can be expressed in pure bracket quotient form.

This chapter studies the applicability of the Dixon formulation when a complete rectangle undergoes isosceles triangular corner cutting at one or more corners. For such a monomial support, the Dixon determinant vanishes if the isosceles triangle has more than three points. But if the isosceles triangle has exactly six points, we are able to identify all the maximal minors; furthermore, each maximal minor is a multiple of the resultant and the extraneous factors are brackets which can be easily predicted.

Our results are applicable for three bivariate polynomials of general bidegree (m, n) having the same monomial support and having the same type of corner cutting at one or more corners. We have proved separately that the results are still applicable when the types of corner cutting at the corners are different [Foo[12]]. An immediate application of these results is the compact implicitization of bicubic $(m, n) = (3, 3)$ toric patches [Krasauska[18]] because their monomial supports can be obtained by a combination of rectangular corner cutting, corner edge cutting, corner point pasting, or 6-point isosceles triangular corner cutting. This is illustrated by the following two examples.

Example 1: A total degree 3 monomial support can be treated as a bidegree $(3,3)$ monomial support with a 6-point isosceles triangular corner cutting at the top right corner as shown:

$$
\begin{array}{cccc}
1 & 0 & 0 & 0 \\
1 & 1 & 0 & 0 \\
1 & 1 & 1 & 0 \\
1 & 1 & 1 & 1
\end{array}
$$

Example 2: A bidegree $(3,3)$ toric patch involving the monomials s^2, s^2t, s^3t, st^2, s^2t^2, t^3, st^3 is a monomial support with a corner point pasting at the bottom left corner, a rectangular corner cutting at the bottom right corner, and a corner edge cutting at the top right corner as shown:

$$
\begin{array}{cccc}
1 & 1 & 1 & 1 \\
0 & 0 & 1 & 1 \\
0 & 0 & 1 & 1 \\
0 & 0 & 1 & 0
\end{array}
\longrightarrow
\begin{array}{cccc}
1 & 1 & 1 & 1 \\
0 & 1 & 1 & 1 \\
0 & 0 & 1 & 1 \\
0 & 0 & 1 & 0
\end{array}
\longrightarrow
\begin{array}{cccc}
1 & 1 & 0 & 0 \\
0 & 1 & 1 & 0 \\
0 & 0 & 1 & 1 \\
0 & 0 & 1 & 0
\end{array}
$$

corner-cut rectangle   bottom-left point pasting   top-right edge cutting

Thus in general bicubic toric patches can be implicitized compactly in pure bracket form. This improves the results of Chionh *et al.*[4] and Zube[22] for bicubic toric patches.

The rest of the chapter is organized in four sections. Section 2 reviews the construction of the Dixon determinant and defines some notations. Section 3 states the 6-point isosceles triangular corner cutting result as a theorem and illustrates the ease of applying the theorem with some examples. Section 4 proves the theorem by identifying all the maximal minors and their corresponding extraneous bracket factors. Section 5 concludes the chapter with some observations on larger isosceles triangular corner cutting and some problems for further work.

2. Preliminaries

This section describes the construction of the Dixon[10] resultant for three bidegree polynomial equations in two variables. Notations needed for the rest of the chapter are also introduced here.

Let the general bidegree (m,n) monomial support be

$$
\mathcal{A}_{m,n} = \{(i,j) \mid i = 0, \ldots, m; j = 0, \ldots n\} = 0..m \times 0..n
$$

which is a complete rectangle. (Note that the cartesian product of two sets of consecutive integers will be abbreviated similarly.) Consider three bidegree polynomials

$$\begin{aligned}
f(s,t) &= \sum_{(i,j)\in\mathcal{A}} a_{i,j} s^i t^j, \\
g(s,t) &= \sum_{(i,j)\in\mathcal{A}} b_{i,j} s^i t^j, \\
h(s,t) &= \sum_{(i,j)\in\mathcal{A}} c_{i,j} s^i t^j.
\end{aligned} \tag{1}$$

The unmixed *monomial support* of (1) is

$$\mathcal{A} = \{(i,j) \mid a_{i,j}, b_{i,j}, c_{i,j} \neq 0\} \subseteq \mathcal{A}_{m,n}.$$

The *Dixon polynomial* of (1) is

$$\Delta_\mathcal{A}(f(s,t), g(\alpha,t), h(\alpha,\beta)) = \frac{\begin{vmatrix} f(s,t) & g(s,t) & h(s,t) \\ f(\alpha,t) & g(\alpha,t) & h(\alpha,t) \\ f(\alpha,\beta) & g(\alpha,\beta) & h(\alpha,\beta) \end{vmatrix}}{(s-\alpha)(t-\beta)}. \tag{2}$$

Our aim is to investigate the matrix form

$$\Delta_\mathcal{A} = \begin{bmatrix} \cdots & s^\sigma t^\tau & \cdots \end{bmatrix} D_\mathcal{A} \begin{bmatrix} \cdots & \alpha^a \beta^b & \cdots \end{bmatrix}^T \tag{3}$$

where the coefficient matrix $D_\mathcal{A}$ is called the Dixon matrix of (1).

The monomials $s^\sigma t^\tau$ (resp. $\alpha^a \beta^b$) that occur in $\Delta_\mathcal{A}$ are called the row (resp. column) indices of $D_\mathcal{A}$. The monomial support $\mathcal{R}_\mathcal{A}$ (resp. $\mathcal{C}_\mathcal{A}$) of $\Delta_\mathcal{A}$ considered as a polynomial in s, t (resp. α, β) is called the row (resp. column) support of $D_\mathcal{A}$. That is,

$$\begin{aligned}
\mathcal{R}_\mathcal{A} &= \{(\sigma,\tau) \mid s^\sigma t^\tau \alpha^a \beta^b \text{ is a term in } \Delta_\mathcal{A} \text{ for some } a,b\}, \\
\mathcal{C}_\mathcal{A} &= \{(a,b) \mid s^\sigma t^\tau \alpha^a \beta^b \text{ is a term in } \Delta_\mathcal{A} \text{ for some } \sigma,\tau\}.
\end{aligned}$$

The ordered pair notation is overloaded to also mean a coefficient row vector:

$$(i,j) = \begin{bmatrix} a_{i,j} & b_{i,j} & c_{i,j} \end{bmatrix}.$$

A *bracket* is a 3×3 determinant which can be obtained as a vector triple product of three row vectors:

$$(i,j) \times (k,l) \cdot (p,q) = (i,j) \cdot (k,l) \times (p,q) = \begin{vmatrix} a_{i,j} & b_{i,j} & c_{i,j} \\ a_{k,l} & b_{k,l} & c_{k,l} \\ a_{p,q} & b_{p,q} & c_{p,q} \end{vmatrix}.$$

Using brackets, we can write

$$\begin{vmatrix} f(s,t) & g(s,t) & h(s,t) \\ f(\alpha,t) & g(\alpha,t) & h(\alpha,t) \\ f(\alpha,\beta) & g(\alpha,\beta) & h(\alpha,\beta) \end{vmatrix} = \sum_{(i,j),(k,l),(p,q)\in\mathcal{A}} (i,j) \cdot (k,l) \times (p,q) s^i t^{j+l} \alpha^{k+p} \beta^q \tag{4}$$

and thus the entries of $D_{\mathcal{A}}$ are linear in the coefficients of each of (1).

Clearly $\Delta_{A_{m,n}}$ is of degree $m-1$ in s, $2n-1$ in t, $2m-1$ in α, and $n-1$ in β. Consequently,

$$\mathcal{R}_{\mathcal{A}_{m,n}} = 0 \mathbin{..} m-1 \times 0 \mathbin{..} 2n-1, \quad \mathcal{C}_{\mathcal{A}_{m,n}} = 0 \mathbin{..} 2m-1 \times 0 \mathbin{..} n-1, \quad (5)$$

and the set cardinalities $\#\mathcal{R}_{\mathcal{A}_{m,n}} = \#\mathcal{C}_{\mathcal{A}_{m,n}} = 2mn$. Thus $D_{\mathcal{A}_{m,n}}$ is a square matrix of order $2mn$. The determinant $|D_{\mathcal{A}}|$ is the classical Dixon resultant of (1) when $\mathcal{A} = \mathcal{A}_{m,n}$.

In the examples, we shall abbreviate the bracket

$$(i,j) \times (k,l) \cdot (p,q) = (i,j) \cdot (k,l) \times (p,q) = ijklpq.$$

For example,

$$|D_{\mathcal{A}_{1,1}}| = \begin{vmatrix} 100100 \ 101100 \\ 110100 \ 110110 \end{vmatrix}.$$

3. The Dixon $\mathcal{A}$-Resultant Quotients

This chapter shows that when the unmixed monomial support $\mathcal{A}$ of (1) is obtained from cutting a 6-point isosceles triangle at one or more corners of $\mathcal{A}_{m,n}$, all the maximal minors and the corresponding extraneous factors can be identified, so that the sparse resultant with respect to $\mathcal{A}$ can be expressed explicitly as a quotient of determinants.

Consider the following subsets of $\mathcal{A}_{m,n}$:

$$
\begin{aligned}
T_1 &= \{(u,v) \mid u+v \le 2\}, & \delta T_1 &= \{(u,v) \mid u+v = 3\}; \\
T_2 &= \{(m-u,v) \mid u+v \le 2\}, & \delta T_2 &= \{(m-u,v) \mid u+v = 3\}; \\
T_3 &= \{(m-u,n-v) \mid u+v \le 2\}, & \delta T_3 &= \{(m-u,n-v) \mid u+v = 3\}; \\
T_4 &= \{(u,n-v) \mid u+v \le 2\}, & \delta T_4 &= \{(u,n-v) \mid u+v = 3\}.
\end{aligned}
$$

$$(6)$$

To relate these subsets of $\mathcal{A}_{m,n}$ to the row support $\mathcal{R}_{m,n}$ and the column support $\mathcal{C}_{m,n}$, we define the following eight translations:

$$\nu_i(x,y) = N_i \oplus (x,y), \quad \mu_i(x,y) = M_i \oplus (x,y), \quad i = 1,2,3,4,$$

where the symbol "$\oplus$" denotes the Minkowski sum and

$$
\begin{aligned}
N_1 &= (0,0), & M_1 &= (0,0), \\
N_2 &= (-1,0), & M_2 &= (m-1,0), \\
N_3 &= (-1,n-1), & M_3 &= (m-1,-1), \\
N_4 &= (0,n-1), & M_4 &= (0,-1).
\end{aligned}
$$

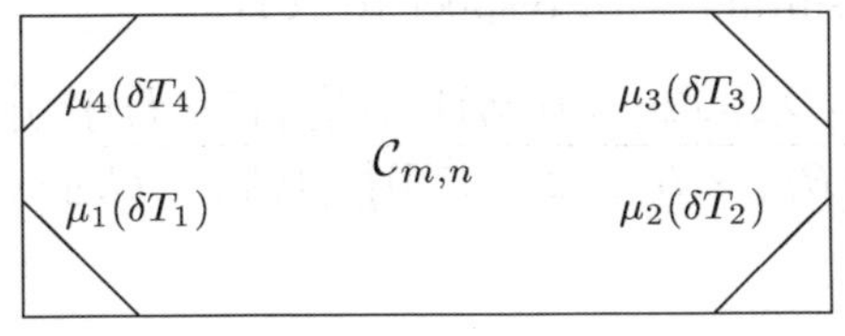

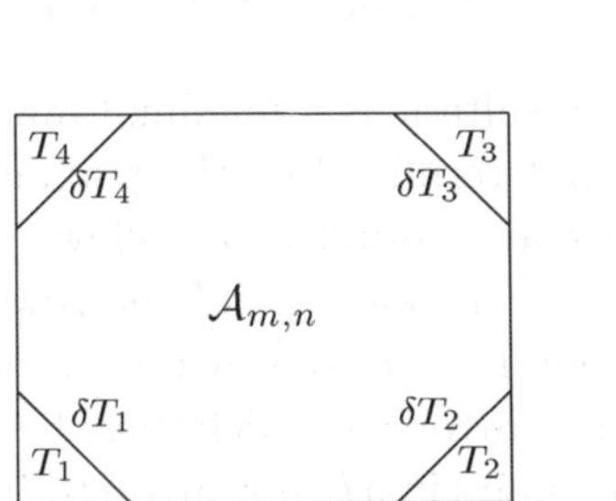

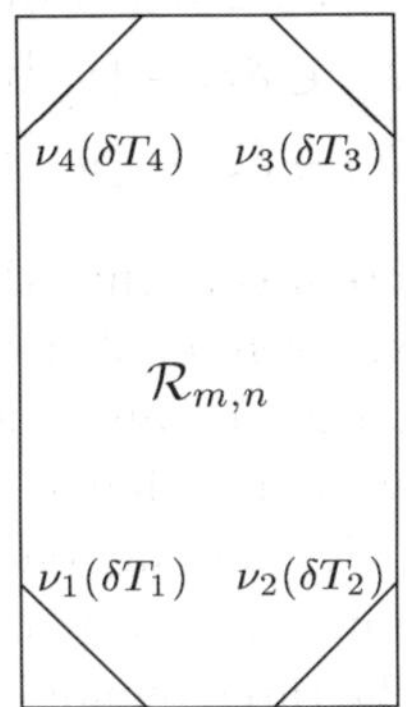

Fig. 1. $T_i, \delta T_i$ in the rectangular monomial support $\mathcal{A}_{m,n}$ (left), $\nu_i(\delta T_i)$ in the row support $\mathcal{R}_{m,n}$ (right) and $\mu_i(\delta T_i)$ in the column support $\mathcal{C}_{m,n}$ (top)

We also let for $i = 1, 2, 3, 4$:

$$\nu_i(S) = \{\nu_i(x,y) | (x,y) \in S\}, \quad \mu_i(S) = \{\mu_i(x,y) | (x,y) \in S\}.$$

The subsets $T_i, \delta T_i$ in $\mathcal{A}_{m,n}$, $\nu_i(\delta T_i)$ in $\mathcal{R}_{m,n}$, and $\mu_i(\delta T_i)$ in $\mathcal{C}_{m,n}$ are illustrated in Fig. 1.

Let $D_{\mathcal{A}}(\{(\sigma_1, \tau_1), \ldots, (\sigma_j, \tau_j)\}, \{(a_1, b_1), \ldots, (a_k, b_k)\})$ be a submatrix of $D_{\mathcal{A}}$ obtained by removing the j rows indexed by $s^{\sigma_1} t^{\tau_1}, \ldots, s^{\sigma_j} t^{\tau_j}$ and the k columns indexed by $\alpha^{a_1} \beta^{b_1}, \ldots, \alpha^{a_k} \beta^{b_k}$.

For any set S, we define $S^0 = \emptyset$ and $S^1 = S$. Thus there is 6-point isosceles triangular corner cutting at none or more corners if the unmixed monomial support of (1) is

$$\mathcal{A} = \mathcal{A}_{m,n} - \cup_{i=1}^{4} T_i^{\epsilon_i}$$

where $\epsilon_i = 0$ or 1, $i = 1, 2, 3, 4$. The following theorem gives the sparse resultant for $\mathcal{A}$.

Theorem 3: If $\mathcal{A} = \mathcal{A}_{m,n} - \cup_{i=1}^{4} T_i^{\epsilon_i}$ and

$$\mathcal{A} \cap (0 \times 0..n) \neq \emptyset, \quad \mathcal{A} \cap (0..m \times 0) \neq \emptyset,$$
$$\mathcal{A} \cap (m \times 0..n) \neq \emptyset, \quad \mathcal{A} \cap (0..m \times n) \neq \emptyset,$$

(7)

then the sparse resultant with respect to $\mathcal{A}$ is

$$\frac{\left|D_{\mathcal{A}}(\cup_{i=1}^{4}\{(\sigma_i,\tau_i)\}^{\epsilon_i},\cup_{i=1}^{4}\{(a_i,b_i)\}^{\epsilon_i})\right|}{\Pi_{i=1}^{4}\left(R_{i,1}\times R_{i,2}\cdot R_{i,3}\right)^{\epsilon_i}\Pi_{i=1}^{4}\left(C_{i,1}\times C_{i,2}\cdot C_{i,3}\right)^{\epsilon_i}}$$

where $\epsilon_i = 0$ or 1;

$$(\sigma_i,\tau_i)\in\mathcal{R}_{\mathcal{A}}\cap\nu_i(\delta T_i);\quad (a_i,b_i)\in\mathcal{C}_{\mathcal{A}}\cap\mu_i(\delta T_i);$$
$$R_{i,j}\in\delta T_i-\{\nu_i^{-1}(\sigma_i,\tau_i)\},$$
$$C_{i,j}\in\delta T_i-\{\mu_i^{-1}(a_i,b_i)\},\quad j=1,2,3;\quad i=1,2,3,4.$$

The theorem says that the sparse resultant is a maximal minor of $D_{\mathcal{A}}$ divided by an even number of brackets determined by the maximal minor. The maximal minor and the brackets are obtained as follows. For each corner i that is cut (that is, $\epsilon_i = 1$), discard any one of the rows indexed by $\mathcal{R}_{\mathcal{A}}\cap\nu_i(\delta T_i)$ and any one of the columns indexed by $\mathcal{C}_{\mathcal{A}}\cap\mu_i(\delta T_i)$. The three remaining ordered pairs in δT_i not involved in deleting the row form a bracket. The three remaining ordered pairs in δT_i not involved in deleting the column also form a bracket. The extraneous factors are the product of these pairs of brackets for all the corners that are cut.

Condition (7) requires that $\mathcal{A}$ has at least one monomial exponent, not necessarily distinct, along each of the four edges of $\mathcal{A}_{m,n}$ and is needed for Proposition 9. There is no loss of generality because degenerate bottom/left edges lead to common factors which should be discarded and degenerate top/right edges mean that the degrees are unnecessarily high.

The following examples illustrate the theorem. In the diagrams, elements of a monomial support are marked 1 and elements of T_i are marked 0. We also abbreviate the ordered pair $(i,j) = ij$ and the maximal minor

$$D_{\mathcal{A}}(\{(\sigma_1,\tau_1),\dots,\},\{(a_1,b_1),\dots\}) = D_{\mathcal{A}}(\sigma_1\tau_1,\dots\,;a_1b_1,\dots).$$

Example 4: Consider the monomial support $\mathcal{A}$ and its row and column supports:

```
                        0 0 0 1
                        0 0 1 1
        0 0 0 1 1       0 1 1 1
        0 0 1 1 1       1 1 1 1      0 0 0 1 1 1 1 1
        0 1 1 1 1       1 1 1 1      0 0 1 1 1 1 1 1
        1 1 1 1 1       1 1 1 1      0 1 1 1 1 1 1 1
            A             R_A              C_A
```

We have $\epsilon_1 = \epsilon_2 = \epsilon_3 = 0$ and

δT_4	00 11 22 33	
$\mathcal{R}_\mathcal{A} \cap \nu_4(\delta T_4)$	02 13 24 35	
$\mathcal{C}_\mathcal{A} \cap \mu_4(\delta T_4)$	10 21 32	

The 12 sparse resultant expressions given by Theorem 3 are

$$\frac{|D_\mathcal{A}(02;10)|}{112233 \cdot 002233}, \quad \frac{|D_\mathcal{A}(02;21)|}{112233 \cdot 001133}, \quad \frac{|D_\mathcal{A}(02;32)|}{112233 \cdot 001122},$$

$$\frac{|D_\mathcal{A}(13;10)|}{002233 \cdot 002233}, \quad \frac{|D_\mathcal{A}(13;21)|}{002233 \cdot 001133}, \quad \frac{|D_\mathcal{A}(13;32)|}{002233 \cdot 001122},$$

$$\frac{|D_\mathcal{A}(24;10)|}{001133 \cdot 002233}, \quad \frac{|D_\mathcal{A}(24;21)|}{001133 \cdot 001133}, \quad \frac{|D_\mathcal{A}(24;32)|}{001133 \cdot 001122},$$

$$\frac{|D_\mathcal{A}(35;10)|}{001122 \cdot 002233}, \quad \frac{|D_\mathcal{A}(35;21)|}{001122 \cdot 001133}, \quad \frac{|D_\mathcal{A}(35;32)|}{001122 \cdot 001122}.$$

Example 5: Consider the monomial support $\mathcal{A}$ and its row and column supports:

$$
\begin{array}{ccc}
 & \begin{matrix} 1\,1\,1\,1\,1\,1 \\ 1\,1\,1\,1\,1\,1 \end{matrix} & \\
\begin{matrix} 1\,1\,1\,1\,1\,1\,1 \\ 0\,1\,1\,1\,1\,1\,0 \\ 0\,0\,1\,1\,1\,0\,0 \\ 0\,0\,0\,1\,0\,0\,0 \end{matrix} &
\begin{matrix} 1\,1\,1\,1\,1\,1 \\ 0\,1\,1\,1\,1\,0 \\ 0\,0\,1\,1\,0\,0 \\ 0\,0\,0\,0\,0\,0 \end{matrix} &
\begin{matrix} 0\,1\,1\,1\,1\,1\,1\,1\,1\,1\,0 \\ 0\,0\,1\,1\,1\,1\,1\,1\,1\,0\,0 \\ 0\,0\,0\,1\,1\,1\,1\,1\,0\,0\,0 \end{matrix} \\
\mathcal{A} & \mathcal{R}_\mathcal{A} & \mathcal{C}_\mathcal{A}
\end{array}
$$

We have $\epsilon_3 = \epsilon_4 = 0$ and

δT_1	03 12 21 30		
$\mathcal{R}_\mathcal{A} \cap \nu_1(\delta T_1)$	03 12 21		
$\mathcal{C}_\mathcal{A} \cap \mu_1(\delta T_1)$	12 21 30		

δT_2	30 41 52 63		
$\mathcal{R}_\mathcal{A} \cap \nu_2(\delta T_2)$	31 42 53		
$\mathcal{C}_\mathcal{A} \cap \mu_2(\delta T_2)$	80 91 a2		

where a represents the integer 10.

The 81 sparse resultant expressions given by Theorem 3 include

$$\frac{|D_\mathcal{A}(03,31;12,80)|}{122130 \cdot 305263 \cdot 032130 \cdot 415263}, \quad \frac{|D_\mathcal{A}(21,53;30,a2)|}{031230 \cdot 304152 \cdot 031221 \cdot 304163}.$$

We are very grateful to a referee who pointed out that the following result is embedded in Theorem 3. Let $(s_i, t_i) \in \delta T_i$ be any of the two interior points. Then we have

Corollary 6: *If* $\mathcal{A} = \mathcal{A}_{m,n} - \cup_{i=1}^4 \left(T_i \cup \{(s_i, t_i)\}^{\delta_i}\right)^{\epsilon_i}$ *and*

$$\mathcal{A} \cap (0 \times 0..n) \neq \emptyset, \qquad \mathcal{A} \cap (0..m \times 0) \neq \emptyset,$$
$$\mathcal{A} \cap (m \times 0..n) \neq \emptyset, \qquad \mathcal{A} \cap (0..m \times n) \neq \emptyset,$$

then the sparse resultant with respect to $\mathcal{A}$ *is*

$$\frac{\left|D_{\mathcal{A}}(\cup_{i=1}^4 \{(\sigma_i, \tau_i)\}^{\epsilon_i(1-\delta_i)}, \cup_{i=1}^4 \{(a_i, b_i)\}^{\epsilon_i(1-\delta_i)})\right|}{\Pi_{i=1}^4 \left(R_{i,1} \times R_{i,2} \cdot R_{i,3}\right)^{\epsilon_i} \Pi_{i=1}^4 \left(C_{i,1} \times C_{i,2} \cdot C_{i,3}\right)^{\epsilon_i}}$$

where $\delta_i = 0$ *or* 1; $\epsilon_i = 0$ *or* 1;

$$(\sigma_i, \tau_i) \in \mathcal{R}_{\mathcal{A}} \cap \nu_i(\delta T_i); \quad (a_i, b_i) \in \mathcal{C}_{\mathcal{A}} \cap \mu_i(\delta T_i);$$
$$R_{i,j} \in \delta T_i - \{\nu_i^{-1}(\sigma_i, \tau_i)\}^{1-\delta_i} - \{(s_i, t_i)\}^{\delta_i},$$
$$C_{i,j} \in \delta T_i - \{\mu_i^{-1}(a_i, b_i)\}^{1-\delta_i} - \{(s_i, t_i)\}^{\delta_i}, \quad j = 1, 2, 3; \quad i = 1, 2, 3, 4.$$

Note that Corollary 6 becomes Theorem 3 when $\delta_1 = \delta_2 = \delta_3 = \delta_4 = 0$. When $\epsilon_i = \delta_i = 1$, the row and column corresponding to (s_i, t_i) are zero, so there is no need to de-select them explicitly when finding a minor of $D_{\mathcal{A}}$. Futhermore, the sets

$$R_{i,j} \in \delta T_i - \{\nu_i^{-1}(\sigma_i, \tau_i)\}^{1-\delta_i} - \{(s_i, t_i)\}^{\delta_i}$$

and

$$C_{i,j} \in \delta T_i - \{\mu_i^{-1}(a_i, b_i)\}^{1-\delta_i} - \{(s_i, t_i)\}^{\delta_i}$$

are identical. The following examples illustrate Corollary 6.

Example 7: We use the monomial support in Example 4 with the interior point $(2, 2) \in \delta T_4$ removed. The monomial support $\mathcal{A}$ and its row and column supports would then be:

$$
\begin{array}{ccc}
 & \begin{matrix} 0\ 0\ 0\ 1 \\ 0\ 0\ 0\ 1 \end{matrix} & \\
\begin{matrix} 0\ 0\ 0\ 1\ 1 \\ 0\ 0\ 0\ 1\ 1 \\ 0\ 1\ 1\ 1\ 1 \\ 1\ 1\ 1\ 1\ 1 \end{matrix} &
\begin{matrix} 0\ 1\ 1\ 1 \\ 1\ 1\ 1\ 1 \\ 1\ 1\ 1\ 1 \\ 1\ 1\ 1\ 1 \end{matrix} &
\begin{matrix} 0\ 0\ 0\ 1\ 1\ 1\ 1\ 1 \\ 0\ 0\ 0\ 1\ 1\ 1\ 1\ 1 \\ 0\ 1\ 1\ 1\ 1\ 1\ 1\ 1 \end{matrix} \\
\mathcal{A} & \mathcal{R}_{\mathcal{A}} & \mathcal{C}_{\mathcal{A}}
\end{array}
$$

We have $\epsilon_1 = \epsilon_2 = \epsilon_3 = 0$, $\epsilon_4 = \delta_4 = 1$ and

$$
\begin{array}{c|c}
\delta T_4 & 00\ 11\ 22\ 33 \\
\hline
\delta T_4 - \{(2, 2)\} & 00\ 11\ \ 33
\end{array}
$$

The sparse resultant given by Corollary 6 is $\frac{|D_{\mathcal{A}}|}{001133^2}$.

Example 8: We use the monomial support in Example 5 with the interior points $(2,1) \in \delta T_1$ and $(5,2) \in \delta T_2$ removed. The monomial support $\mathcal{A}$ and its row and column supports would then be:

$$
\begin{array}{ccc}
& \begin{matrix} 1\,1\,1\,1\,1\,1 \\ 1\,1\,1\,1\,1\,1 \end{matrix} & \\
\begin{matrix} 1\,1\,1\,1\,1\,1\,1 \\ 0\,1\,1\,1\,1\,0\,0 \\ 0\,0\,0\,1\,1\,0\,0 \\ 0\,0\,0\,1\,0\,0\,0 \end{matrix}
&
\begin{matrix} 1\,1\,1\,1\,1\,1 \\ 0\,1\,1\,1\,0\,0 \\ 0\,0\,0\,1\,0\,0 \\ 0\,0\,0\,0\,0\,0 \end{matrix}
&
\begin{matrix} 0\,1\,1\,1\,1\,1\,1\,1\,1\,0\,0 \\ 0\,0\,0\,1\,1\,1\,1\,1\,1\,0\,0 \\ 0\,0\,0\,1\,1\,1\,1\,1\,0\,0\,0 \end{matrix}
\\[6pt]
\mathcal{A} & \mathcal{R}_\mathcal{A} & \mathcal{C}_\mathcal{A}
\end{array}
$$

We have $\epsilon_3 = \epsilon_4 = 0$, $\epsilon_1 = \delta_1 = \epsilon_2 = \delta_2 = 1$ and

$$
\begin{array}{c|cccc}
\delta T_1 & 03 & 12 & 21 & 30 \\ \hline
\delta T_1 - \{(2,1)\} & 03 & 12 & & 30
\end{array}
\qquad
\begin{array}{c|cccc}
\delta T_2 & 30 & 41 & 52 & 63 \\ \hline
\delta T_2 - \{(5,2)\} & 30 & 41 & & 63
\end{array}
$$

The sparse resultant expression given by Corollary 6 is $\dfrac{|D_\mathcal{A}|}{0312\,30^2 \cdot 3041\,63^2}$.

4. A Proof of the Main Theorem

By the theory of $\mathcal{A}$-resultants [Cox *et al.*[7]], we only have to show that the quotient given in Theorem 3 has the following three properties: (1) it is actually a polynomial, (2) it has the right degree in the polynomial coefficients, and (3) its numerator is non-zero in general.

4.1. *The Row and Column Supports of $\mathcal{A} = \mathcal{A}_{m,n} - \cup_{i=1}^{4} T_i^{\epsilon_i}$*

It is essential in the following proofs to know the row and column supports of $D_\mathcal{A}$. They are described in the following proposition proved by the second author.[5]

Proposition 9: *Let $\mathcal{A}$ be as in Theorem 3. The row support of $\mathcal{A}$ is $\mathcal{R}_\mathcal{A} = \mathcal{R}_{m,n} - \bigcup_{i=1}^{4} \nu_i(T_i)^{\epsilon_i}$ and the column support of $\mathcal{A}$ is $\mathcal{C}_\mathcal{A} = \mathcal{C}_{m,n} - \bigcup_{i=1}^{4} \mu_i(T_i)^{\epsilon_i}$.*

4.2. *Dixon Matrix Entries After 6-Point Isosceles Triangular Corner Cutting*

The following entry formula given by the second author[3] will be used to derive simpler entry formulas for some rows and columns of $D_\mathcal{A}$ to exploit the simplification effects of isosceles triangular corner cutting.

Theorem 10: The Dixon matrix entry $D(s^\sigma t^\tau, \alpha^a \beta^b)$ indexed by $(s^\sigma t^\tau, \alpha^a \beta^b)$ is

$$
\sum_{u=0}^{\min(a,m-1-\sigma)} \sum_{v=0}^{\min(b,2n-1-\tau)} \sum_{k=\max(0,a-u-\sigma)}^{\min(m,a-u)} \sum_{l=\max(b+1,\tau+1+v-b)}^{\min(n,\tau+1+v)} B
$$
$$
+ \sum_{u=0}^{\min(a,m-1-\sigma)} \sum_{v=0}^{\min(b,2n-1-\tau)} \sum_{k=\max(0,a-u-m)}^{\min(\sigma,a-u)} \sum_{l=\max(b+1,\tau+1+v-n)}^{\min(n,\tau+v-b)} B
\tag{8}
$$

where $B = (\sigma+1+u, \tau+1+v-l) \times (k,l) \cdot (a-u-k, b-v)$, and $0 \le \sigma \le m-1$, $0 \le \tau \le 2n-1$, $0 \le a \le 2m-1$, $0 \le b \le n-1$.

The following proposition uses entry formula (8) to show that bottom left 6-point isosceles triangular corner cutting simplifies the entries of four columns of $D_\mathcal{A}$.

Proposition 11: *Let* $\mathcal{A} = \mathcal{A}_{m,n} - T_1$, $m \ge 3$, $n \ge 3$. *The entries of the four columns indexed by* $\alpha^a \beta^b$, $(a,b) \in \mu_1(\delta T_1)$, *are given by*

$$
D(s^\sigma t^\tau, \alpha^a \beta^b) = \sum_{l=\max(3,\tau+1-n)}^{\min(n,\tau+1)} (\sigma+1, \tau+1-l) \times (0,l) \cdot (a,b),
$$

where $(\sigma, \tau) \in \mathcal{R}_\mathcal{A}$.

Proof: In equation (8), when $(a,b) \in \mu_1(\delta T_1)$, the ordered pair $(a-u-k, b-v) \notin T_1$ if and only if $u = v = k = 0$. The equation obviously allows $u = v = 0$ and thus simplifies to

$$
D(s^\sigma t^\tau, \alpha^a \beta^b)
$$
$$
= \sum_{k=\max(0,a-\sigma)}^{\min(m,a)} \sum_{l=\max(b+1,\tau+1-b)}^{\min(n,\tau+1)} (\sigma+1, \tau+1-l) \times (k,l) \cdot (a-k, b)
$$
$$
+ \sum_{k=\max(0,a-m)}^{\min(\sigma,a)} \sum_{l=\max(b+1,\tau+1-n)}^{\min(n,\tau-b)} (\sigma+1, \tau+1-l) \times (k,l) \cdot (a-k, b).
$$

Consider the case $\sigma \le a - 1$. The first summation involves positive k and thus sums to zero. The second summation simplifies further to

$$D(s^\sigma t^\tau, \alpha^a \beta^b) = \sum_{l=\max(b+1,\tau+1-n)}^{\min(n,\tau-b)} (\sigma+1,\tau+1-l) \times (0,l) \cdot (a,b)$$

$$= \sum_{l=\max(b+1,\tau+1-n)}^{\min(n,\tau+1)} (\sigma+1,\tau+1-l) \times (0,l) \cdot (a,b)$$

because, when $\tau - b + 1 \le l$, we have either $(\sigma+1,\tau+1-l) \in T_1$ or $(\sigma+1,\tau+1-l) = (a,b)$.

Now consider the case $\sigma \ge a$. Both summations allow $u = k = v = 0$ and equation (8) simplifies to

$$\sum_{l=\max(b+1,\tau+1-b)}^{\min(n,\tau+1)} (\sigma+1,\tau+1-l) \times (0,l) \cdot (a,b)$$

$$+ \sum_{l=\max(b+1,\tau+1-n)}^{\min(n,\tau-b)} (\sigma+1,\tau+1-l) \times (0,l) \cdot (a,b).$$

When $\tau - b \le n$ and $\tau + 1 - b \ge b + 1$, it is obvious that the sums can be combined as

$$D(s^\sigma t^\tau, \alpha^a \beta^b) = \sum_{l=\max(b+1,\tau+1-n)}^{\min(n,\tau+1)} (\sigma+1,\tau+1-l) \times (0,l) \cdot (a,b).$$

It can be checked that when $\tau - b > n$ or $\tau + 1 - b < b + 1$, the combination also holds.

Thus the proposition is proved if we can adjust the lower bound of l to that required by the proposition. For $(a,b) = (0,3)$, the bracket vanishes when $l = 3$; thus the lower bound can be enlarged to $l = \max(3, \tau+1-n)$. For $(a,b) = (3,0), (2,1)$, we have $(0,l) \in T_1$ when $b+1 \le l \le 2$; thus the lower bound for l can be reduced to $l = \max(3, \tau+1-n)$. $\qquad\square$

Remark 12: The proof of Proposition 17 requires the summation ranges for the four formulas to be alike.

Remark 13: Consider the case $\mathcal{A} \cap (0 \times 0..n) = \{(0,3)\}$. The formula produces zero when $(a,b) = (0,3)$. This is correct since the column indexed by $\alpha^0 \beta^3$ does not exist. For the other $(a,b) \in \mu_1(\delta T_1)$, the formula produces zero unless $2 \le \tau \le n+2$; otherwise, it simplifies further to become

$$D(s^\sigma t^\tau, \alpha^a \beta^b) = (\sigma+1, \tau-2) \times (0,3) \cdot (a,b).$$

The following proposition shows that 6-point isosceles triangular top right corner cutting simplifies the entries of four rows in the Dixon matrix.

Proposition 14: *Let $\mathcal{A} = \mathcal{A}_{m,n} - T_3$, $m \geq 3$, $n \geq 3$, The entries of the four rows indexed by $s^\sigma t^\tau$, $(\sigma, \tau) \in \nu_3(\delta T_3)$, are given by*

$$D(s^\sigma t^\tau, \alpha^a \beta^b) = \sum_{k=\max(0,a-m)}^{\min(m-3,a)} (\sigma + 1, \tau + 1 - n) \times (k, n) \cdot (a - k, b),$$

where $(a, b) \in \mathcal{C}_{\mathcal{A}}$.

Proof: In equation (8), when $(\sigma, \tau) \in \nu_3(\delta T_3)$, it can be checked that the ordered pair $(\sigma + 1 + u, \tau + 1 + v - l) \notin T_3$ if and only if $u = v = 0$, $l = n$.

Clearly both sums of equation (8) allow $u = v = 0$. The first sum allows $l = n$ and requires $b \geq \tau + 1 - n$. The second sum allows $l = n$ when $b \leq \tau - n$. Hence, when $b \geq \tau + 1 - n$, equation (8) simplifies to

$$D(s^\sigma t^\tau, \alpha^a \beta^b) = \sum_{k=\max(0,a-\sigma)}^{\min(m,a)} (\sigma + 1, \tau + 1 - n) \times (k, n) \cdot (a - k, b)$$

and, when $b \leq \tau - n$, equation (8) simplifies to

$$D(s^\sigma t^\tau, \alpha^a \beta^b) = \sum_{k=\max(0,a-m)}^{\min(\sigma,a)} (\sigma + 1, \tau + 1 - n) \times (k, n) \cdot (a - k, b).$$

When $k \geq m - 2$, $(k, n) = 0$. When $(\sigma, \tau) = (m - 4, 2n - 1)$, the bracket is 0 when $k = m - 3$. This means that the upper bound of k of both formulas can be written as $\min(m-3, a)$. This proves the proposition when $b \leq \tau - n$.

We can write $(\sigma, \tau) = (m - j, 2n - 5 + j)$, $j = 1, 2, 3, 4$. To enlarge the lower bound from $\max(0, a - \sigma)$ to $\max(0, a - m)$, we need to show that the bracket vanishes for $a - m \leq k \leq a - m + j - 1$ and $j = 1, 2, 3$. This can be checked directly for $\tau + 1 - n \leq b \leq n - 1$. Note that the case $j = 4$ is excluded because there are no values of b such that $b \geq \tau + 1 - n = n$. This completes the proof. $\qquad\square$

Remark 15: The proof of Proposition 20 requires the summation ranges for all four formulas to be alike.

Remark 16: Consider the case $\mathcal{A} \cap (0..m \times n) = \{(m-3, n)\}$. The formula produces zero when $(\sigma, \tau) = (m - 4, 2n - 1)$. This is correct since the row indexed by $s^{m-4} t^{2n-1}$ does not exist. For the other (σ, τ) the formula produces zero unless $m - 3 \le a \le 2m - 3$; otherwise, the formula simplifies further to become

$$D(s^\sigma t^\tau, \alpha^a \beta^b) = (\sigma + 1, \tau + 1 - n) \times (m - 3, n) \cdot (a - m + 3, b).$$

4.3. *Divisibility of Some Minors by Brackets*

Proposition 17: *Let $A = A_{m,n} - T_1$. For any $(a', b') \in \mu_1(\delta T_1) \cap C_A$, a minor of D_A containing all the columns indexed by $\alpha^a \beta^b$, $(a, b) \in \mu_1(\delta T_1) \cap C_A - \{(a', b')\}$ is divisible by the bracket $C_1 \times C_2 \cdot C_3$, where $\{C_1, C_2, C_3\} = \delta T_1 - \{\mu_1^{-1}(a', b')\}$.*

Proof: We examine two cases: $n > 3$ and $n = 3$.

Case $n > 3$. By Proposition 11, any row of the four columns indexed by $\alpha^a \beta^b$, $(a, b) \in \mu_1(\delta T_1)$, can be written as

$$\left[\sum_{l \in L} A_l \times P_l \cdot C_1, \sum_{l \in L} A_l \times P_l \cdot C_2, \sum_{l \in L} A_l \times P_l \cdot C_3, \sum_{l \in L} A_l \times P_l \cdot C_4 \right] \quad (9)$$

where $A_l = (\sigma + 1, \tau + 1 - l)$, $P_l = (0, l)$, $C_i = (a_i, b_i)$ are row vectors, the ordered pair $(a_i, b_i) \in \delta T_1$, $i = 1, 2, 3, 4$, and $L = \max(3, \tau + 1 - n) .. \min(n, \tau + 1)$. The row can be written as a product of matrices:

$$\left[\sum_{l \in L} A_l \times P_l \right] \left[C_1^T C_2^T C_3^T C_4^T \right].$$

This shows that the four columns indexed by $\alpha^a \beta^b$, $(a, b) \in \mu_1(\delta T_1)$, are linearly dependent as they are generated by three columns. Hence $|D_A| = 0$.

Furthermore, we see that any 3×3 submatrix whose columns are indexed by $\alpha^{a'} \beta^{b'}$, $(a', b') \in \mu_1(\delta T_1) - \{(a, b)\}$, is divisible by the bracket $|C_{j_1}^T C_{j_2}^T C_{j_3}^T|$, where $\{C_{j_1}, C_{j_2}, C_{j_3}\} = \delta T_1 - \{\mu_1^{-1}(a, b)\}$.

Case $n = 3$. By Remark 13 of Proposition 11, we can write any row of the three columns indexed by $\alpha^a \beta^b$, $(a, b) \in \mu_1(\delta T_1) \cap C_A = \mu_1(\delta T_1) - \{(0, 3)\}$, in the form

$$\left[A \times P \cdot C_1, A \times P \cdot C_2, A \times P \cdot C_3 \right] = (A \times P)[C_1^T C_2^T C_3^T] \quad (10)$$

where $P = (0, 3)$, $A = (\sigma + 1, \tau - 2)$, $C_1 = (1, 2)$, $C_2 = (2, 1)$, $C_3 = (3, 0)$. Thus the three indexed columns are generated from three other columns whose rows are of the form $A \times P$. Since $A \times P \cdot P = 0$, these three columns are linearly dependent and again $|D_A| = 0$.

We also see that any 2×2 submatrix of any two columns indexed by $\alpha^a \beta^b$, $(a, b) \in \mu_1(\delta T_1) \cap C_A = \mu_1(\delta T_1) - \{(0, 3)\}$, is of the form

$$\begin{vmatrix} A_1 \times P \cdot C_{j_1} & A_1 \times P \cdot C_{j_2} \\ A_2 \times P \cdot C_{j_1} & A_2 \times P \cdot C_{j_2} \end{vmatrix} = (A_1 \times A_2 \cdot P)(C_{j_1} \times C_{j_2} \cdot P).$$

 Foo and Chionh

Thus any minor involving any two of these columns is divisible by $C_{j_1} \times C_{j_2}$. $(0,3)$, where $\{C_{j_1}, C_{j_2}\} = \delta T_1 \cap C_{\mathcal{A}} - \{\mu_1^{-1}(a,b)\} = \delta T_1 - \{\mu_1^{-1}(a,b), (0,3)\}$.

$\square$

We state the linear dependence of the columns indexed by $\mu_1(\delta T_1) \cap C_{\mathcal{A}}$ as a corollary.

Corollary 18: *Let $\mathcal{A} = \mathcal{A}_{m,n} - T_1$. The columns of $D_{\mathcal{A}}$ indexed by $\alpha^a \beta^b$, $(a,b) \in \mu_1(\delta T_1) \cap C_{\mathcal{A}}$, are linearly dependent.*

This divisibility result can be generalized to other corners.

Proposition 19: *Let $\mathcal{A} = \mathcal{A}_{m,n} - T_i$, $i = 1,2,3,4$. For any $(a',b') \in \mu_i(\delta T_i) \cap C_{\mathcal{A}}$, a minor of $D_{\mathcal{A}}$ containing all the columns indexed by $\alpha^a \beta^b$, $(a,b) \in \mu_i(\delta T_i) \cap C_{\mathcal{A}} - \{(a',b')\}$, is divisible by the bracket $C_1 \times C_2 \cdot C_3$, where $\{C_1, C_2, C_3\} = \delta T_i - \{\mu_i^{-1}(a',b')\}$.*

Proof: The case $i = 1$ is Proposition 17. For the case $i = 3$, let $\bar{s} = s^{-1}$, $\bar{t} = t^{-1}$, $\bar{\alpha} = \alpha^{-1}$, $\bar{\beta} = \beta^{-1}$. We have

$$\begin{aligned}
\Delta_{\mathcal{A}}(f(s,t), g(\alpha,t), h(\alpha,\beta)) \\
= s^{m-1} t^{2n-1} \alpha^{2m-1} \beta^{n-1} \Delta_{\overline{\mathcal{A}}}(\overline{f}(\bar{s},\bar{t}), \overline{g}(\bar{\alpha},\bar{t}), \overline{h}(\bar{\alpha},\bar{\beta}))
\end{aligned} \tag{11}$$

where

$$\overline{f}(s,t) = \sum_{i=0}^{m} \sum_{j=0}^{n} a_{m-i,n-j} s^i t^j,$$

$$\overline{g}(s,t) = \sum_{i=0}^{m} \sum_{j=0}^{n} b_{m-i,n-j} s^i t^j,$$

$$\overline{h}(s,t) = \sum_{i=0}^{m} \sum_{j=0}^{n} c_{m-i,n-j} s^i t^j.$$

Obviously we have (1) $(a,b) \in \mathcal{A}$ if and only if $(m-a, n-b) \in \overline{\mathcal{A}}$ and thus $\overline{\mathcal{A}} = \mathcal{A}_{m,n} - T_1$; and (2) $\overline{\alpha}^a \overline{\beta}^b$ appears in $\Delta_{\overline{\mathcal{A}}}$ if and only if the monomial $\alpha^{2m-1-a} \beta^{n-1-b}$ appears in $\Delta_{\mathcal{A}}$ by (11). With these observations it is straightforward to show that (1) $(a,b) \in \mu_1(\delta T_1) \cap C_{\overline{\mathcal{A}}}$ if and only if $(2m-1-a, n-1-b) \in \mu_3(\delta T_3) \cap C_{\mathcal{A}}$, and (2) $\delta T_1 - \{\mu_1^{-1}(a,b)\} \subseteq \overline{\mathcal{A}}$ is equivalent to $\delta T_3 - \{\mu_3^{-1}(2m-1-a, n-1-b)\} \subseteq \mathcal{A}$. Consequently, by applying Proposition 17 to $\overline{\mathcal{A}}$ we prove the desired result for $\mathcal{A}$.

For the cases $i = 2,4$, we let respectively $\bar{s} = s^{-1}$ and $\bar{\alpha} = \alpha^{-1}$, $\bar{t} = t^{-1}$ and $\bar{\beta} = \beta^{-1}$ and prove similarly. $\square$

By using the entry formula in Proposition 14 and imitating the proofs for Propositions 17 and 19, we have the following propositions and corollary.

Proposition 20: *Let $\mathcal{A} = \mathcal{A}_{m,n} - T_3$. For any $(\sigma', \tau') \in \nu_3(\delta T_3) \cap \mathcal{R}_\mathcal{A}$, a minor of $D_\mathcal{A}$ containing all the rows indexed by $s^\sigma t^\tau$, $(\sigma, \tau) \in \nu_3(\delta T_3) \cap \mathcal{R}_\mathcal{A} - \{(\sigma', \tau')\}$, is divisible by the bracket $R_1 \times R_2 \cdot R_3$, where $\{R_1, R_2, R_3\} = \delta T_3 - \{\nu_3^{-1}(\sigma', \tau')\}$.*

Corollary 21: *Let $\mathcal{A} = \mathcal{A}_{m,n} - T_3$. The rows of $D_\mathcal{A}$ indexed by $s^\sigma t^\tau$, $(\sigma, \tau) \in \nu_3(\delta T_3) \cap \mathcal{R}_\mathcal{A}$, are linearly dependent.*

Proposition 22: *Let $\mathcal{A} = \mathcal{A}_{m,n} - T_i$, $i = 1, 2, 3, 4$. For any $(\sigma', \tau') \in \nu_i(\delta T_i) \cap \mathcal{R}_\mathcal{A}$, a minor of $D_\mathcal{A}$ containing all the rows indexed by $s^\sigma t^\tau$, $(\sigma, \tau) \in \nu_i(\delta T_i) \cap \mathcal{R}_\mathcal{A} - \{(\sigma', \tau')\}$, is divisible by the bracket $R_1 \times R_2 \cdot R_3$, where $\{R_1, R_2, R_3\} = \delta T_i - \{\nu_i^{-1}(\sigma', \tau')\}$.*

By combining Propositions 19 and 22, we can assert that the quotient of Theorem 3 is actually a polynomial.

Theorem 23: The product $\Pi_{i=1}^4 \left(R_{i,1} \times R_{i,2} \cdot R_{i,3}\right)^{\epsilon_i} \left(C_{i,1} \times C_{i,2} \cdot C_{i,3}\right)^{\epsilon_i}$ divides the minor $\left|D_\mathcal{A}(\cup_{i=1}^4 \{(\sigma_i, \tau_i)\}^{\epsilon_i}, \cup_{i=1}^4 \{(a_i, b_i)\}^{\epsilon_i})\right|$, where

$$\{R_{i,1}, R_{i,2}, R_{i,3}\} = \delta T_i - \{\nu_i^{-1}(\sigma_i, \tau_i)\}, \quad (\sigma_i, \tau_i) \in \mathcal{R}_\mathcal{A} \cap \nu_i(\delta T_i);$$
$$\{C_{i,1}, C_{i,2}, C_{i,3}\} = \delta T_i - \{\mu_i^{-1}(a_i, b_i)\}, \quad (a_i, b_i) \in \mathcal{C}_\mathcal{A} \cap \mu_i(\delta T_i).$$

Proof: Consider $i = 1$. It is easy to check using Proposition 17 that the submatrix whose rows are indexed by $s^\sigma t^\tau$, $(\sigma, \tau) \in \nu_1(\delta T_1) \cap \mathcal{R}_\mathcal{A} = R$, and whose columns are indexed by $\alpha^a \beta^b$, $(a, b) \in \mu_1(\delta T_1) \cap \mathcal{C}_\mathcal{A} = C$, is a zero matrix. Since the factor $C_{1,1} \times C_{1,2} \cdot C_{1,3}$ arises from the columns of a proper subset of C and the factor $R_{1,1} \times R_{1,2} \cdot R_{1,3}$ arises from the rows of a proper subset of R, by Laplace expansion we see that any minor of $D_\mathcal{A}$ containing these rows and columns is divisible by the product $(R_{1,1} \times R_{1,2} \cdot R_{1,3})(C_{1,1} \times C_{1,2} \cdot C_{1,3})$.

The result then follows from the divisibility proofs of the propositions given above by noting that the divisibility at a corner is independent of the situations at the other corners except when (1) $n = 6$ with $\epsilon_1 \epsilon_4 = 1$ or $\epsilon_2 \epsilon_3 = 1$ or (2) $m = 6$ with $\epsilon_1 \epsilon_2 = 1$ or $\epsilon_3 \epsilon_4 = 1$.

Consider the case in which $n = 6$ and $\epsilon_1 \epsilon_4 = 1$. The left edge of $\mathcal{A}$ has only one monomial t^3. Thus the proof that $C_{1,1} \times C_{1,2} \cdot C_{1,3}$ divides the minor is essentially the same as the proof for $n = 3$ in Proposition 17. The other exceptional cases are dealt with similarly. $\qquad\square$

4.4. *The Quotient Has the Right Degree*

Proposition 24: *If* $\dfrac{\left| D_{\mathcal{A}}(\cup_{i=1}^{4}\{(\sigma_i,\tau_i)\}^{\epsilon_i},\cup_{i=1}^{4}\{(a_i,b_i)\}^{\epsilon_i})\right|}{\Pi_{i=1}^{4}\left(R_{i,1}\times R_{i,2}\cdot R_{i,3}\right)^{\epsilon_i}\Pi_{i=1}^{4}\left(C_{i,1}\times C_{i,2}\cdot C_{i,3}\right)^{\epsilon_i}} \neq 0,$ *it has the correct degree in the coefficients.*

Proof: Note that the entries of $D_{\mathcal{A}}$ and the brackets $R_{i,1}\times R_{i,2}\cdot R_{i,3}$, $C_{i,1}\times C_{i,2}\cdot C_{i,3}$ are linear in each of the coefficients of f, g, h. Thus we need only show that the order of the minor $\left|D_{\mathcal{A}}(\cup_{i=1}^{4}\{(\sigma_i,\tau_i)\}^{\epsilon_i},\cup_{i=1}^{4}\{(a_i,b_i)\}^{\epsilon_i})\right|$ minus $2\sum_{i=1}^{4}\epsilon_i$ is equal to twice the area of the Newton polygon of $\mathcal{A}$.

By Proposition 9, the order of $D_{\mathcal{A}}$ is $2mn - \sum_{i=1}^{4} 6\epsilon_i$. Thus the order of the minor is $2mn - \sum_{i=1}^{4} 7\epsilon_i$. By direct calculation, we see that when $T_i^{\epsilon_i}$ is cut, a triangular area of size $\frac{9\epsilon_i}{2}$ is chipped away from the rectangular Newton polygon of $\mathcal{A}_{m,n}$. Thus the area of the Newton polygon is $mn - \sum_{i=1}^{4}\frac{9\epsilon_i}{2}$. Clearly, we have

$$\text{order of } D_{\mathcal{A}}(\cup_{i=1}^{4}\{(\sigma_i,\tau_i)\}^{\epsilon_i},\cup_{i=1}^{4}\{(a_i,b_i)\}^{\epsilon_i}) - 2\sum_{i=1}^{4}\epsilon_i$$

$$= 2 \times \text{ area of Newton polygon.}$$

Thus the quotient has the expected degree. $\qquad\square$

4.5. *The Quotient Is Non-Zero*

Proposition 25: *The columns responsible for the factors* $C_{i,1}\times C_{i,2}\cdot C_{i,3}$, $i = 1,2,3,4$, *are linearly independent.*

Proof: *Outline.* For each corner i with $\epsilon_i = 1$, consider the columns indexed by $J_i = \mu_i(\delta T_i)^{\epsilon_i} \cap \mathcal{C}_{\mathcal{A}}$. In general there are four columns indexed by J_i; the case of three columns is degenerate and will be handled later. For these $k = 4\sum_{i=1}^{4}\epsilon_i$ columns ordered by i, we will show that k rows can be selected such that the $k \times k$ submatrix of $D_{\mathcal{A}}$ can be written as a $\sum_{i=1}^{4}\epsilon_i \times \sum_{i=1}^{4}\epsilon_i$ diagonal matrix whose diagonal entry is a 4×4 block

$$K_i = \begin{pmatrix} A_i & 0 & B_i & C_i \\ 0 & 0 & D_i & E_i \\ 0 & F_i & 0 & G_i \\ 0 & H_i & I_i & 0 \end{pmatrix} \tag{12}$$

where $A_i, \ldots, I_i$ are non-zero sums of brackets. This shows obviously that columns from different i's are linearly independent. By $B_iE_i - C_iD_i \neq 0$

and the structure of K_i, we see easily that any three columns of J_i are independent.

All the above claims are verified mechanically by a Maple program with the assume facility for symbolic m and n.

Monomials in the support. We need only consider the special monomial support

$$\mathcal{A} = \cup_{i=1}^4 \delta T_i^{\epsilon_i} \cup \{(0,0)\}^{1-\epsilon_1} \cup \{(m,0)\}^{1-\epsilon_2} \cup \{(m,n)\}^{1-\epsilon_3} \cup \{(0,n)\}^{1-\epsilon_4}.$$

This is because if the k columns for this special $\mathcal{A}$ are independent then they will remain independent for a general $\mathcal{A}$.

Column indices. The k columns are ordered and indexed by

$$\begin{aligned}
& \{\beta^3, \alpha^1\beta^2, \alpha^2\beta^1, \alpha^3\}^{\epsilon_1} \\
\cup \quad & \{\alpha^{2m-1}\beta^3, \alpha^{2m-2}\beta^2, \alpha^{2m-3}\beta^1, \alpha^{2m-4}\}^{\epsilon_2} \\
\cup \quad & \{\alpha^{2m-1}\beta^{n-4}, \alpha^{2m-2}\beta^{n-3}, \alpha^{2m-3}\beta^{n-2}, \alpha^{2m-4}\beta^{n-1}\}^{\epsilon_3} \\
\cup \quad & \{\beta^{n-4}, \alpha^1\beta^{n-3}, \alpha^2\beta^{n-2}, \alpha^3\beta^{n-1}\}^{\epsilon_4}.
\end{aligned}$$

Row indices. The k rows needed are ordered and indexed by

$$\begin{aligned}
& \left(\{t^{n+1}\}^{(1-\epsilon_4)} \cup \{t^{n-2}\}^{\epsilon_4} \cup \{t^4, s^1 t^3, s^2 t^2\}\right)^{\epsilon_1} \\
\cup \quad & \left(\{s^{m-1}t^{n+1}\}^{(1-\epsilon_3)} \cup \{s^{m-1}t^{n-2}\}^{\epsilon_3} \cup \{s^{m-1}t^4, s^{m-2}t^3, s^{m-3}t^2\}\right)^{\epsilon_2} \\
\cup \quad & \left(\{s^{m-1}t^{n-2}\}^{(1-\epsilon_2)} \cup \{s^{m-1}t^{n+1}\}^{\epsilon_2} \cup \{s^{m-1}t^{2n-5}, s^{m-2}t^{2n-4}, s^{m-3}t^{2n-3}\}\right)^{\epsilon_3} \\
\cup \quad & \left(\{t^{n-2}\}^{(1-\epsilon_1)} \cup \{t^{n+1}\}^{\epsilon_1} \cup \{t^{2n-5}, s^1 t^{2n-4}, s^2 t^{2n-3}\}\right)^{\epsilon_4}.
\end{aligned}$$

The expression shows that for each corner $i = 1, 2, 3, 4$, one of the four rows needed depends on the cutting configuration of the vertically opposite corner and is indexed by $\{\cdots\}^{(1-\epsilon_{5-i})\epsilon_i} \cup \{\cdots\}^{\epsilon_{5-i}\epsilon_i}$. The vertically opposite corner of the top right, top left, bottom left, bottom right corner is the bottom right, bottom left, top left, top right corner respectively.

Mechanical proving. We describe the mechanical prover for the case when all the corners of the monomial support undergo 6-point isosceles triangular cutting. The other configurations are proved similarly. The program proves that the 16×16 submatrix has a block diagonal structure by actually finding the matrix entries using equation (8) of Theorem 10. Since $\mathcal{A}$ has sixteen monomials, there are $\binom{16}{3} = 560$ distinct modulo sign non-zero brackets $(e_1, e_2) \times (e_3, e_4) \cdot (e_5, e_6)$ to consider. For each of the 16×16 matrix entries, the value of (σ, τ) and (a, b) are known. The program then solves for u,v,k,l by equating $\sigma + 1 + u = e_1$, $\tau + 1 + v - l = e_2$, $k = e_3$, $l = e_4$, $a - u - k = e_5$, $b - v = e_6$. A bracket is in the entry if and only if u,v,k,l satisfy the summation bounds of equation (8). The mechanical prover finally checks that the $k \times k$ submatrix is block diagonal and that the diagonal blocks are given by (12). Finally it checks that the said 2×2 determinant in each block is non-zero.

Degenerate cases. When $n = 6$, we may not need all three columns in a corner to generate an extraneous factor (see Theorem 23). In such cases, we observe that the original $k \times k$ non-singular matrix would shrink to a $k' \times k'$, $k' \leq k$, submatrix which is a block diagonal matrix with 3×3 or 4×4 blocks. The block structure corresponding to those J_i with only three columns would be

$$\begin{pmatrix} 0 & A_i & B_i \\ C_i & 0 & D_i \\ E_i & F_i & 0 \end{pmatrix}.$$

This block structure shows that any two of the three columns are independent. $\qquad\square$

Proposition 26: *The rows responsible for the factors $R_{i,1} \times R_{i,2} \cdot R_{i,3}$, $i = 1, 2, 3, 4$, are linearly independent.*

Proof: The proof is exactly the same as the proof of Proposition 25 except for the selection of rows and columns. The k rows are ordered and indexed by:

$$\{s^3, s^2 t^1, s^1 t^2, t^3\}^{\epsilon_1}$$
$$\cup \quad \{s^{m-4}, s^{m-3} t^1, s^{m-2} t^2, s^{m-1} t^3\}^{\epsilon_2}$$
$$\cup \{s^{m-4} t^{2n-1}, s^{m-3} t^{2n-2}, s^{m-2} t^{2n-3}, s^{m-1} t^{2n-4}\}^{\epsilon_3}$$
$$\cup \quad \{s^3 t^{2n-1}, s^2 t^{2n-2}, s^1 t^{2n-3}, t^{2n-4}\}^{\epsilon_4}.$$

The k columns needed are ordered and indexed by:

$$\left(\{\alpha^{m+1}\}^{(1-\epsilon_2)} \cup \{\alpha^{m-2}\}^{\epsilon_2} \cup \{\alpha^4, \alpha^3 \beta^1, \alpha^2 \beta^2\}\right)^{\epsilon_1}$$
$$\cup \quad \left(\{\alpha^{m-2}\}^{(1-\epsilon_1)} \cup \{\alpha^{m+1}\}^{\epsilon_1} \cup \{\alpha^{2m-5}, \alpha^{2m-4} \beta^1, \alpha^{2m-3} \beta^2\}\right)^{\epsilon_2}$$
$$\cup \quad \left(\{\alpha^{m-2} \beta^{n-1}\}^{(1-\epsilon_4)} \cup \{\alpha^{m+1} \beta^{n-1}\}^{\epsilon_4}\right.$$
$$\left.\cup \{\alpha^{2m-5} \beta^{n-1}, \alpha^{2m-4} \beta^{n-2}, \alpha^{2m-3} \beta^{n-3}\}\right)^{\epsilon_3}$$
$$\cup \left(\{\alpha^{m+1} \beta^{n-1}\}^{(1-\epsilon_3)} \cup \{\alpha^{m-2} \beta^{n-1}\}^{\epsilon_3} \cup \{\alpha^4 \beta^{n-1}, \alpha^3 \beta^{n-2}, \alpha^2 \beta^{n-3}\}\right)^{\epsilon_4}.$$

The block form for this proof is the transpose of that in the proof of Proposition 25. $\qquad\square$

Proposition 27: *The minor $\left|D_{\mathcal{A}}(\cup_{i=1}^4 \{(\sigma_i, \tau_i)\}^{\epsilon_i}, \cup_{i=1}^4 \{(a_i, b_i)\}^{\epsilon_i})\right| \neq 0$.*

Proof: Saxena[19] and Emiris *et al.*[11] showed that any maximal minor of $D_{\mathcal{A}}$ is a multiple of the $\mathcal{A}$-resultant. Since the columns in Proposition 25 and the rows in Proposition 26 are independent, there is a maximal minor M containing these columns and rows. By Propositions 25 and 26, the maximal minor M has the factors $\Pi_{i=1}^{4}\left(R_{i,1} \times R_{i,2} \cdot R_{i,3}\right)^{\epsilon_i}\Pi_{i=1}^{4}\left(C_{i,1} \times C_{i,2} \cdot C_{i,3}\right)^{\epsilon_i}$. Thus $M = \Pi_{i=1}^{4}\left(R_{i,1} \times R_{i,2} \cdot R_{i,3}\right)^{\epsilon_i}\Pi_{i=1}^{4}\left(C_{i,1} \times C_{i,2} \cdot C_{i,3}\right)^{\epsilon_i} N$ for some polynomial N and N is a multiple of the $\mathcal{A}$-resultant. By Proposition 24, the degree of N in the coefficients of the polynomials f, g, h is at least

$$2mn - \sum_{i=1}^{4} 7\epsilon_i - 2\sum_{i=1}^{4} \epsilon_i.$$

That means the degree of M in the coefficients of each of the polynomials is at least

$$2mn - \sum_{i=1}^{4} 7\epsilon_i$$

which is the order of the minor. This means that M and the minor differ by a constant factor and thus the minor is non-zero since M is not. $\square$

5. Conclusion and Future Work

Unlike the case in which the unmixed monomial support $\mathcal{A}$ is a complete rectangle with or without corner edge cutting or a corner-cut rectangle with or without point pasting, the Dixon determinant vanishes when $\mathcal{A}$ is a complete rectangle with 6-point isosceles triangular cutting at one or more corners. But many pure bracket quotient form sparse resultant formulas can still be obtained because we are able to identify all the maximal minors, and for each maximal minor we are also able to predict two brackets per corner such that their product is the extraneous factors.

The proof of our results is quite standard: we show that a certain minor is divisible by a product of certain brackets, the result has the right degree in the polynomial coefficients if it is non-zero, and finally that the minor is indeed maximal. It is pleasant to note that all this can be accomplished with an entry formula (for the divisibility by a product of brackets) and a mechanical prover (for the maximality of minors).

Unfortunately, when we apply this method to 10-point isosceles triangular corner cutting, the quotient formula produces a multiple of the sparse resultant and thus is no longer exact; it can be checked that a quadratic extraneous factor per corner is unaccounted for in this method. Worst, for isosceles triangle having more than 10 points, the quotient formula itself vanishes. Either a generalization of our method or an entirely new method to handle larger isosceles triangular corner cuttings seems worth pursuing.

At this moment our approach seems to be too constructive to be able to deal with systems with more than three equations or mixed monomial supports as we have to know exactly what the entries of the Dixon determinant are. But we have exhibited a class of monomial supports for which the maximal minors are a multiple of the sparse resultant; furthermore, we show exactly how to find the maximal minors and for each maximal minor what the extraneous factors are. As a first step for further generalization of the relationship among sparse resultants, maximal minors, and extraneous factors, we are studying the sparse resultants for monomial supports with arbitrary isosceles triangular corner cutting.

References

1. F. Aries, R. Senoussi (2001). *An implicitization algorithm for rational surfaces with no base points.* J. Symbolic Computation, 31(4): 357–365.

2. L. Busé (2001). *Residual resultant over the projective plane and the implicitization problem.* Proceedings of the 2001 International Symposium on Symbolic and Algebraic Computation, New York, pp. 48–55.

3. E.-W. Chionh (1997). *Concise parallel Dixon determinant.* Computer Aided Geometric Design, 14: 561–570.

4. E.-W. Chionh, M. Zhang, R. N. Goldman (2000). *Implicitization by Dixon $\mathcal{A}$-resultants.* Proceedings of Geometric Modeling and Processing 2000, Hong Kong, pp. 310–318.

5. E.-W. Chionh (2001). *Rectangular corner cutting and Dixon $\mathcal{A}$-resultants.* J. Symbolic Computation, 31: 651–669.

6. A. D. Chtcherba, D. Kapur (2002). *A complete analysis of resultants and extraneous factors for unmixed bivariate polynomial systems using the Dixon formulation.* Proceedings of 8th Rhine Workshop on Computer Algebra (RWCA '02), Mannheim, Germany, March 2002, pp. 136–166.

7. D. Cox, J. Little, D. O'Shea (1998). *Using Algebraic Geometry.* Springer-Verlag, New York.

8. C. D'Andrea, I. Z. Emiris (2002). *Hybrid sparse resultant matrices for bivariate systems.* J. Symbolic Computation, 33: 587–608.

9. C. D'Andrea (2002). *Macaulay style formulas for the sparse resultant.* Trans. Amer. Math. Soc., 354: 2579–2594.

10. A. L. Dixon (1908). *The eliminant of three quantics in two independent variables.* Proc. London Math. Soc., 6: 49–69, 473–492.

11. I. Z. Emiris, B. Mourrain (1999). *Computer algebra methods for studying and computing molecular conformations.* Algorithmica, 25(2-3): 372–402.

12. M.-C. Foo (2003). *Further Results on Dixon $\mathcal{A}$-resultant Quotients.* Master thesis, National University of Singapore.

13. M.-C. Foo, E.-W. Chionh (2002). *Corner edge cutting and Dixon $\mathcal{A}$-resultant quotients.* To appear in J. Symbolic Computation.

14. M.-C. Foo, E.-W. Chionh (2003). *Corner point pasting and Dixon $\mathcal{A}$-resultant*

quotients. To appear in the Proceedings of the Asian Symposium on Computer Mathematics (ASCM 2003), Beijing, China.

15. M.-C. Foo, E.-W. Chionh (2003). *Implicitizing bi-cubic toric surfaces by Dixon A-resultant quotients*. Submitted to Pacific Graphics 2003.

16. J. P. Jouanolou (1996). *Résultant anisotrope : Compléments et applications*. Electr. J. Combinatorics, 3 (2).

17. A. Khetan (2002). *The resultant of an unmixed bivariate system*. Submitted to J. Symbolic Computation.

18. R. Krasauska (2002). *Toric surface patches*. Advances in Computational Mathematics, 17: 89–113.

19. T. Saxena (1997). *Efficient Variable Elimination Using Resultants*. Ph.D. thesis, State University of New York.

20. D. Wang (2001). *Elimination Methods*. Springer-Verlag, Wien New York.

21. M. Zhang, R. N. Goldman (2000). *Rectangular corner cutting and Sylvester A-resultants*. Proceedings of the 2000 International Symposium on Symbolic and Algebraic Computation, Scotland, pp. 301–308.

22. S. Zube (2000). *The n-sided toric patches and A-resultants*. Computer Aided Geometric Design, 7: 695–714.

CHAPTER 14

FACE RECOGNITION USING HIDDEN MARKOV MODELS AND ARTIFICIAL NEURAL NETWORK TECHNIQUES

Zongying Ou and Bindang Xue

School of Mechanical Engineering
Dalian University of Technology
Dalian 116024, China
E-mail: ouzyg@dlut.edu.cn

Compared with other biometric security technologies, automatic face recognition provides a more natural and easier approach for human identification; however, it also presents more technical challenges. There are always variations existing in face photos of the same subject person, which are caused by different lighting conditions, different poses and expressions of the subject person, different orientations and positions of cameras, and other random factors. A human face can be viewed as a Markov chain system first from top to bottom vertically and then from left-hand to right-hand side within each vertical region, and the morphing face photos are observation sequences of the states of this system. Based on the above principle, a hierarchical or embedded Hidden Markov Model (E-HMM) corresponding to a human face can be built through training procedure and act as the basis in face recognition processing. Two new approaches combined HMM with Artificial Neural Network (ANN) are proposed in this chapter. ANNs can be embedded in an HMM based system as probability density estimators, and/or as a post-processing classifier; both will augment E-HMM system recognition performance. Experimental results show that these hybrid HMM/ANN approaches achieved high recognition rate ($>90\%$) and are also robust.

1. Introduction

Biometric identification technologies have received increased attention recently in academic research and practical applications. Compared with other biometric technologies, automatic face recognition provides a more natural and easier approach for human identification and has more attractive application prospects. However, it also presents more technical challenges. There are always variations existing among photo images even taken from the same person. The variations can be caused by many random factors, such as different distances and orientations in photography configurations, different facial expressions, and different lighting conditions.

Research on automatic face recognition dates back to several decades ago. Much effort has been made in this field as reviewed in the survey articles by Chellappa *et al.*[1] and Zhao.[13] The key to the problem lies in selection of the identification feature and recognition mechanism. Based on the recognition principle, diverse existing face recognition approaches can be briefly classified as three catalogues: geometric feature based, principal component analysis (PCA)-like based, and model based.

Geometric feature based approach is the earliest approach to face recognition using separate or combined geometric characteristics directly as matching features. This principle is popularly applied in many geometrical recognition applications; however, it does not work well in face recognition, since real face images always embody significant variations and distortions. PCA based approach views human photo images taken from the same person as a set of pixel arrays in observation and takes the K largest eigenvectors of the covariance matrix of the ensemble of training face arrays as classified features. These K largest eigenvectors sometimes are also called eigenfaces.[10] PCA based approaches offer better recognition performance described in FERET evaluation article[7] by Philips and others. However, many researchers are still working in modified PCA based approaches and other new Factor Analysis based approaches for improving the recognition performance,[4,3,11] which might eventually lead to constitute a comprehensive human face model. Model based approach views variant photo images taken from the same person as different observations generated from a corresponding model. If the model is appropriate, then the recognition approach will work effectively and robustly. To discover intrinsic relations between face images and human face source and to build an appropriate model based on these relations are the key issues in developing model based face recognition technology. Recently, a new type model based approach — Hidden Markov Models (HMM) approach — for face recognition has been investigated and appears to have more promising potential.[9,5,2]

In this chapter, we propose two new hybrid approaches of HMM and ANN, taking advantage of the properties of both HMM and ANN to improve the recognition performance.

                              Ou and Xue

2. Hidden Markov Model for Face

An HMM provides a statistical model for a set of observation data sequences.[8] An observation data sequence denoted as O_1, O_2, O_T is generated by a sequence of intrinsic states in an HMM according to output probability function. The intrinsic states themselves are hidden from observation and associated each other with specified state transition matrix. An HMM can be defined as $\lambda = \{N, A, B, \Pi\}$, where

> N is the number of states in the model,
> $A = \{a_{ij}, 1 \le i, j \le N\}$ is the state transition matrix,
> $B = \{b(O_t)\}$ is the output probability function, and
> $\Pi = \{\Pi_1, \cdots, \Pi_N\}$ is the initial state probability distribution.

A human face can be divided from top to bottom as forehead, eyes, nose, mouth and chin regions sequentially; hence a human face can be viewed as a region chain. In such a way a human face can be defined as 1-D HMM. In essence, a human face image is a two dimensional object which should process as a 2-D HMM. To simplify the model processing and still keep abilities of embedding the transition features from left to right in a human photo image, a specified pseudo 2-D HMM scheme is proposed. Pseudo 2-D HMM extends all top-down sub-regions in 1-D HMM as sub-sequences from left-hand side to right-hand side and uses extended sub-1-D HMM defining these sub-sequences hierarchically. This pseudo face 2-D HMM can be called hierarchical HMM or embedded HMM (E-HMM). In our approach, we take the face 2-D HMM scheme shown as Fig. 1, composed of five super states (forehead, eyes, nose, mouth and chin) vertically, and the super states are extended as {3,6,6,6,3} sub states (embedded states) horizontally.

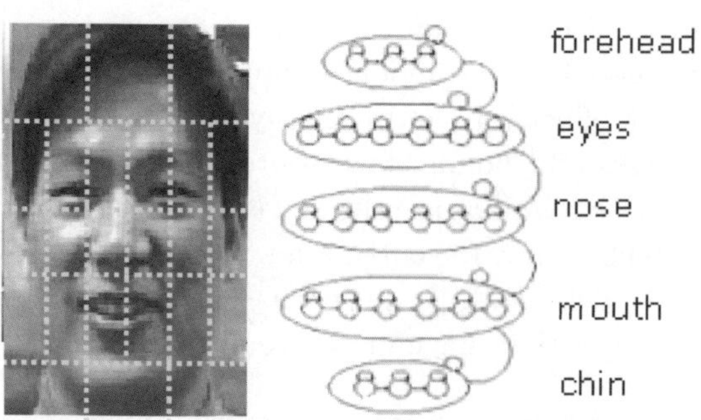

Fig. 1.   E-HMM for face

An E-HMM is defined as $\lambda = \{N,A,\Pi,\Lambda\}$, where N is the number of super states, $\Lambda = \{\Lambda^1, \cdots, \Lambda^N\}$, $\Lambda^i = \{N^i,A^i,B^i,\Pi^i\}$, Λ^i represents the ith super state, and N^i is the number of embedded states in the ith super state.

3. The Observation Vector Sequences for HMM

The observation vector sequence is generated by scanning the image with a $P \times L$ sampling window (image block) left to right and top to bottom as described in the article[5] by Nefian and HayesIII. The overlap between adjacent windows is M lines in the vertical direction and Q columns in the horizontal direction. This technique can improve the ability of E-HMM to model the neighborhood relations between the sampling windows. Figure 2 shows the sampling configuration.

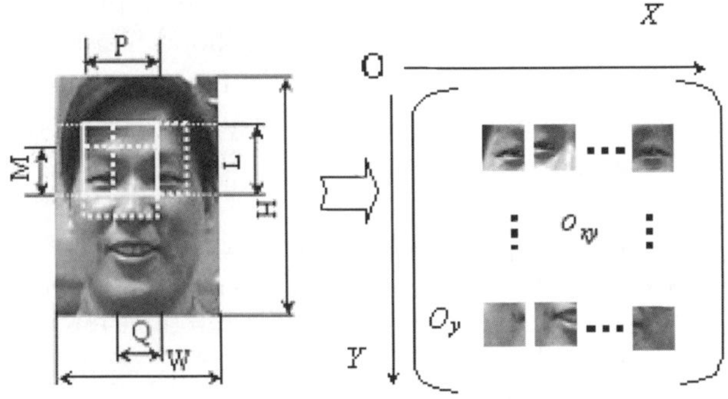

Fig. 2.   Sampling technique for E-HMM

The observation vectors were formed from the 2D-DCT coefficients of each sampling image block. A limited number of the DCT coefficients with larger magnitudes in the upper-left corner (corresponding to the low spatial frequency DCT components) within the sampling window, where most of the image energy is found, were used as the observation vector. Using the 2D-DCT coefficients of an image block instead of the original pixel intensity values as observation vectors has two important advantages. First, 2D-DCT coefficients are less sensitive to image noise as well as face rotations or shifts, and changes in illumination. Secondly, using a limited number of 2D-DCT coefficients reduces dramatically the size of the observation vectors, and therefore decreases the computational complexity of face recognition processing. Increasing the number of DCT coefficient terms and reducing the size of sample windows will generate more detailed data for analysis; however, more noisy distortions will be also involved and an optimal trade-off should be chosen. For our study, we did separate experiments with different sizes of the sampling windows and different 2D-DCT coefficient numbers of the image block. For 100×120 size face image, the experimental results show that $P \times L = 16 \times 16$ block size and six 2D-DCT coefficients for each image block usually yield better recognition performance.

4. Hidden Markov Models Training and Recognition

A human face should correspond to a face HMM. Given a set of face images taken from the same person, model training is estimating the corresponding model parameters and saving them in a face database. Given a test face image, recognition is to find the best matching HMM model within a given face model database and predicting the matching probability. Usually the model corresponding to the maximum likelihood is assumed to be the right choice revealing the identity in the given face database. The general training and recognition process scheme for a typical HMM system can be summarized as shown in Fig. 3.

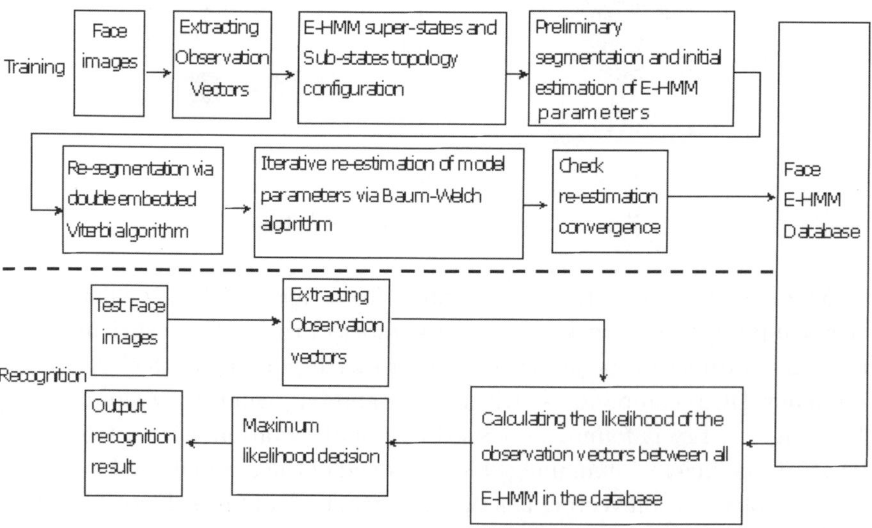

Fig. 3.   The training and recognition scheme for face E-HMM

The important procedures in training and recognition process are resegmentation and iterative re-estimations of model parameters. In a typical HMM system, these classical problems are solved by using the Viterbi algorithm and the Baum-Welch algorithm as described in Rabiner's article.[8] To further upgrade the recognition performance, we propose using ANN techniques to augment the parameter estimation and classifier discrimination in HMM based systems.

5. ANN Estimation of Observation Probability Densities

The properties of HMM or E-HMM are strongly related to the statistical properties of the observation vector sequences. In conventional HMM, the probability density functions associated observation vectors with all states are assumed to be Gaussian distributions. This is a simple and popular method of processing; however, it might not be good enough for all cases. It would be more reasonable if the probability density functions were predicted by analysis of the existing multiple observation sequences. We propose using ANNs to implement this task. As shown in Fig. 4 several modular neural networks are embedded into the E-HMM system to estimate the posterior probabilities of the embedded states; the number of the modular is equal to the number of the super states of the E-HMM system. Specifically, in our recognition system, five super state structures are chosen for an E-HMM, so five MLPs (Multilayer Perceptrons) are embedded in the E-HMM; one MLP is used to estimate the posterior probabilities associated with embedded states in one super state. The sizes of neuron layers of MLP embedded in different super states are different, but the number of nodes of the input layer in all MLPs should be equal to the dimension of the observation vector. The number of nodes of the output layers is the number of embedded states in the correspondence super state, and the numbers of nodes in the hidden layer can be chosen on a trial basis. In our experiments, the numbers of nodes in the hidden layer were chosen roughly equal to three times larger than the numbers of nodes of output layers. Corresponding to given observation vector sequences, the ANN^i can be used to estimate the posterior probabilities for the ith super state.

The system training processing includes two parts: the training of ANN non-parametric estimators of the emission probabilities of embedded states, and the estimation of state transition matrix. A gradient ascent technique is used for training ANN; at the same time the Baum-Welch algorithm is used to estimate the initial and transition probabilities in the underlying E-HMM.

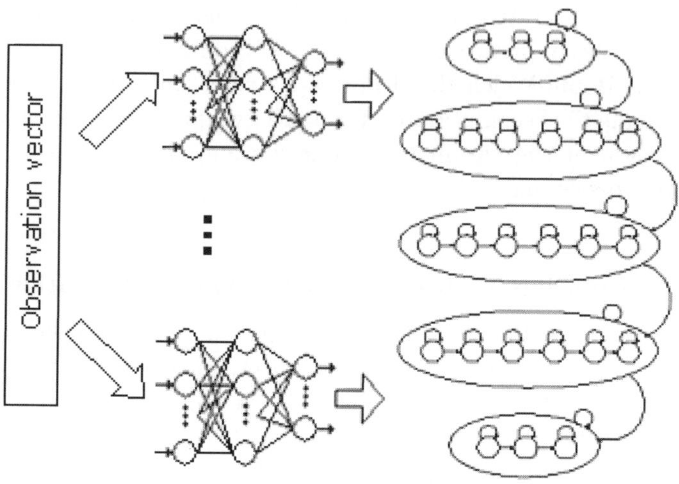

Fig. 4.   E-HMM with ANN density estimation

In model training stage, the optimum super state sequences and the embedded state sequences are obtained from the processing of the double embedded Viterbi algorithm, and the output observation vectors are also labelled with the corresponding super state and embedded state; so we can use the observation vectors associated with the ith super state to train the ANN^i, which will be used in estimating density parameters of the ith super state.

The training formulae for weights of ANN^i can be summarized as follows. Let $O = \{O_y, 1 \le y \le Y\}$, $O_y = \{o_{xy}, 1 \le x \le X\}$ indicate the observation vector sequences, X represent the length of the observation vector sequences in the horizontal direction, and Y represent the length of the observation vector sequences in the vertical direction. The posterior probability of a super state $P(\Lambda^i | O_y)$ corresponding to the given observation vector sequences O_y is chosen as the cost function to be maximized during the ANN^i training:

$$C = P(\Lambda^i | O_y) = \frac{P(O_y | \Lambda^i) P(\Lambda^i)}{P(O_y)}.$$

For a generic weight W of the ANN^i, the learning rule is prescribed as

$$\Delta W = \eta \frac{\partial E_{MAP}}{\partial W} = \eta \frac{P(\Lambda^i)}{P(O_y)} \frac{\partial P(O_y | \Lambda^i)}{\partial W}.$$

Because $P(\Lambda^i)$ and $P(O_y)$ are independent of W of ANN^i, we can rewrite

$$\Delta W = \eta' \frac{\partial P(O_i|\Lambda^i)}{\partial W},$$

where $\eta' = \eta \frac{P(\Lambda^i)}{P(O_y)}$ and $P(O_y|\Lambda^i)$ are calculated by the standard Forward-Backward algorithm. The training algorithm is described in more detail in the reference.[12]

6. ANN Post Classifier

In practical experiments, a face image might present multiple and quite equal high likelihood values with different E-HMM parameters in the system. To augment the discrimination ability of the E-HMM system, an ANN classifier was proposed cascading in the post-processing stage. Figure 5 shows the system architecture.

The artificial neural network used in our system is a feed-forward neural network. The number of nodes in the input layer and output layer is the number of face subjects in the face database, and the number of nodes in the hidden layer can be chosen optionally roughly equal to the number of total sub-states in an HMM.

In our face recognition system, the Baum-Welch algorithm is first used to train E-HMM as described in the references.[9,5] One E-HMM is used to encode one person's face features, so this person's face images appearing under different conditions are used as training samples to train the E-HMM system. The output likelihoods of the E-HMM were encoded to form the input vector and were sent to the ANN in the system training and recognition stage. The output of the ANN classifier is the modified classifying result. In order to ensure numerical stability and fast convergence in the ANN training stage, a normalizing processing procedure is arranged to scale these likelihood values to domain $[0, 1]$ using the following formula:

$$x(n) = \frac{\log P(O|\lambda_n) - \min(\log P(O|\lambda_n))}{\max(\log P(O|\lambda_n)) - \min(\log P(O|\lambda_n))},$$

where $x(n)$ represents the input value of the nth node in the input layer of MLP. The standard BP algorithm is used as the training algorithm. Figure 5 shows the training and testing scheme, where R represents the number of persons in the database, so R E-HMMs are employed and $P(O|\lambda_n)(1 \leq n \leq R)$ denotes the likelihood value of the nth person. All the likelihood values will be sent to MLP after being normalized to domain $[0, 1]$.

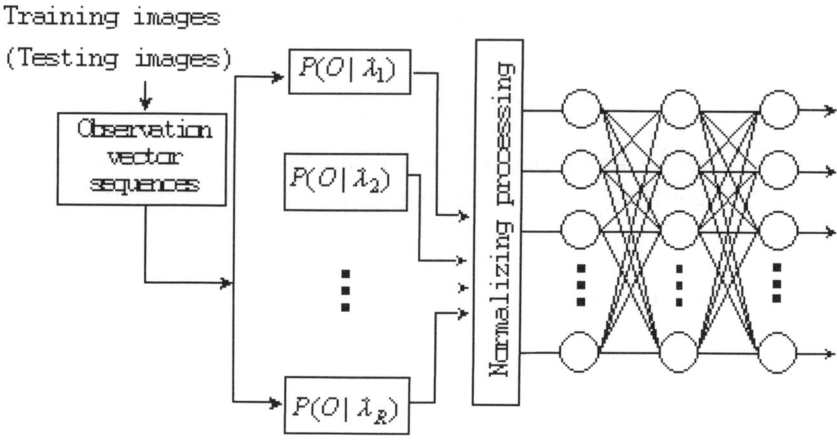

Fig. 5.　The training and testing illustration of the E-HMM with ANN as post classifer

7. Experiments and Results

The face recognition system is evaluated on the Olivetti Research Ltd. (ORL) database.[6] This database contains 400 images of 40 individuals, with 10 images per individual at the resolution of 92×112 pixels. The images of the same person were taken at different times, under slightly varying lighting conditions, and with different facial expressions. Some people were captured with and without glasses. The heads of the people in the images are slightly tilted or rotated. The first five images of each individual are used for training the recognition system; the remaining five images are used for testing the system. Table 1 shows the recognition results of different methods on the ORL face database.

Table 1.　Recognition results of different methods

Methods	Correct recognition rate (%)
Eigenface[10]	90
1D-HMM[9]	85
Pseudo-HMM[9]	90–95
E-HMM[5]	98
E-HMM with ANN density estimation	98.5
E-HMM with ANN post classifier	100

8. Conclusions

For frontal face images, the significant facial regions (forehead, eyes, nose, mouth, and chin) from top to bottom and the local characteristic regions from left to right can be described by the state sequences of E-HMM. A human face appearing under different lighting and pose conditions can be recognized as realizations of the sequences of states of the E-HMM for this person. The E-HMM built from collected face images concisely captures the structure features of two-dimensional face images, and appears to have a more promising potential in modeling and analysis. E-HMM can be used to form a sound basis for face recognition. To further improve recognition performance of E-HMM based systems, ANNs were used as probability density estimator by analysis of collected multiple observation data sequences and as post processing classifier in E-HMM based systems. Testing on the ORL face database, the face recognition rate on the E-HMM system with ANN estimation is 98.5% and achieves 100% on the E-HMM system with ANN post classifier. A comparison with other methods tested on ORL face database shows that the hybrid technique systems have better performance.

References

1. Chellappa R., Wilson C. L. and Sirohey S., Human and machine recognition of face: A survey, *Proc. IEEE*, 83(5): 705–740 (1995).
2. Eiekeler S., Face database retrieval using pseudo 2D hidden Markov models, *Proceedings of the Fifth IEEE International Conference on Automatic Face and Gesture Recognition*, pp. 65–70 (2002).
3. Liu Q., Huang H. and Ma S., Face recognition using kernel based Fisher discriminate analysis, *Proceedings of the Fifth IEEE International Conference on Automatic Face and Gesture Recognition*, pp. 197–201 (2002).
4. Moghaddam B., Principal manifolds and probabilistic subspaces for visual recognition, *IEEE Transactions on Pattern Analysis and Machine Intelligence*, 24(6): 780–788 (2002).
5. Nefian A. V. and HayesIII M. H., Face recognition using an embedded-HMM. *Proceedings of the IEEE International Conference on Audio and Video-based Biometric Person Authentication*, pp. 19–21, Washington D. C., USA (1999).
6. ORL face database, AT&T Laboratories Cambridge, Cambridge, UK (http:// www.cam-orl.co.uk/facedatabase.html).
7. Philips P. J., Moon H., Rizvi S. A. and Rauss P. J., The FERET evaluation methodology for face-recognition algorithm, *IEEE Transactions on Pattern Analysis and Machine Intelligence*, 22(10): 1090–1104 (2000).
8. Rabiner L., A tutorial on HMM and selected applications in speech recognition, *Proc. IEEE*, 77(2): 257–286 (1989).
9. Samaria F., Face recognition using hidden Markov models, *Ph.D. dissertation*, University of Cambridge, UK (1994).

10. Turk M. and Pentland A., Eigenface for recognition, *Journal of Cognitive Neuoscience,* 3(3): 71–86 (1991).

11. Wang H. and Ou Z., Face recognition with independent component analysis and support vector machine (in Chinese), *Journal of Computer Aided Design & Computer Graphics,* 15(4): 416–420 (2003).

12. Xue B. and Ou Z., E-HMM/ANN hybrid network for face recognition (in Chinese), *Journal of Computer-Aided Design and Computer Graphics,* 14(11): 1070–1073 (2002).

13. Zhao W., Face recognition: A literature survey, *CS-TR-4167,* University of Maryland, USA (2000).

INDEX

CANDEMAT 27–29
Castelnuovo theorem 114
Cayley expansion 228
Cayley factorization 230
certified accuracy computation 324
characteristic set 135, 159
class 158, 299, 300
class CGR 267
Clifford algebra 221
Clifford bracket algebra 241
Clifford multiplication 221
clipping curve 22, 120
clipping surface 21, 119, 120
coefficient matrix 377
combinatorial data 351
composite precision 327
computational basis 350
conditionally computable 332
conjugate point 85, 95–97
constant expression 350
constant-coefficient SAS 249
constructible expression 353
contraction 229
control mesh 192
convergent 201
convergent theorem 199
Cremona transformation 81
critical point 15
critical polynomial 251
cross section 113
cubic surface 141
cyclide 35

DCT 399
Dec 301
decidable subset 355
decision problem 333
degree 68, 99, 111, 158
Del Pezzo surface 114, 115
dependent 300
DeriverA 313
DeriverB 316
Desargues theorem 229
Descartes folium 147
dimension 76
dimension-decreasing algorithm 250

dis 251
DISCOVERER 259, 287
Discr 277, 278
discrete Fourier transform 197
discriminant 251
discriminant sequence 277
discrimination matrix 277
DiscrList 277
Dixon determinant 374–376, 393, 394
double rationality 18
dual convolution 193

E-HMM 396, 399, 401, 403, 405
edge-vertex 192
EGC number 323
eigenvalue method 145
embedded hidden Markov model 396
empty word 359
enclosure method 324
enclosure mode 329
Enriques–Manin theorem 114
epsilon-irreducibility 12
epsilon-singularity 12
equation operator 212
essential point 233
evaluation function 350
evaluation problem 351
exact geometric computation 322
exactly computable 337
expanding pseudo-remainder 307
explosion 229
expression evaluation 325
extended magnitude 223
extraneous circle 168
extraneous factor 375, 378, 380, 392–394

face-vertex 193
FERET 397
field of rational functions 79, 107, 111
fine triangular set/system 159
floating point filter 331
floating point number 334
fold point 69

LIST OF AUTHORS